MW01148076

God and Necessity

God and Necessity

BRIAN LEFTOW

OXFORD

UNIVERSITY PRESS

Great Clarendon Street, Oxford, OX2 6DP,
United Kingdom

Oxford University Press is a department of the University of Oxford.
It furthers the University's objective of excellence in research, scholarship,
and education by publishing worldwide. Oxford is a registered trade mark of
Oxford University Press in the UK and in certain other countries

British Library Cataloguing in Publication Data
Data available

Library of Congress Cataloging in Publication Data
Data available

ISBN 978–0–19–926335–6

Printed in Great Britain by
MPG Books Group, Bodmin and King's Lynn

For Dick Trammell, who got me started, and for my parents

PREFACE

This book provides a metaphysic of modality in which God plays the chief part; to locate my position, start at Aquinas and take a half-step toward Descartes. I am writing for theist analytic philosophers, atheist analytic philosophers, and (optimistically) some theologians. Theist analytic philosophers may see at once why my project is worth their time. If you fall into this camp but do not see it, the Introduction and Chapters 2–4 will try to convince you. I offer three things to hook atheists' attention: a chance to bash theism, (part of) a new sort of argument for God's existence, and what I hope is some decent metaphysics that is detachable from the theistic context. The chance to bash arises from the Introduction and first four chapters, which argue that theism brings with it commitment to a particular sort of metaphysics of modality. Here, then, is your chance: theists should believe *that*, and *that*, you may want to argue, is absurd. But to see whether it really is, you will have to go on and consider the theory I offer. The argument for God's existence arises out of the theory, and so if you want to consider that, again, the rest of the book will have a point for you. The detachable metaphysics crops up here and there throughout, but particularly in Chapters 13 and 16. As to theologians—well, for a lot of them this book will be a steep hill to climb. But I hope I have things to say about the doctrine of Creation in the Introduction and Chapters 1–4 that may repay their attention. In Chapter 7 there are what amount to *a priori* arguments for monotheism that may also be of interest. Doctrines of divine ideas have a long history in theology, and Chapters 10–12 offer an anti-Platonist one that may strike their fancies. And again, they may want to make the effort to get through the book to see if the sort of commitment I make about Creation really can be sustained.

Every project starts somewhere. I present a realist account of modality; while I have some things to say against some forms of anti-realism, full discussion of such views must wait. For reasons of length I have also suppressed much I would have liked to say about logic, mathematics, and the history of my topic. Now a word about pronouns. Many philosophers have taken up using 'she' as the generic third-person pronoun. I have not, as I have never heard a reason given for this, and it is not the English I learned at my mother's knee. Some oscillate in the course of a piece between 'he' and 'she'. I have found this distracting as a reader: change of gender suggests that someone else is in view than was being discussed before. 'He or she' will do, but becomes tiresome when used too often. Mostly I try to avoid the issue, but I sometimes try second-person constructions: I am addressing my reader anyway, so why not just do so explicitly, with a friendly 'you'? Some contexts, however, require a different treatment. Sometimes I speak with wide third-person generality of a class to which I belong, when what I really have in mind is myself, or myself as a primary example of the class. On such occasions I am at least in the first instance talking about myself. I am not in doubt as to whether I am he or she, and simply to use 'she' would be literary cross-dressing; I hope readers who avoid the word will excuse my 'he'. I use traditional male language to refer to God: if it was good enough for Jesus, it is good enough for me. I also presume that the human authors of Old Testament books were male. Given the times and culture, the chance that they were not is vanishingly small.

One nice thing about prefaces is the chance to say 'thanks'. I have dedicated this volume to my first philosophy teacher, a man into whose classroom I wandered as a college sophomore—a skinny guy in a rumpled jacket with chalk-dust all over and an infectious grin just to the north. We come to see what our parents did for us when we become parents ourselves: with a 4-4 regular teaching load, he took the time for a senior independent study in which we hacked over *Principia Mathematica* together, and I now know how extraordinary that was. I still remember some of his jokes, and the logic he taught me; I also remember that first moment when it struck me that it would be great to love what I did for a living as much as he obviously did. Thanks, Dick, for my career. To my parents, of course, thanks of a wholly different sort. At various points my thinking has been supported by faculty fellowships at Fordham University, the Center for Philosophy of Religion at the University of Notre Dame, and the Evangelical Scholarship Initiative of the Pew Foundation: to all, my sincerest thanks. I have read papers on some of this to the American Philosophical Association, the Society of Christian Philosophers, the British Society for Philosophy of Religion, and philosophical meetings at Oxford, Cambridge, the University of Birmingham, the University of Texas at San Antonio, Trinity College Dublin, University College Dublin, and Queen's University Belfast. I also had the pleasure of a very active Oxford seminar on the mind of God. The late Phil Quinn, with characteristic generosity, commented on the whole of an earlier version of the MS, and Evan Fales and Bill Alston read substantial chunks of it. I have also learned from reading groups at the Notre Dame Center, and from Jan Cover, Tom Flint, Hugh McCann, Chris Menzel, Nicholas Nathan, Tim O'Connor, Al Plantinga, Mike Rea, Gonzalo Rodriguez-Pereyra, Linda Zagzebski, and Dean Zimmerman. I also thank the referees for Oxford University Press and some journals. Conversations on this topic have spanned my career, so I am quite sure I have forgotten to thank someone; please pardon me if it is you. Joseph Jedwab compiled most of the bibliography. Finally, thanks of another sort: part of the Introduction appeared in 'Why Perfect Being Theology?', *International Journal for Philosophy of Religion* 69 (2011), 103–18, and parts of Chapters 5 and 6 in 'Against Deity Theories', *Oxford Studies in Philosophy of Religion*

2 (2009), 105–60. My thanks to the editors for the reuse of this material, and also my apologies to readers of the latter: a glitch not caught in the proofs made gibberish of part of its argument. You will see here what I meant to say there. My thanks to the Editor and Cambridge University Press for permission to use some of "Swinburne on should be Divine Necessity" (*Religious Studies* 46 (2010), pp. 141–2), which appears in chapter 1. This chapter also drew material from "Necessity." in Charles Taliaferro and Chad Meister, eds, *The Cambridge Companion to Christian Philosophical Theology* (Cambridge University Press, 2010), pp. 15–30, reproduced with permission. Some of chapter 6 appeared in "Aquinas on God and Modal Truth." *Modern Schoolman* 82 (2005), pp. 171–200, and is re-used by permission. Some of chapter 23 appeared in "One Stop Toward God," *Royal Institute of Philosophy Supplement* 68 (2011), pp. 67–104, and is used by permission.

Brian Leftow

Oriel College
September 2011

CONTENTS

INTRODUCTION

CONSIDER the claim that

NC. it is not the case both that $1 + 1 = 2$ and that it is not the case that $1 + 1 = 2$.

Just by understanding this, we 'see' that it is true. If a fully rational person doubts it, the most reasonable explanation is that he or she does not fully understand it. Intuitively, there could not be good reason to reject it: intuitively, it could not fail to be true in any possible situation. It would be true no matter what.[1] (NC) instances a general form, $\neg(P \cdot \neg P)$. We think that any claim instancing this form also would be true no matter what.

Now if a truth would be true no matter what, it is absolutely necessary.[2] So we think that

1. some truths are absolutely necessary.[3]

The general claim

for no proposition P is it the case both that P and that not P

is a thesis of formal logic, and (NC) instances it. So if true, both are in a minimal sense of the term logical truths.[4] Logical truths are not the only

---

[1] Here, 'no matter what' expressly ranges over only possible situations.

[2] Add 'only if' if you do not accept the second, weaker understanding of absolute necessity below.

[3] 'We' of course includes only a majority of philosophers. For denial that the principle of non-contradiction is even true, see Graham Priest, *In Contradiction* (Dordrecht: Kluwer, 1987). For an account of logic as a body of contingent truths see Richard Swinburne, *The Christian God* (Oxford: Oxford University Press, 1994), pp, 106–16.

[4] This minimal sense is not the standard one. For the standard account of logical truth (and an important critique of it) see John Etchemendy, *The Concept of Logical Consequence* (Stanford, CA: CSLI Publications, 1999). Plausibly, not all minimal-sense logical truths are necessary. See Edward Zalta, 'Logical and Analytic Truths That Are Not Necessary', *Journal of Philosophy* 85 (1988), 57–74. Some claim that only fully general propositions are minimal-sense logical truths: see, for example, Bertrand Russell, *Our Knowledge of the External World* (London: Allen and Unwin, 1961), pp. 53–4, 67.

plausible candidates for absolute necessity.[5] Truths of mathematics seem similarly firm to us. So do truths explicating the content of properties, such as *red is a color* and *if anything is a dog it is a mammal*.[6] So do truths expressing exclusions of properties, such as *nothing is red and green all over at once* and *nothing is both round and square*. So do truths expressing supervenience of properties, such as *if anything is a killing in such-and-such circumstances, it is wrong*. There are also necessary truths about particulars. For instance, sets are particulars, and have their members necessarily: necessarily, {Mount Rushmore} contains Mount Rushmore.[7] I am a concrete particular, and necessarily, if I exist, I have or am a soul or contain at least one material part. Any sand-heap is a concrete particular, and for each, necessarily, if it exists, it contains at least two grains of sand. Further, plausibly it is necessary that any sand-heap contain just the grains it contains.

There is also a second, weaker understanding of necessity. A proposition is necessarily true in this sense just if it is true and cannot be false. Suppose that (as many philosophers hold) all of the universe past, present, and future equally exists, 'U' always refers to the whole they compose, and it is always true that U = U. U need not have existed. So suppose that U had not. Suppose too that 'U' is a proper name of U—that is, that necessarily, 'U' refers to U or does not refer to anything. U = U only if something has the property of being identical with U. If there were no U, nothing would have that property. Nothing would be U. Again, an identity-sentence states a truth only if both terms flanking '=' refer to the same thing. Actually, both terms refer to U. Had there been no U, they would not have referred.[8] So had U not existed, 'U = U' would not have said anything true. (This is not to say that U would have failed to be U: there would not have been a U to fail to be U.) But would it be false that U = U? The issues here are complex, but perhaps it would be neither true nor false, or there just would not be such a proposition. If either is correct, that U = U is true cannot be false, but could fail to be true, and so it is weakly but not strongly necessary. Suppose now that not all of the universe's temporal spread equally exists, but instead only the present and perhaps the past do, so that either U is always growing or U always consists of just an instant-thick slice of reality. Then if U grows but 'U' always refers to the whole past and present compose no matter how it is composed, or if 'U' always refers to the sum of all objects existing in the

---

[5] From now on, all modal terms express absolute modalities unless otherwise noted. Chapter 1 provides a detailed account of absolute modality. Here, for introductory purposes, I leave things at an intuitive level.

[6] I now adopt a convention: a sentence in italics is used as if it named the proposition the sentence usually expresses. A predicate in italics names the property the predicate usually expresses. 'P' in such uses as 'necessarily P' abbreviates a sentence. When I do not explicitly introduce a sentence for 'P' to abbreviate, this is because any sentence will do. Thus while 'P' abbreviates a sentence, 'P' is used as if it named the proposition the abbreviated sentence would express. 'Used as if it named' reflects the fact that I am not committed to the existence of propositions. In such sentences as 'L. Leftow exists', 'L.' and '(L)' function as if they named the proposition the sentence expresses.

[7] See James van Cleve, 'Why a Set Has its Members Essentially', *Noûs* 19 (1985), 585–602.

[8] 'Possibilists' (introduced in Chapter 1) would say that if U did not exist, a non-existent object would have the property of identity with U, and 'U' could refer to this object. So they would not concede this.

fleeting present, then if our first case was one of weak but not strong necessity, it is weakly but not strongly necessary that it is or was the case that U = U.

Western theists have reason to believe claims for which

2. God is the ultimate reality

is a convenient shorthand. I shortly show that (1) seems to conflict with some of these claims. One main goal of this book is to show that the conflicts are only apparent. I now explain these claims. One is that God is ultimate in value, or perfect. So explicating these leads me to an account of 'perfect being' theology, of which I do a fair bit in ensuing chapters. Once I have explicated these claims I display their apparent conflicts with (1). I then sketch the road ahead.

Divine Ultimacy

Western monotheists' reason to accept claims we might abbreviate as (2) stems from the sources of Western monotheism, the authorities that Western theists accept—their Scriptures. At least on plausible interpretive assumptions, I now argue, these repeatedly assert that God is ultimate in various ways. If such claims are in Western Scriptures, Western theists who accept these as authorities have *prima facie* reason to accept that God is ultimate in a number of ways. To make my case, I discuss the Old Testament (henceforth OT) and to a lesser extent the New (NT). I focus on the OT because it is common property of Jews and Christians and respected among Moslems:[9] as it is, it lets me make a case that applies to all three Western monotheisms. Let me remind philosophers impatient with discussions of Biblical texts that what I want to set up is a conflict between (1) and things that Western theists have reason to believe. I cannot show that Western theists have reason to believe these things without going to suitably authoritative texts and showing what they say.

Though it is suggestive, (2) is imprecise. 'Ultimate' is from the Latin *ultimus*, whose relevant senses are 'original' and 'last'. So talk of an ultimate reality naturally raises the questions: 'Last or first in what respect?' or 'Relative to what?' Discussion of Biblical texts now suggests some answers.

The ultimate reality

God's uniqueness is a recurrent OT theme. Even OT texts that tolerate talk of other divine beings (such as *Psalm* 82) place God in a unique position of

---

[9] An outsider, noting the *Koran*'s habit of citing, commenting on, and revising OT stories, can find it hard to resist calling the OT a source of the *Koran*.

primacy: He is 'the God of gods.'[10] But the note of uniqueness is of course clearest in texts that assert that God is the only deity of any sort there really is. This is the prophets' consistent refrain. Thus in *Isaiah* God declares:

I am God, and there is no other. I am God, and there is none like me.[11]

I am the first and I am the last; apart from me there is no God. Who then is like me?[12]

To whom will you compare me? Or who is my equal? says the Holy One.[13]

To whom will you compare me or count me equal?[14]

The questions are plainly rhetorical, the expected answer 'no-one'. However exactly one parses these texts, if they make claims about God's nature at all, they assert uniqueness in respect of being 'first', 'last', greatest, and divine, and also some sort of uniqueness *tout court* ('none like me'). Some of these are respects of ultimacy. To be last just is to be ultimate, or perhaps ultimate in duration—that which will outlast any other thing. Being first is also a way to be ultimate—its first member is the last point to which one could trace a series back. Being greatest is being ultimate in value, the last point reached in an ascent along a value-scale.

It is reasonable to read the claim that God is 'the first' as poetic shorthand for claims that God is first in specific ways. One is that God is the first in duration: that is,

FD. before all else existed, God existed, alone, or God and only God did not begin to exist.[15]

(FD) reflects (one reading of) *Genesis* 1: there God is on the scene at the outset, then causes all else to begin to exist. (FD) naturally pairs with a natural sense for 'the last'.[16] For these reasons and because it is conceptually simple,

---

[10] *Ps.* 136:2. All Biblical translations are from the New International Version.

[11] 46:9.

[12] 44:6–7. For other 'first and last' texts see, for example, *Isaiah* 48:12 and *Revelation* 1:17, 22:13. What is first and last—the alpha and the omega—is in one respect at least all-inclusive. So there is a point of contact here with the pantheist's sense of ultimacy, though I will do nothing with it.

[13] 40:25.

[14] 46:5.

[15] It is not clear to me that for present purposes I need provide an atemporalist reading of (FD), for my present concern is with the sense of the Scriptural text, and it is not clear that *Isaiah* commits itself to divine atemporality. However, I think the overall sense of Scripture is either neutral about divine temporality or tilts slightly against it (though my argument on this score must await another occasion). So I provide for atemporalism in the text's second disjunct. The atemporalist can add, 'and would have been there had time not existed', or add that God existed causally prior to all else and this provides an 'analogous' sense in which He is first in duration, or add (if enamored of a view Stump and Kretzmann defend (Eleonore Stump and Norman Kretzmann, 'Eternity', *Journal of Philosophy* 78 (1981), 429–58) that in being simply there at the beginning He is 'already' there because He has an atemporal duration which did not begin when all else began.

[16] In making this point I imply nothing about the relative times of composition of *Genesis* and *Isaiah*. If these texts have only human authors, I am committed only to the claim that material eventually written down or edited into *Genesis* is likely to have been known to the prophet. If (as I believe) they also have a

(FD) likely expresses something the Hebrew author meant to say and did not express so clearly, or did not mean to say, but would likely have recognized as a better statement of what he was trying to arrive at.[17]

'God is the first' also may assert something about God's causal ultimacy. (A causal sense for 'last' pairs naturally with a causal sense for 'first': that is, first which begins all other things, and that is last which ends all other things.) The OT teaches that God creates all else, save perhaps whatever primitive 'material' for creation *Genesis* 1:2's 'waters' and 'deep' might represent. (I discuss this below.) However we construe it, creating is the most basic sort of efficient causality, the one needed if anything else save perhaps the 'waters' is to operate: in *Genesis*, everything other than God save perhaps the 'waters' is there to act only because God first made it. Further, for the OT, God alone creates: the consistent OT refrain is that God is *the* maker of all things.[18] So the OT makes it clear that God has some sort of sole causal ultimacy. So we might see as a clarification of another sense of 'God is the first', or at any rate of the OT's overall teaching about divine creation, that

3. God in some way causally explains all other things' existence,

save perhaps the 'waters' (if these are a thing); and that

4. there is a level of causal explanation at which God alone explains other things' existence,

5. there is no going past this level in any explanation of other things' existence: explanations that reach here, stop here, and

6. all causal explanations of existence eventually reach this level.

Given (6), God is the ultimate explainer of all explained existence.[19] (FD) implies that

7. nothing other than God accounts for God's existence.

For if before all else God exists alone, nothing else was around then to cause Him to exist, and if all things other than God begin to exist, if any of them caused God to exist, He would begin to exist too. (3) implies that, 'waters' perhaps aside,

8. everything other than God has/had a cause of its existence.

The OT's refrain, again, is that God is the maker of all things other than Himself. If this is true, only God is underived, unless 'the waters' represents

---

divine author, my commitment is only that the God who spoke through *Isaiah* did so in light of things He also said or would say through the material in *Genesis*.

[17] I also claim no more than this for (3) and (4).

[18] See, for example, *Ecclesiastes* 11:5; *Jeremiah* 10:16, 51:19. The *Psalms* often call God the Maker of 'heaven and earth' (115:15, 121:2, 124:8, 134:3, 146:6). This is probably intended to cover everything they contain.

[19] If 'the waters' are primitive material, their existence is unexplained.

primitive stuff that does not count as a thing, and so falls outside this locution's scope. (I discuss this below.) Given (FD) and (3)–(8), there is no digging deeper than God; God and nothing else constitutes the basic causal context for the rest of reality.

Actually, (3)–(8) or claims like them have appeal well beyond the bounds of mainline Western monotheism. For some pantheists, God is a unity grounding and manifest in the universe: so, for example, Spinoza, for whom the universe consists of 'modes' inhering in the one substance: God. A substance in which all else inheres is all-inclusive and the most basic reality. Analogs of (3)–(8) hold for a Spinozist deity: it is just that the explanatory relations involved are not efficient-causal.[20] Hindus see their many *vedas* as mere gods and Brahman as God because the *vedas* are finally just manifestations of Brahman, the ultimate reality they reveal: here again, analogs of (3)–(8) hold. And Proclus, a Neo-Platonic polytheist, writes that

God and the One are the same because there is nothing greater than God and nothing greater than the One ... [Plato's] Demiurge is a god, not God. The god that is the One is not a god, but God simply.[21]

---

[20] For other pantheists, the universe is God. As these see it, nothing caused the universe to exist, and so it is (or some of its parts are) causally the most basic thing(s) there is (are). It is also ultimate in the sense of being the most inclusive reality. All else is part of it. It is part of nothing larger. So it is the final context in which all else is embedded. This helps make it divine, or so these pantheists think. Thus Post argues that we can call the universe God because it is *inter alia* the First Cause, metaphysically necessary, eternal, uncreated, and explanatorily independent (John Post, *The Faces of Existence* (Ithaca, NY: Cornell University Press, 1987), p. 357. Cosmological arguers for God's existence do take such properties as at least giving things a long leg up toward deity. But let us run through Post's account of these attributes. For Post, to be the First Cause is to be 'the spatiotemporal sum of all the ultimate explainers plus anything else that has no explanation' (*ibid.*, p. 136). An ultimate explainer explains the existence of something but has no explanation of its own existence: it is an item which is most basic (ultimate) causally. So this is an account of being First Cause theists could easily endorse. For Post, the universe is the First Cause because 'it is an ultimate explainer and the spatiotemporal whole of which everything is a part' (*ibid.*). Post's universe is an ultimate explainer simply because its parts include ultimate explainers (*ibid.*, pp. 133–5). And its parts include ultimate explainers because there are some and the universe is all-inclusive. So the universe is First Cause simply because there are ultimate explainers and it is all-inclusive. (Any ultimate explainer is in an obvious sense a first cause, and so if there are other ultimate explainers of which the universe is the sum, it is not quite kosher to call the universe *the* First Cause. But let this pass.) Again, Post's universe is uncreated and explanatorily independent because (being all-inclusive) there is nothing outside it to create or explain it. It is necessary because it is a final terminus of explanation (*ibid.*, p. 103), which again is so because its parts include ultimate explainers. It is not 'in' time (and so 'eternal') because (being all-inclusive) all time is part of it (*ibid.*, pp. 144–5). Thus for Post, the universe turns out to be God simply because there are ultimate explainers and time and the universe is all-inclusive (and so includes both). Only the last has even a hope of being a reason to call the universe God. Post's God satisfies (2)'s uniqueness condition unless the universe's parts compose two or more universes at once. But if they did, the parts composing any object would add up at once to two or more objects: there is nothing special about universes to generate double-composition. But then for each object thus generated, its parts add up to two or more, and so my parts add up to an infinity of persons, all reading this book with me. There is no good reason to believe this. In any case, I know of no pantheist who has believed in double-composed universes/Gods. Pantheists accept the uniqueness built into (2)'s use of a definite description: for them, God is *the* ultimate reality.

[21] Proclus, *Commentary on Plato's 'Parmenides'*, transl. Glenn Morrow and John Dillon (Princeton, NJ: Princeton University Press, 1983), pp. 32–3.

Proclus calls the One 'God' precisely because he thinks it ultimate in value. He also implies that nothing is *as* great as God—that God is the sole thing with no greater—by refusing to let the One be distinct from God yet share God's property of being unsurpassed. If there is an x such that for all y, if nothing is greater than y, then y = x, there is just one thing than which nothing is greater. So for Proclus, only God is unsurpassed. The One—God— is for Neo-Platonists like Proclus also the ultimate source of all else. (4), (5), (7), and (8) clearly hold for a Neo-Platonic One.

Ultimacy in Value: Perfection and Philosophical Theology

Texts just quoted depict God asserting, in effect, that He has no equal—that He is superior to all others. According to Western Scripture, God is greatest because He is in fact perfect or maximal in various respects. As God has no body, power, knowledge (intellect), character, rationality, will, duration, spatial extent, intrinsic being of some sort and deity are the respects in which He *can* be perfect, as nothing else applies.[22] I consider these in order.

Some texts assert that God's power is the greatest possible: 'the Lord . . . can do all things' (*Job* 42:2); 'Lord . . . nothing is too hard for you' (*Jeremiah* 32:17); 'nothing is impossible with God' (*Luke* 1:37); 'with God all things are possible' (*Matt.* 19:26). 'All things' is the greatest possible range of power. No power can surpass one to which nothing is impossible. So no power can be greater than the one these texts ascribe: they ascribe maximal power.[23]

Some texts assert that God's knowledge is as great as can be: 'God . . . is perfect in knowledge' (*Job* 37:15–6); 'His understanding has no limit' (*Ps.* 147:5). No knowledge can surpass perfect knowledge; an understanding without limit is one that in some sense grasps everything and (obviously) suffers no intellectual limitations.[24]

Some texts assert that God's moral goodness is as great as can be: 'as for God, His way is perfect' (*II Samuel* 22:31, *Ps.* 18:30); 'be perfect, as your heavenly Father is perfect' (*Matt.* 5:48). No goodness can surpass perfect goodness.

---

[22] Or at least nothing else of which we have any ken. Spinoza supposed that God has infinite sorts of attribute (*Ethics* I, df. 6), though we are aware only of two. There is no way to disprove this, of course. But there is equally no reason to believe it. Western Scriptures teach that God is mysterious, but nothing suggests that we take the mystery as having this particular character.

[23] Albeit in a form that needs parsing. Lying is one thing God cannot do, according to *Hebrews* 6:18, and it is 'impossible with God' to make a round square.

[24] But here as with omnipotence, some parsing is necessary. Can God know what I express when I say 'I am Leftow'? Some argue that He can only if He is Leftow.

God is said to possess 'all . . . wisdom' (*Colossians* 2:2). There is no more to have than that. Someone with all wisdom is perfectly wise. Someone perfectly wise is *inter alia* perfectly rational.

One might judge someone's will by its power to get things done or by its habits of choice. As to power, God is omnipotent, so His will can lack none. As to habits of choice, God is perfectly rational and good. Moral perfection is a matter of attitudes and of habits of action, thought, emotion, and will. A will which forms only intentions and attitudes befitting moral perfection and wills only acts befitting perfection is itself morally perfect. Thus implicit in God's moral perfection is part of what we might mean by calling His will perfect. The rest is a consequence of His perfect rationality.

God is said to be eternal (*Ps.* 90:2); His duration is as great as possible.[25] God is said to be omnipresent (*Ps.* 139: 7–10). The sense in which He is present in space is clearly non-standard—we do not think He literally shares our location, and it would be odd to say that He has a size—but if God is present everywhere, then even if He has no spatial extent, the amount of space at which He is present (which in us is what spatial extent measures) is as great as can be given the extent of space.

I use 'intrinsic being' for lack of a better phrase to label what in us is constituted by our bodies and (if any) souls. If God is eternal, He is immortal. What has no body cannot suffer bodily damage, disease, decay, nor entropy. Something omnipotent is able to prevent any other sort of damage, decay, and so on, that there might be. Someone perfectly rational would see no reason to allow any. So God's intrinsic being is as perfect as can be.

There is finally being perfect *qua* deity. Texts that tolerate talk of many deities treat God as supreme among them. Those that call God the only deity trivially imply that He is the best deity. Neither sort says that God is the best possible deity. But there may be a connection between being perfect in these other respects and being as perfect a case of deity as can be.[26] There are at least six ways to connect the two: (a) being divine entails being perfect in these other respects, and so since there are no other respects relevant to being a deity, entails being as perfect a deity as can be; (b) being perfect in these other respects entails being divine, and so, since no other respects are relevant, being as perfect a deity as can be; (c) if one is divine, being greater in those of these respects that are degreed makes one a better deity. If so, being maximal in these respects makes one a perfect deity; (d) if one is divine, being a better deity makes one greater in power, knowledge and goodness. If so, plausibly if God is perfect in these other respects, it is because He is a perfect deity; (e) being a better deity neither accounts for nor is accounted for by being greater in the

---

[25] This does not preclude His being atemporal. If He is, He 'exists forever' not in the sense that He occupies all times but in the sense that at every time, it is timelessly true that He exists.

[26] Kind membership does not come in degrees. Anyone is either divine or not, period. But kinds may be better- or worse-realized. As one cow may be a better cow than another, so it at least makes sense to speak of being a better or worse deity.

degreed respects; all the same, the two co-vary; (f) perhaps to be a deity is to be a personal being sufficiently great in these respects. If this is true, a personal being maximal in these respects must be the most perfect possible case of deity. The disjunction of (a)–(f) is fairly plausible, and so it is fairly plausible that perfections explicit in Scripture carry perfection in deity with them.

Thus God as the Bible depicts Him is perfect in every respect mentioned. There is, of course, no being better than perfect in any respect. I cannot see what could be better to be than a perfect being. If there are other dimensions than spatial and temporal, God can be omnipresent in these too. I can see four possible further respects of perfection. The Bible depicts God as the creator and sustainer of all other concrete things. This or a closely related property might count as one more perfection—one more intrinsic maximum of a degreed attribute it would be good to have, or equivalently one more attribute a being perfect in all respects ought to have. I argue shortly that we should indeed add such a claim to the list. Another candidate perfection concerns God's 'quality of life'. The Bible calls God blessed or happy (*I Timothy* 1:11, 6:15). It does not say that He is perfectly so. If God is perfectly rational, He has *inter alia* a concern for His own happiness. If He is omniscient, omnipotent, and has what I later call the 'GSA-property', He can maximize His own happiness come what may. A rational being would not let Himself be less happy than He could be in His circumstances if He had the choice. Given God's powers and opportunities, He always has the choice. So we can infer that God's life overall will be as happy as we let it be: if there is grief in it, it is due entirely to what His creatures suffer and do, not to anything He has imposed on Himself or failed to do for Himself. God's moral nature imposes on Him perfect moral reactions: if what creatures suffer and do ought to lower His happiness, it does, and lowers it as much as it should. Maximal happiness would not be an admirable property if it were not morally appropriate to have it. The property God has, I suggest, is this: He is such as always to have the maximum morally permissible happiness. This is a reasonable inference from properties which the Bible explicitly ascribes to God, and seems a reasonable candidate for a further perfection. Finally, there are what we might call modal perfections: necessity of existence, necessary possession of other perfections. Scripture is silent on these, save for texts that suggest that it is not possible that God do evil (such as *James* 1:13). I consider these later.

The claim that God is perfect in all respects so far discussed licenses a way to fill out the concept of God: 'perfect being' theology. One sort of 'perfect being' argument would follow this format. Nothing could be a better G (or better in G) than God in fact is. God can be F. God would be a better G (or better in G) were He F than were He not F, precisely because of being F, rather than due to something being F would bring with it. Suppose now for *reductio* that God is not F. Then God is not as good a G as He could be. So if God is not F, it is false that nothing could be a better G than God in fact is. But this is true. So *prima facie*, God is F.[27] If being F is incompatible with some divine attribute initially given from Scripture, this *prima facie* claim is over-ruled. If being F is compatible with all scriptural 'givens' and with all other outputs of this 'first stage' procedure, then *ultima facie* and *simpliciter*, God is F. If being F is compatible with all Scriptural 'givens' but incompatible with some first-stage output H, then if having F and the rest of these is better than having H and the rest, *ultima facie* God has just F. If F and H (plus the rest of the given divine nature) are equal or incommensurable, *ultima facie* God is H or F, but 'perfect being' reasoning does not permit us to choose between them. Perfect-being theologians are rarely this explicit, but what they say can often be fleshed out as or transposed into arguments of this sort. Where Scripture is explicit that God is G, their reasoning tries to show what authoritative statements about God's perfection entail. These arguments' epistemic credentials are as good (or bad) as those of Scripture in conjunction with some of our value-intuitions.

Perfect-being theology is not the same project as showing what, say, a Psalmist would have understood his statements to entail. It is a safe bet that Psalmists would not have parsed their claims as precisely as did Anselm or Aquinas. But it is not clear that only what texts' human authors would likely have understood their words to imply matters to working out a Scripture-based concept of God. A Psalmist asserts that God's understanding has no limit. We need not speculate about exactly what he meant by this. For it is a safe bet too that he would have accepted as representing at least part of it that what it *really is* to have understanding with no limits is true of God. So too, a Psalmist who asserts that God is morally perfect does not have a full ethical theory in mind. But surely he means at least that whatever perfect goodness really is, that is what God has. If we take Scriptural authors to intend at least this much by what they say, what they say licenses the project of perfect-being theology even as its results far outstrip anything they are likely to have understood their own words to imply. For their words have an open texture which their intent licenses us to fill in. So while they doubtless had their own imprecise ideas about what limitless understanding or perfect goodness involve, these represent just the first stage in determining what perfect goodness or limitless understanding really are. Nor is this situation unique to philosophical theology. When an American founding document forbids cruel and unusual punishment, it does not forbid only what an eighteenth-century English colonist would have thought cruel and unusual. The law

---

[27] A different pattern of reasoning begins from the premise that God can be F and would be better (in a sense yet to be specified) were He F than were He not. Such reasoning may come in where we try to fill out the concept of God purely *a priori*.

Again, suppose we ask whether God is F or G, where He could not be both. We must then consider tradeoffs: which would make God better? So we might want to ask whether being F or being G would make God a more perfect being. But while we might, we need not. God falls under kind-concepts: personal being, deity. And we have better intuitions about what makes someone a better personal being or deity than we do about what makes something a better being.

takes 'cruel and unusual' to intend what *really is* cruel and unusual, and so to have an open texture that the best ongoing moral and legal reflection fills in and legitimately takes to be in a broad sense part of the founding document's content. The Framers had their own way of filling in their words' open texture, but this was just a first step toward the full body of Constitutional law. Again, when I call some stuff gold, I do not really know what it is for something to be gold any more than the Psalmist knew what it is for an understanding to be limitless. But if I mean to speak the truth, my 'this is gold' asserts that this block has whatever properties make some stuff gold. And so in a sense, science works out the content of what I have said.

One can raise a worry about resting the perfect-being project on Scripture. We sometimes must claim for God something intuitively a bit less than some texts ascribe to Him.[28] If we do, we may suggest that the texts contain some poetic hyperbole, and are not altogether sober declarations of metaphysical truth—as would also seem plausible from general considerations of context and genre. If some such texts are hyperbolic, why not all? But if all, the Scriptural basis for perfect-being theology is undercut. Perhaps all Scripture really warrants is 'pretty-impressive-being' theology.[29] I reply that a hyperbolic approach to perfection-texts raises a question about authors' intent: what would they have been doing, were they making claims about God they did not think were literally true? Not using metaphor: there is no metaphor in the texts cited. The most plausible view, I think, would be that they were approaching God with the sort of flattery that would curry favor with a despot. But it is reasonable to be charitable in interpreting a text. Part of charity lies in taking authors to be morally earnest where the context makes whether they are so a salient question and nothing explicit casts doubt on it. So I take Scriptural authors to speak sincerely, and make perfection-claims about God not because they thought flattery would get them somewhere with Him, but because they really did think He deserved them. If what they meant to say included the note that God is perfect in these respects, we can pardon them a bit of unclarity about what this involves and get to work. In any case, even if Scripture does not fully warrant the perfect-being project— which I do not concede—perfection-claims have roots in primary religious life. They arguably flow out of Western monotheist attitudes of worship, for arguably to see God as anything less than absolutely perfect would make Him out not to deserve the sorts of attitude Western monotheist worship involves.[30]

Perfect-being theology is inevitably speculative, for it cannot help following our ideas of perfection into detail and into regions about which Scripture is silent. I give many perfect-being arguments in what follows. As I give them,

---

[28] As noted in footnotes above.   [29] A phrase I owe to Phil Quinn.

[30] On this, see as a hostile witness, J. N. Findlay, 'Can God's Existence Be Disproved?', in Antony Flew and Alasdair MacIntyre (eds), *New Essays in Philosophical Theology* (NY: MacMillan, 1955), pp. 47–55.

I have a nagging fear that I am just making stuff up. This is not due to uncertainty about God's being perfect. Rather, our ideas of what it is to be perfect are inconsistent and flawed, and there is no guarantee that they match up with what God's perfection really is. Our intuitions about absolute possibility, again, probably are not wholly reliable; probably we sometimes take as absolutely possible what is merely epistemically possible, possibly true 'for all we know', where we do not know what we would need to know to rule out the candidate possibility. And perfect-being theology is one sort of metaphysics, and so inherits a share of our worries about whether metaphysical reasoning ever shows us more than the insides of our own concepts.[31] But this is not the place to address general worries about metaphysics; if perfect-being theology is epistemically no better off than the rest of metaphysics, it is not obviously worse off either. I have reason to treat God as perfect, but reason also to be hesitant as to what His perfection implies. But the Western theist who seeks not merely to parrot Scripture must overcome this hesitation.

Perfect-being arguments are fallible, not least because our intuitions about perfection are fallible. If they go astray, the one making them has two consolations. For one at least acts reverently in so arguing. And there is also a sort of *tu quoque* to be had. With all its limitations—and there are more than I have mentioned here—the alternatives to perfect-being theology are unpromising. 'Pretty-impressive-being' theology would just be cautious perfect-being theology. It would base itself on perfect-being theology's data (Scripture, religious experience, intuitions about value, and so on). It would treat them in some ways, as does perfect-being theology: it would be careful, for instance, to ascribe no imperfections to God. It would just be less willing to trust certain intuitions. For instance, it might be willing to say that God is morally perfect, but agnostic about whether He is necessarily so. I have shown elsewhere that reasoning about God as first cause or Creator does not provide a second, wholly distinct method for philosophical theology.[32] Nor is negative theology a second viable method. Saying what God is not tells us what God is only if our negations let us close in on some positive partial description of Him. If all I know of X is that it does not fit in any of ten category-boxes, either I have an eleventh in which to fit X or I know nothing of what X is. So theists who criticize particular perfect-being arguments—say, mine—may well wind up offering others of the same sort if they do not either limit themselves to Scripture's explicit claims about God or go silent. If they can do the job better than I, more power to them.

This excursus on method explains a sort of argument I deploy repeatedly. But it also now supports a claim about God's causal ultimacy.

---

[31] My thanks to a referee.

[32] See my 'Concepts of God', *The Encyclopedia of Philosophy* (NY: Routledge, 1998), vol. 4, pp. 93–102, where I also discuss the history and some problems of perfect-being arguments.

Creation *Ex Nihilo*

The OT repeatedly calls God the maker of all things. But just how does He make them? *Genesis* begins this way:

In the beginning God created the heavens and the earth.

Now the earth was formless and empty, darkness was over the surface of the deep, and the spirit of God was hovering over the waters.[33]

There are at least two ways to take these sentences. On one, the first is a topic-sentence telling us what is to come, and the second begins the account of God's creating. On this reading, God *ab initio* faces some initial disorderly reality that talk of the deep etc. symbolizes. God's creating is then His making this into an orderly world. On this reading it is not literally true that God has 'made all things in heaven and earth': He did not make whatever He first faced. Some might suggest that God could have made all things, even allowing divine raw material, were the raw material some sort of *stuff*. For then creating could be making all *things* from this stuff. But stuff is always around in some quantity, and any quantity of stuff is itself a thing, if perhaps an amorphous or scattered one. (A pound of cheese is a quantity of stuff. 'Pound of cheese' is a count-term: we can count pounds of cheese. But we count *things*.) 'The deep' is naturally taken to refer to a thing, which is all the stuff together. Moreover, apart from this, the sense of 'all things in heaven and earth' is likely 'everything in heaven and earth'. 'Everything' includes all the stuff. The sense of Scriptural locutions, then, pushes us toward a different reading—one without a raw material for Creation. Further, if the text depicts raw material for creation, it depicts it as there with God 'from the beginning', and so He is not *the* first in duration.[34] Nor is He *the* first causally: counter to (4), primitively given properties of the primordial material would ultimately

---

[33] 1:1–2.

[34] This is clear if God is temporal. If He is atemporal, then *per* my account of (FD), the sense in which He is first in duration is that at the beginning of all else, He did not begin, but was simply there, never having begun to exist. This could also be true of something temporal, and would on the present reading be true of the raw material: so God would not be *the* first in duration. A footnote offered the atemporalist the chance to make three further additions. As to the second, the raw material would be causally prior to anything formed from it. So God and it would both be causally prior to all formed things. Neither would be causally prior to the other. So neither would count as *the* first in duration in the analogous sense mentioned, and so God would not. As to the third, I do not myself believe that atemporal existence involves duration, so to me it would not help that the raw material likely could not have this. As to the first, who knows? If it was not up to God that He was confronted by temporal raw material, it was not up to Him that there be time. If it was not, I see nothing to rule it possible or impossible that He not be accompanied by time. So it could be that conditionals beginning 'if time did not exist' are counterpossibles. If they are, they are all true, and so do not provide us with a way to distinguish what would have held of God and what would have held of the raw material: we have as much reason to call God first as to call the material first, and so we cannot affirm that either is *the* first. If they are not counterpossible, then it is possible that time not exist. Had time not existed, the actual temporal raw material could not have been there if (as I believe) whatever is temporal is necessarily so. But who is to say whether something atemporal would have been in its place? So with the first addition, we wind up having to be agnostic about whether God is *the* first in duration: we cannot accept that He is, though neither can we deny it.

explain some properties of created things, most properties of created things would trace ultimately to both God and the primordial stuff, and the existence of all else would depend ultimately on God *and* the raw material.[35] Thus the *Isaiah* text discussed seems to treat Creation as not involving pre-given raw material, and if we look to the OT's teaching on creation as a whole, it tilts toward creation *ex nihilo*—not out of any raw material.

On another reading, the first sentence describes an act of creating *ex nihilo*: 'before' this act there was God and nothing else concrete, and by this act heaven and earth came to be, in an initial formless state. One can read the text either way, though I have suggested that other OT material favors the second. In Christianity, the overwhelming tendency has been to take it the second way.[36] One reason, I have suggested, is Scriptural. Another is perfect-being theology. It is more exalted to be the first in duration and causally than not to be. And God's power is greater if He can create *ex nihilo* than if He cannot. So if no conceptual difficulties bar His having this sort of power—which I would argue, given space—there is a perfect-being case that He has it. And if He has this sort of power, it is reasonable to see *Genesis* 1:1 as depicting Him using it.[37] I endorse the *ex nihilo* reading, on both sorts of ground. Further, as I have offered a Scriptural justification for perfect-being reasoning, the perfect-being case for it in the end 'interprets Scripture by Scripture'—a traditional hermeneutic. So I take it that 'in the beginning' God created *ex nihilo* everything outside Him: that is, everything other than God, His parts (if any) or aspects, and His attributes.

Universal creation

We make things: Michaelangelo made *David*. Yet the OT calls God Creator of things that come to be after the universe first appears.[38] There is no sense that

---

[35] The causation here might well be 'immanent' (on which see Dean Zimmerman, 'Immanent Causation', *Philosophical Perspectives* 11 (1997), 433–71): the stuff's being extended, say, would cause the being extended of the thing God made out of it. But immanent causation is efficient causation.

[36] At least some Jewish interpreters favor the first. See, for example, Harry Frankfurt, 'On God's Creation', in Eleonore Stump (ed.), *Reasoned Faith* (Ithaca, NY: Cornell University Press, 1993), pp. 130–2.

[37] Morris offers a different sort of perfect-being argument for creation *ex nihilo*: '…if any contingent being…exists, it must stand in the relation of being created *ex nihilo*. For the Anselmian God is… omnipotent (and) an omnipotent being cannot rely on any independent source for its…products' ('The God of Abraham, Isaac and Anselm', in Thomas Morris, *Anselmian Explorations* (Notre Dame, IN: University of Notre Dame Press, 1987)). But there is an equivocation here. If it is possible to create *ex nihilo*, then an omnipotent being can do so, and so cannot *need* any independent source for its products. But were there some independent stuff just lying around, surely an omnipotent being could rely on it in the weaker sense of putting it to a use it could do without. If not, we would have the odd result that omnipotence would *require* God to go it alone when He had the option of doing otherwise. Moreover, if anything about God precludes a simple's simply popping into being *ex nihilo* absolutely uncaused, it is not obvious that it is His omnipotence: that an omnipotent being could use no pre-given matter, even if true, would not preclude things' coming to be apart from its agency and uncreated.

[38] So, for example, *Psalms* 104:30, 139:13; *Isaiah* 48:7, 54:16.

it is just noticing a few lucky things; the intent seems to be that God in some sense creates everything, no matter when it begins to exist and even if some creature makes it from pre-given material. We must reconcile the OT claim of 'late' creation with the fact that we make things too. I offer four models for this.

On one approach God and a complex of creatures C (Michaelangelo, a chisel, some marble, and so on) made individually insufficient contributions that jointly sufficed for *David*'s existence, but what God does for *David* is so related to His initial act of creation as to count as creating *David* (in a thin sense).

Suppose that the universe has a bottom level of decomposition—parts not composed of further parts; that is, simples. God creates a stock of simples *ex nihilo*, at the universe's origin and perhaps later. These either persist, disappear, or turn into other simples. If one simple turns into another, some sort of partless stuff is common to earlier and later simples, persisting as one turns into another.[39] This must be so if one turning into another is to be distinguished from one disappearing and by so doing causing a new one to appear.

Simples make up *David*'s block of marble. If all of these were created, all *David*'s parts were created. If some arose from created simples, all *David*'s stuff was created. If all parts or all stuff of *David* are created, God made all of *David* appear *ex nihilo*. By so doing He made a creating-*ex-nihilo* causal contribution to *David*: He made the creating-*ex-nihilo* sort of difference for *David* by providing all *David*'s matter *ex nihilo*. This is God's necessary but insufficient contribution to *David*'s appearance.[40] Taken in terms of this, 'God created *David*' is a loose way to say that God created all of *David*, and the latter is a consequence of His making all of the universe begin to exist. C's necessary, insufficient contribution is to arrange parts into *David*.[41] So in a slightly thicker sense of 'creates', God creates *David* with C's help, as C determines that it is *David* God creates, though God made His whole creative contribution to *David* by strict-sense creating all of the universe. That God in this sense created *David* is a consequence of His making all of the universe begin to exist and *David*'s coming to exist.

This model's coherence is enough to show that one can reconcile creation (in a weak sense) of every physical particular with creatures' having robust causal input into what things exist. If the universe has no bottom level of decomposition, this model will not do. But it is easy to remove the model's bottom level; we just say that what we called simples really have parts, and the parts have parts *ad infinitum*. We then have it that each *faux* simple either was

---

[39] I take no stand on whether such stuff is possible, nor, then, on whether simples can turn into other simples. I am just laying out the formally available alternatives.

[40] Some accounts of the relation between stone and statue (on which see Michael Rea (ed.), *Material Constitution* (Lanham, MD: Rowman and Littlefield, 1997)) would require me to adjust my exposition, but would not (I think) affect my overall point.

[41] It is necessary that *someone* do this. It need not have been Michaelangelo.

created with all its parts or arose from an earlier *faux* simple and all its parts. The rest goes as before.

Thicker creation

We can add to this first model to 'thicken' the sense in which God creates items that appear after the universe begins. Suppose, for example, that at the beginning or later, God creates *ex nihilo* some deterministic causal systems, primed to act.[42] He foreknows all that they will bring about. Surely He fully intends some of it. (Perhaps He merely accepts some, as a foreknown but unintended price for effects He wishes: perhaps these effects are unavoidable given these creatures' natures.) By putting these systems in place primed to act as He intends, God causes them to bring about what He intends. So God works through such systems once they exist, even if He is not currently willing their results. So if God creates such a system, He in a thicker sense creates things which appear by its deterministic workings: through it He arranges parts into wholes whose existence He intends. If God has created some deterministic systems *ex nihilo* and intends the existence of at least some things He knows that they will bring to exist, God late-creates some items this way.

   The OT picture of God has Him performing acts of particular providence. These can lead to some rather than other results of otherwise random processes. If God wants you, not someone else, to result from a particular act of sexual intercourse, He can simply make all but one sperm move slowly and one move a bit faster than it might have. This 'thickens' the sense in which He has created you to the one just sketched, as the system consisting of the divine intention that certain sperm move certain ways plus the moving sperm is deterministic: it must evolve just as the intention dictates. God's late-creating some things in this way is fairly likely if He made all the universe begin to exist and acts providentially within it. Another thing falling under the head of 'providential' late creation arises from a natural sense, well expressed in the OT, in which God works through the free acts of creatures He leads to act. If a conductor created in beginning the universe or late-created in some other way an orchestra ready to play just as the conductor wished, then led it, the conductor would make music through the orchestra in a fairly thick sense. If God led Michaelangelo to carve as he did, God in this thick sense made *David* through him. The system consisting of God, Michaelangelo, and the rest of C is not deterministic, but it is close enough to being so to let us say that God creates through Michaelangelo.

---

[42] He could simply create basic particles whose natures guarantee this. My thanks to Hugh McCann here.

These additions yield a second model: God as remote and creatures as proximate causes of late creation. On this model, both God and creatures act in ways that guarantee an effect; that is, are individually causally sufficient for it. But they are not both immediately causally sufficient for it. God 'late-creates' only through creatures.

Immediate late creation

Another model has God and creatures immediately cause the same effects. Suppose that God at Creation wills 'let there be at times t–t* a deterministic system of events S making Mars form.' This is a creative volition. It accounts *ex nihilo* for S's and Mars' existence. By willing it God causes an entire causal sequence including the existence of Mars as its final effect to appear *ex nihilo*, beginning at t. This volition has this sequence as its immediate effect. It does not bring about one part of the sequence by bringing about another. So God has an immediately effective creative volition that Mars exist—God makes the creating-*ex-nihilo* sort of causal difference for Mars—yet creatures have causal input too. For each event in S causes the next, leading eventually to Mars' existing.

Both God and creatures do have a role here. Creatures bring Mars to be by moving matter around or being moving matter. God causes creatures to move matter around. If He does so, it is the creatures that directly move the matter, not God: they have a role, and so does God, as causing them to do it. All it is for Mars to come to exist is for bits of matter to move into appropriate relation to one another. So if God can make creatures move matter, He can make them make Mars. He would not suddenly lose the ability when the effect of that matter's motion is that something new exists. Nor is there any evident reason that God could not make creatures move matter by creating them *ex nihilo* as doing so.

Some may ask whether this would be a case of overdetermination. I think overdetermination can occur, so it would not bother me if it were. But I do not think it is. An overdetermined effect has many causes each sufficient on its own to bring it about. Thus typically, were one cause absent, the others would cause the effect. In this case, both a divine volition and S make causal contributions that guarantee the occurrence of the effect. In this sense, each is sufficient for the effect. But the divine volition is not sufficient on its own. If we remove S, it is not possible that the divine volition still exist, for then it would be an omnipotent volition that failed of its effect. What is true is only that *some* divine volition could bring the effect about without any created sequence doing so—God could have just created Mars on His own—not that this one could have. What cannot produce an effect on its own cannot be sufficient on its own. The most we can say is that were it (impossibly) on its own, willing that S produce Mars, and it did (impossibly) get only Mars, not S, it would have been sufficient on its own. But on the standard approach to conditionals with impossible antecedents (introduced in the next chapter) it is equally true that it would not get Mars, and would not have been sufficient on its own. It is not clear that anything about the volition's actual causal sufficiency on its own follows from the two conditionals. This is enough to show that the third model is not a case of what we usually understand by overdetermination.

I also think that S is not sufficient on its own, though the argument here is weaker. In the model, S appears due entirely to God's creative volition: it has no created cause. Equivalently, it is closed under the created-causal relation. So it is not the case that had God not so willed, created causes would have been there to bring S about anyway. I think that had God not so willed, S would not have been there. Given God's actual responsibility for the contents of the universe, even if it is possible that S pop into being wholly uncaused—ultimately I suggest that it is not—S would not have appeared had God not so willed. If there are possible worlds just like ours save that God does not will S and yet S appears, they are less like the actual world than one in which God does not will S and S does not appear, because they do not violate what appears to be a law in the actual world, that large systems of macro-objects appear only if God so wills.[43] If this is right, then were the divine volition removed, we would not be left with a cause able to bring the effect about on its own. So neither cause would exist without the other. If (as I believe) S could not exist without creation or conservation, then in this case God's volition and S make up an indecomposable single cause, neither part able to act without the other and so neither sufficient on its own for Mars to exist. If S could exist independent of God, God's volition and S are still what we might call a weakly indecomposable single cause, for no possible world with just one is nearer than any possible world without both. But S is in principle sufficient on its own for Mars' existence, though the divine volition is not.

On the third model, if God at the Big Bang willed the existence of all purely deterministic causal sequences extending from the Big Bang, He might thereby immediately create *ex nihilo* tracts of the universe that extend through all of time, yet creatures would have full causal efficacy within these sequences. Further, this model extends to indeterministic sequences, including sequences involving libertarian free choice. We can suppose that God wills 'let there at t be an agent with a libertarian-free choice between doing and not doing act A; if the agent chooses to do A, let the choice initiate a causal sequence which terminates in B's existing, and if the agent chooses not to do A let the choice initiate a causal sequence which terminates in C's existing.' In

---

[43] Those unfamiliar with this way of talking about subjunctive conditionals will find an explanation in the next chapter.

this case the agent will determine what God immediately creates, but it will still be the case that He immediately creates it—with the agent's help.

Nothing Biblical entails or even makes it likely that God late-creates this way. God could be only a remote cause of late creation. Still, if God is able to create *ex nihilo* at all, I see no reason that He would not be able to do this. And there is some reason to read Biblical talk of late creation this way. This model assimilates the sense in which God late-creates to that in which He creates at the universe's origin. It minimizes the difference between what He did for the first creatures and what He does for later ones. This permits a simpler, more elegant reading of the overall Biblical account of creation. Elegance is a virtue in theory construction. And this sort of simplicity is arguably a mark of truth. Further, this model involves God more intimately in making the world, and to many that will itself be another reason to think it correct. So we should accept this model.

Conservation

The NT asserts that God keeps all things outside Him in existence—conserves them—as long as they exist.[44] Expressing this another way, the NT teaches that God causes things to persist. We also cause things to persist: by breathing, I keep myself in being. So we must ask how God's contribution to things' persistence is related to creatures'. God may be able to conserve the universe as a whole by Himself. Having the same ongoing temporal sequence entails having the same universe; if one event occurs after another, they occur in the same universe.[45] If so, God can conserve the universe by Himself if He can cause time to pass without causing anything other than Himself (if He is temporal) to persist. I think this is possible, but the matter would take us too far afield. Apart from the universe, it may be that conservation cannot be a divine solo act. Many philosophers think that something now was something existing earlier only if the earlier thing made an 'immanent' causal contribution to the later thing's existence.[46] If this is true, God can conserve an earlier thing only if it also contributes to its own later existence.

We can extend our last model to the case of conservation and accommodate immanent causation.[47] For suppose that having willed S to make Mars, God also wills 'let Mars' appearance start an immanent causal sequence to its later existence at t**.' God thereby wills that Mars persist, and make the

---

[44] So *Colossians* 1: 17, *Hebrews* 1:3.

[45] If dualism is true, souls are in a broad sense part of the universe, and purely mental events still fall under this point. If only souls existed, they would constitute a universe, and the point would still apply.

[46] See again Zimmerman, *op. cit.*

[47] I take no stand on what this is and whether it is actually needed. My point is only that if it *is* needed, one can believe both in it and in conservation.

causal contribution due to which it persists.[48] God makes the creating-*ex-nihilo* sort of causal difference for Mars throughout its existence. Mars is there at each point in the sequence because God has so willed, and as an immediate effect, the whole sequence appears *ex nihilo*. The sequence consists of nothing but appearances of Mars, each immediately caused by an *ex nihilo* creative volition. Yet Mars also causes itself to persist. Generalizing, any creature persists as long as it does because God wills it to exist *ex nihilo* at every instant it exists. And if God in this way causes all parts of the universe to persist, God causes the universe to persist.

Where created free agency enters, we must complicate the story slightly. If Michaelangelo makes *David*, he arranges marble into *David* but does not account for the marble's existing. If God conserves the marble, God accounts for this: at every time, God makes the ultimate, creating-*ex-nihilo* difference between its being and not being there. So when the marble becomes *David*, God makes the creating-*ex-nihilo* difference between there being and there not being *David*. God does not usurp creature-complex C's contribution. So it is at least partly C's doing that what God makes this difference for is *David*, not something else. But as the stone that makes up *David* is always God's direct creative effect, when that stone becomes *David*, *David* is God's direct creative effect.[49] God directly, immediately creates *David* when *David* first appears, if only by conserving the stone. Thus 'late' creation is a consequence of divine conservation. Late creation by conservation is a natural extension of the last model, which we had some reason to adopt. So we have some reason to adopt it too, and I do. The alternative would be to treat God as a remote cause of persistence, in parallel with the second model.

If God always universally makes the creating-*ex-nihilo* sort of difference, nothing pops into being without a cause. Rather, whatever begins to be is the terminus of a causal chain involving God. So too, nothing continues independent of God. Rather, whatever continues to be is at all times the terminus of a causal chain involving God. Whether or not items *can* begin or continue to be without God's causal input, what I have laid out here suggests that neither actually happens. Rather, God is (directly or indirectly[50]) the Source of All that is 'outside' Him:

GSA. for all x, if x is not God, a part, aspect or attribute of God or an event, God makes the creating-*ex-nihilo* sort of causal contribution to x's existence as long as x exists.[51]

---

[48] I had it independently, but this thought also occurs in David Vander Laan, 'Persistence and Divine Conservation', *Religious Studies* 42 (2006), 173–4.

[49] On some theories of constitution I would have to rephrase this point.

[50] If God conserves B only by conserving A, God conserves B only indirectly.

[51] Classes whose sole ur-element is God might seem to be exceptions. But theists can easily do without classes (see Christopher Menzel, 'Theism, Platonism and the Metaphysics of Mathematics', in Michael Beaty (ed.), *Christian Theism and the Problems of Philosophy* (Notre Dame, IN: University of Notre Dame Press, 1990), pp. 208–29). Alternatively, one could add these classes to the antecedent.

(GSA) makes no claim about God's relation to events because though Biblical authors often say that God causes some event or other, they make no claim about whether God caused and sustains all of them. It is partly Michaelangelo's doing that God makes the *ex nihilo* contribution to *David* rather than a block of stone, but Michaelangelo does not cause Him to make it. Whatever Michaelangelo does, it is up to God whether He makes it, and fully in His power not to make it, but instead let the stone wink out of existence.

My treatment of creation and conservation gives us reason to treat (GSA) as part of the Biblical picture of creation and conservation. (GSA) creates a creation/conservation presumption. Someone who accepts (GSA) and recognizes a sort of non-divine non-event should take it as created and conserved. And someone who accepts (GSA) and suspects that a sort of non-divine non-event could not be created or conserved should seek to eliminate that item from his/her ontology, in favor of entities which do not conflict with (GSA). This presumption soon motivates an expansion of our topic and a rejection of some prominent sorts of metaphysic for necessity.

(GSA) is equivalent to

NG. (x)(if x is not God or a part etc., and is not an event x is not a 'given' for God)

—that is, something God finds rather than helps account for, and must either accept or work around. The move from (GSA) to (NG) is obvious. Nothing God created at the beginning was a 'given' for Him. And His *ex-nihilo*-type contribution to things' beginnings later in history keeps those things from being 'givens'. Though Michaelangelo carved *David* and God did not, God did not find *David* given to Him; He helped make *David*. (NG) is equivalent to

NG*. (x)(if x is is not an event and is a 'given' for God, x is God, part of God, and so on.

The move from (NG*) to (GSA) is also obvious. If only God or what is in God are 'givens' for God, no non-event exists unless He at least helps make it—for if He did not at least help, its existing would be something God just had to accept, and work around or counter, and so a 'given' for Him.

(GSA) and Perfection

I have suggested that (GSA) is part of what the Bible has to say about creation and conservation. It also says that God has the property $\lambda x(y)$(if y is not a part, aspect or attribute of or an event, x and only x makes the creating-*ex-nihilo* sort of causal contribution to y's existence as long as y exists): henceforth the GSA-property. I now argue that the GSA-property is both a perfection and a constituent of other perfections. I take it that a property is a perfection iff it is the maximal degree of a degreed good attribute to have. I premise a supervenience principle:

SP. if being F is a perfection and being F supervenes only on being G, being G is a perfection.

Surely if a perfect being ought to be F, and the only way a perfect being can be F is by being G, then a perfect being ought to be G, so that it can be F. (SP) does not turn attributes like existence, self-identity, or substantiality into perfections. No property supervenes on these unless all existents or substances have it. Nothing common to all things or all substances is the maximal degree of a degreed good attribute to have.

Being a potential ultimate source of some proportion of what benefits things is a good property to have. It is degreed; its maximal degree is the property of being a potential sole ultimate source of all that benefits things. So this is a perfection. The GSA-property gives God this property. This property supervenes only on the GSA-property: the only way something can be the sole ultimate source of *all* that benefits things is by being the sole source *ex nihilo* of all that does so. So the GSA-property is a perfection, by way of (SP).

Again, causal influence on non-divine substances' existence is a good thing to have. It can be misused, but there is value in having it, no matter what one does with it, even if one so misuses it that on balance the world would be better if one did not have it. This property is degreed. Its maximal degree is maximal causal influence on all non-divine substances' existence. The GSA-property gives God this property: either the two are identical or the GSA-property is its supervenience-base. Either way, again, the GSA-property is a perfection. So I suggest that the GSA-property is a perfection (and that we add it to the list of those the Bible ascribes to God). This becomes important in chapters 7 and 13.

The GSA-property is also plausibly a constituent of two other perfections. Developed accounts of omnipresence explicate this partly in terms of God's universal causal influence,[52] and plausibly omnipresence is a perfection. Again, God both has the GSA-property and can exercise the power to give existence freely, with nothing controlling His use of it—which entails that He can take away existence as well as give it. These jointly constitute the property of having complete control over the existence of all non-divine concreta. To control things is to have power over them. It is good to have power over other things' existence, though again this can be misused (and so on). Power over existence is degreed. Complete power over all other concrete things' existence is its maximum, and so plausibly a perfection.

---

[52] So, for example, S. Thomae Aquinatis, *Summa Theologiae* (Ottawa: Studii Generalis, 1941), Ia 8.

Conflicts

I have dallied with the Bible to set up conflicts between (1) and things which Western theists have reason to believe. These conflicts emerge on three assumptions. One is that

9. some strongly necessary truths are not about God and are not negative existentials.

This seems plausible. It is necessary in the stronger sense—unable not to be true—that 2 + 2 = 4. The claim that 2 + 2 = 4 is not a negative existential. And it is on its face not about God. Even if the referents of '2' and '4' are (say) divine ideas, without further premises (that God exists and has ideas, for example), the truth informs us only about arithmetic, not about God, and so it remains plausible that it is not about God. The truth does not wear its ontology on its sleeve. Note in any case that all I am doing here is setting up a problem. One solution to the problem would be to deny (9) on the grounds that such truths as that 2 + 2 = 4 really are about God, divine ideas, and so on.

The next is that

10. it is always the case that if a truth is necessary and not a negative existential, it has an ontology.

Plausibly, truth derives from the world somehow; plausibly it is true that I am bald because I am bald. A proposition represents reality as being a certain way. By so doing it lays down a condition. If reality meets the condition—if it is that way—the proposition is true. In my mouth, 'it is true that Fido is a dog because Fido is a dog' says only that Fido's being a dog meets the condition that *Fido is a dog* lays down, and so the latter is true. I explicate meeting the condition by way of ordinary semantic notions (for example, that Fido is the referent of 'Fido' and Fido satisfies '— is a dog' and so it is true that, etc.). If a truth derives from the world, its ontology is that of the world from which its truth derives—the items that together meet the condition. Stating a truth, *P*'s ontology is giving an account of what real items go into its being the case that P.[53] Perhaps for it to be the case that 2 + 2 = 4 is for there to be numbers, 2 and 4, which stand in relations expressed by '+' and '='. In that case, these numbers and relations are the truth's ontology. Perhaps it is for there to be a proposition true just in itself, not because of anything to which it corresponds, with which it coheres, etc. If so, the truth is its own ontology. Perhaps it is for us to have certain concepts or behavioral dispositions, or for there to be ultimate particles swerving particular ways in the void. The claim that a truth has an ontology makes no commitment as to what that ontology is. I alluded to concepts and dispositions because what a truth's ontology is may depend

---

[53] 'Real' is intended to be broad enough to give philosophers who believe in non-existent objects their day in court.

on what theory of truth is correct; one cannot assume that we should think of this notion in correspondence terms. If it were true purely by convention that $2 + 2 = 4$, that truth's ontology would be whatever goes into the existence of a convention—probably us and our dispositions.

To say that a truth has an ontology is not to say that it has a 'truth-maker'.[54] If truths have truthmakers, their truthmakers are in their ontology, but that they have an ontology is a weaker claim than that they have truthmakers. It does not imply such characteristic truthmaker-theory claims as that anything makes a truth true just by existing,[55] that a special truth-making relation[56] or one of 'grounding'[57] links ontology to truth, that there is a single item which bears this relation to a truth, that a truth's deriving from the world generates any sort of explanation for the truth's being true beyond what might be given in terms of reference, satisfaction, and so on,[58] or that truths assert that their ontology exists or are about their ontology.[59] (There may not be anything the truth 'Santa Claus is a fictional character' is about; there is a *prima facie* case it is about Santa, and there is no Santa. Its ontology may be human stories.)

(10) does not imply that these truths must always have the *same* ontology. The ontology of the claim that some geese are gray may consist in a land only the gray geese, and the population of these varies over time. For the moment I will not discuss the exception for negative existentials. It bears no weight in the current argument, and the reason for it emerges later. Consider the following claim:

> Nothing at all exists, abstract or concrete. Even if there are statuses for non-existents to have—Meinongian 'being' or 'subsistence' or 'pure *aussersein*',[60] merely possible being, whatever—nothing has any such status. All domains philosophers have talked about—the abstract, the concrete, the existent, the non-existent-but-nonetheless-having-attri-butes, and so on—are just empty.

---

[54] For truthmaker theories and their difficulties, see Helen Beebee and Julian Dodd (eds), *Truthmakers* (Oxford: Oxford University Press, 2005), and E. J. Lowe and A. Rami (eds), *Truth and Truth-Making* (Stocksfield: Acumen, 2009).

[55] For which claim see, for example, John Fox, 'Truthmaker', *Australasian Journal of Philosophy* 65 (1987), 189; John Bigelow, *The Reality of Numbers* (Oxford: Oxford University Press, 1988), p. 128.

[56] As in D. M. Armstrong, *Truth and Truthmakers* (Cambridge: Cambridge University Press, 2004), pp. 5–9.

[57] As in Jonathan Schaffer, 'The Least Discerning and Most Promiscuous Truthmaker', *Philosophical Quarterly* 60 (2010), 307–24.

[58] For which see, for example, George Molnar, 'Truthmakers for Negative Truths', *Australasian Journal of Philosophy* 78 (2000), 82; Josh Parsons, 'The Least Discerning and Most Promiscuous Truthmaker', *Philosophical Quarterly* 60 (2010), 309–10; Bigelow, *op. cit.*, 121ff.

[59] For being about truthmakers as a commitment of truthmaker theories, see Trenton Merricks, *Truth and Ontology* (Oxford: Oxford University Press, 2007), pp. 26–34.

[60] For which see Alexius Meinong, 'The Theory of Objects', tr. Isaac Levi, D. B. Terrell, and Roderick Chisholm, in Roderick Chisholm (ed.), *Realism and the Background of Phenomenology* (New York: Free Press, 1960), pp. 76–117.

If it seems to you that if this were so it would not be the case that $2 + 2 = 4$, you accept that the latter claim has some ontology. So I submit that (10) is quite plausible. Finally, I assume that

11. if a necessary truth not about God has an ontology, all of it lies outside God.

From these assumptions I reason as follows.

Let T be the totality of (9)-type mathematical truths. As they are necessary, T's truths have always been true. *Per* (10), there has always been some ontology for these. So *per* (11), there has always been something outside God. If so, (FD) is false. If God is temporal, at no time was He alone. If God is atemporal, something (or things) outside Him never began to be. For mathematical truths never began to be true. So either items in mathematical truths' ontologies have been individually beginningless, or there has been a series of ontologies for them which never began. If the latter, the series is a single, continuing candidate for co-eternity with God. Further, there was always a universe of non-divine things containing this succession, or perhaps just consisting of it, or its current member. If a universe is a single thing, then there has also been a single non-series which is a candidate for co-eternity with God. To evaluate the co-eternity claim we must consider scenarios. God's eternality rules it out that He began to exist, and the alternatives remaining when we eliminate this are:

12. God and what accompanies Him are both temporal and without beginning.

13. Both are atemporal, the 'universe' being an assembly of (say) abstract objects.

14. God is atemporal and what accompanies Him is temporal but did not begin to exist.

15. God is temporal but did not begin to exist and what accompanies Him is atemporal.

On all of these, neither God nor what accompanies Him began to exist, and intuitively (FD) is false, God and His accompaniment are co-eternal. Suppose now that

16. God is atemporal and what accompanies Him is temporal and began to exist.

Nothing eternal began to exist. So on (16), what accompanies God is not eternal, and so God and it are not co-eternal. But (16) faces difficulties. On (11), all ontology for necessary truths not on their surface about God—that $2 + 2 = 4$, for example—lies outside God. So on (16), all the ontology is temporal and began to exist. Thus it began to be true that $2 + 2 = 4$. Just as nothing that begins to exist is eternal, nothing that begins to be true is eternally true. So on (16) there are strongly necessary truths which are not eternal truths, true not from all eternity, but at best from the beginning of time.[61] This is at best incongruous. Further, if the ontologies are there only from the beginning of time, then either

17. had time not existed, $2 + 2 = 4$ would have had no ontology, or

18. had time not existed, $2 + 2 = 4$ would have had an ontology in God.

If (18), this truth would actually have this ontology. The plausible candidates for ontology in God are His nature, ideas, and powers, and God has these. But on (11), $2 + 2 = 4$ has only ontology outside God. So (11) rules out (18). As to (17), if God is atemporal, as (16), time is part of the universe outside God. God can refrain from creating. So on (16) it is contingent that there is time. So on (16) and (17), either it is contingent that $2 + 2 = 4$, or necessarily, if an atemporal God refrains from creating, time springs into being uncreated.[62] This seems false. Surely it is at least possible that an atemporal God not create and there be no universe at all. Thus (17) seems false as well, and so (16) seems ruled out. And so the conjunction of (1) and (9)–(11) entails ¬(FD).

On our assumptions, (1) also seems to conflict with (GSA). Whenever $2 + 2 = 4$, we are assuming, this has only ontology outside God. It is hard to see how the ontology could be only events. If it is not, (GSA) comes into play. If (GSA) is true, then on present assumptions God always makes the *ex nihilo* sort of difference for all $2 + 2 = 4$'s non-event ontology. So its truth causally derives from God. God helps explain its being true. But if it cannot but be true, we may think, there is nothing to explain about its being true. Its being true does not seem to need explaining. It does not seem even to admit of explanation, save if such derivations as it might receive in set theory count as explaining it—and in this case the intuition that what is here does not admit of explanation just transfers to the entire body of set theory involved. Again, on a view that used to be common, the ontology includes the hierarchy of pure sets.[63] It is not easy to see how God might create or sustain the null set; if He could not, nor could He create or sustain any other pure set. On a view now more popular, mathematics is the study of structures instanced *inter alia* by the pure sets. The structures exist either only if instanced or, if not instanced, as pure Platonic objects. If the first, God creates the structure (*simpliciter*) only if He creates all its instances, and so the pure sets. As to the second, many cannot see how God might create an abstract Platonic structure; Platonic objects, they say, just could not be caused to exist. Again, explanations answer why-questions. So if God helps explain it that $2 + 2 = 4$, there are legitimate

---

[61] If they continue from some point later in time, they are only contingently true. The same follows if God is temporal and what accompanies him began to exist.

[62] Or a truth which actually derives from the world could somehow not do so and yet be true—but how could this be so?

[63] That is, the null set, ∅, and all sets of which it is the sole ur-element: for example, {∅}, {{∅}}, and so on.

why-questions about this. But 'why is it that $2 + 2 = 4$?' or the equivalent question about the set theory seem absurd—particularly if read as asking for an efficient-causal explanation. If a question should not arise, it has no correct answer. *A fortiori* it has none invoking God. If $2 + 2 = 4$ has ontology outside God and God does not explain the existence of all of it, (3) and (GSA) are false. Further, if He does not and it includes, for example, pure sets or platonic structures, (1) and (8) are incompatible. God is not the only underived reality. Some of the ontology for $2 + 2 = 4$ also is or was underived. And what does not somehow derive from God is a 'given' for God, counter to (NG). He does not make or shape it. He finds it, and must work within the bounds it sets.

As Western theists have reason to believe (FD), (3),–(8), (GSA), and (NG), these are conflicts between (1) and things Western theists have reason to believe.[64] The (1)–(FD) conflict depends on the ontology being outside God. The rest depend on its being independent of God.

The Project

This book's topic is the challenge that necessary truths (and 'modal' truths more generally, as Chapter 4 shows) pose for the claim that God is the sole ultimate reality. Its basic question is 'How do bodies of necessary (or modal) truth relate to God?' It also briefly takes up a subsidiary challenge, about 'abstract objects', such items as truths, attributes, and numbers: does God account for their existence? Can God create numbers? God can make it true that Fido is a dog (say, by creating Fido), but can He make the truth that Fido is a dog, or the attribute of being a dog? I aim to sketch a theory that rests modal truth on God's nature and mental life, thus defusing its challenge to divine ultimacy. I do not develop it fully. To do so would entail giving full

---

[64] Plantinga suggests that what creates the tension between God and necessary truth is an 'aseity-sovereignty intuition' (Alvin Plantinga, *Does God have a Nature?* (Milwaukee, WI: Marquette University Press, 1980), pp. 34–6). (7) is weaker than Plantingan aseity; Plantinga takes this to imply not just that nothing accounts for God's existence but that there is nothing outside Him whose existence is even a necessary condition of His (*ibid.*, pp. 34–5). The existence of the abstracta Plantinga discusses would jointly account for God's existence only if they jointly composed His nature and His nature's existence would then account for His; both are eminently debatable. Plantinga takes the sovereignty bit of the intuition to be or imply that there are not 'beings whose existence and character are independent of God' (*ibid.*, p. 35). So (3) may imply this. But all Plantinga does to show that any theist actually has this intuition is cite a few arguments from Aquinas (*ibid.*, pp. 28–31). He says nothing of where it comes from or why theists should trust it if they find themselves with it. I have tried to fill in the gaps. Again, Plantinga has it that this intuition's 'central thrust ... is best understood in terms of ... control—of what is and is not up to God' (*ibid.*, p. 83), taking it that something is up to God just if it is fully in His power to have it the case and equally in His power to have it not the case. (FD) and (3)–(8) have nothing direct to do with control. God could be ultimate in their sense even if He had no choice about necessary truths. That He had no choice is the view at which Plantinga ultimately arrives (*ibid.*, p.140ff.), but he seems to see it as involving taking the aseity-sovereignty intuition with less than full seriousness (*ibid.*, pp. 125, 146). I will maintain that God does have options with regard to some, but not all, necessary truths, and take the intuitive basis for giving Him responsibility for necessary truths fully seriously nonetheless.

theories of the truths that are necessary, including those of logic and mathematics. This would require far more discussion than one book can give. What I present instead is a general account of what it consists in for a truth to have a modal status, and an account of what makes modal truths about creatures alone true. Chapter 1 develops some machinery for talking about necessity and possibility. Chapters 2–3 consider solutions to the conflicts developed here, and opt for one. Chapters 4–5 broaden the issue, motivating for theists the claim that God must stand behind not just the truth of necessary truths, but the truth and modal status of all modalized truths. Chapter 6 briefly introduces the broad sorts of theist theory available to explain modal truths about creatures, and considers arguments for the most popular family of theist theories: those basing modal truth on the divine nature. Chapters 7 and 8 argue against such theories. In Chapter 9, I show what the divine nature contributes to my view. Chapter 10 argues that God must think up things to consider making. Chapter 11 discusses how to take talk about divine concepts; I sketch a view on which there are no such things. Nonetheless, chapter 12 discusses God's mental life as if there were so. Chapters 13–21 develop my positive proposal about modal truth. Chapters 22–23 argue that it is true.

Our project concerns the necessary and the possible: modality. So I begin by explaining some basic modal notions.

1

MODAL BASICS

MODAL words indicate ways or modes in which propositions are true: they are necessarily true, contingently true, possibly true. They also indicate ways or modes in which items have properties: the wallpaper may be necessarily, contingently, or possibly red. The two sorts of use are linked, for propositions, if they exist, are items, and truth is a property. Modal words are a family linked to 'can'. I can become a Hindu. I can do this just in case it is possible that I do this.[1] I cannot become a number. I cannot do this just in case it is impossible that I do it. It is impossible that I do it just in case it is necessary that I not do it (that is, it must be the case that I do not). So I can become a Hindu just in case it is not necessary that I not become a Hindu. If it is neither necessary nor impossible that I become a Hindu, I either do so or do not do so contingently. Whichever is the case, the other might have been the case.

The standard logical treatment of 'can' translates sentences such as 'I can become a Hindu' into sentences such as 'possibly I become a Hindu', in which a modal word, 'possibly', modifies an entire sentence, or sentences like 'I possibly become a Hindu', in which a modal word modifies a predicate. 'Must' goes over into similar uses of 'necessarily'. Letting '$\Diamond$' symbolize 'possibly' and '$\Box$' symbolize 'necessarily', one can define either operator in terms of the other:

$\Diamond P =$ df. $\neg\Box\neg P$

$\Box P =$ df. $\neg\Diamond\neg P$.

From these we can derive further modal equivalences, such as

$\neg\Diamond P \equiv \Box\neg P$

or

---

[1] At least, this is so on one use of 'can'. Another implies that not only is this possible, but I also have an ability or power to do it.

$\neg\Box P \equiv \Diamond\neg P.$

The modal words are also connected to 'might' and 'would'. I can become a Hindu just in case I might (in *some* circumstance) become a Hindu. I must be human just in case I would be human no matter what.

Kinds of Modality

There are many senses of 'possible' (and so of the modal words linked to it). Here are three. What is nomically possible is possible given the physical laws there actually are. Equivalently, the nomically possible is what can co-exist with, is compatible with, or is consistent with physical law. What is physically possible is possible given the physical laws plus certain basic physical facts ('boundary conditions'—for example, the total amount of mass–energy in the universe). What is epistemically possible is possible given what we know. Each of these sorts of possibility is compatibility or consistency with some condition. Because each is possibility relative to some condition, we can call these 'relative' kinds of possibility. Each with its correlated kind of necessity, contingency, and so on, is a relative modality.

If we have the concept of a relative modality, we can also form the concept of a non-relative or absolute modality, the concept of being possible (and so on) not relative to some condition, but *simpliciter*. More than this is in fact hinted even in the way I have explained nomic possibility and the rest. For I have said that what is nomically possible is *possible* given so-and-so. There was no evident modifier or condition on 'possible' in this second use: I explained a relative modality by using a modal term in a way not obviously relative. If this was a genuine analysis, then relative modal concepts involve absolute ones. If it was at least a good explanation, then perhaps our understanding of relative modalities depends on an understanding of absolute modalities. We can at any rate see that we can form the concept of an absolute modality as follows.

The operator '$\Diamond_n$,' expressing nomic possibility, is such that a sentence '$\Diamond_n P$' asserts that

1. It is possible that P given that s_1 and s_2 and $s_3 \ldots$

where s_1 and so on state only and jointly state all actual natural laws. (1)'s logical form is $\Diamond(P \cdot s_1 \cdot s_2 \cdot s_3 \ldots)$. The thought in (1) is not that the natural laws make it possible that P or are preconditions that must be satisfied for it to happen that P, but just that one thing that can happen in worlds with the actual laws—one thing the laws allow—is that P.[2] (1) plugs the members of a set of sentences into the schema

---

[2] If one wanted to define kinds of possibility in terms of a subjunctive conditional, one could express (1) using the 'might' connective, $(s_1 \cdot s_2 \cdot s_3 \ldots) \Diamond\!\!\rightarrow P.$

It is possible that P given that __ and __ and ...

We could express the same schema more simply as

2. It is possible that P and __ and __ and ...

We can define each relative possibility operator by plugging the members of a different set of sentences into (2); for example,

$\Diamond_n P =$ df. $\Diamond(P \cdot s_1 \cdot s_2 \cdot s_3 \ldots)$.

Now if we understand the result of plugging the members of one set of sentences into (2), we are just as able to understand the result of plugging the members of another into (2), if we understand them. The null set, $\emptyset$, is a set (*inter alia*) of sentences. So we can understand the result of plugging the members of the null set of sentences into (2). Consider a sort of possibility for which we complete (2) with the members of $\emptyset$. With '$\Diamond$' so read, '$\Diamond$P' asserts that it is possible that P and a null set of other things be so, or more simply that it is possible that P. To say that P could be true given a null set of conditions is to say that P could be true, period. A sort of possibility P has given a null set of conditions is not relative to anything. It is absolute. And absolute possibility is really involved in (2). For (2) does not invoke possibility relative to a set of conditions. It speaks of the non-relative possibility of the conjunction of P and some conditions. This is why its '$\Diamond$' is not subscripted. So if we have relative-possibility concepts, we can form the concept of an absolute sort of possibility.

The operator '$\Box_n$,' expressing nomic necessity, is such that a sentence '$\Box_n$ P' asserts that

3. It is necessary that P given that s_1 and s_2 and $s_3 \ldots$

where the set contains those sentences it contained in (1). (3) is equivalent to $\neg\Diamond$ $(\neg P \cdot s_1 \cdot s_2 \cdot s_3 \ldots)$, $\neg((s_1 \cdot s_2 \cdot s_3 \ldots) \Diamond\!\!\!\rightarrow \neg P)$, and $(s_1 \cdot s_2 \cdot s_3 \ldots) \rightarrow P$. The first instances a schema,

4. $\neg\Diamond(\neg\_ \cdot \_ \cdot \ldots)$.

We can define each relative necessity operator by plugging the members of a different set of sentences into (4); for example,

$\Box_n P =$ df. $\neg\Diamond(\neg P \cdot s_1 \cdot s_2 \cdot s_3 \ldots)$.

One might restrict (4)'s substituends to sentences expressing what I soon call broad-logical possibilities. This would leave us free to define any more restricted sort of necessity. Still, one need not do this. If we do not, among the permissible values will be sentences expressing broad-logical impossibilities, and some sorts of necessity will be definable which are relative to these impossibilities; for example, that

$\Box_I P = df. \neg\Diamond(\neg P \cdot (Q \cdot \neg Q)).$

Every proposition will then be I-necessary. So I-necessity will be vacuous. But this does not mean that there is anything conceptually amiss with it. It is simply not useful. Perhaps this would be a consistent conception to which no real modality corresponds. If there is such a modality, bearing it would not exclude bearing other modalities.

Now consider a sort of necessity for which we enter the members of Ø in (4). With '□' so read, '□P' asserts that it is necessary that P given a null set of other things, or more simply that it is necessary that P. If P must be true given a null set of conditions, P must be true, period. A necessity P has given no conditions at all is not relative to anything. It is absolute. In defining such sorts of necessity, we fill in no blanks. So even if we restricted (4)'s substituends to the absolutely possible, the restriction would not apply to this case, and so no question of circularity would arise in defining absolute necessity. An absolute necessity is relative to nothing, and so to nothing absolutely or in any other way possible.

That we do not fill in the blanks in (4) is one way to cash in the idea that an absolute necessity is so 'no matter what'. Another emerges when we recall that (3) is equivalent $(s_1 \cdot s_2 \cdot s_3 \ldots) \rightarrow P$, and so (4) is equivalent to another schema:

3*. $(\_ \cdot \_ \cdot \ldots) \rightarrow \_.$

Now the result of not prefacing '→P' with a sentence is ill-formed. So we cannot express the absoluteness of a necessity *via* (3*) by not filling in blanks. The closest we can come is to note that it does not matter how we fill the blanks. Thus I note that

ORN. if P has only a relative necessity, it is not the case that with 'P' in the consequent blank, (3*) yields a truth no matter how we fill the antecedent blanks.

Suppose that it is only nomically necessary that P. Then if there are the actual natural laws, it must be the case that P. But change even one law, and it may not be the case that P. If this were not so, P's necessity would not be only nomic, i.e. only relative to the actual natural laws. P could also obtain in situations not involving those laws, and so would have a more-than-nomic necessity. So if P is only nomically necessary, the result of filling the consequent-blank in (3*) with 'P' and the antecedent-blanks with sentences stating all and only the natural laws is true, but some results of filling the antecedent blanks with other sentences are false. Thus (ORN) is true. If (ORN) is true, it follows that if (3*) yields a truth no matter how we fill the antecedent blanks, P does not have only a relative necessity. Instead, the necessity that P is absolute. That (3*) yields a truth no matter how we fill the other blanks is another way to make sense of the claim that a truth is true 'no matter what'.

Narrow-logical Modality

One family of absolute modal concepts arises from the fact that what entails a contradiction just cannot be true, period.[3] Consider the claim that

AB. all bachelors are unmarried.

The contradictory of (AB),

some bachelor is married,

entails a contradiction, that some man is married and is not married. With (AB) in the consequent blank, (3*) yields a truth no matter how we fill the antecedent blanks. Every proposition whose contradictory entails a contradiction likewise passes this test for absolute necessity. To see that (AB)'s necessity is non-relative or unconditional in a slightly different sense, note that if we suppose that some bachelor is married, then as the conditional

If some bachelor is married, all bachelors are unmarried[4]

is true, we can still detach (AB). (AB) comes out true even if we suppose it to be false. So too, if every material conditional with (AB) as a consequent is true, then for any P, (AB)'s truth requires neither that P nor that ¬P. Thus its truth depends on no condition whatever—even the condition that its contradictory is not true.[5] So any modal concepts built entirely on facts about entailing contradictions must be absolute.

Leibniz wrote that 'a necessity which takes place because the opposite implies a contradiction... is called logical.'[6] We can define the Leibnizian narrow-logical modalities this way:

P is narrow-logically impossible = df. *P* entails a contradiction.

So

P is narrow-logically possible = df. *P* does not entail a contradiction.

As that is necessary whose contradictory is impossible,

P is narrow-logically necessary = df. ¬*P* entails a contradiction.

P is narrow-logically contingent just if it is narrow-logically possible but not narrow-logically necessary. There clearly are theses that entail and theses that do not entail contradictions. So there are facts of Leibnizian, and so absolute, modality. This definition employs entailment, which is usually explicated in

---

[3] *Pace* the dialetheists.

[4] Just how to symbolize ordinary indicative conditionals is philosophically tricky, but this can probably be taken as a material conditional.

[5] This is not to deny that if we suppose (AB) false, it winds up the case that (AB) is both true and false. But if it is true and false, it is true.

[6] G. W. Leibniz, 'Fifth Paper', in H. G. Alexander (ed.), *The Leibniz–Clarke Correspondence* (Manchester: Manchester University Press, 1956), p. 56.

modal terms, as strict implication (though most think this at best an imperfect account). I define strict implication in terms of what I shortly call broad-, not narrow-logical modality, and do not define the broad-logical modalities in terms of entailment. I thus avoid circularity.

Other sorts of narrow-logical modality court more controversy. Suppose one says that what entails the contradictory of a thesis of (say) classical propositional or first-order quantificational logic with identity (henceforth just 'classical logic') also just cannot be true, period. Intuitionist logicians, relevant logicians and others will contest this claim. Further, fully supporting it would require defending an account of logical truth *and* of its modal implications. (There is nothing incoherent about the concept of a contingent logical truth.[7]) Still, if we bracket all this we can start from this claimed necessity and define what we might call classical narrow-logical modalities. Since the principle of non-contradiction is a thesis of classical logic, every Leibnizian impossibility is also a classical impossibility, and so too for necessities.

Broad-logical Modality

There are also absolute modalities which are not either sort of narrow-logical modality. Necessarily,

R. nothing is red and green all over at once.

This necessity is more than nomic. The laws strictly imply (R): no matter what, if (for instance) $E = Mc^2$, (R) is true. But equally, no matter what, if $E = Mc^3$ (a different law), (R) is true. And this means that the necessity that (R) is stronger than nomic.[8] In fact, our intuition is that altering natural law, however greatly, cannot affect whether (R). This is a matter independent of natural law. This necessity does not seem relative to any further condition; it seems to rest solely on the nature of color itself, and so to be absolute. But though the matter has been controversial, ¬(R) does not seem to entail a contradiction, nor anything else contra-logical.

---

[7] See Edward Zalta, 'Logical and Analytic Truths That Are Not Necessary', *Journal of Philosophy* 85 (1988), 57–74.

[8] A necessary truth is one that would hold no matter what. 'No matter what' in effect means 'no matter whether this or that or that . . . occurs.' Different sorts of necessity differ by having a different 'no matter what'—because there is a different range of situations such that they would hold no matter whether this or that or that of them occurred. What is nomically necessary, for instance, would be true in any possible situation whose physical laws were just like ours. To say that a claim would be true no matter whether S_1 or S_2 or S_3 obtains is to say that it would be true in all of them. In effect, a '□' is a universal ('all') quantifier over possible situations, saying that the sentence it governs would express a truth in all of these, or that the predicate it governs would be satisfied in all of these. The more situations the '□' quantifies over, the stronger the necessity it expresses. So if every situation with our laws is an (R) situation, but there are (R) situations with laws different from ours, the necessity that (R) is stronger than nomic or physical.

Again, necessarily, Socrates is a substance. As Socrates exists contingently, we must read this as that necessarily

S. (x)(x is Socrates ⊃ x is a substance).

The worst ¬(S) entails is (∃x)(x is Socrates · ¬(x is a substance)). This is not a contradiction, nor does it entail anything contra-logical.

Again, mathematical statements seem to be necessary truths. So consider such contra-mathematicals as that $1 + 1 = 3$ or that $2 = 3$. These are impossible, but the impossibility does not seem to involve violating classical logic. These are inconsistent with mathematical theses: it cannot be the case that $2 = 3$ if, interpreting succession as a relation among the natural numbers,

no two natural numbers have the same successor;

$2 = 1$'s successor; and

$3 = 2$'s successor.

These jointly entail that $2 \neq 3$. So $2 = 3$ entails their joint negation. But their joint negation does not seem to entail anything contra-logical. Again, if mathematics is a body of necessary truth, the widely accepted claim that mathematics in some sense 'reduces' to set theory[9] entails that the axioms of the set theory to which it reduces are also necessary. But the negations of any of these axioms do not seem to entail anything contra-logical. In particular, the Zermelo axioms assert that there are an infinite and an empty set. It does not contradict classical logic to deny these exist.

Our two sorts of narrow-logical modality are built on the claims that

C. necessarily, no contradiction is true, and

CL. necessarily, no contradictory of a classical-logical thesis is true.

Let us ask what (C)'s 'necessarily' can signify. *Per* my treatment of (4), any appeal to an applicable relative modality would simply bring us back to some sort of absolute modality.[10] It would be circular or infinitely regressive to take this as Leibnizian. A regress would not explain at all. It does not seem satisfactory to rest with a circular account here. True, in some families of terms, one cannot break out of such circles, and can only try to explicate terms in the family by making the circle as wide as one can and invoking

---

[9] For a selection of testimonials to this effect see Stephen Pollard, *Philosophical Introduction to Set Theory* (Notre Dame, IN.: University of Notre Dame Press, 1990), p. 1.

[10] Swinburne defines the naturally necessary as 'the fully caused' (Richard Swinburne, *The Christian God* (Oxford: Oxford University Press, 1994), p. 117). This may not apply to (C): we do not at first blush think of it as caused that no contradiction is true. In any case, a full cause just is a cause a statement of whose activity entails the occurrence of its effect by way of statements stating appropriate natural laws. It is a fully explanatory cause, and the sort of explanation involved involves entailment. Entailment is a modal relation: strict or perhaps relevant implication. Swinburne offers a non-modal, conventionalist account of entailment; I argue that it will not do in 'Swinburne on Divine Necessity', *Religious Studies* 46 (2010), 141–62.

examples—for example, moral terms. But when it comes to (C),[11] the circle seems unacceptably narrow. For if (C)'s necessity is Leibnizian, (C) amounts at once to

C*. that some contradiction is true entails that some contradiction is true,

which is vacuous. (C) does not seem vacuous. But (C) is vacuous if (C) means (C*). (C*) does not tell us not to expect to find true contradictions, while (C) does tell us this. And (C) certainly does not *seem* like a case of P→P. Furthermore, on a modal account of entailment (as strict or relevant implication), (C*) in turn amounts to

necessarily, it is not the case that some contradiction is true and no contradiction is true,

which includes (C) and so cannot illuminate it, and then on a Leibnizian account of the modality amounts to

that some contradiction is true and no contradiction is true entails that some contradiction is true,

which is again vacuous. Again, in our definitions of the narrow-logical modalities, the right sides give the meaning of or explain the left sides. So if the impossibility in (C) is Leibnizian, (C*) gives the meaning of or explains (C). But we have already seen good reason to say that (C*) does not give the meaning of (C). Nor can (C*) explain (C). It is hard to see how a case of P→P could explain anything, but in addition it seems instead that we need to bring in (C) again when considering (C*). For when we consider (C*), we think this tells us why (C) is true only if we covertly add that (C): that is, (C*) only seems relevant to why something is impossible if we suppose that contradictions cannot be true and add this to the consequent. So I take it that we have a coherent, contentful concept of Leibnizian modality only if we also have a coherent, contentful concept of at least one other sort of absolute modality, which we can bring in to explicate (C).

  If we put classical modality into this role, things do not improve much. In explicating (C), we get not (C*) but

C**. that some contradiction is true entails that something contra-classical-
      logical is true.

(C**) is not a case of P→P, but still seems nearly vacuous, while (C) does not. (C**) does not tell us not to expect to find true contradictions, while (C) does tell us this. So again, it appears that (C) does not mean (C**). And we think (C**) tells us why (C) is true only if we covertly add (CL), which satisfies us

---

[11] Robert Adams points to this as a problem-case ('Divine Necessity', in Thomas Morris (ed.), *The Concept of God* (Oxford: Oxford University Press, 1987), p. 43), but develops the problem differently.

only if we do not explicate its 'necessarily' *via* either (C) or (CL). On a modal account of entailment, (C**) amounts to

it cannot be the case that some contradiction is true and nothing contra-classical-logical is true,

which still includes (C). Further, once we try to explicate classical modality, the same sorts of questions arise about (CL), with much the same results. Now we could launch an infinite regress of types of narrow modality here: we could have ever richer (and more controversial) logical bases, such as second-order logic, third-order, tense, and so on. But it should be apparent that doing so will not rid us of this sort of difficulty. So eventually we must appeal to a sort of absolute modality which is not narrow-logical.

Plantinga calls this sort of modality 'broadly logical', Kripke 'metaphysical'.[12] To avoid a regress of kinds of absolute modality or a circle, we must not explain this sort of modality in terms of (any modal concept of) entailment. The extensions of broad-and narrow-logical modalities are related this way. It is broad-logically impossible that what entails something contra-logical be true. So whatever is narrow-logically necessary is also broad-logically necessary. But there are (I have suggested) cases of broad-logical necessity which are not cases of narrow-logical necessity. If so, not everything narrow-logically possible is broad-logically possible: if it does not imply a contra-logical that something is red and green all over at once, this is classically possible, but it is not broad-logically possible. If nothing implying a contra-logical is broad-logically possible, everything broad-logically possible is narrow-logically possible.

I use the term 'absolute modality' for broadly logical modality henceforth, as narrow-logical modalities will not concern us. Absolute modalities are objective. That is, whether a thing is (say) absolutely possible is independent of whether any of us do or can conceive, believe, or know it to be so. Absolute modalities do not depend on how we describe things. They are not context-dependent.[13] Other objective modalities are definable in their terms: for example, it is nomically possible that P just if it is absolutely possible that P and s_1, s_2, s_3. Whatever is objectively possible in any other sense is absolutely possible, but perhaps not *vice versa*. Whatever is absolutely necessary is objectively necessary in every other sense: it holds no matter what, period, and so holds in, for example, every possible situation which would include our natural laws.

---

[12] Alvin Plantinga, *The Nature of Necessity* (New York: Oxford University Press, 1974), ch. 1, *passim*; Saul Kripke, 'Naming and Necessity', in Donald Davidson and Gilbert Harman (eds), *Semantics of Natural Language* (Dordrecht: Reidel, 1972), pp. 253–355.
[13] See Ross Cameron, 'What's Metaphysical about Metaphysical Modality?', *Philosophy and Phenomenological Research* 79 (2009), 3–4.

This book is about God's relation to absolute modality. It thus provides an account of God's relation to any other sort of modality definable in terms of absolute modality.

Possible Worlds

Possibilities—'things' which are possible—come in many sizes. It is possible that I become Pope. It is also possible that I become Pope and my wife is surprised. It is also possible that I become Pope, my wife is surprised, and my students are (as ever) unimpressed. Some possibilities are so large that were they realized, for any proposition P, either P would be true or $\neg P$ would be (assuming bivalence) or—if a third truth-value, indeterminate, be allowed— both would be indeterminate. For surely it is possible that truth-values be completely settled. Fully truth-determinate possibilities are the largest ones— wholly complete histories for a possible universe. A 'possibility' Π could be larger than one of these only by being such that for some P, both P and $\neg P$ would be true. Given bivalence, this is clear. Adding indeterminacy as a truth-status does not alter matters. Given three truth-values, Π could also be larger than one of these by having P and $\neg P$ indeterminate but also having the negation of *P is indeterminate* true. This is, of course, just another contradiction. A 'possibility' involving a contradiction being true would not be a possibility at all—it would not be something that could occur.

Thus possibilities have a natural maximal size. In whatever way possibilities are part of reality, maximal possibilities are part of reality. They have as much pre-theoretic claim on us as any other sort. Philosophers sometimes call largest possibilities possible worlds. So possible worlds have a pre-theoretic claim on us; I also express this by saying that they are part of our pre-theoretic modal thinking, though of course we are usually not aware of this when thinking pre-theoretically, and the argument that brought this to light is a bit of philosophy. Any modal metaphysics that is to be adequate to the pre-theoretic modal facts must find a place for them; that is, have something in it about what it is for worlds to be possible.

Every smaller possibility is embedded in at least one largest possibility. For given any smaller possibility, surely it is possible for it to be made actual ('actualized') and also one more proposition to be truth-determinate, and another, and another, and so on until we reach the maximum size. If a smaller possibility is embedded in more than one largest possibility, it is their intersection. The possibility that Leftow become Pope, for instance, is part of the possibility that Leftow become Pope and his wife is surprised, and so on, and part of the possibility that Leftow become Pope and his wife is unsurprised, and so on: it is what they have in common. Because every smaller possibility is part of some largest possibility, giving a metaphysical account of largest possibilities is one way to provide a metaphysic for all possibilities.

Formal Modal Semantics

The standard, Kripkean formal semantics for modal languages deals in possible worlds. A Kripke-style semantics for the modal locutions of a language L involves a sextuple $\langle W, w^*, R, D, Q, V \rangle$. W is the set of all possible worlds, w^* the actual world. R is a relation on the members of W—accessibility or relative possibility between worlds, explained below. D is the set of all possible individuals, Q a function that assigns to each world a subset of D (the individuals that exist at that world, that world's domain of first-order quantification), and V a valuation function that assigns to each predicate an extension at each world, to each constant a denotation at any world at which it has one and to each sentence a truth-value at each world.[14] Given these, Kripkean semantics assigns such truth-conditions to L-sentences as that $\Diamond Fa$ is true just in case there exists a member w of W such that the referent of 'a' exists at w (that is, $V('a') \in Q(w)$) and is in the extension V assigns to F at w (that is, $V('a') \in V('F', w)$). My own eventual proposal modifies this in some ways.

What are Possible Worlds?

Even if possible worlds have a pre-theoretic claim on us, it does not follow that philosophers' candidates for playing the possible-world role in a developed modal metaphysics do. These candidates are of three broad sorts. Start with the objects on which everyone agrees: actual, existing things. If you make do with just these, and say that possible worlds are some sort of actual, existing item, you are an actualist. If you add to your ontology either actual but non-existent or existent but non-actual items, and say that some of these are possible worlds, you are a possibilist.

'Possibilists' take as possible worlds universes enacting complete histories, most of them non-actual or non-existent. David Lewis holds that the actual world is everything spatiotemporally connected to us, and non-actual possible worlds are concrete, spatiotemporal wholes of the same sort as the actual world, but not spatiotemporally connected to us.[15] In his view, both the actual world and these other worlds exist. For Lewis, 'actual' is a token-reflexive term meaning roughly 'part of the spacetime whole of which this token is part.' Because he thinks this, Lewis holds that each world is actual at itself.

---

[14] The *locus classicus* is Saul Kripke, 'Semantical Considerations on Modal Logic', in Leonard Linsky (ed.), *Reference and Modality* (Oxford: Oxford University Press, 1971), pp. 63–72.
[15] David Lewis, *On the Plurality of Worlds* (New York: Basil Blackwell, 1986).

That is, if other worlds contain English-speakers who say of their world 'this is the actual world', they speak truly: they say that this world is the spacetime whole of which their token is a part. Further, anyone at any world who denies that other worlds are actual speaks truly, because in each case this just denies that these other worlds are parts of their own world. For Lewis, there is no other sense for 'actual'. In particular there is no sense in which one world is uniquely, absolutely actual.[16] Lewis is a possibilist for holding that there exist possible items that do not exist in the actual world. For him, other possible worlds exist, but not hereabouts.

Other possibilists hold that other possible worlds are items which do not exist here *or* elsewhere:[17] I will call them Meinongians, though some of them hold only part of the historical Meinong's full view.[18] Consider the phrase 'universe in which Leftow is Pope.' Unless Lewis convinces you, you will think that no such thing exists: I will never be Pope, and the actual universe is the only one that exists. So 'universe in which Leftow is Pope' is a description no existing thing satisfies. If we try to give the name 'W' to one particular Leftow-becomes-Pope world, 'W' will not refer to anything existent. Meinongians, however, would say that 'W' names a non-existent object: non-actual possible worlds, for them, are non-existent objects. (The rest of us are left wondering what this 'are' connotes.) Possibilism avoids contradiction only if '__exists' and '__is actual' express different concepts. For Lewis, all worlds exist, but not all are actual. For Meinongians, all worlds are actual, but not all exist: the actual state of things includes there 'being' many non-existent possible worlds.

Actualists believe only in actually existing objects. So for actualists, merely possible worlds are actually existing things. Thus they cannot be concrete universes, for there is no actual existing universe in which Leftow becomes Pope. But suppose, for instance, that there could have been a talking amoeba. On one actualist view, this is possible because there is at least one proposition 'big enough' fully to describe the content of a largest possibility, such that were it true, there would be a talking amoeba. Such actualists say that the proposition *is* the possible world in which there is a talking amoeba: it is the thing which is possible—that is, possibly true. For actualists, 'world' can apply to two very different sorts of thing: the concrete cosmos surrounding us, and such items as 'big' propositions. For actualists, all possible worlds actually exist: there actually are all the (say) 'big' propositions. Further, for actualists, there is a non-token-reflexive sense of 'actual' in which Socrates was actual and his less talented brother Mediocrates was not. Cognate to this is a non-token-reflexive sense of 'actualized': Socrates' parents actualized it that

[16] *Ibid.*, 92–6.

[17] So, e.g. Richard Routley, *Exploring Meinong's Jungle* (Canberra: Australian National University, 1980), p. 203.

[18] For which see Alexius Meinong, 'The Theory of Objects', in Roderick Chisholm (ed.), *Realism and the Background of Phenomenology* (Glencoe, IL: Free Press, 1960), pp. 76–117.

Socrates exists but not that Mediocrates exists. In this sense, for actualists, only one possible world is actualized.[19] Events actualize the actualized possible world: for example, on the 'big proposition' theory, they make only one big proposition true. I believe in only actual, existing objects, and in a non-token-reflexive 'actual' and cognate 'actualized'. So I use 'the actual world' or 'the actualized world' as if they refer to the abstract possible world which is in the non-token-reflexive sense actualized: for example, the big proposition that is true. I use 'the Actual Cosmos' to refer to the at least partly concrete whole which surrounds us.

Given the language of possible worlds, one can give an easy account of the absolute modalities. The actualist basics are these: a proposition P is true in a possible world W just in case that W is actualized entails that P, and an item exists in W just if that W is actualized entails that the item exists.[20] A proposition is absolutely possible just if it is true in at least one absolutely possible world, absolutely impossible just if true in none, absolutely necessary just if true in all, absolutely contingent just if neither absolutely necessary nor absolutely impossible. The modal operators '$\Box$' and '$\Diamond$' function as if they were quantifiers over possible worlds that $(\exists x)(Fx)$ is true just if at least one object in the domain quantified over is F. '$\Diamond P$' acts as if it quantifies over a domain of possible worlds and is true just if at least one object in the domain is a P-world; that is, a world in which P. So '$\Diamond P$' asserts that in some possible world, P, and '$\Box P$' that in all possible worlds, P.[21]

I do not believe that 'big' propositions or the like are possible worlds. I rather thoroughly do not believe this: I think that if there were such things, they would not be what the modal operators quantify over, and that in any case there are no such things.[22] Still, talk about possible worlds is a useful fiction. For (as I see it) there *are* things the modal operators quantify over, and the truth about them is the truth behind talk involving possible worlds. For no P is there a big proposition according to which P (or some other actualist world-entity). But for every possible P, there is a relevant divine power, and the modal operators, I will suggest, quantify over these. Just as there pretheoretically are largest possibilities, some of these powers have largest scope,

[19] This claim might be a simplification. If the future is as real as the present and past, a single possible world has been actualized, complete in all historical details past and future. But suppose instead that the present and perhaps past are real, but the future is in no way real. Then what has been actualized so far is a segment of history common to many possible worlds. Consider all the ways history might continue from now on. Each way it might continue is represented by an actualist-type possible world containing all of history up to now. The worlds share everything up to now and diverge hereafter. What has been actualized is just the common segment of all these worlds. So just one world has been actualized only when history ends (if it does).

[20] So Alvin Plantinga, *The Nature of Necessity* (Oxford: Oxford University Press, 1974), pp. 46–7.

[21] The *locus classicus* is Kripke, *op. cit.* For alternativee approaches, see, for example, I. L. Humberstone, 'From Worlds to Possibilities', *Journal of Philosophical Logic* 10 (1981), 313–40; John Perry, 'From Worlds to Situations', *Journal of Philosophical Logic* 15 (1986), 83–107; Robert Stalnaker, 'Possible Worlds and Situations', *Journal of Philosophical Logic* 15 (1986), 109–23.

[22] My thanks to a referee here.

and to describe the content of any of these is to describe the content of a complete pre-theoretic possible world.

God, Actualism, and Possibilism

I will set out a theist actualism. God, a realm of existing abstract objects, and a realm of non-existent or non-actual objects compete for many roles in metaphysics. I will try to show what is involved in the claim that God performs some of these roles, and begin an argument that God does a better job than His rivals. There are philosophical reasons to explore theist actualism rather than theist possibilism. These have to do with how hard it is to make sense of something's not existing but nonetheless being (say) a horse, the sheer implausibility of Lewis's theory, and my case (made later) that theist theories can do just by appeal to God all work possibilists do with their other entities: if this is so, theist possibilism would be ontological overkill. There is also a theological reason. I want to give God a large role in the metaphysics of modal truth. As I show in Chapter 4, one can do this on Lewis's view—but then one is left with what I show later to be a lot of needless ontology. On Meinongian possibilism, I now suggest, it is hard to give God a role.

On Meinongian possibilism, merely possible objects are the ontology of all modal truth. So the ontology of modal truth traces back to God only if God is the source of all possibilia. I can think of only four ways to maintain that He is. One is to say that God makes all objects, existent or not. But I do not see how one would go about making a non-existent object. It is not there before one acts, and it is not there after: so what would one's action change? A possibilist might say that in a non-existent but possible world W, a non-existent God creates a non-existent talking poodle, so that it is true at W that God exists and creates it—and so for every other possible world.[23] But this would just be a way to say that God *could* create these other things. It would say not that God is the source of non-existents, but that God could be the source of existents. Without some showing of how God as existing can be the source of non-existents, this claim would leave this non-existent God and the non-existent poodle independent of God's actual being and activity—just brute given parts of the furniture of reality. So it would leave modal ontology independent of God.

A second story might be an attempt at a better answer: non-existents are not sheer nothingness. God has concepts of all possible objects. By conceiving of them, He lends them some sort of 'being' short of actual existence, and

---

[23] A referee suggested this.

thus establishes them as merely possible objects or enables them to establish themselves as such. Variants of this story run throughout the Middle Ages, perhaps most famously in Henry of Ghent and Duns Scotus. Here too I am puzzled: I cannot see what 'being' short of existing would be, or why God's having a concept would impart it. The third story might be seen as an attempt to dispel the puzzle. God has concepts of all possible objects. Some He creates, some He does not. By omitting to create these, He becomes responsible for their non-existence and so 'establishes' them as non-existent objects. But I do not see why God's *failing* to do something would lend anything some sort of positive status. If God has a singular concept C and does not cause it to be instanced, no such thing as C describes exists. It hardly follows from this that there 'is' a C-instance He failed to make. The last story also tries to dispel the puzzle. On this one, we grant God singular concepts before Creation and deny that His having these lends any sort of being to anything. We instead suggest this. God has (in effect) a mental language featuring a body of empty singular terms. Because of this, the true quantificational logic from all eternity is 'free'; that is, it employs non-denoting singular terms and so makes appropriate changes in inference rules (such as denying that if Fa then $(\exists x)(x = a)$, on the grounds that it is true that Holmes is a detective but not that Holmes exists). The impression of a 'merely possible object' is a sort of shadow cast by the fact that there is an empty divine singular term 'a' such that $\Diamond(\exists x)(x = a)$. Meinongians think it is true that Holmes is a detective because there is a non-existent Holmes with some appropriate connection to the property of being a detective. This is chasing shadows. What is really the case is that there is a genuinely singular divine term, 'Holmes', whose substitution into '— is a detective' yields a truth. It is not that terms empty of existent referents are singular because they have non-existent referents, but that they are singular without referents. Theists might be happy with this, but I suspect that Meinongians would not.

Yet suppose there 'are' Meinongian possibilia of which God is not the source. Then from all eternity there was one existent—God—and all the possibilia there ever 'are'. The possibilia do not depend on God. They are all the modal ontology. God then either has no role in grounding modal truth or just overdetermines it. But consider the two overdeterminers. Mediocrates could have existed. This (we are now supposing) is so because Mediocrates himself intrinsically just 'is' and 'is' possible, and because of something about God—say, that He might have made Mediocrates. But God's ability to do so depends on the independent fact that there 'is' a merely possible Mediocrates to actualize. If there were not, He could do nothing about it: there just is not a viable story on which God could 'add' possibilia. So the primary ontology for *possibly Mediocrates exists* is non-existent Mediocrates himself: for it to be possible that Mediocrates exists is for Mediocrates himself to 'be' and bear the attribute of possibility. God is a needless busybody who chimes 'me too' after the argument is over. There may be more to say here, but at least initially it seems that theists who want to give God a role in the ontology of modality should not be Meinongians.

Modal Systems

One can ask about whether it is possible that P—that is, whether in any circumstances, however *outré*, it could occur that P. This is to ask whether in some possible world it is the case that P. One can also ask, 'Given that Q, would it be possible that P?' This question asks whether, were a world in which Q actual, a world in which P would be possible. The question is one of 'accessibility': put very roughly, were a Q-world actual, could its denizens bring it about or have brought it about that a P-world is actual? Its answer depends on what relations of accessibility exist among possible worlds.

There are three popular theories of how accessibility works among absolutely possible worlds, associated with three systems of modal logic: Brouwer (B), S4, and S5. I now supply some minimum information about these three systems.[24] B, S4, and S5 all hold that relative possibility is reflexive: each world is accessible from itself, or in other words, for all worlds W, were W actual, W would be possible. B adds that accessibility is symmetric: for all worlds W and X, if it is the case that were W actual, X would be possible, it is also the case that were X actual, W would be possible. One gets B by adding to the theorems the three systems share the axioms $P \supset \Box \Diamond P$ or $\Diamond \Box P \supset P$. S4 adds that accessibility is transitive: for all worlds WXY, if it is the case that were W actual, Y would be possible, and that were Y actual, Z would be possible, then it is the case that were W actual, Z would be possible. One gets S4 by adding to the common theorems that $\Box P \supset \Box \Box P$ or $\Diamond \Diamond P \supset \Diamond P$. S5 is the union of B and S4. So in S5, accessibility is reflexive, symmetric, and transitive. The S5 axiom is $\Diamond P \supset \Box \Diamond P$. There are *many* other systems of modal logic. These three are of particular concern here because many think S5 to be the correct logic for absolute modality, S4 is among its main rivals, and B makes the difference between the two.

Conditionals

A conditional sentence is (or is equivalent to) one whose main connective is 'if', such as:

5. dinner will be late if the pizza does not arrive soon, or

6. dinner would have been late if the pizza had not arrived then.

---

[24] For full discussion of these and other modal systems see G. E. Hughes and M. J. Cresswell, *An Introduction to modal Logic* (London: Methuen, 1968). I follow them (pp. 46, 49) in stating the axioms below with $\supset$ rather than $\rightarrow$.

In such sentences, 'if' introduces the 'antecedent' clause, that on condition of which the 'consequent' clause will be or would have been true. To stress this relation between the clauses, logicians usually rewrite sentences like (5) and (6) in this form:

7. if the pizza does not arrive soon, dinner will be late.
8. if the pizza had not arrived then, dinner would have been late.

(5) and (7) may be in the indicative, (6) and (8) in the subjunctive mood. But the pairs' difference may not really be in mood. (7) and (8), for instance, are both 'hypotheticals'. Each draws a consequence from an hypothesis, (7) from the hypothesis that the pizza will not arrive by a certain time, (8) from the hypothesis that the pizza did not arrive by a certain time. So perhaps the pairs differ only in tense, not mood.[25] Hypotheses about the future may yet turn out true. Hypotheses about the past have already turned out true or false, but we may or may not know that they have. If we know that P did not occur, a hypothesis that P is counter to the facts. We use subjunctive-sounding sentences like (8) to express 'counterfactual' conditionals, which draw consequences from such assumptions. If we do not know whether P has occurred, we draw consequences from P in indicative-sounding sentences such as

8*. if the pizza did not arrive then, dinner was late.

I follow common practice in calling (7) and its like indicative conditionals and (8) and its like subjunctive conditionals. But in so doing I do not commit myself to saying that they differ in mood.

Some thinkers argue that indicative conditional sentences do not express propositions—that there is not some single thing they 'say'.[26] If this is so, they are not true or false.[27] Instead, these writers argue, indicative conditional sentences express conditional beliefs, or commitments: by saying 'B if A', I do not affirm a truth or falsehood, that if A, B, but instead commit myself to adopting belief B should I learn that A. If indicative and subjunctive conditional sentences are both hypotheticals, differing only in tense, then subjunctives too express just commitments, not truths or falsehoods. All the same, I take it here, without argument, that at least some subjunctive conditionals *are* true.

[25] So Jonathan Bennett, 'Farewell to the Phlogiston Theory of Conditionals', *Mind* 97 (1988), 509–27, and Victor Dudman, 'Indicative and Subjunctive', *Analysis* 48 (1988), 113–22, to whom indicative/subjunctive is a matter of tense, not mood.
[26] See, for example, Dorothy Edgington, 'On Conditionals', *Mind* 104 (1995), 271–80.
[27] So, for example, Alan Gibbard, 'Two Recent Theories of Conditionals', in William Harper, Robert Stalnaker, and C. Pearce (eds), *Ifs* (Dordrecht: Reidel, 1981), pp. 211–47, and Dorothy Edgington, 'Do Conditionals Have Truth-Conditions?', in Frank Jackson (ed.), *Conditionals* (New York: Oxford University Press, 1991), pp. 176–201.

In indicative conditional sentences, 'if' links independent sentences. In subjunctive conditional sentences, this is often not so; in (6) and (8), 'dinner would have been late' does not really make sense as an independent sentence.[28] But logicians usually treat subjunctive conditional sentences like (8) as 'really' pairs of independent indicative sentences linked by a special subjunctive-conditional 'if'-connective, and so read (8) as

8**. the pizza did not arrive then > dinner was late.[29]

Some subjunctive conditionals with false antecedents—counterfactuals—have necessarily false antecedents, such as

9. if there were a greatest prime number, it would be divisible by 5; that is

9*. there is a greatest prime number > it is divisible by 5.

The antecedent of (9) is not just counter to fact but beyond the realm of possibility, and so we term such sentences 'counterpossibles'.[30]

A basic approach to judging whether a subjunctive conditional is true—the 'Ramsey test'—now enjoys wide acceptance. Stalnaker expresses it thus:

First, add the antecedent (hypothetically) to your stock of beliefs; second, make whatever adjustments are required to maintain consistency (without modifying the hypothetical belief in the antecedent); finally, consider whether or not the consequent is then true.[31]

We must read the test in terms of making a hypothesis that P rather than assuming that we *believe* that P.[32] There are such conditionals as 'if nothing existed, nothing would be possible,' 'if there were a round square, it would be round', or 'if I did not exist, my brother would be an only child.' If I believed that nothing existed, that I did not exist, or that there is a round square, my beliefs would be so irrational that there is no saying what else I might believe. But I can certainly examine the hypotheses that nothing exists, I do not exist,

---

[28] If it seems to, this may be because we implicitly construct a context for it. We may, for example, take it as a reply to a question ('What would have happened had the pizza not gotten there by 9?', 'All I can say for sure is that dinner would have been late'). If we do so, we really make sense of 'dinner would have been late' by embedding it in a conditional sentence, such as 'had the pizza not gotten there by 9, dinner would have been late.'

[29] Though there are dissenters, who hold that the same 'if' connective is at work in both indicative and subjunctive conditionals; for example, Brian Ellis, 'A Unified Theory of Conditionals', *Journal of Philosophical Logic* 7 (1978), 107–24; E. J. Lowe, 'The Truth about Counterfactuals', *Philosophical Quarterly* 43 (1995), 41–59. (8) is a would-conditional. There are also 'might' conditionals. These will not concern us.

[30] I believe the term is David Lewis's.

[31] Robert Stalnaker, 'A Theory of Conditionals', in Nicholas Rescher (ed.), *Studies in Logical Theory* (Oxford: Basil Blackwell, 1968), p. 102. For some controversy about the Test, see Peter Gärdenfors, 'Belief Revisions and the Ramsey Test for Conditionals', *Philosophical Review* 95 (1986), 81–93; Sven Ove Hansson, 'In Defense of the Ramsey Test', *Journal of Philosophy* 89 (1994), 522–40; Stephen Read and Dorothy Edgington, 'Conditionals and the Ramsey Test', *Proceedings of the Aristotelian Society* supp. vol. 69 (1995), 47–86.

[32] So Stephen Read and Dorothy Edgington, 'Conditionals and the Ramsey Test', 67–8.

or there is a round square, or think hypothetically about what would be true were these things so.

Possible-worlds semantics for subjunctive conditionals in essence turn the Ramsey test into a broad approach to such claims' truth-conditions.[33] There are many such theories, differing in detail.[34] But they all run broadly along these lines: a subjunctive conditional A>C makes a claim about what would be true if A were true, the world were different in just the ways needed to let A be true, and everything else remained the same. A>C is true iff, supposing A true and given the changes needed to accommodate this supposition, C would also be true. So a subjunctive is true iff in the relevant possible worlds in which A is true and the needed changes are made, C is true. Many propose the A-worlds most like the actual world as the relevant worlds.[35] Thus a subjunctive is true iff the A-worlds most like the actual world are C-worlds; that is, if no A-world most like actuality is a ¬C-world.[36] As counterfactuals' truth-conditions involve other possible worlds, counterfactual conditionals express modal facts.

---

[33] So Stalnaker, 'A Theory of Conditionals', 102.

[34] For a survey, see Donald Nute, 'Conditional Logic', in D. Gabbay and F. Guenther (eds), *Handbook of Philosophical Logic*, vol. 2 (Dordrecht: Reidel, 1984), pp. 387–439.

[35] So, for example, David Lewis, *Counterfactuals* (Cambridge, MA: Harvard University Press, 1973).

[36] Some accounts of vagueness would have to complicate this account, but we can ignore this.

2

SOME SOLUTIONS

THE Introduction set out conflicts between the existence of necessary truths not about God and theses that Western theists have reason to believe. I now consider four broad ways to deal with these conflicts, and suggest that theists endorse the last of them.

Solutions: No Ontology

One could block the argument for the conflicts by denying the Introduction's (10)—that is, denying that the truths discussed there have an ontology. This would deny more than that they have truthmakers. The latter denial is only that some bit of the world distinct from whatever it is that is true (sentences, propositions, etc.) bears an appropriate 'grounding' or explanatory relation to a truth's being true.[1] This leaves it open that this truth's intrinsic character explains its being true—that its truth stems simply from being the proposition it is.

I now argue that there is no way to get such a no-truthmaker view to yield a view in which necessary truths have no ontology. Consider the claim that if anything is round, it is round: perhaps this is true due just to its content. Some philosophers think that its content is necessary. For they think that its content is analytic (however that be explained), and that being analytic explains (or just is) being necessary.[2] But necessity entails truth. So one might infer that in this case content explains truth. One might then try to move from this to a claim that necessary truths have no ontology.

I do not think this will do. The argument that

---

[1] On this see, for example, D. M. Armstrong, *Truth and Truthmakers* (Cambridge: Cambridge University Press, 2004).

[2] I discuss this claim in Chapter 14.

1. S explains it that P,

2. P → Q, so that

3. S explains it that Q

is invalid: that I want to go to the store and believe driving the car will get me there explains my driving my car, and that I am driving my car entails that a car exists, but my beliefs and desires do not explain the car's existing. To avoid this, one might try the argument

4. □P → P,

5. (Π)(ψ)((Π→ψ)→ (that Π explains that ψ)), so that

6. □P explains it that P

But has an obviously false premise, (5): that 2 + 2 = 4 strictly implies that (P) (Q)((P· (P ⊃Q)) ⊃ Q) but does not explain it. The allied premise that

7. *P*'s having its content explains (subvenes) its being necessary that P,

8. its being necessary that P explains (subvenes) its being true that P, so

9. *P*'s having its content explains (subvenes) its being true that P,

Chapter 20 argues that (7) is false for strong necessity, and I shortly argue against (8). But at present I want to make only one point: on (7)–(9), necessary truths have an ontology. It is the truths themselves. It would not be on to disquote them away—to claim that all there is to its being the case that *P* is true is whatever there is to its being the case that P. For on (7)–(9) the truths themselves—their having their content, their being just the truths they are—bear an explanatory burden. They must be there to do so.

If *2 + 2 = 4*'s having its content—that is, being the proposition it is—entails its being true, then since it is essentially the proposition it is, it has being true as an essential property; that is, simply as part of its nature. This suggests an even sparer view along the lines of the last: not that content explains having truth as an essential property, but just that some propositions do have being true as an essential property.[3] There is no explanation for essences being what they are, one might say. With these we hit explanatory rock-bottom. Just as there is nothing to say about why if anything is Socrates it is human, there is nothing to say about why it is true that 2 + 2 = 4. Again, I make only one point. This view too assigns an ontology to the truth that 2 + 2 = 4. On this view, for it to be the case that 2 + 2 = 4 is for something—a proposition,

---

[3] So, for example, Stephen Schiffer, *The Things We Mean* (Oxford: Oxford University Press, 2003), p. 97.

sentence, whatever—to have an essential property: truth. This no-truthmaker view is not a no-ontology view. So it does not provide a way around the Introduction's conflicts.

Some philosophers argue that truths of mathematics are 'trivial', or require nothing of the world to be true.[4] They mean by this that their not being true would not be intelligible to us, this gives them truth-conditions no intelligible state of the world can fail to satisfy, and so there is no particular way the world has to be for them to be true.[5] Even on this account there is something its being the case that $2 + 2 = 4$ consists in: perhaps our being disposed to find it unintelligible that $\neg(2 + 2 = 4)$, perhaps all such homey facts as that these are two apples, those are two, and these and those are four, or perhaps that all the intelligible states are *these*.[6] Thus this too is a less radical claim than that $2 + 2 = 4$ has no ontology.

Some philosophers think that necessary truths get their truth 'for free', without truthmakers just given that they are necessary.

> Consider any necessary truth: let us say, that all triangles are trilaterals. Its truth is due simply to the fact that its denial is impossible. The answer to the question 'Why are all triangles trilaterals?' is simply 'Because it is impossible for plane figures with three interior angles to have some number of sides other than three.' Or one might answer it by presenting Euclid's simple proof that each plane figure has the same number of sides and interior angles. In either case, the answer does not specify... an object it identifies as the truth-maker... for the proposition.[7]

Here a number of points are apposite. The proof certainly convinces us *that* its conclusion is true, but I doubt it would tell us *why* it is true.[8] Not everything that entails a conclusion explains it, as we have just noted, and I doubt that the Euclidean proof's premises are any sort of real basis for its conclusion's truth. More important, this reasoning mistakes the question the truthmaker theorist wants to answer. The truthmaker theorist wants to explain not why all triangles are trilaterals, but why *all triangles are trilaterals* is true. These are distinct propositions even if they are necessarily equivalent, and distinct necessary equivalents can have distinct explanations: all necessary truths are necessary equivalents, but if anything explains it that all triangles are trilaterals, it does not explain it that $(P)(Q)((P \cdot (P \supset Q)) \supset Q)$.

---

[4] Ross Cameron, 'Necessity and Triviality', *Australasian Journal of Philosophy* 88 (2010), 401–15.

[5] So Agustín Rayo, 'Towards a Trivialist Account of Mathematics', in Otávio Bueno and Øystein Linnebo (eds), *New Waves in Philosophy of Mathematics* (Palgrave MacMillan, 2009), pp. 239–60.

[6] I base the latter on Agustín Rayo, 'On Specifying Truth-Conditions,', *Philosophical Review* 117 (2008), 385–443.

[7] So a referee.

[8] I will let the implicit claim that Euclidean geometry is a body of necessary truths pass; perhaps it is all ultimately definitional and so necessary, and if not, a better example could have been chosen.

Explanations of distinct *explananda* are often not in competition, and in particular truthmaker explanation and explanation by necessity or mathematical explanation (if there be such) do not compete. They are different kinds of explanation, and truthmaker explanations (if there be such) are compatible with other sorts even in explaining the same fact, let alone different ones: if its being true that I am writing this has a truthmaker, it is one which my beliefs and desires cause—and so the truth is both truthmaker and causally explained.

A more basic point is that even a truth with no truthmaker and only a mathematical or a sheer-necessity explanation may have an ontology. Its being necessary might have an ontology, and this would on the present view be the truth's ontology. Most basically, it does not seem to me that the impossibility of a contradictory—necessity—explains truth. The following argument, sketched in the quoted passage, is sound for all necessary P:

10. $\Box\neg\neg$P.

11. $\Box\neg\neg$P $\supset$ $\neg\neg$P. So

12. $\neg\neg$P. So

13. P.

Despite this, I now suggest that (10)–(12) do not explain (13).

Necessity does not explain

I begin with some counter-examples. It is widely held that the logic of absolute modality includes S5. In S5, if $\Box$P, then $\Box\Box$P. So in S5, if $\Box$P, then $\Box\neg\neg\Box$P. But that $\Box\neg\neg\Box$P does not explain it that $\Box$P. For it to be the case that $\Box$P is for it to be the case that P in all possible worlds. Given S5, for it to be the case that $\Box\neg\neg\Box$P is for it to be the case that P in just the same worlds. That in reality from which the one's truth derives just is that in reality from which the other's derives. This cannot license explanation in both directions. So as there is no reason to choose just one, it does not provide an explanation either way.[9] To say why $\Box$P, we might say why its ontology is there, and rightly arranged. But nothing explains itself, and so the account of this for $\Box\Box P$ cannot explain why the ontology for $\Box$P is there and rightly arranged. We might explain it that $\Box$P *via* a truth with some sort of conceptual or explanatory priority to the truth that $\Box$P. But it is not plausible that $\Box\Box P$ has explanatory or conceptual priority to $\Box P$. If there is any priority here, it seems to run the other way. Surely it would be odd to explain a necessity entirely by saying that it is necessary. If we are puzzled that $\Box$P, the puzzle might focus on

[9] My thanks to a referee.

its being P that is necessary, or on the necessity. If it is puzzling that P in particular is necessary, it is no less so that it is necessarily so. If the puzzle is that P is *necessary*, that $\Box P$ is necessary will not help: since $\Box\Box P$ is just $\Box(\Box P)$, the *explanans* raises the same puzzle that the *explanandum* does, and so no progress is made.

Again, in S5:

R. the relations of accessibility between possible worlds are transitive.

For (R) to be the case is for there to be among worlds the relations there are. For it to be necessary that R is for these relations to be transitive no matter which world one is looking from (so to speak). For this to be so in S5 is just what it is for (R) to be the case. Again, then, necessity cannot explain truth.

Again, it is widely held that identity-statements are necessary if true. So consider the claim that necessarily, BL = BL. Read as a strong necessity, this asserts that in every possible world, BL = BL. Read as a weak necessity, it asserts that BL = BL and in no possible world is it false that BL = BL. Neither would explain it that BL = BL. An explanation of this would be a good answer to the question 'Why is BL BL?' This does not sound like a question that has a good answer: one wants to reject it with 'Who else would he be?' But 'there was no alternative' just rephrases that rejection, and 'He had to be, didn't he?' just rephrases *that*. None leave us any wiser. What would explain here, if anything, would be an account of why there is no alternative. It will not do to call $BL = BL$ a consequence of a conceptual truth, that $(x)(x = x)$. For this alone does not entail it. It must also be the case that there is such a person as BL (or perhaps such an item as his essence[10]). Perhaps that BL = BL has no explanation at all. If it does, I see only two ways an explanation might proceed. One would appeal to the conceptual truth and the claim that there is, for example, a BL-essence.[11] While both may be necessary, their necessity would play no role in this explanation. It would require only that both be true. The other would run thus. If BL did not exist, nothing would be identical with BL. So it would not be true that BL = BL. Because BL exists, something is identical with BL: namely, BL. So because BL exists, BL = BL.

Again, there are good arguments that if God exists, He exists necessarily.[12] If God is truly the ultimate reality, nothing outside and independent of Him explains why God exists. God's existence is an existential fact than which none is more basic, and if He is *the* ultimate reality, it is one with which none are

[10] See Alvin Plantinga, 'The Boethian Compromise', *American Philosophical Quarterly* 15 (1978), 129–38.
[11] I later give God a role in there being the essence, thus providing a theist version of this.
[12] See my 'Divine Necessity', in Charles Taliaferro and Chad Meister (eds), *The Cambridge Companion to Christian Philosophical Theology* (Cambridge: Cambridge University Press, 2010), pp. 15–30. Even those who think God exists contingently might well grant the text's arguments conditionally—that is, as reasoning correctly about an assumption they reject: see, for example, Richard Swinburne, *The Christian God* (Oxford: Oxford University Press, 1994), pp. 144–6.

equally basic, *per* the Introduction's (4), (7), and (FD). So anyone who claimed that its being necessary that God exist explains God's existing could not both root this necessity in (say) Platonic possible worlds given independent of and outside Him and maintain that He really is ultimate. If necessity always explains truth and the ontology of necessity is in this way Platonic, God's existence derives from the Platonic realm's. It, not He, is the ultimate reality.[13] So if God is truly ultimate, only His nature could contain or explain a necessity that could explain His existence. Perhaps we can flesh out this explanation as follows, letting 'D' symbolize 'there exists a divine being':

14. something is the divine nature $\supset$ $\lozenge$D   (by the divine nature)
15. something is the divine nature   (premise)
16. $\lozenge$D   14, 15
17. $\square$(D $\supset$ $\square$D)   (by the divine nature)
18. $\lozenge\square$D   16, 17, by modal rule
19. $\lozenge\square$D $\supset$ D   instance of Brouwer axiom
20. D   18, 19.

(14) rests on the reasonable thought that attributes are as such things that *can* be had, and so if there is a divine nature, it is possibly exemplified. (16)–(20) are a standard modal ontological argument. If this really does explain God's existence, though, then unless God somehow accounts for (15) and the truth of Brouwer, this derives God's existence from facts independent of His existence, and so God is not the ultimate reality. His nature is more ultimate than He. If it is a kind of constituent of God, as in trope theories and some theories of universals,[14] it will be like a part independent of a whole but included in it. Parts are more basic in reality than their wholes if they are independent of their wholes, for then they do not derive their existence from them, and instead their wholes owe their existence to their parts' existing and being appropriately arranged. This provides an analogous sense in which God's nature would be more ultimate than God.[15] If it is not a constituent, the nature is 'outside' what bears it, linked to it by a relation of 'exemplification' or 'falling under'.[16] Here its priority will simply consist in the fact that it depends for existence on nothing concrete (as if it does not depend on its bearer it will certainly not depend on anything else), while God's existence requires—presupposes—its.

---

[13] Chapter 8 argues this point more carefully.

[14] Universals are shared properties—humanity, for example. Tropes are unshared, individual cases of properties—Socrates' humanity, for example. I explicate these and other theories of attributes shortly. For the general 'constituent' approach to attributes see, for example, Michael Loux, 'Aristotle's Constituent Ontology', *Oxford Studies in Metaphysics* 2 (2006), 207–50.

[15] This sort of consideration is plainly operative in Aquinas' arguments in *Summa Contra Gentiles* (Turin: Marietti, 1909), I, 18.

[16] See, for example, Peter Van Inwagen, 'A Theory of Properties', *Oxford Studies in Metaphysics* 1 (2004), pp. 107–38.

If this is correct, one can hold that God is ultimate and yet His necessity explains His existence only if one can make sense of mutual dependence between God and His nature. It is hard to see how this could work. Aristotelians, thinking in terms of 'formal' and 'material' causes, might say that God accounts for His nature's existence as a subject accounts for that of a non-Platonic attribute it bears, and His nature for God's as an exemplified essential attribute accounts for that of its subject. But on Aristotelian terms there has to be another player in this story. While in one sense it is God who bears His essential attributes, the Aristotelian story requires that something else also bear them in another sense. A particular is not there until its essence is instanced: I am not there until humanity is instanced. So it is not that I receive humanity and so exist, but that something else, my matter, receives humanity and so I exist. For Aristotelians, there must be an underlying item which 'receives' the essence, thus yielding the individual which bears the essence. There is no 'spiritual matter' to play this role in God's case. The notion verges on being contradictory; to be a spirit is precisely not to be composed of stuff. So the Aristotelian parsing of the mutual-dependence option fails.

The only other scenario I can imagine is this. If time had no first instant, perhaps at every instant, God does something which assures that for some further period His nature continues to exist, and then His nature's existing accounts for His existence. Perhaps God at t causes His deity and 'spiritual matter' to persist, to constitute Him later: but this requires 'spiritual matter'. If not, then perhaps God causes deity's later existence and deity later accounts for His. But this surrenders the claim that God's necessity explains His existence. What we have instead is that God's necessity is part of a scenario which, given that He ever exists, explains (only) His continued existence. I conclude that if God is truly ultimate, that He exists necessarily does not explain His existence.

Thus necessity does not always explain. So it is never a full explanation. It is not the full explanation in the cases I have discussed. In other cases—those without the features of my examples which block the claim that in their cases necessity explains—what explains is at least that the *explanandum* is necessary *and* lacks those features or has whatever positive character makes it lack these features. But really, I think it is something else. That it cannot be so that ¬P guarantees it that P. But this does not tell us why P. We do not know *that* until we know why it cannot be so that ¬P. Again, to claim that (10)–(12) explain (13) is to claim that there having been no alternative to P explains it that P. But it is one thing for there to be no alternative and another for P to be so. P might be so in many ways; it could be that what has no alternative is that some one of these many ways obtains. We do not know why P until we know how this sole alternative was realized. The story about this is what really explains it that P. If there is just one way for it to be the case that P, then it is a story about this one way that tells us why P, not the fact that there were no alternatives to it. An explanation from something actual takes precedence over a candidate explanation *via* the character of other possible worlds.

Necessity and supervaluation

One might think to get truth 'for free' from necessity by supervaluationism.[17] This is a semantic strategy to deal with some cases in which claims seem to lack truth-value. Consider a case of vagueness: there is no precise standard for exactly when someone counts as bald. Some people clearly are, some clearly are not, and in many cases we are unsure what to say. It is tempting to say that if one is in the 'unsure' zone, the claim that one is bald lacks a truth-value. Now there are 'unsure' cases because there is indeterminacy about the standard for being bald. Let us oversimplify for exposition's sake, and say that there are 'unsure' cases because there is no determinate maximum number of hairs one can have and still count as bald. If this is what generates 'unsure' cases, we might try to deal with them by stipulation. There are clear cases of baldness and non-baldness, and between the numbers providing clear cases of the one and those providing clear cases of the other are many numbers of hairs which we could with equal legitimacy stipulate to be the maximum for a bald person. The supervaluationist says that if an ascription of baldness would be true no matter which maximum hair-number we stipulated—that is, no matter how we resolved the indeterminacy—then it is true. Applying supervaluationism would treat all possible worlds as of themselves indeterminate as to which world is actual.[18] If P is necessary, P comes out true no matter how this indeterminacy is resolved—that is, no matter which world turns out actual. A supervaluationist could say that this makes P true. Necessary sentences say something true no matter which world comes out actual. So any necessary truth is true by supervaluation, independent of the contents of the actual world. One reply is that the standard modal semantics is not supervaluational.[19] So if we do not have reason to supervaluate elsewhere in our semantics—and I would argue that we do not—it would be too high a price in added semantic complexity (and *ad hocery*) to do so here just to preserve not an inference or a logical truth, but a debatable non-logical move. But even if we took necessary truth as supervaluationally 'true for free,' it would have an ontology. On this approach whatever ontology there is for necessity-claims just becomes the ontology of a necessary truth. I suggest, however, that it is one thing to guarantee truth, and another to be in a truth's ontology. That P is true in all possible worlds guarantees that P is true no matter which world turns out actual, but the worlds are not in the ontology for P.

---

[17] On this see Bas Van Fraasen, 'Presuppositions, Supervaluations and Free Logic', in Karel Lambert (ed.), *The Logical Way of Doing Things* (New Haven, CT: Yale University Press, 1969), pp. 67–91, and Kit Fine, 'Vagueness, Truth and Logic', in Rosanna Keefe and Peter Smith (eds), *Vagueness* (Cambridge, MA: MIT Press, 1996), pp. 119–50.

[18] Here and throughout I use possible-world talk without substantive ontological commitment. We have reason to acknowledge world-sized possibilities in advance of any account of their ontology. So one can acknowledge them without accepting any view as to their ontology. My world-talk is either a convenient fiction or purely non-theoretic (that is, without commitment to any particular ontology).

[19] See Chapter 18.

Truth for free, 2

Again, one might reason, 'if it is true in all possible worlds that P, part of this is that it is true that P in the actual world. So the ontology that provides truth in all possible worlds *ipso facto* provides actual truth. As their actual truth requires no further ontology, they are "true for free."' This argument goes through on Lewis's possibilism, on which the actual world is just one among the possible worlds, all alike concrete existents, and 'actual' is just an indexical picking out the world of the speaker. But reasons to reject Lewis's possibilism emerge later.

The argument fails on most other views of worlds. If the future is unreal, then no matter what non-Lewis view of worlds we take, so far no world is actual.[20] Only a history-segment common to many worlds is. If determinism is fales, this segment might continue in many different ways, and it plus each complete continuation would realize a different possible world. All that history has made determinate is which worlds definitely will not turn out to be the actual world—namely, those not including what has so far happened.[21] If determinism is true, it is determinate which world *is to be* actual. But if the future is unreal, the world is not yet actual. But if the future is unreal, the world is not yet actual. Not all of it exists or has existed; not all that ever will be true has come true. Yet P is necessarily true. So P is true in all possible worlds temporally before it is determined which world is actual. So its truth in all possible worlds does not include its truth in the actual world, since no world is yet the actual world. It only includes truth in the world which will eventually turn out to be actual, or in all worlds not yet precluded from being actual. Without supervaluating, the latter does not give us actual truth.

Suppose now that the future is real. Suppose too an actualism on which possible worlds are abstract. (I explicate this term a little below. For now, if you do not have a working sense for it, take it as just 'not concrete'.) Then there are all the abstract worlds, and in addition the partly concrete Actual Cosmos, whose content 'selects' one abstract world as the one actualized. The worlds include the world which has been selected. So part of P's being

---

[20] If God knows the whole future, the full content of future history is determinate. God's cognitive state might conceivably make the claim that a particular world is to be actual true, but does not make it true that it *is* actual if it is not yet so. Some might reply that if God is temporal, His foreknowledge, existing presently, is enough to 'select' one possible world for actuality. But this equivocates on 'select'. True, if we knew the contents of God's knowledge we would be able to pick out which world is to be actual. But God's knowledge does not make actual all that is part of the actual world: it does not determine the actual world to be the actual world, nor constitute its being actual. God's knowledge instead depends on what *will* determine it to be the actual world.

Given determinism, the contents of the first instant (if any) or of all time before some past determine which world is to be actual. It will be God's knowledge that determines this only if God's knowledge is what imposes determinism, and that world will not yet be actual.

[21] We usually say that it is possible that P just if some world possible from the actual world includes that P. If there is not yet an actual world, the most one can say is that it is possible that P just if some world possible from the so-far actual segment, or from some world including it, includes that P.

true in all worlds is P's being true in the selected, actual world. But it is not true that what provides truth in all possible worlds provides actual truth. What provides actual truth selects one particular world as the actual one. This is the Actual Cosmos's job, and it does this logically posterior to there being all the worlds to select from. So again, what provides necessary truth does not provide actual truth; actual truth requires a contribution from something which is not one of the abstract possible worlds.

On non-existent object—'Meinongian'—possibilism all possible worlds are alike concrete; what distinguishes the actual world is that it exists. Here what provides actual truth is what selects one particular world to exist. The Actual Cosmos, on the Meinongian view, just is the Meinongian world that happens to exist. But even so, the Actual Cosmos or part of it selects a world, itself, as the actual one. This is clear if the future is unreal. The Actual Cosmos began (let us say) with an opening instant whose contents precluded some Meinongian worlds' actuality. On indeterminism, as the Cosmos's history unfolded, each new instant's contents and their causal influence ruled out still further worlds: the so-far-existent Actual Cosmos left less and less of the Meinongian realm in the running. If finally there is no future left, the Actual Cosmos is fully determinate. At that point it rules out all Meinongian worlds but one, itself, from actuality. If the future is unreal but determinism is true, then if there was a first instant, its contents suffice to select the actual world in advance of its being fully actualized; if there was not, then for any t, that of the Actual Cosmos which there has been by t does so. The Actual Cosmos also selects itself if the future is real. Even if past, present, and future are all equally real, if event e had a cause, what explains it that the actual world includes e is some earlier event that brings it about that the actual world includes e rather than some rival outcome. Belief that the future is real does not commit one to denying that events have causes, and this is most of what we need for the self-selection thesis; the rest is that if anything shows up without cause, its doing so *ipso facto* selects for actuality some segment of history in which it does so. Here the overall view comes out enough like Lewis' for the argument to succeed. But the argument's success given some forms of possibilism does not imply that on these, truths that are necessary have no ontology. Instead, it gives these a large possibilist ontology. And we have seen, and will see, reason to reject possibilism.

Finally, one might argue from the claims that an assertion's ontology provides what meets the condition for what it asserts to be true and that if all possible worlds exist and □(Socrates exists ⊃ Socrates is self-identical), all worlds' existence provides what meets the truth-condition of *Socrates exists ⊃ Socrates is self-identical*. But the truth-condition for this is that either Socrates does not exist or he exists and is self-identical.

Disjunctions are true because one or the other disjunct obtains.[22] So either an existent Socrates is this truth's ontology or his absence explains its truth. The worlds do not provide either. They just guarantee that we get one or the other. Thus we have (at least so far) no reason to say that necessary truths get truth 'for free' without ontology. And as the example suggests, what makes a necessary truth actually true can be just part of the Actual Cosmos.

Negative existentials and the no-ontology claim

Certain negative existentials may be truths with no ontology.[23] Plausibly, for it to be the case that there is no Santa Claus is just for it not to be the case that there is one. For Santa not to exist is not for anything to be there, but for something *not* to be there. In particular, it is not for there to *be* an absence of Santa. An absence is not some spooky sort of entity. 'Absence' is just a convenient noun for talking about cases in which there is no entity at all. It is for fans of more commissive accounts of negative existentials' truth to explain why this will not do. If one accepts this account, one might think to get a no-ontology account of necessary truths by taking necessary truths as a sort of negative existential. For it to be necessary that P, one might suggest, is just for there not to be a possible world in which ¬P. One might then argue that the plain unmodalized claim that P is itself a sort of negative existential, true just because there is no possible world in which ¬P: that for necessary truths, being true just consists in being necessary, and so the ontology for $P =$ the ontology for □P.

But there is a problem here. Suppose that as this proposal assumes, a possible-world semantics for modal discourse is correct. Suppose too that there just are no possible worlds at all—or nothing to read possible-worlds semantics as quantifying over. If it is necessary that P, there is no possible world in which ¬P. But on the present supposition, equally there are no possible worlds in which P. It follows then that both *P* and ¬*P* are necessary. So even on the negative-existential move, there has to be at least one possible world to get the distribution of necessity to propositions right. But then its being true that P has an ontology—that world or some portion of it. And if one deals in possible worlds at all, of course, one obtains the wrong results if there is just one of them, for then whatever is not actual is not possible.

---

[22] Though for debate see Stephen Read, 'Ontology and the Disjunction Thesis', *Mind* 109 (2000), 67–79; Gonzalo Rodriguez-Pereyra, 'The Disjunction and Conjunction Theses', *Mind* 118 (2009), 427–43; Mark Jago, 'The Conjunction and Disjunction Theses', *Mind* 118 (2009), 411–15; Dan López de Sa, 'Disjunctions, Conjunctions, and Their Ontology', *Mind* 118 (2009), 417–25.

[23] There is not a vacuum in my room. This is a negative existential in good standing. But it has an ontology. It is true because there is air in the room. For present purposes I need not seek an account of just when negative existentials have and lack an ontology.

Necessary truths, then, have an ontology on this proposal. Still, there may be a nugget of truth here worth noting: even if they have an ontology, necessity-claims may have no truthmakers, even if other sorts of truth do. On the standard semantics, the truth-condition for a claim that $\Box$P is that in all possible worlds, P. So this is how it has to be in reality for the claim to be true; if there are possible worlds, they are in this truth's ontology, and if there are not, whatever world-talk is really about, or whatever there really is that world-talk somehow rests on, is in its ontology. Now for some worlds to be all the worlds is for there to be no other worlds than these. So for it to be the case that in all possible worlds P is for it to be the case that in world W_1, P, in W_2, P, and so on, and there are no worlds other than W_1, W_2, and so on.[24] A conjunction has a truthmaker only if each conjunct does. If negative existentials have no ontology, they have no truthmakers. So this conjunction has no truthmaker, even if all its conjuncts but one do.

If $2+2=4$ has no ontology, its being the case does not even consist in a truth-bearer's being true. Its truth-condition is such that it would be the case that $2 + 2 = 4$ even if (*per impossibile*) all philosophers' domains of reality were empty. So to speak, this would be a fact even if there were no facts. I confess that I just cannot get my mind around this. So it seems to me implausible to deal with our conflicts by jettisoning the claim that necessary truths have an ontology.

Solutions: Restricted Scope

If the relevant necessary truths have ontologies, our conflicts would dissolve if (FD) and (GSA) have restricted scopes and those ontologies fall outside them. Suppose, for example, that the ontology for *if anything is Socrates, it is self-identical* were two properties, being Socrates and being self-identical, bearing certain relations. One might then argue against a conflict with (GSA) in at least three ways. They invoke the property of being abstract, and so I now briefly introduce this.

We call such items as the attribute of triangularity, the number 3 or the proposition that all dogs have fleas abstract, though it is hard adequately to explain that term.[25] Proposed marks of the abstract include being nowhere in spacetime, being in spacetime only derivatively (as Socrates' wisdom may be where Socrates is), being able to be as a whole in more than one place at once without traveling in time and necessarily having no causal powers. Whatever

---

[24] Or that in what talk of world W_1 is really about, or what it really rests on, P, and so on.

[25] For some attempts, see Michael Dummett, *Frege: Philosophy of Language* (London: Duckworth, 1981), second edn, ch. 14, *passim*; Bob Hale, *Abstract Objects* (London: Basil Blackwell, 1987), pp. 45–66; Susan Hale, 'Spacetime and the Abstract–Concrete Distinction', *Philosophical Studies* 53 (1988), pp. 85–102; David Lewis, *On the Plurality of Words* (Oxford: Basil Blackwell, 1986), pp. 82–5; Gideon Rosen, 'Abstract Objects', *The Stanford Encyclopedia of Philosophy* (online).

marks we go by, as abstracta are relevantly like attributes and concreta relevantly like aardvarks, we are usually sure which a given item is. We are also sure that nothing is both at once, and almost as sure that nothing can change status, or be (say) both concrete and possibly abstract.[26] *Prima facie* there are abstract entities of some sort. If three things are triangular, then *prima facie* there is an attribute they share, triangularity, and a number, 3, which is their number. Most philosophers accept abstract objects of some sort—at least sets. Those who deny sets tend to replace them with entities equally abstract.[27] Given the concept of an abstract entity, arguments to defuse the (GSA) conflict include these:

i. Properties and relations are abstract. Abstracta cannot be caused to exist. (GSA) concerns only things of a sort to be caused to exist.[28] So there being abstracta outside and independent of God does not conflict with (GSA).

ii. The Biblical doctrine of creation is not intended to cover abstracta. For (a) it seems implausible that Biblical writers had abstracta in view when they asserted that God has created all things.[29] And (b) the religious significance of the latter doctrine for them was simply to 'ground their conviction that God has a claim on man's praise...worship and religious awe...and obedience', and their belief that God has enough power over what happens that we can rely on Him without fear.[30] If the Biblical

---

[26] The last *has* been denied. See, for example, Edward Zalta and Bernard Linsky, 'In Defense of the Simplest Quantified Modal Logic', in James Tomberlin (ed.), *Philosophical Perspectives 8: Logic and Language* (Atascadero, CA: Ridgeview Publishing Co., 1994), pp. 431–58.

[27] Many 'reduce' sets to attributes (Bertrand Russell, *'Lectures on Logical Atomism'*, in Robert Marsh (ed.), *Logic and Knowledge* (New York: G. P. Putnam's Sons, 1956), pp. 262, 265ff.; George Bealer, *Quality and Concept* (New York: Oxford University Press, 1982); John Bigelow, 'Sets Are Universals', in A. D. Irvine (ed.), *Physicalism in Mathematics* (Dordrecht: Kluwer, 1990), pp. 291–306. Armstrong replaces sets with states of affairs (D. M. Armstrong, 'Classes Are States of Affairs', *Mind* 100 (1991), 189–200). Field replaces sets with spacetime points (Hartry Field, *Science Without Numbers* (Princeton, NJ: Princeton University Press, 1980)). Field thinks points are not abstract (*ibid.*, p. 31). But they are abstract on perhaps the most common way to draw the abstract/concrete distinction: they cannot have causal powers. In General Relativity, if there is such a thing as spacetime, it may be causally involved: it has a curvature that influences matter's path through it. But points cannot have curvature. Only an extended region can be curved. That extended regions of spacetime have causal powers of a sort does not entail that unextended regions do or can. There is such a thing as being too small to have a power: their size makes quarks invisible. Field's argument that spacetime points are not abstract is simply that space's structure is known empirically, not *a priori*. But why think that all knowledge of abstract entities must be *a priori*? We know that there is such an attribute as *being a quark* a posteriori. Field's thought may be that empirical knowledge must have some basis in perception, and so in causal relations. But not everything we know about empirically need have caused our knowledge of it: there need only be *something* which caused our knowledge of it.

[28] So Peter van Inwagen, 'God and Other Uncreated Things', in Kevin Timpe (ed.), *Metaphysics and God* (London: Routledge, 2009), p. 19.

[29] Nicholas Wolterstorff, *Universals* (Chicago: University of Chicago Press, 1970), pp. 293–4.

[30] *Ibid.*, p. 294. Wolterstorff also contends about another sort of abstract object, properties, that 'if God did not exist...the proposition "God exists" would be false. And then the property of being...false would still be exemplified; it would still exist.... this property seems not to depend on God even in the sense that if God did not exist, it would not exist' (*ibid.*, pp. 292–3). But it begs the question of the scope of the Biblical creation doctrine to suppose that propositions (which are also abstract) and properties would exist in some non-deflated sense if God did not. For what we might say instead, see my 'Impossible Worlds' (*Religious Studies* 42 (2006), 393–402). Wolterstorff adds that 'it is presupposed by the Biblical writers that not all

doctrine of creation (and conservation) does not cover abstracta and (GSA) expresses (part of) this doctrine, there is no conflict between (GSA) and abstracta being there outside and independent of God.

iii. (GSA) quantifies over particulars, not properties and relations. So if God is not the source of these, this is compatible with (GSA). (GSA) is thus equally compatible with the existence of any sort of abstract entity outside the scope of its quantifier.

If any of (i)–(iii) succeeds, a parallel move might defuse the conflict with (FD): (FD), one might say, concerns only concrete things, and so does not really conflict with belief in eternal abstracta. The thrust of (i)–(iii) is that (GSA) is meant to range only over the concrete. One might argue similarly for a different restriction, to contingent entities.

Created abstracta

I submit against (i) that God could create some sorts of abstracta. Classes are standard examples of the abstract. But classes in some way just are their members together: there is no more to the class of all apples than the apples. Nor does 'together' signify some special relation elements must stand in to constitute classes. There is none: given the elements, there are the classes, period. So to create the class of all apples, God need only create the apples. The apples' existing entails and *constitutes* the class's. If He creates the apples, an act of *ex nihilo* creation causes the class to appear by causing everything that constitutes it to appear. What else could creating it consist in?

Again, if General-Relativistic spacetime regions are concrete, it begs no questions to say that God can create them *ex nihilo*. But if a region consists of points, as I now assume for argument's sake, God cannot create all of it *ex nihilo* without creating its points. If God did not create the points, there would be nothing of the region left over for Him to create. He could not create just the region and all its extended parts. For at the bottom-most level of decomposition, these all consist exhaustively of points.[31] If they were there in

exemplifications of . . . the property of being . . . true . . . were brought into existence by God, and thus that it was not brought into existence by God. For the propositions "God exists" and "God is able to create" (are) true . . . apart from any creative activity on God's part; in fact, creative ability on his part presupposes that these propositions are true, and thus . . . that there exists such a property as being . . . true' (*ibid.*, p. 292). I cannot resist an *ad hominem*: surely in whatever sense the Biblical writers could manage to presuppose that, they could also manage to include abstract objects in their creation doctrine's scope, counter to the text's (a). More seriously, a proposition's being true presupposes what makes it true, not *vice versa*. So it is not that God's being able to create presupposes that *God exists* and *God is able to create* are true, but *vice versa*. That being so, it would be tenable to claim that God always creates and conserves these propositions—that they always exist because He always makes them exist, and thus always are true due partly to a divine causal contribution.

[31] We have then the oddity that at one level of decomposition, concreta (regions) consist exhaustively of abstracta. This may sound worse than it is. It is usually thought a sufficient condition of being abstract to

advance and God incorporated them in regions, He did not make the regions *ex nihilo*. Instead, He made them out of the points. So either He made the points in making the regions or they appeared uncaused. But if they have no cause, why would they appear together with the regions? That cannot be a coincidence. The only non-divine answer that occurs to me is that given the regions God creates, truths of geometry might require their existence. But if God causes there to be a region whose geometry requires points, God brings it about that the points exist. He wills to make the geometry obtain; He does so by providing its ontology; if the geometry requires points, its ontology includes points. So if points are abstract, they too are abstract entities that God can create.

Turning to attributes, one realist view of them, associated with Aristotle, holds that they exist only 'in' their instances. God can create dogs. If doghood is an Aristotelian attribute, either God creates doghood by creating dogs, or doghood appears uncaused when God makes dogs. If the latter, God wills there to be a first dog, there cannot be a dog unless doghood appears, God does nothing to make doghood appear, but it just does magically appear where and when He needs it: some cosmic force, or sheer luck, or some power of logic to bring it about that Q when P entails Q and it comes about that P, gets God what He needs to complete His task of dog-making. It seems more plausible that God creates doghood by creating the dog. Other sorts of abstracta can be 'logically constructed' from sets, points, and Aristotelian attributes.

Aiming to restrict (GSA) to the contingent, one might argue in parallel to (i) from the premises that properties and relations exist necessarily and necessary beings cannot be caused to exist. But I see no good argument for the latter claim. If something exists necessarily, then it could not have failed to exist, no matter what. But this does not imply that it exists independent of all else. It might instead tell us that something or other would have caused it to exist, no matter what. Effects usually depend counterfactually on their causes. Usually, if something is caused to exist and its cause(s) had not occurred and had nothing take up their causal role, the caused item would not have existed. But this can be true if the effect exists necessarily. If the effect necessarily exists and necessarily is caused, this counterfactual has a necessarily false antecedent and so is true—and as I suggest later, its truth can be metaphysically significant.

---

necessarily lack causal powers, and this, I think, is the sufficient condition points meet. If GTR regions are concrete, it is in part because they have causal powers: their curvature affects the path of matter through them. But it is not unusual for items large enough to be able to have a certain effect to decompose exhaustively into items too small to have that same effect. I am large enough to cause an accurate scale to give a certain weight reading. None of the atoms composing me is, and I decompose exhaustively into these. So perhaps it is a tenable view that concrete regions decompose into items necessarily too small to have the effects regions have.

The Biblical points

Turning to (ii-a), I have already suggested that what Biblical writers had explicitly in mind does not exhaust the content of what they in fact said. But even apart from this, they asserted that God made *all* things. Concrete particulars are things, but in one sense of 'things', so are properties. It is not beyond conceiving that some Biblical writers, at least, contemplated a scope for 'all things' that included the abstract: *Prov.* 8:22 calls wisdom one of God's 'works'—something He made. Be this as it may, 'all things' is also a universal quantification. If Biblical authors meant 'all things' to cover only things of which they knew, then on meeting a kangaroo, they would have concluded either that there were things God had not made (things outside the 'all things' God did make) and yet they were still perfectly justified in claiming that God had made all things (since He made all the things they meant to quantify over), or that previously kangaroos had not been among the things God made, but now that they knew of them, they were. Either reaction would be odd, and so we have reasons of charity not to ascribe either to them. Surely they meant 'all things' to cover things known and unknown: they could not have believed that they knew everything 'all things' ranged over. But once grant this point, and it is hard to see why we should limit its scope to the concrete.[32] Ignorance can extend to whole ontological categories.

As to (ii-b), a doctrine's religious significance to an audience whose mindset we do not fully know can outrun what we have any textual basis to assume, and its content and implications can outrun its religious significance as well as any significance it had to its original audience. But if there are abstracta, plausibly creative responsibility for them would enhance God's claim to our praise, worship, awe, and obedience, and our confidence in His power, and responsibility for all of them would do so maximally. It would deserve awe to be a being for whom not even abstract things like attributes are 'given', one transcendent of even some of the most basic features of the world's ontology. Again, responsibility for things in our environment adds to our reasons to praise and worship God, and for all such things maximally so. If there are abstract objects, they are part of our cognitive environment. Concrete things have properties, relations, types, kinds, and roles. They form sets. They come in numbers. We know about these in knowing about them. Beyond this, on many theories, if there are abstracta, they are as really part of our physical environment as concreta. On many theories of attributes, if red apples surround me, so does redness, or so do their rednesses. And perhaps if the

---

[32] Sticklers might argue this: the phrasing is often 'all things in heaven and earth'. Many putative sorts of abstracta are not spatially located. So they are nowhere in heaven and earth. Only concreta have locations. But the phrasing is sometimes the simple 'all things'. And some putative sorts of abstracta would have locations (tropes, points, immanent universals).

apples surround me, so does the set they form. Moreover, if abstracta exist, some may be valuable. Jones is good because Jones is brave. So having properties contributes to the goodness of good things. Things which help make good things good have value just because they do so. If God deserves thanks, praise, and obedience for making the brave, He would deserve more for making not just the brave but also the property in virtue of which they are brave. Our debt to Him for the bravery around us would be deeper. Again, if it displays God's power to make concrete things, it would display it even more to make abstract ones (the more is made, the more is displayed), and most display it to make all of them. If God makes all sets, for instance, and the ontology of mathematics is that of set theory, then mathematical truths' being true displays His power. If He does not, but sets (or structures they instantiate) are mathematics' ontology, mathematical truth is not a display of divine power. If some other sort of abstract entity provides the ontology of mathematics, the point remains. Again, if God makes doghood, everything in the fact that Spot is a dog displays divine power. If He does not, not everything does so. So if the point of the doctrine is as (ii-a) says, plausibly Biblical authors who came to believe in abstracta would want to hold God responsible for them all. Their idea surely is not that God has done enough to deserve praise and so on (that is, made a big part of reality), but there are realms of reality for which He does not deserve praise and so on. If so, then if we mean to hold to their doctrine, once *we* have abstracta in view, if we uphold the creation/conservation presumption, *we* must take all abstracta to be created and conserved. If we say that the Biblical account of creation is less than universal in scope, the latter claim does violence to its spirit. And if there is much to this at all, any who jib at claiming that God creates abstracta can apply the creation/conservation presumption by trying to do without them. One can make like points against a (ii)-like argument to restrict (GSA) to the contingent.

The quantification move

Turning to (iii), if the last section is on target, the right response might just be that (GSA) expresses only part of the Biblical picture of creation and conservation, and another part is or should be that

> GAO. God creates and conserves all abstract objects outside Him,

and perhaps a parallel claim about necessary entities. Given my response to the Biblical points, the creation/conservation presumption applies to abstracta. Theists can follow it by positing at most sorts of abstracta God can create—sets, points, Aristotelian universals, tropes. Theists do not need sorts of abstracta not constructible from these. A Platonic abstract particular number, for instance, may not be something God could create. But theists do not need these. God's mind can contain the ontology for necessary truths of arithmetic—divine number-concepts, for instance, could do the trick. If God's mind can do the work, why posit more? God's mind is there anyway, if one starts from theism, so eliminating the numbers is sheer profit. Platonic universals can get a similar treatment. It seems right to say that God creates all that exists outside Himself. Abstract entities outside Him (if any) exist.

There are also perfect-being reasons to hold (GAO). We ourselves may cause some abstracta to exist: if I breed puppies, perhaps I cause there to be new sets of puppies, new doghood tropes, even a new Aristotelian universal for a new sub-kind of dog. If we do this, being able to cause some sorts of abstracta is part of what gives us value as agents: it is good to cause a child to be healthy, and if being healthy consists in bearing a health-trope, it is good precisely to be able to cause this trope to exist.[33] It would be a defect in God if He could not manage what we ourselves can manage and there were no explanation of this from some other divine perfection (as, for example, we appeal to God's character to explain the fact that though we manage to do wrong, He cannot). Perfect-being theology denies that God has defects, and it does not seem that some other perfection would explain an inability to cause new tropes to exist. Of course, if we cause tropes to exist, some might think it no big deal, and ask whether ability to do so really contributes to divine perfection. But that we can do something hardly entails that it is not a perfection to be able to do it—we can be morally good. In any case, God's perfection in this respect may consist partly in ability to do a great deal more of it than we can. And 'we can do it too' does not apply to necessary-being parallels to (GAO) or to necessary abstracta, making which would be God's sole prerogative. More generally, given things to have power over, it seems a perfection to have power over them.[34] If (GAO) is true, God has power over the existence of the abstract as well as the concrete, including anything necessary and abstract. *Ceteris paribus*, more power-over is better to have than less. Again, to be transcendent of and unlimited by the abstract as well as the concrete seems a perfection. So if (GAO) is a coherent claim, unless (GAO) would be incompatible with God's having an at least equally weighty perfection, God is a perfect being only if (GAO) is true.

---

[33] This applies to tropes and universals. One may wonder about sets: it is good to make three children healthy, but we do not give extra credit for making a set of three healthy children. But the only way to have power over the set is to have power over the health, and power over the set is a necessary by-product of this. So it is better to have power over the set than not to have it, though not precisely because it is power over a set. If God gets credit for sets precisely as sets it is because He provides most mathematical ontology and gets there first with it, I think.

[34] Though again, in the case of sets, this may be at least partly because it is a perfection to have power over other things and this brings power over sets with it.

Solutions: Safe Ontologies

If necessary truths not about God have ontologies and we cannot dissolve our conflicts by scope-restriction, we could defuse them by giving these truths ontologies that do not conflict with (FD) and (GSA).

Conventionalism and conceptualism

Some sorts of conventionalism hold that human conventions make necessary truths true: it is (they say) true due only to how we use words that a bachelor is an unmarried adult male.[35] These, then, might say that for it to be true that a bachelor is an unmarried adult male just is for humans to use words in particular ways. Conventionalism is compatible with (FD): our conventions began to exist long after Creation. It is also compatible with (GSA): God creates and conserves all that goes into adopting and maintaining conventions. In fact, conventionalism can bring necessary truths under God's sway. For God creates us and gives us our powers. So God can limit the conventions we can adopt by giving us only limited powers of language use. If God wants to bring it about that by convention, P, He can so construct us that any conventions we adopt will have us so use words that P. On conventionalism, then, necessary truth is no challenge to God's ultimacy.

On conceptualism, what makes it necessary that P is that P is true and $\neg P$ or some claim closely associated with $\neg P$ is in some appropriate sense inconceivable to us or idealizations of us, or perhaps (paralleling one sort of conventionalism) simply that $\neg P$ or the related claim is inconceivable.[36] It is sometimes not clear whether a conceptualist wants to say that absolute necessity *just is* inconceivability—to make a claim about the ontology of necessity-claims, and 'reduce' necessity to inconceivability—or say that necessity is one thing, inconceivability another which brings about, explains, or subvenes it. God creates and conserves all that goes into things' being inconceivable to us or our idealizations, and we came to be long after Creation. So conceptualism yields a safe ontology for necessary truths if it holds that inconceivability is sufficient to determine truth, and if not, it does so if conjoined with any safe proposal about what makes it true that P, e.g. a 'trivialist' thesis that if it is inconceivable that $\neg P$, there is no particular way the world has to be for P to be true. So conceptualist

---

[35] A. J. Ayer, *Language, Truth and Logic*, second edn. (New York: Dover Publications, 1952), p. 77. This is not the only conventionalist thesis that Ayer advances.

[36] So, for example, Nicholar Rescher, *A Theory of Possibility* (Pittsburgh, PA: University of Pittsburgh Press, 1975); Stephen Leeds, 'Possibility: Physical and Metaphysical', in Carl Gillett and Barry Loewer (eds), *Physicalism and its Discontents* (Cambridge: Cambridge University Press, 2001); 'Physical and Metaphysical Necessity', *Pacific Philosophical Quarterly* 88 (2007), 458–85. One could read Simon Blackburn this way ('Morals and Modals', in Simon Blackburn, *Essays in Quasi-Realism* (Oxford: Oxford University Press, 1993), pp. 52–74). Peter Menzies endorses a biconditional linking possibility and conceivability by an ideal conceiver, but not the claim that being conceivable *makes* a state of affairs possible ('Possibility and Conceivability', *European Review of Philosophy* 3 (1998), 255–77).

theories are or can be made compatible with (FD) and (GSA). And on this sort of view, God can determine what comes out necessary (and true) by determining what we are able to conceive.

But conventionalism and conceptualism about the truth of necessary truths sit ill with Western theism. It did not wait upon us that red is a color or that $2 + 2 = 4$. God had an opinion on these first. He was not wrong. And it beggars belief to suppose that His opinion was about what we would probably say if He made us, or what our cognitive limits would be. Even if (*per impossibile*) it were not possible that anyone other than God think or speak, God would have known that red is a color. Again, there are necessary truths about God, and it would be a defect in a theory of necessary truth to have one account for truths not about God and another, rather different account for truths about God; any theory that could plausibly bring both sorts within the scope of a single account would automatically be preferable just for being simpler. But if we extend conventionalism or conceptualism about necessary truths' truth to theism, God exists because we say He does or because His non-existence is (supposedly) in some sense inconceivable. If we extend conventionalism or conceptualism about necessity to the theist case, God's essence depends on us—perhaps He is omnipotent independent of us, but we made Him necessarily so, or He made Himself necessarily so by so making us that we make Him so. This is not plausible.

Stepping back from theism, it is possible that no humans exist. If conventionalism or conceptualism could not allow for this, that would simply be a large strike against these views. But on these views, with no humans around, nothing is necessary.[37] So on these views, possibly no truths are necessary. If so, all necessary truths are only contingently so. But to the extent that we have intuitions about iterated modalities, such truths as that if something exists, it is self-identical do not seem able to fail to be necessary. Further, $\Diamond\neg\Box P$ entails $\Diamond\Diamond\neg P$. Given S4, this entails $\Diamond\neg P$. So if we assume conventionalism or conceptualism and that S4 governs absolute modality, from any putatively necessary P we can infer that $\Diamond\neg P$: necessity disappears altogether. Thus any intuitions we have in favor of the claim that absolute modality's logic includes S4 and there are absolute necessities tell against conventionalism or conceptualism. Finally, a point specific to conceptualism: on such a view, actuality is tailored to our or our idealizations' cognitive limits. If failing a conceivability condition suffices for being impossible, whatever is possible meets that condition. So if only what is possible is actual, on conceptualism, the actual world consists wholly of states of affairs meeting the conceivability condition. But there is little reason to think that the world is in this way transparent to our minds.

---

[37] Unless (in the conceptualist case) there are facts about what ideal humans' or ideal conceivers' cognitive limits would be whether or not there are humans. But then these facts or whatever established them would be the most basic modal ontology; we would no longer be doing conceptualism.

Safe ontologies: non-divine powers

On 'non-divine powers' theories, all necessity is due to actual non-divine things' causal powers.[38] For it to be the case that $\Diamond P$ at t is (to a first approximation) for non-divine causes on the scene at or before t to have or have had the power and opportunity to bring it about that P or else to contribute causally to there being non-divine causes with the power and opportunity to bring it about that P, or contribute causally to there being non-divine causes with the power and chance to contribute causally to there being non-divine causes with the power and chance to bring it about that P, and so on.[39] This does not require that anything cause it that P if it happens that P. For it does not require that causes whose powers make it possible that P also bring it about that P. But if there neither is nor has been such a power, $\neg\Diamond\neg P$. Since $\Box P \equiv \neg\Diamond\neg P$, we might then say that its being necessary that P just *is* there not being or having been such a power. But this would not be quite right. Powers will still be the ontology of many necessary truths. For as I show later, 'powers' views are S5 views. In S5, all possibility-claims are necessary. But on 'powers' views, if possibly P, the ontology for this is a power appropriately related to its being the case that P. Further, suppose that there were no non-deities. Then there would be no non-divine powers to 'anchor' power-chains, and so no such chains. So for any P, there would be no chain containing a non-divine power to bring it about that $\neg P$, and so all propositions would come out necessary, and so true. Thus a non-divine-powers view delivers only the necessary truths we want only if there are enough powers to rule out necessary truths we do not want. So to speak, we need powers to push the boundaries of the impossible to where they should be. But this means that even if some necessary truths individually have no ontology, the whole body of necessary truths has the whole body of non-divine powers as its ontology. For just these truths to be necessary and those propositions to be impossible is for there to be just these powers and no others.

Non-divine-powers views sit ill with theism. It is contingent that God decided to create. But there has not been a non-deity able to bring it about, bring it about that another can bring it about, and so on,[40] that He never did. So on a non-divine-powers view, this contingent fact comes out necessary. Again, suppose that no non-divine power could ever bring it about that no quarks exist—perhaps God has a protection order on them. Then on a non-

---

[38] See, for example, Andrea Borghini and Neil Williams, 'A Dispositional Theory of Possibility', *Dialectica* 62 (2008), 21–41. Conventionalists and conceptualists hold 'non-divine powers' theories on which not all such powers count. On their views, a theist should hold, God delimits the necessary by determining what the relevant non-divine powers can and cannot bring about—only in this case, the bringing-about is of descriptions or conceptions.

[39] A better version would begin from Chapter 13's more elaborate account of causal possibility, then restrict the relevant causes to created ones.

[40] From now on, take this sort of addition as read where appropriate.

divine-powers view, necessarily there are quarks. But it does not follow that there are quarks. For God can bring it about that there are no quarks. So for a theist, a non-divine powers view cannot provide that necessity entails truth. Again, God can perform miracles within the power of no non-deity. On a non-divine-powers view, it follows that God can do the metaphysically impossible. But it cannot be correct so to treat metaphysical modality that the impossible can be actual. Again, no non-divine power could ever bring it about that God exists. So on the view we are examining, this is impossible. Yet God exists.

Stepping back from theism, no non-divine power could ever bring it about that there is no round square: at any time, it is too late, for there are already none apart from that power's causal input. So on a non-divine-powers view, it is impossible that there is no round square, and so the impossible is actual. Further, if it is impossible that P just if there is and has been no non-divine power able to bring it about that P, then since there has never been a non-divine power able to bring it about that there is or that there is not a round square, a proposition and its negation are both impossible. Again, corresponding to every power-chain moored in the actual world are what we might call non-divine-causally possible branches off actual history. If there actually is a power that can have (say) just effects 1, 2, and 3, there are three branches: one in which it has 1, one for 2, one for 3. If 1 has the power to lead to the existence of a power which can have effects 4, 5, and 6, there are branches from 1: 1 + 4, 1 + 5, and 1 + 6. Talk of these branches, carried through 'to the end' (if there is one) is what corresponds within such a view to talk of complete possible worlds. Here are some things true in every non-divine-causally possible branch off actual history (if there is no backward causation):

— there is or has been some non-divine concrete thing;
— there is or has been a Big Bang singularity;[41]
— there was no universe before our Big Bang (if there was none),[42] or
— there were one or more (if there were);
— temporal, spatial, and spatiotemporal relations are or have been exemplified (if the singularity counts as a point of spacetime[43]);
— there are or have been events;
— some events occur or have occurred which do or did in fact actually occur;
— the set of events that has occurred at some actual spacetime point has occurred;
— there have been items in spacetime;
— some mass/energy exists or has existed;

---

[41] Or the zone of quantum expansion with which some cosmologies replace it, or whatever else might take its place in alternative physical theories. From here on take this qualification as read.
[42] Whatever 'before' can mean here: perhaps only 'causally prior to or causally disconnected from.'
[43] If it does not, there will be some transform of this point.

— there has been the amount of mass/energy there at some time has
   actually been;
— the natural laws have at some time been what they at some time have
   actually been.

Intuitively, all these things are contingent. But on this view, if they occur in all
branches, they are all necessary. I add that if the world is deterministic, then at
the Big Bang singularity all future history was determined. This is good
reason to say that at that point a set of future-tensed propositions was true
which described all of history. But then on the present view these would all be
absolutely necessary. To reach the same point in another way, note that if the
world is deterministic, powers present at the Big Bang could produce only
what has actually occurred: there was no non-divine power to have things
otherwise. But surely, were the world deterministic, other histories would be
absolutely possible.

It is possible that there never was a Big Bang singularity. There was (we can
well suppose) nothing non-divine before the singularity; if time begins at the
singularity this is particularly clear. At the singularity, it is already too late (so
to speak) for this to be possible because actually so. Nor can the powers of
anything after the singularity ground this possibility. But the singularity has
no power never to have existed. Even if it did, or if we extended the view so
that non-divine things' natures could also ground possibilities and the singularity's nature made it the case that it need never have existed, nothing about
the singularity could make it the case that it need not have been replaced by
another such object. The singularity cannot have an effect on what might or
might not have taken its place had it never existed. This leaves only angels and
such as possible bearers of a power to bring it about that there is never a
singularity. I doubt that someone who wanted to avoid the divine in modal
metaphysics would feel better about angels; an angel would be relevantly like
a limited deity. In any case, this would require an angel around in time to
prevent the singularity, and so prior to it in some way. But if time begins at the
singularity, only a timeless being could be causally prior to it. Angels are
temporal, as standardly conceived. So a non-theist 'powers' approach seems
unable to ground this possibility.

Again, there could have been a physical universe distinct from any there
actually is. This need not entail replacing any actual universe: perhaps there
just could have been one more in addition to the rest. If we take 'universe' in a
sense which lets there be more than one of them, universes must be causally
isolated from other universes; plausibly if goings-on in one part of physical reality
can affect another part, those parts are parts of one universe. Given universes'
causal isolation, no power of any actual universe or universe-part can produce
another universe. Thus no power of any actual physical thing can make another
universe possible. A non-physical concrete thing can do this only if it can create *ex
nihilo*, for if it took matter from one universe to make another, the resulting

universe would not be causally isolated from its parent. But there is no reason to ascribe any such power to anything non-divine.

Again, it could have been the case that there are non-divine concreta, but none that actually exist. No power of any actual non-divine concrete thing could ever have made this possible, as no such power could have made it the case that there never were any non-divine concreta there actually have been. Nothing can make it the case that it itself never existed. So were any actual non-divine concrete thing around to try, it would be too late for it to succeed. Like reasoning applies to the claim that it could have been the case that there were from the inception of any universes there are only natural laws distinct from any that actually ever obtain anywhere.[44]

I do not claim to have disposed conclusively of any view I have discussed. But I think we now have at least some reason to think that these will not do. If they will not, theists must take another route. There is, for instance, an easy way to remedy the last defect of the non-divine-powers view: add divine powers. If there is an omnipotent God who has or had the power to bring about the negation of any state of affairs that should not have turned out necessary, they are all contingent. And perhaps it is true that $2 + 2 = 4$ because there is no power, not even in God, to bring about the negation of this.[45] Such a view is of course compatible with (FD) and (GSA). If God has not created, God is its entire ontology of necessary truth: as with the non-divine-powers view, it delivers the right necessary truths only given the right powers. I now turn to distinctively theist approaches to the Introduction's conflicts.

---

[44] For a similar point see Alexander Pruss, 'The Actual and the Possible', in Richard Gale (ed.), *The Blackwell Guide to Metaphysics* (London: Basil Blackwell, 2002), p. 330.

[45] I had the thought independently, but it is also in Jonathan Jacobs, 'A Powers Theory of Modality', *Philosophical Studies*, DOI 10.1007/s11098-009-9427-1 14.

3

THEIST SOLUTIONS

DESCARTES saw the ultimacy issue necessary truths pose:

> to say that... the mathematical truths which you call eternal... are independent of God is to talk of Him as if He were Jupiter or Saturn and to subject Him to the Styx and the Fates.[1]

Bayle took up Descartes' thought:

> If... propositions of eternal truth... are such by their nature and not by God's institution, if... he has recognized them as true of necessity, because such was their nature, there is a kind of *fatum* to which he is subjected; there is an absolutely insurmountable natural necessity.[2]

As Descartes and Bayle see it, either God is ultimate or 'eternal truths' are. There is no third option. If the eternal truths are ultimate, it is as if we stand with God under a sky not of His devising. If God is the truly ultimate reality, either God somehow includes that sky, or it is one more thing He brought to be. And while both speak of truths, the problem they raise is equally one about ontology.

Leibniz held that God includes the sky: 'This so-called *fatum*, which binds even the Divinity, is nothing but God's own nature, his own understanding.'[3] If God's nature is necessary truths' ontology, these truths derive from Him, for they are true because their ontology is as it must be for them to be true, and God's nature is as it is just if it exists. So these truths do not challenge His ultimacy. It does not matter that He cannot be otherwise. The point is that they rest only on what He is. Descartes, on the other hand, asserts that

---

[1] Anthony Kenny (tr. and ed.), *Descartes' Philosophical Letters* (New York: Oxford University Press, 1970), p. 11.

[2] Pierre Bayle, *Historical and Critical Dictionary*, p. 111, quoted in G. W. Leibniz, *Theodicy*, sec. 150, tr. Diogenes Allen in his *Leibniz: Theodicy* (Indianapolis, IN: Bobbs-Merrill, 1962), pp. 104–5.

[3] Leibniz, *Theodicy*, sec. 151, tr. in Allen, *op. cit.*, p. 105.

God is no less the author of creatures' essence than he is of their existence; and this essence is nothing other than the eternal truths.[4]

Descartes also said that

with (an item) existing outside thought ... essence and existence are in no way distinct ... in Peter himself, being a man is nothing other than being Peter.[5]

In short, for Descartes, eternal truths about creatures are creatures' essences, and the only reality creatures' essences have outside the mind is as the creatures themselves. If these things are so, these truths themselves are creatures—somehow, it seems, the creatures whose essences they are. Thus Descartes writes that

God established the eternal truths ... by the same kind of causality as he created all things ... as their efficient and total cause ... God is the author of everything and ... these truths are something and consequently ... he is their author.[6]

The mathematical truths which you call eternal have been laid down by God and depend on him entirely no less than the rest of his creatures.[7]

This would also explain Descartes' notorious claim that

just as (God) was free not to create the world, so He was not less free to make it untrue that all the lines drawn from the center of a circle to its circumference are equal.[8]

In the Aristotelian logic Descartes inherited, universally quantified conditionals have existential import. So if all lines drawn from the center of a circle to its circumference are equal, in this logic, it follows that there are circles. If this did follow and this truth existed only as the creatures which are its subjects—as circles—then had God refrained from creating, and so brought it about that there are no circles, this eternal truth would have been untrue. God was free not to create. So (Descartes may conclude) God was free to make the geometric truth untrue. On this reading, for Descartes, eternal truths about creatures are contingently necessary, as all creatures exist contingently.[9]

---

[4] Descartes to Mersenne, 23 May 1630, in Kenny, *Letters*, p. 14.

[5] Descartes to an unknown correspondent, 1641 or 1642, in Kenny, *Letters*, pp. 187–8.

[6] Descartes to Mersenne, 23 May 1630, in Kenny, *Letters*, pp. 14–15.

[7] Kenny, *Letters*, p. 11.

[8] Descartes to Mersenne, in Kenny, *Letters*, p. 11.

[9] Eternal truths about God Himself have a different status: 'the existence of God is the first and most eternal of all the truths which can be, and the one from which alone all the others derive' (Descartes to Mersenne, 2 May 1630, in Kenny, p. 13. See, for example, Norman Wells, 'Descartes' Uncreated Eternal Truths', *New Scholasticism* 12 (1982), 141–55; E. J. Curley, 'Descartes on the Creation of the Eternal Truths', *Philosophical Review* 53 (1984), 152–3). I cannot take up Descartes' account of logic here.

The conflicts between the existence of necessary truths not about God and important theist theses depend on the assumption that all these truths' ontology lies outside and independent of God. Leibniz moves it within God. Descartes leaves it outside but denies its independence. Both hold that God provides all necessary truths' ontology, though they differ on how He provides it. Leibniz' move should commend itself to theists who take Ockham's Razor seriously. For theists come to their thinking about necessary truth with God already in hand. If they can give an adequate account of necessary truth with no more than Him, any richer metaphysic of modality is for them otiose. Leibniz' metaphysic of the necessary is broadly Platonist. For 'Platonism' is our name for any theory which sees necessary truth as independent of human thought and language and of physical objects, and if modal ontology lies within God, necessary truths' truth is settled independent of these. But Leibnizian theism avoids a problem other sorts of Platonism face, noted by Paul Benacerraf.[10] One can summarize this in the present context as follows:

> If the ontology of necessary truths consists in things linguistic, conceptual or physical, we can come to know these truths, by grasping our own thoughts and language or by how the objects affect us. To Platonism, necessary truths' ontology is independent of thought and language and causally inert. As inert, it cannot affect us; as independent of thought and language, our access to these is not access to it. So we have no good account of how we could know necessary truths if they have Platonist ontologies: we can have an acceptable modal epistemology only by sacrificing Platonism.

Leibnizian theism blocks the argument by denying a premise: God is not causally inert. Now someone might reply that even if God can have effects, the effects He can have cannot constitute a knowledge-yielding causal path from the ontology of necessary truths to us, and so the Benecerraf problem survives the loss of this premise. But on a theist modal metaphysic this is not so. Suppose the ontology of a necessary truth P is something about God. God has cognitive contact with this, and it contributes to His knowing that P. Knowing that P and wanting us to know it, God brings it about that we believe that P—say, by hardwiring us innately to do so given suitable thought-experiments. Then our belief rests on a causal path from the ontology of the truth we know, just as it does when we know by sense-perception that a particular apple is red. For God has cognitive contact with the truth's ontology, this conditions His action and His action leads to our beliefs. How to build from this beginning to the conclusion that by our standard methods of belief-fixation we come to know that truth will depend on what account of knowledge we work with, but many sorts of account will let us complete the story. Yet the theist need not complete it to have a response to the revised Benacerraf argument. The theist need not say that God does ride to the rescue of modal belief. It is enough that He *can* do so: this lets the theist deny the revised argument's key premise.

---

[10]   See Paul Benacerraf, 'Mathematical Truth', in Paul Benacerraf and Hilary Putnam (eds), *Philosophy of Mathematics*, second edn. (New York: Cambridge University Press, 1983), pp. 403–20.

The Benacerraf problem is in effect that Platonism threatens us with skepticism about modal belief. Theists can go beyond blocking the argument to a broadly Cartesian reply. General belief in God's goodness favors the claim that He would want us to have largely correct beliefs. If there is a God who contains or creates all modal ontology and wants us to have largely correct beliefs about the necessary, this is reason to take our methods of modal belief-fixation as reliable and to think we can know necessary truths. So it would be a Cartesian response to modal skepticism to argue for a God who both determines or grounds necessary truth and gives us access to it. One such argument might start right here. The conjunction of modal non-skepticism and the claim that some form of necessary-truth Platonism is true can be persuasively backed. The more reason we have to believe it and the less credible the alternative responses to the Benacerraf problem, the more support a theist theory of the necessary gains, and so the more theism gains.

Note finally that theism without a theist theory of the necessary faces something like the Benacerraf problem: if necessary truths' ontology were independent of all *divine* thought, uncreated and causally inert, how could we make sense of *God*'s knowing necessary truths? So theists need a theist modal metaphysic to make sense of God's modal knowledge. This suggests, incidentally, that appeal to God cannot defeat Benacerraf's problem if the ontology of modal truth consists in Platonic entities He did not create and does not sustain.

Consequences of Divine Ultimacy

I suggest that God provides all necessary truths' ontology, and soon offer a position embodying this thesis. The Introduction's (FD) conflict depended on necessary truths' having ontology outside God from all eternity. So theists should hold that necessary truths have no such ontology. This rules out eternally created/sustained abstract entities. The (GSA) conflict depended on necessary truths' ontology being neither created nor sustained. The (GSA) conflict would arise no matter when this ontology existed; it did not depend on its being there from all eternity. So theists should hold that necessary truths never have non-divine ontology not both created if it begins to exist and sustained if continuing to exist. This rules out uncreated/unsustained abstracta, and if there is no way to create and sustain non-existent objects, rules these out too.

(GSA) has a lacuna. It does not cover events, and events have a strong claim to be part of our metaphysics. They plausibly are causes: plausibly the ball's striking the glass causes its shattering. They plausibly are effects: the shattering is caused. We seem to perceive them: we can watch the glass shatter. Perceptible items with causal relations have a strong claim to be real. If there are no events—that is, if the true metaphysics does not include them, even though we seem to see and talk about them[11]—we need not worry about how God relates to necessary truths about them. But if there are events, there are necessary truths about them, and plausibly the events are in those truths' ontologies. If 'd' names Napoleon's death, it is strongly necessary that either d does not exist or d = d. It is true that d = d just if d *is* identical to d. So d itself is part of the ontology of *d = d*. It is an item that goes into the world's meeting its truth-condition. So if there are events, events are in the ontology of some necessary truths. As there may be events, I now argue that if there are, they too fall within the scope of divine causation. The Bible is full of claims that God causes particular events and entire classes of events (for example, those involved in the continued orderly function of nature). But it is true of every event that it is in the ontology of necessary truths about it. So I can claim that God is responsible for all of all necessary truths' ontology only if I can claim that God is in some way responsible for all events. I now argue this.

God and Events

Events are concrete particulars which continue through time (a football game, say, for three hours) and have causal relations. So are we: not only is my existence (an event) caused, but I am caused to exist. Thus there is an argument by analogy here: events are in relevant respects enough like the paradigm items (GSA) covers that we should delete (GSA)'s clause excluding events. Again, if the point of the Biblical creation doctrine is as the last chapter's (ii-a) says, plausibly if they considered the matter, Biblical authors would want to extend (GSA) to events. For points like those made earlier about abstract entities apply here. If it displays God's power to make all concrete substances, it would display it even more to cause all events. Responsibility for all events would maximally enhance God's claim to our praise, worship, awe, and obedience. Responsibility for all things in our environment would particularly add to our reasons to praise and worship God, and if there are events, they are part of our environment—a part that affects us causally. Again, consider a simple event: a ball's rolling across a table-top from t to t*. The ball occupies a series of places, beginning with its place at t and ending with its place at t*: either at every instant it is in a distinct minimal place—one whose boundaries are those of the ball—or (if there are

---

[11] Perhaps the antecedent should be 'if the true metaphysics includes no events at its fundamental level.' On the plausible assumption that how things are at the fundamental level determines what is the case at higher levels, we need only worry about God's relation to a metaphysics' fundamental level and the principles which determine how the fundamental settles what is true at derivative levels. For accounts of the fundamental/non-fundamental distinction and its significance see, for example, J. R. G. Williams, 'Fundamental and Derivative Truths', *Mind* 119 (2010), 103–41, and Alexander Paseau, 'Defining Ultimate Ontological Basis and the Fundamental Layer', *Philosophical Quarterly* 60 (2010), 169–75.

no instants) over every period t–t* includes, it is in a four-dimensional analog of this. Its being in a place, and its state of motion while there, cause its presence and state of motion in later places. There is no more to the event than this. Now at every time from t to t*, God is conserving the ball in being. This is necessary to its persistence. If He did not conserve it, the ball would wink out of existence. Just by conserving the ball, then, He is conserving the event. He is making a causal contribution to its continuance—one such that if He did not make it, the event would cease (because the ball would disappear). So (GSA) leads us directly to a conservation thesis for events involving conserved particulars, and (GAO) to one for events involving conserved abstracta. But given (GSA) and (GAO) every non-divine item which persists is conserved.

Events not only occur but exist. (They fall within the range of existential quantifiers.) So at t our event began to exist. At t, God either created the ball *ex nihilo* or late-created it or was conserving it. So He contributed causally to the event's beginning to exist. If God both created or conserved the ball and was the sole cause starting it rolling, only He began the event, though perhaps He did not alone determine which event began. (It would not have been that event had it happened to a different ball. If God conserved the ball, the ball might have made a causal contribution to its own persistence—causal theories of identity over time insist on this. If it did, the ball played a role in the ball's being there to begin to roll, and so in the identity of the event.) We call God's causal contribution to the beginning of any non-divine item's existence creating it. So I suggest that there is a legitimate extended sense in which God creates such events when they begin. For events with created causes, the story parallels the Introduction's story about Michaelangelo and *David*: over time, Michaelangelo arranges his arm and a chisel into various positions and so into a particular event of carving, and at every time, God makes the ultimate, creating-*ex-nihilo* difference between this event's being and not being there by doing so for the particulars it involves, though the event's created causes account for its being a carving, not (say) a whittling to which He contributes. If this is right, then again there is a legitimate if still more extended sense in which God creates the event when it begins.[12]

My arguments drew on ordinary thinking about events, but developed philosophical theories of events create no problem for my conclusion. For Quine, for instance, an event is 'the content, however heterogenous, of some portion of spacetime, however disconnected or gerrymandered.'[13] This could just as easily describe a (four-dimensional) created/conserved object or congeries of such, and Quine in fact identifies events and 4D objects.[14] If this is the right story about events, (GSA) applies to them. If we

---

[12] Those who resist these suggestions can just say that some ontology of some necessary truths is only conserved, not created, and rephrase various claims in the rest of the book accordingly.

[13] W. V. O. Quine, *Word and Object* (Cambridge, MA: MIT Press, 1960), p. 171.

[14] Ibid.

transfer the Quinean view to a 3D universe, then every instantaneous temporal part of a Quinean event is identical with some part(s) of some 3D object(s) at that time, and so if (GSA) is true, God creates and conserves all temporal parts of all events by creating and conserving objects. Some take events as a kind of abstract entity: Chisholm, for instance, as a species of state of affairs[15] (a sort of entity he later 'reduced' to properties[16]), Montague as a property,[17] Lewis as a class,[18] Bennett as a trope.[19] Whatever these views' merits, they simply bring events under (GAO), and so universal divine causation follows. For Kim, an event is a subject having a property at a time;[20] for Lombard it is a temporally continuous change from a subject having a property at one time to its having a property at another, or some compound of these.[21] (GSA) gives us God's responsibility for the subjects, (GAO) His responsibility for the attributes. If there are times, they are abstract if they are temporal points or intervals of these, and so fall under (GAO). If they are not points or intervals of points, they count as concrete extended things, and so fall under (GSA). So God is responsible for everything that goes into an event on these views. And as we can easily parse our ball example in terms of these views, they pose no problem for my thesis about events.

I need not argue a theory of events here. Whatever their nature, I take it that God should be taken to be among events' sources—that is, that we should delete (GSA)'s exception for events. From now on, take this deletion as read. Abstract-entity theorists can accept this, for (GAO) follows from (GSA) thus modified. As to how God is causally responsible for events, for those with only God as cause this is no more (or less) problematic than divine causation generally. For events with both divine and non-divine causes, the additional question arises of how God and creatures may both causally contribute to their beginning and continuing. As we have seen, answers to this may resemble models of late creation and conservation discussed earlier, and such answers were elaborately discussed by the scholastics under the heading of how God 'concurs' with created causes.[22] Creaturely events with no non-divine cause may still have a divine cause. Given (GSA), if an electron E comes to exist without physical cause, E was created, and so God caused this event.

This leaves just creaturely events with no cause at all, divine or creaturely. I am a bit skeptical that there can be any, and by arguing to extend

---

[15] Roderick Chisholm, *Person and Object* (LaSalle, IL: Open Court, 1976), p. 126.

[16] Roderick Chisholm, *On Metaphysics* (Minneapolis, MN: University of Minnesota Press, 1989), p. 148.

[17] Richard Montague, 'On the Nature of Certain Philosophical Entities', *Monist* 53 (1969), 159–93.

[18] David Lewis, 'Events', in David Lewis, *Philosophical Papers* (Oxford: Oxford University Press, 1986), vol. 2, p. 245.

[19] Jonathan Bennett, *Events and Their Names* (Oxford: Oxford University Press, 1988), p. 90.

[20] Jaegwon Kim, 'Events as Property-Exemplifications', in Jaegwon Kim, *Supervenience and Mind* (New York: Cambridge University Press, 1993), pp. 33–52.

[21] Lawrence Brian Lombard, *Events* (London: Routledge and Kegan Paul, 1986), pp. 171–2.

[22] On which see Alfred Freddoso, 'God's General Concurrence with Secondary Causes: Pitfalls and Prospects', *American Catholic Philosophical Quarterly* 68 (1994), 131–56, and 'God's General Concurrence with Secondary Causes', *Philosophical Perspectives* 5 (1991), 553–85.

(GSA) I have argued that there are none. But let us suppose that there are some. If there are, each is essentially self-identical. So there are necessary truths about them. If (GSA) is true they cannot be Quinean; if (GAO) is true they cannot be abstract. They must instead be complex, as in Kim or Lombard, and the attributes they involve must be real abstract entities, else they will not be distinguishable from Quinean events. *Per* (GSA) and (GAO), they would not be anything beginning to exist; as I have argued, what begins to exist is created, and so its beginning to exist is caused. Nor could they be anything continuing to exist; absent created causes, divine conservation would cause persistence. (If a causal theory of identity over time is true, further, an item persists only if its earlier existence (immanently) causes its later, and so if such a theory is true, persistence without created causation is impossible.) I would argue that if a thing ceases to exist without created cause and (GSA) and (GAO) are true, God causes its ceasing to exist. For if without non-divine cause an item ceases to exist at t, God also ceases to conserve it, and this, I would argue, accounts for its ceasing to exist. If this is correct, uncaused events would have to be a persisting item's changing or continuing to be as it was. *Per* (GSA) and (GAO) the item would be conserved. If the change is an attribute's first appearing without physical cause, *per* (GAO) the attribute will be created, and this will be the event's cause. If the change is gaining an attribute which already existed, the attribute is conserved throughout, as it is through continued possession. If the item loses an attribute, *per* (GAO) the attribute was conserved until then. So the event's being uncaused can only mean that it has no sufficient causal condition. God contributes to it causally, but His contribution is only necessary, not sufficient. Such events occur only if God promotes their occurrence. He does so in a number of ways.

One is that He does not prevent them, though He could. If such events are possible, none occur with absolute necessity. God creates and sustains freely. It is in His power not to do so. (GSA) tells us that God creates and sustains all non-divine concreta, (GAO) all such abstracta. Thus every non-divine thing could have failed to exist: none exist necessarily. And so no event happening to them happens of necessity either. So a causeless creaturely event would have to happen contingently, because there only contingently are non-divine things for it to happen to. Now if God is omnipotent, God can bring about—at a very rough first pass—every contingent state of affairs.[23] If an event occurs contingently, one possible state of affairs is its never having occurred. So if God is omnipotent, God can prevent any contingent event. This gives us a thin sense in which God

---

[23] For a full account see my 'Omnipotence', in Thomas Flint and Michael Rea (eds), *The Oxford Handbook of Philosophical Theology* (Oxford: Oxford University Press, 2009), pp. 167–98. 'State of affairs' has an ordinary language use, which philosophers render slightly technical: as a philosophical term, 'state of affairs' denotes something a grammatical sentence would describe. The sentence 'The cat is on the mat' describes the state of affairs *the cat's being on the mat*. A state of affairs is (supposed to be) a way for things to be; one way for things to be is that the cat be on the mat. I do not think there are such entities as states of affairs, in the end. I use the term for convenience. In state-of-affairs lingo, all possible and impossible states of affairs exist—there are all these ways for things to be. They do not all *obtain*. A state of affairs obtains just in case things are that way; *the cat's being on the mat* obtains just if the cat is on the mat.

promotes any wholly uncaused event: He knew that it might occur and was able to prevent it, but instead let it occur. Still, the real meat of divine promotion lies elsewhere.

We have noted another sort of promotion: God contributes causally necessary conditions for such events' occurrence. Again, for any causeless event, God establishes natural conditions which promote its occurring. Such events occur only in accord with natural law. God determines the laws.[24] His putting these laws in place promotes any uncaused event that occurs even if the laws make the event very unlikely, because He could have put in place laws which would not have permitted it at all, or would have made it even less likely. Further, suppose we take the passing of a unit interval of time as a chance for a type of uncaused event to occur and take these chances as statistically independent. Say that the laws make the chance of *not* getting that type of event in the unit interval .999. Then the chance of not getting such an event in two unit intervals is .999 × .999, in three is $.999^3$, and so on: as time goes on, the chance of not getting one declines, and so the chance of getting one increases. So by continuing to sustain the universe and the laws that establish the unit-time probability, God raises the probability of eventually getting an event of such a kind, promoting it in a further way. Beyond these things, God prevented or permitted the preventing of anything that would have prevented the event. If God did all these things because He intended the event to occur, it might even be fair to say He had brought it about that an uncaused event occurs, without causing it. If He did all these things merely envisioning such events' occurring and accepting this as a by-product of something else He intended by maintaining the laws for such a period, we might still find this fair to say, though we might say that He had not done so fully intentionally.

Thus even if an event is without cause, there is a significant, thick sense in which it is from God: God promoted it without violating its causeless character, and without His efforts it would not have occurred. And so there seems no real obstacle to bringing events—even events without cause—within the scope of our claim about God and the ontology of necessary truths. So theists who believe in propositions, attributes, and states of affairs should hold that

1. (P)(P is necessary ⊃ ((x)(x is in P's ontology ⊃ x is God or an item in God or God creates and sustains x as long as it exists or x is an event to which God causally contributes[25]) · (F)(F is in P's ontology ⊃ God has F or an

---

[24] Just how to cash this out will depend on what laws are. If they are just Humean regularities, God settles what the regularities are to be in scripting His providential plan. If (at the other extreme) there being a law consists in there being some kind of lawmaking or necessitating relation between properties (a view associated with Armstrong and Tooley), God decides which properties are to be so related. And so on.

[25] The Western religions appear to teach that everything outside God began to exist. Current cosmology seems to concur. So these pose no problem for the claim that anything sustained was also created. Something non-divine which never began to exist could be sustained through all its existence. It is a delicate question whether it could count as created. If it could not and there were such things I would have to complicate this clause.

attribute that has F or an attribute that has an attribute that has F (and so on) or God creates and sustains F as long as it exists) · $(S^{26})(S$ is in P's ontology $\supset S$ is God's or a divine attribute's having an attribute or God creates and sustains S as long as it exists))).[27]

Those who think other sorts of item figure in necessary truths' ontologies should add appropriate clauses. Those who disbelieve in attributes or states of affairs can delete clauses or say under their breaths that if there are none, there are none in any P's ontology, and so none any P's ontology of which the consequents of these conditionals are not true, and so the relevant clauses are trivially true.[28] (1) is phrased as quantifying over propositions. I cannot let this domain be empty, as I intend (1) to be non-trivial. But I make no commitment as to what is in it. 'Platonists' about propositions take them to be abstract entities of some sort; 'nominalists' about propositions try to get by without the abstract, or even without entities at all to play their role. But any adequate nominalist substitute for Platonic propositions will have some ontology. If nominalistically acceptable items abc are the reality behind talk of a Platonic proposition P, we can take 'P' to refer plurally to abc, or refer to their sum, or the like, and take (1)'s quantifier to range over these pluralities, sums, and so on. (1) quantifies over *whatever* realities stand behind our proposition-talk. (1) does not restrict itself to truths not about God, because if a truth is about God, its ontology must be God, items in God, divine attributes, divine states of affairs, and so on—the states of affairs perhaps including items to which God is related, and these, consonant with (FD) and (GSA), must be non-eternal items God creates, and so on. (1) is non-modal. It deals only with actual necessities. On S4 and S5, these are the only necessities there could be, and so nothing more need be said. If the true logic of absolute modality does not include the S4 axiom that $\Box P \supset \Box\Box P$, there are contingent necessities, and perhaps there could be necessities there are not. So if the true logic of absolute modality does not include the S4 axiom, we must ask whether the claims motivating (1) are contingently true. I argue later that theists should hold (GSA) to be necessary. If I am right, this sets up the (GSA) conflict in all possible worlds, and should move theists who believe in contingent absolute necessities to accept (1)'s necessitation.

Some necessary negative existentials appear to be truths without ontology, such as

---

[26] This is a state-of-affairs quantifier.

[27] (1) quantifies over propositions. The idea of quantification over all propositions faces a Cantorian problem. Consider a supposed set of all propositions, S. By the power set theorem, S has more subsets than elements. To each subset corresponds a proposition; for example, that the empty set is a member of *that* subset. So there are more propositions than are in S, and so S cannot be the set of all propositions. (This argument modifies one from Patrick Grim, *The Incomplete Universe* (Cambridge, MA: MIT Press, 1991), pp. 91–4.) So if quantification requires that there be a set over whose members one quantifies, one cannot quantify over all propositions. I think there can be such a thing as all propositions without there being a set of them all, and so I think this problem can be met. My account of what it is for there to be an 'all' emerges later.

[28] Of course, the conditionals whose consequents contradict these consequents are also trivially true.

S. nothing both is and is not square.

But there do not just happen to be no square non-squares. There is a reason for this—one which some theories of modality try to articulate. What provides this reason may be (S)'s ontology. If it is, (1) covers it. If it is not, still the plausible candidate explanatory stories do not invoke absences 'all the way down'. Sooner or later, what provides the explanation turns out to be something—for example, the natures of the properties of being and of not being square, or Platonic facts about logic, or conventions for the words 'and' and 'not'. If the explainer(s) from all eternity is (are) something, analogs of the Introduction's problems arise. To deal with this, theists should embrace a stronger thesis than (1), □-Ontology, that

> (P) (P is necessary ⊃ ((x)(x is in P's ontology ⊃ x is God or an item in God or God creates and sustains x as long as it exists or x is an event to which God causally contributes) · (F)(F is in P's ontology ⊃ God has F or an attribute that has F (and so on) or God creates and sustains F as long as it exists) · (S)(S is in P's ontology ⊃ S is God's or a divine attribute's having an attribute or God creates and sustains S as long as it exists))· (P has no ontology ⊃ God is, contains, has or arranges for all that truth-explains P))).[29]

Truth-explainers are absences and items playing the role just ascribed to properties, Platonic facts, or conventions. If God provides a truth's truth-explainers, He or His action explains its being true: if a lack explains a truth, what explains the lack explains the truth, and so does what explains the presence of what explains the lack. So in the case of necessary truths without ontology (if any), God does not only account for the lack of an ontology. He accounts for the truth's being true. I now argue that He also accounts for the truth of necessary truths not about God which do have ontologies, and in addition, in a sense I explain, He provides their truthmakers.

If a truth has an ontology, its truth-conditions are satisfied iff its ontology is such as to do so. Suppose that the ontology for *Fido is brown* is Fido, brownness, and a relation between them. Then its truth-conditions are satisfied iff Fido is brown, which consists in Fido and brownness standing in that relation. If Fido, brownness, and the relation do satisfy the truth-condition of *Fido is brown*, I say that these items together make that truth true—equivalently, that they are its truthmaker. I speak so in a thin sense. I am not adopting a 'standard' truthmaker theory featuring any truthmaker-theory claim which the Introduction mentioned. To say that a truth has a truthmaker in my sense is just to say that its truth-conditions are met, by its ontology being such as to do so. A truth can have a truthmaker in my sense, then, even if there is no single entity which is the truthmaker it has. As I use

---

[29] Again, ontological scruples might lead one to add or delete clauses here.

the term, that *Fido is brown* has a truthmaker says little more than that *Fido is brown* is true. Take all subsequent talk of truthmakers in this thin sense unless I indicate otherwise. Nor does use of 'truth-explainers' imply that there are single truth-explaining entities, a single specialized truth-explaining relation, and so on: this is a thin term paralleling my thin-sense 'truthmaker'.

I now introduce a further technical term, 'from eternity' (short for 'from all eternity'). God is eternal, and I say that something exists from eternity if its duration or lack of it equals God's. So if God is atemporal, to exist from all eternity, or from eternity, is to exist atemporally. Even if time is infinite pastward, if God is atemporal, something which existed through all past time would not have existed from all eternity. If God is temporal, something exists from eternity just if it has existed as long as God has. Now as necessary, our target truths are true from all eternity. If these have an ontology from all eternity, given (FD), it must be God, in God, divine attributes, and so on: there was nothing else from all eternity. From eternity, then, this ontology is as it is intrinsically and extrinsically by God's nature or some divine activity. If the ontology of our target truths from all eternity is just God, then just by being as He is, He satisfies these propositions' truth-conditions. If it is items in God, they satisfy them by being as they are (which may be as some divine activity made them be). And so on. Given (FD), then, theists should accept in addition to □-**Ontology** that

> (P)(P is made true from all eternity ⊃ (x)(P's from-eternity truthmakers include x ⊃ x is God or an item in God) · (F)(P's from-eternity truth-makers include F ⊃ God has F or an attribute that has F (and so on)) · (S) (P's from-eternity truthmakers include S ⊃ S is God's or a divine attribute's having an attribute)).

I later explain at some length just how non-God-involving (henceforth "secular") God or these items make such truths true. It remains to discuss truthmakers for necessary truths.

Let us say that God provides a *proposition*'s ontology if He provides those entities that would go into making it true were it true.[30] God can provide a proposition's ontology without thereby bringing it about that it is true. Suppose that God creates Fido and the color brown,[31] and the relation of exemplification exists first in His having His nature. If so, He provides the ontology for Fido to be brown. But it does not follow that Fido is brown. However, the story for necessary truths differs. Here, providing ontology provides truth-makers. The least controversially necessary truths are identities, logical truths, and mathematical truths. More controversial are essential truths and truths about

---

[30] The Introduction spoke only of a *truth's* ontology, as those items from which its truth derives.

[31] This is unproblematic if the color is not a Platonist universal. We can make sense of it even if brownness is Platonic, as long as we do not take being Platonic simply to entail being uncreated. For instance, if it entails only being able to exist unexemplified, it could still be that brownness does not exist till something first has it, and so God could create it in creating something brown. If being Platonic in addition entails existing necessarily, then the claim that there are Platonic universals falls foul of (FD). It might be compatible with (GSA): see my 'God and Abstract Entities', *Faith and Philosophy* 7 (1990), 193–217, and 'A Leibnizian Cosmological Argument', *Philosophical Studies* 57 (1989), 135–55. I do not, however, now stand behind everything in these papers.

other attribute connections, and truths of modal logic. If the logic of absolute modality includes S4, there is another category: necessary truths are necessary necessarily. If it includes S5 there is one more: what is possibly so is necessarily possibly so. I now discuss the first six sorts. The next chapter takes up the last two, without taking a stand on whether they are in fact necessary.

Identities

For it to be true that Moses = Moses, all that is required is that Moses exist. There is no further, special way he has to be. He meets the claim's truth-conditions just by existing. Consider the predicate __ = Moses. All that is required for Moses to satisfy it is that Moses be there. If Moses satisfies it, it is true that Moses = Moses. So God gives identity-statements their created truthmakers just by creating and sustaining what He does. God gives this sort of necessary truth its secular truthmakers just by giving this sort its ontology.

Essential and Attribute-connection Truths

Essential truths assert the possession of essential properties. Assume for the nonce, if only for argument's sake, that things do have such properties. Then sample essential truths might be that water = H_2O, that tigers are mammals, or that Moses is human. Essential properties can be thought of in two ways: modal and definitional. On the modal conception, F is an essential property of A just if F is a property and $\Box Fa$, and is an individual essential property (a haecceity) of A just if in addition, $\Box(x)(Fx \supset x = a)$. On the definitional conception, F is an essential property of A just if F is a property and being F is part of what it is to be A: that is, A is A at least partly in virtue of being F.[32] Any property definition-essential to A will also be modally essential to A: necessarily, if A exists, A is a case of what it is to be A, and necessarily, what it is to be A is what it actually is to be A. There are not alternatives, which are what it only might be to be A. A word with a definition cannot have alternative definitions—different definition entails different word—and if there are definitional essences, they are relevantly similar. Plausibly there are some definitional essences. Plausibly, to be the set {a, b} is just to be a set and have as members just a and b. Perhaps to be water just is to be H_2O. But perhaps not everything has a definitional essence: is there really something it is to be Richard Nixon?

---

[32] For this approach to essence see Kit Fine, 'Essence and Modality', *Philosophical Perspectives* 8 (1994), 1–16.

Given the two conceptions of essences, the essential-truth sentences above might express at least the following propositions:

2. being water = being H_2O;

3. $(x)(x$ is a body of water $\equiv$ x is a body of H_2O);

4. being a tiger includes being a mammal;

5. $(x)(x$ is a tiger $\supset$ x is a mammal);

6. being Moses includes being human;

7. $(x)(x$ is Moses $\supset$ x is human); or

8. Human$_{Moses}$, a predication.

(2) falls under my treatment of identities. That is, God gives this its truth-maker just by creating and sustaining an attribute. Of course, what this amounts to depends on just what attributes *are*.

Attributes

If I say that Fido is a dog, I apply to Fido token words expressing a concept. By so doing I ascribe to Fido membership in the extension of '— is a dog', which is a class. I do this because I notice something(s) about Fido. Now the claim that Fido is a dog attributes being a dog to Fido. Attributes are things that are attributed. One may wonder precisely *what* we attribute to Fido in calling him a dog. Theories of attributes answer this question. Their answers amount to different selections of bits of what goes into our making attributions. There are at least six basic sorts of theory of what attributes are:

a. Asserting that Fido is a dog says of Fido just that he satisfies '__ is a dog'. What makes it true is that token words or concepts apply to Fido.[33] 'Fido is a dog' attributes just that some token word or concept applies; attributes are words or concepts.

b. Fs satisfy '— is F' because they belong to the class of Fs. Predications thus ascribe class-membership. What makes a predication true is having the relevant attribute. So on this view, to have an attribute is to belong to a class; the 'having' relation is membership, and the attribute is the class.[34]

---

[33] So, for example, Bruce Aune, *Metaphysics* (Minneapolis, MN: University of Minnesota Press, 1985), p. 55. Strictly, in each case, we attribute or predicate a *token* of '__is a K,' a particular utterance or inscription. If we predicate a token, we in some way predicate a type. Talk of types raises the attribute problem all over again. For being of a certain type is an attribute of a word, and types are kinds. Thus a friend of (a) must apply (a) to word-types too. Further, if the ontology of word-types were richer than (a), there would be no principled reason to avoid this richer ontology. And so for (a) to have a point, the ontology of predication must be strictly in terms of concept—or word-tokens.

[34] So W. V. Quine, *Word and Object* (Cambridge, MA.: MIT Press, 1960), p. 267; Lewis, *Plurality,* pp. 50–69; Anthony Quinton, 'Properties and Classes', *Proceedings of the Aristotelian Society* 58 (1957–58), 33–58.

c. A similar view is possible, which substitutes mereological sums for classes.[35]

d. Items are all dogs because they are like each other or some paradigm dog in the right way or degree.[36] Asserting that Fido is a dog ascribes the right likenesses to Fido. But Fido and Rover make it true that Fido is like Rover. This view parses attributes away.[37]

e. Ks satisfy '__ is a K' because they have a *sui generis* entity, Khood, 'in common.' Each K has a K-making relation to one and the same thing, Khood: that is, what constitutes it a K is having this relation. Asserting that Fido is a dog ascribes to Fido the right relation to Khood. Platonists hold that these common *sui generis* things—universals—can exist uninstanced, Aristotelians that they cannot. On this view, attributes are universals.

f. Each K satisfies '__ is a K' because it has a 'trope' of Khood. A trope is a K-making *sui generis* entity unique to each individual K, an individualized Khood. On this view, attributes are tropes.

For reasons that need not detain us, (a)–(d) are called forms of nominalism, and (e) realism. (d)–(f) base their views on the 'noticing something(s) about Fido' bit of what goes on in attribution. Each of these views yields an account of what it is for God to make an attribute. On concept nominalism, God need only make those realities which stand behind talk of concept possession: He can think, and so come to be in states we speak of in terms of concept possession, or create language-users with certain linguistic dispositions. On class nominalism He need only make classes, and He does this by making their ur-elements; so similarly mereological nominalism. On resemblance nominalism He need only make particulars. On realism and trope theories, God must make universals or tropes. It may sound odd to say that He can, but consider: surely God can create the first quark ever to exist. He can do so no matter what the ontology of attribution is. So if to be a quark is to bear a quark-trope, He can make a quark-trope appear, and if to be a quark is to bear an Aristotelian universal, He can make such a universal appear. Of course, it is hard to imagine how He does this, but it is equally hard to see how He makes particulars: if 'let there be' works in the one case, why not the other? As to Platonic universals, my own preferred move is to dissolve them into the realities behind talk of divine concept-possession: theists simply need not deal in them with the mind of God available to do the work instead. Thus

---

[35] D. M. Armstrong mentions this (*Nominalism and Realism* (Cambridge: Cambridge University Press, 1978), pp. 34–5), but to my knowledge no-one has held this view.

[36] See, for example, H. H. Price, *Thinking and Experience* (Cambridge, MA: Harvard University Press, 1953).

[37] So do recent forms of fictionalism about abstract entities, which are not relevant here.

there is (I submit) no bar to taking (2) in terms of my treatment of identities. (2) can be so taken no matter what the true non-platonic theory of attributes is.

Further Essentialist Truths

Given (2), God brings it about that (3) is true just by making water. Given (2), for (3) to be true, water need only exist: every body of water has the property of being water, and that just is being H_2O, so every body of water is a body of H_2O and *vice versa*. So God gives (3) its truthmakers just by creating and sustaining, and (GSA) takes us directly to the claim that the secular truthmakers for (3)-type truths come from God. Further, God gives (3) its truthmakers by providing its ontology.

(4) represents something a believer in definitional essences might say. So we cannot gloss its talk of property-inclusion in terms of entailment—of its merely being the case that being a tiger entails being a mammal. Rather, the thought is that as a definition of the word 'tiger' includes (let us suppose) the word 'mammal', the definitional essence of being a tiger includes the property of being a mammal. As the word is part of the definition, the property is some sort of part or constituent of another property. Well, if this is how it is, all God has to do to make (4) true is cause there to be the property of being a tiger, with the property of being a mammal as part of its makeup. Plausibly, He could not make *that* property without giving it that makeup; a property which had the property *being a fish* where *being a tiger* has *being a mammal* would *ipso facto* be a different property, just as a definition invoking a different, non-synonymous word would be a different definition. So (GAO) takes us directly to the claim that God gives (4)-truths any secular truthmakers they have (and so for (6)-truths too). He does so just by providing their ontology.

If there are definitional essences, then as (2) yielded that to give (3) its created truthmakers all God had to do is make water, (4) yields the conclusion that to give (5) its secular truthmakers, all God must do is create tigers. If something is a tiger it has the property of being a tiger, and *ipso facto* any properties that property definitionally includes; thus it suffices to make (5) true that there be tigers (and so for (7)). If there are no definitional essences, (5) is a truth of attribute-connection, not fundamentally different from truths which are not intuitively candidates for being definition-essential—for example, that (x)(x is water ⊃ x freezes at 32° F at sea level). Regardless, though, we are supposing that (5) represents the actual-world instantiation of a necessary connection of properties. So it seems natural to say that had God not made *being a tiger* a property that necessarily brought *being a mammal* with it, it would not have been *that* property. For the relational property is not its arbitrarily. Rather, being a tiger entails being mammalian due to something about its intrinsic content, and it is not plausible that this something is merely accidental to it, as it is hard to see how a property which entailed being a fish instead of being mammalian could be *that* property. I suggest, then, that if there are no definitional essences, all God had to do to give (5) a truthmaker is make the attributes as they actually are (and must be), with the relational as well as intrinsic properties connected to their identity set as they are. For (2)–(7), then, (GSA) and (GAO) take us not just to claims about ontology, but to claims about created truthmakers.

It is unclear whether to count (8) weakly necessary. If its copula is tenseless, it is equivalent to a claim that it is or was or will be the case that Socrates is (present-tensed) human. Either this was always true or, if there are no singular truths about not-yet-existent individuals, before Socrates existed there was no such proposition. If its copula is present-tensed, it is now false. So perhaps (8) fails the Introduction's account of weak necessity. On the other hand, it is common to gloss claims of weak necessity this way: with "$\square$" expressing strong necessity, weak-necessarily Fa = df. $\square(x)((x =a) \supset Fx)$.[38] On this definition, weak necessity that Fa is compatible with possible falsity (if the non-existence of a makes it false that Fa). If (8) does have this sort of weak necessity, one cannot treat it without discussing the ontology of essential predication. Some nominalists would say that all God need make to make Moses human is Moses himself: Descartes was such a nominalist in saying that Peter's humanity is just Peter. Others might add His making a class of humans, a concept of humans, or other humans; on these views, these are part of the ontology for *Moses is human*. But if God makes Moses and makes a class of humans, *ipso facto* Moses is in the class and so (on this sort of nominalism) it is true that Moses is human; if God makes Moses and a concept of being human Moses *ipso facto* falls under the concept and so (on this sort of nominalism) it is true that Moses is human; if God makes Moses and other humans, they *ipso facto* resemble *qua* human and so on this sort of nominalism too, it is true that Moses is human. In all these cases, then, by providing ontology, God provides truthmakers. If nominalism is false, God would in addition to Moses have to make or have made a universal, humanity, or a trope, an individual case of humanity. Tropes and on some views universals are constituents (in a broad sense) of their bearers.[39] An essential property is on such views an essential constituent—one such its bearer cannot exist without. If so, then if God in making Moses makes all constituents of Moses or puts in place previously existent universal constituents, here again, in providing ontology God provides truthmakers. If universals are not con-stituents of their bearers, they stand in a relation to them—'exemplification'. If God makes Moses and Moses is essentially a man, He makes Moses a man. It is part of making Moses that God make him a man, whatever the proper ontology of doing so—that is, even if that involves making him exemplify

---

[38] So, for example, Saul Kripke, 'Identity and Necessity', in Milton K. Munitz (ed.), *Identity and Individuation* (New York: NYU Press, 1971), p. 137.

[39] On this see Michael Loux, 'Aristotle's Constituent Ontology', *Oxford Studies in Metaphysics* 2 (2006), 207–50.

humanity. If so, then even on this assumption, providing Moses includes providing a truthmaker for (8). No matter what the ontology, then, God gives essential and attribute-connection truths their secular truthmakers in providing their ontology.

Logical Truth

Some say that logical truths are trivial, not requiring that the world be any particular way to be true.[40] This seems false to me. We can clearly conceive circumstances in which the truths of classical logic would not be true. Their being true requires of the world that these circumstances not obtain.

Logical truths are either theses of which logical systems consist, or instances of these. On standard accounts, a logical formula is logically true just if it comes out true in all models—that is, on all admissible substitutions for its variables and assignments of objects to its referring expressions (if any) and extensions to its predicates.[41] If a formula has this property, every sentence which interprets it says something true, and since this includes all and only the sentences with that formula's logical form, all such sentences express truths. On this account, logical truth guarantees actual truth of a class of propositions expressed by sentences sharing a logical form. Given a classical semantics, the principle of non-contradiction—henceforth PNC—is a logical truth. But given a non-supervaluational semantics that lets propositions lack truth-value (have 'truth-value gaps')—henceforth a 'simple gap' semantics—it is not. One can use a 3-valued truth-table to speak of truth-value gaps, letting '___' symbolize a truth-value gap rather than a third, non-classical value. Then in the 3-valued logics of Kleene and Lukasiewicz, the truth-table for '$\neg$' runs thus:

P	$\neg$P
T	F
F	T
—	—.[42]

Their truth-table for '$\cdot$' adds to the classical possibilities that a conjunction has no truth-value if at least one conjunct has none. Given these truth-tables, if P has no truth-value, nor does $\neg(P \cdot \neg P)$.[43] On a simple gap approach, that is all

---

[40] So Agustin Rayo, 'Towards a Trivialist Account of Mathematics', in Octavio Bueno and Øystein Linnebo (eds), *New Waves in Philosophy of Mathematics* (Palgrave MacMillan, 2009), pp. 239–60.

[41] So John Etchemendy, *The Concept of Logical Consequence* (Stanford, CA.: CSLI Publications, 1999), *passim*.

[42] Graham Priest, *An Introduction to Non-Classical Logic* (Cambridge: Cambridge University Press, 2001), pp. 119–21.

[43] Nor does $P \cdot \neg P$: on these truth-tables, contradictions can fail to be false. On these tables, logical form is not enough to guarantee a truth-value (though it can guarantee against some truth-values: nothing contradictory can turn out true): the world must also contribute, by contributing a truth-value for P. We think that contradictions must be false because we take it that '$\neg$' reverses truth-value and so

there is to say: PNC has instances without truth-value if any proposition lacks a truth-value, and so if there are gap propositions, PNC is not a logical truth.[44] So either PNC is a logical truth, or a simple gap semantics is true and there are gap propositions and so it is not—period. And if PNC has gap instances, it is not true (or false).

Our language contains vague predicates. One sort of treatment of vagueness adopts a simple gap approach. If this sort of treatment is correct and there are gap propositions, then, PNC is not true (nor false).

Vagueness

Vague predicates—tall, hot, red, bald—admit of borderline cases. Some shades of color are definitely reds. Others are definitely not. Still others are not definitely red and not definitely not red.[45] They fall on the border between red and non-red, and so are borderline red. Some men are definitely bald. Some are definitely not. But some are not definitely bald and not definitely not bald. They fall on the border between bald and non-bald, and so are borderline bald.[46] Typical vague predicates generate sorites series, in which one moves from cases in which the predicate definitely applies, to borderline cases, to cases in which the predicate definitely does not apply, by gradual change in some relevant property—for example, by gradual decrease in the number of hairs on a man's head. If a man is borderline bald, it may seem to us that more is the case than that we simply do not know whether he is bald. It may seem to us that he falls in an in-between zone objectively. If a predicate F is vague, we are at least tempted to say that for some a it is not true that Fa and not false either: that is, it is at least initially plausible that a language with vague predicates generates truth-value gaps.

It is controversial what logical and semantic sense to make of languages with vague predicates. One approach to vagueness is simple-gap.[47] I have already shown that on the K–L truth-tables, PNC is not a logical truth if there are gap propositions. Nor is anything else—an appropriate placement of gaps can always generate an instance without (classical) truth-value. So the simple-gap response to vagueness just gives up the claim that there are logical truths. Thus the clearly conceivable circumstances in which the truths of classical logic would not be true are these: the world contains objective indeterminacies. In some cases it

guarantees a false conjunct to a conjunction, but this guarantees a false conjunct only if a conjunct has a truth-value to reverse.

[44] Unless being a logical truth is being guaranteed (by form) non-false— that is, guaranteed true if truth-valued.

[45] 'Definitely' can bear different freights. For present purposes I need not decide between them.

[46] Further, if a predicate is vague, not only is no sharp border evident between cases in which it definitely applies and cases in which it definitely does not, none is evident between cases in which it definitely applies and cases in which it neither definitely does nor definitely does not. The 'boundary' of its indefinite zone is itself indefinite.

[47] So, for example, Michael Tye, 'Sorites Paradoxes and the Semantics of Vagueness', in *Philosophical Perspectives* 8 (1994), 189–206.

just does not settle a classical truth-value for sentences involving vague predicates. And a 'simple-gap' semantics for sentences appropriately employing these predicates is correct. Thus the truths of classical logic are not true by their content alone. They require something of the world to be true. They require either that it not contain such indeterminacies or that its truths—whatever truths are—have a supervaluationist semantics, which provides logical truths with classical truth-values even if some propositions have none. They also require, of course, that the logical constants have the content they do—and whatever the ontology of this, it is part of the world.

Here (to a theist) God enters the picture. Supervaluationist semantics has an ontology, involving, for example, meanings or sets.[48] It is true only if the ontology is there, and on the present account it is there only if God makes His contribution. God creates sets by creating their members, if there are sets; I myself would argue that there are no sets, but certain divine mental events take their place.[49] If meaning is something we shape, then as noted earlier, God determines our meaning-shaping capacities, and can also (of course) influence our use of them as He pleases. This also entails that to the extent that we determine the semantics of our talk, and in particular whether it is supervaluational, God can settle this through us. As to the non-semantic part of the picture, one can show, I think, that from all eternity there were no indeterminacies in God.[50] From all eternity, the only state 'outside' God was there being nothing other than God. This contained no indeterminacies either, and it obtained because God so wished: had He wanted to create from all eternity, He could have done so. Further, the only reality whatever determines the content of logical truths could have had from all eternity, consistent with (FD), was in the mind of God. So from all eternity the mind of God settled the content of logical truth and the divine being and the upshot of a divine refraining satisfied the worldly requirements for logical truth. Thus from all eternity the mind of God and a state of things He established made logical truths true, including providing any needed semantic machinery. (Logical truths are about everything. So everything figures in their truthmakers.)

Now let us turn to Creation. If Creation contains no indeterminacies, that is God's doing. He made and sustains it. He permits the instancing only of attributes which do not bring indeterminacy with them; He supports all events in which Creation avoids generating indeterminacies, and prevents others. So if there are logical truths, God does not just provide their ontology. They are true because all propositions have (classical) truth-values, reality's being fully determinate makes this so, and God brings this about. Given the right semantic machinery, everything helps make logical truths true. So if there

[48] See, for example, Kit Fine, 'Vagueness, Truth and Logic', in Rosanna Keefe and Peter Smith (eds), *Vagueness* (Cambridge, MA.: MIT Press, 1996), pp. 119–50.

[49] See, for example, Christopher Menzel, 'Theism, Platonism and the Metaphysics of Mathematics', in Michael Beaty (ed.), *Christian Theism and the Problems of Philosophy* (Notre Dame, IN: University of Notre Dame Press, 1990), pp, 208–29.

[50] I do so in 'God, Vagueness and Logical Truth' (forthcoming).

are logical truths, God makes them true just by thinking and being Himself before He creates; by creating and sustaining, He gives them their full ontology and the rest of their truthmaker.

Mathematical Truths

To take a view about the relation of mathematical ontology and mathematical truth, one must take a view of what that ontology is. Defending such a view is a larger project than I can undertake in a book primarily about something else. So I simply say how I see it. Mathematical Platonists take mathematics to be a body of truths about real abstract entities, be they sets, structures sets for instance, or substitute items (such as properties) able to mimic the relevant structures of set theories. If Platonism is correct, any mathematical sentence with an '=' in the right place expresses an identity-proposition about these items. So if Platonism is correct, all mathematical identities fall under my treatment of identities. For Platonists, anything in set theory not expressed as an identity of some sort is a truth about the universe of sets. The standard Zermelo–Fraenkel (ZF) axioms of set theory capture independent mathematical reality. But if the ZF axioms are true, they are true just because certain sets exist or do not exist.[51] If Extensionality holds, that is because there is just one set for every plurality of elements. If Null Set holds, that is because there is a null set. If Pairs holds, that is because there are all the pair-sets; if Unions holds, that is because there are all the union-sets; if Power Set holds, that is because there are all the power sets; if Infinity holds, that is because there is a set with an infinite number of members; if Regularity holds, that is because there are only well-founded sets; and if Replacement holds, that is because the right sets exist. Thus if Platonism is correct and God provides the sets or set-substitutes, He thus provides truthmakers for ZF, and with it for all mathematics derivable in ZF. Geometry and topology also study sets; if these have elements God provides them, and again, in providing the sets, He validates the relevant axioms. My own account of pure mathematics would be broadly Platonic, but with set-substitutes in the mind of God.[52] Thus I do not consider how the story would differ on non-Platonic approaches to mathematics, and it is by providing these set substitutes—the ontology of mathematics—that God provides truthmakers for pure mathematical truth. There are also impure mathematical truths—for example, that one cat, Tom, plus one mouse, Jerry, are two animals. These have a further ontology, for example, as Tom and Jerry themselves. To cause them to be true, all

---

[51] For the following axioms see any work on set theory; for example, Stephen Pollard, *Philosophical Introduction to Set Theory* (Notre Dame, IN: University of Notre Dame Press, 1990).

[52] See, for example, Christopher Menzel, 'Theism, Platonism and the Metaphysics of Mathematics', in Michael Beaty (ed.), *Christian Theism and the Problems of Philosophy* (Notre Dame, IN: University of Notre Dame, Press, 1990), pp. 208–29.

God had to do was make Tom, make him a cat and an animal, make Jerry and make him a mouse and an animal, and make the pure truth true.

Modal Logic

Taken in terms of the standard modal semantics, theses of modal logic make claims about possible worlds and relations between them. The S4 thesis that $\Box P \supset \Box\Box P$, for instance, asserts that if in all worlds possible relative to the actual world P, then in each world W of those worlds, in all worlds possible relative to W, P. So either the ontology of these theses consists of worlds, relations among them, domains, and the rest of what a face-value reading of the standard semantics posits, or it consists of whatever modal reality stands behind talk of these.[53] And so if theses of modal logic are necessary and **□-Ontology** or a suitable extension is true, God is, contains, or is the source of all possible worlds (and impossible ones, if any), domains, and the relation of accessibility. Again, it is a necessary truth that a world has the content it does. So if God is responsible for all ontology for all necessary truths, then if a truth about a world's content has an ontology, God is responsible for it. But the truth that in W, P has an ontology: it is W and perhaps P. So for every W, God is responsible for W's existence.

If God is responsible for worlds' existence, He is also responsible for their content. That is, if God is responsible for W's existence, and in W cats fly, God or something about God brings it about that in W cats fly or explains this or is its ontology. For it is a necessary truth that a world has the content it does—that just certain propositions would be true were it actual. Intuitively, if Puff cannot be Boots, a world in which Puff flies cannot be a world otherwise the same in which Boots flies. If possibilities 1 and 2 are identical, then were 1 actualized, things would be just as they would were 2 actualized. So consider a maximal possibility 1, that $P \cdot Q \cdot \ldots \cdot R$, and a maximal possibility 2, that $P \cdot Q \cdot \ldots \cdot \neg R$. If it could be that $1 = 2$, one of two things could be true. One is that things' being such that $P \cdot Q \cdot \ldots \cdot R$ and things' being such that $P \cdot Q \cdot \ldots \cdot \neg R$ could be exactly the same. But this cannot be true. That R is true and that instead ¬R is true suffices to make the state of things different. The other alternative is that 1 could survive alteration into 2—that is, that a possibility in which R could turn into one in which ¬R. I cannot quite make sense of this. If there is anything coherent here, it would flout intuitions very near that about Puff and Boots above, and also create sorites worries. If 1 could survive one alteration, into 2, why not two? And so on. Where could we draw the line? In other sorites cases, there is clearly a point where the series of changes has gone too far: remove too many grains and we clearly no longer have a heap.

---

[53] I will not repeat the latter disjunct or claims like it; take it or these claims as added where appropriate.

But if we allow even a first alteration in the content of a world, we set aside the main or only intuitions we could call on to reject the claim that 1 could survive alteration into a possibility that $\neg P \cdot \neg Q \cdot \neg \ldots \cdot \neg R$. So it cannot be that $1 = 2$, and so worlds have their content necessarily. If in a world W, P, it is necessarily true that in W, P.[54] Thus God brings it about that there is a world W only if He brings it about that in W, P—a non-P world could not be W—and He contains W only if He contains a world in which *inter alia* P. Just as if Moses is necessarily a man, to make Moses, God must make a man, so if necessarily in W, P, to make or contain W, God must make W a P-world or contain a P-world.

If God is responsible for a world's content, He is responsible for which counterfactuals are true in it. A world if possible is a maximal possibility, and so every proposition including counterfactuals must have a determinate truth-status in it. That God accounts for worlds' contents also implies that God is responsible for particular accessibility relations. For part of a world's content concerns what is possible relative to that world. If W is possible relative to W*, this truth is itself necessary. It could differ only if the contents of W and W* could differ. So if God is responsible for necessary truths' truth, He is responsible for particular accessibility relations. If God determines worlds' content and also which worlds are possible relative to which, He *ipso facto* determines which worlds among those possible relative to any world are the closest ones in which a given counterfactual's antecedent is true. And if the worlds are possible, this determines which counterfactuals are true.[55] So if God accounts for the possibility of the possible, as the next chapter argues, God is responsible for counterfactuals' truth, *simpliciter*, and if God does not account for the possibility of the possible, He still makes the largest contribution to it.[56]

I specified that the worlds be possible and alluded to God's responsibility for possibility because of the truth-conditions of counterpossibles. On the standard approach they are all trivially true, just because their antecedents are impossible.[57] If the standard approach is correct, God is responsible for counterpossibles' truth just if God accounts for the possibility of the possible: by rendering candidate worlds possible, God determines what is impossible. For once there are possible worlds, anything included in none is impossible: to be impossible is to fall outside the possible worlds. However, the standard approach is not beyond question. It is correct for worlds including contradictions in which all laws of logic are just as they actually are. For given these laws, if a contradiction is true, anything follows:

---

[54] If there are worlds in which there is no W, it is true in every world in which there is a W that in W, *P* is true, and this truth has the weaker sort of necessity mentioned in the Introduction.

[55] So David Lewis, *Counterfactuals* (Cambridge, MA.: Harvard University Press, 1973), *passim*.

[56] Molinism holds that counterfactuals about what free creatures would do in all possible circumstances are true entirely independent of God. (See, for example, Thomas Flint, *Divine Providence* (Ithaca, NY: Cornell University Press, 1998).) Plainly, then, Molinists must reject or qualify much of what I have said about God's modal role.

[57] So Lewis, *Counterfactuals*, 24–6.

i.   P · ¬ P   premise;

ii. P   simplification;

iii. P v Q   addition;

iv. ¬P   simplification;

v.   Q   iv, v, disjunctive syllogism.

So in such a world, every proposition is true. For this reason there is just one such world. Were it actual, every subjunctive conditional would be true. But there might also be impossible worlds which are impossible because in them some logical law invoked in (ii)–(v) fails, or which are impossible for other reasons than containing a contradiction. The standard approach looks less plausible in such cases. Consider a set of impossible worlds which differ from the possible worlds only in this: in some world possible relative only to these worlds, there is a flea not identical with any actually possible flea. Actually, let us say, P > Q and possibly P. The only difference between the worlds which make this so and the corresponding impossible worlds is that in the latter there is or can be this particular flea. Should that really make it the case that P > Q and P > ¬Q? What about this flea should make it the case that a perfectly possible state of affairs implies a contradiction? If there are non-contradictory impossible worlds, the standard approach to counterpossibles is not plausible: we want to say that some are non-trivially true and others false. For such worlds it might be that if God sets worlds' content and accessibility relations, He accounts for the truth in them of all their counterfactuals.

If God is responsible for all particular accessibility relations, He *ipso facto* is responsible for every generalization about accessibility. If God brings it about that W is possible relative to W* and *vice versa*, and does this for every pair of worlds, He *ipso facto* brings it about that accessibility is symmetric. Again, if God provides an accessibility relation, He provides a determinate relation, one whose properties are set: if it is a symmetric relation, then accessibility is symmetric. God's responsibility for accessibility relations entails that He is responsible for making true all theses of the true logic of absolute modality (henceforth 'the true modal logic'). Thus God provides modal logic's truth-makers by providing modal logic's ontology—the worlds, domains and so on, and the relation(s) of accessibility. Truths are true because reality is as they represent it.[58] If they have ontologies, God makes reality as these truths represent it by providing the relevant ontology. I submit, then, that beyond □-Ontology, theists should hold □-Truthmaker, that in my thin sense of 'truthmaker', where *P* is of the first six sorts discussed.

> (*P*)(□*P* ⊃ God is, contains, has, has attributes that have (and so on) or produces all truthmakers or truth-explainers for *P*).

---

[58] For discussion of the difference between this truism's being true and the truth of a 'standard' truthmaker theory, see Trenton Merricks, 'Truth and Freedom', *Philosophical Review* 118 (2009), 29–31.

4

THE ONTOLOGY OF POSSIBILITY

I have suggested that to preserve divine ultimacy, theists should hold □-Ontology. I now argue that theists should maintain two further theses. One of them is ◊-Ontology: the claim that $(P)(\lozenge P \supset$ God is, contains, has, or produces all of $\lozenge P$'s ontology). I now explicate ◊-Ontology.

The Claim Explained

◊-Ontology is non-modal. It deals only with actual possibilities. On S4 and S5 these are the only ones there could be, and so no more need be said. Modal systems not including S4 permit states of affairs that might have been possible, but are not. Should some such system be the true modal logic, we would have to ask whether what motivates ◊-Ontology holds of necessity. ◊-Ontology is deliberately general. It does not intend to select among theist views. As we shall see later, Aquinas' modal ontology was God's nature, which He identified with God Himself. Leibniz placed the ontology for modal truth about non-deities in the divine intellect, Descartes in creatures. All three could accept ◊-Ontology. ◊-Ontology takes truths of possibility to have ontologies. They do on the standard semantics, on which that ◊P has as its truth-condition that there *is* a possible world in which P. On what I believe to be the correct semantics, its truth-condition is also existential. So on the standard approach or my own, possibility-claims are true because something(s) exist(s). Even if some entities are to be paraphrased away, or are not part of the fundamental level of reality (thus Van Inwagen would let us say that there are chairs, but deny that the ontology of this claim really does involve chairs[1]), this does not affect my point. If an entity is to

---

[1] So Peter van Inwagen, *Material Beings* (Ithaca, NY: Cornell University Press, 1990).

be paraphrased away or is at a non-fundamental level, a claim's ontology is not what it seems on the surface. But if it is genuinely existential it has one nonetheless, which is given in a paraphrase or a fundamental-level account. If possibility-claims really are existential, then, every truth of possibility has an ontology. If they are not, still, the thesis that truths of possibility have no ontology would (I submit) ultimately be as implausible as the thesis that necessary truths have none, and for much the same reasons. In fact, if the true modal logic includes S5, as many believe, the first thesis would be just an instance of the second.

◊-**Ontology** speaks of *all* ontology, so it has particularly wide import if the Ontology Inclusion claim is true:

OI. $(P)(P \supset$ all ontology for P is ontology for $\Diamond P)$.

For ◊-**Ontology** and (OI) jointly imply that God provides all ontology for actual truths. One might be tempted to add to (OI) that if P has no ontology, all ontology for P's truth-explanation is ontology for $\Diamond P$'s truth-explanation. For one might think that whatever truth-explains it that there are no round squares, truth-explains it that possibly there are none. But as I use these terms, a truth has a truthmaker only if it has an ontology and a truth-explainer only if it does not. So no truth has both, and as just noted, that possibly there are no round squares has an ontology. I now argue (OI).

Ontology Inclusion

(OI) is easiest to show on possibilism. It is true that $\Diamond P$ just if there is a possible world in which P. P's ontology in a world is just all items in that world which go into its being the case in that world that P. Lewis holds that merely possible items exist. For Lewis, in other possible worlds non-actual existing objects go into its being the case there that P, and in the actual world actual existing objects go into its being the case actually that P. Possible worlds all alike exist. Each P-world's objects contributing to its being the case that P in that world are part of the ontology for $\Diamond P$ across all worlds. There is nothing special about actual objects in this. They are just some of those that go into its being the case that P in some world. So the ontology for P in the actual world—the ontology for P—is part of the ontology for $\Diamond P$. On existent-object possibilism, then, (OI) is patent.

Now consider Meinongian or non-existent-object possibilism. Here non-actual possible worlds are non-existents, though perhaps some of their objects and properties exist (they are also in our world). Non-existents are in possible worlds' domains. So while actual existing objects are ontologically special, they and non-existents are equally part of the ontology for $\Diamond P$ across all worlds, as in Lewis: the (existent) dogs of our world and the dogs of other worlds (some non-existent) are all in worlds' domains and all alike contribute to its being the case that in some possible world there are dogs. So P's ontology is again part of $\Diamond P$'s; the logic of getting from possibilism to (OI) is much the same.

Let us now consider actualism. One sort of actualism gets to (OI) as possibilism does. Linsky, Zalta, and Williamson hold that for any x, if x could exist but there is no concrete object x, x exists, but is an abstract object—and that all abstract objects exist necessarily.[2] If this is correct, there actually are all the items that in various worlds contribute to making it the case in those worlds that P, and those making it the case actually that P are just some of the actual items that make it the case that P in some world or other. But this is an atypical sort of actualism. Assume now, with most actualists, that if x is possibly concrete, then if x is not concrete, x does not exist. Such actualists divide over whether there are singular truths about x if x has yet to exist.

Suppose first that there are, with such as Plantinga. On the standard semantics it is true that possibly Fido is a dog iff in some possible world it is true that Fido is a dog. Suppose now that the future is unreal. If it is, then if Fido has not yet existed, Fido just does not exist. Suppose too that there 'are' no non-existent objects. Then if Fido does not exist and it is true in some possible world that Fido is a dog, this' being true in that world does not involve Fido himself, though it is a truth about him. If Fido does not actually exist and there are no non-actuals or non-existents, Fido is not in the domain of any possible world. Rather, associated with possible worlds are proxies for Fido—on Plantinga's proposal, for instance, his individual essences.[3] There are Fido-truths in possible worlds because the proxies have attributes—for Plantinga, it suffices for it to be true in W that Fido is a dog that his individual essences bear to doghood in W the relation __is co-exemplified with__.[4] That is, W represents that Fido is a dog by assigning Fido's essences and doghood to the extension of __ is co-exemplified with __, or perhaps W just represents that Fido is a dog—but this is what one must do with the semantics of the representation, given that Fido himself is not there to be in W's domain. Once Fido exists, though, there is another way for it to be true that possibly Fido is a dog. There are still Fido-proxies, and these still have whatever attributes previously made it true in W that Fido is a dog. But Fido himself now exists and satisfies 'possibly __ is a dog'. That is, now Fido himself is in

---

[2] See, for example, Bernard Linsky and Edward Zalta, 'In Defense of the Simplest Quantified Modal Logic', *Philosophical Perspectives* 8 (1994), 431–58; Timothy Williamson, 'Bare Possibilia', *Erkenntnis* 48 (1998), 257–73.

[3] See Alvin Plantinga, 'Actualism and Possible Worlds', *Theoria* 42 (1976), 139–60.

[4] *Ibid.*, 159–60; see also Thomas Jager, 'An Actualistic Semantics for Quantified Modal Logic', *Notre Dame Journal of Formal Logic* 23 (1982), 338. (Plantinga says that Jager's system reflects his general approach (Alvin Plantinga, 'Self-Profile', in James Tomberlin and Peter van Inwagen, eds., *Alvin Plantinga* (Dordrecht: D. Reidel, 1985), p. 92).)

W's domain (that is, a set including Fido now replaces the set which previously served as domain) and its extension of '__ is a dog'. Thus the truth-in-W of *Fido is a dog* is now overdetermined, and so is the truth of *possibly Fido is a dog.*

The ontology for *Fido is a dog* is just Fido and the predicate '__ is a dog' or a property it expresses. The latter get assigned extensions in worlds, and so before Fido existed they were in the ontology for *possibly Fido is a dog.* Now that Fido is here, he is in the latter ontology too: he is in the domain of worlds in which he is a dog. So if Fido is a dog, the ontology for *possibly Fido is a dog* includes the ontology for *Fido is a dog.* The logic of the situation does not change for attributes or states of affairs (if any): either these exist necessarily (so Plantinga) or there are proxies for them in worlds in which they do not exist or there are worlds in which there are no truths about them unless and until they come actually to exist; if the last, then again ontology for P about them is ontology for ◊P, for only by there being ontology for the former does the latter come to be true. Generalizing this gives us (OI). So given actualism, an unreal future and no non-existent objects, the standard semantics delivers (OI). Note now that this does not depend on the future's being unreal. If future items exist, then they are always in non-actual worlds' domains, and so if they figure in the ontology for P, equally they figure in the ontology for ◊P. Actualism with non-existent actual objects is structurally just like the Linsky–Zalta–Williamson view above, so we get (OI) without denial of non-existents too. Finally, we assumed above that there are singular truths about the not-yet-existent. If we deny this, with such as Prior,[5] we still get (OI). For then no world's domain contains either non-actual future individuals or proxies for them to generate singular truths. There are no singular truths about them till they exist; once they exist, they become part of possible worlds' domains, and so again we get (OI). Thus really, all we need to get (OI) are actualism and the standard semantics. Of course, if I am right, then on actualism the truth of *possibly Fido is a dog* may wind up overdetermined. But truths can be overdetermined; it takes only one cat to make it true that there are cats, but every new kitten adds a new overdeterminer which contributes as much as older cats to there being cats. There is nothing special about truths of possibility that would keep them from being overdetermined.

Regardless of ontology—whether actualism or possibilism be true—we get (OI). The argument used the standard semantics. So if this sort of semantics is correct, (OI) is true, and to the extent that it is a good regimentation of our modal intuitions, modal intuition favors (OI). But nothing in this argument requires that we be realists about possible worlds. All that is needed is the *form* of the standard semantics—that is, that talk about worlds, domains, and so on, provides an adequate semantic account.

---

[5] A. N. Prior, 'Identifiable Individuals', *Review of Metaphysics* 13 (1960), 684–96.

The Range of ◊-Ontology

I take it, then, that (OI) is true. If (OI) and **◊-Ontology** are true, again, God provides all ontology for all actual truths with ontologies. This implies that if Bob chooses with incompatibilist freedom, God provides Bob's choosing, and even Bob's initiating his choice, and that might seem to rule it out that Bob chooses freely. But it is standard Western theism that God conserves Bob and his powers throughout the choice. If He does, He provides the choice and the initiation in a sense sufficient for us; **◊-Ontology** does not imply that God causes either immediately, and merely conserving Bob and his powers does not plausibly create a difficulty for freedom.[6]

If God plays the role **◊-Ontology** specifies for all actual truths, He plays this role for every P such that □P. Thus **◊-Ontology** entails **□-Ontology**. Also, on **◊-Ontology** God provides all ontology for all necessary truths' being necessary or for what truth-explains this. We can see this in three ways:

—not just that P but that □P is an actual truth.

—He provides all ontology for all truths of absolute possibility, and as we see shortly, His providing no more accounts for their being all the possibilities. If He provides the ontology for all the world-sized possibilities—that is, the worlds or what stands behind talk of them—and accounts for their being all, He provides all that goes into any proposition's being true in all possible worlds, and so necessary.

—if □P, then ◊□P. That ◊□P is a possibility-claim, that ◊(□P). Given (OI), what provides ontology for □P does so for ◊□P. So God provides all ontology for all truths of absolute possibility only if He does this for □P.

On **◊-Ontology,** God provides all ontology for (or for the truth-explanation of) all truths in a proper symbolization of which:

S. the first symbol is '◊,' '¬,' or '□,' some sequence of tokens of these prefixes a sentence,[7] the sequence includes at least one occurrence of '◊' or '□,' and all the rest of the symbolization lies within the scope of the prefixed operators.

For **◊-Ontology** quantifies over all propositions, and so over propositions expressed by sentences (S) describes.[8] Thus prefixing '◊' to any (S)-type sentence yields a sentence expressing a proposition to which **◊-Ontology** applies, and so no matter what the sequence of these operators with which a sentence begins,

---

[6] This is not to say that Western theists have no such worry. (GSA) is part of standard Western theism, and I have argued that on the latter, God immediately conserves Bob's choosing and initiating his choice. My point is only that **◊-Ontology** is not what creates the worry.

[7] Counting a single occurrence of '◊' or '□' as a (degenerate) sequence.

[8] My thanks to a referee here.

prefixing these with '◊' yields a sentence expressing a proposition to which ◊-Ontology applies. Again, as just shown, ◊-Ontology entails that God provides all ontology for (or for the truth-explanation of) truths that □P, for any value of P. This too holds for values of P expressed by (S)-type sentences. As to claims properly symbolized as (S)-type sentences which begin with '¬,' given double negation elimination we need worry only about sentences starting with one '¬,' and so with '¬◊' or '¬□.'

In a standard Kripkean semantics, the truth-condition for claims of the form ¬◊P is that there is no possible world in which P. This is a negative existential. As I see it, negative existentials are true without ontology. They are true because there is not something. On ◊-Ontology, what there is not is appropriate God-provided ontology for ◊P. For on ◊-Ontology, God provides all possibility-ontology. There is no other candidate source. On ◊-Ontology, that there is no other candidate is God's doing too: on ◊-Ontology, God provides all ontology for there being (or for truth-explaining it that there are) no other candidates. (He neither makes any nor permits any to show up without Him.) If God provides all possibility-ontology and makes it the case that there are no other candidate sources, God explains it that there is not the possibility-ontology there is not: it is not there because He did not provide it or provide anything else to provide it, and explains it that there are not other sources He did not provide. Thus divine action or inaction explains the absence that truth-explains it that ¬◊P. So on ◊-Ontology, God provides for the truth of every claim the first two symbols of whose proper symbolization are '¬◊': the licit values for P in the sentence '¬◊P' include sentences (S) describes. Finally, on the standard approach, the truth-condition for claims of the form ¬□P is that it is not the case that in all possible worlds, P. Again, on ◊-Ontology, God provides possibility-ontology with this feature. So God provides the ontology for every claim the first two symbols of whose proper symbolization are '¬□.'

Call the claims so far discussed simplest modal truths. On ◊-Ontology God provides all ontology for (or for truth-explaining) all simplest modal truths and all non-modal truths. So on ◊-Ontology, God provides for the truth of

a. conjunctions all of whose conjuncts are non-modal or simplest modal truths. What provides for the truth of *P* and provides for the truth of *Q* provides for the truth of *P · Q*.

b. disjunctions all of whose disjuncts are non-modal or simplest modal truths. What provides for the truth of *P* and provides for the truth of *Q* provides for the truth of *P* v *Q*.

c. negations of (a)- and (b)-claims. This is not just because □(¬(P · Q) ≡ (¬P v ¬Q)) and □(¬(P v Q) ≡ (¬P · ¬Q)). Rather, I am following a principle of economy. Given the equivalence, for instance, (b) can cover negated conjunctions. If we let (b) do so, we get more bang for our ontological buck. It would be up to fans of any more commissive account to explain why this will not do.

d. conjunctions and disjunctions of (a)–(c)-claims, and of these or (c)-claims with (a)- or (b)-claims, non-modal or simplest modal truths, and negations of these, and so on recursively.

e. quantifications of simplest modal truths and of (a)–(d)-claims. If one simplest modal truth is that □Fa, its first-order existential quantification is that (∃x) (□Fx). On ◊-Ontology, God provides for the latter, because what meets the truth-condition of *John is a necessarily man* meets the truth-condition of *something is necessarily a man*. The universal quantification of □Fa, that (x) (□Fx), is true just if ¬(∃x)¬(□Fx). If nothing existed, the latter would be true. But as God exists necessarily (so I hold), it is not possible that (x)(□Fx) come out true because nothing exists. If something exists, it is true that (x)(□Fx) just if (i) each particular a, b, c . . . is necessarily F; and (ii) there are no particulars other than a, b, c . . . God provides the ontology for or for truth-explaining (i) by filling out the content of all possible worlds and either creating or refraining from creating. By not adding anything not necessarily F, God provides for (ii)'s truth without providing any ontology.

f. conjunctions, disjunctions, and negations of (e)-claims, and conjunctions and disjunctions of these and of (e)-claims with (a)–(d)-claims, non-modal or simplest modal truths, and negations and quantifications of these, and so on recursively.

g. modalizations of (a)–(f)-claims, and so on recursively.

h. negations of (a)–(g)-claims, and so on recursively.

So ◊-Ontology provides for the truth of all modal truths.

A Second Thesis

Thus ◊-Ontology entails **All Modal Ontology**, the claim that

> (P)((◊P is true ⊃ God is, contains, has or produces all of ◊P's ontology) and (P is true ⊃ God is, contains, has or produces all of P's ontology or all ontology in its truth-explanation) and (□P is true ⊃ God is, contains, has or produces all of □P's ontology or all ontology in its truth-explanation)).

To explicate **All Modal Ontology**, I now bring in the standard distinction between *de dicto* and *de re* modal claims. An unquantified modal sentence says something *de re*-modal just if in it a modal operator governs the ascription of some property to some thing(s) to which the sentence refers; equivalently, just if in it a modal operator has within its scope a non-logical constant used to refer.[9] That God is necessarily omnipotent is *de re*. It says of one particular thing that it has a property necessarily. A quantified modal sentence says something *de re*-modal just if in it a modal operator occurs within the scope of a quantifier, as in $(x)(\Box Fx)$. Iff a quantified modal sentence is *de re*, its instances are *de re*. **All Modal Ontology** entails that God provides all ontology for (or for the truth-explanation of[10]) every *de re* modal truth. So **All Modal Ontology** entails that God does so for all actual and possible truths ascribing possible careers and essential properties.

Everything is the subject of at least trivial *de re* modal truths. For all y, y necessarily is self-identical—that is, necessarily has $((\lambda x)(x=x))$. On suitably liberal views of properties, self-identity is then a trivial modal-essential property, one absolutely every particular has. I believe that every item has substantive modal-essential properties, ones not shared with all items. This is clearly so for items with definitional essences. As to items without them (if any), if modal intuition is any guide to reality, I could not have been a set or a sneeze. I have at least the substantive modal-essential properties of being concrete and substantial, if these are properties. If there is not something it is to be me, this is not definition-essential. The same will hold for all concrete substantial particulars, and the like for items either non-particular, non-concrete, or non-substantial. Again, I am essentially identical with Brian Leftow, and if this is a property, nothing else can have it. But I do not insist on either modal or definitional essentialism. I aim to show *inter alia* how God relates to essence if some kind of non-trivial essentialism is true, and so I discuss how God would account for there being substantive essential properties. But if nothing can have essential properties, the motivation for my overall theory will not change: there are still necessary truths, and even apart from this, as I show shortly, ultimacy and other concerns would still drive us to ◊-**Ontology**. Nor would what I say about God's relations to the content of possible worlds change: only these would determine not substantive essences, but just possible careers which in all cases vary so widely as to rule out non-trivial essential properties, or essential properties *tout court*.

A modal claim is *de dicto* just if it is not *de re*. On **All Modal Ontology**, God provides all ontology for all *de dicto* modal truths. Necessary connections between properties—as perhaps that necessarily, any body of H_2O is liquid between 32° and 212° Farenheit—are asserted in *de dicto* modal claims. Thus if **All Modal Ontology** is true, God provides all ontology for or all necessary connections between properties. These will include connections that follow from the contents of kind-essences, if any—such as the claim about H_2O just

[9] One might want to say that a modal sentence says something *de re* if in it a modal operator has within its scope a free variable. But such a sentence does not express any particular proposition. It is like sentences in which 'it' ought to have an antecedent but does not, so that 'it' refers to nothing determinate.
Predicate-constants do not refer to properties. Rather, they express and predicate them.
[10] I will not repeat this disjunct; take it as read where appropriate.

mentioned—and connections that constitute kind-essences such as that between *being water* and *containing oxygen*.

So far all I have done is explicate ◊-**Ontology** and **All Modal Ontology**. I now introduce one question they answer. I then argue the two.

The Question of Modal Status

For every necessary P, □-**Ontology** makes a claim about the truth that P. We can also ask about the ontology of modal status—being necessary, contingent, and so on. □-**Ontology** says nothing about this. On □-**Ontology**, God determines the true modal logic. If logical theses are necessary if true, this settles it that this logic's theses are necessary. Thus □-**Ontology** also implies that God supplies all ontology for these theses—but it does not imply that God supplies all ontology for their modal status. On □-**Ontology**, God is responsible for the existence and contents of worlds (or what lies behind world-talk). So given (OI), on □-**Ontology** He also at least partly accounts for its being possible that worlds exist and have these contents. Again, worlds have their contents necessarily; if (as is plausible) this truth is itself necessary, □-**Ontology** entails that God provides its ontology, and so provides the whole ontology for the modal status of truths about worlds' contents. Beyond those mentioned (granting the assumptions made), □-**Ontology** does not of itself make God responsible for propositions' modal status. Nor does □-**Ontology** of itself make God responsible for any world's modal status.

□-**Ontology** traces modal logic to God, but modal logic does not settle the modal status of any particular world. If God settles modal logic, He is responsible for whether accessibility is reflexive: that is, for whether every world is accessible from itself, such that if actual it would be possible. But that a world would be possible if actual does not determine its modal status. Every possible world would be possible if actual, but if we speak for the nonce as if there are impossible worlds, a world can be both impossible and such that it would be possible if actual. All that is required is that in the impossible circumstance of its being actual, it would be possible. If there are impossible worlds, then some impossible world W includes its being the case that W is possible, since, one sort of impossibility is that an impossible state of affairs be possible, and there is no reason to restrict this to the non-world-sized. If so, then W is impossible, but were W actual, W would be possible. Again, on the standard treatment, all counterpossibles are trivially true. So for all worlds W, if W is impossible, *W is actual* > *W is possible* comes out true (though *W is actual* > *W is impossible* does too). Again, if we consult intuition case by case, theists may well want to say that some impossibilities' being actual would not cancel the truth that P→◊P. There may be worlds whose sole reason for impossibility is that God's goodness would not let Him permit the amount of suffering they contain, no matter what. Nothing in the supposition that one of these is actual would require us to deny that $P \rightarrow \Diamond P$.

Again, on **☐-Ontology**, God determines accessibility relations between different worlds. But this does not entail that He determines their possibility: that W is actual $\rightarrow$ W* is possible does not imply that either is possible. Thus given **☐-Ontology** it is a further question what God's relation is to the modal status of modal truths.

From ☐-Ontology to the Answer?

Given **☐-Ontology**, the question has a quick answer if the true modal logic includes S5. For if it, does then on **☐-Ontology** God provides the ontology for all modal status. In S5, there are just four modal statuses: $\Diamond$, $\neg\Diamond$, $\square$, and $\neg\square$.[11] $\neg\Diamond$ is just $\square\neg$, and $\neg\square$ is just (($\Diamond$ and $\Diamond\neg$) or $\square\neg$)). So in S5, what gives claims the status $\Diamond$, $\square$, $\square\neg$, or (($\Diamond$ and $\Diamond\neg$) or $\square\neg$)) gives all claims their modal status. Of course, $\square\neg P$ is just $\square(\neg P)$ and $\Diamond\neg P$ is just $\Diamond(\neg P)$, so really we have only the statuses $\Diamond$ and $\square$ to worry about. In S5, all $\Diamond$ and $\square$ modal status is necessary: $\square P \rightarrow \square\square P$ and $\Diamond P \rightarrow \square\Diamond P$. $\square\square P$ is just$\square(\square P)$ and $\square\Diamond P$ is just $\square(\Diamond P)$. So given S5, if **☐-Ontology** is true—that is, God provides all ontology for necessary truths—God provides the ontology for its being the case that $\square P$ and $\Diamond P$, for all necessary and possible P. Thus, given **☐-Ontology** and S5, God provides the ontology for all modal status and the truth of all modal truths. Given S5, **☐-Ontology** entails **◊-Ontology** and **All Modal Ontology**.

Given **☐-Ontology**, if the true modal logic includes S4, the S4 axiom that $\square P \rightarrow \square\square P$ gives us that God provides all ontology for the modal status of any truth with a proper symbolization beginning with '$\square$,' *per* the argument just given for S5. He does so if **◊-Ontology** is true. I do not see how He could if it is not. On the standard semantics, for it to be necessary that P is for all possible worlds to include that P. That is, it is for it to be the case that W_1 is actual $\rightarrow$ P and W_1 is possible and W_2 is actual $\rightarrow$ P and W_2 is possible, and . . . and there are no possible worlds other than $W_1, W_2 \ldots$ On **☐-Ontology** and S4, God provides all ontology for this truth. So He provides all ontology for all its conjuncts. So He provides all ontology for worlds' possibility. So given S4, **☐-Ontology** entails **◊-Ontology** and **All Modal Ontology**.

Even apart from S5 or S4, it is plausible that God is responsible for the ontology of modal status. For on **☐-Ontology** God provides the worlds (or, again, what lies behind talk of them). Perhaps these *are* the whole ontology of their being possible: perhaps they just are possible (or not) purely by virtue of their own content. If not, possibility is (so to speak) an extra property

[11] See G. E. Hughes and M. J. Cresswell, *An Introduction to Modal Logic* (London: Methuen, 1968), pp. 49–50.

externally affixed, and (GAO) gives us that God provides it. If so, **□-Ontology** and (GAO) entail that God provides all that goes into worlds' being possible; anything else is possible by being actual or by its relation to worlds; (GSA) and (GAO) entail that God provides all that is actual and any relations involved; so **□-Ontology**, (GSA) and (GAO) give us **◊-Ontology.** Add the relation of accessibility, courtesy of (GAO), and we have **All Modal Ontology.**

I have argued that theists should adopt (GSA), (GAO) and **□-Ontology**. If these are true, **◊-Ontology** follows. So theists have (I claim) good reason to adopt **◊-Ontology** and **All Modal Ontology.**

Ultimacy and Modal Status

If we do not trace to God all ontology for modal status—that is, adopt **◊-Ontology** and **All Modal Ontology**—we court ultimacy problems. The only plausible way for theists to deny **All Modal Ontology** is to hold that there is outside God independent of any divine act a full panoply of worlds whose content settles their modal status.[12] These will have to be abstract—e.g. 'big' propositions. For it is not independent of God what concrete existents there are.[13] If there are such worlds, **□-Ontology** is false. (The necessary truth that there are worlds is actually true, and God does not provide the worlds in its ontology.) Unsurprisingly, then, the Introduction's ultimacy problems resurface. The worlds are co-eternal with God, leaving Him not *the* first in duration. They are also underived, and so conflict with (GSA) and (GAO).

There would also be a problem beyond those in the Introduction. There are necessary truths about God's nature. If the worlds their necessity involves are independent of God, these determine what God must be and do. The worlds' truths of possibility determine what He can be and do. The worlds in no way depend on God, and He in no way explains them, but they explain or at least delimit much about Him, and God in a variety of ways depends on them. So on the most plausible way to maintain that modal status' ontology is independent of God, the deepest level of reality belongs to worlds. They, not God, are the ultimate reality.[14]

---

[12] I discuss only this case, but the extension to the case of God's not being responsible for only some modal status should be plain. If God is not, there will have to be at least parts of some possible worlds independent of Him, and the reasoning will be much as in the case of partial Platonism discussed below.

[13] This suggests something I show below, that the conjunction of theism and Lewis's views is a coherent if odd position.

[14] None of these things would follow if God had the sort of extreme omnipotence some think Descartes ascribed to Him. Then even if God had not determined what the worlds or His nature were, it would be in His power to do so. The worlds would be what they are only on His sufferance. God would control them and so they would not really control Him. So this further problem does connect with the extent of God's control, as Plantinga's account of the 'aseity-sovereignty intuition' and its relation to modal metaphysics (Introduction, fn. 65) suggests. But I do not see how to make the claim that God controls His entire nature

Partial Platonism

Even partial Platonism would challenge God's ultimacy. Imagine a Platonic Heaven of partial possible worlds, that include no necessary states of affairs other than those about their own contents and existence. They are partial because apart from states of affairs like *in W, P is true, there are possible worlds,* and (if the true modal logic includes S5) *W is possible,*[15] no one state of affairs figures in each. Save for those about worlds or their contents, the states of affairs they contain are all contingent. If God can complete these partial worlds, He can be responsible for the truth and necessity of whatever is necessary and not about Platonic Heaven's contents, and the possibility of all of the possible that He did not inherit. But such partial Platonism still leaves a challenge to divine ultimacy, even leaving aside the necessary truths for which God does not account. Partial Platonic Heaven would be a realm of items of some sort. These would be co-eternal with God. They would be underived and a 'given' for God.[16] If they made true any truths about God, these would at least partly determine what He can be and do. Truths about possibilities for creatures would partly determine creatures' natures. So to secure divine ultimacy, theists must reject even partial Platonism and show that God provides the ontology for all modal status—that is, that **All Modal Ontology** is true.

From (GAO) and (GSA)

If modal truths' ontology lies within God, this accords with **All Modal Ontology**. If it does not but is all actual, then as every actual entity is either concrete or abstract, (GSA) and (GAO) tell us that God accounts for its existence. So actualism, (GSA), and (GAO) jointly entail **All Modal Ontology**.

Modal ontologies sort exhaustively into actualist and possibilist, and the latter into existent-and non-existent-object possibilism. We also get **All Modal Ontology** if we conjoin Lewis' existent-object possibilism with (GSA) and (GAO). The short version of the reason why is that (GSA) and (GAO) deal in existing objects, without restriction to actual existing objects. Some might jib at taking Lewis' distinctive ontology to lie within their scope, but arguments like those given earlier for (GAO) are available here: for example, that if the Biblical authors had become convinced of Lewis' views—now *there* is an unlikely scenario—what they did say and the

---

plausible, and if He has only partial control over His nature, He has only partial control over the contents of worlds. There are bits of worlds that remain more ultimate than He, namely those that determine Him to have that of His nature which is beyond His control, and so too modal facts that are beyond His sway.

[15] And their necessitations, and theirs, and so on, if the true modal logic includes S4.

[16] Meinongian non-existents would not *exist* as long as God, since they do not exist at all. But non-existent Santa would be human, or such as to be human if actual, for as long as God is divine, and would be understood and a 'given' too.

significance it probably had for them suggest that they would probably have wanted (GSA) and (GAO) to cover the extra ontology.

Lewis' views are these. Merely possible objects exist as truly as we do. All possible items including worlds are spacetimes,[17] their parts, concrete particulars, and sets. A possible world is just a spacetime and its inhabitants. Lewis' worlds are discrete from one another in that none of their parts bear spacetime relations to any other world.[18] Non-sets AB belong to the same world just if each part of A stands in some spacetime relation to each part of B.[19] Presumably a set belongs to a world if all its members do. There are also transworld sets, which do not meet this condition; Lewis says that transworld sets of individuals play some property roles[20] and sets of worlds play the role of propositions.[21] As he holds that properties exist in every world in which they have instances, late Lewis may think that transworld sets exist in every world in which they have members. Early Lewis, quoted below, thought that such sets exist *in* no world, but equally from the standpoint of all. Either way, what makes a set merely possible is that none of its members have spacetime relations to us. What makes a non-set merely possible—that is, part or all of a merely possible world—is that it bears no spacetime relations to us.[22] All non-sets either exist in just one possible world or are cross-world sums of such items, as nothing can have all of its parts exist in each of two spatiotemporally unconnected spacetimes. Possible non-sets have their parts all in one world; transworld sums of these count as impossible—though they exist—or as possible in a more liberal sense.[23]

It is not at first obvious that God can fit into this picture. For Lewis, anything concrete and temporal has all its parts in just one possible world, or has parts in more than one. Nothing concrete and temporal all of whose parts exist in just one possible world has made anything in any other world, one might think, as its causing something to exist would cause there to be a temporal relation between itself and its product. And (it can seem) nothing with parts in more than one world has as a whole created anything in more than one world. (It is certainly true that impossible objects do not cause anything.) But (it seems) anything that has not as a whole created most of concrete reality is not God. So it seems that on Lewis' account, nothing temporal in any possible world is God. But for Lewis, nothing atemporal is a possible non-set, since for Lewis, to be a possible non-set is to be part (proper or improper) of a world—that is, a spacetime system. If many worlds have

[17] Or systems relevantly *like* spacetimes (David Lewis, *On the Plurality of Worlds* (Oxford: Basil Blackwell, 1986) pp. 75–6). Take this qualification as read where appropriate.

[18] Lewis, *Plurality,* pp. 70, 78.

[19] *Ibid.*

[20] *Ibid.,* pp. 55–6.

[21] *Ibid.,* p. 105.

[22] And what makes a set merely possible is that all its members are.

[23] Lewis, *Plurality,* pp. 210–20.

counterparts of our God, none is responsible for the existence of all concrete non-divine reality—each is one world's god, numerically distinct from all the rest. So it can seem that Lewisian theists would be stuck at best with an odd sort of polytheism, unless they held that there is a deity in just one possible world.[24]

But it is false that nothing with parts in more than one world can have as a whole created anything in more than one world. It could be this way: its part in W created the rest of W. Its part in W* created the rest of W*. And so on through the rest of Lewis' universes: thus if God were a sum of Lewis' worldbound individuals, and Lewis is content to let such sums be possible in a broad sense, God could be a sum which as a whole has created every concrete thing that is not part of Him, by having parts that created smaller bits of all this. Still, Lewisian theists might not be happy to say that God is in the stricter sense an impossible individual. Lewis himself suggests some ways forward. In an early paper, he took seriously the thought that not everything that exists is in spacetime:

> Nothing... inhabits more than one world (but) some abstract entities ... inhabit no particular world but exist alike from the standpoint of all worlds, just as they have no location in time and space but exist alike from the standpoint of all times and places.[25]

Consistent with Lewis' general approach, a world could be a spacetime *plus non-spatiotemporal items*. Why not? Why think it necessary that all that exists, exists in spacetime? This would complicate Lewis' account of the worldmate relation only slightly. Lewis' basic view is that non-sets AB are worldmates—parts of the same possible world—just if every part of A is spatiotemporally related to every part of B.[26] The revised basic view would follow 'just if' with a disjunction. One disjunct of this would be the original biconditional's right side. The other would be 'or A or B is non-spatiotemporal'. On this revision, the worldmate relation is no longer transitive. Instead, only spatiotemporal worldmate-hood is transitive. Worlds' sharing a non-spatiotemporal part would not violate the spacetime discreteness Lewis builds into his account of worlds: it would not entail that they share any spatiotemporal parts or stand in any spacetime relations.

Suppose, then, that as on standard classical theism,[27] God is non-spatiotemporal. That such a God had causal relations to many spacetimes would

---

[24] For some of this see Robin Le Poidevin, *Arguing for Atheism* (London: Routledge, 1996), p. 30. The next few paragraphs *inter alia* respond to Le Poidevin's arguments. See also Paul Sheehy, 'Theism and Modal Realism', *Religious Studies* 42 (2006), 315–28. I am one of the referees whom Sheehy acknowledges; some of what is in the next few paragraphs also appears in his article, but only because it appeared in my comments on his earlier draft.

[25] David Lewis, 'Counterpart Theory and Quantified Modal Logic', in Michael Loux (ed.), *The Possible and the Actual* (Ithaca, NY: Cornell University Press, 1979), p. 126.

[26] Lewis, *Plurality*, p. 70; for elaboration and qualification, pp. 70–8. The wrinkles introduced after the basic account have no bearing on the present matter. I therefore ignore them.

[27] So, for example, S. Thomae Aquinatis, *Summa Theologiae* (Ottawa: Studii Generalis, 1941), Ia, qq. 8–10.

not entail that anything in one spacetime was so much as causally relevant to anything in any other. Nor would it entail that there are any spacetime relations between them. For as I have argued elsewhere, an atemporal God can have effects in spacetime without becoming spatiotemporal.[28] So if an atemporal God causes something to exist in spacetime, no spacetime relation comes to link it to God. Now if God causes George to exist and yet there is no spacetime relation between Himself and George, and God causes Georgette to exist and yet there is none between Himself and Georgette, it is possible that God cause them both to exist without there being any spacetime relation between George and Georgette if it is possible that there be none between George and Georgette. Thus a classical-theist God could fit into the modified Lewis picture nicely, and could create all Lewis-worlds. By so doing, He would create the entire ontology of modality: God would create the space-time portions of all Lewis-worlds from His position outside them all. He might represent them to Himself (logically) first, but they would not be *possible* (existent) worlds until He creates them. His knowledge of their contents would not depend on their existing spread out before Him, and their status as possible (existent) would depend on the exercise of His will. Thus (GSA), (GAO), and a Lewis-style possibilism allowing the non-spatio-temporal entail **All Modal Ontology**, if God is atemporal. On this picture, God has contingent relational attributes. From the standpoint of any world, in Lewis' terms, God has created all that is not Himself, but might instead have so created that the result was a different world. This Lewisian picture is not compatible with God's having contingent intrinsic attributes: God as outside all worlds is intrinsically just as He is no matter which world He is viewed from. But the claim that He has none is part of doctrines of divine simplicity which are themselves part of classical theism.[29] Many theists have been and are willing to bite this particular bullet.

Nor are matters hopeless if God is temporal—and if temporal, a Lewisian God can have contingent intrinsics. Lewis suggests that though individuals exist in but one world, other worlds represent possibilities for them, by containing simulacra which represent them by resembling them.[30] The theist, then, can say that other worlds' deities represent possibilities for our God by way of simulacrum. So the theist can say that there is just one God—ours—in the picture. Every other world's theists will make the same claim about *their* world's God—and be correct, in Lewis' terms.[31] This is just as monotheists in our world would want if (as they want to say) each world's God just represents the one God there is (who is *inter alia* ours). So a mono-theist could consistently believe in Lewis-worlds and divine counterparts.

[28] See my *Time and Eternity* (Ithaca, NY: Cornell University Press, 1991).
[29] So for example, Aquinas, *ST* Ia 3, 6.
[30] Lewis, *Plurality,* p. 194.
[31] Lewis, *Plurality,* p. 195.

A Lewis-monotheist would say that God has created all actual concreta other than Himself, plus spacetime, thereby created all sets in this world alone, and would have created the other worlds had He chosen differently—as any other monotheist would. Where things become distinctively Lewisian is in the claim that if God might have created differently, there exist the worlds He would have created and the God He would have been had He created them, and the allied claim that the existence of sets with members in more than one world depends on a joint effort by the actual God and the Gods He might have been.

On Lewis' account, a temporal God's pre-creative situation can be just as theist common-sense would say. Actually He represents all the possibilities to Himself and chooses one;[32] possibly He represents them all and chooses another. God's actions across all worlds account for the existence of all non-divine portions of Lewis' worlds. In each world, God knows what He might have done (does in other worlds)—that is, in each world, God knows the contents of all possible worlds. All possible worlds are such that God might have created (did create) their non-divine parts and providentially helped actualize them, and this is *why* they are possible (existent) worlds. In each world, God exists causally before the rest of that world, but not causally before the existence of other worlds. Nor does He exist causally after or simultaneous with other worlds, so there is no bar to the claim that in each world He has knowledge which presupposes the existence of those worlds. In no world does God's knowledge of what is possible depend on causal relations with other worlds—and this is fine, for no-one has ever maintained that God knows what is merely possible by having it cause Him to know it, or by actually causing it to exist.

Whether temporal or atemporal, God's creating all non-divine concreta and by so doing creating all classes is His establishing the full Lewisian ontology of modality, and so providing all modal ontology.[33] Thus if possible

---

[32] This is too simple a picture, but the complications needed for a full account do not matter for present purposes.

[33] Richard Davis argues that Lewis' views and theism are incompatible. For Lewis, a proposition is the set of worlds at which it is true (Lewis, *Plurality*, p. 53). Thus all necessary truths are identical with the set of all possible worlds—call it S. Davis writes that for Lewis, 'S contains only concrete, physical objects ... (But) God could have refrained from creating *anything* physical ... if He had, then ... S would have been the empty set! Thus the conjunction of theism and (Lewis' view) implies that it is actually possible that a necessary truth ... have been false' (Richard Davis, 'God and Modal Concretism,' *Philosophia Christi* 10 (2008), 42). Now if S is actually not the empty set, it could not have been the empty set: nothing is contingently identical with anything. What Davis means is that the empty set would have played the S-role, and the set that actually plays it would not have existed. But suppose that God actually had not created. On Lewis' terms it would not have followed that the empty set played the S-role. There would still have been all other Lewis-worlds, for on his terms it is not the case that an actual (this-worldly) creative act provides all physical objects for all possible worlds. Davis has covertly slipped actualism into his argument—which renders it irrelevant to whether theism is consistent with ontological views Lewis held. But there is a more basic issue here: God is free not to create anything physical only if there could have been nothing physical. So how can we square the belief that there might have been nothing physical with Lewis' view? Or, to put it another way, how can Lewis provide for a physically empty world? Lewis himself did not provide one

worlds are as Lewis holds, we have **All Modal Ontology**: God creates all in the ontology of modality that He does not contain.[34] This is a variation on Descartes' view. It need not include all claims some think Descartes made— for example, that some necessary truths are as they are because God so wills and God might have willed otherwise. God could also create all non-divine modal ontology on existent-possibilia views more liberal than Lewis' about abstracta, as long as the liberality did not extend to (say) existent non-actual Platonic particulars (*per* earlier argument). But these are eliminable; theists can use divine number concepts (say) in place of non-actual Platonic numbers. So I suggest that (GSA) and (GAO) yield **All Modal Ontology** on any existent-possibilia view.

Let us now take up the last sort of view: non-existent-object possibilism. Non-existents are nowhere in space or time. Quine's non-existent fat man in the doorway is not really in the doorway. Though he has the property of being in the doorway, if he does not exist there, the doorway is just one particular place where he is not.[35] Rather, he is such that if he did exist, the doorway is

---

(*Plurality*, p. 73); here we are in the realm of sympathetic extensions to Lewis' view. Gonzalo Rodriguez-Pereyra suggests that a broadly Lewisian view could allow a world consisting entirely of abstract objects, the pure sets: this would be a world at which nothing physical exists, a physically empty world ('Modal Realism and Metaphysical Nihilism', *Mind* 113 (2004), 683–704). The strategy adapts nicely to the move which lets a temporal God count as part of a world and tolerates God-counterparts, for then there might be as many physically empty worlds as we please containing just a God-counterpart. Each such counterpart might have created, but (in His own world) does not: so there is nothing physical *in that world*, and yet there is the full ontology of modality to provide the very set which constitutes all necessary truths, on Lewis' terms. On the view that sees just a single God outside all Lewis-worlds, what is needed is a counterpart relation which lets part of one world count as a counterpart of another world. But nothing in Lewis' setup rules this out. Lewis' counterpart relations are just relations of similarity: an item is your counterpart in a world under a particular counterpart relation just if nothing in that world more resembles you under that relation (Lewis, 'Counterpart Theory and Quantified Modal Logic', in David Lewis, *Philosophical Papers*, v. 1 (Oxford: Oxford University Press, 1983), pp. 27–8). Thus almost anything can be the counterpart of almost anything else, under an appropriate counterpart relation, for almost anything can count as most similar to almost anything else under some weighting of similarities. Now an area of pure vacuum in a world without substantival spacetime is an absolute nothingness. There is nothing physical in it; it is part of a physical world only because other parts of that world surround it. Suppose that there is at least one such vacuum, V, somewhere in Lewis' plethora of universes. Then we can say that under one counterpart relation, V counts as a counterpart of the physical portion of every world. A counts as a counterpart of B just if B might have been as A represents it as being. So if a physical world-portion has V as a counterpart, it might not have existed. If all physical world-portions have V as a counterpart, every possible complex of physical things might not have existed and not have been replaced. If so, there might have been no physical things at all. Thus in every possible world it will be true that God could have existed without physical accompaniment instead of having things as in that world. But this is true along with S's being suitably full, even were things as God + V represent. For were the actual world God + V, physically full worlds would still be possible.

[34] Sheehy suggests that Lewis-style views make the modal problem of evil particularly acute: if overall-evil possible worlds exist, God has caused them to exist, and so is not perfectly good (*op. cit.*, 321–4). Fair enough, but the theist has the modal problem anyway, and if there are resources in theism to handle it at all, Lewis-style views do not rule out their use. So this is no more an objection to the conjunction of Lewis' view with **All Modal Ontology** than to any other version of theism. I note *contra* Sheehy (*ibid.*, 323) that if God *conceives* evil worlds, it does not follow that He creates them, i.e. renders them possible: so if we can conceive of these, it does not follow that we can conceive of something God cannot, but only that we can conceive of something He has not willed to be possible.

[35] Terence Parsons sorts out the senses in which the fat man is and is not in the doorway in *Non-Existent Objects* (New Haven, CT: Yale University Press, 1980).

where he would be. Nor can non-existents act on anything as long as they do not exist.[36] So non-existent objects count as abstract on two standard ways of drawing the abstract/concrete distinction, though many would be concrete if they existed. But non-existents are not the sort of thing God could create, as creating a thing is causing it to exist. So (GAO) dictates rejecting non-existents, at least if they have no sort of being at all. Meinong says that his non-existents 'subsist'. He does not explain what this means. We can take it for the nonce to imply that they have some sort of 'being' though not the sort existents have (and pretend that we understand what this means). What 'subsists' might depend for its 'subsistence' on God. This was no uncommon thought in the Middle Ages; one finds variants of it in Henry of Ghent and Scotus.

Giving up pure non-existents is no problem for theists. The divine mind can provide substitutes, as far as modal metaphysics goes: in place of non-existent Santa, that in God which lets us speak of a Santa-concept.[37] Thus (GSA) and (GAO) yield **All Modal Ontology** in conjunction with two broad sorts of modal ontology. (GAO) rules out the third broad sort (which is rather implausible in any case). So if we follow (GSA) and (GAO) without stint, they yield **All Modal Ontology** *simpliciter*. So theists have good reason to accept **All Modal Ontology**. Further, the argument to this point suggests how theists should satisfy **All Modal Ontology**.

Abstract entities eternally outside God which eternally depend on Him would conflict with (FD), which for reasons like those developed for (GSA) covers the abstract as well as the concrete. So Western theists should not believe in these. They should instead limit their modal ontologies to God and created non-eternal concreta and abstracta. Any modal truths true from eternity must have their first ontology in God somehow. If one can make do here with items in God, eternal abstracta outside Him are otiose. But surely one can make do with items in God. If there were (say) eternally an attribute of caninity outside God, there would also be God's concept of this attribute's content.[38] God's natural omniscience guarantees that this concept would be complete in

---

[36] What about the non-existent fat man in the doorway who is kicking out the non-existent thin man in the doorway? (So a philosopher at the University of Birmingham.) Well, at the very least, he cannot act on anything that *exists*. But this restriction would be hard to motivate if the fat man could kick in every sense I can: I certainly have no problem kicking existing things. On Parsons' sort of view, the fat man *simpliciter* cannot kick, but is such that if he existed, he would be kicking.

[37] I do not claim that the divine mind will do for all purposes. Meinongians take non-existents as intentional objects of certain sorts of mental states. If items in the divine mind can play the same role—which I doubt—they would certainly not do so as naturally. But for this to be a problem for (GAO), theists would need good reason to think that there are decisive advantages to Meinongian accounts of intentionality. I doubt that there are any.

[38] Thomas Morris and Christopher Menzel identify the two ('Absolute Creation', in Thomas Morris, *Anselmian Explorations* (Notre Dame IN: University of Notre Dame Press, 1989), pp. 161–78). In so doing, they claim that God creates His concepts (*ibid.*, pp. 166–7), or perhaps His concepts' contents (*ibid.*, p. 166). If the identification really just reduces such abstract entities to divine concepts, I have no quarrel with it now (though I purge the divine mind of concepts later). If the claim is really that God's concepts have an 'external' content which God creates by thinking as He does, it seems to me simply unmotivated; the

every respect. But then this concept can be put to any philosophical use to which we might put the attribute.[39] So Ockham's Razor too bids theists seek any from-eternity ontology of modal truths in God, and this is where our attention will focus.

standard motivations for externalism do not apply in this case, and by moving to a purely internal or 'narrow' conception of divine mental content one avoids conflict with (FD).

[39] See my 'God and the Problem of Universals', *Oxford Studies in Metaphysics* 2 (2006), 325–56.

5

MODAL
TRUTHMAKERS

I now argue that theists should hold that

POSS. $(P)(\Diamond P$ is true $\supset$ God is, contains, has, has attributes that have (etc.) or produces all its truthmakers), and

NEC. $(P)(\Box P$ is true $\supset$ God is, contains, has, has attributes that have (etc.) or produces all its truth-explainers).

These yield God's responsibility for all modal truthmakers as ◊-**Ontology** did God's providing the ontology of all modal truths. Like **All Modal Ontology,** (POSS) and (NEC) speak only of actual truths and do not select among theist views. (POSS) deals in truthmakers because on the standard modal semantics and my own, $\Diamond P$'s truth-condition is existential. If it is, every truth of possibility has a truthmaker: it is true because something exists. (NEC) deals in truth-explainers because necessity-claims are true partly because there is not something (if $\Box\neg P$, because there is not a world in which P), and absences are not truthmakers.[1] Again, as I use these terms, no truth has both a truthmaker and a truth-explainer.

From -◊Ontology

If worlds are possible just in virtue of their content, this and ◊-**Ontology** implies (POSS). For on this assumption and ◊-**Ontology**, God is the *locus* or source of all possible worlds (or whatever stands behind talk of these[2]). Due to

---

[1] I take it that if there are worlds in which P, these are part of the ontology for $\Box P$, and contribute to its being true.

[2] Take this addition as read where appropriate.

God, there exist all possible worlds in which P. But that there exist a possible world in which P is the standard truth-condition for the claim that $\Diamond P$.[3] So given this thesis and $\Diamond$-**Ontology**, God provides all truthmakers for every possibility claim; once again, God provides modal truth just by providing modal ontology. (POSS) is almost enough on its own to get us (NEC). For given argumentation in Chapter 4, if God provides all the possible worlds, God explains it that there are not possible worlds there are not: they are not there because He did not provide them or provide anything else to provide them, and explains it that there are no other sources for them He did not provide. (The explanation includes that He has the GSA-property and a cognate GAO-property; at another level, whatever about Him gives Him these.) So God is responsible for all worlds' being all the worlds. Further, on $\Box$-**Ontology**, God accounts for all accessibility. So on (POSS) and $\Box$-**Ontology**, God's doing or being settle which worlds are possible, and which are accessible from possible worlds. But if there are some worlds possible from the actual world in which P and no other worlds, this makes it true that $\Box P$. Even if the worlds are 'big' propositions, that there are some such propositions and no other 'big' propositions satisfies $\Box P$'s truth-condition. So on the assumption noted and theses already argued, God also accounts for all necessity, which is (NEC).

It is good to have independent arguments for a conclusion. So I now argue (POSS) and (NEC) independent of the considerations that have so far driven the discussion.

Modality and God's Power

Let us first think about God's power. Intuitively, if God is omnipotent His power is unlimited. Philosophers add at once, though, that God can bring about or help establish only what is absolutely possible.[4] This is well motivated. Were God able to bring about the absolutely impossible, it would not *be* impossible. It would be something God possibly brings about.[5] Yet when philosophers introduce such claims to (say) first-year university students, the frosh tend to reply, 'surely that "only" limits God's power? If God is omnipotent, how can there be things He cannot do?'

---

[3] We later see that God's existing also makes it true that possibly God exists. I would argue that God Himself is the sole ontology for the truth that God exists—that God meets its truth-condition, rather than its truthmaker also involving some further item which is existence or His existence. If this is correct, the case of God's existence does not provide a counter-example to $\Diamond$-**Ontology**'s implying (POSS).

[4] 'Help' allows for facts God cannot establish on His own: for it to be a fact that I feed some fish, I must do the feeding. For a full discussion of omnipotence, see my 'Omnipotence,' in Thomas Flint and Michael Rea (eds), *The Oxford Handbook of Philosophical Theology* (Oxford: Oxford University Press, 2009), pp. 167–98.

[5] I take it that absolute possibility is the 'outermost' sort of possibility—that it could not be the case that something is absolutely impossible, but possible in some further, weaker sense: say, 'divinely possible'— that is, able to be brought about, but only by the power of God. I built this into the concept of absolute possibility in introducing it, by claiming that whatever is objectively possible in any other sense is absolutely possible. For an argument that this is so for 'logical modality' that adapts readily to what I call absolute modality, see Bob Hale, 'On Some Arguments for the Necessity of Necessity', *Mind* 108 (1999), 23–52.

Some try to meet the students' concern by arguing that there are no 'things God cannot do', because if a state of affairs is absolutely impossible, there is no act or task of bringing it about. Actions or tasks (they say) are by definition things someone *can* do. If a state of affairs is absolutely impossible, nobody can bring it about. So there is no act or task of doing this[6]—and so, the argument concludes, no act or task God cannot do. But students tend not to feel comfortable with this. And perhaps there is something to their feeling. For one thing, the frosh may be groping toward the thought that if there were an omnipotent being, nothing would *be* impossible.[7] That is not an absurd thought. The no-task response supposes that some things are impossible, and so does not address it. Again, it is now more usual to define omnipotence in terms of the range of states of affairs God can bring about.[8] Discomfort with acts or tasks God cannot do may well transmit itself to talk of states of affairs He cannot bring about. To address this with an analogue to the act/task move, one would say that there are no impossible states of affairs to be brought about. But this is implausible. Reasons to say that there 'are' possible states of affairs have parallels for impossible states of affairs: for example, just as it is intuitive to say that there are ways things could be, it is intuitive to say that there are ways things could not be, for instance, such that, '2 = 3' says something true when all its terms are used normally. Perhaps neither possible nor impossible states of affairs exist—that is my preferred view, in fact. My point is that there is little or no asymmetry in their intuitive support, and there would have to be a fair amount of asymmetry for this move to appeal. Moreover, perhaps the modal part of our description of an act or task ('*can* do') smuggles something in illicitly.

We have the sentence

RS. It is not the case that something is both determinately round and
     determinately square.

(RS) says something true.[9] The contradictory of a truth is not nonsense but a falsehood. So (RS)'s contradictory,

---

[6] So Richard Swinburne, *The Coherence of Theism*, rev. edn. (Oxford: Oxford University Press, 1993) p. 153.

[7] So a referee.

[8] So, for example, Joshua Hoffman and Gary Rosenkrantz, 'Omnipotence Redux', *Philosophy and Phenomenological Research* 49 (1988), 283–301; Thomas Flint and Alfred Freddoso, 'Maximal Power', in Alfred Freddoso (ed.), *The Existence and Nature of God* (Notre Dame, IN: University of Notre Dame Press, 1983), pp. 81–113; Edward Wierenga, 'Omnipotence Defined', *Philosophy and Phenomenological Research* 43 (1983), 363–76.

[9] By contrast, 'it is not the case that slithy toves gambol in the wabe' does not say something true. It is nonsense, like what it 'negates'. If this does not seem so, this may be because you are confusing it with 'it is not the case that "slithy toves gambol in the wabe" says something true.' This does say something true. It does because this claim follows from the truth that it is not the case that 'slithy toves gambol in the wabe' says something. This latter is something we can say truly, because we are mentioning the letter-string rather than trying to use it to say something. Those who try to assert that it is not the case that slithy toves gambol in the wabe do not say something true, because they try to use the string, as assertions that ¬P use rather than mention "P." 7.

¬RS. something is both determinately round and determinately square

says something false—and so it says something. It is not nonsense. We understand what it says, though not in the fullest possible way. (We cannot picture what would make it true.) If we do, there is something it says. If ¬(RS) says something, so does

¬RS*. something is determinately round and determinately square and made by someone.

For it too contradicts a truth, and we understand it in whatever way we understand ¬(RS). (¬RS*) describes the result of performing a task. In whatever sense we can conceive of this, we can conceive of the task being performed. So *prima facie*,

SM. someone makes it the case that ¬(RS)

says something—something closely related to (¬RS*). If (SM) says something, it describes the doing of an act or task, if not one whose results we can picture, or one someone possibly does. So to the extent that we understand (SM), we may be conceiving (in some sense) an act or task no-one can do. Coming at this another way, *prima facie*, if a sentence S says something, so does 'someone makes it the case that S.'[10] So again, *prima facie*, (SM) says something describing an act.

To allow for this we could just say that an act (task) is something an act - (task-) description would describe, and an act - (task-) description is a sentence-frame whose main verb is a verb of agency, which yields a comprehensible sentence if one fills its gap with a term for an agent (such as '__ is feeding a bird'). 'Would describe' brings non-actual actions under this rubric, and the notion of an action can be understood without a modal element: an act is something of a sort to be done, or such as to be done, and so agency-verbs express things of a sort for someone to do, and so on.[11] If we say only this, the bare form of an act—(task-) description does not rule out impossible actions (tasks). '__ is making a round square' yields comprehensible sentences given the right terms in its gap, though not sentences possibly saying something true, or saying something whose truth we can picture, or sentences we understand in the fullest way. So it is not as if there is no alternative to saying that an action (task) is a thing someone can do. And so it is worth asking why the notion of an action (task) must have a modal element. Might there be something question-begging in that?

---

[10] That is, we have at least a general intuition in this direction, which may or may not survive further reflection.

[11] Some might say they cannot understand this save by tacitly introducing the modal 'can do' or 'could do' again. If this is your plight, approach this in terms of conditionals. All possible tasks are tasks someone can do just if (RS) is false. Impossible tasks are those someone can do just if (RS) is true. If this latter claim makes sense, the bare form of an act - (task-) description does not rule out impossible actions (tasks).

Still, the idea of acts an omnipotent being cannot do may not be what disturbs the frosh; many are, after all, content to say that God is omnipotent but cannot do evil (that is, that if in the circumstances doing a certain act would be evil, God cannot then do that act, though He might be able to do acts of that precise type in circumstances in which doing so would not be evil). One source of the feeling that it limits God's power if He can do only what is absolutely possible, I think, may be that talk of absolute possibility has no obvious connection with God. The limits of the possible seem wholly independent of God. So if they are the boundaries of His power, these boundaries seem imposed on Him from without. So it seems that what God can and cannot do is determined from without—and this, I submit, may be the real root of the frosh unease.[12] The Frosh Intuition, then, is that on a good account of omnipotence,

FI. if God is omnipotent, nothing independent of Him determines what He can do.

One way to respect (FI) is to adopt (POSS). On (POSS), what states of affairs are possible is not independent of God. Instead, God as it were stretches out the realm of possibility, and its having a certain extent is just His stretching it so far and no further. The extent of the possible just expresses God's own nature, power, or activity. So if God can bring about only the absolutely possible, this does not fence God in from without. Given (POSS), God can bring about only what is possible because God can bring about just what He makes it possible that He bring about. That is, something about God makes possible what is possible. Given this something, there is a distinction between possible and impossible states of affairs. Given this distinction, the only possible divine acts bring about possible states of affairs. By delimiting the possible, God determines what it is possible for Him to bring about—what the possible actions of bringing-about are. Further, if God puts in place a modal logic containing S4, what is impossible is necessarily so, and so acts of making it possible are not possible. Thus if God puts such a logic in place, it is not true that given a boundary between the possible and the impossible, God can still do the impossible, because He can make it possible. On the view I adopt later, God puts such a logic in place. On (POSS), then, it is not the possible that places limits on God, but God who delimits the possible.

(POSS) gives us (I claim) the best account of the relation between God's omnipotence and absolute possibility. We have two intuitions, (FI) and that God can do only what is absolutely possible. These seem to clash. (POSS) lets them co-exist harmoniously. For God's nature, power, and action are not

---

[12] At any rate, it is the most cogent root I can ascribe to it. Worries based on Biblical texts like 'with God all things are possible' (*Matthew* 19:26) seem to me misplaced. For nothing in such texts suggests a particular reading of 'all things'. Reading them along the lines 'with God all doable things are doable' seems to me plausible, and plausibly the medievals who crafted our classic accounts of omnipotence read it thus.

matters independent of God. If only these bound God's power, God meets (FI)'s condition on omnipotence. Thus we can preserve both intuitions if we adopt (POSS). The harder it is to find other ways to do so, the more of these two intuitions' force (POSS) inherits.[13]

I now argue (POSS) in a second way.

(POSS) and the Modal Problem of Evil

Theists hold that

1. God exists and is omnipotent, omniscient and perfectly good.

'Logical' arguments from evil claim that evils exist with which (1) is not compatible and infer that (1) is false. Many theists hold not just (1) but

2. Necessarily, (1).

Friends of (2) face a modal analogue of a logical argument from evil.[14] We seem able to describe evils a perfectly good God could not permit: for instance, that

E. there is a universe consisting entirely of sentient beings who forever suffer horribly and pointlessly against their wills.

If a perfectly good God could not permit it that (E), (1) and (E) are incompatible. So the modal problem of evil lies in the incompatibility of (2) and

3. Possibly (E).

If (2) is true, in no possible world is (E) true. (E) makes perfect sense. So it *seems* to describe a genuine possibility. But if (2) is true, it does not: (3) is false. Thus friends of (2) need to undermine (3) somehow. It is hard to see how to make a case against (3) unless God has a hand in what is possible: unless worlds can fail to be possible by lacking theological credentials—that is, because God's nature or activity rules them out. (POSS) lets God rule out

---

[13] (FI) is not the only intuition we have in this vicinity. We might also think that:

O. if God is omnipotent, His power is unlimited; and

U. if God's power is unlimited, He does not limit it Himself.

(O), (U), and (POSS) are co-tenable, for it is co-tenable with (POSS) that God have placed every state of affairs in His power's range. Had He done so, He would have set no limits to His power, and everything would be possible. Conflict emerges if we conjoin (O), (U), (POSS), and the claim that some states of affairs are impossible. But in this conflict, if there are any impossibilities, (O) or (U) should lose. If we reject (POSS), God's power is limited from without by facts of impossibility—and intuitively limits imposed from without, over which one has no control, are worse than self-imposed limits whose extent one in some way controls. Again, there being just a certain stock of states of affairs to which to give modal status, whose content is not up to God, would be a non-self-imposed limit. If so, then equally by setting up any particular stock and no more, God would self-limit His power. As one or another must be the case, it would seem to follow that any extent of divine power involves some limitation—in which case either (O) is false or omnipotence is impossible. I incline to reject (O).

[14] See Theodore Guleserian, 'God and Possible Worlds: the Modal Problem of Evil', *Noûs* 17 (1983), 221–38.

evil worlds, and embeds this in a global theory about God and possibility, without which denying (3) would seem hopelessly *ad hoc*. So (POSS) seems likely to be part of the best defense of (2) against the modal problem of evil. Friends of (2), then, should accept (POSS).

I now take up objections to (POSS).

More about Evil

Evil can seem to cut against as well as for (POSS). For standard replies to 'logical' arguments from evil premise that various things just are not possible. For instance, one 'logical argument' contends that God would not permit moral evil. An all-good God, some say, would make only free creatures who would do no evil no matter what—that is, who do not even possibly do evil. If this is true, then if we do evil, God does not exist. A common response to this argument runs this way. Necessarily,

4. the best sort of freedom for creatures includes the all - things - considered ability to do evil.

If (4) is necessary, God does not have the option to make free creatures, give them their best sort of freedom, and yet render it impossible that they do evil. And so if God has good enough reason to make free creatures and give them their best sort of freedom, making creatures able to do evil will turn out compatible with His perfect goodness, and so His existence. This story depends, obviously, on a claim that something is impossible. But if God determines what is possible, perhaps no appeal to impossibility can excuse Him.[15] For instance, perhaps it was in Him to make (4) non-necessary and then false, letting our best sort of freedom exist without the possibility of evil. If by so doing He could have avoided allowing moral evil while incurring no worse cost for His creatures, He should have. So it can seem that given (POSS), there is no blocking this argument from evil—in which case there is no God. So it can seem that if a God would if actual set the limits of the possible, there is no God. If this is correct, there is a God only if the limits of the possible are independent of Him.

If this objection seems persuasive, it may be because we stop a bit short in thinking through what would follow if it is entirely up to God what is possible. If it is, it is up to God whether necessarily one should not allow moral evil one is able without cost not to allow, whether it can be better to be imperfectly than perfectly good, and whether perfect goodness is compatible with allowing evil one could prevent with no effort, cost, etc. If it is entirely up to God what is possible, it is in Him so to reshape the moral universe that

---

[15] So Earl Conee, 'The Possibility of Power Beyond Possibility', *Philosophical Perspectives* 5 (1991), 447–73.

He comes out in the best moral state no matter what evils He allows. For that matter, if it is entirely up to God what is possible, it is in Him to have things be possible of which we have no ken, which He then renders actual and which are such as to provide a successful theodicy within the constraints of the moral universe we now inhabit despite the falsity of (4). Or God can handle the argument by invalidating the inference-rules it uses.[16] So—precisely because all bets would be off were the limits of the possible entirely up to God—accepting both (POSS) and that God has it in Him to have the bounds of the possible other than as they are would not be reason to think the problem of evil worse than it might have been.

But more basically, (POSS) is silent on whether it is in God to have the bounds of the possible other than as they are, and if it is, whether it is in Him to have them other than as they are in all respects. (POSS) does not entail that it was entirely up to God what is possible. I submit that even if (POSS) is true, it is not up to God who He is, whether He is divine, what it is to be divine or to be Himself, or that these things are not up to Him. That these things should be up to God seems to me dubiously coherent. The ultimacy concerns that move me do not require these claims, and the rationale I give later for what I say about God's power over necessary truths about creatures does not extend to necessary truths about Himself. So I am free to reject these claims, and I do. Thus in my view, if the theist can make it out that the divine nature determines (4)'s truth or necessity, the theist can have (POSS) and also have it the case that it was not up to God whether (4) would be true. The theist can say that the bounds of possibility are set at least partly by what God is.

If true, (4) is necessary. It is necessary what properties do or do not include, and that a certain sort of freedom is *simpliciter* best for creatures takes into account all possible kinds of creatures that might be free, and so is true in all possible worlds, if in any. Almost all who have held (POSS) have held that God's nature somehow encodes truthmakers for all necessary truths about creatures. On such a view, (4) is true due to the divine nature if (4) is necessary. So most historical accounts including (POSS) give theists what they need to handle evil despite (POSS). I, however, argue later that God's nature does not encode such truths. So I now argue in a different way that if true, (4) is true due to the divine nature.

If an attribute F is part of God's nature, it is no more up to Him what it is to be F than it is what His nature is. Now one thing God is by nature is free. So it is no more up to God what freedom is than what His nature is.[17] And so if in conjunction with further premises whose truth is not up to God a suitable

---

[16] So a referee.

[17] A referee counter-argued: on the view I go on to argue, it is up to God what the natures of creatures are. So it is up to God whether necessarily, a creature is free only if it is libertarian-free. If so, it seems that God determines to some extent the nature of freedom. A short reply is that my claim is that if God is by nature free, *what freedom is* is determined at the level of His nature. Not every necessary truth about freedom is part of what it is to be free. The claim about creatures is really one about the possible extension of freedom and of one kind of freedom, not what freedom is.

account of freedom gives us (4), it is not up to God whether (4) is true. One not implausible story involving freedom goes this way.[18] An act or omission is free only if its agent is its ultimate source, and so only if the agent was not determined to do or not do what it did by something external. If true, this is true due to the divine nature; its truth is not up to God. God gave creatures natures not including all-things-considered ability to do evil, He by imposing natures on them would be the ultimate source of their not doing evil. Thus their not doing evil would not be free, though they might be free to choose between doing good and doing the morally indifferent, or choose which good to do. So because creatures get their natures from God (a truth not up to God), they can freely not do evil only if they are able to do evil. Suppose, then, that the best way to do good rather than evil is freely, and the best sort of freedom for creatures is one which lets them do good rather than evil in the best way. Then (4) is true, and if the two last 'best' claims also trace to things not up to God, (4)'s truth is not up to God, (POSS) notwithstanding. This account is worth serious thought. But rather than explore it fully, I offer another story that would yield (4), which turns on something else not up to God.

God is by nature unsurpassably loving, wise, generous, compassionate, and faithful, possessed of all knowledge and power He needs to express these things in the ways best for those He loves, strongly disposed to bless those He loves, and powerful enough to do so beyond all measure. Beyond all this, He is such by nature that the greatest joy creatures can know, the Beatific Vision, consists simply in a loving 'sight' of Him, however we understand this. So God is by nature a being loving relationship with whom is the best thing that could happen to creatures. Now there are many forms of love-relationship. Creature–God love is (I suspect) *sui generis*, no more reducible to another kind than parent—child love is to romantic. But the OT calls those God seems to have loved best—Abraham and Moses—God's friends.[19] Aquinas defines *caritas*—the distinctively Christian form of love—as friendship with God.[20] So friendship is a model our authorities suggest.

By His nature, God would make a surpassingly great friend. Part of the reason for saying this has already been laid out. To go further, let's note some salient traits of friendship. Being a friend is a way of loving: God is by nature perfectly loves us all. At its best, friendship is a relation in which each friend has a non-self-interested concern for the other: values the other, but not for what he/she can get out of it. God's perfect love and goodness guarantee a perfect form of this attitude; again, if His love conforms to the Christian

[18] Here I am indebted to conversation with Eleonore Stump, and to Thomas Williams and Sandra Visser, 'Anselm's Account of Freedom', in Brian Davies and Brian Leftow (eds), *The Cambridge Companion to Anselm* (Cambridge: Cambridge University Press, 2004), pp. 179–203. Much of this story is stated in Wesley Morriston, 'What's So Good About Moral Freedom?', *Philosophical Quarterly* 50 (2000), 349–50. Morriston rejects it, but as I am not committing to it, I need not discuss his arguments.

[19] *Exodus* 33:11, *II Chronicles* 20:7, *Isaiah* 41: 8.

[20] *ST* II–IIae, 23, 1.

conception of it, as ἀγάπη, it is by nature not self-seeking.[21] Still, true friends also enjoy one another's company; we read that God delights in those who love Him.[22] True friends promote their friends' good for their friends' sakes, not their own: God provides for all and (so we read) seeks their ultimate joy, and again, His perfect love and goodness guarantee both providential action and His perfect motives. True friends feel sympathy for their friends' sorrows and happiness for their happiness. Some doctrines of divine impassibility would deny this, but it is certainly Biblical. Friends trust each other to do these things, and so trust each other to understand each other well enough to do so: God is omniscient and His character makes Him supremely worthy of trust. Friends share interests: if God is perfectly good, any good we wish to promote is also one He wishes to promote, at least *ceteris paribus*. Friends spend time together and share activities: God is always with us, being by nature omnipresent if there is space to be present to, by nature shares our activities at least by providing all things that promote them, and concurs with all we do. Friends value their shared history; God's perfect goodness guarantees a love of all that is good in it. God's nature, then, guarantees that He is maximally ready to be a perfect friend to any creature able to be a friend. His nature makes Him one terminus of a friendship-relation. That is, God's nature makes it the case that whether there will be friendship between us depends only on how we respond to God's availability. To the extent that we love God at all, we will approximate to some attitudes and acts characteristic of a good friend, due just to the natures of love and of friendship. That will be all that is needed to constitute a friendship between God and ourselves. And again, this is all just a function of the natures of God and of friendship. God's nature is not up to Him. This nature includes that of love—perhaps a specific mode of love (ἀγάπη), perhaps a univocal general nature if love has one, but at a minimum the divine nature guarantees a general pattern of acts, attitudes, and (perhaps) affects such as to come out by 'family resemblance' as a perfect instance of love given other cases of love to which to compare it. To be a friend is just to love in a particular way; that God so loves as to be a friend is again part of His nature, as just shown. So it is not up to Him that He is ready to befriend, what love is, that any love between Him and a creature will count as a form of friendship, or that therefore the fullest flowering of this love, our highest good, will be the fullest development of a friendship.

Most of our friendships begin in an involuntary response: we are attracted. And perhaps they always have an involuntary component; Harry Frankfurt suggests that

It is a necessary feature of love that it is not under our direct and immediate voluntary control. . . . a person . . . cannot affect whether or how much he

---

[21] So Anders Nygren, *Agape and Eros* (London: SPCK, 1939).
[22] For example, *Deuteronomy* 30:9, *Isaiah* 5:7. 65:19.

cares about (his beloved) merely by his own decision. The issue is not up to him . . . There are . . . things that people cannot do . . . because they cannot muster the will to do them. Loving is circumscribed by a necessity of that kind: what we love and . . . fail to love is not up to us.[23]

But friendship also has a voluntary component. One chooses whether to follow up the initial attraction. If one does, and a friendly sort of love develops, it is at every step open to one to break the relationship instead of continuing it. One can break even the strongest friendship: one can walk away and cease to do anything about whatever caring is in one. Love-*relationships* are under our control, because it is up to us what we do about what we care about. Further, even if one cannot just decide not to love someone and make it work, one can control love to some extent indirectly, since one can control one's exposure to the beloved and what one dwells on in thinking about the beloved, and come to care less by directing one's attention elsewhere. Whether we tend our loves or choke them off is up to us.

Beyond this, there is at some point in the growth of a friendship a commitment one can make, withhold, maintain, or cut off, and without which the fullest form of friendship is impossible. Implicitly, we commit to standing by our friends, and the deeper the friendship the deeper the commitment. Intuitively, this commitment cannot be coerced. Nor can the rest of a friendship. We can be forced to act as if we were someone's friend. But we cannot be forced to love beyond a minimal level; in fact forcing destroys the chance to do so, may destroy even the initial basis for attraction, and so may make us cease to care altogether about the person coercing us. Friendly acts not motivated by friendly love or genuine commitment do not constitute a friendship. The result of coercion is an imitation friendship; in particular, the commitment in question has to be made without coercion if the genuine article is to result. Perhaps it can only be made without coercion. It amounts to forming a complex of stable, sincere intentions, and it is not clear that coercion can produce these. Nor can brainwashing produce genuine commitment and friendship. If Demon brainwashes Pythias into thinking he is Demon's friend and believes he thereby has a friend, Demon is deluded. Pythias is Demon's puppet, and puppets are not friends. True friendship is a response that emerges ultimately from one's friend.[24] Pythias' response to Demon emerges ultimately from Demon. So too, a coerced response emerges ultimately from the one coercing, to the extent that it *is* coerced.

If God gave creatures natures which guaranteed that they would be His friends, He would impose 'friendship' on them. This would be relevantly like brainwashing or coercion: it would be clear that our response emerged

---

[23] Harry Frankfurt, *The Reasons of Love* (Princeton, NJ: Princeton University Press, 2004), pp. 44, 46.

[24] Libertarians will so read this as to entail that if determinism obtains, there are no true friends. But one need not take it so; the point would survive given a reduced sense of 'ultimate' that allowed friendship within determinism.

ultimately from God, not us. So God can create friendship between Himself and creatures only if He leaves creatures all-things-considered able to reject His friendship. Unlike my first story, this one depends on no broad thesis about the nature of freedom. It makes instead a claim about what is required for one sort of love-relationship. Note that this story does not require that God be able to reject friendship with us. Creatures must be able to reject God's friendship because God imposes their natures on creatures. It is not up to God that they must, because it is not up to Him that He imposes natures on items He creates. We do not impose God's nature on Him, and so the story does not require that He be able to reject friendship with us. So the story would be unaffected were it to turn out that God simply could not reject us. However, everything I have said may be compatible with at least one way for an unsurpassably loving, compassionate etc. being to reject friendship with us: perhaps He could do so if He knew that we had so rejected friendship with Him as to guarantee that no matter what He did, we would not relent. This would leave Him as loving and generous to us as we allow Him to be, compassionate, and so on. It would simply be an acknowledgement that it takes two to tango, and we had decided never to dance.

It makes good sense, then, that our authorities liken creature–God love to friendship. Due to His nature, it is not up to God what love is, that He is such as to befriend creatures, that His relation to them will be what we know as friendship if they respond appropriately, or that the possibility of creatures' fully developed friendship with God requires that they be all-things-considered able to reject it. So if creatures' highest good is the fullest development of a friendship with God, this highest good is not possible unless we are able to reject it—and it is not up to God that this be so. I now argue that it is morally evil to reject this relationship. If this is true, then we are not able to have our highest good unless we can do at least this sort of evil. I then suggest that it is not up to God whether this is morally evil. If this is so, it is not up to God that we cannot have our highest good without being able to do evil. But necessarily, if we have a highest good, what is best for us is that we attain it. So necessarily, for all x, if we have a highest good, it cannot be better for us to have a sort of x that would not let us attain this than to have one that would. Thus the best sort of freedom for us is what lets us attain our highest good. And so necessarily, if it is evil to reject a loving relationship with God, the best sort of freedom for us includes all-things-considered ability to do evil—that is, necessarily (4). And if I am right, it is not up to God whether this is so.

It is Evil to Reject God's Friendship

I now turn to my case that it is a bad act to reject God's friendship. Consider George, who is kind, funny, wise, sympathetic, upright: in every way a good companion. Unknown to me, George has helped me greatly all my life, simply because from afar, he likes me. Everything he has done for me is something which, had I known, I would have been glad to have him do. Finally I learn all this, and we meet. George asks me to have a beer with him. It is obviously an invite that could lead to becoming his friend. This is something he wants, it is a fitting response to his kindness to me, and he will be mildly disappointed if I decline. I have nothing else to do that afternoon. There is no moral reason not to acquire another friend. I even like beer. Surely I owe it to a good man who has greatly helped me to give him a chance. If I do, it would be a bad act to decline. Someone who habitually responded in relevantly similar ways would surely count as having some constellation of moral shortcomings, and this is true only of bad acts. Plausibly this response would be ingratitude, an evil. Now change the setup: George has done just as much for me, but I do not know of it when he makes his invitation. In this case I can decline blamelessly. My ignorance excuses me. But I have done something that needs excusing—a bad act. For suppose that once George dies, I learn what he did for me. I will at that point keenly regret snubbing him. This will be a distinctively moral regret, for I will know that I inadvertently denied kindness an appropriate response, that I owed him better treatment—that I unknowingly did what I ought not to have done, that without meaning to, I did a bad act. Further, the more I learn that George did for me, the worse I will rightly feel. The rightness of the feeling indicates that the more he did, the worse I did. And God has done much more for us than any human could. So if God acts as a hidden friend to me, I do evil if I reject His initial offer of friendship.

It is not a bad act, once one has given someone as many chances as he deserves, to reject his friendship if he gives one reason to do so. But God's character guarantees that He never in fact gives one such reason. A morally perfect creator always so acts to each friendship-capable creature as to deserve friendship. Of course, it does not always seem to all of us that God is acting this way. Many Western theists would concede that some may only in the afterlife be able to see how God has been good to them: they may sheepishly say that that is part of why faith is required. And if it does not seem to one that God is being friendly, this may be morally sufficient reason to reject divine friendship even if in fact, God is then acting as a friend would. Arguably ignorance of a divine benefactor is in some cases not intellectually or morally culpable.[25] One is not ungrateful if one non-culpably does not think anyone is behind the scenes acting as a friend would, or that one has anything to be grateful for. Lack of gratitude because one does not believe one has a benefactor seems to differ from the vice of ingratitude.

The possibility of ignorance of God may be irrelevant to my argument about the initial offer. If one does not think someone seeks one's friendship,

---

[25] There are deep, tangled issues here. I cannot broach them. This claim represents what most parties to the relevant disputes would concede.

or sincerely thinks that no-one does, perhaps one does not count as rejecting a friendship. Perhaps one has not met a condition of doing so: one does not believe the potential friend is there to reject. So even if it is evil to reject God's friendship, perhaps those in such epistemic positions are not doing that evil. At any rate my argument does not require the claim that they are. What matters, or so I have argued, is that we be able to reject this relationship—not that every failure to love God count as doing so. This also gives us a way to think about ceasing to be God's friend after one has embarked on this. If God is supposed to be by nature perfectly good, loving, and so on, then there are at least two possible negative responses to apparent evidence of His not so acting, or lack of evidence of His so acting. One is to reject His friendship: perhaps we continue to believe that He exists, but react more negatively to His current treatment of us than we should, or fail to give Him as many chances as He deserves. Another is to cease to believe that He exists. One rational response to a sincerely formed belief that something has happened which a God of the character I have described could not have allowed is to believe that there is not such a God. If not believing that God exists entails that not taking up a divine offer of friendship does not count as rejecting that offer, then ceasing to believe that God exists does not constitute rejecting friendship with God. If I have thought Santa was my friend and then learn that there is no Santa, I have not rejected a friend I had previously had. I have come instead to believe that there was never any friendship to be had there. If I think George Bush is my friend and then mistakenly come to believe that there is no George Bush, I do not count as rejecting a friend. I instead mistakenly come to believe that there was never someone there to befriend. Again, it is no part of my argument that every failure to love God count as rejecting divine friendship (or that this not be so).

God and the Standard of Evil

The last bit of my argument is that it is not up to God whether it is evil to reject His friendship. It is up to God whether it is morally evil to reject this relationship just if the standard for the relevant sort of moral evil is in His control: if the non-moral facts are set (offer of friendship, nature of potential friends, and so on), only that is still a variable. I cannot give my full story about value here, but I do not believe that it is up to God what is morally good or evil. As I see it, the ultimate standard of moral goodness is God's own nature: God is good purely of Himself, and others are good just if they stand in the right relation to His nature. If this is so, God controls what is good or evil only to the extent that He controls what there is to stand in such relations. It is (so I will suggest) up to God whether there is such a thing as courage. There is such a thing only because He thought it up, and it was in Him never to do so. Given that God has thought it up, though, it is not up to Him whether courage is evil. Rather, its relations to His nature determine this. The relations are at least like resemblance in a key respect. Two humans resemble in being human. We can make no sense of the idea that they should both be human, resemblance be what it is, and yet they not resemble *qua* human: this is just an incoherent supposition. So too given the nature of God and (say) a character-trait, it is determinate that it is good, indifferent, or evil, and it is not a coherent supposition that it be otherwise.

Only divine command and cognate theories place some moral properties in God's control.[26] Recent divine command theorists limit the extent of God's control to the distribution of rightness, wrongness, and cognate properties such as being obligatory and being permitted.[27] They do so because it helps such views overcome problems. I will mention two.

It is a fundamental premise of divine command theories that I should obey divine commands. But a divine command cannot create an obligation to obey divine commands. For if God commands me to obey His commands, why should I obey this initial command? Either when I receive this command I already ought to obey, or it is not the case that I ought to obey. If I already ought, it is too late for the divine command to create the obligation. It already exists. If it is not the case that I ought to obey it, then I do no wrong if I disobey it. But if I do no wrong if I disobey it, then even given the command, I have no obligation to obey that command or any other.[28] Any moral case that I should obey divine commands, then, will have to rest on moral facts not involving obligation: on divine command theories, all relevant obligations are created by divine commands, and so simply raise the question of why I should obey once more. This pushes us into the realm of good and evil, not right or wrong. But if facts about good and evil were themselves created by divine command, a variant of the 'why obey' question would arise. Suppose that all that makes an act morally good is that God commands or wills that it be done. Then we must ask why it is morally good to do acts God wills. 'Because God wills it' just raises the question anew, and if God's will is the source of the good as well as the right, there are no other moral

---

[26] Philip Quinn, 'Divine Command Theory', in Hugh LaFollette (ed.), *The Blackwell Guide to Ethical Theory* (Oxford: Basil Blackwell, 1999), pp. 53–70, and Edward Wierenga *The Nature of God* (Ithaca, NY: Cornell University Press, 1989), pp. 213–32 hold that what matters to meta-ethics is God's willing something, not His issuing an explicit command. So their views are strictly speaking only cognate to divine command theories, unless we use 'divine command' as a generic term for any form of theological voluntarism.

[27] So, for example, Robert Adams, 'A Modified Divine Command Theory of Ethical Wrongness', in Paul Helm (ed.), *Divine Commands and Morality* (Oxford: Oxford University Press, 1981), pp. 83–108; Edward Wierenga, *op. cit.*; William Alston, 'Some Suggestions for Divine Command Theorists', in *Divine Nature and Human Language* (Ithaca, NY: Cornell University Press, 1989), pp. 253–73. Philip Quinn defined goodness in terms of divine commands in *Divine Commands and Moral Requirements* (Oxford: Oxford University Press, 1978, pp. 67–71, 83–6), but abandoned this move in 'Divine Command Theory', *loc. cit.*

[28] This somewhat reworks an argument of Richard Price quoted in William Wainwright, *Religion and Morality* (Aldershot: Ashgate, 2005), pp. 82–3.

resources to draw on. So it seems that divine command theories can make a moral case that we should obey divine commands only if they leave a suitable domain of facts about good and evil independent of God's will. The natural point of division will be this: what God wills us to do becomes obligatory, and whatever its other moral qualities, thenceforward it is also good to do it because it is good to meet one's obligations, and bad not to do it because it is bad not to meet one's obligations. All other cases of good and evil are independent of God's will—and the motivations that push one to a divine command theory (divine independence and sovereignty, as well as motivations that push one to ground moral modal truths in a theist modal theory) push one to ground them in God's nature.

Another reason to leave good and evil partly outside the scope of God's will arises from an objection to divine command theories. If nothing is good in advance of God's setting His will or issuing commands, many argue, then God might command literally anything, and on a divine command theory, that would make it good: so God might command that all puppies be roasted live on spits, and it would then be good to do so. Recent writers reply with an appeal to God's character.[29] If God is (say) loving in advance of issuing His commands, He would issue only commands a loving being would issue. If He is loving by nature, it is not possible that He issue any other sort of command. So if it could not be loving to have all puppies spitted, it is false that God might issue this command, as it would be contrary to His nature or character, though it is true nonetheless that if (counterpossibly) He did so command, this would make puppy-spitting good. Wierenga appeals to the virtues of being loving, merciful, just, and faithful as constraining God's commands—and does call them virtues.[30] So does Adams.[31] It matters that these be understood as moral virtues: otherwise they provide no guarantee that God's commands will in fact stay within the realm of the good. (Love unmoored to the good might lead one in very odd directions.) But a virtue is precisely a stable character-trait leading reliably to attempts to perform (and perhaps success in performing) what the agent understands to be good acts, or what are in fact good acts. Whether attempts are enough and whether what matters is just the agent's understanding are matters of debate. But to deal with God we need not take them up. God's beliefs about the good will be accurate if there are facts for them to capture, and His understanding is coextensive with the moral facts. God's attempts to do good will fail only if they depend on our co-operation and we do not give it, and such things do not impugn one's virtue. If the good involved in the acts typical of a given virtue is good only by God's willing it to be so, the puppy-roasting problem looms again: if God made it

[29] *Op. cit.*, nn. 26, 27.
[30] *Op. cit.*, pp. 203, 222.
[31] *Op. cit.*, pp. 101–2.

good to roast puppies, it would then be an act to which the appropriate virtue would incline Him, and so would once again be a live option for a divine command. The appeal to virtue only works if the relevant goods and evils are so independent of His will.

I began this argument because I had used the modal problem of evil to support (POSS), and it seemed that evil could also be used against (POSS). I have argued that it cannot. I now consider three other objections to (POSS).

Regress?

I cash (POSS) out partly in terms of ontology in God, and such talk of ontology raises a difficulty.[32] If a proposition's ontology is there and is such as to make the proposition true, the proposition is true: if for it to be the case that P is for A to exist and have attribute F, then if A has F, it is true that P. This is a case of strict implication. That relation is modal. That P strictly implies that Q just if $\Box(P \supset Q)$. So for (say) God's being divine to be what makes it true that P is for it to be the case that $\Box$(God is divine $\supset$ P). But then there must be ontology for this too, and a further modal relation, and so *ad infinitum*. If we keep getting modal relations between truths and ontology, the objection goes, we do not explain how God stands beneath all modal truth: there is always some modal truth left outside the *explanandum*.

If there is a problem here, it is not unique to theist modal metaphysics. I say eventually that God's total state from all eternity is from eternity the ontology of all absolute-modal truths, and indeed the totality of their truth-makers. Any other ontology as a whole—all Lewisian worlds, for instance—would have the same role. So I am no worse off than anyone else who believes in modal ontology. But I am not sure there really is a problem here. If God's total state is the ontology for/makes true/truth-explains all modal truth, no one item in God is so or does so for all of modal truth. This does not entail that some part or aspect of God's total state is not the ontology or truthmaker or truth-explainer for whatever particular modal truth we are discussing. As to the conjunction of all modal truths, divide and rule: the plurality of the conjuncts' ontologies/truthmakers/truth-explainers does the trick.

Omnipotence

Another objection goes this way:

5. If (POSS) is true, God could have been able to bring about each state of affairs He now can bring about, plus more He cannot now bring about.

---

[32] My thanks here to Thomas Flint.

6. If God could have been able to bring about more, He could have had a larger range of action than He has. So:

7. If (POSS) is true, God could have had a larger range of action than He has.

8. There could not have been a larger range of action than an omnipotent being has. So:

9. If (POSS) is true, God is not omnipotent.

But suppose that the logic of absolute modality does not include S4. If it does not, there could have been other possibilities than there are. If there could have been, perhaps in some possible world there are more, in some sense of 'more'. If there are, then for this sole reason, an omnipotent being, able (speaking roughly) to bring about or help bring about anything absolutely possible,[33] could have had a greater range of action if it could have been omnipotent in such a world. This is no scandal. So whoever held both (POSS) and that the logic of absolute modality does not include S4 could deny (8) with equanimity. There could have been such a range, given the S4 denial—and further, this does not entail that any actually omnipotent being, with a lesser range, is not in fact omnipotent, since omnipotence is defined in terms of ability to bring about possible states of affairs, not ability to bring about what only might have been possible. On the other hand, if the logic of absolute modality includes S4, then even if (POSS) is true, (5)'s consequent is false. In S4, every possibly possible state of affairs is possible. So there are no more states of affairs, such that God might have been able to bring them about, but is not. So if absolute modality is an S4 modality, (5) is false. Whatever the truth about S4, then, the argument fails.

In any case, it is co-tenable with (POSS) that (5)'s consequent be false. (POSS) lets the divine nature determine all modal facts. On a divine-nature version of (POSS), (5)'s consequent would be true only if God could have given Himself a different nature. It is not up to God what His nature is. So divine-nature-theorist friends of (POSS) can deny (5). It is also co-tenable with (POSS) that it be up to God to some degree what is possible, but God do all it is in Him to do in regard to establishing possibilities, even though His nature does not impel Him to do so. If God did so, again, (5)'s consequent would be false. So, again, it is co-tenable with (POSS) that (5)'s consequent be false. If it is (5)'s antecedent does not *a priori* or analytically imply its consequent. But then it is unclear what reason there is supposed to be to believe (5).

Omnipotence again

Another objection to (POSS) is that it trivializes omnipotence or could expel it from God's nature altogether. Suppose that God is omnipotent and so can

---

[33] This needs to be tweaked and supplemented to get near being a fully adequate necessary condition on omnipotence, but none of the required changes matter for present purposes.

bring about or help bring about anything absolutely possible. Suppose (POSS) too, and that it is in God to have the entire range of the possible consist of (say) His existing, being as He is, setting His power and there being one apple. Then God could count as omnipotent even if all He could do is set the range of His power and make an apple. But this would trivialize omnipotence: an omnipotent being must be able to do more. Suppose on the other hand that omnipotence precludes a range of power this limited, but on (POSS) it is in God to have the range of the possible come out this small. Then (POSS) entails that it is in God to bring it about that He is not omnipotent. If so, being omnipotent is not part of His nature. Further, it is in Him to bring it about either that omnipotence is not part of deity or that He is not divine. As it is not clear that properties can have inessential parts—that deity could contain omnipotence in some possible worlds but not all—it seems to follow that it is in Him not to be divine.

The shortest answer here is that (POSS) says nothing at all about whether it is in God to have the range of the possible other than it actually is. So (POSS) carries none of the suggested consequences. Further, if (POSS) is true *and* it is in God to make the range of the possible other than it actually is, it does not follow that it is in God to make the range of the possible so small as to threaten His omnipotence. Even if it is in God to have the range of the possible be other than it is, His nature could constrain the way He could vary its range. We must accept one such constraint if God is by nature good, for then, however He filled out the possible, He would not include in it any possible world too evil to permit to be actual. Perhaps His natural omnipotence imposes another constraint. So I answer as follows.

God has no power over what His nature is. This is compatible with (POSS), which does not require that it be up to God what it is possible for Him to be. This is also compatible with the Introduction's ultimacy concerns. These are met if (GSA) and (FD) are true, there is a level of causal explanation at which God alone explains other things' existence, there is no going past this level in any explanation of other things' existence, nothing other than God accounts for God's existence, and everything other than God has/had a cause of its existence. The claim that God has no control of His own nature is just irrelevant to these things. Nor is the claim that God has no power over what His nature is a threat to divine aseity: it does not make God depend on anything outside Himself. It is part of God's nature to be omnipotent; so God has no power over the fact that He is omnipotent. Further, what omnipotence *is* thus is also part of God's nature and beyond His control. The nature of omnipotence (say I) includes a non-trivial range component: simply put—as we need no more—one is omnipotent only if one can bring about a *lot*. So whatever God does with the range of the possible must be such that He comes out able to do a lot.

In any event, if there is a problem here, it arises as we consider restricted ranges for the possible, whether or not God is the reason for them. For be

(POSS) as it may, it could be true that to be omnipotent includes being able to bring about or help bring about all that is absolutely possible even if the only possible state of affairs beyond God's existing and having His nature were one apple's existing. If the real problem is making God's power hostage to the range of the possible, one could be pardoned for seeing (POSS) precisely as an antidote to this.

(POSS) has intuitive backing and survives the objections I have brought against it. So theists have reason to accept it independent of the main line of argument I have pursued. I now turn to (NEC).

A Perfect-being Argument

It would be an awesome thing to be unconstrained even by modal truths and facts of modal status—to be a being to whom even these are not 'given', save insofar as its own nature is given. A being whose power is not externally limited even by these would seem more powerful than one whose power was subject to such constraint. (NEC) secures this awesome lack of constraint. So if (NEC) is viable, theists have 'perfect-being' reason to adopt it.

The intuition to which I am appealing is of course Cartesian. But it need not lead us where it (may have) led Descartes.[34] It need not lead us to give God power over the truths of logic, for instance, if these have a foundation in God's own nature and it is not up to God what His nature is. It need not lead us to say that it is up to God what His nature is. It cannot be up to anything what its nature is; it must have a nature to be there to have anything up to it. The claim that the less limitation, the more power, is compatible with the claim that certain limitations (if that is what they are) cannot be avoided. Again, it can be true both that some truths are necessarily necessary and that they are not a 'given' for God, if God gave them that status. I show later that this can indeed be so on my approach.[35]

---

[34] For the main interpretations of Descartes' theory, see Alvin Plantinga, *Does God Have a Nature?*, (Milwaukee, WI: Maquette University Press, 1980), p. 95ff.

[35] Necessary necessity is also compatible with the main alternative to mine, on which the divine nature makes all modal claims true from eternity true. For plausibly God's nature is necessarily as it is. If it is so, so are any necessary truths whose necessity is grounded on it.

6

MODALITY AND THE DIVINE NATURE

I now turn to the task of constructing a modal metaphysic incorporating (POSS) and (NEC)—one on which facts about God, His acts, or His products account for all modal truth and status. An easy way to see that such theories can be had is to see that there is a theist transform of a well-known theory. On one Platonist view, possible worlds are attributes entire universes could exemplify, such that if one were exemplified, one possible history for an entire universe would be enacted.[1] The first Platonist account of attributes was, of course, Plato's theory of Forms. Augustine provided a theist transform of this by turning Forms into ideas in the mind of God.[2] One can do this with universe-attributes. If God is omniscient, then (one might say) for every Platonic universe-attribute there will be a divine concept whose content is just how a universe would be were that universe-attribute instanced. As the Platonist would say that $\Diamond P$ just if there is a universe-attribute F such that $\Box$(F is instanced $\supset$ P), the theist can say that $\Diamond P$ just if there is a universe-concept C such that $\Box$(C is satisfied $\supset$ P). As F's being as it is might make it true that $\Diamond P$, so might C's. The theist can parse talk of possible worlds into talk of satisfiable divine concepts, eliminate the universe-attributes, and relocate their content to the mind of God. So however well universe-attributes fare at the tasks for which philosophers posit worlds, their theist transform should fare at least as well.

I now briefly set out the options for theist theories. I then consider arguments in favor of what has been the dominant sort of view. I contend that none work; many just beg the question against the sort of view I think theists should

[1] As in Robert Stalnaker, 'Possible Worlds', in Michael Loux (ed.), *The Actual and the Possible* (Ithaca, NY: Cornell University Press, 1979), pp. 225–34.

[2] St Augustine, *Eighty-three Different Questions*, tr. David Mosher (Washington: Catholic University of America Press, 2002), pp. 225–34.

prefer. *En route* I consider how God might acquire creature-concepts. I contend that He could not derive all of them from His own nature by rational means we can imagine. If He could not, either God was by nature stocked with creature-concepts, so that He never had to acquire them, or His nature led Him to come up with them by rational means of which we have no ken, or His nature brutely compelled Him to come up with them, not by any sort of rational means, or He came up with them in some way His nature did not determine.

Theist Options

I begin with the possible sorts of theist theory. A theist account of modal truthmakers might appeal to God, anything in God, any attribute God has, and so on, and so what sorts of theist theory are possible depends on what theist resources there are. God has, to begin, a nature. Let us call it deity. If deity is a property, it is the property having which makes God divine.[3] Beyond deity, perhaps there are also in God necessary attributes distinct from deity, contingent attributes, activities His nature determines or activities not so determined; the latter might be contingent or necessary.

Contingent divine attributes

God's having attributes contingently might account for the contingency of truths about the non-divine: if God preferred bosons to fermions contingently, this might account for the contingency of *there are more bosons than fermions*. Nothing distinctively modal rules out contingent truthmakers for even necessary truths. A necessary truth of the sort to have a truthmaker necessarily has some truthmaker or other. It does not follow that it necessarily has any particular truthmaker. Some necessary truths have contingent truthmakers and may even have only contingent truthmakers. To show this, I suppose two plausible principles about truthmakers, that

EX. every F's existing makes it true that something is F;[4] and that

DISJ. whatever makes it true that P makes it true that P v Q.

Given (EX), every existing thing's existing makes it true that something exists (is an existing thing). Now consider the necessary truth that

SN. either something exists or nothing exists.

---

[3] Perhaps deity is not a property. Aquinas held that God is identical with His nature (*ST* Ia 3, 3). If He is, 'God' and 'deity' refer to the same thing. If they do, either God is a property or deity is not a property.

[4] Be clear, again, that I am using 'truthmaker' in my thin sense. I do not take an F's existing to be some entity bearing a special truthmaking relation to the claim that something is F. The point is simply that there being an F (which I do not take to be some entity, a state of affairs, either) satisfies the truth-condition of *something is F*.

Given (EX) and (DISJ), every existing thing's existing makes (SN) true. It is either necessary or contingent that something exists. If it is contingent, there are no necessary beings. If there are none, (SN) is a truth which though necessary has only contingent truthmakers. Suppose now that necessarily something exists. Then either there are or there are not necessary beings. If there are not, (SN) still has only contingent truthmakers: it does not necessarily have any particular truthmaker. If there are, still (SN) has *inter alia* contingent truthmakers. But though it is possible to ground even necessary truths on contingent truthmakers, I know of no-one who has appealed to God's having a contingent intrinsic attribute to truthmake or explain the modal status of modal truths. The lack of candidates is (I suspect) primarily because doctrines of divine simplicity from Augustine through Descartes ruled against the claim that God *has* such attributes, and theist theories of modality fell out of favor after Leibniz.[5] Nor do I know of anyone who has appealed to contingent divine extrinsic attributes. The problem here is surely that these come too late in the game. For God to have a contingent extrinsic attribute, there must be something contingent to which He is related. So He must have made that thing, and so causally prior in the story of that extrinsic attribute will be a contingent divine activity and the created thing itself. Either might figure in a more basic truthmaker, leaving the extrinsic attribute otiose.

Contingent divine activity

Descartes may trace necessary truths to a contingent divine act. He holds that

> it was free and indifferent for God to make it not be true that . . . contradictories could not be true together . . . God could have made [this] possible, but . . . has in fact wished to make [it] impossible . . . God cannot have been determined to make it true that contradictories cannot be true together, and therefore . . . he could have done the opposite.[6] The . . . truths which you call eternal have been laid down by God and depend on Him entirely no less than the rest of his creatures.[7]

> From all eternity he willed and understood them to be, and by that very fact he created them.[8]

---

[5] For Aquinas' doctrine, see *Summa Theologiae* (Ottawa: Studii Generalis), 1941, (henceforth *ST*), Ia, 3. For Descartes, see Jean-Luc Marion, *Sur la théologie blanche de Descartes* (Paris : Presses universitaires de France, 1981).

[6] Descartes to Mesland, 2 May 1644, as quoted in Alvin Plantinga, *Does God Have a Nature?* (Milwaukie, WI: Marquette University Press, 1980), pp. 100–1.

[7] Descartes to Mersenne, 15 April 1630, in *Descartes: Philosophical Letters*, tr. Anthony Kenny (New York: Oxford University Press, 1970), p. 11.

[8] Descartes to Mersenne, 27 May 1630.

For Descartes, God created and made necessary all necessary truths not about Himself. Descartes may think that God did so by a contingent act. Within this picture, God's act may also count as a truthmaker. Suppose that we say with Descartes that it is not true that

SI. if anything is Socrates, it is self-identical

until God does His bit,[9] and suppose for *reductio* that His bit is to concentrate really hard for a full minute. God firmly intends (SI) to be true: He makes up His mind in a way which guarantees that He will not change it. He then starts concentrating. Must we really wait the full minute for (SI) to be true? Just because God has made up His mind, will not change it, and cannot slip up, things cannot turn out otherwise than that nothing is Socrates or else Socrates is self-identical: this disjunction describes all the alternatives God's decision leaves for reality. If things *cannot* turn out otherwise, then once God makes up His mind it is inevitable or (say) really or causally necessary that (SI).[10] Such modalities N are such that $\Box_N(SI) \supset (SI)$. So (SI) is true from the point of divine decision on. God's decision brings it about that $\Box_N(SI)$ and (SI).

A Platonist about worlds might say that whatever the causal story, its being the case that $\Box_N(SI)$ *consists in* only (SI)-worlds remaining N-possible after the decision—that is, in the fact that (due to God's decision) no $\neg(SI)$-world represents the future course of history or is still a way things N-can be. Cartesian nominalists might call worlds idle wheels. They might suggest that its being the case that $\Box_N(SI)$ just consists in God's having decided that no matter how things go, it shall not be the case that $\neg(SI)$: that this necessity just is a cause's preventing something. If so, a divine decision makes it true (thin sense) that $\Box_N(SI)$. The nominalist might then go further: it is part of (SI)'s being prevented that (SI) is not the case. So the concrete preventing act making it true that $\Box_N(SI)$ makes it true that (SI). The Cartesian nominalist might conclude that not just God's products but His act make this true.

The temporal example is there to pump intuitions about a causal rather than temporal sequence: the intuition I am looking for is that in the causal sequence, 'as soon as' God wills (SI) to be true, it is true, even 'before' Socrates shows up. If this is right, then though Descartes does not appeal to contingent divine acts (or God's doing them) as truthmakers, they are truthmakers in his theory.

---

[9] This may seem implausible; nothing was Socrates even 'before' the divine act, and so 'before' it, you may think, either nothing was Socrates or Socrates was self-identical. This might also seem a true no-ontology necessary truth. But recall that for Descartes (SI) has existential import. And note too that for (SI) to be true there must be (so to speak) something that specifies what there is not as Socrates and the property he would otherwise have as self-identity: if not, properties of being Socrates or self-identity, or a particular proposition built of concepts of these, then something else playing this role. These items are in (SI)'s ontology. And those accepting (GAO) might not find it implausible that such items as wait on some divine act to exist.

[10] I explicate causal modalities later at length. For real modality see, for example, Harry Deutsch, 'Real Possibility', *Noûs* 24 (1990), 751–5.

Deity

Deity's existing or having its character might well truthmake necessary truths about God. There are many plausibly necessary truths such as

O. if something is a divine being, it is omnipotent.

(O) looks like a truth about a kind-essence: about what is required for, is constitutive of, or follows upon belonging to a kind. Plausibly kind-properties make such truths true (by having the content they do—just being the properties they are). If so, plausibly deity makes (O) true. Again, many hold that

N. if a divine being exists, it exists necessarily.

(N) makes a claim about conditions under which a deity would exist: namely, that if there is one, it would exist no matter what. Items' natures determine the conditions under which they would exist. It is due to what it is to be a dog that a dog is what results if (say) a certain mutation takes place in some sequence of DNA. As for dogs, so for deities; any nature does the same metaphysical jobs as any other. So deity's existing or having its character makes (N) true.

One might think too that deity gives claims like (O) and (N) their modal status. (O), for instance, tells us that something follows from being divine, just as such. If deity makes this true, seemingly deity grounds an entailment. If it does, deity makes it true that □(something is a divine being ⊃ something is omnipotent). So it seems that deity gives (O) its modal status.[11] Still, there is (so I will argue) a distinction to be made between making a truth the right sort to come out necessary once what is needed for truths to be necessary is in place and providing what's needed. The reasoning just given suggests that deity does the first. I soon argue that it does not do the second.

Aquinas treats deity as the truthmaker for all claims of possibility and necessity about non-divine beings. He writes that

> all creatures, before they existed ... were possible beings ... only through the divine power, inasmuch as God was able to produce them in being.[12] God knows things which neither are, nor were, nor will be as possible to His power. Therefore He knows them ... as existing in the divine power.[13]

Possibly there is a Tony Blair just if Tony Blair is a possible being. On Thomas' account of God's omnipotence, every possible non-divine being is a possible

---

[11]   Assuming, of course, that (O)'s 'if' is adequately rendered as a modalized '⊃'.

[12]   S. Thomae Aquinatis, *ST* Ia 9, 2, 47a49-b5.

[13]   S. Thomae Aquinatis *Summa Contra Gentiles* (Turin: Marietti, 1909) (henceforth *SCG*) I, 66, p. 60. See also *Aquinas's Quaestiones Disputatae de Veritate* 2, 8, *ad* 5, in *Sancti Thomae Aquinatis Quaestiones Disputatae* (Turin: Marietti, 1927), v. 3, 52.

divine product.[14] So whatever makes claims about possible divine products true *ipso facto* makes claims about possible non-divine beings true. Thomas asserts that God's possible products 'exist' in His power. He thus commits himself to the claim that all possible non-divine beings 'exist' there. There being a possible non-divine being is a truthmaker for a possibility-claim. So what provides the 'existence' of possible non-divine beings makes possibility-claims true. So for Thomas, God's having His power provides truthmakers for truths about the possibility of non-divine beings.

For Thomas, God's power extends not just to the existence of non-divine beings but to everything whose being produced does not entail a contradiction: God can bring about at a time every state of affairs producible at that time.[15] So every producible state of affairs 'exists' in God's power. But for Thomas, all possible states of affairs involving non-divine beings are producible. So all such states of affairs 'exist' there. Given all facts about what is possible (including that they *are* all the facts), all facts about what is necessary follow. Thus for Thomas, God's power contains the full stock of possible and necessary facts about possible non-deities. But talk of God's power is really shorthand, for Thomas. In Thomas' eyes, God has no attribute of power distinct from deity.[16] Instead, every divine essential attribute is identical with deity, and in particular 'God's power... is the divine essence itself.'[17] Deity includes power by being identical with it. Thus Aquinas' thought is really that truthmakers for all modal truths about the non-divine are somehow within deity. One might vary his view by treating deity as a conjunctive property including omnipotence or a property on which being omnipotent supervenes. Either would base all modal truth about the non-divine on God's having necessary properties distinct from His nature. But one could still fairly call either a deity theory.

Natural activities

For Plotinus, necessary truths are truths about Platonic Forms, which he sees as necessary beings.[18] Plotinus gives the name '*Noûs*' to a deity which is the sum of all Forms.[19] For Plotinus, another deity, the One, is the source of *Noûs*. Plotinus describes the One-*Noûs* relation this way:

---

[14] See, for exxample, *ST* Ia 25, 3.

[15] *ST* Ia 25, 3-4. For Thomas, God even brings it about that creatures act freely: He sustains creatures in their free actions, and sustains the actions themselves insofar as they are beings.

[16] *Quaestiones de Potentia Dei* 1, 1 *ad* 9 *et* 14.

[17] *ST* Ia 77, 1, 463b.

[18] Plotinus, *Enneads* V, tr. A. H. Armstrong (Cambridge, MA: Harvard University Press, 1988), 8, ll. 1–4.

[19] *Ibid.*, V, 1, 4. For Plotinus, only Forms are necessary, and so *Noûs* is the sum of all necessary beings. Unsurprisingly, then, *Noûs* is itself a necessary being: Plotinus writes that ' "happened to be" does not... apply to' *Noûs* (*ibid.*, VI, 8, 9, l. 24), and what does not just happen to be (exist accidentally or contingently) exists necessarily. In fact, Plotinus calls *Noûs* a necessarily necessary being: he writes that it 'does not... just happen to be a thing which does not happen...' (*ibid.*, VI, 8, 9, ll. 24–31).

the One . . . produces everlastingly . . . If anything comes into being after the One . . . it necessarily does so . . . without the One being moved . . . without any . . . act of will . . . on its part.[20]

The One produces necessary beings by nature, involuntarily. These and their relations truthmake necessary truths. Because the One has a certain nature, there are these modal truthmakers, 'outside' it. Western monotheists think it was in God's control whether He ever produced anything outside Himself. So Western monotheists appealing to natural divine acts have spoken instead of God's necessarily producing entities within Himself. Leibniz appealed to God's intellect:

the divine understanding . . . makes the reality of eternal truths: although His will have no part in it . . . these very truths . . . would not exist if there were no divine understanding wherein they are realized.[21]

God's understanding is the realm of the eternal truths, or of the ideas on which they depend.[22]

On this account, God just thinks modal truths into (intra-mental) being, naturally and automatically. For Leibniz, in creatures' cases, He does so by thinking up concepts ('ideas'), whose contents dictate modal truth. Actually, the claim that a divine mind thinks up necessary entities and they exist in it is there even in Plotinus. For Plotinus, the generation of the necessary has two distinguishable aspects. One is the One's production of 'pre-*Noûs*', an unformed ability to think. The other is pre-*Noûs*' 'turning' (by the nature the One gave it) to the One, and conceiving the panoply of Forms as its representation of the One's content.[23] Augustine collapsed the One and *Noûs* into a single being; Leibniz inherited the resulting picture.

By denying God's will a part in thinking up His ideas, Leibniz, like Plotinus, offers a 'natural/involuntary act' theory. By denying the will a part, Leibniz implies that this does not involve decision, selection, or anything with respect to which God has an alternative. For Leibniz, God thinks up His concepts by nature—, the ideas of creatures are linked with the divine essence.[24] Aquinas saw things similarly. He wrote of the Son's generation within the Trinity, which is *inter alia* the generation of all God's ideas:[25]

the will can in no way be the source of the divine generation . . . a will, just because it is a will . . . can act or not act, do such or such, will and not will . . . whence it is clear that whatever has will as its source . . . is able to

[20] *Enneads* V, 1, 6, ll. 18-34; tr. A. H. Armstrong.

[21] G. W. Leibniz, *Theodicy*, secs. 184, 189, tr. in Diogenes Allen (Indianopolis, IL: Bobbs-Merrill, 1962), 107, 109.

[22] G. W. Leibniz, 'Monadology', in Nicholas Rescher (ed.), *The Monadology: An Edition for Students* (Pittsburg, PA: University of Pittsburgh Press, 1991), sec. 43.

[23] On this see A. C. Lloyd, 'Plotinus on the Genesis of Thought and Existence', *Oxford Studies in Ancient Philosophy* 5 (1987), 155–86.

[24] See Robert M. Adams, *Leibniz* (New York: Oxford University Press, 1994), p. 170.

[25] S. Thomae Aquinatis, *Quaestiones Disputatae de Veritate*, q. 4.

be or not be (and so is) a creature . . . For this reason . . . Catholics say that the Son is begotten not by will but by nature.[26]

Just as the intellect's act is seen to follow the will's, in that the will commands it, so conversely the will's act is seen to follow the intellect's, as the intellect presents the will its object . . . whence there would be an infinite regress, unless a halt were posited in an act of the intellect or the will. But we cannot posit a stop in an act of will, because its act presupposes an object. Whence one should posit a stop in an act of intellect, which it does naturally, not by the will's command. And in this way the Son of God proceeds as Word.[27]

The Son, being God, is a necessary being.[28] But whatever exists by will exists contingently. So it must be a matter of God's nature that the Son exists. He must in particular exist by a natural act in which God's intellect produces all of His thought-contents.

Here we can contrast Descartes:

The mathematical truths which you call eternal have been laid down by God . . . as a king lays down laws in his kingdom.[29]

A king lays down a law by an act of command—essentially, by declaring his intent that this be the law. So the point of this simile is that a use of God's will determines mathematical truths. Thus Descartes continues:

It will be said that if God had established these truths He could change them as a king changes his laws. To this the answer is 'Yes He can, if His will can change.'[30]

As we have seen, Descartes holds that God by will *creates* modal truths.[31] But the primary difference between Descartes on the one hand and Aquinas and Leibniz on the other is not in respect of creation. Nor is it a matter of the faculties involved.[32] Descartes insists on the identity of God's intellect and will:

In God willing and knowing are a single thing in such a way that by the very fact of willing something he knows it and it is only for this reason that such a thing is true.[33]

---

[26] S. Thomae Aquinatis, *Quaestiones de Potentia Dei* 2, 3, in *Sancti Thomae Aquinatis Quaestiones Disputatae*, v. 1 (Turin: Marietti, 1931), 27–8.

[27] *Ibid*, 2, 3 ad 3, p. 28.

[28] Whatever its defects as an argument, the Third Way ascribes to God a sort of necessity that amounts to being unable to come into or go out of existence. Given Aquinas' modal theory, this suffices for something very close to our notion of absolute necessity. On this see my 'Aquinas, Divine Simplicity and Divine Freedom,' in Kevin Timpe (ed.), *Metaphysics and God* (London: Routledge, 2009), 21–38.

[29] Descartes to Mersenne, 15 April 1630, tr. in Anthony Kenny, ed., *Descartes: Philosophical Letters* (Minneapolis, MN: University of Minnesota Press, 1970), p. 11.

[30] *Ibid.*, 11.

[31] Descartes to Mersenne, 27 May 1630, in Kenny (ed.), *Letters*, p. 14.

[32] As Leibniz suspects: *Theodicy,* sec. 188.

[33] Descartes to Mersenne, 6 May 1630, in Kenny, *op. cit.*, pp. 13–14.

If God's knowing = God's willing, God's setting up the eternal truths is as truly an act of intellect as an act of will. The real dispute between Descartes and Leibniz is over whether the activity involved is natural or voluntary and free.

Natural acts and deity

Let us now ask just how the divine nature guides the divine intellect on monotheist natural-act views. Suppose that necessarily, God so thinks that

CATS. normal cats have four legs.

One thought would be that (CATS) is just written into deity and God reads it there and affirms it: what is so guides the affirming of a being whose nature is to affirm just what is so. On this account, God does nothing to make (CATS) true. What makes (CATS) true precedes any divine activity. Talk of divine activity just adds an epicycle to a deity theory: natural-act theories are really deity theories.

Another thought would be that His nature impels Him to think up cats and gives Him such powers of conception that He can only conceive of normal cats as having four legs, and because He must so conceive them, normal cats have four legs. Conceptualist modal theories hold that absolute-modal truths not about what we can and cannot conceive acquire their modal status due to facts about what we (or our idealizations) can and cannot (or could not) conceive. On this alternative, then, a natural-act view is a deity theory plus theist conceptualism. The divine nature determines God's powers of conception. This is the 'deity' portion of the view. The conceptualist portion is what makes facts about God's powers of conception determine modal truth about the non-divine. On this account, once it is set in deity that God cannot but conceive that (CATS), (CATS) is true. God's having powers of conception are the real modal truthmakers. But again, God's nature sets God's powers of conception. So this take on a natural activity theory resembles Aquinas, but places in the basic modal truthmakers not all of God's powers but a subset of them.

We may ask why deity prescribes affirming (CATS). This could be because:

a. (CATS) already is true, from all eternity, and deity requires God to recognize the truth. The theist version of this has to locate this truth in God somewhere. If (CATS) is necessary, it must then necessarily be written into something in God. This will be deity, a conjunct of it or something supervening on it (and so determined by it). So this alternative reduces to a deity theory.

b. Deity makes God morally perfect and ideally rational, and God ought to affirm (CATS). But let's ask what grounds this 'ought'. If it is useful that

(CATS) be so (say, in constructing a universe), rival ideas about cats would be just as useful. If four-legged cats are pretty, other numbers of legs could be just as pretty. That God would by so doing affirm something true is the only candidate I can fathom. If God grasps that (CATS) is true, a theist modal theorist will insist, (CATS) is true prior to this grasping due to something in God. So there is a necessity in God that there be some truthmaker for (CATS). If that necessity did not stem from deity, the divine acts appealed to would not be entirely natural—from God's nature. That given, the intuitions that push us to say that (SI) is true at the point of divine decision push us to say that the content of deity makes (CATS) true. So here again we wind up with a variant deity theory.

c. It would be appropriate to His perfect goodness to do so. But why? This will run as in (b), I think, and so this is just one more epicycle on a deity theory.

d. For no reason at all. But then God does so under brute compulsion. The whole realm of modal truth about the non-divine then has the status of a divine nervous tic imposed by nature.

Thus it is fair to sort natural-act theories under the broad heading of deity theories. For as far as I can see, on these the content of deity determines the content of modal truth. The only question is whether modal truths are written into deity in the indicative or the imperative.

The missing option

The necessary options so far considered all count as deity theories, though in different ways. The one option not yet considered is a theory appealing to a divine act that is necessary but not determined by God's nature. In the tradition stretching from Plotinus through Leibniz, there is no conceptual space for this. The influence of Aristotle is one large reason for this, for on Aristotle's view, things' attributes sort into natures, 'proper' necessary accidents natures determine, and the contingent. I think there is such space. Much of this book explores such a view.

Whether theists should adopt the view depends, of course, on how its costs and benefits compare with those of deity theories. One cost of any theory consists in the commitments one must take on to block arguments for its rivals. So it would be good to turn to arguments for deity theories. But one does not find explicit arguments for them in (say) Aquinas or Leibniz. This may be because deity theorists' positions were consequences of other commitments. To Aquinas, for instance, Platonism was 'against the faith' for reasons closely tied to (GSA),[34] so modal truthmakers from all eternity had to be theist. For Aquinas, God's simplicity implies that

---

[34] *ST* Ia 84,5.

everything in Him is identical with deity.[35] So for Aquinas, anything in a theist modal theory not resting on divine products must rest on deity.[36] Again, the lack of explicit argument may have to do with a lack of formulated alternatives to argue against, or may be because where an alternative offered itself (Descartes, in Leibniz' case), it seemed obviously objectionable. Be this as it may, I am left to try to reason out on deity theorists' behalf, from the outlines of their theories, considerations that may have motivated them. I hope I am fair to them in doing so. I begin with an argument from a general consideration about necessity.

Necessary Truths and Truthmakers

A basic thought behind Plato's theory of Forms is that eternal truths require eternal truthmakers. Plotinus clearly picks up on this. The Platonic thought's modal transform would be that

1. if a truth is necessary, its truthmaker exists necessarily.

From this one might argue:

2. God's nature includes or determines everything necessary in God. So if necessary truths' truthmakers lie in God, God's nature includes or determines them.

But as we have seen, (1) is false. If a truth is necessary and of the sort to have a truthmaker, necessarily it has some truthmaker. But it need not be the same one in every possible world. As to (2), we now commonly use 'nature' for the conjunction of an item's necessary attributes. With 'nature' so taken, (2) is trivially true but does not preclude the missing option, for with 'nature' so taken, God's nature may include things deity neither includes nor determines. Medievals would have taken 'nature' to refer to deity. So taken, (2) begs the question against what I have called the missing option. I now consider arguments that the contents of deity provide a domain over which '□' quantifies.

Nature and Necessity

One might reason this way:

3. God has deity and deity is God's nature.
4. Any nature is had necessarily. So

---

[35] ST Ia 3, 3–7.
[36] For Aquinas, whatever is not identical with the divine essence is a creature (ST Ia 28, 2 sc).

5. Necessarily, God has deity.
6. God includes all it takes to give (3)'s first conjunct its modal status. So:
7. Deity includes or subvenes the entities semantically required to do so.
8. These are the possible worlds, their domains, and so on.
9. If there are possible worlds, their contents make true or just are all modal truths. So:
10. Deity brings with it the full range of modal truth.

I reply that the move from (6) to (7) is a *non sequitur*. The entities could just as easily lie or have a supervenience-base elsewhere in God.

Actuality and Possibility

Again, if God actually has deity and what is actually so is possibly so, there is at least one possible state of things—one possible world. So (one might infer) having deity brings possible worlds with it. I reply again that even if necessarily, if God has deity, there is a world, this does not entail that God's having deity accounts for the world's existence. Something else about God could do so instead. I now turn to arguments from divine attributes.

Creating and Refraining

God's nature determines that God is able to create and able to refrain from doing so. Thus (one might argue) God's nature determines that there are possible worlds in which He creates and possible worlds in which He does not.

I submit that the premise does not imply the conclusion. Even if God's nature has a role in there being worlds in which God creates and worlds in which He does not, it does not follow without further premises that that role is providing worlds. For something else could be true instead, given only the claim about God's nature. It could be like this: God's nature and something in God other than His nature both have a role in setting up the realm of possible worlds. God's nature determines that there are two ways for things to be, that God creates and that He does not. But these ways for things to be do not count as worlds in the standard sense, because they do not include all that would be true in either case. That God creates includes nothing about *what* God creates. But there would have to be something He created. That God refrains from creating includes nothing about what He does not create. But again, there would have to be such things. If there were not, there would be nothing to create, and so no possibility of choosing not to do so. God's nature determines that if there are worlds, some but not all will be worlds in which

God creates, and that's that. All God's nature settles is that there be two sorts of world. Something else in God determines what sorts of creatures He might create and so fleshes out worlds' contents. It takes the fleshing-out to have worlds. It is as if God's nature provides world-schemata—as it were, templates for worlds in which God creates and worlds in which He chooses not to create—but God's free creativity fills out the schemata to obtain possible worlds. '□' quantifies over worlds, not schemata. Thus this argument's premise does not yield its conclusion; it does nothing to rule out this alternative.

Divine Freedom

Again, God by nature has a freedom involving all-things-considered power to do other than He in fact does. And God by nature has alternatives to His state before deciding whether to create which need not be filled out with creaturely content. He actually enjoyed self-awareness blissful to some particular degree. He could have brought Himself to enjoy it to some other degree. But then even apart from creature-content, God by nature faces alternate possible worlds.

I reply that God's freedom does not guarantee that He always is able to do otherwise. Insofar as it does not involve creature-content, His pre-decision state could not have been otherwise: He grasped all there was to know perfectly, and maximally enjoyed all that was enjoyable about it. Further, a pre-decision state is not sufficient for an entire possible world. As God's nature gives Him the alternative of creating, He would have to at least go on to choose whether to create, and if so, what to create. So even if God's nature outfitted Him with alternatives to His initial state, it would remain the case (say I) that something other than His nature would have to chime in to fill out the content of possible worlds.

Omnipotence

One could run indefinitely many instances of this argument-form:

11. Due to the content of deity, God is omnipotent.
12. God is omnipotent ⊃ possibly God brings it about that P. So:
13. Due to the content of deity, possibly God brings it about that P.
14. Possibly God brings it about that P ⊃ possibly P. So:
15. Due to the content of deity, possibly P.

Given such an argument for every possible P about the non-divine, plus something about deity entailing that they *are* all the possible Ps about the non-divine, necessary truth about the non-divine will rest on deity. So given the latter, a deity theory of such truth is true, and of course we can have one for modal truth about the divine.

I reply that the move from (11) and (12) to (13) is invalid. It can be the case that because of P, Q, and that Q ⊃ R, but not be the case that because of P, R. Because of the rocket's propulsion, I go to the moon, and if I go to the moon, the moon exists, but it is not the case that because of the rocket's propulsion, the moon exists. Still, one can get around this. Suppose that deity is a complex property including omnipotence, and the latter is a conjunction of fine-grained abilities, such that for every possible P about the non-divine, there is a discrete ability to bring it about that P. Then in place of (11)–(15) we can run indefinitely many instances of this argument-form:

16. God's having deity includes God's being omnipotent.

17. God's being omnipotent includes God's being able to bring it about that P. So:

18. God's being able to bring it about that P includes its being the case that possibly P. So:

19. God's having deity includes that possibly P.

But (17) begs the question. Omnipotence need not have a specific range of effects—what *is* in fact possible—written into itself. Perhaps omnipotence receives its range from some other source in God. Even if God is able to create quarks, perhaps He did not have this ability as part of His nature. Perhaps He had as part of His nature only the ability to create, and this was specified as an ability to create quarks by something else in Him—say, a free thinking up of quarks. Being a police officer includes being empowered to enforce the law. It does not have within itself what the laws are, or what they govern: police receive the laws from elsewhere. So the police power to enforce laws does not have its range of enforcement activity as part of its very nature. Rather, its range is specified—and often changed—by legislation. Every power has a range of effects it can bring about. But a power's very nature need not determine that range. In fact, it usually does not. I have by nature, let us say, the power to jump. But this power's nature does not determine on its own how high I can jump, or over what sorts of obstacle. Many animal natures bestow the power to jump, along with a particular range of degrees of strength that animal may attain: so each animal nature bestows a power with a different range. Even if we specify that it is a human's (or my) power to jump, factors like the gravity of the item from which I jump are also relevant, as are (for more *outré* possibilities) how far it is technically feasible to change my makeup, alter the physical conditions in which I act, and so on. Plausibly, none of these are part of the power's very nature. Now in God's case there is, of course, no external environment not of His own making. But the conceptual point about powers and ranges stands. It could be up to God to determine the range of omnipotence—what abilities His natural omnipotence gives Him—by determining what states of affairs are producible. It is not controversial that God can at least partly specify what He can do. It is up to God whether He makes anything that cannot survive the loss of any part. So it is up to God whether He is able to destroy something by removing just one of its parts—as vs being able to be able to do so, in virtue of being able to create such a thing.[37]

Rationality

Another divine-attribute argument begins from the claim that God is ideally rational. It is a reasonable thought that a believing is not epistemically rational unless it is truth-aimed—that is, unless the believer adopts the belief because the believer thinks it true or has grounds so to think or the belief is the output of a truth-aimed mechanism. God cannot merely *think* something is true, nor have grounds He is not aware of, nor can anything truth-aimed in Him fail of its target. So for all P, God believes that P only because *P* is true: and so if □P, God's belief that P presupposes that *P* is true, and this truth helps explain His having it. God has this belief from all eternity. (FD) and (GSA) dictate that its truthmakers from all eternity lie in aspects of God given in advance of His beliefs—and so within deity or some attribute it brings with it, since it is hard to see what else of this sort there could be.

One reply here is that if I am successful in laying out a coherent position below, this itself blocks this argument. For my position will be that some modal truth is determined by something in God in advance of His modal beliefs but not determined by deity. I argue that what I call secular modal truth rests on something like a divine stipulation. A stipulation could be logically prior to a divine modal belief—God might stipulate (CATS), know that (CATS)'s truth depends solely on His stipulation, and therefore believe (CATS). Still, even if I can make this out, it raises an issue.

If God does something relevantly like stipulating (CATS), what reason could He have to make one stipulation rather than another? If He has none, He seems to act arbitrarily and so irrationally. On a deity theory, on the other hand, either the reason for God's belief that (CATS) is that He perceives the truth written into His nature, or He has this belief due to compulsion by His nature of a sort that requires no rational justification (as it does not to breathe). Advantage deity theories, it seems. This is a large matter. I take it up later. But I note at present that sheer stipulations which are not truth-aimed need not be irrational. It is sheer stipulation that American law requires driving on the right side of the road. The left would have been just as good. But it does not follow

---

[37] 'Able to be able' does not entail 'able'. I am not now able to play a piano concerto, because I cannot now play the piano. But I am able to be able to play a concerto, because I am able to learn to play the piano.

that the law which so rules is irrational. There was good reason to make some law: it is safer if everyone drives on the same side. And if there was no reason to prefer either side, that just means that we had good reason to 'just pick'. Again, it was sheer stipulation that Sherlock Holmes' friend Watson be a doctor. He could as easily have been a lawyer. But it was not irrational for Conan Doyle to stipulate this. It did make for a good story.

Omniscience

The simplest argument from omniscience would be this:

20. It is part of God's being divine that He is omniscient.
21. It is part of God's being omniscient that He know all modal truths.
22. It is part of God's knowing all modal truths that all modal truths are known.
23. It is part of all modal truths' being known that there are all modal truths. So:
24. It is part of God's being divine that there are all modal truths.

I reply that (21) is ambiguous. One can read it as claiming that it is part of omniscience to know the particular modal truths there are, treating 'all modal truths' as referring to $P, Q, R \ldots$, so that the sense of (23) includes that there are $P, Q, R \ldots$ This simply packs $P, Q, R \ldots$ into the divine nature. So read, (21) begs the question in favor of a deity theory. One can also read (21) in the sense that it is part of God's omniscience to be such that (p)(P is a modal truth $\supset$ God knows that p). So read, (21) is compatible with there being no modal truths packed into the divine nature, and so begs no questions. But then 'all modal truths' does not refer. So if we so read (23) as to preserve the argument's validity, 'all modal truths' does not refer there either, and so (23) does not say that there are $P, Q, R \ldots$ So a conclusion that God's being divine contains these does not validly follow. Further, (23) may not be well formed on this reading.

Range of Knowledge

An argument that by nature God thinks up specific sorts of creatures runs this way:

25. God does not think up elephants > God knows less than it is in Him to know.
26. God knows less than it is in Him to know $\rightarrow$ God is less than maximally perfect cognitively.

So:

27. God does not think up elephants > God is not maximally perfect cognitively.

28. By nature God is maximally perfect cognitively. So:

29. By nature God thinks up elephants.

Let us first consider (25). To pursue the discussion, I need a term fit to name a property, though there neither is nor can be a property for it to name. So I say that there is no such property as *being a zog*. I do not take *being a zog* to refer, obviously, but I will use it as if it did. There being no such property, it is not possible or impossible that something be a zog, i.e., have a property which neither is possible nor is impossible because it does not exist to bear either modality.'

As I see it, if God does not think up elephants, *being an elephant* no more names a property than *being a zog* now does. There are then no facts about elephants—not even that God has not thought them up. If God never thinks up elephants, He grasps certain facts. If He does think up elephants and all else is the same, He grasps these and also facts about elephants. Even if the two sets of facts are same-order infinite, the first is a proper subset of the second.[38] In one legitimate sense of the word 'less', proper subsets contain less than their supersets. So it is legitimate to say that God knows less if He knows a, b, c . . . but does not think up elephants, than if He knows up a, b, c . . . and facts about elephants too. *A fortiori*, if there would be no facts about any creature had God not thought up creatures, God knows less if He does not think up creatures.

However, this does not give us (25). (25) requires that He thinks less *and* it is in Him to know more. As I see it, had God not thought up elephants, it would not have been in Him to think up elephants. If He does not think up elephants, there is no property of being an elephant, and so nothing to be in God to think up. Thus God brings it about that it is in Him to think up elephants only by doing so. So it is not the case that had He not thought up elephants, He would have known less than it was then in Him to know. He would have known less than it is *now* in Him to know, but as it is at that earlier point up to Him whether there will ever be such a thing as an elephant to be in Him to know this is irrelevant. Further, it is not then in God to bring it about that it is in Him to know about elephants, as that too would require the property *being an elephant*. All that is true then is that it is in God to think up creatures. So again, it is false that He knows less than it is then in Him to know if He does not think up elephants. It is in God by nature only to know the facts about some sort or other of possible creature—or particular individual possible creatures, if it is in Him before creating them to

---

[38] These would be sets of all facts. There are problems with talk of such sets (see Patrick Grim, *The Incomplete Universe* (Cambridge, MA: MIT Press, 1991), pp. 91–124). I speak so here only to simplify exposition.

have singular concepts of creatures[39]—since the concept of a possible creature is the only creature-related content that is in Him by nature. (By nature He can create, so by nature there can be such a thing as a creature.) If the only fact about possible creatures were that He had the power to think some up and had not done so, He would know all the facts about possible creatures just by knowing this. So it is not even the case that if God thinks up no sorts of creature, He knows less than it is in Him to know—for had He thought up none, it would not have been in Him to know any more than this. So as I see it, (25) is false.

I also reject (26). The relevant divine cognitive perfection is omniscience. Knowing less need not involve not being omniscient. If we take it for the nonce that being omniscient includes knowing all truths, God might be omniscient and yet know less, if the reason were that 'all truths' included less. In the same way, He could be omnipotent yet able to do less, were the reason that less was absolutely possible to do. Nor need knowing less involve not being infallible, perfectly rational, maximally well justified in all He believes, and so on—that is, of less than maximal excellence as a cognitive agent—if again the only reason is that there is less to know. Knowing less need not involve losing any cognitive faculty. Nor need it involve any faculty's being intrinsically less perfect: God needs no practice to improve His cognitive skills, but is *ab initio* perfect in the use of His powers. Nor need knowing less imply having a lesser record of accomplishment, from one point of view: being omniscient, having only infallible, best-justified knowledge, and so on, is as good as it gets, even if omniscience involves knowing less. From another point of view, God's record *is* lesser if He knows less. But nothing forces us to consider this relevant to God's perfection, as long as the reason He knows less is simply that there is less to know. It is relevant if one develops one's dispositions by practicing—but God does not. In any case, even an agent who needs to practice can be as good dispositionally with a lesser record as another with a greater: some people pick up knacks easier than others. It can even be the case that an agent with no record surpasses in disposition any with a record. Suppose that all parts of humans are material, and imagine that someone produces an atom-for-atom perfect replica of Babe Ruth. Dispositions supervene on or are identical with pure categorical attributes, and if all parts of humans are material, Duplicate Ruth duplicates all of Ruth's pure non-relational categoricals. So if all parts of humans are material, Duplicate Ruth has all of Ruth's dispositions to action. Duplicate Ruth thus is exactly as good a hitter, even though he has never swung a bat. If not all parts of humans are material, Ruth had a soul. But if there are souls, plausibly God could create a Duplicate Ruth Soul—why not?—and it is in any case not clear that

---

[39] For arguments that He cannot, see, for example, Christopher Menzel, 'Temporal Actualism and Singular Foreknowledge', *Philosophical Perspectives* 5 (1991), 475–507, and Christopher Hughes, 'Negative Existentials, Omniscience and Cosmic Luck', *Religious Studies* 34 (1998), 375–401.

Ruth's hitting ability would depend on his soul. Suppose then that we have Duplicate Ruth in 1927, and the original Babe dies: then there is a home-run hitter with no record of hitting whose ability to hit surpasses any home-run hitter's who has a record.

No matter what, it is in God to think up more. So there is no such thing as a divine cognitive record perfect in respect of how much God thinks up. And so God's perfection in quantity of knowledge is to be defined where perfection does make sense—getting all of it, or as close to this as is compatible with, for example, His being one person and not another.[40] I submit then that if knowing less would leave God omniscient, infallible, amd so on, and with cognitive faculties as perfect as it is in them to be, it simply would not leave God less perfect. Nor does knowing less entail having less perfect mental contents: a few very valuable mental contents might well be more valuable than many of little worth.

Omniscience Again

I now turn to a more complex argument. Suppose that God has distinct essential attributes of power, goodness, knowledge, and so on, and an occurrent mental life involving distinct states of knowledge, volition, desire, and so on.[41] If so, God naturally has concepts of all these, since He naturally grasps His nature. These let Him represent to Himself 'diminished' versions of His properties.[42] To begin, God sees that He knows that P and Q. This attribute—knowing that P and Q—involves a lesser amount of knowledge than He has. He also sees that He knows nothing other than *these*, where 'these' ranges over all the truths He knows. So He finds in Himself the materials to conceive a diminished version of His propositional knowledge: knowing that P and Q and having no other of God's knowing-some-propositions attributes and knowing nothing other than these, where 'these' refers to P and Q. If God has some sort of perceptual knowledge of concrete reality, He can 'diminish' this conceptually in a similar way, by conceiving of being able to grasp only some exemplified properties or parts of reality perceptually. Again, God can produce many effects. Powers are relevantly like functions from 'firing' conditions to states of affairs brought about. So if God has a stock of states of affairs He can bring about, He can represent to Himself in like manner being able to bring about just that P. This conceives a lesser range of power than He has.

---

[40] If 'I am Brian Leftow' expresses a truth only I can know, then if God creates other people, He brings it about that He cannot know all truths.

[41] These are not trivial assumptions. Aquinas would deny them all in the name of divine simplicity.

[42] Aquinas speaks of God as understanding the natures of creatures insofar as they participate in His nature, by being like it in various ways to various degrees (*ST* Ia 15, 2). Diminishment generates concepts of lesser degrees of properties whose maximal degree God has naturally. So this account is one way of explicating Aquinas' view, though within a view of the divine nature he would not accept.

God by His natural omniscience notices all the subsets of effects He can bring about, truths He knows, etc. So He is naturally set up to conceive diminished versions of His own attributes. Further, He does conceive all these. For He can, and as omniscient, He knows He can. So God knows that He can form exactly these concepts. He cannot know this without knowing what the results would be. So He knows what these concepts would be. As omniscient, He also knows everything about what it would be to have full command of them. So He has full command of these concepts: one cannot know *everything* about what it would be fully to command the skills needed to ride a bicycle without knowing how to ride a bicycle. The deity theorist will contend, then, that God's nature determines that He conceives these. Some attributes cannot thus be diminished: there are not plausibly degrees of being live, conscious, or a person.[43] But God has concepts of these naturally, since He is naturally omniscient and without them He would fail to know things about Himself. He also has the concept of a creature (a created item) naturally, as He naturally understands His power to create and so knows that it would have a product. So it seems to follow that God by nature can form (and so has) such concepts as 'conscious creature less powerful than I.' Some sorts of creature-concept, at least, are a natural result of such operations—such as concepts of finite spirits (angels and souls).

Further, we can well suppose that God naturally knows all logic and all of mathematics. This might get us still further.[44] Geometry, we can say, gives God the idea of spatial extension. If God is temporal, His life has a temporal location and has or has had a duration. A naturally omniscient God will naturally notice these things, and so have naturally concepts of duration, temporal location, and persistence. So given what we have already seen, He naturally can form the representation of a spatially extended substance with finite causal powers that persists through time, and of systems of these. Moreover, God can then conceive of a spatial thing that at different times occupies different spatial positions (if only by bearing different spatial relations to other spatial things in its system). So God naturally can conceive of motion. (If God is temporal and time passes, He is aware of something at least like motion.) So God naturally can also conceive of spatial things able to cause other spatial things to move, and so of some causal powers material things have, for example, those associated with mass, charge, impenetrability, solidity, and liquidity. If God's inner life has any phenomenal content—a difficult point—He can conceive of related sorts of phenomenal experience. If He can, He naturally can conceive spatial things whose powers include powers to

---

[43] There are borderline cases of these things. But they are, for example, borderline cases of being *simpliciter* a person, not of being to some degree a person. The right treatment of borderline cases does not involve degreed possession of properties or degreed truth of propositions. This last seems widely agreed among theorists of vagueness, but for a defense of a degree approach to the vague, see Nicholas Smith, *Vagueness and Degreees of Truth* (Oxford: Oxford University Press, 2008).

[44] Chris Shields inspired this line of thought.

cause phenomenal experiences in other things. This gives us matter, *modo* Locke. If God can conceive of conscious spatial things, He can conceive kinds of goodness He Himself cannot possess. He can, for example, conceive spatial things that can suffer damage and feel pain, if His conscious experience gives Him a way to conceive the latter. He can use this, perhaps, to construct an idea of bravery, and do the like for chastity. God does not know by sense-perception; He has no senses. But He could conceive of knowledge obtained by performing mental operations on phenomenal qualities caused in the perceiver in certain ways. So natural concepts of embodied beings like ourselves seem also to fall out of the story.

I now argue three points about this story. The mathematical part, I submit, fails to get us natural concepts of material things, irrespective of how the rest fares. More basically, the story does not get us the full concept of any possible creature, because it does not give a basis for God naturally to have kind-concepts for creatures. Because of this, the story does not even show that there is a basis in God's nature for truths to the effect that certain diminished divine attributes are possibly exemplified. It is possible that something know just that P and Q only if possibly there is a fully determinate concrete particular with this property. If God's nature does not make the latter possible, then, it does not make the former possible either. Finally, I argue, even if the story gave us full representations of candidate creatures, the deity theorist has not shown that God's having these would suffice to make it possible that something satisfy them. God's will plays a role for which the deity theorist has not made a place.

From mathematics to matter?

To begin, mathematics would not really yield God spatial concepts. Mathematics speaks of intervals of number and continuous number series, but there is nothing literally extended in either: understanding what a continuous number series is would not entail having any idea of another sort of continuum points in which might pair 1:1 with numbers. Geometries are satisfied in abstract mathematical 'spaces' involving no spatial extension.[45] So having geometry in mind does not entail having the concept of extension: something more would be needed, some interpretation of the mathematics. Nor does knowing geometry entail having other spatial concepts. If God is not spatial, He has nothing in His own being to give Him an idea of a spatial way of being extended. If God is timeless, nothing in His own being gives Him an idea of a temporal way of being extended, or indeed of being extended at all. So if God is timeless, He cannot get the concept of matter from mathematics. Deity theorists have been almost unanimous that God is timeless; for these, this

---

[45] Here I am indebted to Oliver Pooley.

would end the matter. I have argued that God *is* timeless, and so as I see it this does end the matter.[46] But if God is temporal, there is a bit more to say.

If God is temporal He naturally has temporal concepts, and if He naturally has the logical concepts, perhaps He can also then form the concept of non-temporal extension and location. But space and spacetime have positive traits of their own.[47] There is more to being a spatial (or spacetime) extension than being a non-temporal extension; we know this if only because string theory is able to conceive of dimensions that are neither spatial nor temporal. The concepts of non-temporal extension and location do not give God any of this positive content. There is nothing in them to tell Him what space or space-time would be like positively and intrinsically. Given only these, all God would have in mind is an abstract notion of something which is not time but realizes some geometric and metric properties somewhat as time does. He would not have the concepts of space, spacetime, matter or material things. The rest of the story, then, should be parsed *via* not the idea of a spatial substance but that of a non-temporally extended substance. God could still then perhaps conceive based only on material 'given' with His nature of an extended thing that at different times occupies different positions in the non-temporal dimension (s) through which it extends. So God can perhaps conceive in this way of motion, though not motion through space. All this gives us not Lockean matter, though, but abstract mathematical schemata physical worlds could instance if He somehow got the ideas for matter and space. Further, none of this gives us what the matter-analogue in these abstract schemata *is*, but at most what it is empowered to do, at the abstract schematic level. Material things do not have only powers: powers supervene on or are identical with categorical monadic properties. Nothing in the content we have so far yields these; if powers and their categorical bases are identical, nothing we have said so far gives God concepts under which to grasp what they are when described categorically. So even given natural mathematical knowledge, God is far from being able to get full representations of material creatures out of His natural endowment.

I now take up a way His endowment falls short of giving Him full concepts of creatures which applies even to immaterial creatures.

Natural divine kind concepts?

Let us make some assumptions least favorable to my case. Take it that being divine, a spirit, a person, a substance, conscious, alive, powerful, free, and good, and having knowledge and other mental states, are distinct realities in

---

[46] Brian Leftow, *Time and Eternity* (Ithaca, NY: Cornell University Press, 1991).

[47] I speak as if space, time, and so on, are substantival just for ease of exposition. The same sorts of point could be made about spatial or spatiotemporal relations.

God prior to His conceiving. Take it too, against Aquinas' and other analogical accounts of theistic predication, that God and creatures fall under the concepts of these univocally.[48] If this is so, then just by noticing these things in Himself, God has concepts of attributes available to form creature-concepts. So on present assumptions, God would naturally have concepts of these.[49] Even so, I now argue, God would not find within Himself sufficient material to come up with full creature-representations by any means we know. All possible creatures belong to kinds, in a somewhat Aristotelian sense of the term. Their kind-properties provide answers to the question 'What is this?' If they are spatiotemporal, kind-properties determine their distinctness-conditions at and identity-conditions across times: because Fido is a dog, Fido is distinct at t from anything not wholly overlapping him, and identical with objects at earlier times iff (say) there is a continuous spacetime path between Fido at t and these other objects, every point along which is occupied by an item in certain animal kinds (dog, perhaps dog-zygote) with appropriate causal relations to Fido at t. If there can be creatures extended or located in non-spatiotemporal dimensions (think again of string theory), analogous points apply to their kinds.

If all possible creatures have kind-properties, then if God's natural endowment does not give Him the resources to frame creaturely kind-concepts, it does not let Him conceive of any particular possible creature.[50] So it does not, by enabling God to conceive such creatures, make it possible that there be any. And so, as noted above, it does not even establish on its own that any diminished divine perfection is possibly exemplified. Now a naturally-generated divine representation gives conditions for distinctness at a time for anything spatial only if God naturally has spatial concepts. He does not. So such a representation could not have the content we ascribe to concepts of material kinds. For like reasons, they could not have the content kind-concepts for creatures existing in non-temporal, non-spatial dimensions would need. A naturally generated divine representation gives conditions for identity over time only if God naturally has temporal concepts. If He is atemporal, He does not. So there is at least a substantial question about whether a naturally generated divine representation could have the content even of kind-concepts that we would apply to purely temporal creatures (angels, souls). Thus if kind-concepts are of kind-attributes and kind-attributes

---

[48] Aquinas contends that God is not a substance (*Quaestiones de Potentia Dei* 7, 3 *ad* 4) and is not in any kind, so that even *deity* is on his terms not a kind (*ibid., corpus*). Thomists, following him, argue that such terms as 'person' and 'spirit' apply to Him only by analogy (cf. *ST* Ia 13, 5).

[49] He would also have concepts of kinds of entity He finds in Himself—states, events, and so on. Points I make about substances apply to kinds of non-divine states, etc. *mutatis mutandis*, and so I do not discuss them.

[50] Or if there cannot be or are not such divine pre-creative concepts anyway, completely conceive of a purely general type of creature. If He cannot do the latter naturally, He is not naturally set up to create any fully determinate particular creature. Rather, He must first complete the relevant concept in a way His nature does not determine.

determine persistence- and distinctness-conditions, the only sort of non-divine kind God's concept of which uncontroversially could be natural would be one whose instances are spaceless, timeless, and so on—without location in any dimension. It is unclear whether there are any such kinds. The primary candidates here are certain sorts of abstract entity. Theists have reason to look askance at these—they conflict with (FD)—and as we saw earlier and will see at more length later, theists have both Ockhamist reason and theist resources to prune them away. They have these resources necessarily if God exists necessarily, whence they can and should hold it not so much as possible that there be such entities. If this is not possible, there is no kind-attribute for them to exemplify. Attributes are things that *can* be instanced.

Be this as it may, on present assumptions, the kinds under which God falls are *substance, person, spirit,* and *deity.* I now argue that even on the favorable assumptions made, none of these helps, or helps enough, in forming creaturely kind-concepts, and so the deity theorist's picture of God's natural conceptual repertoire fails when it hits kind-concepts.

Substance

Substance is too general to be any good on its own. Creatures are various *kinds* of non-divine substance; we need to get concepts of such kinds. It would not be plausible to claim that *substance* builds its sub-kinds in: that if one somehow sufficiently grasped what it is to be a substance, one would 'just see' that there could be such things as elephants. I see only one way to leverage *substance* into full creature-kind concepts, and that is to claim that to be of every more specific kind is to be a substance with certain kind-defining attributes which are not themselves kind-properties: that is, that for all creaturely kinds K, to be a (normal) K is to be a substance with non-kind attributes F, G, and so on. But even if we grant this, God naturally has available from His natural endowment for kind-defining attributes only degrees of attributes God naturally has or naturally has in His experience. So this would imply that each possible kind of creature differs from every other in range of possible power or knowledge or in respect of some other attribute God has in some degree, some quality God experiences, etc. This seems unlikely. Plausibly there could be a different kind of bug just like ladybugs in these respects. Plausibly there could be bugs with minds by nature just like ladybug minds, just the divine powers-in-degrees ladybugs have, amd so on, whose only (and kind-defining) differences from ladybugs lie in or stem from that in their bodies on which mental properties do not supervene. Such bodily differences would yield differences in powers. But the powers involved would not be powers God would have by nature. If one kind of bug naturally has a red shell and the other naturally has a blue shell, just the one has naturally the power to appear red to normal perceivers in normal conditions. God is not naturally colored.

I have seen only one way to try to show that His nature makes it possible that there be physical properties fit to cause experiences of phenomenal colors. I have argued that it fails.

If (as I have argued) God cannot naturally have concepts of physical properties, the present proposal cannot give God a natural concept of any kind with a physical kind-defining attribute or one which supervenes on a physical attribute. But plausibly the kind-defining attributes for every sort of physical thing are physical and those for every embodied person supervene on the physical. Even if they do not, if it is part of an embodied person's kind to be embodied, then if every body is physical, the present proposal still falls short. And if a person's kind permits it to be embodied, then still, the natural powers and liabilities that kind confers cannot be explicated without bringing in physical attributes, and so again this proposal falls short.

This leaves non-divine persons whose kind does not let them be embodied. It is unclear that there can be any: what would keep an angel, say, from taking on a body as a Platonic soul is supposed to? But we know so little about angels and the like that we can hardly rule it out that this is possible. Still, even angelic kinds might differ only in respect of conferring a quality God neither naturally has nor naturally has in His experience. Perhaps the kinds *being a seraph* and *being a cherub* confer all the same attributes save different natural appearances. Though they are immaterial, seraphim naturally signal their presence to God by causing in Him one sort of quale and to us by appearing to have six wings. Cherubim naturally signal their presence to God by a different quale, and seem to us to have eight wings. But God has no natural appearance. He does not naturally cause any quale in anyone when present, nor naturally appear winged. He can do either if He chooses, being omnipotent. But this does not suffice for having a natural appearance: that requires that the item by nature signal its presence in a particular way, given appropriate conditions.

Of course, even if angels can have natural appearances, perhaps there can also be angels without them. But we are in no position to deny the following: every angelic kind differs from every other in some attribute it confers which God neither naturally has nor naturally has in His experience. So even a deity theorist willing to settle for a deity theory of modal truths about necessarily bodiless angels could not (I submit) give us a good reason to believe it. We would have to settle for agnosticism here, even on assumptions favorable to deity theories.

Problems about spirit

Spirit and *person* provide all creaturely kinds only if every possible thing is some sort of spirit or person. The concept of God we began with resembled Leibniz's; if we held that every possible thing was a spirit of some sort, we would have a broadly Leibnizian picture of the world. But Leibniz was wrong. Some things are neither spirits nor persons; so these concepts do not provide kinds for all actual creatures, let alone all possible ones. It may even be that *spirit* is not a kind.

Plausibly, a spirit is just an immaterial substance (Aquinas) or a bodiless person (Swinburne). That is, plausibly being a spirit consists in being a substance and not being material or being a person and not being embodied. Even if we accept the determinable-plus-determinant model of kinds conceded for argument's sake above, it seems a reasonable constraint that the determinant be something positive. For even if there could be just two species of animal—dogs and cats—it would not seem that to be a dog is to be an animal that is not a cat. If we ask 'What is it?', the reply 'It is an animal and it is not a cat' seems a riddle, not an answer. Being an animal does not determine sufficiently precise persistence and distinctness conditions, and not being a cat provides nothing positive to determine these more precisely.

Moreover, on almost any theory of attributes, there is good reason not to believe in negative properties. For one can easily provide truth-conditions for predications of negative predicates without them: if Fido is not a cat, this is not because he has the property of being a non-cat, but because he lacks the property of being a cat. So they are unnecessary entities, and Ockham's Razor bids us shave. Thus if the concept of a spirit is, as it seems, a negative one, on most attribute-theories there is no good reason to believe in a property of being a spirit. There just is not and cannot be such a kind-property as *spirit*, unless it has some positive content of which we have no ken. If there is not, the concept of being a spirit is not a concept of a kind-property, and so is not useful in trying to show how God could have concepts of creaturely kind-properties.[51]

Beyond this, there are questions about how God could have this concept by nature. If a spirit is just (say) a bodiless person, being a spirit consists in being a person and not being embodied. If this is so, having the concept of a spirit depends on having the concept of matter. I have argued that the only story I know on which God could naturally generate the concept of matter by conceptual operations we grasp fails. If it does, and no other story offers itself, we should conclude that God does not have the concept of matter by nature unless (a) it is part of an innate stock He does not acquire; or (b) He acquires it by a natural brute compulsion; or (c) He acquires it by conceptual operations on His natural endowment of whose nature we have no idea. Whichever we choose, the same would apply to the concept of a spirit. The deity theorist who takes up (a) or (b) sacrifices a line of argument for preferring deity theories to my own, as emerges later. Further, (a) is just implausible: it is not

---

[51] Note that if there is no kind-property *spirit* in the strong sense of kind-property with which I am working, this does not entail that spirits are not a natural kind—that is, that the class containing all and only spirits is not maximally natural.

plausible that I innately have the concept of matter, and I do not see why it should be more so in God's case. (c) cannot be ruled out; of course, there is much about God we will never know. But equally, there is no good reason to embrace it. In the context of an argument to make a deity – theory plausible, the deity theorist has to give us some reason to think that God would have acquired His natural matter-concept in this way if we are to rule for (c) or (b), and I do not see what that could be.[52] If God does not have the concept of matter by nature, either there is purely positive conception of a spirit, of which we have no ken, or God would not by nature have the concept of a spirit at all. Deity theorists who want us to believe the first must give good reason to do so: good luck to them.

I note finally that if there is no property of being a spirit, God could be naturally omniscient even if He did not naturally have the concept of a spirit. If there is no such property, then if the concept did not yet exist, a God without it would not miss any property He has—though once the concept existed, He would see that He fell under it.

The problem with persons

Person, I now suggest, cannot be the only kind under which something falls, if indeed it is a kind. Consider the major accounts of what it is to be a person which do not simply reduce it to being something else (such as a human organism). These define personhood in terms of capacities: to be a person is to be rational[53] (a dispositional matter) or capable of self-consciousness,[54] moral responsibility,[55] second-order volitions,[56] or mental states generally.[57] Possession of these capacities does not seem able to determine persistence- and distinctness-conditions, as a kind-property should. If one of these accounts is true, then, that might suggest that *person* is not really a kind, or that if it is a kind, it is necessarily a kind something falls under only if it also falls under some other kind that provides such conditions. As we consider cases, we do find kinds beneath personhood. God is a person because He is divine. We are persons because we are human. If apes are persons it is because they are apes—that is, because they naturally have brains of the right sort to underwrite the required capacities. If more than one kind of thing can be a person, *person* cannot be the only kind anything falls under. If it is a kind, it is

---

[52] General appeals to perfection will not do. There is no reason to think that having innate concepts would be an imperfection.

[53] Locke, ultimately following Aristotle and Boethius.

[54] John Locke, 'Of Identity and Diversity'. reprinted in John Perry (ed.), *Personal Identity* (Berkeley: University of California Press, 1975), p. 39, ultimately following Aristotle and Boethius.

[55] Locke, *An Essay Concerning Him on Understanding* (Oxford: Oxford University Press, 1975), Book 2, ch. 27. Most would consider this to follow from being rational.

[56] Harry Frankfurt, 'Freedom of the Will and the Concept of a Person', *Journal of Philosophy* (1971), 7, 10.

[57] P. F. Strawson, *Individuals* (London: Methuen, 1959), pp. 101–2.

not an ultimate, basic kind. So *person* cannot be the only kind-concept for persons; it does not suffice to specify the kind of any possible creature. One might ask here whether God would have it in Him to think up persons for whom *person is* an ultimate, basic kind. I think not. He is personal by nature, and so His nature sets what it is to be a person. He has no control over what His nature contains, and He is Himself a person because He belongs to another kind.

Deity to the rescue?

We come finally to deity. We are trying to argue a deity theory rather than simply assert that somehow, we know not how, God gets creature-concepts out of deity. So it will not do here simply to suppose that God has some unknown way to get creature-concepts out of deity. We must show that He can by way only of operations with which we are acquainted. There is a way if deity is a conjunctive property: if, say, to be divine is to be a substance, omnipotent, omniscient, and . . . If it is, God can negate or detach a conjunct and get a representation of a substance which is omnipotent but not omniscient—a substance with these powers but not those (if omnipotence is a conjunction of powers), and so on. But I do not think deity is a conjunctive property.

Conjunctive properties have their natural home only in certain theories of attributes. On resemblance nominalism there are no attributes, and so there are no conjunctive attributes. If attributes just are concepts or predicates, some attributes certainly are conjunctive. But I soon argue that deity cannot be a predicate or concept. Some take attributes as classes of items satisfying predicates. If there are classes, there is a class of all and only things both hairy and fierce; within this theory, then, there is the conjunctive property of being hairy and fierce. I argue elsewhere that this theory of attributes faces massive objections.[58] On the other main theories, attributes are universals or tropes. I now argue against the existence of conjunctive universals or tropes.

Armstrong argues for conjunctive universals this way:

> It is logically and epistemically possible that all properties are conjunc-
> tive properties . . . so (if) there are no conjunctive properties . . . it (is)
> logically and epistemically possible that there are no properties at all.
> I take this to be a good reason for . . . admitting conjunctive properties.[59]

There are two arguments here. One is:

30. It is logically possible that all universals are conjunctive. So:

[58] 'One Step Toward God', Royal Institute of Philosophy Supplement 68 (2011), 67–104.

[59] A Theory of Universals (Cambridge: Cambridge University Press, 1978), p. 32. Earlier discussions of Armstrong's case overlook part of this argument, and so substantially misread him; see Albert Casullo, 'Conjunctive Properties Revisited', Australasian Journal of Philosophy 62 (1984), 289–91, and Eric R. Kraemer, 'Conjunctive Properties and Scientific Realism', Analysis 37 (1977), 85–6.

31. If there are no conjunctive universals, it is logically possible that there are no universals.

32. It is not logically possible that there are no universals. So:

33. There are conjunctive universals.

The other is:

34. It is epistemically possible that all universals are conjunctive. So:

35. If there are no conjunctive universals, it is epistemically possible that there are no universals.

36. It is not epistemically possible that there are no universals. So:

37. There are conjunctive universals.

If (30) implies (31), then if in some possible world all universals are conjunctive and actually none are, it is logically possible that there are no universals. But even if in some possible world all universals are conjunctive and actually none are, I do not see why it could not still be the case that in every possible world there are universals. What would follow if this last is so is at most that the population of universals varies world-to-world, since no conjunctive universal can be non-conjunctive. But only someone who thought all universals exist necessarily could find a varying population objectionable—and if we added their necessary existence to (30)–(33) as a premise, it would follow that *actually* all universals are conjunctive: if all universals exist necessarily and there is a possible world in which all universals are conjunctive, all universals are present in the world in which all universals are conjunctive, and since no universal can be conjunctive in some world and non-conjunctive in others, all universals are actually conjunctive. But I doubt that all universals are conjunctive. For one thing, if we resolve a property into two other properties, I do not see what reason we could ever have to think we had found a conjunctive property rather than a conjunction of properties.[60] Waiving this, I note that there is no ontological work a conjunctive property could do that could not be done by its conjuncts unconjoined. So even if we think we have found a conjunctive property, at any level of resolution at which we think we find it, we can simply posit the conjuncts without the conjunction: for any conjunctive property we actually think we need to recognize, we need not recognize *that one*, and Ockham's Razor counsels no posits without need. Eventually, being finite, we will find a level of resolution at which we can go no further, at which we seem to have a conjunctive property and so commit to just non-conjunctive properties. As we can go no further, we have no reason to believe that these properties might themselves be conjunctive. One might reply: how about induction over past resolutions into conjunctive properties, and the suspicion that saying that the ultimate level is non-conjunctive makes our metaphysics merely an artifact of our cognitive limitations? Any

---

[60] Here I am indebted to Casullo, *op. cit.*, 290.

metaphysics we will ever have reason to believe in will be a function of our cognitive input, which is limited. In that sense, there is no escaping the possibility that we believe what we do only due to our cognitive limits. Just because this cannot be escaped, it is no reason not to believe any particular thing which on full consideration seems true to us. We can only do as well as *we* can do. If induction were an all-things-considered determinative reason not to believe in complexity below the level at which we can resolve an item into components, we could never have good enough reason to believe we had reached (say) the fundamental level of physicals theory. But surely we can have such reason.

Nor do I see a way to get (35) from (34). If (34) does imply (35), then if for all we know, all universals are conjunctive and yet it is also the case that there are no conjunctive universals, then for all we know, there are no universals. But that we do not know that it is not the case that all universals are conjunctive just does not entail that we do not know that it is not the case that there are no universals. It seems possible that someone possess a very strong argument for universals together with no principle at all for deciding what kinds of universals there are. And this seems possible even if in fact there are no conjunctive universals. As far as I can see, that it is compatible with S's knowledge that

>   UC. all universals are conjunctive

and its being a fact that there are no conjunctive universals entail that it is compatible with S's knowledge that there are no universals only if (there are no conjunctive universals) ⊃ (S knows that there are no conjunctive universals). For if there are no conjunctive universals, the only way (UC) could be compatible with this would be that there be no universals. So if S knows there to be no conjunctive universals, the only way (UC) could be compatible with what S knew would be for there to be no universals. So if S knows that there are no conjunctive universals and it is epistemically possible for that (UC), it is epistemically possible for S that there are no universals. But Armstrong gives us no reason to accept that (there are no conjunctive universals) ⊃ (S knows that there are no conjunctive universals), and as a claim about any random S it is not at all plausible.

I can see only two other kinds of consideration favoring conjunctive universals. One appeals to structural universals. Molecules have complex structures: they consist of numbers of various sorts of atoms. Plausibly, then, the property of being a particular sort of molecule—say, methane—in some way involves the properties of being a hydrogen atom, being a carbon atom, and so on, and so is 'structural'. So if there are universals, plausibly there are 'structural' universals. Structural universals involve higher-order relations: the property of being a methane molecule is the property of having a part with the property of being hydrogen, and having another part with that property, and so on. Talk of higher-order relations lends itself to the forming of conjunctive properties: there is a property F&G, we might say, just if there is a higher-order relation between them that links two properties just if they can be co-instantiated. So realists about structural universals can easily believe in conjunctive universals.[61] The short answer—one we all heard at mother's knee—is that 'you can' does not imply 'you should'. Belief in structural universals is justified (if at all) because there is a distinctive line of ontological work they can do.[62] Again, there is no distinctive work for conjunctive universals to do.

Some, however, are willing to let universals be layabouts. 'Abundant' theories of universals posit a universal for (almost) every predicable, and so (in effect) infer conjunctive universals from conjunctive predicables. So arguments for such theories might be a third sort of backing for conjunctive universals. George Bealer presents an argument with these main premises:

38. All terms which seem to refer to attributes are singular.

39. Conjunctive predicables should be understood as referring.

40. They refer to necessarily existent abstract entities.[63]

The argument supposedly gets us an 'abundance' of universals because (38) concerns *all* such terms, including, for example, 'being red and round'. But even if we grant (38), the argument does not in fact yield abundance. Terms which are *grammatically* singular may nonetheless refer to many things which do not compose anything. Bealer's case for (38) is built on the claim that an argument like this is valid:

Whatever is a universal is an abstract entity.

Being red and round is a universal. So:

Being red and round is an abstract entity.[64]

If the argument is valid, it is plausible that in it 'being red and round' functions as a singular term. But now suppose for a moment that Van Inwagen is correct: there are no chairs, merely clouds of particles arranged chairwise.[65] Even if Van Inwagen is correct, this argument goes through:

Whatever is in the corner is dimly lit.

The chair is in the corner. So:

The chair is dimly lit.

---

[61] So John Bigelow and Robert Pargetter, 'A Theory of Structural Universals', *Australasian Journal of Philosophy* 67 (1989), 1–11.

[62] On which see David Lewis, 'Against Structural Universals', *Australasian Journal of Philosophy* 64 (1986), 25–46.

[63] George Bealer, 'Universals', *Journal of Philosophy* 90 (1993), 5–32. Actually, Bealer executes the argument only for propositions, and leaves the analogous argument for attributes as homework for the reader. Bealer notes that theism provides a viable alternative to (40) (*ibid.*, 27–8).

[64] Only 'like' because he states such an argument only for the case of propositions (*op. cit.*, 9).

[65] Peter Van Inwagen, *Material Beings* (Ithaca, NY: Cornell University Press, 1990).

Again, we can use 'the Supreme Court' to refer not to an institution but to the Justices plurally. But this is still a valid argument:

> Whatever is a group of nine people contains at least one idiot.
>
> The Supreme Court is a group of nine people. So:
>
> The Supreme Court contains at least one idiot.

For all Bealer shows us, then, 'being red and round' may not refer to any one thing.

Chisholm argues for abundant (and Platonic) universals by paraphrase considerations:

> There are many things we seem to know about properties... If (this) knowledge... were just a kind of knowledge about individual things, then we could paraphrase our ostensible property statements into statements (whose) individual terms and variables (take) only individual things as their values... (But) such paraphrase is not possible in every case.[66]
>
> We ... have a good reason for believing that there are attributes (if) a belief for which we have good reason... can be adequately expressed in statements... that contain terms purporting to designate attributes and... in that use are subject to existential generalization (and) we cannot express the belief in question without using terms that thus purport to designate attributes.[67]

Typical of Chisholm's allegedly resistant statements is 'There are shapes that are not exemplified.'[68] Whatever the worth of such arguments as support for belief in *some* universals, they do not support belief in conjunctive universals. For we *can* paraphrase statements ostensibly referring to these into statements not doing so, with no apparent loss of content (beyond the appearance of commitment to such universals). With the property of being red and round in mind, let us try 'There are shapes-and-colors that are not exemplified.' For this we might offer 'There are shape–color pairs whose members are not co-exemplified' (pairs are classes, not universals) or 'There are shapes that are not exemplified and there are colors that are not exemplified.' What is lost, beyond the appearance of commitment to a conjunctive universal? Van Inwagen offers a similar sort of argument, based on the (claimed) ineliminability of quantification over properties.[69] But that we must quantify over some properties, if true, hardly entails that every appearance of an apparent property name constitutes a place over which we should quantify.

I see no other bases for belief in conjunctive universals, and so I do not think they have anything to recommend them. Further, there is reason not to believe

[66] Roderick Chisholm, *On Metaphysics* (Minneapolis, MN: University of Minnesota Press, 1989), p. 141.
[67] *A Realistic Theory of Categories* (Cambridge: Cambridge University Press, 1996), p. 20.
[68] *On Metaphysics*, pp. 141–2; see *A Realistic Theory of Categories*, p. 21.
[69] Peter van Inwagen, 'A Theory of Properties', *Oxford Studies in Metaphysics* 1 (2004), 107–38.

in them, even apart from the Razor. For one thing, if there are any, there must be something in reality to distinguish one's presence from the presence of its conjuncts, for the conjuncts could be there though the conjunctive universal is not: if Fa and Gb and there are no other particulars, something has F and something has G but nothing has the conjunctive property F&G. Even if something has F&G, something must make being F&G different from just being F and also being G. So there must be some kind of property-combiner *in reality*, something corresponding to the '&' in 'F&G'—perhaps the higher-order relation mentioned above. But there are no good candidates.

The combiner cannot be any kind of causal relation. Talk of supervenience would be off-target; it does not give us the difference between having F and having G and having F&G. I suspect that ordinary composition and mereological summation apply only to particulars. But leaving that aside, if there are composites, composition is either restricted (that is, not all groups of items compose a further item) or not. If it is restricted, there must be something that distinguishes groups which compose something from groups which do not, some *reason* composition takes place in just some cases, some condition only composite-forming groups meet. Composition surely cannot just be 'brutal'.[70] But I see no prospect of finding such a condition for attributes. If composition is unrestricted, either there is or there is not something about any group which makes it compose a further thing—some condition the group must meet beyond just existing. It is hard to see what such a condition could be, particularly for attributes. But if all it takes to compose something is to exist, then other than the existence of the composites, there is no difference between a world in which universal composition holds and one in which it does not: composition is 'brutal' but on a grand scale. Further, it is hard to escape the impression that this view of composition differs only verbally from a denial that composition ever really occurs.[71] For it is hard to escape the impression that the only real import of the claim that my nose and Alpha Centauri compose an object is that one can use a singular term 'the mereological sum of my nose and Alpha Centauri' to refer to the two together, and if the universality of composition entails that nothing is composite in any 'thicker' sense than my nose and Alpha Centauri are, then composition generally is just the shadow of possible language use—which is to say that there never really are, apart from our thinking, any composite objects. So I doubt that composition is unrestricted, for particulars or anything else.

The property-combiner cannot be set-formation if attributes are universals: a set of universals is not a universal. Perhaps one might suggest that conjunct properties constitute a conjunctive property. But the going accounts of the constitution relation either involve spatial coincidence and so just do not

---

[70] *Pace* Ned Markosian, 'Brutal Composition', *Philosophical Studies* 92 (1998), 211–49.

[71] On which see Eli Hirsch, 'Physical-Object Ontology, Verbal Dispute and Commonsense', *Philosophy and Phenomenological Research* 70 (2005), 1–30.

apply to abstract entities, or involve relative identity or near relations thereof, and so both incur a heavy theoretical burden and fail to apply in this case.[72] For the conjunct properties remain completely distinct, and if we think of the relative identity as between the conjuncts and the conjunction, still any relative-identity relation is 1:1, not one–many. Some properties realize others (of which more anon): being of such and such shape, composition, and so on, realizes the property of being a car. But we are looking for a relation between conjunct properties that would explain the presence of a conjunctive property—something to add to their being there to yield the latter. Realization is just wrong for that: it is not a relation between realizers, but one between realizers and the realized. Armstrong offers 'partial identity' as the relation, but cannot give another case of it which does not obviously boil down to ordinary part–whole relations not involving anything which is other than wholly identical with or wholly distinct from anything else.[73] So the property-combiner would have simply to be a brute, mysterious primitive—something we would need good reason to introduce. We sometimes do have good reasons for this, as (I submit) in the case of modality. Modal locutions are deeply embedded in ordinary thought. We find some modal judgments strongly intuitive. Modal locutions, however, seem to resist analysis in terms of non-modal locutions, and reductive projects (of keeping modal locutions in the language but assigning them wholly non-modal truthmakers) have not produced plausible results. So I think we have good reason to accept some modal locutions as conceptually primitive and specifying something equally primitive in reality. Nothing like this holds for 'partial identity'. So I do not see adequate reason to introduce a property-combining primitive. This is so *a fortiori* because, again, the conjuncts can do any ontological work a conjunctive universal could do. Finally, the case against conjunctive tropes is in most respects parallel to that just laid out for universals.

Thus it seems to me that deity is not conjunctive. Nor is it disjunctive (a thesis which Ch. 8 rejects at length), nor negative (what would that mean?). If so, God cannot by decomposition obtain creature-kind-concepts from *deity*. Getting them by logical or mathematical operations seem a non-starter: e.g., conjunction—because anything which is a deity and something else is divine, and disjunction, because our whole question is how God would get any suitable concept to disjoin with that of deity. Intensive augmentation does no better: I am not more intensely divine than God is. So God could work with *deity* only by diminishment, among the conceptual operations of which we have any ken. But diminishing *deity* yields only diminished degrees of *deity*. Were this how God

---

[72] For the various accounts see Michael Rea (ed.), *Material Constitution* (Lanham, MD: Rowman and Littlefield, 1997).

[73] Armstrong, *A Theory of Universals*, pp. 36–9. Armstrong acknowledges that this leaves 'partial identity' looking like just an alternative way to talk about ordinary part-whole relations (*A World of States of Affairs* (Cambridge: Cambridge University Press, 1997), p. 18).

came up with creatures' kinds, all creatures would be minor gods: a low-degree deity is a deity. Surely rocks are not even a little bit divine. Further, I doubt that possession of kind-properties admits of degrees. In the evolutionary past, no doubt, there were borderline cases of birds, but it seems better to say that they were almost but not quite birds than to say that they were partly or to a low degree birds.

Further, even if we waive all this, diminishment of deity has to be along some scale. God can conceive naturally of a deity less powerful or wise than He, but it would need argument that such a deity is *ipso facto* less divine: the Greeks acknowledged greater and lesser Olympians as equally gods, and do not seem to have made any conceptual mistake in doing so. It seems conceptually proper to say both that any being that deserves worship at all is simply divine and that some beings deserve more worship than others. So associated properties are not obvious candidates for providing a scale; absent argument that degrees of these do provide degrees of deity, we must look to deity itself. How would God come to have a deity scale? I see four ways to think of this:

41. God's deity comes only with something like a set of numbers with which to pair lower-degree versions of deity.

42. God's deity comes with a set of imperative directions, 'diminish 10%', 'diminish 20%', or the like. This generates the scale by generating the items ranked along it.

43. God's deity comes with, and the scale consists of, an ordered set of ever-lower-degree versions of deity.

44. God's deity comes with gradations built in, as if God starts out with a full tank of deity with volume-marks along its side: 3/4-full, half-full, and so on. Constructing ideas of items at various points on the scale (lower-degree versions of deity) consists in (as it were) mentally emptying the tank to various degrees.

Turning to (41), we must ask what there is to pair with each number. If the lower-degree items to be paired are there in the divine nature, with only the pairing still to do, there is no diminution, no real obtaining of anything out of deity: there is just deity primitively full of its lower degrees, and so creatures' natures, and God noticing what their natures are. To assert this would be just to assert a deity theory without argument, and we are seeking precisely a way to argue one. If the lower-degree items are not there to be paired, they will have to be invented, then paired with numbers. If the given scale is what (41) says it is, this inventing cannot be a matter of diminution along a scale. God has to make creatures up in some other way, and (41)'s idea of diminution does no work in explaining how He does it. And if creatures really are creative inventions, any deity theory is false.

(42)'s directions either do or do not spell out just what is involved in diminishing 10% (and so on). If they do not, (42) is too thin a model to give the idea of diminution real bite. For if they do not, then unless God's deity comes with inner gradations, as on (44), there is nothing to say just what diminishing 10% would take. God would have to decide without guidance what that operation involves—that is, purely and simply make up what counts as diminishing 10%. But if He makes up the operation, *a fortiori* He makes up the result. His nature would be an original, the diminished result something like an imperfect copy conceived creatively. There is some sense in which the original has some of the copy's content within itself—but everything which makes the copy distinctive, makes it other than a mere duplication of the original, would in no sense be part of the original's content. So one could not really say in this case that God's nature contained the content of the lesser-degree deity-concepts, nor that He had them naturally. One would have to grant that some degree of sheer creativity figured in His coming up with them. So read, (42) would hardly differ from (41). If, on the other hand, the directions spell out just what it is to diminish 10%, they fully determine the operation's result, and in effect they spell out in the imperative mood the sort of 'volume mark' (44) speaks of in the indicative— and so (42) winds up a slight variation on (44).

As to (43), if a contentful scale is given along with the divine nature, there is no diminishing for God to do to come up with creaturely natures. The lower-degree sorts of deity are all there, along the scale; we have simply a primitive-contents-of-deity theory. As the idea that God diminishes deity conceptually does no work, it cannot help a deity theorist argue that creature-natures really are packed into deity. And even if we granted the deity theory that God's deity has packed within itself what it is to be divine to degree 0.9, 0.8, and so on, the deity theorist making the present move on creaturely kinds would have to explain why being 0.9 divine amounts to being a dolphin, 0.8 divine to a chicken, and so on, or more generally why it should be that any created nature really correlates with one particular degree of deity. I have no clue as to how such accounts would go. Turning finally to (44), note that a volume's parts are present in the whole: if one has a full tank of gas, one has two half-tanks. So (44) is really just the claim that the items to be paired with numbers are given in the divine nature, but without even the pairing left for God to do. On (44), then, again, the idea of diminution does no work in accounting for the natures of creatures. God does not diminish deity conceptually; it is just a given fact that deity contains within itself other natures equivalent to diminished versions of itself. Again, we want to know how it is set what degree of deity is to be a fish, a fowl, and so on. In sum, then, (41)–(44) do not provide a way for diminishment of deity to yield creaturely kind-concepts, nor *a fortiori* a way to argue for a deity theory.

In sum, God's kinds do not seem to give Him the resources to generate by any means we know representations of creaturely kind-properties; if I am right about *spirit* and *person*, they do not get Him *any* set of properties sufficient fully to conceive even a single possible creature.[74] Though God has a perfect mind, the material He has to work with does not let us explain His possession of these concepts in this way. Thus while He might naturally have (or be primed to develop) representations of candidate attributes for creatures, we so far have seen no reason to credit Him with natural concepts of possible creatures to have them.

The role of will

I have argued, then, that the story under discussion does not in fact get God full concepts of any candidate creature. I now argue that even if we granted that it does, it would not get us the conclusion that God's nature, of itself, grounds any modal truth about creatures. God's representing (say) angels to Himself, even if He does so naturally, does not suffice to make any angel possible: for He could naturally represent combinations of attributes just discussed to Himself, have the combinations in all ways internally proper as candidates for possibility (such as not containing any F and G such that for all x, Fx and Gx entails a contradiction), and then have it the case that no matter what, He would not permit them to be instanced.

The story I have been discussing either does or does not extend to giving God a natural conception of pain and suffering. If it does not, the story fails in another respect. If it does, then on the story, God can naturally represent to Himself something He would not possibly permit to be: an angel whose only power, save those that constitute its being a person, is to feel searingly intense pain. Such a being could achieve nothing and could not be rewarded in any way for its suffering. It could exist only to provide some good to others, and my intuition is that no such good could neutralize the evil its existence entrains or right the wrong of treating a person entirely as a means and not at all as an end in itself. If God is necessarily perfect morally, He does not possibly permit such a thing to exist. Yet there is nothing *intrinsically* impossible about the suffering angel. We can vividly conceive it, its concept surely harbors no hidden contradictions, etc. It is impossible purely because God would not let it exist, no matter what: that is, because God actually makes none and wills to prevent any, and is so disposed that He would so will, no matter what.

Nor is God's moral perfection the only thing that might intrude here. Plausibly, God also finds in Himself natural materials for a representation of evil, though He does not find in Himself any inclination to do it. For if God naturally has the representations just noted, He also naturally will grasp degrees of unlikeness to Himself in a respect, as He can see that creatures who know less would be more unlike Him in one respect than creatures who

---

[74] Or, again, maximally determinate creature-kind, if there are no pre-creative concepts of particular creatures.

know more. He will know many truths with a general form, which He would also grasp:

GF. to have attributes—and—and . . . includes being unlike God to degree—in respect of—.[75]

If this is correct, it would be inexplicable if He did not also have naturally every representation He could form by plugging in to (GF) values whose representations He has naturally. So He also naturally represents degrees of unlikeness to Himself in respect of goodness. Thus He naturally represents to Himself being maximally unlike Him morally, or infinitely unlike Him, if there is no maximal degree here. Something thus unlike Him would more incline to choose an act the less likely God is on moral grounds to do it, more desire to do it the less God would desire to and more incline to frustrate God's purposes the more it can grasp them and see a way to do so. It would be God's inverse morally. 'Evil' could be explicated in terms (roughly) of what such a being would be most likely to do.

God can conceive near-omnipotence (ability to bring about every state of affairs God can, save one) and near-omniscience (knowing all that God knows, save moral truths by the means sketched). Thus if the general story we are scouting is true, God could naturally represent a being near-omnipotent, near-omniscient, and maximally or infinitely evil: a maxi-devil. As far as we can see, there is nothing intrinsically impossible about a maxi-devil. It would take a long hard slog to show that near-omnipotence and omniscience and creatureliness entail not being maximally evil *apart from* a necessary disposition of God preventing maxi-devils. Yet even if this combination of attributes did not run foul of God's moral preferences, He might have other relevant preferences. If these are contingent, it might be that had He not had these, He would have had still others that would also have ruled them out. For instance, there would be risk in making a maxi-devil. Perhaps God could also see a chance of great good in it. But how much risk is He prepared to assume? Even if God has different degrees of risk-aversion in different possible worlds, perhaps God necessarily is sufficiently risk-averse that He would not risk a maxi-devil. If so, in no possible world would He make one or let one appear— and this is why maxi-devils are impossible. So even if representations of candidate creatures were somehow built into God naturally, creaturely *modal truths* could well still depend on God's will and dispositions. Even if it is not up to God that there is a representation *maxi-devil*, it could still be up to God whether it is possible that there be a maxi-devil. Nor is there anything unique about *maxi-devil* that gives God's will a look-in. If it is vulnerable (so to

---

[75] The degree-talk would just be an application of natural mathematical knowledge, but those skeptical here could substitute a comparative form, 'to have attributes—and—and . . . includes being more unlike God— in respect of—than to have attributes—and—and . . .'. I could run my argument in terms of this, *mutatis mutandis*.

speak), so is every other creature-representation: if others win through to possibility, it is because a God who could prevent this does not.

One might rejoin here that this is not enough to show that if the story succeeded otherwise, God's nature would not be the ground of modal truth. I have appealed to necessary divine preferences—against a certain degree of risk, for instance—as keeping certain representations from representing possibilities. But (one might argue) God's nature contains or determines His necessary preferences. So perhaps the story should be that God's nature determines a field of divine representations and also determines which ones of these turn out to express genuine possibilities: and so it is deity all the way, although the story is a bit complicated. But here I protest. One point at issue between the deity theorist and what I have called the neglected option is precisely whether everything necessary about God is in or determined by deity. On the view I set out later, there are necessary divine volitions and dispositions which the content of deity does not explain.

I now take up another argument.

Imitation and Self-understanding

Aquinas argues that God understands His nature perfectly, and this includes understanding all the ways He can be imitated.[76] Had God not understood some way He could be imitated, He would have fallen short of perfect self-understanding. For Thomas, everything other than God imitates Him in some way.[77] If we extend this to a claim that every possible creature would imitate God, it will follow that that in God's nature which produces His perfect self-understanding requires Him to come up with concepts of all possible creatures. So His nature would impel Him to form these and determine the way they come out (as originals determine how things formed to be copies come out).

Leaving aside the ways originals do not determine the content of imperfect copies, this argument begs the question. Even if God must understand all the ways He can be imitated to understand Himself fully, it is compatible with this that He determine what those ways are rather than finding them all written out within His nature. Perhaps God first understands Himself, then creatively thinks up the ways He can be imitated, and by so doing adds to His self-understanding a grasp of how other things can imitate Him. Suppose that this is how things are. Then if He does not think up some way to imitate Him, there is nothing about how He can be imitated that He misses. For only His thinking it up would establish that He could be imitated this way. So on this

---

[76] *ST* Ia 15, 2.   [77] *ST* Ia 4, 3.

alternate picture, nothing in God's nature requires Him to come up any particular creature-concept. The argument just given gives us no reason to adopt its picture of creatures and imitation of God rather than this other.

Thomas also held that God knows all the ways He *cannot* be imitated.[78] This permits an epicycle on the present argument, but it should be clear from the foregoing how I would deal with it.

Cognitive Perfection

Another argument might run this way. By nature, God is cognitively perfect. Suppose that there is a unique best set of creature-concepts to be formed. If by nature God is cognitively perfect and there is a best set of creature-concepts to be formed, God forms these. So God forms these. And so God's nature guarantees that He hits on the best concepts: they again emerge as in an appropriate sense natural. A short answer would be: why should we think there is a unique best set to be formed?

Deity theories have dominated the scene in theist modal metaphysics. But I at least have not been able to find a good argument for them. I next offer an argument against them.

---

[78] For Thomas, all God's knowledge of evils falls under this heading.

7

DEITY AS ESSENTIAL

I have blocked arguments for deity theories. I now argue against deity theories. I begin by arguing a needed lemma, that deity is essential to whatever has it: that is,

> DE. (x)(x is divine ⊃ necessarily x is divine).

I also argue that deity is in fact an individual essence—that if possibly something has deity, it is not possible that any other individual have it. 'Deity' again refers to that having which makes *God* divine, where God is understood as in the Western monotheisms. Because it does, I take having deity to have some sort of necessary connection to having the traditional divine attributes. I make below such claims as that having deity entails being eternal. There have obviously been things various cultures took to be gods but did not take to be eternal. This is just irrelevant for present purposes.

A Natural-kind Argument

I begin my case for (DE) as follows:

1. The concept of deity is an 'Aristotelian' natural-kind concept.
2. If anything is a deity, it has always been a deity.
3. If something has always been a deity, there is no natural-kind concept under which it fell before it fell under deity.
4. If there is no natural-kind concept something fell under before it fell under deity, deity is among the first natural-kind concepts it fell under.
5. Nothing could have failed to fall under the 'Aristotelian' natural-kind concepts it first fell under. So:
6. If anything is a deity, it could not have failed to be a deity.

7. If anything is a deity, it cannot cease being a deity. So:

8. If anything is a deity, it could not have failed to be one and cannot cease to be one.

9. For all x and F, if x could not have failed to be F and cannot cease to be F, necessarily x is F, and so being F is modal-essential to x. So:

10. (DE).

I first argue (1). It seems that to say that God is a deity is to say what kind of thing He is: that God is a deity and that Rover is a dog seem the same kind of claim. One can imagine polytheists treating deities as a kind distinct from mortals. They would not cease to do so if they subsequently found that there is just one, nor would they make a conceptual mistake in this. Deity could be a kind-concept even if there has only ever been one deity: the concept of a dog would be a kind-concept, a concept fit to sort things into a kind, even if the first dog had died before reproducing. Deity could be a kind-concept even if only one possible individual could satisfy it. For one might mistakenly believe that many things could, and shape one's concept accordingly. Moreover, it just does not seem impossible that there be a fact about what kind of thing something is, but just one possible item can be of that kind. If *number* is a kind, *prime number* is a sub-kind, and *even prime number* seems an *infima species* or lowest kind even though only one thing can satisfy it. So I submit that 'deity' expresses a kind-concept.

If the concept of deity is a kind-concept, it is surely a natural-kind concept. I do not mean by this that deities are found in nature. Rather, deity meets generally accepted conditions for being the same kind of kind as kinds whose instances are found in nature.[1] Whether something is a deity is wholly independent of whether we think it is. There are properties having which is necessary and sufficient for being divine, and what these are, again, is independent of us. Deity has explanatory value: His being divine explains a great deal about God. Its possession imparts characteristic causal powers, those of omnipotence. Deity is intrinsic, if the West has its content roughly right, for the West holds that God could have been divine even had He created nothing at all, and so nothing outside Him is necessary for His being divine.[2]

---

[1] I cull the following typical properties of natural kinds from Joseph LaPorte, *Natural Kinds and Conceptual Change* (Cambridge: Cambridge University Press, 2004), pp. 19–20, and T. E. Wilkerson, *Natural Kinds* (Aldershot: Avebury, 1995), pp. 29–35. If the Western monotheisms have it right, deity is a kind that does not admit borderline cases. (Greek polytheists might have disagreed.) But being a kind does not analytically imply having borderline cases: we can make sense of kinds of abstract object, and there are no borderline cases of being, for instance, a number or a property.

[2] A Platonist might cavil: to be divine, God must be omniscient. To be omniscient He must know the necessary truths. And these are and/or are made true by Platonic entities outside Him. I am of course in the process of arguing *inter alia* that theists should not be Platonists about necessary truth. But just what it could mean to say that Platonic entities exist 'outside' God when neither of them is spatial is an interesting question. And on plausible accounts of the intrinsic (for example, Stephen Yablo, 'Intrinsicness', *Philosophical Topics* 26 (1999), 479–505), relations to necessary entities come out as one and all intrinsic.

And deity is a 'sparse' property—the sort that would figure in a minimum basis for constructing a world that would look and act just like ours.[3]

'Aristotelian' natural kinds (as discussed earlier) determine persistence—and distinctness-conditions. Plausibly deity does so. Deity makes a deity eternal. If being eternal is being atemporal, then deity determines the only fact about a deity's persistence conditions—that strictly speaking it has none, since only temporal things persist. But one might add this: if a deity is atemporal, then though there is no time at which its existence is located, every time is one at which it is true that timelessly, a deity exists. This is a persistence-condition in an extended sense. If being eternal is having an unlimited temporal existence, then since (as I argue elsewhere[4]) deity makes its bearer a necessary being, deity determines that a deity persists, no matter what. This is straightforwardly a persistence condition. Further, deity determines conditions under which one deity is distinct from another existing at the same time: as I will argue, they are null, because there cannot be more than one deity.

Turning to (2), as Western monotheism understands deity, necessarily, any deity is eternal, and so such that there is no time before it exists.[5] An eternal deity could fail always to have been a deity only if it always existed, was first non-divine, and later became divine. The Western religions deny that this has occurred. Thus the Western religions commit themselves to (2): for them there is just one deity, and He has always been divine. This will suffice for those who take the standard beliefs of one of these faiths as normative. Again, if being eternal is being atemporal, then nothing can become a deity. No atemporal being could become one, as becoming divine would be an intrinsic change. A thing changes intrinsically only if it first has a property and then—later—lacks it. Anything that earlier has a property and later lacks it is *ipso facto* in time. Nor could something temporal become both atemporal and divine. What is atemporally so is so equally from the standpoint of any time. If it is now the case timelessly that P, it is the case timelessly that P at any other time, because atemporal states of affairs cannot cease to obtain: a state of affairs ceases to obtain only if first it does and then later it does not, and any state of affairs that has another state of affairs later than it is *ipso facto* in time. So nothing could first not be and then be atemporal. If it was ever atemporal, it was so from the standpoint of any time, including those before it supposedly became atemporal. This will suffice for atemporalists. My further arguments, then, suppose that a deity's eternality is temporal.

An argument against its being possible to become a temporal deity may begin from a definition: let 'being F is a better state than not being F' mean

---

[3] For the connection between sparseness and naturalness, see David Lewis, *On the Plurality of Worlds* (Oxford: Basil Blackwell, 1986), pp. 59–69.

[4] 'Divine Necessity', in Charles Taliaferro and Chad Meister (eds), *The Cambridge Companion to Christian Philosophical Theology* (Cambridge: Cambridge University Press, 2010), pp. 15–30.

[5] There is no time before a deity exists if it is atemporal. This is also true if it is temporally eternal—for then its past existence extends as far as time itself does.

that being F is objectively and intrinsically such that someone ideally informed and perfectly rational would prefer *ceteris paribus* being F to not being F, or is objectively and intrinsically such that something F is more worthy of respect, admiration, honor, or awe than something not F, *ceteris paribus*. Let us also say that if something is a deity, then just *qua* a deity, it intrinsically and objectively is an appropriate object of greatest worship, and if something is not a deity, then just *qua* not a deity, it intrinsically and objectively is not an appropriate object of greatest worship.[6] Now plausibly,

W. anything deserving greatest worship is in a better state than anything that does not.

I argue (W) thus. Greatest worship is the attitude of greatest respect, admiration, honor, and awe, or the activity of expressing this attitude. So something intrinsically and objectively is an appropriate object of greatest worship only if it intrinsically and objectively deserves more of these than anything not an appropriate object of greatest worship. If so, *per* our definition of being a better state, something intrinsically and objectively is an appropriate object of greatest worship only if it is in a better state than anything that is not: which is (W). But if something is a deity, then just *qua* a deity, it intrinsically and objectively is an appropriate object of greatest worship. So if something is a deity, then just *qua* a deity, it is intrinsically and objectively in a better state than anything that is not. And so by way of our account of 'better state,' we have

D1. being a deity is a better state than not being a deity.

We can also give a 'perfect being' case for (D1). Being divine as Western theism understands it implies having what we might call the Biblical perfections—those discussed in the Introduction. Non-Biblical perfections might fall into three broad categories. Some fill out Biblical perfections. One Biblical perfection was to have 'understanding without limits'—that is, no intellectual limitations. So if there is an intellectual property lacking which would involve suffering some intellectual limit, perfect-being theology will infer that God has it, *ceteris paribus*. Call these specifying perfections, since they provide more detailed content for Biblical perfections. Perfect-being theology holds that God has a best compossible set of perfections—a set S of compatible perfections such that having any other such set would be a state equal with, lesser than, or incommensurable with having those in S. S includes many specifying perfections.

---

[6] This claim is compatible with polytheists' appropriately offering some degree of worship to many gods. It insists only that (so to speak) God outranks the gods. The Introduction noted that the main historical polytheisms happily agree.

Again, there are the modal perfections mentioned earlier. I argue elsewhere that necessary existence is a better state than contingent.[7] If it is, then if existing necessarily is compatible with having the Biblical and specifying perfections and doing just what God has done—as certainly seems the case[8]—then if God exists contingently, it is possible to deserve more worship than God in fact deserves or more deserve worship than God in fact does, not due to (say) doing more than God has done, but due solely to being a sort of being superior to God. Something of which this was true would be in a better state than God is in, and have a set of perfections superior to God's. Perfect-being theology will not accept this, and any Western theist will jib at it. It does not fit with the unqualified praise Western theistic worship offers to have in the back of one's mind a reservation: You are great, but I can think of greater. The same will apply to necessary possession of perfections if that is also better. (I argue below that it is.) So Western theists and perfect-being theists should grant that S includes at least some modal perfections.

Finally, there might be perfections neither Biblical, specifying nor modal—perfections in categories these do not cover. We have no idea what these further categories could be, and no reason to believe that there may be any beyond a general cognitive humility. For these to give reason not to accept (D1) we would need reason to be nearly agnostic—to have a confidence approaching 0.5—about the thesis that

MP. there are 'mystery perfections' better to have than those in S and incompatible with some of S, or some possible being could and a divine being could not have all those in S plus some mystery perfections,

and to think that (MP), if true, is reason to deny (D1). But S is the best compossible set of perfections. If F is initially in S and incompatible with mystery perfections, and the latter are better to have than F and compatible with the rest of S, the mystery perfections take F's place, and being a deity is still better than not being one. If those so far in S are compatible with extra mystery perfections, it follows that the mystery perfections are in S, and a deity would have them, as it has whatever is in S. We can see that (MP) gives us no reason to doubt (D1).

If (D1) is true, then if a deity is temporal,

D2. having been divine longer is a better state than having been divine for less time.

For if (D1) is true, an ideally informed, perfectly rational being would prefer *ceteris paribus* having been divine for longer to having been divine for less time. One can deserve present respect for what one was and no longer is: past Presidents of the US and aging sports heroes are in a sense has-beens, yet we

---

[7] Taliaferro and Meister, 'Divine Necessity'.
[8] At any rate, assuming an adequate response to the modal problem of evil—which I believe can be had.

think it right to honor them. One can also deserve present respect for what one was and still is: a President who is finishing a long, successful term of office is the more impressive for it. This would apply to presently having been divine longer. Again, if one has been divine longer, then even if one's past and one's having had it deserve no present respect at all, still, when the divine parts of one's past were present, one was in a better state. It is rational to prefer that more of one's life when present be in a better state. Suppose one were behind a veil of ignorance, choosing how much of one's life would be spent divine. If ideally informed and perfectly rational, one would choose more over less. This would remain so, *ceteris paribus,* were one told that upon 'insertion' into this life, much of the divine part would lie in one's past.

This brings me, finally, to the perfect-being argument for (2). Something becomes divine only if it first is not and then is divine. Consider, then, any time at which a non-deity becomes divine, by changing or coming to exist. Suppose it could have done so a bit earlier. Then it could have been divine longer. If the past has been finite this is true in a straightforward, ordinary sense. If the past has been infinite, it is true in a different but still legitimate sense: the times at which it was divine are a subset of the times it could have been divine. So by (D2) it is in a lesser state than it could have been in by then. So it does not have a best compossible set of perfections that could be had by then. So it is not in a state a temporal deity would be in by then. So a being cannot succeed in becoming divine unless it could not have done so sooner. But if it could not have become divine sooner, but has not always been divine, plausibly there could be something else just like it save for becoming divine sooner. So whether or not our first being could have become divine sooner, if it was not always divine, plausibly there can be a more perfect deity—one with a better compossible set of perfections by then. But any temporal divine being has a best such set. So our first being that supposedly became divine was in fact not divine at all. Thus something is divine only if nothing could have been divine sooner. But it is possible always to have been divine. So it is not possible to become divine. If it is not, (2) is true.

(3) and (4) are obvious. If the logic of absolute modality includes S5—a widely shared view—then (5) follows. 'Aristotelian' natural kinds determine persistence conditions, and so determine a range of truths sharing the form *possibly condition C obtains and __ still exists* or *it is impossible that C obtain and __ still exists.* If a thing first falls under an Aristotelian kind, then, it begins to exist with such truths true of it. Given S5, all such truths are necessary. If a thing first falls under an Aristotelian kind, then, it could have failed to have these truths true of it only if a necessary truth could have failed to be true. Given S5, this is impossible (and given only S4, this is impossible of the impossibility-truths). So given S5, a thing could have failed to fall under its first Aristotelian kind(s) only if it could have instead fallen under some other

kind(s) its falling under which would make true precisely these truths. But suppose that two kinds determine precisely the same persistence conditions. Then they allow to every member of each at all times in all worlds all and only the same further states: every K_1 always has open to it (as states into which it can persist) all states then open to a K_2, including being a K_2, and *vice versa*. So each member of each has open to it being a member of the other. Moreover, suppose there is a K_1 at t, and given the conditions then, among the states open to it is continuing to be a K_1. Then necessarily, any K_2 at t under those conditions has open to it continuing to be a K_1. Nothing can continue to be a K_1 unless it *is* a K_1. So necessarily, any K_2 at t under those conditions is a K_1. This applies to all possible members of each kind in all possible circumstances at all possible times. So the kinds are necessarily co-extensive. But then it is not the case that a K_1 could have *instead* fallen under another kind, K_2, making true precisely the truths about possible states into which it could persist. It *did* fall under this kind. And it is not the case that it could have failed to be a K_1. Necessarily, if it is 'instead' a K_2, it is also a K_1. So I suggest that (5) is as plausible as the thesis that S5 is the logic of absolute modality—and even apart from argument it is fairly plausible.[9] (5) allows that I could have started out blue-eyed—instead of brown-eyed.[10] Blue-eyed humans are not an 'Aristotelian' kind: while 'human' tells us what I am, blue-eyed humans are not an Aristotelian sub-kind, as they have no distinctive persistence—and distinctness-conditions. (5) allows that caterpillars change kind, into butterflies. But how could a caterpillar have started out as a stone instead? What would have made it that same individual? If an Aristotelian-kind-member in one world is identical with an Aristotelian-kind-member in another, there are informative necessary conditions on such identities.[11] It is plausible that one such necessary condition is identity of initial Aristotelian kinds.

I take (7) in this sense: any actual deity not only does not cease to be a deity in any continuation of actual history, but does not cease to be a deity in any continuation of any possible history. The Western religions agree that necessarily, a deity is eternal. But they do not mean by this merely that a divine being lasts forever in *some* state or other. Told that God was divine for an hour, then turned into a turnip and lasted forever in that state, Western theists would not reply 'Yup, that's just what we meant—God exists eternally.' The

---

[9] Penelope Mackie provides strong sustained criticism of views including (5) in *How Things Might Have Been* (Oxford: Oxford University Press, 2006). But one need not endorse any view Mackie discusses to find (5) appealing enough to make one suspect that *some* view including it must be correct. My argument bypasses her criticisms of the specific views she takes up, and so does not require addressing them.

[10] Or if I came to be before my eyes did, with some other change in appropriate property.

[11] Kripke's 'spinning disc' argument that some transworld identities are bare is not to the point. Even if the identity of this bit of the disc in this world with that bit in another world is bare, this bit cannot be identical with a flea in another world, and this states one informative necessary condition on cross-world identity.

As I see it, if there are such informative conditions, this tells us something about how God's mind works in establishing these identities, rather than representing independently grounded constraints He must respect.

Western religions mean, surely, that necessarily, whatever is divine is eternally so. They mean (I submit) to commit themselves to (7).

We can also argue (7). Suppose first that a deity's eternality is temporal. Then something ceases to be divine only if it first is and then is not divine, or else time ends. As to the latter, any divine being is as such eternal. If time ends, nothing temporal is eternal, for a temporally eternal existence does not end. So if time ends, nothing temporal was ever divine, and so nothing temporal ceases to be divine. But if something ceases to be divine with time yet to run, it never was guaranteed to be divine for all time. Having this guarantee seems a possible property. One thing we could mean by calling a temporal deity eternal is that it has it. The property is compatible with the rest of the divine perfections, and better to have than to lack. So a being without it is not perfect, and so not a deity, and so cannot cease to be one.

Suppose now that God is atemporally eternal. Again, no atemporal being changes intrinsically 'while' atemporal, and ceasing to be divine would be an intrinsic change. So no atemporal being can cease to be divine, unless it can become temporal and at its first temporal instant not be divine. (This would not be a case of a temporal deity ceasing to be divine, since it would never have been both temporal and a deity.) But nothing atemporal can become temporal. *Per* earlier argument, if from the standpoint of any time it is atemporal, it is so from the standpoint of all, including those after its supposedly becoming temporal. Its 'atemporal phase' (oxymoron) could not simply disappear. That would be relevantly like an intrinsic change in it. First it would be there; later it would not; anything of which this was true would be temporal. Again, if something were to become temporal, its 'atemporal phase' would be over. What is over is in the past, and so not atemporal. So what supposedly became temporal would never have been otherwise.

Another argument for (7) runs this way. A divine being could cease being divine only voluntarily or against its will. But plausibly it could not do so voluntarily. A divine being, as such, is omniscient, omnipotent, and perfectly rational. So a divine being could cease to be divine voluntarily only if it believed correctly that it had sufficient reason to do so voluntarily. But giving up divinity would be giving up a great good, moving into what would likely be a much lesser state. Someone perfectly rational would thus require very good reason for this. But what reason could there be? What good would be great enough to justify this and such that even omnipotence could not achieve it without ceasing to be divine? 'Kenotic' Christologists offer the only reply that comes to mind: the good of becoming incarnate and saving humanity.[12] But it is highly controversial whether this (or doing this in the best way) requires a deity to cease to be divine. Even if one thinks that *some* sort of 'kenosis' is necessary, this need not involve ceasing to be divine. It could be

---

[12] For discussion see C. Stephen Evans, (ed.), *Exploring Kenotic Christology* (Oxford: Oxford University Press, 2006).

full-blooded and theologically adequate understood only as voluntarily giving up the *use* of divine properties which nonetheless are still possessed. If it is possible that God become incarnate and save humanity (or do so in the best way) without literally giving up divine properties, these goals do not justify doing so. (This applies equally to related suggestions—for example, that the good be showing solidarity with the human condition, expressing supreme love for humanity, or showing oneself willing to labor under the same conditions one imposes on creatures.) Now anyone sympathetic to 'skeptical theism', as I am, must allow that there may be goods wholly beyond our ken.[13] But the skeptical theist need allow only for goods great enough to justify a large finite amount of suffering and moral evil, which moreover need be only unfamiliar instances of familiar categories.[14] The traditional Western view would be that having deity is a good of infinite value, however hard it is to conceptualize this, and any other sum of possible goods would be less. If that is right, there could not be a good large enough to justify this change, and so someone omniscient and perfectly rational could not have sufficient reason to undergo it voluntarily.

Let us now consider the thought that a divine being ceases being divine against its will. As omnipotent, something like the following is true of it: for all P, if at the time of willing it can come about that P, then if the divine being wills with executive will (the sort that brings things about) that P, it is the case that P. An omnipotent will can simply overrule non-omnipotent causes. So an omnipotent being could be forced against its will to cease being divine only by another omnipotent being who wills that it not be. But there cannot be two omnipotent beings whose wills contradict.[15] Suppose that there are two and their wills are wholly unconstrained. If it is possible at t that it come about that P and that it come about that ¬P, one omnipotent being, able to will whatever it pleases, could will at t that P, and the other, equally uncon-strained, could will at t that ¬P. So if it is possible that there be two unconstrained omnipotent beings, it is possibly possible that a contradiction be true. But it is not. Hence there could be two omnipotent beings only if at least one's will were somehow constrained, so that it could not will that P if the other has willed or is willing that ¬P. To work, this constraint would have to remove the possibility of contradictory volitions. But then for at least one of them, for some P at some time, it would be possible that it come about that P, and yet due to being unable then to will executively that P, that being could not bring it about that P. Thus at most one of the beings would always be able to will to use power constitutive of omnipotence, or at most one would have a

[13] For 'skeptical theism' see Michael Bergmann, 'Skeptical Theism and Rowe's New Evidential Argu-ment from Evil', *Noûs* 35 (2001), 278–96.

[14] The point about categories is why skeptical theism and my attitude to mystery perfections are compatible.

[15] What follows is just the latest variation on a thought that goes back at least to Lactantius, but was most famously put by Duns Scotus (*Ordinatio* I, d. 2, q, 3, n. 180).

will nothing could overrule. Either way, there could not be a second omnipotent being able to force a divine being against its will to cease being divine.

(7) appears true. (9) is obvious. (5) is plausible. So plausibly (DE) is true.

A Perfect-being Argument

Another argument for (DE) runs as follows:

11. If any x is divine, then if being F would be compatible with the rest of x' attributes and being F is a better state than its complement, x is F.

12. It is possible to be essentially divine. So:

13. Being essentially divine is compatible with at least one complete set of attributes a divine being could have.

14. It is better to be essentially than to be contingently divine. So:

15. (DE).

(11) is a basic premise of perfect-being theology and expresses a basic move it uses to fill out its concept of God. So (11) has indirect support by way of the plausibility (and, I have argued, virtual inescapability) of the method and its results. In (11), F's complement is the disjunction of all possible attributes (and conjunctions of attributes) incompatible with being F. (11) lets us infer that God has an attribute only if there is no at least equally good attribute in F's complement: in a tie, perfect-being theology does not decide between claimants. This makes it plausible that perfect-being theology does not yield creature-involving divine mental states or relational attributes. Consider whether, if universe U would be better than universe U*, it would be better to know that U exists than to know that U* exists, to have willed U than to have willed U*, or to co-exist with U rather than U*. If none of these is a better state, perfect-being theology yields none of them. If any is a better state, this presumably is due to the value of U. But for every universe, a better is possible. So if a greater universe yields a greater state, no possible state of knowing, willing, or being related to a universe is better than its complement, and so perfect-being theology cannot infer God's being in any such state.

(12) is the thesis that $\Diamond(\exists x)(Dx \supset \Box Dx)$, not $\Diamond(\exists x)(\Box Dx)$. Thus whether it is possible to be divine is irrelevant to (12): something could be such that if it were divine it would be so necessarily even if it were not possible to be divine. In fact, if this were not possible, everything would trivially have this property. So there is something to discuss only if we assume that it is possible to be divine and focus narrowly on whether it is in addition possible to be so necessarily. We thus can ignore arguments over whether divine attributes are individually exemplifiable or are compatible. The question is simply whether, if compatible, they can also be had necessarily. (12) is false if it is

possible to be divine but having deity entails having attributes which either cannot be had essentially or cannot be had essentially by something with some other divine attribute. Some argue that moral perfection cannot be had essentially; I defend elsewhere the claim that it can.[16] Some argue that nothing could be both essentially morally perfect and omnipotent, for someone essentially morally perfect would not have an ability an omnipotent being should have, to do a bad deed. I rebut this elsewhere.[17] I know of no other plausible argument from non-creature-involving divine attributes that would cause trouble here. And creature-involving states cannot cause trouble. I would suggest that essential deity rules out only those having which would require having made a morally unacceptable universe.[18] But if it rules out more, it surely does not rule out all, and if no other creature-involving state is perfection-enhancing or all are equally so or all are incommensurably so or each has a better, then for any such state essential deity might rule out, there is another not less good to take its place. I take it, then, that nothing bars asserting (12). If (12) is false, every possible deity exists in at least one world in which it is not divine. We see below that this is an uncomfortable conclusion. So it appears below that (12) is true.

(14) forces us to ask whether it might on the contrary be better to have some standard divine attribute contingently rather than essentially. Again, the only plausible candidate I know of is moral perfection. Theodore Guleserian has argued that the free-will defense against the problem of moral evil commits theists to divine contingent moral perfection. The defense claims that our having the sort of freedom that lets us do evil is of such great value that God's permission of all evil we do is justified by being for the sake of allowing us such freedom. This makes most sense (Guleserian argues) if such freedom is just better to have *tout court*, even in God's case.[19] Guleserian's claim is false if there are reasons it is valuable or better that *we* have this sort of freedom which do not apply to God, or reasons it is better for God not to have it which do not apply to us. I provide both elsewhere.[20] Stephen Davis, Guleserian, and William Rowe offer another argument involving moral perfection, which we can put thus: if God is essentially perfect morally, it is impossible that He do evil, or not do the best available action if there is one. If this is impossible, God cannot refrain from doing any good not doing which would be evil, or doing a best available action. If God cannot refrain from doing some good, there is no good reason to praise Him for doing it. Yet surely it is better to be morally praiseworthy for the good one does than not

[16] 'Necessary Moral Perfection', *Pacific Philosophical Quarterly* 70 (1989), 240–60.

[17] 'Omnipotence', in Thomas Flint and Michael Rea (eds), *The Oxford Handbook of Christian Philosophical Theology* (Oxford: Oxford University Press, 2009), pp. 167–98.

[18] In which case, if I am right that deity entails necessary existence, essential deity is possible only if there is an acceptable reply to the modal problem of evil—as I have suggested there is.

[19] Theodore Guleserian, 'Divine Freedom and the Problem of Evil', *Faith and Philosophy* 17 (2000), 348–66.

[20] *Divine Freedom*, forthcoming.

to be.[21] I reply that even if perchance it is necessary that God create, it is not necessary that He create precisely this universe, with us in it.[22] He was free not to do so, if only because He could have created another instead. Suppose as a worst case that once creatures exist, God cannot refrain from doing them any good He in fact does: what He has made places on Him moral demands to which He must respond. Even so, He put Himself in this position voluntarily and with full knowledge of what the results could or even would be. He made Himself unable to refrain. If I took a pill which forced me to do various good acts, foreknowing the good I might or would be forced to do and intending to do whichever good things situations force me into, it would be true that I did those acts because I chose to (conditional on being in the forcing situation), with full ability to refrain. The only oddity would be that I also brought it about that at some point between the choice and the performance I voluntarily lost my ability to change my mind. Surely I would deserve praise for doing those acts, even though at the time of performance, I could not refrain. Moreover, I would deserve praise for the antecedent moral goodness which led me to impose on myself the necessity of doing these acts. God's case would be similar. I submit then that the argument of Rowe *et al.* fails.

To develop a case for (14), I note that whatever possibly lacks any divine perfection actually has a modal property: it is possibly imperfect in that respect. All divine perfections are better states to be in than their negations. As it is possible (I assume) to have each divine perfection, anything possibly imperfect is possibly surpassed in the relevant respect. Either it itself can surpass it, or something else can. If someone contingently divine, Zeus, can surpass himself, he can fail to be the best he can be in this respect. Surely it is better to be unable to be less than one's best. If there were no best, but instead just ever-ascending levels of perfection to reach, we could not call ability to fail to be one's best a flaw. But we are speaking of divine perfections—properties which are maximal levels of some attribute, or at least better to have than their negations. So we need not consider this. Where there is a maximum to be had, it is a flaw to able to fall short of it. This is true even if being able to fall short is a prerequisite of something good. Not every necessary condition of a good is itself good. In some cases it is better to able to fall short but have the good thing which requires this than to lack both the flaw and the good which requires it. I argue below that this would not apply to a deity's case.

Suppose now that Zeus does not have this flaw—he is necessarily as good as he can be in all respects and so cannot surpass himself—but that someone

---

[21] Stephen Davis, *Logic and the Nature of God* (Grand Rapids, MI: William B. Eerdmans, 1983), pp. 94–5; Theodore Guleserian, 'Can God be Trusted?', *Philosophical Studies* 103 (2001), 296; William Rowe, *Can God Be Free?* (Oxford: Oxford University Press, 2004), pp. 141, 150.

[22] Unless every other world feasible for God is straightforwardly less good than this one. But I see no reason to believe this.

else, Mars, can surpass him in some respect. Then Zeus is necessarily imperfect in at least one respect. This is not a good property to have, *ceteris paribus*. Further, Zeus either can or cannot co-exist with a Mars surpassing him. Suppose that he cannot. Zeus cannot surpass himself in Fness. In any world, his F-state is his maximal and only state across all worlds. If Mars can surpass him, then in some world w, Mars surpasses Zeus' only F-state. But then if Zeus exists necessarily, Zeus and Mars exist in w, and Mars F-surpasses Zeus there. Thus if Zeus cannot co-exist with someone surpassing him and his only F-state can be surpassed, Zeus exists contingently. It cannot be that Zeus exists necessarily, Mars can surpass Zeus, but Zeus cannot co-exist with someone surpassing him. As I argue elsewhere, necessary existence is superior to contingent.[23] So if Zeus cannot co-exist with Mars, being surpassable brings a second imperfection with it. Further, I would argue that all standard Western divine perfections are compossible. If they are, what can be imperfect in even one respect can be surpassed *tout court*, by a deity otherwise like it but perfect in the relevant respect. So plausibly just because Zeus has some divine perfection contingently, Zeus is less than a perfect being. If then it truly is possible that there be a perfect being, it is better to have no divine perfection contingently.

If Zeus can co-exist with someone surpassing him, Zeus need not be contingent, but Zeus could look or could have looked up to Mars as his superior in some respect, or even *tout court*. If this is not compatible with deity, Zeus co-exists with Mars only if he is not divine. Problems with this scenario emerge below. If this is compatible with deity, then still a deity who can look up to a superior deity is a second-class deity, if only perhaps by a small difference. Even if Zeus has no superior, it is partly by a lucky break that he is top dog, not wholly by his own intrinsic merits. It would be better to be a first-class deity—one that needed no luck to be best.

These are perfectly general considerations. We can think more specifically about the implications of being contingently divine given a list of deifying attributes—attributes distinctive of deities lacking one of which would entail not being divine. These prominently include the Biblical and specifying perfections. God may have deifying attributes of which we know nothing. But suppose we see reason to say of the Biblical perfections that it is better to have them necessarily. If it is, then it is better to have the specifying perfections necessarily: if, for example, it is better to have 'understanding without limit'—to be intellectually perfect—necessarily, and one is not intellectually perfect unless one has specifying perfection F, then it is better to have F necessarily. If both are true, God has all known modal perfections save necessary existence, for whose superiority I have argued. If S5 is the logic of absolute modularity, as I argue later, He has *these* necessarily. So if we see reason to say of the Biblical perfections that it is better to have them

---

[23] Taliaferro and Meister, 'Divine Necessity'.

necessarily, this will give (quasi-inductive) reason to expect this to hold for any deifying attributes beyond our ken. So let us work with the Biblical perfections—being perfectly wise and good, omnipotent, omniscient, eternal, such as to be omnipresent if there is any space, such as to be source of all other things if there are any, and incorrupt—that is, without defect in purely categorical intrinsic non-mental properties.[24] In each case, I now argue, it would be better not to possibly lack the attribute.

Perfect wisdom provides the clearest case. Surely it is better to be unable than to be able to be less than ideally wise. This would not rule out being (say) passionately in love; it can sometimes be wise to let oneself be irrational in certain respects. What can be less than ideally wise can act with less than ideal wisdom. Such acts may cause harm, do evil unintentionally, or fail of their aim or what is best: the claim that someone can be a little unwise but cannot be unwise when these are the stakes would be hopelessly *ad hoc*. Surely it is better not to be able to fail in these ways.

If one is not necessarily perfect morally, one can fall short morally. Surely it would be better to be immune to this. Guleserian points out that being able to fall short morally is a precondition or component of our sort of moral freedom, and such freedom is a great good.[25] But again, not every precondition or component of a good is itself good, and I have already noted my suggestion elsewhere that a case for such freedom's being among our best goods need not carry over to God.

Being able to lack some power an omnipotent being would have lays one open to lacking the power to accomplish one's goals: if I can lack the power to bring it about that P, surely it is possible that I lack it and want, or see that it would be best, to bring it about that P, and that I have the chance to do so. Again, we could ourselves wish to be safe from this. One might reply that there are virtues which if one is rational require at least belief that one lacks some powers, such as bravery, Stoic endurance, self-sacrifice. An omniscient, perfectly rational being could have these beliefs only if they were true. So perhaps an omniscient, perfectly rational omnipotent being could not have such virtues,[26] and so (one might argue) as it is morally better to have the chance to have such virtues, it is morally better not to be omnipotent necessarily. Now such virtues are not small things. But there are moral achievements omnipotence makes possible: benevolent creation of wonderful universes, unlimited exercise of perfect justice, acts of mercy on

---

[24] It is not easy to see what these could be in a spirit's case (so Ernest Sosa, 'Persons and Other Beings', *Philosophical Perspectives* 1 (1987), 164–6)—other than a kind. But kind-properties will not tell us much here, because we do not know what such defects in, for instance, a soul would be.

[25] Guleserian, 'Divine Freedom'.

[26] This raises questions about what it can mean for God to be perfect in virtue, and about whether perfect goodness (which presumably includes perfection in virtue) is compatible with the full range of other Biblical perfections. To address these here would be too large a digression; I hope to deal with this elsewhere. But I note that a divine being able to become incarnate as a human and so act under certain temporary cognitive and power limits would also be able to have the virtues of human finitude.

stupendous scales. Even on a smaller scale, having powers one must lack to self-sacrifice, be brave, and so on, can make possible moral achievements one could not manage without these powers. I can rationally sacrifice myself if I believe I lack the power to gain without doing so and without unacceptable side-costs what the sacrifice achieves. It is rational to fall on a grenade if I believe I cannot get it away from my squad-mates in time. If I believed I were quicker and stronger and that time permitted, I would try to grab the grenade and throw it back at the enemy. If I had the powers I believed I did, I would succeed. This would not be self-sacrifice, but it would be brave, make my squaddies safer and bring about a better result for us. If I have the power and chance to throw the grenade back and believe I do, to fall on the grenade would be irrational. Just because it would be irrational, it would not be a perfect moral act. (Arguably it would not even be brave, but instead reckless or impetuous.) If that is right, I can be in a position to have self-sacrifice be a maximal moral achievement or one in which tossing back the grenade is, but not both. An act of bravery which brings about a better result is no worse than an act perhaps of greater bravery (in the one case I act with certainty that it will cost my life, in the other not) with a lesser. Again, I can act bravely only if I can believe I am in danger. I can believe I am (and correctly) even if I can eliminate the danger safely—the charging tiger is dangerous till I shoot it. But I am more profoundly in danger, and so can act with deeper bravery, if I lack the power to eliminate the danger. On the other hand, if I can eliminate the danger, I can save others from it, an act of benevolence. Arguably it is better to be able to be more benevolent than to be able to be braver, in this case, and in any case a being powerful, knowledgeable and rational enough not to be able to act bravely can achieve a level of benevolence lesser beings cannot hope for. It is dubious that the virtues of finitude are great enough goods to outweigh the moral achievements open to omnipotence. If so, the moral argument for being able not to be omnipotent is at best a wash, leaving intuitions that it would be good to be unable to fail through lack of power to carry the day.

If one is not necessarily omniscient, one can lack knowledge an omniscient being would have. It can be good not to know things too painful to know, things we are better off not knowing, or things it would violate others' right to privacy to know. But it is hard to see how ability to be ignorant could be limited to just such cases. Absent such *ad hocery*, ignorance opens one to failure to accomplish good goals: if I can not know that P, surely I can both not know and need to know that P. It is better not to be able to fail than to be able to fail to do good. As to problematic knowledge, a being with the other traditional divine attributes could not find some things too painful to know, or better off unknown. For no truth about God alone is either, He knows only God is perfectly rational, and He knows only contingent truths He permits to be true, apart perhaps from some truths about Him alone.[27] Knowledge painful to have can be worth having. If it is, it is not too painful to have—it is worth having despite the pain. If it would be too painful to know that P, a perfectly rational, in-control God can and will make sure that it is not true that P. If it is worth it to God to suffer knowing that P, then just for that reason, it is not *too* painful to know that P. The like applies to knowledge one is better off without.

As to violating our privacy rights, if God is by nature omniscient, it is absolutely impossible that He not know all about us.[28] No-one can be obligated to do what absolutely cannot be done. So God cannot be obligated not to know things about us, nor then not to know them without our consent. We have a right of privacy against God only if He is obliged not to know certain things about us without our consent. So we have no right of privacy against a necessarily omniscient God. If His omniscience is contingent, perhaps there might be such a right. But one could not use any supposed moral superiority in this alternative scenario to recommend contingent omniscience.

In one respect there is nothing to be gained morally by making His omniscience contingent: if we do not have a privacy right, God does not violate it, if we did have one He would respect it, and so either way He would have clean hands. However, one can still ask whether God would be *better to us* if He did not know what we wished to keep private: whether it would be more benevolent to run the world so.[29] This, of course, would raise the question of whether it would be better to have restricted omniscience necessarily, but I will not pursue this. Instead, I argue that theists should not qualify omniscience at all here, because on balance it is morally preferable that God have it.

It is a morally admirable state of affairs that there be a match between goodness and happiness—so much so that Kant called this the 'highest good'.[30] This is obviously not the case in this life. Western religion teaches that it happens in the next because there is a God who is a perfect moral judge, before whom every act finally receives its due. Making the highest good available to us is part of God's being good to us. For that matter, so is His merely judging. It is good for us that we live in a cosmos kept in moral balance, that there is judgment for those who wrong us, that the thought of it can deter some from wronging us, that we in being judged are judged with perfect fairness, that there is perfectly fair reward for any good we do, and so

---

[27] Further, I am in the process of arguing that it is up to God what necessary truths about possible non-divine concreta He knows. So if any candidates for these might count as painful to know, similar points would apply.

[28] There is an issue here about propositions involving 'I', but as it does not bear on this argument, I omit it.

[29] Here I am indebted to Margaret Falls-Corbit and F. Michael McClain, 'God and Privacy', *Faith and Philosophy* 9 (1992), 382.

[30] Immanuel Kant, *Critique of Practical Reason*, tr. Lewis White Beck (Indianapolis, IN: Bobbs-Merrill, 1956), p. 115. The Christian doctrine of justification by faith does not threaten this claim, since it partly concerns how we achieve goodness.

on. Even the obvious downside to being judged may come under the heading of being good to us—being fair to us is one way to be good to us, and this way is compatible with also being good to us in ways perfect mercy and benevolence dictate. (Feeling vengeful, we may feel less pleased that God should be thus good in judging to those who wrong us, but we ought rationally to restrain this feeling in light of the fact that others have it about us and God has no reason to honor it only in some cases.) God could not be a perfect moral judge without a full grip on all circumstances of our actions and every relevant thought, feeling and intention. For one thing, thoughts, attitudes, desires, and so on, are themselves morally evaluable: the Sermon on the Mount deals in the moral importance of not lusting and being poor in spirit and pure in heart. There is no way to assess who is pure in heart without looking at all within. Again, the evil would likely wish to hide their thoughts etc., from God—but not only they. Were God to honor such wishes, He would be least able to judge precisely where it is morally most desirable that He do so. It would not be more benevolent to victims for God to be unable fairly to judge their victimizers, nor better morally that some have the highest good granted or withheld on inadequate grounds. Nor could God wait to see if apparent evil is done and then peek at, for example, governing intentions if needed. If He is atemporal, He cannot change from not having read one's mind to having read it. If He is temporal, then if He did not read a thought when present, He cannot later remember it, and if the universe has no temporal extension, but is instead the zero-temporal-thickness of the present, what is past can no longer be accessed in any other way. Even if the past exists, so that past thoughts are there to be read, and 'seeing' in the past what one did not look at when it was present is a possible cognitive achievement for a temporal being, the fact remains that not all morally discreditable thoughts, desires etc. lead to evil external actions, and even less do all morally credit-worthy thoughts ever lead to overt action. So if God's policy were only to peek when overt action provides evidence that peeking is needed, He would miss much that is morally relevant. If we ought morally to approve it that the Kantian highest good is available and evil will face a full moral accounting, we ought morally to approve it that God has the access these require. All this in fact suggests that being such as to be a perfect moral judge if there are other agents might be a moral perfection perfect-being theology ought to ascribe to God. It may count as a Biblical specifying perfection. If so, then even on moral grounds, perfect-being theology should not qualify omniscience here.[31]

---

[31] Falls-Corbit and McClain suggest a variety of moral goods that would be served if God 'respected our privacy.' This would emphasize that we belong to ourselves (*op. cit.*, 375): but we also belong to God, who made and sustains us. It would let us be free to think even the most repellent things (*ibid. et* 379). But we are free, in fact, to do so whether God sees or not, and psychologically free to think the repellent as long as we are not constantly aware of divine monitoring, as is so. This does not require the false belief that we are not monitored (*contra* 381), merely that we are not always aware of all we know, and that even when we are aware of this, it is not psychologically 'live' for us, not something that really feels constraining. (God might

I turn now to non-personal deifying attributes, and first to eternality. Being irenic, let us say that being eternal is having a temporally unlimited existence and that one way to do so is to be atemporal. (Limits of time do not limit the existence of a being not *in* time.) If something is possibly non-eternal, then, it possibly has a temporally limited existence. If a being can have a temporally limited existence, either there can be time before or after it exists or its existence can be coterminous with a time that begins or ends. The first implies contingency of existence. If the second is true, than had that time lasted longer, the non-eternal being either would or would not have lasted longer with it. If the second, this being can fail to exist at some time: it is contingent. If the first, this being can fail to exist as long as it might. This implies failing to be divine as long as it might, and so an earlier argument comes into play here. Further, this is a defect if the being's existence is guaranteed to be good, for then it can miss out on additional good it might have had. And if something has the rest of the divine attributes, this guarantees that any period of its existence will overall be good and worth having. If its existence is not guaranteed to be good, that is itself a defect best done without, and possible only if it has other defects. So it is better to be necessarily than contingently eternal, at least given the rest of the divine attributes (recall that we are discussing only whether someone with these should have them necessarily). Again, if it is better to have necessarily the attributes which guarantee that further existence would be good, it is better to be necessarily eternal.

Omnipresence is typically cashed out in terms of having the power to control and knowledge of what goes on in all places.[32] So something can be not such as to be omnipresent given space only if it can fail to be omniscient or omnipotent. I have already discussed those failures. So I turn to being such as to be the source of all concrete existents other than oneself—the

---

well design us not to feel thus.) God's 'respecting our privacy' would allow for intimacy based on voluntary self-disclosure (*ibid.*, 377–8): but as long as our awareness of divine 'monitoring' is not psychologically 'live', we can feel in our disclosures to God just what we would in our disclosures to someone to whom what we said was not previously known. It is a psychological fact that believers can passionately pray petitions even while believing that God already knows what they will ask, and in any case, the disclosure can become voluntary if we appropriately endorse God's presence to our thoughts, just as (say) it can become voluntary to rob a bank with a gun at our heads if we come somehow to identify ourselves with and be glad we are acting for the person with the gun. God's 'staying out of our thoughts' would let Him trust us (*ibid.*, 378–9), respecting our 'unique responsibility' for our thoughts (*ibid.*, 380). But our responsibility for our thoughts remains unique: we are the ones who generate them, not God, and they are our psychological states, not God's. And God trusts us (in one sense) even though He knows us thoroughly, for He leaves us free to act as we will. Finally, should we *feel* violated if we feel constantly observed by God, whether or not the feeling corresponds to a violated right? God has no prurient interest in us. He sees us only with kindness and love. It is for our own good that He sees us. People who would ordinarily be embarrassed to be seen naked by a stranger often do not feel this way when the stranger is a doctor who must examine them to make them well and approaches them with a professional manner. This seems rationally appropriate. And God is the physician of our souls.

[32] So, for example, S. Thomae Aquinatis, *Summa Theologiae* (Ottawa: Studii Generalis, 1941), Ia 8.

GSA-property.[33] If (say) God has this necessarily, it is not possible that He co-exist with something He does not create and sustain. Necessarily, every being with which He co-exists depends on Him for its being. This seems possible. It is an awesome status, and so better than its negation. A deity would be in a better state with it than without. And having it does not seem to conflict with any other candidate divine perfection. If we add that a necessary being necessarily has this property, it follows that in no possible world does any concrete thing not owe its existence to it—that nothing can exist independent of it, that every other possible concrete being depends essentially on it for existence. This is an even more awesome status, seems possible, seems perfecting, and does not seem to conflict with other candidate perfections.[34]

There is finally being incorrupt. We have no idea what non-mental non-power defects in spirits could be. If there are none, any spirit is necessarily incorrupt. But let us assume for argument's sake that there can be some. If a deity is incorrupt but not necessarily so, it either could have had or can still have such a defect. It is better not to have than to have a defect, *ceteris paribus*. But the *cetera* can fail to be equal. This is so iff the defect is a necessary condition of a 'makeup' property that leaves the defective being on balance better off than it would have been without both, and the defective being has the 'makeup' property. (Note that a 'makeup' property does not remove a defect. It only compensates for one.) One might think there is a second possibility here, that having a defect be a necessary condition not of a makeup property but simply of having some nature better to have than its complement. But any such attribute can be treated as making up for having the defect. Consider first, then, being still able to have a defect.

It is not better for A not still to be liable to defect only if for all defects to which A is liable, A's having that defect would entail A's having a 'makeup' property good enough to at least balance off the defect. In God's case, the 'makeup' properties could not be mental, moral, a matter of power, duration, presence to some area, or the like. For God already has the Biblical and specifying perfections. No improvement in these respects is possible for Him, and so none could compensate for any defect. Someone might say that His having some perfection *is* a compensation for a defect—that is, includes the relevant improvement—or that the defect is just a necessary condition of having some perfection, but I cannot see how to *argue* this. So apparently a 'makeup' property would have to be some way of making a spirit better precisely *qua* spirit—something analogous to improving the non-power physical attributes of a physical being—or else fall into some 'mystery perfection' category. We have no clue what would improve a spirit in that way, even as we

---

[33] Which if earlier argument was sound entails a GAO-property, which I will not discuss separately.

[34] One might argue that if universes it would be evil to create are possible, it conflicts with divine impeccability. But here the conflict is not with impeccability as such, but with the conjunction of impeccability and that possibility.

have none what a spirit's non-mental non-power defects could be, and no idea what a mystery perfection's category might be. So we ought to doubt that a makeup property is even possible in God's case. If none are, it cannot be better for God still to be able to have a defect. Further, if it is not better *ceteris paribus* to be unable than to be able to have a defect, that is because it is not better *ceteris paribus* to have neither defect nor makeup than to have both. (If it were worse to have both, the ability to have both would be opening one to a worse state, and so *ceteris paribus* would be worse to have than the inability.) If this is true, being incorrupt in this respect is not a perfection at all. For *per* (11) above, being F is a perfection, an attribute God's having which is an output of perfect being theology, only if it is better to be F than to have any attribute incompatible with being F. If in fact being incorrupt in some respect is not better, this is not plausibly a contingent fact. It is just a function of what the defect and the makeup *are*. So if God is not in all respects necessarily incorrupt, the right conclusion to draw is not that He is contingently so. It is that being incorrupt in all respects is not after all a perfection, and God necessarily has what is a perfection—which includes some complex of defects and makeups. So if being incorrupt in all respects is a perfection, it is one better had necessarily.

I ask finally whether anything similar is true not of being still liable to defect but of being such that one could have had one. Well, suppose that on your twenty-first birthday your parents tell you a dark family secret. There is a streak of hereditary insanity among your ancestors: many of your great-great-great-grandparents, great-great-grandparents, and great-grandparents were institutionalized. However, the common thread is that they were all hopelessly mad by age 16. So you yourself are in the clear; you might have had the fatal gene, owing to who your parents were, but if it has not manifested by now, you do not. You could have had a defect, but did not receive it. You would not greet this with blank indifference. You would be thankful. And though you had not known of your danger, you surely would feel that it would have been better to be safe. The rest of the dialectic goes as it just did: you would overrule this intuition only if there were some makeup for the vulnerability, and so on.

An Essential-perfection Argument

I put my next argument for (DE) into symbols for clarity. Letting 'Dx' denote 'x is divine', and 'Px' denote 'x is perfect', it is:

16. $\Box(x)(Dx \supset Px)$.   premise
17. $\Box(x)(Px \supset \Box Px)$.[35]   premise

---

[35] This does not without further assumptions entail that any perfect being made perfect *inter alia* by being F is necessarily F. For we cannot rule it out that there is not just one consistent set of perfections for a maximally perfect being to have. Even if all those we have surveyed are consistent, we cannot rule it out

18. $\square(x)(Dx \supset \square Px)$.   16, 17
19. $\square(x)(Px \supset Dx)$.   premise
20. $\square(x)(\square Px \supset \square Dx)$. So: 19, conditional proof
21. $\square(x)(Dx \supset \square Dx)$.   18, 20.

The conditional proof of (20) is just this: given (19), assume $\square Pa$, for any a, and $\square Da$ follows by modal rule. Perfect-being theology premises that whatever is divine is perfect; the Introduction assembled one sort of case for this claim, the method's plausibility gives another, and I believe we could develop a third by explicating what it would take to deserve the unqualified praise involved in monotheist worship. If whatever is divine is perfect, it is surely because of the attributes being divine implies having. It necessarily implies having these, by its necessary content. So (16) is true. (17) rests on a perfect-being inference from two premises, that

22. it is possible to be necessarily perfect

and that

23. it would be better to be necessarily than to be contingently perfect.

As to (22), we need not consider 'mystery' perfections, modal perfections can of course themselves be had necessarily, and specifying perfections go with Biblical, as noted earlier. Of the Biblical perfections only moral perfection raises any difficulties for (22), and I have already cited my treatment of this. (23) is intuitive, but has also in effect already been argued: I argued (14) above by arguing (23). We can also argue this way: if necessarily whatever is divine is perfect, necessarily whatever is securely and permanently divine is securely and permanently perfect. So if it is possible to be securely and permanently divine, it is possible to be securely and permanently perfect. But the former is indeed possible: an omniscient, omnipotent, perfectly rational being can maintain its deity, and so its perfection, if it chooses. It can render this permanent, and its perfection will be secure if the basis on which it chooses to be permanently perfect is secure. But this is so: as omniscient it chooses based on the best available information, as perfectly rational it makes the

that there are other perfections of which we have no ken, which are not consistent with each other or with some member of the set with which we have been dealing. The following is at least epistemically possible: There are two sets of attributes AB, A is {F, G, H}, B is {F, G, I}, and H and I are incompatible. Anything having all members of either would be a more perfect being than anything not having all members of either, but anything having A would be equally perfect or incommensurable in perfection with anything having B.

Now if this were so, a perfect being would have to have F, G, and HvI, but H and I would be 'optional'—a perfect being could have either and still be perfect. If so, perhaps the perfect being could be necessarily HvI but only contingently I. However, if we have some consistent sets of perfections for a maximally perfect being to have, all of them include F, and we see no equal- or incommensurable-value alternative being F, we can defeasibly infer that any perfect being will be necessarily F if anything can have F necessarily. If there is just one set of perfections for a maximally perfect being to have, then if (17) is true, any perfect being has all of them necessarily.

most rational choice, and as omnipotent it is able to assure that things do not work out in ways that undercut its bases for making this choice. So it is possible to be securely and permanently perfect. If it is possible, being so is compatible with being perfect; it would be better to be so than not to be so; so by (11), perfection must be possessed securely and permanently. Now it is possible to be more or less permanently perfect—if both A and B are perfect at all points in their lives, but A has a longer life, A is more permanently perfect than B. It is also possible to be more or less securely so. And by the same token, plausibly it is better to be more rather than less securely and permanently perfect. So perfection must be had with the maximum security and permanence it can be had with.

The maximum of security and permanence in perfection would be having perfection necessarily, if as (22) asserts this is possible. One way to have a property insecurely is to be able to lose it; the corresponding maximal degree of security is to be unable to lose it. Another way to have a property insecurely is to be able never to have had it: it was then not secure that one would ever have it. Consider the property of existing. We need never have been. We owe our lives to a lucky meeting of sperm and egg. In some moods we can feel gooseflesh at the thought that we might have missed it all. We do so because the thought makes us feel vulnerable. It was not a secure thing that we would ever be. Once we exist, we are no longer vulnerable to never having been, but still it is true of us once we exist that before we existed we *were* vulnerable to this—though this is not the best way to put it. Something that was never vulnerable to not existing exists more securely than something that was, for there was never a chance that it would fail to exist. If one neither could have failed to have nor can lose a property, one has the property necessarily, and so with maximal security. So given (11) and (22), we have (23).

I now argue (19), from (D1). If being divine is better than its complement and compatible with the rest of a suitable bundle of attributes, perfect-being theology will ascribe it to a perfect being. It is better than its complement unless it is incompatible with some better, equally good or incommensurably good alternative perfection. We see no candidates for these. Further, plausibly being divine entails the Biblical and specifying perfections, and it appears compatible with the modal ones. So plausibly perfect-being theology makes deity itself a perfection, an attribute a perfect being will have *qua* perfect.

Again, consider the Biblical perfections: in all personal attributes, intrinsic being, duration, spatial extent (we can add, too, in presence to any other dimensions there may be) and power, including having the GSA-property. Anything which lacks one of these is less perfect than God. We do not see a way to make something more perfect than this, because we do not see other respects in which personal beings could be perfect, nor anything better to be than personal. We do not see a different way to be equally perfect, because we do not see other respects of perfection incompatible or incommensurable with these, such that there could be two perfect beings, one with the rest of the standard divine attributes plus one of these and the other with the rest plus the other. But if anything has all these attributes, it is divine. It is just what we conceive God to be. There does not seem to be anything else it could be. If it walks like a duck and quacks like a duck... But if, given that something is perfect, it could only be divine, (19) is true.

Bruce Langtry has suggested that it might be possible to be as perfect as a deity but not divine.[36] Perhaps there could be two beings, A and B, both omniscient, omnipotent, and so on, but such that A made and sustains both B and the universe. Were this so, he suggested, A and B would be perfect but only A would be divine—only A could have the GSA-property, and so count as God. This would assume that the GSA-property is not one a perfect being ought to have. But a perfect being ought to have a maximally valuable set of compossible perfections. I argued earlier that the GSA-property is a perfection. As far as we can tell, it is not incompatible with any candidate perfection, and so plausibly it is a member of any maximal-compossible-perfection set. Again, there cannot be two omnipotent beings whose executive wills contradict. So on Langtry's scenario, either B comes into existence with its freedom restricted—with it not so much as possible that B will that P if A simultaneously wills that ¬P—or A restricts A's freedom in willing that B exist, or both. It is hard to see how A could make it absolutely impossible that A or B have the wrong volition without limiting one or the other's power or knowledge; given such a limit, though, the limited one would not be omnipotent or omniscient, nor as perfect as a deity. Further, even if somehow still omnipotent and omniscient, the limited one would have a lesser range of choice and volition, and so be less free, so less perfect, and so not perfect. If both are thus limited, neither is as free as it could be without the other, nor then as free as deity is supposed to make God. So neither is perfect unless it is impossible that A exist without B and impossible that there be instead of either a different perfect being, C, just like A save for being able to exist without B or anyone B-like. (On these conditions, A or both A and B could be most perfect possible beings despite the limitation.) Further, A can assure that B does not come into existence willing the contradictory of something A is willing only if A brings B into existence with its initial volitions at least partly determined by A. So B comes into existence with its will determined by another—which (or the liability to which) arguably is enough to constitute a difference in perfection between them. But if B is less perfect than A, B is not perfect. Again, we can ask whether A makes B contingently. I have argued that necessary existence is a perfection.[37] If it is, then if B is contingent and A necessary, B is less perfect than A, and so not perfect. But if A makes B necessarily, A's creative freedom is restricted, and so arguably A is less than

---

[36] In correspondence.   [37] Taliaferro and Meister, 'Divine Necessity'.

perfect.[38] A is certainly so if a C-type being is possible. B will be more weakly omnipresent than A, since one note of the standard account of omnipresence is that God is omnipresent in virtue of His sustaining causal efficacy.[39] Again, this is arguably a difference in perfection. Finally, ontological independence is also generally seen as a perfection; the medieval consensus for this was so strong that it led even to widespread acceptance of now-controversial doctrines of divine simplicity.[40] Being uncreated and uncreatable is one form of ontological independence. If it is indeed a perfection, B is not perfect. Thus Langtry has a significant burden of argument if he wants to convince us that his scenario is a genuine possibility.

Three Further Arguments

Again, if Yahweh is only contingently divine, then if Yahweh exists necessarily because He is divine, we have the oddity that in a world in which Yahweh is not divine, His existence could be explained by the fact that in another world He is divine.[41] ('Why do you exist?' 'Well, I could have been God.') Further, in this case, Yahweh's necessity is itself contingent. If so, the logic of absolute modality does not include S4. Strong intuitions favor the claim that it does.[42]

If Yahweh can be non-divine, He if non-divine either can or cannot co-exist with someone divine. If He cannot, there is a possible concrete, non-divine being which no possible divine, supposedly omnipotent being can create (unless creating Yahweh would cause the creator to go out of existence before Yahweh arrived: but this is ruled out if deity entails eternality). But then either omnipotence confers less power than we thought, or omnipotence is just impossible. Suppose, however, that non-divine Yahweh can co-exist with another deity. Then He either can or cannot be created by this deity. If He cannot, we have seen the consequences. If He can, possibly Yahweh, our God, is a creature and owes someone else worship. It is true even now, while He is divine, that He is creatable and could owe another worship. This is unintuitive. It is flat ruled out if being uncreatable is a perfection.

---

[38] This is not a case against the Trinity; as I read this—along with the Latin tradition generally—it is not the case that one divine or perfect substance makes or sustains another; see my 'A Latin Trinity', *Faith and Philosophy* 21 (2004), 304–33.

[39] So, for example, Aquinas, *ST* Ia 8; I say 'more weakly' because B meets another sufficient condition for omnipresence in Aquinas' account.

[40] See Alvin Plantinga, *Does God Have a Nature?* (Milwaukee, WI: Marquette University Press, 1980).

[41] This need not be the only available explanation, but it would be *one* available explanation.

[42] Though see to the contrary Nathan Salmon, 'The Logic of What Might Have Been', *Philosophical Review* 98 (1989), 3–34.

Another Problem: Explaining Deity

Again, if Yahweh is only contingently divine, there is or is not an explanation that He is actually divine. Suppose first that there is not. Then we need not have had the God we do rather than another or none, and there is no reason we do have Him. So if we like the God we have, it is just good luck to have Him. We can thank our lucky stars that we have Him. This metaphor expresses our sense that it would make sense to thank something other than Yahweh that Yahweh is God, even if there is nothing to thank. That is, if He is only contingently divine, His being divine seems to us the kind of thing that could be explained, even if *de facto* it is not. This does not befit a genuine ultimate reality. There should not be (so to speak) a more basic role in reality (deciding what is divine) that just happens to be unfilled. To say that there is makes Yahweh rather like Zeus, living under the sway of the Fates, but a Zeus who can thank his lucky stars that there are no Fates to live under. Such a Yahweh can also be relieved and happy that he gets to be God. It does not befit deity to be divine by a lucky break.

Swinburne objects to talk of luck here:

> [God's] existence is . . . *the* ultimate brute fact . . . There is no chance here, because the nature of things is that what is and what is not depends on the will of God, and that can only be if he exists. But then is it not fortunate chance that this is the nature of things? Fortunate, maybe. But not chance, because this is how the world works . . . the ultimate principle of its operation.[43]

The thought seems to be that a claim involving God's existence qualifies as something like an ultimate natural law, and such laws cannot be said to obtain by chance. But why not? They cannot do so if obtaining by chance is having only a partial law-governed causal explanation or obtaining in accord with a statistical natural law, but we have a more basic concept of chance that does not require explicating in these ways.

Talk of luck might also seem out of place if we were likely to get Yahweh as God (for example, Yahweh is God everywhere in logical space save for one possible world). But if it did seem out of place, that might well be because it seemed that what established this high probability, or the probability itself, explains it that Yahweh is God. If something explains it that Yahweh is God, that something denies Yahweh at least part of the 'ultimate reality' honors. The Introduction suggested that it is part of God's ultimacy that nothing accounts for God's existence. If something explains it that Yahweh is God, then even if Yahweh's existence has no further explanation, His being divine does, and so *God's* existence—the existence of something having the divine nature—has an explanation. Again, even if nothing more basic explains

---

[43] Richard Swinburne, *The Coherence of Theism*, rev. edn. (Oxford: Oxford University Press, 1993), p. 277.

Yahweh's existence, there is something explanatorily more basic than His being divine. So any explanation tracing a fact back to the existence of a being having the divine nature can be pushed further, to a more basic explanatory level, and God's being divine is not at the explanatorily ultimate level of reality. Ultimacy concerns, then, rule against this.

But we have assumed for the moment that it is just a brute unexplained fact that Yahweh is God. If it is, that it was likely to be so does not explain this; it is unexplained that what was probable happened. One might perhaps argue that if it was highly probable that Yahweh be God, this of itself provides an explanation and makes talk of luck inappropriate. I think not. If I buy one ticket in a million-ticket fair lottery, the probability of my winning is one in a million. If I do not win, it might seem that the mere fact that the probability against winning was so high explains it, and it was not bad luck that I lost. But really, it is my ticket purchase and the actual causal sequence which led to the lottery draw which explain my losing. All the probability tells us is that there was likely to be some such explanation for the actual course of events if I bought a ticket. And it was bad luck that what was likely to happen did in fact happen. It was luck, genuine chance, if the drawing was not rigged, and it was bad for me—that it is luck I should have expected to have is why my saying this would violate a certain conversational implication. That I should have expected it does not entail that what generates the expectation explains the outcome. One might have expected Obama to win the 2008 election because certain groups were highly likely to vote for him—and in the event, he might have won because other groups voted for him instead. So I submit that my talk of luck is legitimate even if Yahweh was likely to be God.

Suppose, on the other hand, that it is contingent that Yahweh is God and there is an explanation for His deity. I take it, as just argued, that sheer probability does not provide the explanation. Suppose, then, that some cause accounts for Yahweh's being God. It can do so only by either giving a Yahweh already existent the divine nature, or causing Yahweh to exist and making Him divine.[44]

Making Yahweh Divine

Let us consider the first scenario: Yahweh is not made. He existed prior to being God, lacking some divine attribute, and some other thing contributed it and so made Him divine. In examining this scenario I assume that deity is a conjunctive property no conjunct of which entails all of the rest. I do not believe this, but do so because it is the assumption least favorable to my case.

---

[44] If you think that causation requires the existence of causal laws and that God, if He exists, determines what the laws are, you will doubt that these alternatives are possible. You should then conclude, of course, that there cannot be a causal explanation for Yahweh's being God.

I will take it, then, that to be divine includes being immaterial, personal, eternal, morally perfect, able to create *ex nihilo,* omnipotent and omniscient, and having the GSA-property. Arguments I give about moral perfection cover rational perfection and being incorrupt *mutatis mutandis.* Omnipotence and omniscience yield omnipresence, on the standard account of the latter,[45] so I need not discuss that separately. Let us examine the main divine attributes, to see whether they really could be given to another who already existed.

Something could make a previously existing Yahweh immaterial only by making a previously material being immaterial. This has not actually made Yahweh God. For an initially material being to have a shot at deity in this way, it must have not begun to exist—only so could it be eternal. But the universe began to exist. So then did every material thing. I suspect that making something material immaterial is not so much as possible. Consider a thing wholly composed of material parts. If it became immaterial, first it would consist of certain parts, then all at once it would consist of none of those parts. Personal-identity theorists who consider the Star Trek transporter-beam widely report an intuition that a material object could not survive simultaneous replacement of all parts with other parts. If this intuition is correct, I do not see how one could survive simultaneous replacement of all parts with nothing at all. Still, perhaps some material things are only partly composed of matter: a body–soul composite is only partly composed of material parts. If you are a body–soul composite, and your soul survives death, part of you is available after the loss of all material parts, and so the transporter objection does not apply. But if your soul survives, there are three options. Perhaps you do not survive as an immaterial being. Rather, you cease to exist, leaving behind just a soul. If not, then perhaps you come to be identical with your soul. This would be a case of contingent, temporary identity, and so is a non-starter. If neither, then you and your soul remain distinct, but your soul wholly constitutes you, as a block of marble wholly constitutes a statue. This raises the question of what the constitution relation is. On some accounts, constitution is a case of spatial coincidence between distinct things.[46] These cannot apply here, and what is left of them when the coincidence conditions are deleted is too weak to plausibly capture constitution. Other accounts involve what amount to relations of relative identity.[47] There are good reasons to think that there is no such thing.[48] So probably the constitution relation would have to be primitive. Thus the

---

[45] Aquinas, *ST* Ia 8.

[46] For example, Lynne Rudder Baker, *The Metaphysics of Everyday Life* (Cambridge: Cambridge University Press, 2007), p. 161.

[47] For the main alternatives, see Michael Rea (ed.), *Material Constitution* (Lanham, MD.: Rowman and Littlefield, 1997).

[48] See, for example, John Hawthorne, 'Identity', in Michael Loux and Dean Zimmerman (eds), *The Oxford Handbook of Metaphysics* (Oxford: Oxford University Press, 2003), pp. 110–28.

third will not appeal to anyone suspicious (as I am) of primitive relations of constitution.[49]

Something could cause a previously existing Yahweh to be personal only by converting some non-person to a person. A non-person would lack most divine features, and so this could not be the only divine feature something gave Yahweh. As to eternity, something could make Yahweh to have existed timelessly only if it accounted for Yahweh's existence. Something could make Yahweh to have existed through all of a beginningless past time only if it had always sustained His existence. Neither is compatible with deity, which implies being neither created nor sustained.

If something gave Yahweh moral perfection at t, He either did or did not exist beforehand. If He did pre-exist, He either was or was not morally perfect then. We can eliminate the option existing beforehand/imperfect then. If Yahweh was initially morally not perfect, Yahweh can never be made morally perfect, for a *perfect* being would not have even a brief spell of non-perfection on its record. True moral perfection would have at least three components: perfect current virtue, a perfect history of virtue, and a spotless record of acts (never having done anything evil). The argument for this is straightforward: three-component perfection seems perfectly possible. If it is—one- or two-component perfection is obviously a lesser good—and so neither counts as being perfect in this respect, because it is surpassable. Now, a spell of non-perfection would have to consist in having either a spotted record or no record at all for some period, or in lacking perfect virtue for some period. Nothing capable of moral agency ever has no moral record. As soon as one becomes morally responsible, either there is or there is not a good or a bad act for which one is then responsible. If one is then responsible for neither sort, one still has a record, though an empty one. One might have done good or done bad, but did neither: that's the record. It is impossible to have a spotted record for only a time: spots may be repented, forgiven, atoned-for, but do not literally wash out, as it never ceases to be the case that (say) you did in fact tell that lie. And nothing which for some period lacked perfect virtue ever has a perfect history of virtue: there is always that blank or imperfect spot.

The options left to consider are existing beforehand/perfect then and not existing beforehand. We can eliminate not existing beforehand. On this option Yahweh is non-eternal (thus non-divine) or is made eternal (which we have eliminated). Again, if something makes Yahweh morally perfect as soon as He exists, and Yahweh is timeless, then it is never the case that Yahweh is perfect without outside aid. If so, Yahweh can never be morally perfect, for it is better

---

[49] On my parsing of the Incarnation, an incarnate God who ceased to be incarnate would not be a material or partly material object who ceased to be material, but an immaterial object ceasing to be part of a certain whole (see 'A Timeless God Incarnate', in Daniel Kendall and Steven Davis (eds), *The Incarnation* (New York: Oxford University Press, 2002), pp. 273–99).

to be perfect unaided, and this is certainly possible, and so a morally *perfect* being would not receive moral aid for its entire life. If Yahweh is temporal and never began to exist, then if Yahweh was morally perfect as soon as He existed, the cause that made Him so must have done so for all of some beginningless period; there was some beginningless period during which Yahweh was not unaidedly perfect. Perhaps this period ends, and after that, Yahweh preserves His moral perfection unaided. But then no matter when it ends, it could have ended sooner, and so again, His actual moral state is surpassable.

We are left, then, with the hypothesis that Yahweh existed beforehand and was then morally perfect, but at t, something else so acted as to suffice for His being morally perfect. It either is or is not the case that had outside help not been given, He would have been morally perfect at and after t. If He would not have, then He needs help to be morally perfect for part of His life. If so, He is never fully morally perfect, since a *perfect* being would not need the help. Suppose now that Yahweh would not need the help: He was already morally perfect and would have continued to be so without this other cause acting. Then this other cause is an overdeterminer: either it and Yahweh jointly produce Yahweh's further perfection, though either could have produced for it alone, or one of them accounts for it alone, and the other is just a 'fail-safe' available to take over should the one falter. If the other is the fail-safe, it does not make Yahweh morally perfect. If Yahweh is the fail-safe, He is never morally perfect, for it would be better not to owe one's perfection to another for any period. If the two account for it together, then again it would have been morally superior for Yahweh to be the sole source of His moral achievements. I suggest, in short, that absolute moral perfection is not an attribute that anything can receive from without.

If something made Yahweh able to create *ex nihilo* and Yahweh did not make this other thing, (GSA) is false. If Yahweh made something that made Him able to create *ex nihilo*, He could not have created it *ex nihilo*. He made it out of something. If He made it out of something He did not make, (GSA) is false. But if Yahweh never began to exist, and time had no beginning, another scenario needs to be considered: perhaps for all t, Yahweh made all things existing at t out of prior things. On this scenario, Yahweh makes every thing at every time without having created any *ex nihilo*, and eventually makes one that somehow gives Him this power. This does not preserve (GSA) and then (FD) is also false: the cross-time series of made things and the universe are co-eternal with Yahweh, as we have seen. It is also puzzling how someone not able to create *ex nihilo* could make something able to give Him this power. One wants to say: if this power is not in the nature of things *ab initio*, then it just cannot be in the nature of things (and say this too of the GSA-property). Further, on this alternative, Yahweh never has the GSA-property and so is never divine.

Again, any Western theist will insist that Yahweh accounts for the fact that there ever are things other than He. But if He does so in this scenario, *when* does He do it? At any time, if He has done it, He did it earlier, not then. Nor can Yahweh have done this over the whole of time down to the present, or some other beginningless period. For it did not take the whole of this period to account for this. If He did it at all, He managed to do it completely in an earlier period—one earlier because it ended earlier. If Yahweh is always temporal, He can only account for this at some time. But on the scenario outlined, there can be no time at which He does so. I conclude that Yahweh cannot have made in a non-creative way something able to give Him the power to create.[50]

In any case, nothing could give Yahweh the GSA-property, $\lambda x(y)$(if y is not God, a part, aspect or attribute of God or an event, x and only x makes the creating-*ex-nihilo* sort of causal contribution to y's existence as long as y exists). If Yahweh has already made this difference for everything, He already has it, and so nothing can give it to Him. If He has not, but there is something there to give it to Him, it is not something for which He has made this sort of difference, so it is too late for Him to acquire the property, and so again, nothing can give it to Him.

Turning now to omnipotence, (GSA) requires that Yahweh make the thing that makes Him omnipotent. But if Yahweh could make Himself omnipotent in this way, why could not He just make Himself omnipotent directly? Why the middle-man? Further, omnipotence is a set of intrinsic powers.[51] So to make something omnipotent is to give it intrinsic powers. But nothing can just be given intrinsic powers without being changed in some other way: things have intrinsic powers because they have other, non-dispositional intrinsic attributes, or else their powers are identical with attributes we could describe in non-dispositional terms. So we must ask what the base-property for omnipotence is: what attribute could ground its acquisition, or *be* it

---

[50] One might object that if this argument is sound, a like one will show that a temporal God could not account for His being in any state He is in eternally: knowing, for instance, that $2 + 2 = 4$ or intending to create other things. Since I think God is atemporal, I would be happy with this, and take it as an argument for His atemporality. But Bruce Langtry (who raised the point about intention in correspondence) suggests that either God accounts for His having the intention at every time before He acts on it or in this case 'When?' needs no answer. The latter is true only if the question is somehow inappropriate. I can make little of the claim that it can be inappropriate to ask *when* something done in time has been done. So perhaps Langtry's point is that nothing has been done—the intention is a dispositional state, God never began to have it (so too His belief that $2 + 2 = 4$), nor then was there any time at which such an event took place. If that is what these cases involve, they are not good analogies to God's making there be other things, which He does by causing an event. If having the intention (say) does involve causing an event, the cases are still dissimilar. If it is not just a disposition, God accounts for His intention at every time before He acts on it because He constantly maintains it (and so one might say of His beliefs, if one holds with, for example, Aquinas (*Summa Contra Gentiles* I, 56) that all of God's knowledge is occurrent, none dispositional). If so, every time prior to His act is a new time at which He brings it about that He has it. His bringing this about is complete at every time, as Langtry suggests. Having made other things is not an ongoing state God maintains. It is not (as it were) done new at every time. Once God has made other things, His bringing this about is complete. There is no more to be done. It is complete not at but before any time, on this scenario; so any time is too late for it to have been completed then.

[51] See my 'Omnipotence', in Thomas Flint and Michael Rea (eds), *The Oxford Handbook of Philosophical Theology* (Oxford: Oxford University Press, 2009), pp. 167–98.

described non-dispositionally? The only plausible answer, and perhaps the only conceivable one, is deity. This would contradict our favorable assumption that deity is a conjunction including omnipotence. More to the point, where the question at issue is whether something can be made divine, it would beg the question to assert that this is possible. So barring some other candidate base-property for omnipotence, it would beg the question here to assert that Yahweh could be made divine by being made omnipotent. Omniscience in the sense in which it is part of the divine nature is similarly dispositional: it is the disposition to know whatever is to be known.[52] So the same point applies here, and so it seems that the claim that something could make Yahweh divine in the end just cannot be supported.

Arguments from Perfection

If Yahweh is made divine but not made to exist, then either He was initially perfect but not divine—which we have ruled out—or in being made divine, He is also made perfect. This yields a further reason why Yahweh cannot be made divine: nothing could be made perfect. The Western monotheisms hold that God is divine but was not made so. I premise that this is possible and (16).[53] Given these premises, it is possible to be perfect and not owe perfection to another. Now though the intuition is hard to explicate, intuitively, it would be better to be perfect independently than to be made so by something else. If this is true, then if it is possible to be perfect independently, it is not possible to be made perfect by something else. Any owed property is not perfection. But anything made divine would owe its perfection to another unless it also, simultaneously underwent some change caused from within sufficient to make it perfect. Even then, the cause of its being perfect would include both itself and some other thing, and an argument parallel to that just given will conclude that it is not possible to owe perfection to a joint cause including anything external—since it would be better to be entirely independently perfect. The upshot is that nothing can be changed into a deity.

Again, there are three ways Yahweh could owe perfection to another: by being made to exist, perfect, or made and then perfected, or by existing without having been made and then perfected. The first two are not compatible with having the (GSA)-property. But as I have argued, a perfect being

---

[52] This might be a disposition that cannot be unmanifested. But that makes it none the less dispositional. If there were a diamond which could not exist save when something was trying to scratch it, its hardness would still be a dispositional property.

[53] Since this entails that it is possible to be divine, if this were a treatment of the ontological argument, this premise would be too controversial simply to drop in casually. It would require argument. The present context, though, is a discussion of the nature God would have if there is a God. In that context this assumption is trivial: of course, if there were a God, one property He would have is being possibly existent. This is true even if it in fact it is impossible that there be a God.

would have this. So on the first two, what came to be would not in fact be perfect. So on the first two options, it is not possible to owe perfection to another. On the third, Yahweh receives perfection as a contingent property: were it necessary, He would owe His existence, not just His perfection, to what perfected Him. (17) rules this out.

I have argued that nothing could account for Yahweh's being God by giving a Yahweh already existent the divine nature. The other alternative mentioned above was causing Yahweh to exist and making Him divine. Now something that did this, or for that matter made an already-existent Yahweh divine, might deserve worship for doing either—it would be the lucky star we could thank for having our God. So it is not clear that either is compatible with Biblical monotheism. Further, if Yahweh was made, His maker existed at least as early as He did, and so (FD) is false. And if Yahweh was made, He depends on His maker for existence and not *vice versa*, and so (GSA) fails.[54] So (FD) and (GSA) rule this out. If He was made, further, Yahweh is straightforwardly a creature, which seems incompatible with deity. I conclude that it is not the case that something else could account for Yahweh's being God. Now if Yahweh is contingently God, either something else accounts for this or nothing accounts for it. As shown above, unacceptable consequences also flow if nothing accounts for it. I conclude that it is not the case that Yahweh is contingently God. There are no such problems for the claim that He is necessarily God. What is necessarily the case is not so by a lucky break, and so the 'nothing accounts for it' option brings nothing suspect with it. There are, then, many reasons to accept (DE).

Deity as an Individual Essence

We can in fact argue a stronger conclusion: not only is (DE) true, deity is in fact a haecceity, an individual essence, of Yahweh: nothing else could have had it. Deity's being an individual essence is compatible with *deity* being a kind-concept. An attribute is an individual essence expressed by a kind-concept just if it is a kind with just one possible member expressed by a kind-concept. There may well be cases of this. I have already mentioned *even prime*. Transforms of that reasoning apply to any ontology of number. Again, *set* is plausibly a kind-concept. *Null set* plausibly restricts it. 'It is a null set' seems to say what kind of thing something is, but expresses an individual essence.

---

[54] There might seem to be an odd scenario to consider: suppose that time never began, and at every t it is the case that Maker causes Yahweh to exist at t and Yahweh, existing, causes the existence of Maker for a period after t open toward t (that is, some period we would get by deleting t from the interval t–t*). Would this be a case of mutual dependence for existence? I would say that it is mutual dependence for continuation of existence, but that really, in this scenario, neither accounts for the fact that the other ever exists at all. If so, (GSA) still fails.

(DE) is part of the individual essence thesis.

So we need only argue that

24. no-one other than Yahweh is divine in any possible world.

Perfection and Supremacy

One argument for (24) is perfect-being. Perfect-being theology tells us that

25. there cannot be something wholly distinct from Yahweh and greater than He actually is.

But there is also a case that

26. there cannot be something wholly distinct from Yahweh and as great as He actually is.[55]

This is not because Yahweh would have any intrinsic perfection by being unequalled, any more than He does by being unsurpassed. But consider a comparison with a field of possible rivals. For simplicity, suppose there is just one, Schmod, whose perfections would be commensurable with Yahweh's. If (25) and (26) are true, they are true due to both Yahweh's intrinsic character and that the competition would have if actual. If (25) is true, Yahweh's intrinsic perfection equals or surpasses Schmod's. (26) entails that Yahweh's surpasses Schmod's. Schmod is the same in the two comparisons: say, intrinsically perfect to degree n. A being intrinsically perfect to a degree greater than n is intrinsically greater than one perfect to a degree not greater than n. So Yahweh is intrinsically greatest among His commensurable possible rivals only if (26) is true. Now one basic form of perfect-being argument for a divine attribute is roughly this: if it would be better to be F than not to be, and being F does not conflict with having some at least equally perfection-conferring constellation of attributes, then God is F. It would be greater to be intrinsically such as to be the greatest possible being among commensurable rivals than not to be. No constellation of attributes could confer more perfection than one that made one thus greatest. Being thus greatest entails (26). And nothing of a perfect-being sort can rule (26) out. Since it does not assert any specific first-level divine attribute, (26) is not the sort of thing to conflict with conclusions of perfect-being theology which assert such attributes, and that God has an equal or a superior is hardly likely to be a perfect-being conclusion, or to follow from one. Hence perfect-being theology must accept (26).

Now, being divine entails being perfect. If this is so and someone else could have been divine, there could have been another being as perfect as Yahweh

---

[55] As I understand the doctrine of the Trinity, (26) does not rule it out, for as I read it, the Persons are not wholly distinct from Yahweh. See my 'A Latin Trinity'.

actually is or else incommensurably perfect. So if (26) is true, there could not have been someone divine distinct from Yahweh but commensurable in perfection: that is, (26) implies ((24) v there can be someone divine and perfect but incommensurable in perfection with Yahweh). But the possibility of incommensurable perfections Yahweh does not have seems to hinge on the availability of 'mystery' perfections: we do not know of candidates. This gives us weak reason to infer (24).

Another argument for (24) has as premises (DE), that being divine entails existing necessarily, and that the true modal logic includes Brouwer. This last is plausible, though to show why I would have to canvass intuitions in favor of S5, and I must defer doing so. Given these things, (24) is false only if Yahweh co-exists with another deity. But He does not.

Again, if (24) is false, in some possible world there is a deity who is not Yahweh. So either Yahweh exists contingently, or Yahweh is contingently divine, or in some world there are two deities. Being divine entails existing necessarily. (DE) rules out the second. As to the third, being uncreated and such as to have created any other concreta follow from being divine. There cannot in one world be two uncreated beings who have created every concrete thing other than themselves. For then each would have created the other. But if one is there first to create the other, it was not created by that other, and it is impossible that the two simultaneously bring each other into being.[56] So the third is impossible.

Again, if (24) is false, we can ask why Yahweh is God rather than this other candidate, or perhaps neither.[57] There is or is not an explanation for this. I have argued that unacceptable consequences follow no matter which we pick. I take it, therefore, that (24) is true and so deity is a haecceity.

Some might object that in the context of my theory, on which God determines what apart from Himself is possible, (25) and (26) make God out to be jealous and grudging: why would God not let things equal or surpass Him? I suggest that it is not in Him to do so, for His control of what is possible does not extend to modifying His nature. God is by nature uncreated, necessarily existent and the source of any other concrete things there are. He gains some increment of perfection from the first and third. If God is all three by nature, no other being in any possible world is both uncreated and the source of all else concrete. Thus even if some possible being matched God's perfection in all other respects, it would come out below God on balance.

---

[56] Note that the point here concerns creation specifically. It is another matter whether two beings might eternally sustain one another, neither having begun to exist.

[57] I have already ruled out 'both' as an option.

8

AGAINST DEITY THEORIES

WITH my lemma in hand, I now present my main argument against deity theories. It has two premises, that

1. deity theories commit us to the claim that God's existence depends on there being truthmakers for particular necessary truths about creatures, and

2. theories that did not so commit us would *ceteris paribus* be preferable,

and concludes that it would be preferable *ceteris paribus* to avoid a deity theory.

The Argument for (1)

I now state my argument for (1). Consider a necessary truth about creatures alone, such as one expressed by 'water = H_2O'. This sentence may state a property-identity, that being water = being H_2O. It may also state that

(WATER) (x)(x is a body of water $\supset$ ($\exists$y)(y is a body of H_2O and x = y)) · (x) (x is a body of H_2O $\supset$ ($\exists$y)(y is a body of water and x = y)).

(WATER) is a strong necessity: in every possible world, either there are no bodies the stuff 'water' actually is or H_2O, or there are and every body of the one is identical with a body of the other. Now consider a particular impossibility, that (WATER) is untrue. To suppose this is not to suppose that water has a different nature. This latter may be not just impossible but inconceivable. Plausibly 'being water = being H_2O' expresses *being H_2O = being H_2O*. If it does, to say that water has a different nature is to say that something other than *being H_2O* is identical with *being H_2O*. It is hard to make coherent sense of this, and it is *a priori* false: it is in these senses inconceivable. But (WATER) would be untrue were H_2O not possible nor so much as impossible, but instead just not a denizen of logical space. We can coherently suppose (WATER) to be untrue by supposing that logical space so differs that there is in it no such property as being H_2O, nor any such proposition as (WATER), nor anyone, even God, able to imagine such a stuff as H_2O.[1] Philosophers consider alternative logical spaces routinely, in considering metaphysical theories involving different systems of necessary truths: for example, theism vs atheism or absolute idealism vs physicalism. That there is no such property as being H_2O is not nonsense, nor is it *a priori* false. It was a significant empirical discovery that there is such a stuff as H_2O. If there is in fact an associated property *being H_2O*, that was a partly empirical discovery, the rest lying in philosophical arguments about the nature of properties and when we are entitled to infer properties' existence from empirical results. The property probably was not conceived of before there was empirical evidence of its existence; Gay-Lussac and Humboldt may have imagined models of it (or what it is to have it) before their 1805 work gave the first such evidence, but whatever they imagined was probably so inaccurate and broad-brush that it could not count as modeling the property there really is. If the content of such propositions as (WATER) involves the property *being H_2O*, it was in the same way a partly empirical discovery that there is such a proposition as (WATER), and (believers in God would add) that it is in the power of an omnipotent God to conceive it. In the no-property/proposition situation (WATER) is not false. It is not there to bear a truth-value. But because it is not, we, with (WATER) to hand, can truly say that it is not true there.

My argument emerges if we consider the simplest sort of deity theory, that of Aquinas. On this, if something is divine, deity's being as it is makes true all necessary truth about water—what it is to be water, what is necessary to be water, how water can change, what water can do, and so on. It encodes its nature, in short: the nature of water is in some way in the nature of God. If the nature of water is in deity, then if (WATER) is untrue, there are consequences for deity, and this has consequences for God's existence. The argument runs this way. On a deity theory,

3. (WATER) is untrue → either nothing has deity or deity contains no attribute from a set of attributes of which it necessarily contains some member.

4. Deity contains no attribute from a set of which it necessarily contains some member → deity does not exist.

So:

[1] I hold it conceivable that God not have had this ability, even if it is *a priori* true that if anything is God, it is omnipotent. Just how this can be emerges later.

5. (WATER) is untrue → either nothing has deity or deity does not exist.

6. Nothing has deity → God does not exist.

7. Deity does not exist → God does not exist.

And so:

8. (WATER) is untrue → God does not exist.

(8) is unintuitive. It does not seem that God's existence should depend on facts about water. Surely deleting a chemical property from logical space should not affect whether God exists. It seems irrelevant to God's existence, so it seems that it should not alter this. I now consider three replies to this initial pumping of an intuition:

If the impossible is actual, *everything* follows. So we should expect that even a chemical impossibility would carry with it the non-existence of a necessary God.

But that the impossible implies everything is usually called a paradox of strict implication precisely because we think some things should not follow from any given impossibility. That being so, our intuition that chemistry should not thus affect theology is not undercut: it is just one more reason to consider this paradoxical. That is, it is one more reason to think that strict implication does not quite capture what entailment really is, though we use it *faute de mieux*.

Well, even if it should not imply *everything*, the impossible should strictly imply every other impossibility, so again, it is not surprising that deleting a chemical property also deletes God.

But this too is a paradox of strict implication. We have persistent intuitions that 'entails' should express some relation more discriminating than this, and such a relation might well not link (WATER)'s untruth to God's non-existence.

Someone who cannot imagine water is not omnipotent and so not God. So supposing that there is in logical space not being able to do this does involve supposing God's not being there.

But this assumes that power to imagine water must be part of what omnipotence confers. So Chapter 6 has already blocked this argument: it could be up to God whether He has this power, though it is not up to Him whether He is omnipotent. The theory I soon develop shows how this could work.

With this promissory note issued—and another, to say more to pump this intuition below—it does not seem that (8) should be true. Of course, it *is* true, because if (WATER) is necessary, (8) has an impossible antecedent. But this is irrelevant. I do not claim that (8) is false. What matters for my purposes is that (8) is counter-intuitive and deity theories commit us to it—that (8) follows from a deity-theoretic premise, (3), in conjunction with truths. Even if all impossible-antecedent conditionals are trivially true, they are not all counter-intuitive. And even if all such conditionals are true for semantic reasons, some may also reflect important facts: truths can be overdetermined to be true. I argue below that on a deity theory, (8) is such a case. It reflects a substantive, objectionable dependence that would exist were a deity theory true; it is a counter-intuitive consequence that reveals something counter-intuitive in the theory, not just an oddity of conditional semantics. We can ignore (8)'s oddity only if the *only* reason we have to affirm (8) is semantic. I show below that deity theorists have other reasons.

It is natural to read (3)–(8) in the vocabulary of transworld identity, supposing that the very item which plays the God-role in our world plays it too in other worlds. Nothing turns on this. Counterpart theorists deny it.[2] On counterpart theories, any possible item exists in just one world, but other worlds represent possibilities for it by containing items like it which play its role—its counterparts. An item A^* counts as A's counterpart in a world relative to ('under') a particular counterpart relation—that is, by weighting most certain respects of similarity between A and A^*.[3] On counterpart theory, then, we might say that Δ and Yahweh play the roles of deity and God in our world, exist in no other, and have counterparts in other worlds. In a counterpart vocabulary, the argument through (5) runs this way:

3* (WATER) is untrue $\rightarrow$ either nothing has a Δ-counterpart under any relevant counterpart relation or no Δ-counterpart under any relevant counterpart relation contains an attribute from a set of attributes some member of which each of Δ's counterparts under any relevant counterpart relation contains.

4*. No Δ-counterpart under any relevant counterpart relation contains an attribute from a set of attributes some member of which each of Δ's counterparts under any relevant counterpart relation contains $\rightarrow$ nothing is a Δ-counterpart under any relevant counterpart relation. So:

5*. (WATER) is untrue $\rightarrow$ either nothing has a Δ-counterpart under any relevant counterpart relation or Δ has no counterpart under any relevant counterpart relation.

Modulo their commitment to counterpart theory, (3*)–(5*) should be as plausible as (3)–(5). If (3)–(5) are plausible and (3*)–(5*) prove less so, it might be more appropriate to lower our confidence in counterpart theory than to hold either (3*)–(5*) or (3)–(5) with the lesser confidence (3*)–(5*) inspire. But it will be clear that my arguments would have equal force if framed in counterpart terms.

---

[2] The *locus classicus* is David Lewis, *On the Plurality of Worlds* (Oxford: Basil Blackwell), p. 192ff.
[3] As we assess counterparthood, context determines which respects we weigh most; such contexts can shift from one sentence to the next.

One might raise an epistemic problem for the argument to (8) this way:

9. $7 + 5 = 13 \rightarrow$ God believes that $7 + 5 = 13$

and

10. God believes that $7 + 5 = 13 \rightarrow$ God is not omniscient

entail that

11. $7 + 5 = 13 \rightarrow$ God is not omniscient.

But nonetheless, it is not plausible that

X. ($7 + 5 = 13$ and God believes that $7 + 5 = 13$) $\rightarrow$ God is not omniscient,

and this might suggest that (9) and (10) do not in fact provide good reason to accept (11). So perhaps we need more than just the transitivity of entailment to accept that (3) and (4) provide good reason for (5).[4] Note, then, what the epistemic flaw of (9)–(11) actually is. The truth of a conditional with an impossible antecedent can be overdetermined. Sometimes they are true not just because their antecedents are impossible, and sometimes these over-determining grounds of truth give us reason to believe them independent of their antecedents' modal status. When we accept (9), we suppose that $7 + 5 = 13$ for the sake of seeing what follows and hold fixed that God is omniscient; that (9)'s consequent then follows is an overdetermining reason (9) is true and is for most of us, I think, the reason we incline to accept (9). We accept (10) because its consequent follows if we suppose it is not the case that $7 + 5 = 13$ and hold fixed that God is omniscient and an omniscient being believes no falsehoods—that is, *inter alia* because we reject what we suppose in evaluating (9). (X)'s implausibility reminds us that if we continued to suppose that $7 + 5 = 13$, and reasoned within the supposition, we would not have overdetermining good reason to accept (10). (X)'s implausibility raises the question of whether it is licit to suppose both that $7 + 5 = 13$ and that this is false in supporting (11). We must therefore ask whether the same sort of problem crops up for (3)–(5).

As we shall see below, the deity theorist accepts (3) *inter alia* because (WATER) is true and (he/she supposes) so is a deity theory. This reason is independent of our reasons to accept (4). (4)'s antecedent makes a claim about the constitution of a property. (4) instances a general truth about the nature of properties. (3) and (4) provide overdetermining reason to accept (5) if we have reason to hold this truth fixed in thinking about properties in impossible situations. But we do. Treating deity as containing other attributes amounts to treating it as a set or a conjunctive property. We would not know what to

---

[4] Bruce Langtry raised this difficulty.

make of the claim that {a} = {b} though a ≠ b; it would leave us with no grip on what a set is supposed to be. Similarly, we would not know what to make of the claim that (F · G) = (H · I), though these are four distinct attributes; it would leave us with no grip on what conjunctions are supposed to be. We have to assume that {a} = {b} iff a = b and (F · G) = (H · I) iff there are appropriate identities among the conjuncts to keep a grip on the content of impossible suppositions—and we ought to think about them in ways that keep our grip on their content, unless the supposition itself will not permit this. The supposition that (WATER) is untrue permits this. So we should continue to suppose what gives us reason to accept (4) even within the scope of an impossible assumption.

I now argue (3)–(8). I discuss just the most basic sort of deity theory, on which the divine nature's existing or being as it is makes true the full modal truth about creatures. This eases exposition, and it should be clear how to transform the argument to apply to more complex forms. But transformation may not even be needed. Consider a natural-activity deity view. On this, deity is such that due to having it, God by nature gives rise to a truthmaker for (WATER). Plausibly, a natural-activity view should hold that God's having deity also makes (WATER) true. Suppose that as in Leibniz, having deity makes God such as to conceive of water. Then this is due to part of deity's content. Being such as to conceive of water includes water, the object of conception, being H_2O. If it did not, then if water is H_2O, it could not dictate that God conceive of water. But then deity encodes the nature of water. It is set within it that God is so to think that water = H_2O. In some way, the content that water = H_2O is there. Now we are taking it that *water = H_2O* needs a truthmaker to be true. God's conceiving either does or does not produce entities to truthmake modal truth. If it does not, God's actually thinking that water = H_2O adds nothing to what is there to make it true that water = H_2O, and so is not plausibly what makes the difference between its being and not being true that water = H_2O. So if due to God's thinking having the content that water = H_2O, *water = H_2O* is true, it ought equally to be the case that this is true due to God's nature somehow embodying that same content. If God's thinking does produce entities, the question will be why the content's being in them rather than the divine nature is crucial. It is hard to see why it should be. God's concept (if that is what He produces) and deity contain the same content. If they did not, God's concept would not have produced the content deity dictated. And deity, like God's concept, is an entity encoding this content. So a natural activity theory should grant that God's having deity, or something about deity itself, makes (WATER) true. If so, every deity theory incorporates the simplest, and my discussion of the simplest theory suffices for the rest.

I now display the move from a deity theory to (3) more clearly. I start by laying down some theses about attributes. I then apply them.

Attributes

If attributes are universals or tropes, they have a content. There is a way things are in virtue of having them; there is a character they confer on their bearers. Their content determines what a thing's having them makes true: it is because being a dog makes something a mammal that Rover's being a dog makes it true that there are mammals. A universal or trope's intrinsic character or makeup determine what it confers on its bearers. (What else could do so?) So if what it conferred on its bearers somehow changed, its intrinsic character or makeup would have changed too.

On predicate / concept nominalism or class or mereological nominalism, these things are not true. Belonging to the class of all and only dogs does not give Fido his doggy character or constitute his having it. Rather, it is because he has his doggy character that he belongs. On these forms of nominalism, the truth is instead this. Attributes have a content. That is, there is a way things are in virtue of which they have an attribute; there is a character having an attribute entails that its bearers have, though having the attribute does not account for their having the character. Attributes' content encapsulates what a thing's having them makes true in virtue of its being such as to have them. If attributes are predicates or concepts, it is because being a dog entails being a mammal that Rover or his being a dog makes it true that there are mammals. If attributes are classes or sums, associated with each is a predicable which just its members satisfy, its intension, and this expresses the attribute's content.

On predicate / concept nominalism, an attribute's intrinsic character determines just what about its bearers makes it the case that they have it. It is because '__ is a dog' means what it does or the concept of a dog includes what it does that being thus-and-so qualifies Fido to be a dog. So if what character the bearers have *qua* having an attribute somehow changed, the attribute's intrinsic character would have changed too. But plausibly predicables have their meanings essentially different meaning, different predicable and so too concepts their contents. Predicable tokens' physical makeup can differ world-to-world but is just irrelevant to their function in theories of attributes. If so, on concept nominalism, attributes and their content cannot differ in any relevant way world-to-world. So too, classes have their members and sums their parts essentially.[5] Since only classes can have members, they are also classes essentially; similarly, sums are sums essentially. There is nothing more to a class's (sum's) intrinsic character than its being a class (sum) and having the members (parts) it does. So if attributes are classes (sums), they and their content cannot differ world-to-world either. Still, it is also substantively true that if what character the bearers have *qua* having an attribute somehow changed, the attribute's intrinsic character would have changed. It is because a

---

[5] On classes see James Van Cleve, 'Why a Set Contains Its Members Essentially', *Noûs* 19 (1985), 585–602.

class or sum contains what it does that its intension is what it is: because a class contains just dogs, '__ is a dog' is its intension.[6] So if somehow what character bearers have *qua* having an attribute somehow changed, the attribute's makeup would have changed too.

I now apply these claims.

From a Deity Theory to (3)

Necessarily, an unchanged truthmaker truthmakes the same set of truths if it is present. If its being the case that P truthmakes just P, how could this in other worlds truthmake other truths or not truthmake P? So if someone's having deity actually makes (WATER) true, necessarily, if someone has deity, this makes (WATER) true, if deity's content is unchanged. Suppose now what I will shortly argue, that deity's content does not change world-to-world.[7] If it does not, that someone has deity is the same truthmaker no matter what: since the truthmaker is that *someone* has deity, it does not matter who it is. Then on the simplest deity theory, necessarily, if someone has deity, this makes (WATER) true. So deity necessarily contains some property (perhaps itself) such that necessarily, if something has this property, this makes (WATER) true. Perhaps this is the same property in all worlds. But perhaps not: perhaps in one world the property is F, in another G, and so on. If that is so, then F, G, and so on make up a set at least one member of which deity contains in every possible world in which someone has it. There is also such a set if it is the same property in all worlds: namely, that property's singleton set. So necessarily, if someone has deity and deity contains some member of a set of attributes (the (WATER)-truthmaking set) of which it necessarily contains a member, (WATER) is true. This is so not just because this conditional's antecedent and consequent are necessary, but because necessarily, God's having a member of this set is a (WATER)-truthmaker. So by contraposition, necessarily, (3). We now have a reason to affirm (3) that is independent of its having a necessarily false antecedent: (3) reflects a fact about truthmaking and a truthmaker a deity-theory assigns (WATER).

To complete my argument I must argue the premise that deity's content does not differ world-to-world. Its content differs just if its makeup or character differ. I discuss first makeup, then character, on the initial assumption that deity can have no constituents.

---

[6] It is also true that because '—is a dog' means what it does, the class of dogs is its extension. These claims are compatible. The one tells why, if we start from classes, classes pair with predicates as they do. The other tells why, if we start from predicates, predicates pair with classes as they do. The one tells how intensions are determined, the other how extensions are.

[7] If I am right about the three forms of nominalism just discussed, this needs arguing only for realism and trope theories, but my argument will be perfectly general.

Suppose first that deity is necessarily a simple property, entirely without constituent properties. Then its makeup cannot differ world-to-world, for there would be nothing to underwrite a transworld property-identity—a simple property could have no constituent properties in common with any property not fully identical in makeup with it. Granted, some identities, and some cross-world identities, may be brute, ungrounded, not further explicable. Even so, the more puzzling the identity, the less we incline to credit it without some explanation. Explanation seems needed if we're told that simple doghood in W and simple cathood in W* are the same property, and appeal to a property-haecceity, if there are such, would in this case be theft, not honest toil. The point carries over to a counterpart-theoretic context. There it is just that a counterpart-relation which made simple doghood in W simple cathood in W*'s counterpart could not be plausible. For this counterpart claim to be plausible, there would have to be some intuitive basis for a claim that the two resemble sufficiently. Just being properties could not be it, as this would render all W*-properties counterparts of all W-properties under the same counterpart relation: each property would 'be' every property in the other world, and so every item in W* would have every property in W: every cat would also be a dog, a sneeze, and a square root. Just being mammal-properties could not be it, as this would render all W*-mammal-properties counterparts of all W-mammal-properties under the same counterpart relation, and so every cat would also be a dog, an ape, a woolly mammoth, and so on: in each case, the preferred basis for resemblance will bring too many counterparts with it. If counterpart theory is to be plausible, surely it must try to avoid one item in a world 'being' multiple items in another world. But even if a counterpart theorist does not see this as a general *desideratum*, we want there to be just one counterpart in *this* case, and so failure to secure this is still a problem. Resemblance with respect to being the property had in W just by all dogs or the property in W* had just by all cats does give us just one counterpart. But everything resembles everything with respect to some similar disjunctive property, and so if we allowed it, there could be no principled reason not to let everything in W be a counterpart of everything in W* in just the same way simple doghood is supposedly a counterpart of simple cathood—not under the same counterpart relation but under one relevantly precisely similar. That being so, this is a vacuous resemblance. It is in any case not grounded in anything intuitively common, and so provides no *intuitive* basis for a claim that the two resemble sufficiently.

I now turn to character. While something necessarily simple cannot differ in constituent from world to world, nor (obviously) in necessary features, it could differ world-to-world in contingent features or attributes—a simple particle might move one way in one world, another in another. On the simplest deity theory, not deity's having attributes but God's having deity truthmakes modal truths. Only the content of deity matters. But we could consider a variant deity theory, which based modal truths on attributes rather than contents of deity, and let these vary world-to-world. This deity-based view might yield deity-based truthmakers for different sets of truths in different worlds even if deity is internally necessarily simple. If (WATER) is necessary, though, it would still have to be the case that deity had in each world some attribute its having which made it such that if someone has deity, (WATER) is true. So this would yield a relative of (3), that (WATER) is untrue → either nothing has deity or deity has no attribute from a set of attributes of which it necessarily has some member, and we could revise the rest of the argument accordingly. This argument would not need the claim that deity's content does not differ world-to-world, since the content (or something's having it) would no longer be what makes (WATER) true. Since the same argument about an attribute's character would work if its makeup did differ world-to-world, I do not discuss character further.

If Deity can have Constituents

Thus if deity is necessarily simple, my argument from a deity theory to (3) goes through. Suppose, on the other hand, that deity has constituents in some possible world. Then either it has all of these necessarily or it has some contingently. If necessarily, deity's makeup is the same in all worlds, and so the argument proceeds as on the assumption that deity is simple. I doubt that attributes can have the relevant sort of constituents contingently. Classes have members and sums parts essentially. Concepts have component concepts necessarily—nothing not containing the concept *animal* is the concept *rational animal*—and if token concepts have any other sort of constituent, they are not relevant. Predicables have component words necessarily—a parallel example suffices—and again, if predicable-tokens have other sorts of constituent, they are just irrelevant to issues of content. Nor does it seem that tropes or universals can have constituents contingently. If a trope or universal has tropes or universals as constituents, presumably this is because it is logically complex. Conjunctions and disjunctions (for instance) have their members necessarily; I can make nothing of the claim that the proposition P · Q could be the proposition P · Q · R · S. Why should conjunctive or disjunctive tropes or universals differ in this respect from propositions?[8]

If a complex trope or universal had constituents contingently, then (say) trope or universal F · G could in another world be trope or universal F · G · H—its cross-world identity would depend only on its containing F · G. (Again, I am taking it that there must be some ground for such an identity, and that appeal to attribute-haecceities would be cheating.) We usually think of attributes' identity-conditions in terms of intensions or extensions. If F and G are

---

[8] The question will seem particularly pointed to those who think that propositions are structured entities containing properties as constituents.

cross-world identical, the intension of w's F · G = that of w*'s F · G · H only if being F · G entails being H. If it does, the two intensions have precisely the same entailments, and so it is hard to see why the boundary between intension and mere entailment would fall differently in different worlds. If it does not, then considered intensionally, the w-attribute identical with w*'s F · G · H is w's F · G · H, not w's F · G, or else the identity links the F · Gs of the two worlds. So only something about their extensions could make plausible an identity between w's F · G and w*'s F · G · H.

Now extensional identity-conditions more coarse-grained than that necessarily coextensive properties are identical are not plausible: if mere co-extension sufficed we would get contingent identities of properties. So if F · G is not necessarily co-extensive with F · G · H and their intensions are not identical, there is nothing to make a cross-world identity between the two plausible. Thus we need only consider what to say if F · G and F · G · H *are* necessarily co-extensive. If they are but they necessarily differ in intension, any reason we have to say that H is not included in the property in one world is there in any other world. So it does not seem that a trope or universal can have a constituent only contingently. So too, if the two are necessarily co-extensive and necessarily have the same intension, H is not only contingently a constituent of the property: any reason we have to say that it includes H in one world is there in any other world. There is another option to consider only if at least one property has its intension contingently. But I can make nothing of the claim that a property might have its intension contingently. That would be like saying that in some worlds the definition of *being a dog* (if it has one) is that of being a cat, while yet the property was the property of being a dog. So the more usual approaches to property-identity militate against contingent constituents, unless there is some other way than logical complexity for a trope or universal to have constituents. Again, if F · G and F · G · H can be identical, why not F and F · G · H, I and F · G · H (where none of the four mentioned are identical), or I · K and F · G · H (where none of the five are)? If we allow this sort of cross-world identity at all, there seems no non-arbitrary stopping-point before we reach cases where we simply lose our grip on what a conjunction is supposed to be.

The closest we can get to deity's having constituents contingently, I think, is to say this: items have different deifying properties in different worlds. There is also a disjunctive property whose disjuncts are all and only these properties. A divine being has in different worlds different disjuncts of this disjunction but the same disjunction. If deity is the deifying property something has in all worlds in which it is divine, then deity is this disjunction. Having deity is sufficient for being divine. So is having any disjunct of deity. On this approach, in any world God has two sorts of nature, the disjunctive property He has in all worlds in which He is divine, and a particular disjunct, His most determinate nature (MDN) in that world. He has His MDN contingently. Deity is the disjunction, though, so again, deity has its actual makeup in every possible world in which God has it.[9] So I submit that whether or not deity has constituents, deity's makeup does not differ world-to-world. *Per* argument above, nor does its character, nor then does its content.

Bruce Langtry suggests another sort of disjunctive deity theory.[10] Suppose that there are no disjunctive properties: there are only disjunctive predicates which apply in virtue of non-disjunctive properties. Thus there would be no property of being a human parent; there would be properties of being a human mother and being a human father, and '__ is a human parent' would apply in virtue of one of these. On this assumption, there could be a deity theory on which '__ is divine' is a disjunctive predicate, and something is divine just if it has $F \cdot G$ or it has $F^\star \cdot G^\star$. Then one might suggest that the content of deity differs world-to-world (since it applies in virtue of different conjunctions) and yet the content of deity necessarily makes (WATER) true (if, say, both F and $F^\star$ do so). However, our operating account of deity has been that it is the property having which makes God divine. If we stick with this, then on this proposal, there are just different deifying properties in different worlds—deity is not disjunctive. The predicate is disjunctive, but the predicate is *ex hypothesi* not a property. And it will not do to shift ground, and claim that the disjunctive predicate is a property; we see later that deity cannot be just a predicate. Further, if it *were* a property, either the conjunctions that do the work would or would not themselves be predicates. If not, we have different theories of attributes true of the two different kinds of deifying property: but why on earth would we believe *that*? If they would, we have just a variation on the MDN story, MDNs are in no real sense the content of disjunctive deity, and so it is false that the content of deity differs world-to-world.

A related proposal involves property-realization. Some properties realize other properties: a thing's being of a certain shape, composition, and so on, realizes the property of being a carburetor. This happens when the realized property specifies a causal role, and a thing is fit to play (or have its parts play) the role just in virtue of having the realizing property. The realized property—such as being a carburetor—might be a second-order functional property realized by first-order conjunctive properties involving shape, composition, and so on. Or it might be a subset of causal properties which figures in all property-sets possessed by all and only carburetors.[11] The proposal, then, would be that deity is a property different properties realize in different

---

[9] One might ask here whether different divine beings could have different disjunctive deifying attributes. I have argued that there could not be a divine being not identical with Yahweh. But in any case, this would not affect my argument: we would just substitute for (3) a claim that: (WATER) is untrue $\rightarrow$ either nothing has Yahweh's sort of deity or Yahweh's sort of deity contains no attribute, etc., so alter the rest, and continue as before.

[10] In correspondence.

[11] See Sydney Shoemaker, *Physical Realization* (Oxford: Oxford University Press, 2007), pp. 11–18.

worlds, its realizer in a given world is its content in that world, and so deity is a property whose content, the realizer, differs world-to-world even if deity is simple. Now one way to think of realized properties is as disjunctions of their realizers.[12] Taking realization this way, this is just the MDN scenario above. If deity is not disjunctive but is multiply realized—I will assume that this is possible, though one could question it—deity is then in effect a determinable, and determinables (again debatably) are not just disjunctions of their determinates. On these assumptions, deity's content is the same world-to-world. Only the determinates differ. So again, the claim that deity's content does not differ world-to-world stands.

Playing Favorites?

(3) is true, but since it is impossible that (WATER) is untrue, so too is

12. (WATER) is untrue →God has deity and deity contains some attribute from a set of attributes of which it necessarily contains some member.

You may wonder, then, why I should be allowed to ignore (12). Well, that all strict conditionals with impossible antecedents are true is an artifact of their semantics. A strict conditional is true just if there is no possible world in which its antecedent is true and its consequent false. An impossible antecedent is true in no possible world, and so every strict conditional whose antecedent is impossible is such that in no possible world is its antecedent true and its consequent false. Some strict conditionals are true only because their antecedent is impossible. But again, truths can be true not just for general semantic reasons but because of how certain other facts are. These are the impossible-antecedent conditionals to use in philosophical argument.[13]

---

[12] See, for example, John Heil, *The Nature of True Minds* (Cambridge: Cambridge University Press, 1992), p. 64.

[13] Much the same point applies, of course, to counterpossibles, and one could run the argument at least as well with counterpossible analogues of (3), (5), and (8)—I have argued with strict conditionals simply to eliminate a few pages' worth of technicalities on how counterpossibles and strict conditionals interact. Arguing *via* counterpossibles would not change matters on their standard treatment: for on this, all are true, just as all strict conditionals with impossible antecedents are, and the key issue, again, is just which ones we have a right to ignore. Even adopting a non-standard treatment of counterpossibles would not affect the argument. Suppose first that all counterpossibles are false or truth-valueless. (8) could still follow from the premises, since these include counterpossibles, false premises can entail false conclusions, and on a suitable account of entailment premises some of which lack truth-values can entail truth-valueless conclusions. One could not hold it against a deity theory that it implies false/truth-valueless conclusions in conjunction with such premises, or indeed that some non-true claims are 'the right thing to say' despite their non-truth if the theory is true. (Any other theory will also have non-true 'right things to say' associated with it.) But such implications could still be reasons to reject theories due to the conclusions' implausibility or failing to reflect the facts—which is to say, that my overall argument would work as well. If on the best semantics all counterpossibles are non-true, I can just say that the semantics and the particular facts about God and (WATER) overdetermine the non-truth of (8)'s counterpossible analogue. My argument, then, would begin from a non-true premise a theory leads us to endorse ((3)'s counterpossible analogue) and take us to a non-true conclusion we would prefer not to endorse. Finally, if counterpossibles

(3) reflects how truthmaking works. For (WATER) to be untrue given Yahweh with deity, deity as above and a deity theory, a (WATER)-truthmaker would have to fail to make (WATER) true, which violates the whole notion of truthmaking. The hypothesis that (WATER) is untrue does not inherently involve this oddity. So (12) involves a gratuitous additional impossibility that violates the notion of truthmaking. That is, (3), not (12), best reflects how things actually are.

A Way Around the Argument: Junk DNA

However, if deity is disjunctive, a reason to favor (12) over (3) beckons. Junk DNA is that of an organism's DNA which has no biological function. One could suppose that deity contains something *like* junk DNA: that it has disjuncts which possibly have a function, providing an MDN for God in at least one possible world, but also disjuncts with no possible function, which would be His MDN in impossible circumstances. A deity theorist could suggest that if deity contains junk DNA, whether (WATER) is true is a matter of which disjunct of deity is God's MDN: deity is disjunctive, according to some disjuncts (WATER) is not true, and there is nothing on the scene prior to God (in any sense) to settle whether (WATER) is true before the disjuncts weigh in. If deity contained the right junk DNA, then were (WATER) untrue, deity would be just as it actually is, but an appropriate junk disjunct would be God's MDN, and God's having this MDN would truthmake *(WATER) is untrue.* So it seems that if deity contains appropriate junk DNA, (12) rather than (3) reflects the facts: the reasoning about truthmaking no longer favors (3), because God's having His MDN, not His having deity, is the relevant truthmaker. So a deity theorist might consider blocking my argument by positing divine junk DNA and so rejecting (3)—not as false, but as less reflective of the facts.

But junk DNA is not actually compatible with a deity theory. The presence of a truthmaker for P determines whether P or instead $\neg P$ is true. On the simplest deity theory, God's having deity is the first available truthmaker for (WATER). There are no Platonic entities to compete for this role, and any other truthmakers are divine states presupposing that God has deity, items God creates or their being in certain states. So on the simplest deity theory, God's having deity determines whether (WATER) is true. But if deity contains junk DNA, it cannot. If deity contains junk DNA, whether (WATER) is true is a matter of which disjunct of deity is God's MDN. So if deity contains junk DNA, God's having deity determines whether (WATER) is true only if it

are not all true or all non-true, they can differ in truth-value. Then my subsequent argument would amount to a case for calling the counterpossible analogues of (3) and (8) false, and so rejecting deity theories for committing us to them.

determines which of deity's disjuncts is God's MDN. But if deity contains junk DNA, God's having deity cannot determine this: God's having the disjunction cannot determine which disjunct is His MDN.

Consider, to begin, possible worlds. If God's having deity determined God's MDN, it would (putting it crudely) trim deity of all *possible* disjuncts save one. God actually has deity, and we are taking this to determine His actual MDN. In every possible world, God would have deity, deity would be just as it is, and so God's having deity would determine that God had the MDN He actually has. So there would be just one MDN in deity for all possible worlds. There would be no determining of MDN to do in possible worlds, unless God's having deity determined that He has His possible MDN rather than any impossible MDN and so determined that some possible rather than any impossible world is actual. But now let us consider impossible worlds. (Junk DNA is there just to be God's MDN in impossible circumstances. In whatever sense there 'are' impossible circumstances, there are world-sized (and even larger) impossible circumstances: one impossible circumstance is that an entire impossible world be actual. So if we deal in junk DNA, we cannot jib at talk of impossible worlds.) In any impossible world in which God's having deity achieves just what it does actually, God would have His possible-world MDN. But in some impossible worlds, God has deity, deity is just as it actually is, this is sufficient to determine God to have His actual MDN, yet deity does not manage to determine this. (After all, this is impossible, and nothing justifies not positing impossible worlds for it once we've begun to traffic in impossible worlds.) In this sort of impossible world, God's having deity does not determine God's MDN.

If there are impossible worlds in which God's having deity does not determine God's MDN though deity is as it actually is, we must ask what determines whether we have the possible (and 'normal' impossible-world) or the odd-impossible case.[14] If it is God's having deity, we lose deity's odd-impossible disjuncts: God's having deity itself determines that no disjunct is needed to cover this odd sort of impossible world, since it determines Him to have a possible-world MDN, and the junk-DNA view posits only disjuncts that 'cover' at least one impossible world. And as we have already seen, if God's having deity determines God's MDN, there is just one possible-world disjunct. So if God's having deity determines whether we have the possible/normal-impossible case, deity turns out non-disjunctive, unless it includes disjuncts that do not even provide an MDN in the odd-impossible case: but a disjunct that does not even *impossibly* have a function would be too junky to have any reason to posit. If deity is not disjunctive, it does not include junk DNA. On the other hand, if it is not God's having deity that determines whether we

---

[14] One might reply, 'this does not need determining—it is just a necessary truth that some possible state of affairs, not any impossible one, is actual.' But this necessity must itself be grounded in God, on a theist view, and deity on a deity view.

have the possible/normal-impossible case, then after all, God's having deity does not determine God's MDN. And so either deity turns out not to include junk DNA or God's having deity does not determine God's MDN and so does not determine whether (WATER) is true. If God's having deity does not determine this, we've left the simplest deity theory, and so arguably left all deity theories. So the junk DNA proposal is not compatible with the simplest deity theory—such a theory could not add junk DNA to block (3)—and if every deity theory contains the simplest is compatible with no deity theory.

Now, some might reply 'so much the worse for the simplest deity theory, or any deity theory, but grounding (WATER)'s truth or untruth on God's MDN still counts as a divine-nature theory, since an MDN is a sort of divine nature. So if there is some acceptable way to account for God's having His MDN, the junk DNA proposal can still count as an acceptable divine-nature theory.' But this just brings us to the last reason junk DNA will not do. Either God accounts for His having His MDN or nothing at all does so: from all eternity, God is the only available candidate. There is an unacceptable consequence either way.

I have been supposing that (WATER) is untrue because the property *being* H_2O and (WATER) itself are just not there in logical space—not so much as impossible. If whether (WATER) comes out true depends on which disjunct of deity is God's MDN, the nature of water is in deity, though not in every disjunct of deity. If it is in deity, it is in logical space that *being water = being* H_2O. If *being* H_2O is there in logical space, it is up to whatever accounts for God's having His MDN whether (WATER) is true if only if it is up to this whether if *being water = being* H_2O, being a body every molecule of which is a water molecule = being a body every molecule of which is an H_2O molecule —control of which would seem to require control over some substitution principle—or what the property *being* H_2O is identical with: that is, whether being H_2O = being H_2O or instead being H_2O = being triangular.

The claim that God has control over logic is unacceptable Cartesianism. But *being* H_2O = *being triangular* renders false what we would have thought was a thesis of logic. For if *being* H_2O = *being triangular*, every property of *being triangular* is a property of *being* H_2O. One property of *being triangular* is non-identity with *being* H_2O; others imply non-identity with *being* H_2O, e.g. being a geometrical property or being a shape-property. A world in which *being triangular* lacked all such properties would be impossible not because of the identity of *being* H_2O and *being triangular* but because it would be a world simply without *being triangular*. Thus in a world in which this property exists and is nonetheless identical with *being* H_2O, *being* H_2O has at least one property implying non-identity with *being* H_2O. So even if *being* H_2O = *being* H_2O, in this world it is also the case that *being* H_2O ≠ *being* H_2O and so presumably that ¬(*being* H_2O = *being* H_2O). If this does *not* follow, then still it is presumably a logical truth that $(F)\neg(F \neq F)$, and so one way or another we have an instance falsifying an apparent logical truth.

On the junk-DNA proposal, then, if it is up to God what His MDN is, it is up to God whether what are in fact truths of logic turn out false. This goes beyond accounts of modal truth about creatures alone—our stated purview— since logic is not about creatures alone. It is wild Cartesianism. To me there nothing is to be said for such a view. If the only way to have a theist theory were to hold that it is up to God whether some instance of $(F \neq F)$ is true, we would have to conclude that theist theories were not finally even coherent, since they require positing as an alternative open to God a scenario which is not. But a theist modal theory can consistently and with good motivation draw up short of this. Deity theories always have. On the other hand, suppose that nothing at all determines what God's MDN is. There were in some sense open alternatives for it to be otherwise: if it was in no sense open for some other disjunct of deity to be God's MDN, the other disjuncts would not be His MDN even in impossible circumstances, and so would again be too junky to believe in.[15] And what God's MDN is determines whether a *de facto* logical truth is in fact true. Where there are no alternatives to an outcome, even if the outcome has no cause, it does not seem right to call it a matter of chance. But where there are alternatives and there is no cause for what eventuates, it does. So on this view, it is up to chance whether what is in fact a logical truth turns out true. That does not seem right either. It is constitutive of the identity relation to be reflexive. Nothing that was not reflexive could be that relation. So if there is such a property as *being H_2O*, what that relation is dictates that *being H_2O* = *being H_2O*. That $((P \cdot (Q \supset \neg P)) \supset \neg Q)$ is a logical truth, or at least a logical non-falsehood. It is constitutive of conjunction, negation, and material implication so to interact that this comes out logically true (non-false). Again, it seems constitutive of negation that if $\neg Q$ is true, Q is false. It does not seem in any sense a matter of chance that these things are so—how could it be up to chance what is constitutive of identity?—or that there *are* such things as identity, conjunction, etc. But all this dictates the falsity of *being H_2O* = *being triangular*. If non-chance facts dictate a conclusion, the conclusion is not so by chance either.

Finally, let us just compare the 'chance MDN' theory with a rival. On the 'chance MDN' view, it is not up to God what disjuncts deity contains, nor which disjunct winds up His MDN. These jointly determine the modal truth. So God has no power over the content of modal truth. The view I shortly offer does not involve disjunctive deity, but does involve God producing a range of alternative candidates for the body of modal truth. On my view, God then selects among these. This gives Him real power over the content of

---

[15] I leave as homework for the reader what 'open' might mean here. I am just sketching a view I do not accept. If you cannot make sense of 'open' here and are not willing to play along, that will simply be another reason to reject the view—which is fine with me.

modal truth—and yet, as I show, the view yields an S5 modal metaphysics and avoids Cartesianism. This latter simply has to be a more attractive view for theists, particularly those inclined to perfect-being reasoning: it gives us a God with more power over the content of reality, at no intuitive cost (or so I argue).

(4) is patent: if it is the case that necessarily, if deity exists, it contains an attribute from set S, then if deity does not contain an attribute from S, deity does not exist. So then is (5). My argument for (6) and (7) invokes the lemma the last chapter argued. Nothing can exist without one of its essential properties. So if (DE) is true, (6) and (7) are true. I now consider a form of objection to (6) and (7).

Counterparts and (6)

(6) might look less than obvious to a counterpart theorist. A counterpart theorist might reason this way, again letting 'Δ' and 'Yahweh' denote the actual players of the deity and God roles:

In counterpart metaphysics, (6) becomes

6a. Nothing has Δ → Yahweh does not exist and has no counterpart under any appropriate counterpart relation.

Consider a property Δ* just slightly different in content from Δ. Suppose that in another world, Δ* plays the deity-role and some being has Δ*. An item's counterpart in another world is the being in that world most like it under the counterpart relation in question. The being with Δ* could be just like Yahweh in every respect save those following from the slight content-difference between Δ* and Δ, and there might be no other being in this world with any divine attribute. If this is so, surely the being with Δ* is Yahweh's counterpart. If it is, this world represents a possibility for Yahweh, not some other being. So Yahweh could have existed but not had Δ, provided that such alternate properties are available. So (6) is false, because (6a) is.

The short answer to this is that it is just bad counterpart theory. In the scenario, Δ* is Δ's counterpart. The claim that it plays the deity role asserts this, and many theories of attributes allow it: if attributes are token concepts, token predicates or tropes, single-world classes or sums of particulars or tropes, single-world universals,[16] or parsed in terms of resemblances among

---

[16] Lewis suggests that if properties are universals, then as there is qualitative duplication between worlds, universals occur in many worlds (*Plurality*, pp. 204–5). This argument succeeds only if single-world universals could not explain such duplication. But my duplicate in another world might be just like me because he has properties just like mine, where this latter resemblance is primitive, as it is among duplicate tropes. Appealing to primitive resemblance at this point might undercut the argument for universals from their ability to explain resemblance, but would not undercut all motivations for universals, since these serve many other purposes. Trans-world universals would provide a point of overlap between Lewisian possible

any of these, they have counterparts. If Δ has a counterpart, the counterpart-theoretic rendering of (6) is not (6a) but

6b. Nothing has Δ or a Δ-counterpart under any appropriate counterpart relation $\rightarrow$ Yahweh does not exist and has no counterpart under any relevant counterpart relation.

(6b) is true, and so gives us no reason to think (6) is false.

So we can dismiss the counterpart sally. Still, it is just one version of a more general and perhaps less easily dismissed move.

Understudies

Suppose that in addition to the actual divine nature, Δ, there is or might be another property which in other worlds serves as the divine nature—an understudy, which takes up the role when Δ is indisposed. If a deity theory let Δ have understudies, it could hold that God's existence requires only that He have some divine nature, not Δ. We can make sense of the idea of a role of being a certain attribute, and the idea that more than one item might play it, without recourse to counterpart theory. Any sort of thing just mentioned as an other-worldly counterpart for Δ could also serve as an understudy. On one sort of class nominalism, for instance, for any attribute F and world W, F-hood in W is the class of W's Fs.[17] On this, different classes play the F-hood role in different worlds. We understand this claim; it is part of the theory, but this does not seem an objection to the theory. On this sort of nominalism, a cat may have a different cathood in different worlds, yet still be itself and a cat, because its being a cat implies only that some class plays the role of its nature. Again, Leibniz thought that God had before making Socrates a concept of him which included every attribute Socrates ever would have—this being, expressing, or determining Socrates' nature—and also seems to have held that had God instanced a concept whose content differed even with respect to a single accidental property, the result would have been not Socrates but someone else.[18] Thus Leibniz held that our Socrates had just one possible nature. Now it is not implausible that God has such concepts, nor even that they might be, express, or determine an individual's nature. But it is rather more plausible that had God chosen to instance a concept differing in one accident, the result would have been a slightly different version of our very

worlds, albeit not in a concrete world-part. So they sit at best uneasily with Lewis' other views. So it could be that on balance, Lewisian counterpart theorists who are realists should believe in counterparts of universals.

[17] So Quinton, 'Properties and Classes', *Proceedings of the Aristotelian Society* 58 (1957–58), 33–58.

[18] For texts and discussion see J. A. Cover and John O'Leary-Hawthorne, *Substance and Individuation in Leibniz* (New York: Cambridge University Press, 1999), 87–131.

Socrates—same Socrates, different nature.[19] We could see this in terms of a disjunctive Socrateity and MDNs distinguished by contingent properties: perhaps there are distinct sufficient conditions for being Socrates, and Socrates' MDN in a world is whichever of them is satisfied there. I do not endorse this view. My claim is only that it has at least some appeal. If it does, so too should the idea that some natures have understudies: for on this view, the MDNs do.

Once understudies come into view, we must ask whether Δ has or might have an understudy according to which some modal truth's truth-value is not what it actually is. Perhaps it is only contingently possible that there are quarks, and had an understudy been the divine nature, *there are quarks* would have been impossible. Or perhaps had an understudy been the divine nature, there would have been no such property as *being H_2O* (other divine natures involving such a property would also have been deleted from logical space, then) and so (WATER) would not have existed. If there were or could be such an understudy, 'deity' in (3)–(8) would at best be ambiguous, between different players of the deity role. This would suggest two courses of action. In one, we disambiguate to, for example,

3**. (WATER) is untrue → either nothing has Δ or Δ does not contain some member of a set of attributes such that it necessarily contains a member of that set,

(3**) yields not (5) but

5**. (WATER) is untrue → nothing has Δ or Δ does not exist.

To get to (8), the argument would need

6c. Nothing has Δ→ Yahweh does not exist,

and

7a. Δ does not exist→ Yahweh does not exist.

But given understudies, these claims are just false. If Δ did not exist, Yahweh could exist but have an understudy. And in fact, with understudies in the picture, (DE) does not support (6c) and (7a): it is not an essential property to have Δ in particular, but at most to have it or an understudy. So on this alternative the argument fails. On the other approach, we replace (3) with

3***. (WATER) is untrue → either nothing has Δ or any of its understudies, or neither Δ nor any of its understudies contains some member of a set of attributes such that every player of the deity role necessarily contains a member of that set.

---

[19] There are complexities here about singular possibility and individuation which I cannot take up. My only claim is that *intuitively*, this is a tenable view.

Suppose that (WATER) *were* untrue. On the understudy hypothesis as now construed, it would not be the case that nothing had Δ or an understudy: something would have an understudy making (WATER) untrue. Nor would it be the case that neither Δ nor an understudy contains some member of a set of attributes such that every player of the role necessarily contains a member of that set. That set would include at least one attribute such that if someone had the understudy conferring it, (WATER) would be untrue. So if we took it to be possibly the case that (WATER) is untrue, we would call (3***) simply false. If we took (WATER)'s untruth to be impossible, deity theorists could still reject (3***) in favor of some other truth, for not best reflecting the facts. Thus the availability of appropriate understudies could block my argument. And it would make (1) seem questionable. If there could be understudies providing truthmakers for different modal truths than we actually have, then since God's existence would depend only on His having some deifying property, not on His having Δ, it would not be obvious that His existence depends on there being a truthmaker for any particular modal thesis about creatures.

However, even if some natures have understudies, it does not follow that all can, or that they can be of a sort to make the understudy move available.

Deity has no Understudies

Δ's understudies either would or would not co-exist with Δ. If they would not, either they would be Meinongian non-existent possibilia, or they would be Lewisian existent possibilia, and the claim that they and Δ do not co-exist would be true just if we restrict the existential quantifier to what exists in *my* world.[20] Non-existents are in general dubious, and theist modal theories make them otiose. A Lewisian understudy such that (WATER) has no truth-value or quarks are impossible would be part of a concrete existing impossible world. If there were such a world W, though, no Lewisian sense could be given to its being impossible. For Lewis, to be possible is just to be a (proper or improper) part of a world: worlds are as such possible. As we have seen, Lewis is willing to tolerate existent impossible individuals (cross-world fusions of world-bound items), but this is at best an oddity of his view, and existent impossible worlds would surely be an oddity too far. Again, no sense could be given in Lewisian terms to there being no such property as *being water* in a world other than one involving a restricted quantifier—there being no such property *there*. But this is not enough to bring it about that (WATER) has no truth-value, if the property exists in or across other worlds. And for Lewis, properties exist

---

[20] If we do not thus restrict the quantifier, an item in a different Lewisian world co-exists with me.

across worlds, and so their existence involves a quantifier not restricted to individual worlds' domains. With the quantifier unrestricted, there would be such a property as *being water*: the set would exist, though it would not exist *there*. Again, no sense could be given in Lewis' terms to quarks' being impossible in a world. In W, it would be the case that there is a world with quarks (our own)—what exists, with the quantifier taken unrestrictedly, does not vary world-to-world.

On actualism, the claim that everything is actual does not involve a restricted quantifier: all there is to existence, taken unrestrictedly, is what exists actually—that is, in my world. On actualism, if Δ's understudies would co-exist with Δ, the claim that Δ has understudies (henceforth the Understudy Thesis) is closely related to the junk-DNA view. If Δ has co-existing understudies, then if there are disjunctive attributes, there is also a disjunctive attribute whose disjuncts are Δ and its understudies, of which God has some disjunct in every world in which He has Δ or one of the understudies. So the Understudy Thesis is really a disjunctive account which insists that deity is always the MDN, not the disjunctive attribute. And to have a disjunct available to serve in impossible worlds, the disjunctive attribute would have to include junk DNA. Thus if there are disjunctive attributes and deity and its understudies co-exist, the Understudy Thesis is really the junk DNA proposal rephrased, and so should be rejected. If there are no disjunctive attributes, still analogues of arguments against the junk DNA proposal apply. And though I have questioned a parallel claim about acts and tasks, there is something to be said for the view that attributes just are things that can be exemplified. If they are, understudies that make (WATER) untrue are ruled out. For nothing in any possible world is such that (WATER) is untrue.

Given my argument that there cannot be a deity distinct from Yahweh, another argument against the Understudy Thesis opens up, based on what an understudy would turn out to be on various theories of attributes.

Concept Nominalism

On concept nominalism, attributes are just concepts.[21] Concept nominalism tells us that to be divine is just to fall under the concept *deity*. If this is true, God made Himself divine by thinking up *deity* to fall under, or by so classing himself correctly. But surely His being divine is not His falling under the concept *deity*, but that about Him in virtue of which He falls under it. Nor is His being divine His being correctly thought of as divine; rather, what constitutes Him divine is that about Him in virtue of which the thought of Him as divine is correct. Deity is God's kind. Being of this kind makes Him

---

[21] Predicate nominalism is in all relevant respects parallel and so does not require separate discussion.

omnipotent; omnipotence is one of the properties He has in virtue of being divine. Surely God did not make Himself omnipotent by coming up with a concept. I take it, then, that concept nominalism just does not apply to deity.

Armstrong dubbed a related view 'ostrich nominalism'.[22] The ostrich shares concept nominalism's ontology and denial that anything need make Ks Ks (they just are Ks, primitively). But the ostrich does not offer a theory of attributes. Rather, the ostrich says we need only worry about what makes predications true; according to Devitt, this account need only speak of reference and satisfaction.[23] This last, though, confuses truth-conditions with truthmakers: as an account of truthmaking ontology, ostrich nominalism holds that only concrete particulars are needed. On ostrich nominalism, where 'K' is an intrinsic predicate, each K itself is that in virtue of which 'K' applies.[24] There is no Khood in an ostrich ontology, but if we use 'Khood' to express a functional role, of being that in virtue of which 'K' applies, the ostrich will say that the K itself plays the Khood role. So God plays the Δ-role, on this account, and so what plays the Δ-role has understudies only if God does—that is, only if someone else could be God. But no-one else could. So ostrich nominalism does not provide a co-existing or a possible Δ-understudy. Nor are there Lewisian impossible deities, and a theist modal theory has no truck with Meinongian impossibilia.

The Other Nominalisms

On one class nominalism, attributes are classes of their actual, existing instances. So Δ is the singleton {Yahweh} and on this view, Δ has an actual understudy iff Yahweh co-exists with someone else who could be divine: if A could be divine, {A} could be deity. But no-one else could have been God. So on actualist class nominalism, Δ has an understudy only if it co-exists with a class which does not contain Yahweh alone, but could. Classes, though, have their membership essentially.[25] No class could have other members than it actually has. So on actualist class nominalism, Δ has no understudy. On Lewis' or Meinongian class nominalism, attributes are classes of their actual and possible instances.[26] But if no other individual could be divine, deity still remains Yahweh's singleton or a class containing only Yahweh and His appropriate counterparts, with no understudy in any possible world. On

[22] D. M. Armstrong, *Nominalism and Realism* (Cambridge: Cambridge University Press, 1978), p. 16.

[23] Michael Devitt, '"Ostrich Nominalism" or "Mirage Realism"?', *Pacific Philosophical Quarterly* 61 (1980), 436.

[24] As noted earlier, Descartes held a version of this: see his letter to an unknown correspondent, 1641 or 1642, in Anthony Kenny (ed. and tr.), *Descartes' Philosophical Letters* (New York: Oxford University Press, 1970), pp. 187–8.'

[25] Van Cleve, *op. cit.*

[26] Lewis, *Plurality,* pp. 50–69.

mereological nominalism: given that there are no other possible deities, Δ is just Yahweh, or a sum of Yahweh and the right counterparts: again, no under-studies.

On resemblance nominalism, there is no such entity as the divine nature: being divine is just resembling either all deities or a paradigm deity to the right degree. On resemblance nominalism, the Understudy Thesis could take two forms. One is that there actually is or at least could have been some other degree to which (or perhaps way?) God could have resembled Himself. But God could not have failed to resemble Himself to the maximal degree, or to do so in virtue of being identical with Himself. The other is that there is or could be someone else resemblance to whom could have constituted being divine—someone else who could have been paradigmatically divine. I have ruled this out.[27] So on resemblance nominalism, there are no understudies for deity in any possible world.

Trope Theories

Tropes are 'thin' particulars. There is nothing to Fido's doghood but its being a case of doghood, or perhaps also its belonging to Fido. So a non-deity trope could not have been a deity trope. There is nothing 'in' (say) a doghood trope to make it identical with a deity trope in another possible world. (Fido is not possibly divine, so its belonging to Fido is not a candidate.) While we may let some cross-world identities be brute, we wouldn't let this one: we would demand an explanation. And we could not appeal to a common role different entities play in different worlds. Tropes have intensional content, or just are reified intensional contents. The role of a doghood trope is to have doggy intensional content and so 'make' something containing it a dog. So tropes have their characters essentially: a trope of doghood could not have been a deity trope.[28] So an understudy for Δ that could block the case for (3) would have to be a deity trope differing in content from Δ enough to make (WATER) untrue.

We do not meet cases of properties that are not *something's* case of the property: if we meet a case of doghood, it belongs to a dog. So trope theories tend not to allow 'free-floating' or ownerless tropes. If there are none, an understudy for Δ would have to belong to someone other than Yahweh, who would then be divine but such that (WATER) is untrue. Again, there cannot be someone divine but distinct from Yahweh, and no-one in any possible world is such that (WATER) is untrue. So if trope theory is true and tropes

---

[27] And so matters would not differ even if we held with Rodriguez-Pereyra that to be F is to resemble all possible Fs (Gonzalo Rodriguez-Pereyra, *Resemblance Nominalism* (Oxford: Oxford University Press, 2002), pp. 99–101).

[28] Trope theories divide over whether tropes can swap owners—that is, whether A's trope of doghood could pass to B. So on some trope views, the ownership-relation of a trope, if there is one, is not essential. But this does not matter for my argument.

cannot float free, in no possible world is there an understudy for Δ which makes (WATER) untrue.

Suppose on the other hand that we let tropes float free. With no bearer, a deity trope does not carry with it a competitor for Yahweh. And a free-floating trope which would make (WATER) untrue could share a possible world with a deity-trope that would make (WATER) true: this would not generate a contradiction. Consider a free-floating trope of baldness. It is a baldness, a being-bald, not a bald thing. If nothing has it, and it is the only one, then it is not the case that anything is bald. Similarly, a free-floating trope of being *inter alia* such that (WATER) is untrue is a being-such, not a thing such that. If nothing has it, nothing is such that (WATER) is untrue. And if nothing is such that (WATER) is untrue, it is not the case that (WATER) is untrue, and so no contradiction of (WATER)'s having a truth-value ensues. Still, if we let tropes float free, this gives an ontological priority to tropes of essential properties: the trope can exist without a bearer, but not the bearer without some trope. The priority is there anyway, on trope views—they claim it as an advantage that one can 'construct' ordinary particulars out of groups of tropes[29]—but it is particularly vivid if the tropes need not be grouped to exist. So even if we let tropes float in general, we could not let deity-tropes float, else we would be creating a class of entities such that God requires one of them to exist, but these do not require God to exist—'constructing' God from entities more ultimate in reality than He. Ultimacy considerations rule this out.[30] So free-floating-trope theories cannot apply to deity.

Realism

Aristotelian realism is no more congenial to the Understudy Thesis. Universals are as 'thin' as tropes, or perhaps thinner: universals have nothing 'in' them about which particulars have them. Like tropes, they have (or are) intensional contents: cathood, say, somehow encodes what it is to be a cat. So as with trope theory, it seems implausible that a property which is not deity in one world could be deity in another. There is a looser sense in which one property can 'be' another—one property can realize another—but I ruled out realizer-versions of an understudy view above. Now if properties exist in a world only if instanced in that world, there is an understudy for Δ in a world only if someone in that world has this understudy property. But then again, in

---

[29] So, e.g., Keith Campbell, *Abstract Particulars* (Oxford: Basil Blackwell, 1990), and John Bacon, *Universals and Property Instances* (Oxford: Basil Blackwell, 1995).

[30] The medieval doctrine of divine simplicity was largely motivated by repugnance to this sort of construction (see, for example, Aquinas, *Summa Contra Gentiles* (Turin: Marietti, 1909), I, 18). Morris and Menzel would redress the balance by having God create the deity-tropes ('Absolute Creation', reprinted in Thomas Morris, *Anselmian Explorations* (Notre Dame, IN: University of Notre Dame Press, 1987), pp. 161–78), but this courts the problems I discuss in 'God and Abstract Entities', *Faith and Philosophy* 7 (1990), 193–217.

no possible world has Δ an understudy which makes (WATER) untrue. Nor is there any other sort of actual Δ-understudy: nothing which failed to make its bearer divine could be one, and there are not two Gods. Nor has Δ an understudy in another world borne there by a deity other than Yahweh. Δ has an understudy in a possible world only if Yahweh Himself possibly bears this understudy. If He did, in every world He would have a disjunctive nature and an MDN—which we have seen will not do—or arguments like those against this view would apply.

Platonist Realism

Platonism, I now argue, is just an unacceptable account of deity. The standard way to explicate Platonism about attributes is to say that Platonic attributes exist whether or not exemplified. If God exists contingently, Platonism gives deity ontological priority over Him: it can exist without Him but not *vice versa*, and He depends on it, not *vice versa*. If God exists necessarily, deity does too. If both exist necessarily, the standard explication cannot mean that there are possible worlds in which God does not exist but deity does. Rather, it must mean that deity is intrinsically indifferent to exemplification: it does not draw its being or content from the God who has it, and even if God did not exist, it would exist and be as it is—this last being a conditional true both for purely semantic reasons and because of the nature of deity.

Whether God is necessary or contingent, then, if deity is Platonic, its existing and being as it is are explanatorily prior to God's having it. For its content does not derive from God but characterizes God: God is divine because He has deity, and so His characteristics include just what the property contributes. On realism, a property K has a K-making role: a property is an entity the right relation to which is constitutive of being K. The property contributes K-hood to the K; it makes the K what it is. Thus deity's being as it is explains God's being as He is—God is omnipotent, perhaps, because deity entails or contains omnipotence. God's being as He is does not explain deity's being as it is, for as we've seen, if deity is Platonic, it does not draw its being or content from the God who has it. Thus on Platonism as on a free-floating trope theory, God depends on essential attributes more ultimate than He. But there is more: let's now ask which truths deity makes true explanatorily prior to God's actual existence if deity is Platonic. One, surely, is that possibly God exists: this is made true by deity's being exemplifiable. Suppose too that if God exists, He exists necessarily. If this is true, it is true due to His nature. Powerful intuitions also favor the claim that the true modal logic includes Brouwer. On a deity theory, truths of modal logic have truthmakers in deity. And so if the true modal logic includes Brouwer, on a deity theory, deity makes this so.

So on a deity theory and the assumptions noted, deity's existing and being as it is make true the premises of a standard modal ontological argument:

◇(God exists).

□(God exists ⊃ □(God exists)).

◇□(God exists)⊃ God exists (instance of Brouwer axiom).

From the first two follows by modal rule that ◇□(God exists), which with the third yields that God exists. Because deity's existence is explanatorily prior to God's, these premises are true explanatorily prior to God's existence. They entail it. And the existence of their truthmaker(s) seem(s) to explain the conclusion. That is, it seems that on these assumptions, God exists because deity exists (independent of Him) and contains what it does. It does not cause Him to exist. But it explains His existence non-causally: God's existence supervenes on deity's.[31] Now on a deity theory, deity encodes the entire Platonic realm: deity *is* the entire Platonic realm, collapsed into one entity. So on this account, God's existence supervenes on that of the entire Platonic realm. First it is there and is as it is, and 'then' God exists because of this. On this picture, then, God derives His existence from deity/the Platonic realm and not *vice-versa*. So deity/the Platonic realm, not God, is the ultimate reality.[32] Ultimacy considerations, then, rule Platonism out as a theory of deity, particularly but not only if God exists necessarily. One could opt for Platonism and a deity theory by denying a premise above, of course, but theist philosophers tend to favor both divine necessity and Brouwer, and in fact tend to think modal ontological arguments sound, and this would in any case leave the problem of dependence intact. Finally, given Platonism, understudies could threaten monotheism. Their natures would make it possible that they have bearers. We already have a truthmaker for Brouwer in God's having Δ. If the understudy attribute would also make its bearer a necessary being, then, we would have two deities.

I submit, then, that on no theory of attributes considered does the Understudy Thesis provide a viable objection to my argument.

---

[31] This is one entity's existence supervening on another's. We do not usually think of supervenience calling things into existence, but consider a case of property supervenience on a trope theory: because this event is a neuron's firing with a particular functional role, it is a thought of the word 'dog'. Even if tropes can exist elsewhere and then transfer to new owners, that does not happen here: nothing in this mind, we can suppose, was just previously a thought of 'dog'. So this trope appears (as it were) *ex nihilo*. So if properties are tropes and this is a case of supervenience, in it one entity's existence supervenes on another's.

[32] Rationalists have sometimes said that God's nature accounts for His existence (see Benedict Spinoza, *Ethics*, tr. E. Curley, in *The Collected Works of Spinoza*, tr. E. Curley (Princeton, NJ: Princeton University Press, 1985), pp. 408, 409, 415; G. W. Leibniz, 'On the Ultimate Origination of the Universe', in *Leibniz: Monadology and Other Philosophical Essays*, tr. Paul and Anne Schrecker (Indianapolis, IN: Bobbs-Merrill, 1965), p. 85; Samuel Clarke, *A Demonstration of the Being and Attributes of God* (London: John and Paul Knapton, 1738), pp. 15, 17, quoted in William Rowe, *The Cosmological Argument* (Princeton, NJ: Princeton University Press, 1975), pp. 182–3). But none of these writers were also Platonists, and so none actually embraced this consequence. For them, rather, it was the case that God explained His own existence by way of His nature: thus Clarke called God 'self-existent' as a way to express His necessity, while Spinoza, in the *Ethics'* first definition, spoke of a necessary being as 'cause of itself'. I do not say that there is a coherent thought here in the end. I say only that given writers' views, they would likely not have thought the conjunction of their claims with Platonism acceptable.

And now to (1)

(6) and (7) are true. Thus a deity theory is committed to (8). The argument shows that on a deity theory (8) is not just an artifact of the semantics of conditionals. It also derives from the basic deity-theoretic claim that God's having a deity which is as it is makes (WATER) true, *via* premises which at no point trade on the oddity that having an impossible antecedent makes any conditional true. Thus (8) shows us that on a deity theory, (WATER)'s being true is a substantive necessary condition of God's existing. Further, the argument could have run just as plausibly *via* counterfactual conditionals to a substantively as well as trivially true counterfactual conclusion, and (8) is at any rate strong, substantive reason to infer a corresponding counterfactual.[33] So a deity theory generates at least two conditionals expressing that God's existence substantively depends on there being a truthmaker for (WATER), and if this is so, (1) is true.

Now there are ways to downplay (1)'s dependence. Some deity theorists—such as Aquinas—hold that God = deity and deity has no constituents.[34] On these assumptions, there is no worry here: God's depending on there being a truthmaker for (WATER) is just deity's existence depending on deity's existence, which is trivial, not substantive. But the simple-property claim is in tension with a deity theory: it is hard to see how a property without internal complexity could contain all the content deity theories say deity does.[35] Yet without the simple-property claim, if God = deity, uncomfortable ultimacy questions arise about the dependence of God (= deity) on His (deity's) constituents.

If God ≠ deity, and there is such a thing as deity, what it is might affect our view of the dependence in (1). I have argued that deity is neither a Platonic entity nor a concept. It cannot (I think) be a class, on a deity theory: a class lacks the sort of intensional content to be part of making true all necessary truths about creatures. If deity is a trope or an Aristotelian universal it may derive its being from what has it—that is, exist not just only if exemplified but because exemplified. If it does, (1)'s dependence (one might suggest) is trivial

---

[33] Certainly for any *possible* P, $(P \rightarrow Q) \rightarrow (P > Q)$. On the standard approach to counterfactuals this should also be true for impossible antecedents. If no possible world is a $(P \cdot \neg Q)$-world, no possible world is a $(P \cdot \neg Q)$-world closer to actuality than any $(P \cdot Q)$-world. This is so even if (as it is impossible that P) we also have that $(P \rightarrow \neg Q) \rightarrow (P > \neg Q)$. For even so, no $(P \cdot \neg Q)$-possible world is closer to actuality than any $(P \cdot Q)$-possible world, and if we speak fictionally in terms of impossible worlds, it is a very reasonable thought that the impossible world closest to actuality is one in which all propositions are true (and false). For failures of logic surely have to weigh extremely heavily in judging impossible worlds' closeness to actuality, and if logic continues to 'work' in an impossible world, any impossibility strictly implies a contradiction, and thence implies everything.

[34] For the first claim, *ST* Ia 3, 3. For the second, note that God, who is identical with deity, is Himself said to be entirely simple (*ST* Ia 3, 7).

[35] I criticized what is in effect one of Aquinas' main ways to suggest that it does in Chapter 6. I reject his other ways to try to make this claim out in 'Aquinas on God and Modal Truth', *The Modern Schoolman* 82 (2005), 171–200.

and merely counterfactual. And on my own argument, if God ≠ deity, deity must be one of these. But as we see below, even counterfactual dependence is enough to cause trouble. Further, if deity does derive its being from God, all that means is that there is real mutual dependence between deity and God: God supports deity in existence, as bearers do attributes, and it enables Him to do so, as the nature which constitutes Him in existence. Chapter 2 argued that to explain God's existence, this story requires another player, 'spiritual matter,' but if we do not try to explain God's existence in that way, we simply have two real eternal dependencies of different sorts. The sorts' difference may keep the scenario from entailing some kind of objectionable self-dependence. If this is right, God's dependence on there being a (WATER)-truthmaker remains real and substantive even on derived-being deity theories, for it is founded on His real dependence on deity and its real inclusion of a (WATER)-truthmaker. If the sorts' difference does not block objectionable self-dependence, it cannot be both that God depends on deity for His existence and deity depends on God for its. As the first is obvious, we must then reject the second: if it exists and is not identical with God, deity must be Platonic, or an Aristotelian attribute which is somehow indifferent to exemplification. I have already argued against Platonism. On the variant Aristotelian view—if it really is coherent—there remains a substantive dependence on deity and so on there being a (WATER)-truthmaker. Finally, on resemblance nominalism there is no such thing as deity. Talk of a divine nature is just a way to talk about what is true of God just *qua* divine, i.e. (I suppose) just in virtue of satisfying '— is divine.' So a deity theory becomes a claim that (*inter alia*) just because God is divine, (WATER) is true, and so God is divine → (WATER) is true. For reasons below, this conditional is objectionable.

I turn now to a case for my main argument's (2).

A Case for (2)

If (WATER) is necessary, (8)'s antecedent is impossible. So (8) is true—but it does not seem that it ought to be. There is a number of reasons for this. One is the intuitive irrelevance of (8)'s antecedent to its consequent: (WATER)'s truth-value seems to have nothing to do with whether God exists. Where a conditional's antecedent is intuitively not relevant to its consequent, as in

were Louis XV King of France, watched pots would seldom boil,

we incline to reject the conditional. We override this inclination only for general semantic reasons (which are irrelevant here, since my argument concedes that there are such in this case) or if given some reason to see antecedent and consequent as connected—for example, some background theory which makes the antecedent relevant to the consequent. Now one might reply that a deity theory makes the one relevant to the other. But this will not do. Deity theories do not make (WATER) *appear* relevant to God's existence, and lack the claim on our acceptance which (say) a well-confirmed background scientific theory has. On a deity theory, (8) is a substantive truth reflecting the content of the divine nature. Deity theories have the intuitively false consequence that in (8), antecedent is relevant to the truth of consequent. As the consequence *is* intuitively false, it really counts against them. Further, a divine-nature theory commits us to the intuitively false claim that (WATER) and (8) reflect the content of deity. All these are equally problems for the counterpossible

8*. (WATER) is untrue > God does not exist,

even if it asserts a mere counterfactual dependence, as it would for Aquinas, as long as the story behind that counterfactual dependence is deity-theoretic.

Again, recall (5): on deity theories, if (WATER) is untrue, nothing has deity or deity does not exist. If nothing has deity, either deity is an unexemplified Platonic universal or deity does not exist. I have argued that deity cannot be Platonic. Further, the ultimacy considerations that motivate deity theories rule against Platonic entities. So it seems to me that on deity theories, if (WATER) is untrue, deity does not exist. Deleting deity deletes all that deity contains. So on deity theories, if (WATER) is untrue, some truthmaker of every necessary truth does not exist. Further, there is nothing special about (WATER)'s being untrue: on a deity theory, any necessary falsehood substantively commits us to deity's non-existence. Now if some truthmaker of a necessary truth does not exist, either that truth is not true, or it is true due to a truthmaker it would have if that truthmaker did not exist. So deity theories force us to endorse not just (8) but, for example, that

Hydrogen contains two protons → it is not true that 7 is prime, or there is a truthmaker for 7 *is prime* that would be there if deity did not exist,

and

it is false that if anything is Socrates, it is human → it is not true that *modus ponens* is valid, or there is a truthmaker for this that would be there if deity did not exist.

All such conditionals are vastly unintuitive, simply because intuitively, what would make their antecedents true has no connection with what would make their consequents true. What makes each true, given a deity theory, is that

a truthmaker for both *P* and *Q* does not exist → *Q* is not true, or *Q* has a truthmaker that would exist in this circumstance.

This is strongly intuitive. If a strongly intuitive truth generates unintuitive consequences when conjoined with a deity theory, this is reason to consider deity theories unintuitive, and so reason to think them false.

Again, if deity does not exist, nor does God. Subtract God, and plausibly we must subtract everything else concrete. Deity theorists reject independent abstract objects. So given a deity theory, if deity does not exist, nothing is left to make anything true. And so deity theorists who agree with me that absent God there would be no non-divine concreta must endorse as a substantive truth reflective of the facts that

hydrogen contains two protons → it is not true that 7 is prime.

But insofar as we have any intuitions about relevance, here consequent seems irrelevant to antecedent. Why should a change in chemistry mess up the numbers?[36] Note again that this would equally be a problem for (8*), *mutatis mutandis*.

The last argument premised that without God there would be nothing concrete: I now support this. *Per* (GSA), God at all times makes for every concrete thing a creating-*ex-nihilo*-type causal contribution. Plausibly, if we remove God, we remove His effect, the universe's existence. For plausibly, if an effect has a non-probabilistic, non-overdetermining cause, had the cause not acted, the effect would not have occurred. God's creative causation is not probabilistic. If He says 'let there be' there is no chance that there not be. It is overdetermining only if either (a) He and something(s) else actually co-produce the universe, each cause or set of causes' contribution being individually sufficient; or (b) this is not so, but something(s) else would have made His causal contribution if He did not. Western theists deny (a) for Creation: God alone produced the universe. Subtract the universe and there is nothing to sustain, so the question of whether (say) God and sustained things each causally suffice for the universe's continued existence cannot arise. Western theists also deny one way (b) could be true, that there was anything else at Creation that would have created if God did not, as they hold that at Creation there was nothing concrete but God. If there was no backstop for God at Creation, waiting to act if He did not, (b) could also be true if

13. God does not create > another creator appears uncaused and creates.

In the nearest possible worlds in which God does not create, He does or does not exist. If in some He does not exist, God exists contingently—as I deny elsewhere.[37] If (13) is true and in some He exists, it was up to God whether there was a universe (as theists think) only if had He existed and not created, the *reason* He would have not created would have included (13) and reason to let another item create instead. This may be possible if the other item is, but it is implausible. Further, if a state of affairs obtains, then absent any specific

[36] The theory I eventually offer avoids this consequence, as it does not claim that (WATER)'s truth is in any sense written into the divine nature.

[37] 'Divine Necessity' in C. Taliaferro and C. Meister (eds), *The Cambridge Companion to Christian Philosophical Theology* (Cambridge: Cambridge University Press, 2010), pp. 15–30.

knowledge of how likely it was, it deserves more confidence that it was likely to obtain than that it was not. So if (13) is true and in some non-creating worlds God exists, it deserves more confidence that there is than that there is not a possible world in which God exists and if He did not create, it is likely that someone else would. But theists would (I believe) confidently deny that it could be the case that God's role is likely to be taken up by someone else. Further, if in the nearest world in which God does not create someone else would, it is possible that some creature owe worship elsewhere. Then either someone else could be sole deity or monotheism is only contingent: there could be two proper objects of some degree of worship. Again, I think standard Western theists will jib at this. Again, if (13) is true and it is possible that God exist and not create, it is possible that He exist and not have the GSA-property. If, as I have argued, this is a perfection, it follows that He is only contingently perfect and so (if I am right that necessary perfection is possible) not perfect at all. So I conclude that plausibly (13) is false and so plausibly, if there were no God, there would be nothing else concrete.

Again, creaturely modal truth bears no marks of being written into deity. (WATER) appears in no way shaped by the fact that it is written into deity. What there is to deity aside from water-nature does not explain this being true, as far as we can tell. But given a deity theory, it is reasonable to expect such explanation and such marks—and would be even on Aquinas's view.

Again, deity is the property having which makes God divine. So it should contain just things that help make one divine.[38] Intuitively, facts about water do not help make God divine—and this intuition persists even on Aquinas's view. Now the deity theorist might reply that omnipotence helps make God divine and implies being able to actualize on His own all possible worlds not involving creaturely libertarian-free agency,[39] and so worlds in which (WATER) holds, and so since omnipotence helps make God divine, so do facts about water. But if we stop this story before (WATER), it is no worse, and we understand omnipotence no less. In an alternate logical space in which there were no such property as *being H_2O*, God could satisfy any definition of omnipotence we find in the literature. This suggests that it is irrelevant to being omnipotent what worlds' precise contents are—for omnipotence is precisely ability to actualize such worlds *whatever* their content. If we can understand what it is to be omnipotent adequately if we stop before 'and so' in the story just given, it seems simply to beg the question to push the story further. Facts about water are irrelevant to the job the property *deity* does, and should not be packed into it without more justification than this story gives. Again, the deity theorist might say that if God has a full grasp of His nature and knows of His power that He can make all possible water and

[38] Which is an additional reason to avoid junk DNA.
[39] If a world contains my taking a walk with libertarian freedom, I must help God actualize it, since it is I, not God, who determine whether the walk that world contains becomes actual.

cannot make any that is not H_2O, God can read (WATER) off the content of His power. So His power's existing must somehow make (WATER) true. Again, the deity theorist may say, if God cannot make water that is not H_2O, then if He is omnipotent, the mere fact that He has no such power truth-explains it that $\square\neg$(water $\neq H_2O$). But neither point requires that (WATER) have been written into deity *ab initio*, as deity theories state. It could be that what powers God has with respect to H_2O is to some extent up to Him.

An Objection: (8) is Inescapable

A deity theorist might argue that no other theory can avoid (8), that thus one might argue, it is not a distinctive problem for deity theories that they commit us to it, and that therefore the commitment should not count against them. Platonism, for instance, seems no less than a deity theory to commit us to (8)—were the Platonic Form of water absent, so that (WATER) were not true, deity would lack a feature it necessarily has, that of co-existing with a Form which makes (WATER) true. This is not an intrinsic feature, but an intrinsic feature is not needed to derive (8). So too, if not God's nature but a Cartesian decree of His will provides the from-eternity truthmaker, and God had made no decrees about water, deity would have lacked a relational feature it has necessarily, that of co-existing with a divine decree rendering (WATER) true.

I reply that while (8) cannot be escaped, its import differs depending on the kind of feature involved. On a deity theory, (8) expresses a real, intrinsic, substantive and objectionable dependence. If God brings the truthmaker to be, Descartes-style, plainly He is in the driver's seat: the truthmaker really depends on Him, not *vice-versa*, and the counterfactual dependence $(8^\star)$ records is just a deceptive shadow of this, as cannot be said on a deity theory. In a sense we can ignore the Platonist story: if my earlier arguments were sound, theists should have no truck with Platonism for reasons independent of (8). But even if theists dance with this particular devil, all deity derives from co-existing with (say) the Form of Water is an extrinsic property. It may even be a 'mere-Cambridge property' of being such as to be said truly to co-exist with it. Deity in the Platonic scenario is really, intrinsically as it is no matter what Form it happens to co-exist with. Why should the theist object to dependence for mere-Cambridge properties? It is true that

$4^\star$. deity lacks a mere-Cambridge property it has necessarily → deity does not exist,

because $(4^\star)$'s antecedent and consequent are true in no possible world. But $(4^\star)$ does not at all reveal the underlying metaphysics, since lack of a mere-Cambridge property cannot explain the non-existence of anything. So a

Platonist theist can happily ignore it. So too, it does not seem that lack of a mere property of co-existence could explain the non-existence of deity.

Consider the arguments I have given for (2) against a Platonist and a Cartesian metaphysical backdrop. Platonism embodies the intuitive irrelevance of (8)'s antecedent to its consequent, by separating the pre-Creative truthmaker for (WATER) entirely from God. Cartesianism does so too: for Descartes, (WATER) is true due to truthmakers which do not exist from all eternity and consist entirely in entities wholly discrete from God, and also (though Descartes does not seem to notice) to a free decree of God, one not in any way dictated by His nature—and so one whose deletion from reality should have no effect on His nature. Platonism and Cartesianism can gladly agree that creaturely modal truth bears no marks of being written into deity and that deity should contain just things that help make one divine. Cartesianism lets God have any creaturely truthmakers He pleases, and so does not commit us to anything like *hydrogen contains two protons → it is not true that 7 is prime*. For Platonism the situation is less clear, but I suggest that it is similar, because (again) lacking a mere-Cambridge property is not the sort of thing that can explain non-existence. The background metaphysics of these other views, in other words, gives us reason to ignore (3)–(8). Deity theories stand alone in telling us that we should be happy with (3)–(8).

Partial Deity Theory?

If the argument to this point is sound, a deity theory cannot be the whole truth about creaturely modal facts. But perhaps a partial deity theory is true. Chapter 6 considered one route to this conclusion. For God has naturally any creature-representations that would result from operations He is naturally able to perform on mental content He naturally possesses, and so one might suggest that a deity theory holds for modal truths established by creature-representations God has naturally. Chapter 6 argued that there are none, but perhaps a partial deity theory could have another source. Suppose that some predicates true of God by nature apply to God and creatures univocally. Then it might seem that there are attributes God has by nature which creatures also have. If creatures have the very attributes God has by nature, then it could seem that a deity theory must hold for these attributes. If a creature can be omniscient, for instance, it might seem that the divine nature determines the truth about at least one possible creaturely attribute. Further, this would escape this chapter's main argument: it would not be counterintuitive that the divine nature should determine the truth about omniscience, an attribute God has essentially. So a deity theory holds for any divine attribute creatures can also have.

I concede that some predicates true of God by nature apply to God and creatures univocally. We think we can understand talk about God's mental life non-metaphorically. We could not do so were there no univocal core to it—that is, were no entailments involved in talk of created minds preserved, and in the same sense, in our talk about God's. God can think by nature. Suppose, then, that I say that God is thinking. You ask, 'Is He conscious of His thinking?' 'No.' 'Does His thinking process any information?' 'No.' 'Is there anything He's thinking *about*?' 'No.' 'Is the thinking an act He is doing?' 'No.' At this point, I think, you will have no clue what I meant by saying that God is thinking. The statement will appear to have no literal content at all, though it might be a metaphor for something. But there is just no good reason to reduce this claim to a metaphor. We know what we mean to ascribe to God in saying that He thinks, at least on an abstract level, and there is no good reason to think that it is not literally true of Him.[40] Nor does the analysis of mental concepts militate against this conclusion. Most philosophers of mind now treat most of these in functional terms: to be a belief, say, is on such accounts to be a mental state with a particular sort of role in an economy of other mental states which as a whole has certain sorts of relation to informational input and behavioral output. Characterizing mental states functionally makes no claims at all about how they are implemented or realized, and leaves open the possibility that in some cases they are not physically implemented or realized at all.[41]

I grant the univocity thesis. Still, it is a legitimate question whether predicating the same term univocally of God and creatures ascribes them the same attribute. Once we take account of what attributes are, I now argue, we see that the univocity thesis does not yield an argument for even a partial deity theory.

Concept Nominalism

On concept nominalism, to have the same attribute is just to fall under the same concept. So if we can speak univocally of God and creatures at all, they have the same attributes. But concept nominalism seems to me false. Its stronger versions ascribe a K-making role to attributes—that is, concepts. But again, what makes God divine is not His falling under a concept, but that about Him which makes Him do so. Stars are stars mind-independently: we do not make them stars by so forming concepts that they come out as stars. On concept nominalism without K-making attributes, that the whole concrete K, not any part or aspect or constituent of it, falls under '__ is a K,'

---

[40] Fans of Aquinas's account of theological predication as 'analogical' (see e.g. *ST* Ia 13) may jib at what they may take as an overly quick dismissal. My response is that properly understood, Aquinas himself concedes that we make some positive, literal, and true predications about God. But I must postpone exegesis to another day.

[41] So William Alston, 'Does God Have Beliefs?', in *Divine Nature and Human Language*, (Ithaca, NY: Cornell University Press, 1989), pp. 39–80.

makes it true that it is a K. This runs up against fairly potent intuitions. Consider some bronze being hammered into a statue intended to represent Zeus. The bronze does not initially fall under *statue intended to represent Zeus*. The hammering shapes it, and at some point in the process, the bronze is so shaped that it does. But the mass of bronze seems to fall under *statue intended to represent Zeus* in virtue of its shape: the shape, not just the mass, seems to have a part to play. There is more to say here, but I think we can safely bid goodbye to this version of nominalism too.

In any event, even if we accepted concept nominalism and univocity, we could not get a deity theory out of the two. To show this it suffices to show that one can tell a consistent story involving univocity, concept nominalism and the falsity of a deity theory. My story is this. As no deity theory is true, where God and creatures are both F, nothing in God dictates how or whether any possible creature falls under '__ is F', even if perchance God's nature determines Him to have this concept. Rather, God first exists on His own. He grasps all that He is, forms, for example, the concept *alive,* and sees that He falls under it. What He knows then is just that about Him which makes Him fall under it and that He does fall under it. It is up to God whether any other possible thing also falls under it. God in designing horses makes sure that they would fall under it too, and so (in concept nominalism's terms) have the same attribute. But God can no more read out of Himself what it is for horses to be alive than He can what it is for them to be horses, for their being horses includes life's taking a particular form in them and is what makes '__ is alive' apply. A concept applies univocally in such cases only once God has creatively come up with a creaturely kind. To design a horse, God must design the way life is realized in horses. The bare univocal concept *alive* gives no clues to this. God and horses satisfy it, but nothing in God's nature determines in advance how horses realize life.

Class Nominalism

I have already mentioned my critique elsewhere of class nominalism. But even if this critique were wholly unsuccessful, this view would not support a deity theory. On class and mereological nominalism, God can have attributes in common with creatures: they can belong to the same classes or sums. But there is a consistent story including class or mereological nominalism and univocity that avoids a deity theory. Suppose that no deity theory is true. God has all attributes He has by nature prior to creating.[42] So on class or mereological nominalism there are classes or sums before God creates. But there are none to which creatures can belong. For no creatures do belong to

---

[42] Causally prior, at least, and also temporally if He is temporal.

them. They contain only God. Classes have their members and sums their parts essentially, so there is no attribute God has then which creatures can also have. If God has His nature before creating, then, it does not 'contain' any attributes possibly common to Himself and creatures. Once creatures exist, there are sums and classes containing both. But as nothing in God's nature dictates what creatures He might make, so nothing in it dictates what classes and sums He might belong to once creatures exist. So nothing in God's nature dictates what the attributes common to God and creatures turn out to be. So class and mereological nominalism conjoined with univocity do not yield a partial deity theory. This is an actualist story, but it has a transform for Lewisian possibilism—*per* my earlier point that this plus a theist theory can be a version of Cartesianism, on which God creates all modal ontology—and for any possibilism dealing in 'subsistents' with 'being' but not existence. Non-existent-object possibilism is dubiously compatible with a deity theory—how could the divine nature account for there 'being' the non-existents there 'are'?—and so we need not worry about extending the argument to this view (which theists, again, do well to avoid anyway).

Resemblance Nominalism

Resemblance nominalism would not support a partial deity theory. On this view, there are no attributes; '__ is F' applies to different items just if they appropriately resemble some other F(s). This is surely how concepts come to apply to new items, and so the concept-nominalist story applies here. Again, if this is true, God is an original, and anything that comes out enough like Him to satisfy the sense of '__ is F' He satisfies is a copy designed to be like the original. We have already seen that originals' natures do not determine how copies turn out to realize likenesses to them. Thus on resemblance nominalism, the divine nature does not settle the content of creaturely possibility and necessity.

Universals and Tropes

I approach what I want to say about realism *via* trope theories. Within these, 'quasi-universals' are easily defined: a perfect quasi-universal is a class of perfectly similar tropes. Things have the same perfect quasi-universal just if they bear perfectly similar tropes. An imperfect quasi-universal is a class of imperfectly similar tropes similar enough to make univocal predications true of their bearers, and things have the same imperfect quasi-universals just if they bear tropes belonging to such a class.[43] Not just perfect but

---

[43] One could do the like within resemblance nominalism.

also imperfect quasi-universals can support univocal predication, for items can fall under the same concept due to imperfectly similar tropes. Sometimes this is so because the concept, being shaped by our finite capacities, is insufficiently discriminating. If things have real inhering physical color-properties, these vary continuously: they are properties of being disposed to reflect and absorb light of various frequencies, and so strictly, the physical color a thing is if it reflects light of wavelength 4000 Ångstroms differs from the physical color it is if it absorbs that but reflects wavelengths of 4000.00001 Ångstroms. Our visual systems are not sensitive to differences this small, and so our concept of violet covers both. More generally, any vague concept F will apply to items clearly F, items near the F/non-F border, and perhaps even borderline cases of F (if they did not have a claim to be Fs, they would not qualify as borderline cases). But it is plausible that attributes making a thing a borderline (or nearly so) F differ from attributes making one clearly an F.

Quasi-universals do not yield a partial deity theory. For they are determined by what tropes there are, and even if a trope theory and univocity are correct, there is a consistent non-deity-theoretic story to tell: that nothing in God's nature dictates a particular scheme of creaturely tropes, any more than it does any scheme of creatures. But just as nothing in God's nature would dictate a particular scheme of quasi-universals, nothing in God's nature would dictate a particular scheme of purely creaturely universals. The remaining question is whether anything in God's nature itself, prior to thinking up creatures, would itself be a universal (or a trope foundation for a perfect quasi-universal). For it would be only if it could be shared by something other than God in some possible world (or there could be perfectly similar tropes): if it could not be, it would be not a universal (foundation) but a haecceity. The non-deity theorist can say, I think, that just as it is up to God what non-divine things there can be, so it is up to God whether some things in His nature are universals (foundations). This does not require any strange metaphysical contortions. What is in His nature is an attribute regardless. The only question is whether it is a *universal* (foundational) attribute, or instead a haecceity. Now haecceities come in at most three varieties. Perhaps there are non-qualitative identity-properties like *being identical with Socrates*, which in some way include an individual in their makeup. Again, perhaps there are qualitative identity-properties like *Socrateity*. It is not up to God whether properties of these sorts are haecceities. But perhaps there are also qualitative properties which are not identity-properties but nonetheless are haecceities: I have argued that deity is one of these. If there is one, perhaps it is up to God whether there are others. For qualitative properties which are not identity-properties, the difference between haecceities and universals is just over what can have them—which is in at least some cases up to God, on a non-deity view. A non-deity theorist can consistently hold that while it was never up to God whether some haecceities are haecceities, it was up to God whether any universal would be a universal. So to get common attributes out of realism and univocity, one must also add the premise that some qualitative attributes in the divine nature are universals rather than haecceities independent of divine action.

But any argument for this thesis would have to be an argument for at least a partial deity theory. Any universal is something at least two possible items can have. Any possible item not identical with God would be non-divine. So an argument that something in the divine nature is a universal independent of divine action is precisely an argument that independent of divine action, an attribute that is part of God's nature can be had by something non-divine, and so implies that some modal truths possessing that attribute makes true are about God and non-God alike, based entirely on God's nature. This tells us that realism plus univocity cannot provide an independent route to a partial deity theory, for an attempt to use them so must be supplemented by a further, independent argument for such a view. If there is no such argument the move *via* realism fails. If there is one, it is otiose. My discussion to this point should cast doubt on the claim that such a further argument can be had. And in any event, I have argued elsewhere that precisely *qua* theists, theists should reject universals.[44]

If not Deity, What?

It emerges later that there is a thin partial deity theory I cannot avoid. This concession is compatible with what I have argued here, for that thin theory applies to no substantive modal truth about items other than God or His attributes—no truth involving any item or kind of item other than these having any particular attribute. Once that thin theory is on the table, I will continue to speak of mine as a non-deity view, meaning by this that it is a non-deity theory of modal truths other than the very abstract ones noted there. Now all I have argued is that it would be preferable *ceteris paribus* to avoid a (thicker) deity theory. To see whether the *cetera* really are equal, we need to compare with (thicker) deity theories the costs of a sample non-deity theory. I next construct one and make the comparison. If God's having His natural endowment does not make a modal truth true, the truth must rest at least partly on something beyond God's having this endowment or doing acts His having it guarantees that He does. The only facts there are about God, beyond these, concern acts and states deity does not dictate. If modal truths about creatures are not written into deity but have some basis in God, we must look to these for their truthmakers.

---

[44] 'God and the Problem of Universals,' *Oxford Studies in Metaphysics* 2 (2006), 325–56.

9

THE ROLE OF DEITY

I now begin to construct a non-deity modal theory. Its main part deals with a particular sort of modal truth. I begin by at least partially delimiting that sort. I next explain a further locution I use in setting out my view. I then set out deity's place in the theory and sketch the full theory.

Secular Truths

I have objected to the divine nature (God's having it, its being as it is, and so on) truthmaking modal truths about creatures alone, without specifying very precisely just what truths I have in mind. I aim to offer a theory of such truths' truthmakers. So I must first give at least some indication of what this class of truths includes. My term for the target truths is 'secular'. I now try to say just what about a truth makes it secular. Not sentences but things they state are true, false, or secular. In what follows, to avoid cumbersome phrases, I sometimes call sentences true, false, or secular: this is just shorthand for claims that they state something true, false, or secular.[1]

A secular sentence is roughly one whose content when used assertively in normal circumstances, on its own, on the surface, taken at face value, provides no information about God if it is true.[2] Thus a true secular sentence states no truth about God. A maximally informative verbal expression of what it says would contain no term which refers to God if God exists or to

---

[1] There is a further advantage to speaking of sentences. There is no doubt when sentences are atomic, molecular, and so on. But there is room for doubt when propositions they express are. Sentences atomic in form may express propositions that are not atomic: 'the room is empty' might really say that there is nothing in the room. (My thanks to Mike Rea here.)

[2] One might argue that if God exists, any sentence purportedly not about God provides a truth about God. Take one such sentence S. Since S is not about God, it is true that S is not about God, and this provides the truth about God that S is not about Him. (So a referee.) However, unless S asserts that it itself is not about God, it is not S's content that provides this information.

attributes only God has if He exists. Neither God nor such attributes are in the domain of any of its quantifiers, or in secular truths' ontologies. Now a normal assertion that P asserts just that P. It takes inference for us to access other information it provides. But it is not the case that that for all PQ, if P $\rightarrow$ Q, that P informs us *inter alia* that Q; if Q is necessary, anything strictly implies it,[3] but not everything informs us that Q. Thus secular truths can strictly imply (or be strictly equivalent to) truths about God and yet be secular; what is required is just that the implication (equivalence) hold *only* because the truth implied is necessary. I suggest that if true, 'P' provides the information that Q just if *P* in conjunction with at most definitional and logical truths strictly implies that Q and this is not a paradox of strict implication.

Now let us get more precise.

Atomic sentences

A term is apt to refer to God iff it is relevantly like 'God', 'the Creator', and so on. That is, it is apt to refer to God if either it is used as if it made direct reference to God (by way perhaps of a historical chain extending from a 'baptism' in which God introduced and named Himself) or it has a sense fitting it to pick out God in normal usage. A term is apt to refer to an attribute just if either it is used as if it directly referred to it or it has a sense fitting it to pick the attribute out in normal usage. An attribute involves God just if a maximally informative verbal expression of its content would contain a term apt to refer to God (as with __ is related to God). Predicates do not refer to but express attributes. A term is apt to express an attribute involving God or an attribute only God has iff its sense fits it to do so. An attribute involves an attribute only God has just if a maximally informative verbal expression of its content would contain a term apt to refer to or express such an attribute (as with __ is related to an omnipotent being). Taking events Kim-style, as items' having attributes at times,[4] an event involves God just if what it happens to includes God or an attribute involving an attribute only God has. It should be fairly clear how to extend this sort of account to other ontological categories.

An atomic sentence states something secular, I will say, just if

A. none of its terms is apt to refer to God, attributes that involve God, attributes only God has, attributes involving such attributes, events involving God or attributes only God has or attributes involving such attributes, and so on, unless the term occurs within the scope of

---

[3] A strict conditional is true just if it cannot be the case that its antecedent is true and its consequent false; thus every strict conditional with a necessarily true consequent is true. Correspondingly, every proposition strictly implies every necessary truth.

[4] Jaegwon Kim, 'Events as Property-Exemplifications', in Jaegwon Kim, *Supervenience and Mind* (New York: Cambridge University Press, 1993), pp. 33–52.

a non-factive propositional-attitude verb—that is, a verb V such that S' V-ing that P does not entail that P; and

B. none of its terms is apt to express an attribute involving God, attributes only God has, or attributes involving such attributes, unless the term occurs within the scope of a non-factive propositional-attitude verb.[5]

Even if God exists, 'Smith hopes that God exists' passes (a) and so counts as secular.[6] It should, for this does not inform us that God exists. (a) and (b) do not exempt referring terms within the scope of factive propositional-attitude verbs, those such that S' V-ing that P entails that P. 'Jones knows that God exists' fails (a). This should not count as secular, for it informs anyone who believes it and grasps the definitional truth that P is known → P that God exists.

Molecular sentences

Turning to molecular sentences, a conjunction one of whose conjuncts provides information about God (His distinctive attributes, and so on) if it is true provides information about God (and so on) if it is true. So a conjunction is secular just if all its conjuncts are. Disjunctions one of whose disjuncts provide information about God (and so on) if true provide information about God (and so on) if true. The claim that either trout are fish or God is perfect informs us that about God that either He is perfect or trout are fish. So a disjunction is secular just if all its disjuncts are. A negated sentence is secular just if the sentence negated is. Thus a material conditional is secular only if both its antecedent and its consequent are.

Quantification

Universal quantifiers quantify over everything in a domain. So if (x)(Fx) and God is in the domain, God is F. That (x)(Fx) says that something is true of all the items in the domain, and one of them is God. So I say that any universal quantification quantifying *inter alia* over God provides information about God if true, though we must know that He is in the domain to extract it: a universal quantification is secular just if God is not in its domain. If (∃x)(Fx) and the domain is just abc, it follows that Fa v Fb v Fc. So if God is in the domain, it is not secular; any existential quantification quantifying *inter alia*

---

[5] Perhaps there could be languages that express truths about God without using terms referring to God, predicates expressing attributes only God has, and so on. (My thanks to Mike Rea for this worry.) If so, relativize this account to languages *we* have, which (as far as I know) cannot manage this.

[6] I take it that such claims as this or that S knows that P predicate a property of S, and so are atomic.

over God provides information about God if true, though again we must know that He is in the domain to extract it. An existential quantification is secular just if God is not in its domain. Thus if God does not exist, all quantification is secular.

Odds and ends

General truths explicating properties God has are not secular. They have the form $(x)(Fx \supset Gx)$, and should quantify over all the Fs; thus they are universal quantifications with God in their domain. For all P, that P is true is secular just if *P* is. That P in W is secular just if what 'P' states in W would be secular were W actual. That $\Diamond P$ is secular just if in every accessible world in which P, what 'P' actually states is secular. That $\Box P$ is secular just if in every accessible world, what 'P' actually states is secular. The treatment of simple modal operators should suggest how to deal with iterated modalities.

If God exists, pure logical and mathematical sentences are not secular. Consider, for instance, the Principle of Non-Contradiction. It is appropriate to state it as $(x)(\Phi)\neg(\Phi x \cdot \neg\Phi x)$, with both domains unrestricted. So stated, if God exists, it quantifies *inter alia* over God. So it is non-secular. It makes a claim about *everything*, that none of it has both a property and its complement. So it carries as much information about God (if He exists) as it does about anything else. Much the same holds of pure mathematical truths. For it is plausible that, for example, the truth that $1 + 1 = 2$ really involves variables—for example, that it is really that $(xy\Phi)(((\Phi x \cdot \Phi y \cdot (z)(\Phi z \supset (y=z$ v x =z)) $\cdot$ (x$\neq$y)) $\supset$ (2w)(Φw)). So if God exists, sentences of pure logic and mathematics are not secular. As I assume that God exists and my main concern is a theory of secular truths, I say little about logic and mathematics here. Secular necessary truths chiefly explicate essences of individuals and attributes; they may also include natural laws; if S5 is the true logic of absolute modality, they include secular necessities and possibilities. World-indexed truths are also modal; *P in W* is plausibly explicated as $\Box(W$ is actual $\supset P)$. So secular world-indexed truths also lie in my purview. If it is secular that zebras are possible, it is non-secular that possibly God co-exists with zebras. My theory will also apply to such non-secular truths.

Secular States of Affairs

I also speak (without commitment) of secular states of affairs. My account of these builds on the foregoing. Take any secular atomic sentence, S is P: S's being P is a secular state of affairs. Take any molecular secular sentence, e.g. S is P or S* is P*: S's being P or S*'s being P* is a secular state of affairs. And so on.

Thus my target truths and states of affairs. I have gone into some detail to suggest that one can say sensible things to develop my 'secular' notion and to explain why pure logic and mathematics are tales for another day. The most important sorts of claim I discuss are of simple forms. If God can make claims of the form $\Diamond(P \cdot Q \cdot R \ldots)$ true He can account for the possibility of entire possible worlds. If He can make true claims of this form where each proposition asserts the existence of a particular non-divine being, He can make it possible that worlds have the domains the standard modal semantics associates with them. If He can make true claims of the form $\Box(P \supset Q)$, He can institute natural laws of even the strongest sort. If He can do this where the antecedent asserts that a particular exists and the consequent asserts that it has a property, He can fill out the essences of particular non-divine things. I now introduce another technical locution.

What It is in God to Do

We sometimes say things like 'I did not have it in me to disagree.' We usually mean by this e.g. that we did not have the power or motivation to do so. To have it in me to do something is usually to have the power and some motivation to do it. I am going to use this phrase differently. I say that God has it in Him to do A if He has the power to do it. I also sometimes say this if He does not. Sometimes the only reason God does not have the power to do something is that He has brought it about that He does not. Suppose that God has the power to make items of just ten kinds. Then He does not have the power to make things of an 11th kind. As I see it, the only reason He does not have it is that He has not thought up an 11th kind and done certain other things consequent on that. By not doing so, He has denied Himself the power to make things of an 11th kind. This is the *only* reason He does not have it. So I say also that though there is no 11th kind, God has it in Him to make things of an 11th kind. I define the locution in my technical sense this way:

> God has it in Him to do A = df. God is intrinsically such that (God wills to have the power to do A) $\supset$ (God has the power to do A).

This yields, of course, that God has it in Him to do what He has the intrinsic power to do. I use 'It is in God to do A' and 'God is such as to do A' as notational variants for 'God has it in Him to do A.' A third context in which I use these locutions is this: suppose that God is considering whether it shall be possible that P, but has not yet decided. (Later chapters explicate what is going on here in detail.) Power is to produce what is possible, so at this point it is not the case that

God has the power to bring it about that P. But He is such that if He wills to have it, He will have it, it will be possible that P, and it will be possible that He bring it about that P. So I say that at this point He has it in Him to bring it about that P. Be clear, then, that when I use this locution, I am not saying that God can bring it about that P. I mostly use it when He cannot, or cannot yet. And as emerges below, sometimes, when it is true that it is or was in God to bring it about that P, God has rendered it impossible that P.

One might wonder whether 'it is in God to bring it about that' is a new sort of modal operator.[7] If so, it is not a very exciting one. Letting 'I' symbolize it, the main truths involving it would be just that $\Diamond$P, P, and $\Box$P entail IP, IP entails none of these, I 'collapses' (IIP entails IP), (IP · IQ) ≡ I(P · Q) and (IP v IQ) ≡ I (PvQ)). If there are worlds, there are no I-worlds as a layer beyond possible worlds unless for reasons having nothing to do with I, there are impossible worlds. At no time in any possible world has anything *only* status I. As I argue later, God's assignment of ordinary modal status takes no time at all; as soon as a content is in His mind, it has an ordinary modality. The basis on which I argue this makes it plausible that this is necessarily so. So I-status is necessarily equivalent to a disjunction of ordinary modalities, and if 'I' does introduce a distinct modal status, a 'modal collapse' immediately negates this: its character as a distinct modal status collapses away. What is left when this occurs is a point about God's endowments. It is in God to think up a kind He has not actually thought up.[8] It is (so I later argue) impossible that He do so—that is, He does it in no possible world—but He is so endowed as to do it, and the only reason it is impossible is that He has not done so. Its impossibility is a result of His action rather than an external constraint upon it. As it is impossible, that God thinks up such a kind has an ordinary modality. Its bearing the status 'I' just indicates that its impossibility is a product of something God has done, not a function of lack of strength in or external constraint on God. It notes a way in which His natural endowment runs beyond the realm of possibilities He has established. If either the stock of states of affairs or their modal status is up to God, one needs to say something *like* that God has the power to bring about states of affairs that are not in fact possible, without actually saying it and so suggesting that they are after all possible. We can say that it was in God to bring about something that (now, given what He has done) cannot be so. This does not imply that these states of affairs are possible or that He possibly so acts as to effect them. Finally, if 'I' is an operator, I do not offer a deity theory for I-truths. It is in God to make dogs, but it is not by His nature in Him to make dogs, since it is not part of His nature that there be such a property as doghood.

---

[7] Thomas Flint and Michael Rea have pushed this point with me.

[8] Morris and Menzel ('Absolute Creation', repr. in Thomas, Morris, *Anselmian Explorations* (Notre Dame, IN: University of Notre Dame Press, 1987), pp. 161–78) would say that thinking up a kind amounts to creating an abstract entity *ex nihilo*. That is, on their view of God's contentful mental states, there are abstract entities which are their contents. I deny this latter, and so deny that this 'thinking up' creates anything. I sketch my alternative view in Chapters 11 and 12.

Thus my two special locutions. I now turn to deity's role in my theory. First, a general point. Platonism is not the correct account of deity. I suggest that Aristotelian attributes, if any, exist because their instances exist. It is not a fluke or a brute fact that doghood exists only if there are dogs; this is so because dogs' existing accounts for doghood's. If it does, then if there are no non-existents and we leave God out of the picture, nothing settled what doghood's content would be before dogs appeared. There just were no facts about this at all. If that is right, then how dogs concretely are somehow accounts for the content doghood has. The same applies to tropes on the only sort of trope theory that might apply to deity, one which does not 'assemble' God from ontologically more basic tropes. So I suggest that whatever sort of attribute deity is, what it is to be divine is not set independent of God. Instead, how God actually is determines what it is to be divine. If there is such a thing as deity, not only does it exist only because God does, but the way God concretely *is* determines its content. This claim is compatible with an Aristotelian theory of universals, a trope theory or nominalism.

Deity as Truthmaker

There are necessary truths no divine act can explain—for instance, that

DP. whatever is divine is personal.[9]

These require truthmakers. There are reasons to find them in deity. Truths like (DP) in effect state requirements to be divine. To be divine is to bear the divine nature. Natures include what it takes to bear them. So the divine nature includes what it takes to bear *it*—and so its content, or its having that content, renders these truths true. It does not make them necessary. If they are necessary, this is God's doing, or so I contend. His nature may guarantee that they come out necessary, but it does not provide the worlds in which they are necessary: these worlds involve creatures, and their creaturely content is not part of His nature. Further, (DP) involves the property of being personal. There are necessary truths about what it is to be personal. These need truthmakers. If God is to be the sole ultimate reality, these truthmakers must involve God in the right way. For if what it is to be personal has nothing to do with God, for instance, one can press some explanations (e.g. of what being personal is, and why God counts as personal) deeper than God, His nature, and His activities. So divine ultimacy presses us to a theist account of what it is to be personal. If deity (its having its contents, and so on: from now on I will just say 'deity' to smooth exposition) makes (DP) true, it makes true

---

[9] Morris and Menzel trace the existence of God's nature to divine activity. If its existence makes (DP) true, as I suggest, then they would explain (DP)'s truth by divine activity. I argue against them in 'God and Abstract Entities', *Faith and Philosophy* 7 (1990), 193–217.

a truth involving being personal. So deity involves what it is to be personal somehow. If *only* deity equips God to function as God, and a functioning God must be personal, deity must determine what it is to be personal. So theists will do well to hold that the divine nature is the deepest place in reality at which there are any facts about being personal—that what makes (DP) true not just involves but settles what it is to be personal. So too, if God is by nature good, what it is to be good is determined by the way God is morally.[10]

Gilbert Fulmer asks us to consider a (presumably necessary) truth that may express part of what it is for God to be omnipotent, that

GW. (φ)(if God wills that φ, and φ meets further conditions S, then φ).[11]

Fulmer suggests that (GW)'s being true

> cannot itself be the product of [God]'s will; for if it were not a fact, his will could produce no effects whatever—and to make his will effective would be to produce an effect . . . (GW) is logically more fundamental than [God]'s choices: his acts presuppose (GW).[12]

It is false that were (GW) not true, God could have no effects. God might have effects were it true instead that $(\exists\phi)$(if God wills that φ, then φ). But theist causal explanations that P may run by way of (GW) and a premise that its being the case that P meets conditions S and God wills that P. (GW) cannot have such a causal explanation. Still, one might give it another sort. One could, for instance, introduce a hierarchy. Suppose that there is an infinity of levels of divine activity, starting at level n and descending to n–1, n–2, and so on, and suppose that at each level n, typed versions of (GW) hold: for example,

GWn. (φ)(if God executively intends that φ, and φ meets further conditions S, and bringing it about that φ is an n-level task, then φ).

Given such levels, theists could claim that at each level n, (GWn) holds due to a divine act at level n–1. (GW) would then have the status of untyped assertions within a typed set theory: it would be systematically ambiguous between assertions of different type-levels, and so 'true' only in that all disambiguated theses like (GWn) are true. Given such a hierarchy, at any level n, God would have established the conditions for His own agency at a deeper level n–1.

Nothing in this picture is formally inconsistent, I think, and if anyone could do an infinity of tasks, God could. But it is strange and vertiginous to say that

---

[10] For a look at a full theory of attributes incorporating this, see my 'Divine Simplicity', *Faith and Philosophy* 23 (2006), 365–80.

[11] Gilbert Fulmer, 'The Concept of the Supernatural', *Analysis* 37 (1977), 113–16. Fulmer calls (GW) a 'natural law' and does not include the clause about S. But most theists do not think that if φ entails a contradiction and God wills that φ, then φ is the case. The S-clause lets theists make such exceptions.

[12] Fulmer, 'The Concept of the Supernatural', 114. For a like point see J. L. Mackie, 'Omnipotence', in Linwood Urban and Douglas Walton (eds), *The Power of God* (Oxford: Oxford University Press, 1978), p. 81.

any divine act presupposes an infinity of other divine acts (prior conceptually if not in time). So it seems most plausible that the content of deity, or God's having it, makes (GW) true. Being divine—having deity—gives God all the equipment needed to outfit someone as a functioning God. (GW) must be true for God to act as God (that is, act, and have some reasonable version of omnipotence). So the contents of deity must make (GW) true.

Here is one way deity might underwrite (GW). Suppose with Tooley and Fales that causation involves higher-level attributes linking attributes, so that e.g. baseballs' striking glass with enough force causes glass breaking because a primitive __ causes __ relation links the relevant event-types.[13] Now consider state-of-affairs attributes C and A: C is a state's being conceived by God, meeting appropriate conditions, and being executively intended by God to be actual and A is its being actual. Deity might underwrite (GW), then, by including being such that the __ causes __ relation links the event-type __ comes to have C to the event-type __ comes to have A. This does not include a specific range of mental contents linked to executive intentions or results. Rather, the connection is between attributes: being divine, being conceived by x, being intended by x, being actual, the causal relation. On a non-deity theory, the domain of mental contents involved is not determined by God's nature, and so a connection at the level of God's nature cannot involve a specific such domain.

Deity and the Causal Relation

Mention of the causal relation raises another issue. Suppose that God's acting to bring anything about entails His making a causal relation obtain between Himself and some effect. The causal relation is a relation. So per (GAO), God must account for its existence. He cannot do so causally if His causing anything to exist presupposes that there is such a thing as the causal relation. So how?

One suggestion, just mooted, would be that the causal relation is part of the divine nature, existing due to God's having His nature. On this view there is such a thing as causation only because God is divine and so such as to cause. God does not cause the causal relation to exist. Rather, God's having His power includes the causal relation, for His having His power includes His nature's establishing a causal-relation connection between event-types. So the causal relation depends non-causally on God. To bring about effects, God uses an already-given causal relation located in His nature. This relation is like a Platonist universal: it would exist even if nothing were ever caused.

---

[13] Michael Tooley, *Causation* (New York: Oxford University Press, 1987); Evan Fales, *Causation and Universals* (New York: Routledge, 1990).

An alternative would be to say that the causal relation exists because it is instanced, deriving its being from its instances. While the Platonist says 'there can be cases of causal connection only because the causal relation already exists', the causal Aristotelian reverses the priority and says 'there is a causal relation only because there are cases of causal connection.' So the Aristotelian might say that God creates the causal relation itself, and 'puts' it between His willing something and its being so, in and by actually willing some particular thing and having it be so. Compare: the Platonist would say that God can be good only if there is such a thing as goodness for Him to have. The Aristotelian would insist that instead, there is such a thing as goodness only because God is good. So too, the Aristotelian would have it that God's actually causing certain things is the most basic reason that there is such a thing as causal connection. There is an analogy here too (though not as close) to theories of space. Substantivalists are spatial Platonists, insisting that there must be such a thing as space for there to be cases of spatial relatedness among items other than parts of space ('every case of spatial relation requires a space already in existence'). Relationalists are spatial Aristotelians, suggesting that instead, in whatever sense there is such a thing as space, it exists only because there are cases of spatial relatedness among items which are not parts of space, that spatial relatedness establishes rather than presupposes space. Perhaps God causes the causal relation to exist in (say) causing things to exist, and His nature does not contain this relation as a constituent, but outfits Him to cause it to exist. In this case, deity solves the causal relation problem by letting God cause this relation to exist. Deity also still underlies (GW), but not due to any inner complexity involving the causal relation. It instead just makes it true as some sort of brute fact. For present purposes, we need not choose between Platonist and Aristotelian approaches to the causal relation problem. It is enough to see that there are not unpromising ways to handle it.

God and Causal Necessitation

On most non-Humean accounts, causation involves real necessitation of an effect (whether or not necessitation is part of an *analysis* of causation).[14] It would be good to keep our theory of necessity simple, and so parse this in terms of absolute necessity rather than introducing a second form of necessity. If we do so, then if God is the source of absolute necessity, He is the source of causal necessity. If causation does involve necessity, I go Aristotelian at this point. As I see it, God's activity accounts for some of what a Platonist would call its preconditions. As spatial facts (for a spatial Aristotelian) account for the existence of the space a Platonist would consider their precondition,

---

[14] For what follows I am indebted to discussion with Evan Fales.

causal facts (for a causal Aristotelian) account for the logical space—the realm of possible-world-talk-truthmakers—a causal Platonist would call their precondition. God produces what lies behind possible-world talk. If this involves necessitating that it exist, God produces this necessity (and world-talk-truthmakers) by producing that underlying reality. God's activity clothes itself in that by reference to which it can count as necessitating anything. What accounts for the necessity in causal production is this activity's product, not its presupposition. So the necessity involved is as it were retrospective. God's producing worlds, or whatever lies behind world-talk, does not count as necessary until it is complete. Then what makes it necessary is its relation to a framework for whose existence it accounts.

This is actually an easy position to hold. Begin with a truism: relations relate things. That is their job. They can do the job only if the things are there to relate. Thus a dyadic relation is exemplified only if both its terms exist. They are its prerequisites: the relation cannot be exemplified unless both are given. The causal relation links a cause to its effect. But the effect a cause produces does not exist until the cause has produced it. So the causal relation cannot be exemplified until the cause *has* produced its effect. So to speak, it is not that one has the cause, then the relation, then the effect.[15] Instead, one has the cause, then the effect, then the relation between them by which the cause accounts for the effect, or else the cause and then the effect and the relation together. In these claims, 'then' carries a temporal sense where the cause is temporally before the effect. Where it is not, 'then' does not. Instead, 'then' expresses a relation of precondition or presupposition: there being a relation between cause and effect has as a precondition the effect's occurring, which has as a precondition the cause's action, or else the relation does not presuppose the effect but occurs along with it, and the two jointly have as a precondition the cause's action. In God's causation of the reality behind possible-world talk, then, either we first have God, then the reality behind world-talk and then the causal relation between them, or else first God, then the reality and the relation together. In general, the production relation either presupposes or occurs along with the product. So the product which gives necessity either is a presupposition of or occurs along with the relation which involves it. Even if causal relations just *are* forms of necessitation, God causally accounts for what is needed for them to be so, and so to be exemplified.

God, Causation, and Counterfactuals

Let me now note how my approach to causation plays out with regard to counterfactuals. Suppose that God causes there to be the reality behind

---

[15] One does often have the cause, then a causal process, then the effect. But a causal process is not a relation, though one's occurring may bring about the exemplifying of a relation.

possible-world talk. Then there being counterfactual truths presupposes His doing so, assuming the standard semantics. At the level in the order of preconditions at which God is making His contribution, there are no counterfactual truths about God and this reality. It is not the case either that were God not to act, the reality behind world-talk would not be there, or that were God not to act, it would. God acts to produce the reality behind world-talk causally prior to the establishing of counterfactual facts. This reality provides for the semantics of counterfactual truths once it is there. Once it is there, it is the case that were God not to act, it would not exist. By causing it, God brings into existence the machinery needed for it to depend on Him counterfactually. Just as God's activity clothes itself in what it takes for it to necessitate, it clothes itself in what it takes for it to support counterfactual truths. If causal relations do not consist in relations of counterfactual dependence, as I believe, there is no bar to this. Even if they do, if I am right that a dyadic relation's obtaining presupposes that both terms exist, this is still a coherent claim.

God existing causally before there is this reality is not a possible world, if there is nothing for possible-world talk to be about till this reality is there. Nor is it an actual world. It is not a world at all. In every possible world, God exists and this reality is there. And God never exists save in a world. But we're analyzing just how that comes to be so.

Natural Powers

The divine nature determines some modal facts involving only God. By nature God is all-things-considered *able* to imagine or conceive, know, form attitudes and preferences, choose, will, bring about external states of affairs, create, and sustain. All-things-considered abilities factor in everything that might in other circumstances block an ability's use: if, for instance, I could jump vertically ten feet iff I were on the Moon, but I am not on the Moon, I do not have the all-things-considered ability to do so. So having such abilities has modal content: one is thus able to do act A only if one can do A—that is, possibly one does A. I grant that God by nature has such abilities due to the explanatory project I am taking up—to account for there being secular modal facts, and being the ones there are. Suppose that there is nothing modal in the divine nature logically before there are these facts. The 'ingredients' in their explanation can only be divine attributes, representations, and acts. I do not want to *reduce* secular modal facts to non-modal facts involving these. So I need to show how secular modal facts can emerge from these. If there is nothing modal in any of these, any combination or function of these alone will contain nothing modal. So there will be no natural, toil-rather-than-theft way to get secular modality to emerge from them. Given only non-modal 'ingredients', the only way to get modality into the picture will then be by sheer divine *fiat*: God considers His representation of Moses existing, says 'Let that be possible', and so it is. Perhaps someone omnipotent could have it in Him to produce possibility by sheer will. But this smacks of magic. To rest my account of the origin of secular modality on this kind of simple *fiat* would surely make it less plausible than it might be. So I suggest that God does indeed have the natural powers mentioned. This lets me treat the emergence of secular modal facts as involving a particular way in which God specifies His very general natural powers to produce more determinate creature-directed powers—a 'shaping' of a pre-given modal element rather than its injection *ex machina* into a modally flat landscape. It lets me explain rather than simply posit—at the cost of a posit one step further back, of course, but a posit most would want to make anyway.

Commit to a theist modal theory, pack into the divine nature abilities to make zebras, ponies and so forth, and the result is a deity theory close to Aquinas's. One could move away from this in two steps. One would make secular modal status up to God, but not the stock of secular states of affairs to which He gives modal status. It would then be (say) natural to God to think up zebras, but up to Him whether zebras are possible. The second would add that secular states of affairs are things He simply dreams up, not dictated by anything that is naturally in Him. On the second, God's nature determines that He can think, create, etc: it gives Him a range of action-types, not any range of determinate actions, and God establishes His range of actions by dreaming up creatures and possible worlds. I offer a theory that makes the second step. It is this sort of theory that my argument against deity theories motivates, for if we make only the first step, we still have it that zebras and the rest are written into deity. They are there without a determinate modal status, but it was not their having a modal status that generated the oddities I tried to highlight. Part of what makes Aquinas' a deity theory is that He packs God's nature primitively with highly specific powers. I instead pack in only the most general powers. And I treat the emergence of secular modality as God's giving Himself further powers, by specifying powers He had initially.

Powers are real, inhering attributes which are *like* functions from circumstances—opportunities to act and perhaps triggers for action—to effects.[16] A power is something which, given an opportunity and a 'trigger', produces an effect. The reference to opportunity matters. Powers can be masked, blocked from acting: if one first swallows an antidote, then swallows the poison it counters, the poison remains poisonous—that is just part of its nature—but its power to kill cannot manifest itself.[17] Masked powers lack the opportunity to act. When a power is masked, it is not the case that all things

---

[16] Some *all-things-considered* powers may not be intrinsic. Something has such a power only if there are all things needed to give opportunity for the power to act. Some opportunities depend on items outside the thing with the power: I have the opportunity to make an unaided 10-foot vertical jump only if I am not on Earth.

[17] On this see Alexander Bird, 'Dispositions and Antidotes', *The Philosophical Quarterly* 48 (1998), 227–34.

considered, it *can* produce an effect. It could have produced one—had it not been masked. And this is true only because it could have not been masked. Again, powers can be present only when they do not have an opportunity to act. A glass might be fragile—have the power to break easily when struck—but it might be that whenever something is about to strike the glass, God melts it, and so it ceases to be fragile.[18] Powers thus 'finked' are kept from having chances to act. A 'finked' power too all-things-considered cannot produce an effect, because it lacks opportunity, but it could have done so if there could have been circumstances in which nothing 'finked' it. To say that a power has the opportunity to act is to say *inter alia* that it is not finked, masked, or in any other way interfered with—that all conditions are propitious, including (if need be) the presence of a specific trigger for its action. If a power can have opportunity, it can act. *A fortiori* if a power does have opportunity, it can act. This is why powers are intrinsically modal attributes. So where there is power and opportunity—equivalently, where there is all-things-considered power—there is possibility. It is possible that the power act, and so possible that its effect obtain.

God has powers by nature. They are not finkish: they will not disappear when needed. There is nothing within or without God to impede their use. God's merely existing establishes the opportunity to use them. They are primed to act; God need only call on them. The presence of powers of this sort, in circumstances of this sort, is enough to make possibility-claims true. These powers and possibilities come earlier in the order of explanation than the full possible worlds we usually take modal operators to quantify over. The possibilities do not constitute worlds on their own, for if they did then, they would now—possible worlds have their contents essentially, and what God could do then, He still can do—and there is no possible world in which the only possible actions are those I now set out.

The extent of possibility God's natural powers determines is extremely limited. God uses a power to imagine or conceive to think up creatures, and has the power to choose between imagined alternatives. There is (so I soon argue) no alternative to God's using these. By God's nature, then, there is just the one possibility—that He use them. Nothing in God's nature dictates how He uses them. They have no determinate uses written into them, nor even any 'slots' for a determinate number of kinds of use. All facts about how He could use them are determined by how He does use them (of this more anon), and His nature does not determine this. Again, God by nature makes some uses of other powers—He knows about Himself, approves of Himself, etc. There are no alternatives to His doing these things. Here too there is just the one possibility. As to all other possible uses of these powers, again, there is nothing determinate written into His nature. He is naturally able to know

[18] This slightly alters an example in C. B. Martin, *The Mind in Nature* (Oxford: Oxford University Press, 2008), p. 13.

about creatures, but there are no sorts of creature it is natural to Him to know about. The only possibility naturally given is that He know about some creature or other. Divine powers purely *ad extra*—to create, sustain, and bring about external states of affairs—are just 'two-way' powers naturally. All that holds of God due to His very nature is that He can use or not use them. By His nature, it is just possible that He create (etc.) and that He not. If no deity theory is true, His nature determines no specific facts about what He could create (and so on). But as we shall see, God's natural two-way powers *ad extra* are all that is needed to generate secular modal facts.

I speak of divine natural powers, but I cannot appeal to actions in possible worlds to make sense of the modal content of natural-power locutions. For I allow that God has powers prior in the order of explanation to there being possible worlds. Moreover, as emerges later, I do not really believe in possible worlds, but instead parse possible-world-talk in terms of powers: the reality behind the claim that there is a possible world in which God creates two hydrogen atoms and thereafter just sits on His hands—that is, what would make it true but for its existential commitment to a world, or makes it a good fictional way to express a truth *modulo* that commitment—is that God has the powers and had opportunity to create two hydrogen atoms and refrain from creating anything else. As I see it, the truthmakers for modal truths from all eternity were are that there were/are divine powers of various sorts. Talk of possible worlds is just a fiction which gets at a reality which consists in divine powers more specific than those God has by nature. So I face a question of how to explicate the modal content of powers. I incline to stand pat, and say just that powers' modal content is primitive, not further to be explicated. Every non-reductive theory of modality involves some sort of primitive modal fact: compatibility, exemplifiability, actualizability. Just on the score of being primitive, appeal to powers is no worse. We later see some ways it may be better.

The divine nature alone does not fill out the content of any possible world. It does not provide the creaturely content of any world—even a world in which God exists alone, since in any such possible world, He has thoughts He does not have by nature. What I have isolated in my talk of natural powers is not a sort of possible world containing God alone, but the source of the distinctively modal content in possible worlds containing both creatures and God. God has indefinite powers by nature. Secular modal facts emerge from His rendering His powers fully definite—giving Himself specific powers He does not have by nature: for example, the power to create ocelots.

God determines what definite non-natural powers He has. As I suggest later, it is in Him to have had, and perhaps to have, a different set, as it is in Him to have thought up other bearers of secular modal status than He has. It does not follow from this that God could have had or did have the power to have a different set. Recall my parsing of the 'in Him' locution: that it is in God to bring it about that P *means* that God is intrinsically such that (God wills to have the power to bring it about that P) ⊃ (God has the power to bring it about that P). That these things are in God, then, does not involve anything modal, including the existence of the power in question. All power is to do or bring about what is possible. So the only determinate, non-natural powers God could have had are those He has, unless He has made some modal system weaker than S4 true: only if He has could there have been a range of possibility other than the one there actually is. The range of possible possibility, possible possible possibility, and so on for as many iterations as one likes, is God's doing. God gives Himself not just the range of non-natural power He has, but the range of ranges He might have had, and so on. If God could have had other powers, this is an option He gave Himself. And if it is hard to see what point there could be to bringing it about that one could have had a different range of determinate power, that may be some reason to think He has not done so. If God could not have had other powers, this was wholly His doing. He did not deny Himself possible courses of action He would otherwise have had. He just determined what the possible courses of action *are*. It is not the case that God loses power by instituting necessary truths, i.e. determining that there are things He cannot bring about. He instead sets His only range of power.

My overall picture, including the role of the primal divine powers, is this. God thinks up a secular state of affairs S. Having done so, He has an opportunity to render S possible and one to make S impossible, by making one or another decision. He can decide: this is a natural power, present prior to possible worlds in the order of explanation. He can decide whether S is possible: this is a specified power, one God came to have by conceiving S. Again, this is prior in the order of explanation to there 'being' possible worlds. He can make S possible, by deciding. It is in Him (we can suppose[19]) to bring it about that S, once He has thought S up, but it is up to Him whether to have the power to do so. It is in Him both to give Himself this power and not to do so. At this point the power does not exist; it does not exist unless and until He has it. So while it is in Him to give Himself the power, there is no power such that it is in Him to give Himself *that*. (Compare: I owe you a dollar, but there is no dollar such that I owe you that one.) It is not the case that the power is possible or that it is not. It is not there to bear any attribute, including that of possibility.

Nor then can we say that at this point S can be possible. It is not even the case that there can be a power to bring S about, and (we can suppose) S is of a sort not to come about unless something brings it about. '◊◊S' quantifies over worlds, speaking fictionally. Quantification over worlds is licit only once God *has* His specific powers, since—to get way ahead of myself—they are the reality behind world-talk, the entities '◊' and '□' really quantify over. If it were

---

[19] For the present example only. There are secular states of affairs God thinks up such that this is not in Him—horrors too great to allow, contra-logicals, and so on.

the case that $\lozenge\lozenge S$, the power to bring it about that S—the reality making it true that $\lozenge S$—would be there to bear the attribute of possibility, to be a thing God has the power to give Himself. It is because we cannot 'yet' use '$\lozenge$' that my picture does not imply that every S God conceives is at least possibly possible, and so nothing is more than contingently necessary.

S initially has no modal status at all. God has the power to make S possible. It does not follow that S is possibly possible; that, again, would entail the existence of a power before the divine decision that brings it to be. It is possible that God make S possible only if there is a possibly possible world in which S comes about. At this point, God has power and opportunity not to establish such a world. God has the power to make S impossible. It does not follow that S is possibly impossible. Lacks of power establish an impossibility only if suitable powers are already on the scene (recall Chapter 2 on created-powers theories). Without God's specified powers there are not, and (as emerges) these arrive all at once. Rather, God's decision renders an amodal state of affairs modally determinate.

Scotus held that God's thinking produces creatures in 'intelligible being', and the content of the creatures thus produced renders them possible (or not). Ockham argued against Scotus that logically before God thinks the creature up, it

> is possible ... or ... not possible. If it is possible, then it is possible before it is produced in intelligible being. If it is not possible, then it is incompatible with existence.[20]

'Logically before' God thinks up Rover, he is either possible or not possible. If Rover is then possible, this is not God's doing: God has not yet even conceived him and (Ockham assumes) does nothing unintentionally. If Rover is then not possible, Ockham infers, he is then impossible. Not even God can make the impossible possible, and so Rover would remain impossible despite any divine attempt. So (Ockham concludes) God does not account for facts of possibility. As I see it, God thinks up Rover and it is then up to Him whether Rover shall be possible. So there is for me as for Scotus a point in the explanatory story prior to Rover's being possible. But there is for me as for Scotus no *time* at which Rover's status is ever unsettled, and that being so, it is not clear why there being such a point in the story of how it comes to be eternally settled should create a problem. That story does not (so I argue) describe a temporal process. It is just a way of pointing out what eternally presupposes what. As long as the whole chain of presupposing and presupposed facts is eternally in place, Ockham's argument raises a pseudo-problem: in any sense that matters modally—at all times in all worlds—there *is* no 'before' God thinks up Rover. Rover is eternally possible, but that is because God eternally does something. As we *consider* Rover at the pre-modal stages of the explanatory story, the

---

[20] William Ockham, *In I Sent.*, d. 43, q. 2, in *Opera Theologica* v. 4, p. 647.

right thing to do is abstain from modal talk. Rover is never really other than possible. But when his being possible is the fact to be explained, that fact should not enter the story before its conclusion, and as the explanation serves to rule out his ever having any other modal status, no other modal status should apply to him at any point in the story either. At earlier stages, we should not say that Rover is possible, nor that he is impossible. In so doing we are not saying that he has some strange third status that would require us to treat being possible and being impossible as contraries rather than contradictories. We are just refusing to speak till the appropriate point in the story. As soon as God thinks Rover up, he is possible. But His thinking Rover up does not suffice for this, and explanatorily posterior parts of the story I tell presuppose it. *Just qua thought up by God*, Rover is neither possible nor impossible. The *qua*-locution keeps us from having to do anything fancy with the modal semantics. It serves to refer the claim 'Rover is neither possible nor impossible' to a particular point in the explanatory story, and with this restriction, all the claim does is remind us not to apply modal words to Rover at this point.

The claim that

NC. it *was* not the case that God could have made it possible that P

concerns God just *qua* considering whether to make it possible that P. At this point in the story, the only modal facts are those determined by God's nature. God's nature does not suffice to assign a modal status to the act of making it possible that P. If God has not yet determined P's modal status, the act of making it possible that P has no modal status yet. If it has none, it is not yet the case that God could or could not have made it possible that P. We express this, looking at that point in the story, in (NC). What makes (NC) true is simply that *qua* considering whether it is to be possible that P, God has not yet decided on this.

Powers God Cannot Use?

I have said that it is in God to have or have had other powers than He in fact has, and to think up other secular states of affairs than He has, but I will say that He cannot do so—that is, does so in no possible world. This may sound like I will ascribe to God an in-principle unusable power, to have there be other powers and states of affairs than there are. I do not. For one thing, the 'in Him' locution does not ascribe a power. It ascribes at most only a basis for having a power. Again, to come up with more states of affairs, God would use just what He uses to come up with those there are. On the story I eventually tell, God simply thinks things up, then either permits or prevents them; what He permits is then possible. God would do the same if He permitted more.

His coming up with more would involve nothing He does not actually use. So having it in Him to have more does not entail having an unusable power.

One might reply that there is still something here that God cannot use: He cannot use that of His endowment that would bring forth more states of affairs than there are. But God *has* used what it takes to add states of affairs to what there are: He has added those there are to an initial situation without them. I doubt that on the right way to individuate powers, God has in addition an unusable power to have there be more than *these*. Further, the fact that God Himself has made it impossible that there be other states of affairs should tip us that there is something wrong with the reasoning. It is *in Him* to manifest what it is in Him to do to this further degree. Otherwise there would have been nothing for Him to do—the limit on its use would have been set by His nature. He has not done so. His not doing so made it the case that He could not have done so. But at the point at which He did not do it, it was not impossible that He do it, and it was in Him to do it.

Questions naturally arise about how much that is impossible it is or was in God to bring about. I maintain that it was in God not to think up each secular state of affairs He has in fact thought up (otherwise they were written into Him, either in the indicative or in the imperative). I also hold that for any range of these He thought up, it was in Him not to think it up. It was in Him to add to the stock of bearers of modal status there actually are, or substitute for ones there are ones there are not. For it is not in His nature for His imagination to be exhausted; there is not some inbuilt limit to how much God can conceive, setting (so to speak) an outer boundary beyond which He could not extend the realm of secular states of affairs. I do not hold that there are particular secular states of affairs it is in Him to think up such that He has not thought these up: were this true, there would be secular states of affairs whose being such did not depend on God's thinking them up. I also maintain that secular modal status was up to God. I do not believe it was in God to have mathematical and logical truths come out false, to bring it about that there never was a God, that He was never God, that someone else was God, or that the divine nature be other than as it is. Saying that secular truths depend on divine activities does not commit me to saying that other sorts do.

God had it in Him to think up more than He has, and perhaps to permit more of what He has thought up. He did not. But nothing blocked His doing so, and His endowments to do so did not disappear when it was up to Him whether to do so. So what explains it that He did not do so? In the case of permission it is a simple choice, and to be explained as choices are. Further, I would argue that there is a limit to what can be explained about some cases of choice. Reasons may incline without necessitating, or barely incline at all. In such cases, finally all there is to say may be that the agent just did so choose. God's nature may partly explain His not thinking up more: perhaps He did not think up more horrors than He has because His nature kept Him from even conceiving things worse than are currently possible or impossible. But beyond this, all there is to say is that He did not. If this is acceptable in the case of choice, where fairly specific reasons can bear, it is more so in the case of dreaming up concepts of creatures, where perhaps there can be no reason at all to think up (say) quarks rather than schmarks. Causation may provide another parallel. There may well be probabilistic causation. On one reasonable gloss, what makes it probabilistic is that even given the most conducive circumstances, certain powers are not determined to fire, but may do so or may not, and over a series of opportunities do so with a particular frequency. Probabilistic causation may involve powers which simply do or do not fire, with no further explanation of why they do not if they do not. These cases, of course, raise difficulties for certain sorts of principle of sufficient reason, but it is no part of theism to be committed to one of these, though *de facto* some theists have been.

I now turn to a point about what deity endows God with mentally.

Deity and Preference

God surely has preferences, which at least partly account for His choosing what He does. He has some by nature, such as His preference for moral good over moral evil. But if secular states of affairs are not 'in' the divine nature, God cannot by nature have preferences involving these. So God cannot by nature prefer chocolate to vanilla, or courage to cowardice. As God does prefer courage to cowardice, He has preferences He had not by nature, but only once He thought up creatures. His natural preferences can involve only states He is in and values He realizes by nature, none of which are creature-involving. So God might by nature prefer good to evil, moral to aesthetic value, His knowledge of Himself to His knowledge that nothing other than He exists, knowledge to volition (or not), and so on. If any of these are straightforwardly better or worse than one another, there is in each such comparison a best. So God's purely natural preferences cannot differ with respect to these, as God cannot have an imperfect preference, and one which flew in the face of a fact of bestness *in this case* would be imperfect.[21] If any of these are of equal or incommensurable value, on the other hand, it would seem odd for God's nature to home in on just one: why would deity dictate a preference that is no more a matter of acknowledging superior value than that for chocolate over vanilla? In this case, it seems, the most God's nature could provide would be a power to form alternate sets of preferences, given content among which to prefer. We could represent this as His nature

---

[21] Robert Adams has famously argued that gracious love for creatures could legitimately trump God's preference for the best ('Must God Create the Best?', in Thomas Morris (ed.), *The Concept of God* (Oxford: Oxford University Press, 1987), pp. 91–106).

providing templates for sorts of possible world—worlds in which God prefers the one, in which He prefers the other, and in which He has no preference. Templates are not worlds, nor do these templates determine how many worlds of each sort there might come to be. Nor do the templates yet represent possibilities. I shortly argue that God's nature dictates that He think up creatures. The templates do not represent any creatures. Things' being only as templates represent, then, is not a possible state of affairs. But what they represent comes to be incorporated in possible worlds: there are possible worlds in which God prefers one, another, or none of items of equal or incommensurable value.

A further question is whether, once God has creatures in mind and forms preferences concerning them, His nature uniquely determines what He prefers. I suggest that it determines only a range of preference-sets He *might* have, and does not account fully for His having the actual preference-set He has. If God's nature determines every detail of His preferences once He has secular states of affairs in mind, then it is not possible that He have any other preferences than He has, given those He has conceived. If that is how things are, it is harder to explain how it is that He might seek to actualize the wide variety of possible worlds He might. Let us consider the ways one might suppose God to choose which world to seek to actualize. Among these might be: reasons to seek to actualize a possible world uniquely determine one world as the ideal one to try for, and God simply chooses as reason dictates, or instead: reasons uniquely determine one and God chooses it because He prefers to be reasonable. I set these aside. God probably does have reasons for features of the world that are utterly beyond our ken. What I cannot believe is that He has one for every little bit of it—that there is some transcendent rationality to there being, at this instant, n quarks rather than n + 1. Again, it is enormously plausible that there is no uniquely best possible world. But if there is not, then for any congeries of goods G about a world that could provide a reason to seek to actualize it, there is either a world with a better, or a world with an equal set, or a world whose goods are just incommensurable with G's. If this is true, sheer reason, regarding goods, cannot uniquely determine God's choice. Moreover, if (as is plausible) only something God regards as worth choosing for can provide a reason for Him to choose a world, it is not enough that worlds offer arrays of goods: God's *preferences* about those goods will determine His reasons. To the extent that the goods have an objective ordering, perhaps His preferences will mirror this—but as there seem to be many incommensurable sorts of value, it is plausible that God's preferences cannot simply mirror any such ordering, and so we must consider another sort of role for preference in divine choice, a role not simply determined by abstract rational considerations or an objective ordering of values.

God has created our universe, U, and brought us to be within it. A much less interesting and valuable universe would be U*, containing just two atoms and the void. U* certainly seems possible.[22] So does the conjunction *God exists and U* exists*. If it is possible, God might at least permit U*. If I'm right that God is perfect by nature and the GSA-property is a perfection (and perfections are such by their intrinsic contents and so not contingently), then if possibly God exists and U* exists, God might have created U* instead of our own universe. Now if all God's preferences are His by nature (once He has envisioned a range of universes), if God created U*, He would have picked U* given the preferences He actually has. But either God's actual preferences converge on a fairly narrow sort of universe, leading Him to uniquely prefer a range of worlds rather like U, or they leave His choice relatively unconstrained. The more they converge on a world very like U, the less they would have rendered His choice of U* rational. If God's preferences make it highly satisfactory to have a universe very like U, and less satisfactory the further a universe is from being like U, and nothing constrains God's choice, and U* is in the relevant respects very unlike U, it would be rather irrational to pick U* rather than U. So on this account of God's preferences, He might have made a rather irrational decision. But if He is necessarily perfectly wise, this is false. We could push this in another direction: if God's natural preferences favor a universe very like U, and He cannot decide save with ideal rationality, U* and many other universes that intuitively seem possible or compatible with God's existence turn out not the latter, and perhaps not the former. I am willing to exclude possible-seeming universes from possibility—I do so on moral grounds—but it would be better to do as little of this as we can. The more we overrule intuition, the less plausible the resulting position.

Suppose, on the other hand, that God's nature determines every detail of His preferences once He conceives creatures and His preferences do not converge on a world rather like U, but are instead broad and indefinite enough to make U and U* not unacceptably different in the degree to which they satisfy God's preferences. Then the last paragraph's problems do not arise. But we get others. A set of preferences so indefinite as to make U and U* almost equally satisfactory does not well recognize and respond to the radical differences in value between U and U*. This does not befit perfect goodness and rationality. Again, such preferences give little guidance to God's choice. If despite the great difference between U and U* God did not prefer one or the other, His preferences did not guide His choice. Instead, there being no other basis to choose, He simply picked a world in the U–U* range arbitrarily, or created and set in motion some non-deterministic mechanism to do this for Him.[23] (If He made one, made it deterministic, and set it in motion, He would determine the result and so just be picking by indirect means.) As to the first,

---

[22] If for some reason this does not seem possible to you, substitute your own example of a much less valuable universe.

[23] This, of course, would raise the question of how He would pick a mechanism. I am not claiming that such questions are finally answerable or that this really turns out in the end to be a possibility: but in the abstract it seems like an option, and so I include it for completeness.

some arbitrary choice may be involved in any universe-selection. (Could there be a unique best number of stars to have?[24]) And perhaps where there is no basis to choose, if one has good reason to make a choice, one has good reason to 'just pick', it being better to have some result than none. Still, the more arbitrary the choice God makes, the less rational (in another sense) the choice. For there is more about the universe for which He has no reason at all. And the more arbitrary the choice, and the less responsive to the actual values of the alternatives, the less easily God's making it sits with His being perfectly rational and ideally wise. This applies *a fortiori* if God farms His choice out to a mechanism. In this case there is literally no divine reason for anything about the universe save those features common to every world in the U–U* range. This could make the problem of evil intractable—in which case it is not a genuine possibility. Believers would like to see the world as manifesting divine wisdom, but could not do so for any part or aspect of the world if they believed this procedure had operated unless they knew what the U–U* range was and what features were universal within the range.

If we allow that God's nature does not determine every detail of His preferences given conceived creatures, but instead God might have had other preferences than He did, we can allow that God might have had preferences that would make U* more satisfactory to Him than U. This allows for God's choice of U* and avoids the consequences I have sketched. We need not say that God might have made an irrational choice in creating either, or that He might have been insensitive to the values of U and U*, or that there might have been a universe for most of which He had no good reason (as there might were it possible that He choose our universe from preferences that would have made U* almost equally satisfactory). Rather, He could have preferred U* and so chosen it.

Of course, this move raises another question: how could a being ideally rational by nature prefer U* to what seem like obviously better universes? Well, there are good things about U*. It would not distract a deity with some thinking to do. It is elegantly simple. To someone with a taste for (say) Japanese minimalism it could be beautiful, and even more beautiful than something more baroque. And it is possible to have almost any aesthetic taste, because even if there are objective aesthetic qualities—which is highly debatable—there are many sorts of beauty. U* contains no suffering or moral evil. It is certainly possible that someone be so highly averse to sin and suffering as to prize highly universes without them: atheists often wonder why God does not evince this trait. Again, Western orthodoxy holds that God is able not to create. If this is possible, it is possible that He prefer on balance a situation with nothing but Himself. Now there are at most three ways God might

---

[24] Even if there is a best possible universe—which hardly seems likely—it does not follow that there is a best possible number of stars. For a best universe is best *overall*, and this is compatible with its being non-best in any particular feature.

determine what to create.[25] Either He picks in accord with some preference, or He 'just picks', or He farms the choice out to a non-deterministic picking mechanism. So either it is possible that He simply prefer not to create, or it is possible that He 'just pick', wind up picking a world with Himself alone, and accept it—preferring not to create not initially, but on balance once He has changed the situation by 'just picking'—or it is possible that He set up a mechanism that turns out to yield 'create nothing', and He prefer to let that stand rather than rerun the procedure, once again preferring not to create on balance within a changed situation. If that is possible, and U* is in some sense an improvement on it, it is also possible that God wind up creating U*, either because He can have on-balance preferences that initially yield a choice of U*, or because He can have them after a 'just pick' choice or the operation of some selection mechanism.

I suggest, therefore, that even given the creatures He envisions, God's nature determines only a range of preference-sets He might have (some elements of which doubtless occur in all sets), not the full set He actually has. Why does God then see all candidate creatures and (say) prefer quarks to schmarks? He just does. There is nothing more to say. So too, when someone libertarian-free makes a choice, while there might be factors that incline him/her to it, in the end, he/she just does so choose, though he/she could do otherwise. If God's nature does not wholly determine His preferences, as I have argued, there must be some brute preferences in Him. The less scope for brute preference in God, the greater the scope for brute choice unrationalized by preference. There is no imperfection in being such as to just like something once you see it, if it is your nature to develop likes and there is nothing irrational about the likes you develop (as I assume in the quark/schmark case: what I have in mind is that there is no objective merit either preference fails to do justice to). But the less one's preferences rationalize one's choices, the more the risk that one's choices come out arbitrary and so imperfectly rational. So I hold that God develops 'brute likes' undetermined by His nature once He has creatures in mind.

So, it is possible that God be in alternative states of brute liking. If it were not, worlds He could rationally choose only if He were in these states would not be possible. By allowing alternative divine preference-states, we allow worlds to be possible which would not be as rational as U for Him to pick, given His actual preferences, and allow too He could have both been ideally rational and picked them.

---

[25] Perhaps one or more of these is in the end not a way things could go. I am not committed to all three genuinely being possible; I am allowing all apparent options for the sake of completeness.

10

THE BIGGEST BANG

I now begin to explain the non-deity component of my theory of secular modal truth. This part of the story begins with God thinking up all secular states of affairs. I first argue that God's nature requires Him to think some up. I further argue that He thinks up all He thinks up at once, in the Biggest Bang of all. I finally maintain that God's nature imposes only the weakest constraints on what He thinks, and discuss implications of the claim that it is in Him to think up more than He has in fact thought up.

Must God Think up Creatures?

Being by nature omniscient, by nature God knows all there is to know about Himself. So He knows what it is to be something He has made—a creature.[1] For in fully comprehending Himself, God fully comprehends the whole of what He is naturally able to do. So God knows that He naturally can create and what it is to create. Knowing the latter, He knows that any act of creating has a product. Further, one does not fully understand a productive power without fully understanding what it is a power to produce.[2] So if He fully understands the power to create, He fully understands what it is to be something created, for 'something created' is almost the least one can say about what the power to create is a power to produce. (That it would be something created is also the most God could know about creation's product prior to thinking up specific sorts of creatures.) So as God is by nature omniscient about His own nature, He by nature grasps what it is to be something created—a creature. Further, God by nature knows that He has the power and opportunity to create, and so knows that it is possible that there be creatures: this possibility is given with His power

---

[1] Here I am indebted to Joseph Jedwab.
[2] Here I am reworking Aquinas.

and the opportunity to use it which His existence provides. And as God by nature knows that creatures are possible, God by nature has the concept of a possible creature. The question, then, is whether in addition God by nature thinks up specific sorts of possible creature.

A moral consideration

One argument that by nature God does so runs thus: God is by nature perfectly good. This includes perfect generosity. One kind of generosity consists in being willing to give if asked. Another kind does not wait to be asked, but actively seeks to give. The latter is surely the better form. So perfect-being theology rules that God has it, and naturally has a supremely generous disposition. It is hard to see how such a disposition could fail to drive Him to at least consider giving something to someone. Within the Trinity, the Father in some sense gives all He is to the Son and Spirit. But on what I think the correct view of the Trinity, this is in a fairly strong sense God giving to Himself.[3] If a view broadly along those lines *is* correct, it is reasonable to think that a generous impulse would lead God to at least consider further giving. God's natural knowledge equips Him with the general concept of a possible creature. He knows that He cannot give further unless He creates. It seems to me, then, that natural generosity would incline God to think about the sort of giving He cannot do unless He creates others to receive. Now He has naturally the general concept of something created. He could think about giving the gift of Himself to something created without dreaming up any particular sort of thing other than Himself. But it is reasonable to think that God's generous impulse would carry Him further, to think of some specific sort of thing to give to. Here there is the threat of an extension, to an argument that God's generosity requires Him actually to create. This can be dealt with, though, as I treat the extensions considered below.

Creativity arguments

Two perhaps stronger arguments that God thinks up creatures by nature rest on His creativity. One can distinguish two forms of creativity. Some will come up with something creative if set a task or asked for an idea. Others do not wait to be moved from without, but are irrepressibly creative, new thoughts springing up just out of their own inner drives. The latter is surely the better form. So it is the form we should ascribe to God. But it is hard to see what in a divine psychology could block this sort of impulse. So it appears that if God

---

[3] So 'A Latin Trinity,' *Faith and Philosophy* 21 (2004), 304–33.

has it, He will be creative, i.e. think up creatures to make. And so God's by-nature perfect creativity guarantees that He thinks up creatures.

Again, plausibly the overall creative state of someone dispositionally creative who has a good record of creativity is better than that of someone equally creative dispositionally who has no record. *Some*thing valuable accrues to the creator, if not a further degree of dispositional creativity. If so, a God who never thought up creatures would be in a less perfect overall creative state than one who did, and so if God by nature is perfect creatively, God by nature thinks up creatures.

A step too far

Having said this, I must head off possible extensions of the argument. One begins from the claim that

1. If God is in a better creative state for just thinking up creatures, then He would be in a still better creative state if He actually made some,

detackes the conditional, and continues that

> God can actually make some. So:
> God can have actually made some. So:
> God can be in a more perfect creative state.
> God is perfect only if He cannot be in a better state. So:
> God is perfect only if He creates. But
> God is essentially perfect. So:
> God is not free not to create.

Here I reject (1). In God's case, a conceived work is guaranteed to come out exactly as conceived (its execution is guaranteed to be perfect), and its execution requires but a word. If so, all marks for a record of creativity are earned in the planning. So it is not plausible that actually creating improves God's creative state—having created more would not give Him more of what thinking up creatures gives Him, or more of something else relevant to being creative. He would have a longer record as a *cause*, but that's another issue.

Again, some might contend that if God is better for thinking up some creatures, He would be better for thinking up more than for thinking up less, and so in parallel for making more than for making less. So I note against the first that if doing something is better than doing nothing, it does not follow that doing more is better than doing less. It is good to give presents, but too-large presents can be more trouble than they are worth. The second again confuses record as cause with record for creativity; it also ignores that making more might mean making matters worse.

Another extension might be

2. God makes a good creature in W and no creature in W* → God has a better record as a maker in W.

3. God has a better record as a maker in W → God is in better state as a maker in W, and

4. God is in a better state as a maker in W → God is a more perfect being overall in W.

5. It is possible that God make a good creature.

6. It is not possible that God be more a more perfect being than He is. So:

7. It is not possible that God not make a good creature.

(2) and (3) parallel the second creativity argument. But (6) is ambiguous. Perfect-being theology usually deals in such attributes as omniscience, omnipotence, and so on: it fills out our concept of God's nature. (6) is true if God's being perfect consists merely in His having His nature, and so such perfections as these. But in this sense of 'perfect being', (4) is false: having made more has no effect on God's being omniscient, omnipotent, etc. Suppose, on the other hand, that God's being more perfect includes His being in specific creature-related states (like having created a, b, and so on). Then (4) is plausible, but (6) so taken is false. If being in a better state of this sort is part of being more perfect, then if a better record is possible, it is possible to be more perfect. If we treat perfection this way, then as there is no best record of making universes to have—for any God might make, a better would have been possible—there cannot be a maximally perfect being. God can be perfect *tout court* only treating perfection in the first way.

I submit, then, that God by nature thinks up definite candidate creatures (if it is in Him to have pre-creative singular concepts of creatures otherwise, maximally definite sorts of candidate creatures). Further, it is at least plausible that His nature guarantees that some of these turn out possible—that God might permit them to exist. Part of His motivation for thinking them up, I have suggested, is a generous impulse. If this is so and He nonetheless comes up with nothing He could stand to let exist, there would be a mismatch between His natural desire to be generous and His cognitive power: His power would not suffice to serve His (entirely good) desires. This would obviously be a defect. Again, it would be a defect in His creativity if it were insufficient to serve a desire that leads Him to grant it free play. But if we rule these defects out, God's nature guarantees that some creature turn out possible. These conclusions suggest that I cannot after all escape at least a very thin partial deity theory. That there is something non-divine is a secular truth. That possibly there is something non-divine is a secular modal truth. It appears that God's nature is sufficient to make it true, or at least to guarantee the production of a truth-maker for it (as in Leibniz). If that is right, then as God necessarily has His nature, this modal truth is itself necessary, and its necessity stems from God's nature. Again, even if one rejects the last step, to a natural guarantee of possible creatures, God's nature makes Him so think that the claim that there is something non-divine bears some modal status. This is a secular truth, and it seems that God's nature guarantees that it comes out true and necessary. I concede these things, and henceforth ignore the concession. I cannot avoid all deity elements in my view, but I continue to call it a non-deity theory, on the grounds that it does not involve the divine nature in making true any but this sort of abstract secular truth. On my view all *substantive* secular modal truth remains outside what deity makes true or guarantees to come out true.

God by nature thinks up definite candidate creatures. I now argue that He thought up all such items at once—which is why I call His doing so the Biggest Bang.

For a Bang

God is either temporal or atemporal. If God is atemporal, He thinks up nothing later than anything else. All His thoughts are there in the same temporally unextended part of His life. So we can say they all are there at once, though we cannot in this case read this as 'at one *time*.'

Suppose on the other hand that God is temporal. If God naturally can represent to Himself a particular creature before it actually exists, then I now argue that He thinks up all creatures, worlds etc. at once (that is, from all eternity). If He cannot, the closest He can come is to represent some individual with just the purely general attributes that (say) I have—a maximally detailed type I instance, a concept of someone just like me, but not of me. If this is correct, the argument will suggest *mutatis mutandis* that He had at once all His general representations for types of possible creatures (someone just like me, like you, and so on), worlds (complete save for the identities of the individuals they contain), etc.

Consider any delay in thinking up a (type of[4]) creature or world. Unless there is some reason to delay—that is, where only getting to the goal matters—it is better to get to a goal sooner rather than later. So unless there was reason to delay, it would have been better to think it up sooner, or sooner than *that*, and so on till the delay is pared to zero.[5] And so this is how it naturally would have been for God, unless there was reason to delay. Reasons for delay prior to Creation would have to come from within God, since there is then nothing outside Him to provide one. But what reason could there be? It is not as if He needs examples to jog His mind or inspiration

---

[4] From here on, take this insertion as read where appropriate.

[5] If God is temporal and eternal, He exists without beginning, throughout a past without beginning: an eternal being by definition cannot have begun to exist. (For discussion, see my 'Eternity and Immutability', in William Mann (ed.), *The Blackwell Companion to Philosophy of Religion* (New York: Basil Blackwell, 2004).) Suppose, then, that if an item's existence had a first instant or first finite period, then it began to exist. (I am not sure this is true—a necessarily existing God *might* provide an exception—but many people seem to believe it.) It follows that if God was temporally eternal, past time was infinite, and so the only delay that could be involved would be one infinitely long, since before any point in time there would have been an infinite time.

from something He's already thought up, or has a finite mind capable of generating only so much content at once. A perfect being would not need to add something later to rectify defects in His first effort; a perfect God gets it in one. Might He save some thinking to do later, to have something to pass the time? God has Himself to contemplate. If our imperfect grasp of Him in the Beatific Vision is (so we are told) the greatest joy of which we are capable, it is dubious that God's perfect grasp would leave Him bored. In any case, there is much else a deity could do given things He had already thought up—for example, create some of them and interact with them—which at least if our own experience is any guide would be rather more interesting. Might God draw out the process to enjoy anticipating His next move? Either God does or He does not exhaustively foreknow what He will think up next, in perfect detail. If He does, He cannot enjoy the sort of anticipation whose flavor depends on not knowing what is coming next. Now it can make sense to enjoy anticipating even an event whose content one fully grasps, if the event will bring about some real-world change one desires (such as full foreknowledge of one's wedding). But merely thinking up creatures does not change the real world outside God. So it is not clear that anticipation would make sense here. But in any event, it does not seem to be possible. If what God foreknows in full detail is what creatures He will think up, He already has them fully in mind, in His foreknowledge. If He has them in mind, it is too late to anticipate thinking them up. On the other hand, if God cannot fully foreknow His next creative burst, it is still an odd picture: God rubbing His hands with glee, thinking 'My oh my, what will I come up with next?' God dreams up creatures to enjoy contemplating the possibilities, but even if all He is doing is contemplating, better to have more to contemplate sooner. But this is not all He is doing. More fundamentally, God dreams up creatures and worlds to consider what to create. This is goal-oriented thinking. This being so, it would be better to have at once the full range of options He is to consider. So there is no delay involved: God thinks up all creatures from all eternity, whether He is timeless or temporal. Further, while the moral and creativity arguments do not entail this, I suggest that they also lend it some support.

One might wonder why—given a first pass at a 'full range'—He would not add still more, however many and great those He first comes up with. After all, He would know that it is Him (if temporal) to do better next time; only on a deity theory could He have thought up everything creaturely it was in Him to think up. But God's reason to take a second pass would have to be either some desire or purpose His first pass did not ideally satisfy or His knowledge that He could on a second pass think up worlds better than any He had thought up on His first pass. The relevant desires or purposes divide into those He had before He had worlds in mind and those evoked by first-pass worlds. If His first pass contained no worlds ideally satisfying the desires and purposes He had before He had worlds in mind, His mind would have imperfectly served His initial motivations. Liability to this would be an imperfection. If His first pass evoked desires and purposes no first-pass world ideally satisfied, God would have failed to envision any world good enough to satisfy ideally all desires and purposes any first-pass world would evoke in Him. This would imply a failure of fit between that in Him which generates His desires and purposes and that in Him which generates ideas that could satisfy them. Liability to this too would be an imperfection. So a perfect being would in His first pass think up many worlds ideally suited to both sorts of desires and purposes.[6] If they are ideally suited, it does not seem that He should *want* to consider more.

If He nonetheless thought up more, He would do so because He knew that it is in Him to produce still better if He sets Himself to surpass His prior effort. But He would know this no matter what He did. Further, no matter what He did, this knowledge would have the same rational and motivational force. There would be nothing to lessen it, as He could not tire, find thinking harder, come to the end of His resources, etc. So if He ever had sufficient reason to add possibilities, He would have it no matter what He added. And so ceasing to add new possibilities would have to mean failing to do what He had sufficient reason to do, and doing what He had sufficient reason not to do. If He never stopped adding, though, He would never create, frustrating one motivation He has to be thinking up creatures at all. This might mean that it would be more rational to stop at some point than never to stop. But halting at any particular point would be arbitrary. If any stopping point would be arbitrary and would leave Him knowing as He did at the outset that He has to choose among alternatives He could surpass if He thought further, there is no reason to proceed to a second set of worlds. He has as much reason to choose to seek to actualize a world from His initial array of alternatives[7] as He will ever have to choose to pursue a world from any array,[8] and so there is no point to delay, particularly if His initial array contains worlds ideally satisfying all His purposes and desires. I take it, then, that even if He is temporal, God's representations of creatures and worlds arrive all at once. Those who think God temporal but disagree can relativize the relevant parts of what I say to sets of representations that have arrived as of a given time.

As I see it, the content of deity does not determine what God thinks up in the biggest Bang. Instead, God invents the very natures of things. God's nature did not require that there be such a thing as redness. Nor does redness result

---

[6] This implies, of course, that a surpassable world could ideally suit God's desires and purposes. I see no reason to doubt this; for discussion of some of the issues, see my 'No Best World: Moral Luck', *Religious Studies* 41 (2005), 165–81, and 'No Best World: Creaturely Freedom', *Religious Studies* 41 (2005), 269–85.

[7] If the world does not contain created incompatibilist freedom, then God need not merely seek to actualize it: He can just will it and have it. If it does, then we have seen why trying to actualize it is all He can do.

[8] Of course, if He stops with array $W \ldots W_n$, He will not have any reason to choose of the form '*this* world is better than any world in $W \ldots W_n$.' But He will have reasons of precisely similar forms. If W^* is in $W \ldots W_n$ and is a better world than any in sub-array $W \ldots W_m$, He will have among other reasons to choose to pursue W^* that W^* is a better world than any in $W \ldots W_m$. Further, no matter where He stopped in adding possibilities, He would not have any reason to choose of the form '*this* world is better than any world in $W \ldots W_o$,' where $W \ldots W_o$ is the full array He has thought up and $o \neq n$.

from deliberate choice. One chooses deliberately among alternatives one has in mind. So to choose deliberately to think up color, He would have to have first thought up thinking it up, and He could not do so without thinking it up. Rather, God spontaneously comes up with redness. Doing so is a feat of sheer imagination. Red is a color because that is how God thinks of it. It is necessarily a color because He does not possibly think of it any other way. Some might respond here, 'If this is so, there is no reason for there to be such a property as redness. It just happens. There is no reason for red to be a color. It just is. This turns necessary truths into sheer surds. This is at least as bad a problem as any developed for deity theories or Platonism.'[9] But on the contrary, if this is a problem, it is just as fully one for deity theories or Platonism.

Consider first the question why there is such a property as redness. I have argued that sheer necessity (equivalently, lack of an alternative) does not explain. If it does not, Platonists cannot answer the question by appeal to redness' necessary existence, nor deity theorists to the necessity of God's nature's existing and containing redness. Nor could either answer by (say) pointing out that other creaturely properties' existence entails redness. For this would just push our interest back a step, to why there are *those* properties: the same sort of question would arise. In any case, those other properties entail redness's existence only (so to speak) given that there is such a property to entail. The entailment fact is just that of co-presence in all possible worlds, and we are asking why possible worlds are stocked with the particular co-present items they are. I do not see that the Platonist can say more than that it is just an ultimate brute fact that there is, and is necessarily, such a thing as redness. Nor can the deity theorist say more than that it is an ultimate brute fact that there is redness (in the divine nature, which necessarily exists just as Platonic redness would). For me, there is no such thing as a Platonic property, redness. There is just a divine thought contentful in a particular way, such that if it is appropriately involved in a divine action, red things result. For me, as just seen, there is nothing more to say about this divine thought than just that it is there, as a brute fact. Brutality for brutality, my view is no worse than Platonism or deity theories (or possibilism) here. *Mutatis mutandis* the same will be true for red's being a color. The Platonist and deity theorist will just say that this is just part of what it is: there is no explanation to be had. I say that it is just part of what it is and equivalently, just part of how God thinks of it. So again, no disadvantage accrues to my view.

One might instead try to push a problem from the opposite direction. Platonism and deity theories (one might argue) do not make it look like there is something to say about why there is such a thing as redness. They do not suggest that this is a good question. My view, on the other hand, seems to make the similar question about a divine thought a good one. For it answers the question, with a brief causal story. If my view makes it look like there is

---

[9] So a referee. I note but will not contest his Platonist assumption that properties exist necessarily.

something to explain when really there is not, that is a disadvantage vis-à-vis its rivals. However, there would be a problem here only if the question I make good and answer were the same question that is not a good one on the rival views. *Their* question concerns the existence of a necessary, abstract property. I can agree that if there were such things, asking for a causal story behind their existence would not be apt. But I do not believe in these. My story concerns the occurrence of an episode of divine thinking. Events *are* the sorts of things for which this question is appropriate.

'Given' Material

If it is natural to God to think up some creature or other, the next question is whether there are sorts of creature it is natural to God to think up. God's natural state provides Him some 'given' material to think about, and He naturally has or acquires any concepts needed fully to comprehend it. If this material could in principle be used to think up items other than He, His natural omniscience will not miss this. So we can ask whether His 'found' material makes it natural to think up sorts of creatures appropriately based on it. Earlier arguments suggest that on a non-deity view, this 'found' material leaves Him great scope for creative thinking.

It is little help with kind-concepts. The only kinds it is plausible to see God as belonging to are *particular, substance, spirit, person,* and *deity.*[10] So if God naturally has or acquires just the kind-concepts He needs to comprehend Himself, plausibly He will naturally have or acquire just these. As noted earlier, it is not plausible that *substance* (or *particular*) build its sub-kinds in. Further, if other kinds exist only if God thinks them up, then independent of God's creative thinking, *particular* and *substance* have no sub-kinds other than God's. So *particular* and *substance* give God little toward thinking up kinds of non-divine substance. We've seen that *person* cannot stand alone, that there is no such kind-property as *spirit* and that it is questionable whether a God without the concept of matter could have the concept of a spirit. Finally, creatures are not lesser deities and their kinds are not sub-kinds of *deity.* So the most God could be is a partial kind-paradigm for creaturely substances. And nothing in Him would dictate any particular scheme of the sort of distant likenesses to Him that stones and stars have. 'Found' material *could* not dictate what God does with it. 'Found' pictures do not determine how we read them; directional signs (arrows) are not self-interpreting; deconstructionists can read chemistry texts as poetry. This is not a matter of our cognitive limitations—well, perhaps the last is—but of the natures of pictures and signs. So it seems

---

[10] For some of what makes something a kind-concept, see Chapter 7.

unlikely that God's 'found' material can dictate a unique way of reading it, as a sign or clue as to what other sorts of things to think up.

Non-kind concepts

One sample non-kind intrinsic divine state will let me make the points I want to make about these, so let us focus on a state of knowledge. If omniscient, God knows that He has knowledge. His full self-comprehension will give Him a grasp of what knowledge is. Let us examine how far God's grasp of His knowledge takes Him toward conceiving creatures.

God is by nature omniscient. So He is naturally aware of Himself. His having His full natural endowment is a precondition of doing anything He does not do by nature: if He did not have it, He would not exist, and existing is a precondition of doing anything. So in what I will call the order of preconditions, He is aware of Himself before He thinks up creatures. When[11] He is aware only of Himself, God has not yet thought up other states of knowledge than He Himself has. Thinking about these would constitute turning away from Himself, so to speak. If God has not yet thought up other things, but simply is aware of Himself, no such state has yet been conceived. Nor is any such state possible, since only a deity theory or Platonism could provide the possibility. Nor is one even conceivable, as only a deity theory or Platonism could provide the possibility of its being conceived. Nor is one so much as inconceivable. To be inconceivable is to be conceived in no possible world, given that there are worlds or the realities behind world-talk. God's conceiving creatures is the first step toward establishing the reality behind world-talk. Thus only if creatures have been conceived is anything inconceivable. At the point in the order of preconditions at which God is aware just of Himself, God has it in Him to conceive non-divine states of knowledge only in the weak sense that it is in Him to conceive non-divine states. There are then no non-divine states such that it is in God to conceive *them*. So before God conceives creatures, there are no modal- or I-facts about particular creaturely states at all.

If no states of knowledge other than God's are yet possible or conceivable, then if God develops a concept, *state of knowledge*, to comprehend something in Himself, this concept applies to no possible or conceivable non-divine state. It is not, as first developed, a concept which can have instances other than God's (no other instances being then possible). But if the same concept is turned later to creatures, it does not preclude this extension either. So it is initially a concept *indifferent* to further extension. Having the concept includes being such as to apply it to any state of knowledge. Because of this, if non-divine states of knowledge become possible, God becomes able to apply it to

[11] That is, at the particular point in the order of preconditions at which . . . Context will make clear when 'when' and like terms should be so read.

them. But nothing in the concept as God has it in comprehending Himself demands this further application.

Thus God's having the concept *state of knowledge* does not guarantee that when He turns to thinking up creatures, He will think up creatures like Him in respect of having states of knowledge. If He wished it the case that nothing other than He could have knowledge, there would be nothing in the concept to say Him nay. This reasoning generalizes. On a non-deity theory, nothing in God's nature or natural grasp of Himself dictates that God come up with creatures like Him in any particular way. If He brings it about that His concepts come possibly to apply to both Himself and creatures, that is just His creativity in action. And even if God models what He thinks up on Himself, the nature of an original, purely of itself, does not determine how it can be imitated, for it determines nothing about what media and styles are available, nor do the contents of concepts originally framed simply to be adequate to the original.

If God's material and initial concepts do not dictate what He does with what He 'finds', still some inbuilt way of dealing with it might. But on a non-deity theory, God's nature does not constrain the results of His thinking up creatures and worlds save in that it must result in things morally acceptable to think up. If deity contained a natural imperative to think up conscious creatures, for instance, a partial deity theory would be true for the claim that P. possibly or impossibly there are conscious creatures. But we have seen reason to reject even partial deity theories, save for the abstract sort mentioned earlier. The most God's nature could impose on Him if no deity theory is true is an imperative to think up items like Him in some respect to some degree. This would not determine Him to think up any particular sort of creature. This directive, in fact, would be fully satisfied if God thought up things which would if He made them exist—since existing would be a way they would resemble God. But one thing God knows of possible creatures, just as such, is that if He made them, they would exist. So just in having the concept of a possible creature, God has a concept of something which would resemble Him in existing if He made it. So the 'directive' is satisfied just by God's having a concept He has naturally—as one would expect, if it is indeed natural.

What about Omniscience?

If nothing in God's nature determines Him to think up any particular sort of creature, then for any creature-concept He actually has, it was in Him never to have had it. This can sound counterintuitive, for it can seem that

8. necessarily, if God lacks a quark-concept, He is not omniscient.

If (8) is true, His natural omniscience entails His naturally having the concept. But if (8) seems plausible in this context, this is because it seems that without a quark-concept, God would be missing something, namely the possibility of quarks. That is, it is because we are tacitly taking it that

NCP. God exists and has no quark-concept > quarks are possible.

But the best theist view will not endorse (NCP). Necessarily, if God exists and has no quark-concept, God does not know that quarks are possible. As necessarily, God is omniscient,

9. God exists and does not know that quarks are possible > quarks are not possible.

So necessarily,

NC¬P. God exists and has no quark-concept > quarks are not possible.

(NC¬P) and (NCP) are both trivially true if (as shortly emerges) God necessarily has a quark-concept. So at best we ought to be agnostic about making any substantive philosophical use of (NCP) and (8). But in fact (9) reflects the nature of God: it reflects that it is part of God's nature to be omniscient. (NCP) is true for *only* trivial semantic reasons. Its truth reflects only those. So the best theist theory should endorse (9) and so (NC¬P)—that is, base its reasoning on (9) and (NC¬P). Even if (NCP) is true, not every truth is relevant to every problem. That its truth reflects only general semantics makes it irrelevant to this one.[12] If neither (NCP) nor (NC¬P) is more relevant to the problem than the other, then the most we learn from them is that were the impossible actual, a contradiction would be true. This tells us little about God and quarks. If one is more relevant, it is (NC¬P), and so we should ignore (NCP): less relevant implies not relevant at all, in this instance. (8) and (NCP) take it as a fixed point that quarks are possible. But surely for theists, God's omniscience is a firmer, deeper fixed point. God is omniscient by nature, and God's existing and having His nature are the deepest-lying facts in all reality: deeper than any facts about quarks, if these are not facts about God's nature. When we take God's omniscience as fixed, we assure that whatever set of creature-concepts God frames misses nothing—it is not in God to fall short—but we assure that this is true however many or few concepts God frames. God must have concepts of all possible creatures. But this does not imply that it is not in Him not to have the concept of a quark. With His omniscience as our fixed point, had He not had a quark-concept, He

---

[12] One could make at least some case for treating counterpossibles instead as all false or all truth-valueless, or discriminating among them on the basis of an 'impossible worlds' semantics. If they are all false, (NCP) is false, and so an objection resting on it will fail. If they all lack truth-value, this would create no problem for my argument against (NCP). Nor would the third, for if my argument faces no other objections, intuition will tell for (9)'s truth and (NCP)'s falsity.

still would have had concepts of all possible creatures. For then quarks would not have been possible creatures. Taking God's omniscience as the fixed point dictates (9) and (NC¬P).

One could suggest that (9) is true because God's omniscience must catch whatever the facts of possibility might be, and so the possible determines what concepts God has. But if we said this, we would be treating the content of the possible as the independent factor, the fixed point. We would just be adding that God necessarily adjusts Himself to the fixed point. Further, this offers no account of how God catches the facts of possibility or why He is so good at tracking the possible. If we treat an omniscient God as the fixed point, we can say that facts about possibility really emerge from facts about God's mental life: that (say) quarks are possible because God conceives of them and permits them to exist. This claim affords a satisfying account of both. It also provides a satisfying explication of the claim that God's being omniscient is a firmer, deeper fixed point than modal facts. So I suggest that if necessarily God has His actual concept of a quark, and necessarily quarks are possible, the first is explanatorily prior to the second.[13] And so I suggest that (9) and (NC¬P) reflect that this is the true order of priority.

I have claimed that had God no quark-concept, quarks would not have been so much as possible—there would have been nothing God was missing. If this line does not convince, this may be because as we in our quarky world consider God's having no quark-concept, we think we see a quark-sized hole in God's knowledge: the quark *is* possible, we think, but God does not know it. But in thinking this way, we treat a world in which God has no quark-concept as if our quarky world were possible relative to it. This is where we go astray. If God can have no quark-concept, no quark-containing world is accessible from any world in which He lacks it: relative to no-quark-concept worlds, our world is not possible, even though our world is in fact possible. In no-quark-concept worlds, God lacks the concept of no possible creature, even though actually, quarks are possible.

But there is a still more startling consequence. If in some possible world W God has no quark-concept, our world cannot be an impossible world relative to W either. Suppose that our world were so much as an impossible world relative to W. Then in W He would lack a concept needed to know that quarks are impossible. So there would be a truth about the impossible that God did not know, namely that quarks are impossible. So God would not be omniscient in W. But it is impossible that God not be omniscient, and we have stipulated that W be a possible world. Thus God having no quark-concept is a situation *nowhere in any logical space (considered as including even impossible worlds) containing a quarky world.* To consider God having no quark-concept is to consider the hypothesis that there be an entirely different system of worlds, possible and perhaps impossible, in which quarks figure nowhere. Were there such a system *instead of* our system, it would not be possible that

---

[13] Just how having a concept relates to divine permission emerges later.

there be a quark, and a God with no quark-concept would be missing no possible creature.

Further, if a God omniscient by nature has no quark-concept, quarks are not so much as conceivable. No matter how we parse conceivability, any conceivable item will have some modal status. It will be either possible or impossible. But if God has no quark-concept, quarks are neither. If God had no concept of them and nonetheless they *were* conceivable, they would be so because either God or someone else conceives them in some other world. But then God would fail to be omniscient about the content of the possible or the impossible. Again, if quarks were conceivable, a God with no quark-concept could not know this, since one can know that quarks are conceivable only if one has a quark-concept. We do not know that zogs are conceivable, even if they are. We can read the string 'zogs are conceivable', but to us, it does not express a proposition, and so if the string expresses a truth, we cannot know that truth. Moreover, if quarks were inconceivable, a God with no quark-concept could not know this either. God can know that it is impossible to conceive of a quark only if He has some quark-concept. But if God has a quark-concept, it is not impossible to conceive of a quark. So it is impossible that God know this. Thus if God cannot conceive of a quark, it cannot be so much as impossible that quarks be conceived: quarks do not rise to the level of being inconceivable. There are no facts about quarks at all, even that they are inconceivable.

Nor could a God who cannot conceive of quarks think up creatures able to do so. If He did, He would have in mind possible worlds whose kinds He did not fully know. He would know, say, that in world W Leftow thinks up some kind of sub-atomic particle or other, but have no concept of what it is that I think up. He would lack knowledge of my possible kind-thoughts. He would also have given me a nature whose powers He does not fully comprehend. So it is not in Him to think up creatures who can conceive kinds He cannot. Rather, for God to think up a creature able to conceive of a K, God must have a representation of Ks, to assign them as possible objects of conception to others. If God has not conceived of a certain sort of object, God cannot render it conceivable for anyone else.

What about Qualities of Experience?

If it is the case that for God to think up a creature able to conceive of a K, God must have a representation of Ks, seemingly it will also be the case that for God to think up a creature able to have a quality of experience, God must have a full representation of experience with that or a relevantly similar quality. Perhaps one can fully represent to oneself qualities of experience one cannot oneself have: if so, nothing else needs saying. But if not, then God is able to have either every possible quality of phenomenal experience or some set of phenomenal qualities such that He can conceive of every other possible quality on their basis (as we might conceive of Hume's missing shade of blue). The Psalmist asked, 'Is the inventor of the eye unable to see?' Whatever the right answer, there cannot be anything about visual experience that's inconceivable to Him: else He designed our visual systems in partial ignorance, and even now does not know what it is like for us to see. And that He has no sense-organs does not entail that He does not have the kinds of experience our organs give us.

The argument about experience applies even to pain. So if one cannot fully represent to oneself qualities of experience one cannot have, God can feel pain. Now it is hard to see how one might conceive or understand pain fully on the basis only of non-painful experiences (or one's understanding of one's power to have them): phenomenologically, nothing else is quite like it. And God had better have known *some*thing pretty revealing about what pain feels like before creating. Otherwise it might seem plausible that perhaps He allowed so much pain because He did not know any better. Though ignorance excuses, we do not want to think of God as acting in ignorance of what He was making—that seems a far from perfect way to create, particularly when the consequences for creatures are so dire. But surely we ought to be tentative when it comes to speculating about what God can feel. God can have some quality of experience whence (or merely from His understanding of His power to have it) He can fully conceive of pain. Perhaps it is pain, but perhaps not. Even if our own experience contains nothing which is not pain and yet could let us fully conceive or understand pain, when it comes to the quality of God's experience, the qualities of our own are probably a poor guide.

What about Propositions?

I have spoken of kinds of object and qualities of experience. Let us now ask whether a line of argument like this might go through for propositions. If God cannot express a proposition, He cannot think it, and if He cannot think it, it is hard to see how He could assign it as a possible object of conception for someone. Yet perhaps I can conceive a proposition God cannot. When I say 'I am Brian Leftow' I express something I know. If you say 'I am BL,' meaning to assert something of yourself, you speak falsely. This might be because when *I* say 'I am BL' I express a true proposition only I can express. If it is, God cannot express this truth. But plausibly, if a language L is sufficient to express a proposition P, anyone perfectly competent in L who can conceive that P can express P to him/herself in L. So as God perfectly knows English, it seems to follow that if 'I am BL' expresses a truth only I can express, God cannot conceive the truth it expresses. What I intentionally express, I conceive. So on these assumptions, God has thought up someone who can conceive a proposition He cannot—He has assigned the proposition as an object of conception without being able to conceive it. So if only I can express what I express by 'I am BL,' what God conceives is not the limit of the conceivable.[14] This might suggest by analogy that after all I could conceive of quarks even if God could not or that God could make me able to feel pain even if He could feel nothing remotely like it.

Now if there are not private-access truths, there is no difficulty here at all. And there might not be. Perhaps when I token 'I am BL' I express a truth that God and I can both know: for example, that this is BL. I express this by tokening first-person sentences. God cannot, but can express it by, for example, 'This is BL.' Perhaps if I ask God what I said, and he replies 'You said that you are BL,' he tells me the very thing I said, not just something close in content to it.[15] But as there might be private truths, it is worth seeing what we can say if there are. Even if there are private truths, so that God has placed within someone's cognitive range a proposition He cannot express, the parallel between kinds of object or qualities of experience and propositions breaks down: God can have a thick sort of indirect access to private truths with no strong parallel in the other cases. If this is correct, conceding that God can make others able to conceive propositions He cannot would not place my earlier arguments in jeopardy.

I know that I am BL. God knows of me that you (as it were pointing at me) are BL—a claim enough like what I say by 'I am BL' to make it at least somewhat plausible that 'You said that you are BL' reports the very thing I said—and that he knows that he himself is BL (which also has that property). He knows that if I token 'I am BL' I express a truth just like the one He would express by 'I am God' save for being about me. He knows that this is BL and is an 'I' and that the referent of 'I' for BL is BL. 'I am BL' expresses my being BL, a state of affairs or event in which I have the property of being BL. I am a public object and even if that I am BL is a private truth, being BL is a publicly accessible property—you know that I have it. So God completely perceives my being BL. He misses nothing about it. He knows the entire state of affairs 'I am BL' expresses, and that and how the private truth would express it, and that the truth is exactly like one He knows about Himself. God cannot express this truth, but what He does know adds up to a pretty meaty indirect grip on it. Given all this, perhaps His conceiving it indirectly, as the truth 'I am BL' would express, is enough to let Him conceive of my conceiving it and bring it about that I can conceive it.

---

[14] It would not follow from this, though, that the limits of the conceivable are independent of God. For God would then set them partly by determining His own range of action and conception and partly by thinking up other beings.

[15] My thanks to a referee for the example.

But suppose, on the other hand, that God could not experience phenomenal color. He could then know about color only what an omniscient physicist blind from birth could. I believe that He would therefore be ignorant of genuine facts, those about what color looks like.[16] If He would, He might then think to Himself of the experience Leftow would have if confronted in appropriate conditions by an apple reflecting just light of certain wavelengths, but there would be nothing in His own experience such that He would know that my experience is just like His save for being mine, not His—and plausibly not even anything that would be much like it, such that He could have some indirect grip on the content of an experience of phenomenal red. His knowledge about my seeing a red apple would not really add up to any indirect grip on my phenomenal experience. He could have no sort of access to some states of affairs involved in my seeing the apple. And suppose that God could not conceive of the kind *quark*. Then there would be blanks in His knowledge of the sub-atomic. If I could conceive it, He could refer to the kind of object I conceive of, under such descriptions as 'The object-kind Leftow's tokens of "quark" express . . .' If there are properties constitutive of being a quark, then even if He could conceive of them individually, He could not conceive of them conjoined. If there are properties not constitutive of but following from being a quark, He could perhaps conceive of their conjunction as entailed by something, but not conceive of what it is that entails it. Given these limits, we would not be much tempted to ascribe to Him a meaty indirect grip on what it is to be a quark. So perhaps private truths would not be an insuperable objection to my line of thought, for perhaps the analogy between God's indirect access to such truths and anything He could have in the case of kinds of object or experience is not strong.

Let me finally note something my conclusions here do not imply. If I am right, God has in every possible world a representation of every actually possible creature.[17] I argue later that God has a concept of Fs iff there can be Fs.[18] If this is true, then if in every possible world God has the same concepts, in every possible world, the same creatures and creature-attributes are possible. One might think, then, that unless the ways these combine into states of affairs or the possibilities for God Himself differ from world to world, it follows from my account that S5 is the logic of absolute modality. But it is equally true on my account that God has in every possible world a representation of every possibly possible creature, even if there are possibly possible but not actually possible creatures. And that God has a representation of every

---

[16] This commits me to a particular stance on Frank Jackson's 'knowledge argument'. So be it. For the argument and the main range of responses, see Peter Ludlow, Yujin Nagasawa, and Daniel Stoljar (eds), *There's Something About Mary* (Cambridge, MA: MIT Press, 2004).

[17] Or type of creature, if the possible is irreducibly general. Again, take this qualification as read throughout this paragraph. And as emerges later, my talk of representations is only a *façon de parler*.

[18] The concept-talk too turns out to be a *façon de parler*.

actually possible creature in every possible world does not entail that in every possible world this representation is a concept, something that can be satisfied.

Weaker Constraints

Deity does not dictate God's creature-concepts. It may, however, have a weaker effect: if it would be imperfect or wrong to have a certain sort of concept, then God does not have it. This does not imply that He reflects on its imperfection or wrongness and therefore does not have it. One's nature may sometimes operate without conscious thought. Perhaps the perfectly virtuous sometimes are not even tempted to do other than the good, never consider doing otherwise, and flow into good action easily, with nothing to overcome. So it would be with God in this case: His basic nature would simply set His mind in a certain sort of path. But *if* some such 'constraint' operates in His concept-formation, it is certainly not so narrow as to dictate thinking up (say) quarks rather than not. As far as we can tell, there is nothing evaluatively significant in this option.

Creative Thinking

Before all Creation,[19] nothing causally constrains God's thinking, as before Creation there is nothing concrete other than God. Nothing outside Him epistemically constrains His thinking either. There are then no concreta whose natures He must catch. Nor (I claim) are there outside Him independent Platonic facts about the natures concreta would have were there any. If (as I claim) a story about God alone suffices as a modal metaphysic, it would be otiose to believe both in God and in these. If God forms the concept *quark*, then, there is thus nothing outside Him He would have missed had He not done so. God's nature does not determine what creature-concepts He forms. As there is nothing else to determine this, it follows that what creature-concepts God has is wholly up to God. Nothing dictated that God form the representation of a quark. He simply did so. Being a quark consists in whatever God thinks it does, solely because God thinks it does.

This raises the question whether, had God thought of *quark* differently, quarks would be a different sort of particle. Well, perhaps they would have. We can distinguish the role a sort of thing plays in a world from the thing that plays the role. There might be a world just like ours save that in it, particles just like quarks in most ways but intrinsically different in one play the role quarks play in nature. Are these other particles quarks or schmarks? It is not obvious

---

[19] Causally and perhaps also temporally.

that they have to be schmarks. Perhaps to be a quark is to play a particular role in nature, and what it consists in to be the thing that plays that role can vary. Again, suppose that God's actual quark-concept includes being F. Had God not had this concept in any world and instead had in every world a concept just like it save that it also included being ¬F, and made it the case that no-one else in any world had the former, it would not be unreasonable to say that He had rendered *quark* an inconsistent concept. But perhaps if He had packed some concept with different notes, it would not have been the concept of a quark. Perhaps it would have been a different concept, *schmark*. We need not resolve this. If they would have to be schmarks, I say that it was in God to think up schmarks and leave quarks unconceived, but if they would be quarks, I say that it was in God to have made quarks a different sort of particle. It is true that being a quark consists in whatever God thinks it does, solely because God thinks it does, even if a slight alteration would have to have produced a schmark- rather than quark-concept. For it is still the case that God's unconstrained thought determines what features are packed into the concept *quark*, so as to be those slight variations in which are inconsistent with having the same concept.

'Relationalism'

I have said that what creatures (and secular states of affairs) God conceives determines what creatures (and secular states of affairs) are conceivable. So on my account, what God does—His actual conceiving activity—accounts for some of what a Platonist or deity theorist would call its preconditions. As for a relationalist actual facts of spatial relation help account for there being possibilities of location (which are really possibilities of spatial relation), actual facts of divine conceiving determine what God's possible conceivings are. God's mental activity determines what worlds are possible. Possible worlds include possible divine activities. So on my account God's mental activity determines what divine activities are possible. Conceiving is one divine activity. So God's mental activity determines what divine conceivings are possible—that is, what is conceivable for God. If God is by nature omniscient, the facts about what He conceives necessarily track those about what is conceivable. The only question remaining is of the direction in which the explanation of this tracking runs. That what God conceives determines what is conceivable, even for Him, explains why and how God's conceiving tracks the conceivable.

Might More be Better?

If nothing constrained God's conceiving, it was in Him to think up good creatures in addition to those He has actually conceived. This would be so no matter what He conceived. As this is so, His effort could not but be such as to have it in God to be surpassed. One might argue that this is incompatible with God's being perfect.[20] Suppose that

10. it is in God to think up just what He has, plus a good thing not identical to any of these things.

A good thing not identical to any of these would be an item which actually is neither possible nor even impossible. This description cannot be satisfied: there is nothing in any possible world of which God has no concept. But it is in God to have thought up something to satisfy it. That is, it is in God to do something impossible—where the only reason it is impossible is that He did not do it. Let a zog be this good thing. Of course, neither He nor we can describe what God has not thought up—if God cannot, we cannot, and if God could, He would have thought it up. But we can suppose that something in a box is good even though we have no idea what the box contains. Seemingly:

11. Had God thought up just what He has, plus a good thing not identical to any of these things, His thoughts would've been better than they actually are.

12. Necessarily, for all xy, if x and y do acts of the same type in relevantly similar circumstances and x produces a better product, x does a better act than y,

13. Necessarily, for all xy, if x's and y's records for actions of some kind are indiscernible save that one act of x is better than the corresponding act of y, x has a better record for acts of that kind than y, and:

14. Necessarily, for all xy, if x's and y's records of action are indiscernible save that for one sort of action, x has a better record than y, x is a more perfect being than y. So:

15. Necessarily, if it is in God to have thought up something good He has not thought up, it is in God to be more perfect.

Perhaps, then, (15) is why lacking the thought of a zog would leave God less great. Further, plausibly a perfect being is as perfect as is in it to be. It is such as not to be surpassed even by itself.[21] So if (10)–(14) are true and yield (15), God is a perfect being only if it is not in Him to add something good to the content of possibility. If so, then as this is in God if my story about the possible is correct, if God is perfect, something is amiss in my views.

I reject (14). Consider Gabriel the Slacker Angel. He never does much—just sits around Heaven watching TV. Lincoln had a better record for courage and

---

[20] The argument has obvious debts to William Rowe's main line of attack in *Can God Be Free?* (Oxford: Oxford University Press, 2004).

[21] *Pace* 'process' theism (see, for example, Charles Hartshorne, *The Divine Relativity* (New Haven, CT: Yale University Press, 1947)).

being generally helpful. So too for wisdom (TV did not help what Gabriel has in place of a brain) and (we can suppose) every other virtue. All the same, Gabriel is a more perfect being than Lincoln was; angels' powers are immensely greater than ours, however little they use them, and this outweighs the difference in record. Again, one intuition behind (14) is that a perfect being is *inter alia* one that always does its best, so that we can read back from its effect to all that it is capable of doing. But another intuition is that something perfect in (say) power is literally inexhaustible in power: is such that no matter how much or how well it does, it is able to do still more. If we go with this intuition, something is perfect in power only if it cannot do its best because there is no such thing as a best to do. If this is how it is, we cannot infer from effect to capacity, nor then to intrinsic perfection. What can perfect (say) bravery be, if not a virtue which leads to a best possible record for bravery? Perhaps perfect bravery is a virtue such that any defect or surpassability in the actions of the one who has it will not be due even partly to a lack of or defect in bravery.[22] Someone perfectly brave might do only surpassably brave acts and assemble only a surpassable record of courage. Perhaps there can be only such acts and records if perfection in bravery is of the inexhaustible sort. What follows from being perfectly brave is only that the reason one's acts or record could've been better is not that one is defectively or incompletely brave.

So too for God and zogs. Perhaps it is in God to have thought up more kinds than He did, including *zog*: perhaps the perfection of His cognitive power or imagination is of the inexhaustible sort. He thought up just so many kinds. Despite this, He is perfectly and so inexhaustibly wise, creative, and so on. His not thinking up a zog is not explained by lack or defect of wisdom, creativity, etc. Perhaps nothing explains this. He just did not. Why should we expect an explanation here? God has the full natural endowment He would use to think up zogs, whether He so uses it or not. The greatness of His wisdom, creativity, and so on, depends on His inexhaustible natural endowment, not on having an unsurpassable product: wisdom, creativity, and so on, are dispositions, not records of achievement. Lesser record does not entail lesser endowment: Slacker Gabriel might have exactly the powers of the better-known Gabriel, as Duplicate Ruth had Ruth's. A lack of cognitive power, and so on, is not the reason God stopped where He did. He just did stop; perhaps His nature was to produce some determinate domain or other—it is hard to see what else it could be in Him to do—and there was no reason to stop in one very good place rather than another, given in particular that there is no best for Him to do.[23] In this case, there cannot be

---

[22] This parallels a definition of omnipotence by Erik Weilenberg ('Omnipotence Again', *Faith and Philosophy* 17 (2000), 42).

[23] Here we are skating at the edge of Rowe's *a priori* argument for atheism (*Can God Be Free?*, 88–150). I show why the argument fails in 'No Best World: Moral Luck', 165–81, and 'No Best World: Creaturely Freedom', 269–85.

a quantitatively maximal record due to God's very perfection, and so if we are to call God's record maximal, we must explain this in other terms. One might, for instance, say that His record in thinking up creatures is perfect qualitatively. Nothing about them traces to a lack of wisdom, creativity, or cognitive power. There could not be a better executed set of possible creatures, as there could not be a better executed set of whittled dolls than those a perfect whittler made. Perhaps it does not seem so to us (why nature red in tooth and claw?). But I am not offering an argument that it *is* so. I am merely explaining the claim that it is.

One might think that God has (as it were) passed up His chance to think up some good thing He has not thought up—again, let us play the game of calling it a zog. There *was* an opportunity to think up zogs, and if it sounds odd to say that there was an opportunity to do something that is now impossible, bear in mind that this was precisely a chance to determine whether it would be impossible.[24] But now (we may think) it is impossible, and so there is no longer a chance to do it. Still, even if He has made it necessarily necessary (and so on) that there is no such thing as a zog, rather than saying that He has passed His chance up, we might better say that He *is* passing it up. As one is passing up a chance, not only has one not lost any power, one has not yet even lost the chance. There is a rough analogy to this if God is timeless. If He is temporal, then once the past is past, God has lost His chance to have it other than it was. It is now too late for Him to have the Poles defeat the Germans in 1939, for nothing can alter the past. But if God is atemporal and ever has the chance to have the Poles defeat the Germans, He cannot lose it. For if God ever has the chance, it is not at all points in His life too late for Him to bring this about. But if at only some points in His life it is too late, there is a part of His life in which it is not yet too late, and this part is at some point over. What is over lies in the past. And if it is not yet too late, the part when it is over is still to come—it is future. So if God ever has this chance and is atemporal, He cannot lose it. And so God retains both all needed power and the opportunity, and so the all-things-considered power, to make the past be other than it in fact was. He will not use the power and take the chance, because He has not done so and an atemporal being cannot change intrinsically. But He has both.

Again, suppose that at t I choose to do A with libertarian freedom—freedom to choose otherwise. If at t I have lost my chance to choose not to do A, it is not in my all-things-considered power at t so to choose. I still have the strength, know-how and abilities needed, but I no longer have the opportunity, and so all things considered, I can no longer make this choice.

---

[24] It is now 'accidentally necessary' that the Giants won the 2009 Super Bowl. (For an account of this modality see Alfred Freddoso, 'Accidental Necessity and Logical Determinism', *Journal of Philosophy*, 80 (1983), 257–78, and 'Accidental Necessity and Power Over the Past', *Pacific Philosophical Quarterly*, 63 (1982), 54–68.) So it is accidentally impossible that they did not. But they had the chance to determine whether it would be thus impossible. So talk of having a chance to determine impossibility makes sense in at least some contexts, and I claim in this one too.

Now I have lost my chance to choose otherwise if it is too late to do so. Up to t, the time of choice, it is not too late. At t, I choose to do A. It cannot be too late to choose otherwise at t, though. If it were, I would not have at t the chance to do otherwise, and so this choice would not be in my all-things-considered power. So if at t it was too late, at t I was not free to choose otherwise. But I was. So at t, I have not yet lost my chance. I am rather in the act of passing it up. Prior to t I have not yet lost it; after t I have lost it; at t I *am losing* it.[25]

Suppose now that God acts with the sort of libertarian freedom involving being all-things-considered able to choose otherwise as He chooses. If God is timeless, the passage of time cannot make it too late for Him to do A. If at t it was not too late for Him and then at t+1 it was, at t He had a future, in which it was to be too late for Him, and so was in time. God actually said 'Let there be light.' And so there was light. But God is timelessly in the very act of saying 'Let there be light.' Nothing in His life is after this act, and if it is timeless, it is never over. (Again, what is over lies in the past.) If God speaks with strongest libertarian freedom, then even as He says 'Let there be light' it is in His all-things-considered power to refrain. It is not too late for Him to do otherwise as He does it, just as it was not too late for me to choose otherwise. But it is now timelessly the case that He is doing it. So God now timelessly has the all-things-considered power to refrain from saying this. Had He refrained, reality would've been lightless. So God now timelessly has a power such that had He used it, there would have been no light. It is not too late for Him to use it. Rather, He is timelessly passing up His chance to use it. If one *is* passing up the chance and *has not yet* passed it up, one still has the chance. The chance to use this power cannot be gone for a timeless God: if God is timeless, nothing in His life is ever gone. So God still has the chance to make the universe lightless, though He is not taking it.

I now suggest a parallel. As it is, at all times, there is light (let us say); in parallel, let us say, in all possible worlds there is no such thing as a zog. This is not because God is thinking up zogs and then saying no. He is simply not thinking up zogs. But as at all times God is saying 'Let there be light', so in all possible worlds it is as if God says 'Let there be just these kinds and no others', where these kinds do not include *zog*. This is as close as one can get to saying 'Let there not be such a thing as a zog' without having the concept. Then just as God retains the ability and chance not to say 'Let there be light', so God still has the general, unspecified ability and chance to say instead in all possible worlds 'Let there be such a thing as a zog.' He *is* passing up the chance, rather

---

[25] Thus my choice at t is contingent: I believe in the contingency of the present. On the other side, apparently, is the Aristotelian dictum that what is, when it is, is necessary (Aristotle, *De Interpretatione*, 19a24–5). This seems true of the present, in one sense of 'necessary': what is presently can no longer be averted. But this is compatible with contingency in a different sort of modality: what cannot be averted includes that my choice is contingent in this other way.

than *having* passed it up. In this sense, He is such as to make a zog, though He has no specific power to do so, nor is it in Him to do specifically that.

In saying that though there was light, God can make it the case that there was none, we want to assert that

> God can make it the case that: there never was light. *And* it is the case that there was light,

not

> God can make it the case that: there never was light and it is the case that there was light.

So in the modal case, I want to say that

> God is such as to make it the case that: there is such a thing as a zog. *And* there is no such thing,

not

> God is such as to make it the case that: there is such a thing as a zog and there is no such thing.

Nothing in my views commits me to the latter.

Finally, let us look at how the claim that God is such as to make more states of affairs possible interacts with divine omnipotence. For a simplest case, assume a constant stock of secular states of affairs to bear modal status: that is, that there would be just these regardless, and it is up to God whether some of them are possible. Then God makes more of these possible only if He makes less impossible. Let us say that God makes a secular state of affairs impossible by preventing it, possible by consenting to causally contribute to it. The more He prevents, the less to which He consents, and *vice-versa*. God has sway over all these states of affairs regardless. He can prevent or consent to each. The only question is whether by consenting to more He gives Himself more He can bring about. This does not mean that it is up to Him whether He is omnipotent. Rather, He is by nature such that He will be omnipotent whatever the precise range of states of affairs omnipotence empowers Him to bring about. He is simply determining what that range is.

Some states of affairs' intrinsic content rules out God's bringing them about, such as *a quark's popping into being with absolutely no cause*. If S is not one of these, but God cannot bring S about, that is because He has prevented S' coming about. He has as it were made S a stone too heavy to lift. But God's 'inability' to effect S is actually an assertion of power over whether S occurs. God's use of His power to prevent, to render states of affairs impossible, limits His opportunities to use His power to bring about. But to limit the opportunities one power has is not to limit God's power *simpliciter*. Where God puts the boundary between the impossible and the possible is a fact about how He uses one power and limits His chance to use another. Loss of a chance to use a power does not change the power intrinsically at all. And if the same states of affairs bear modal properties whether or not they are possible, and in either case, the distribution of modal properties is God's doing, one distribution does not leave God less power over whether states of affairs occur than another would, though one may leave Him less He might do than another would. Further, if it is impossible that God 'lift' S, this does not entail that God is not omnipotent. God would not be omnipotent only if it were possible that S be 'lifted' and He could not do it. Again, God has merely set the range of omnipotence

If God renders S's occurring impossible, He is still intrinsically such that (God wills to have the power to bring S about) $\supset$ (God has the power to do so). This is not just because the material conditional's antecedent is impossible—that is not enough to make God any particular way intrinsically—but because He does not change Himself intrinsically by deciding that no matter what, S shall not occur, in any other way than the occurrence of the decision itself. 'Before' deciding God had it in Him to bring it about that S. He has opted not to have the power to do so, but this does not change that about Him that made it the case that if He so willed, He would have the power. So even if God renders S' occurring impossible, it is in God to have S come about. But this is no scandal: it does not entail that He might do so, or that it is possible that He do so. It means only that the only reason He lacks the relevant power is that He has decided to lack it. As that is always true, it always remains in God to have wider-ranging power than He has. Each state of affairs He prevents is one He has it in Him to consent to. If He consents to it, He is ready to help bring it about: nothing more is needed. Preventing S is passing up the chance to bring S about, not altering His intrinsic readiness to do so given the chance. But again, that it is *in* God to have such a power does not entail that the power is possible, nor then that God is not omnipotent (due to lacking a power He might have). There is no such power for God to lack. The point is just that this is God's doing, and His nature did not dictate it.

If it is in God to bring about things that are in fact impossible, then where P is impossible due to divine activity, some conditionals of the form *if God wills to have the power to bring it about that P and then wills that P, then P* are true. As this conditional's antecedent is impossible, the conditional is trivially true. But the antecedent is impossible only because God has done something: He has made P impossible. It is not a trivial truth that God has done this if He had it in Him not to do it. So the conditional is not *only* trivially true. Beneath its triviality lies a non-trivial act of God that made its truth trivial: God has set the range of His own power, and of omnipotence.

Let us now consider what to say if the stock of states of affairs is inconstant. As it is, certain states of affairs are possible, others impossible, but let us now suppose that God is able to add to the stock of possible-or-impossible state of affairs further states of affairs that now do not exist, and so are neither possible nor impossible. For example, suppose that God has thought up a determinate set of candidate humans. If none of them would if actual be Santa Claus, then there is no state of affairs *Santa's being human*. But God can think up a Santa. He has the natural ability to think, without constraint. There is no Santa for Him to think up unless He does so, and if He does not, there is no specific power to think up Santa. But we, with Santa in mind, can say of God truly that even if He had not thought up Santa, He would have had the natural, unspecific power which is all it takes to do so. If He does think up Santa, there will be states of affairs there now are not, e.g. *Santa's being human*. So too, there is no state of affairs *something's being a zog*. Had God thought up a property for '__ is a zog' to express, in addition to the actual modal facts, it would have been possible or impossible that there be zogs. So if it is in God to add to the stock of states of affairs, it is in God to give the possible a wider extent without subtracting from the range of state of affairs He prevents. It is in God simply to add to the states of affairs over which He has power.

Still, if God thinks up more properties, He does not give Himself more power. He just gives Himself more chances to use His natural power. By not thinking up zogs, God has denied Himself not a natural power, but a specified power. But specified powers are in one respect not additions to God's natural powers. Having a specified power consists in having a natural power plus there being something that gives God a chance to use this power in a specific way. The same degree of power can accomplish more if it has more opportunities. There is just no inference from more opportunity to more power. If God thinks up *being a zog* and renders zogs possible, He has the power to make zogs. But it is possible to have more powers of this sort—powers that in effect build into their description a specific opportunity to use a more basic sort of power—without being more powerful—that is, having more strength or force to put behind whatever one does. One is not less powerful for having fewer chances to use the power one has. To think of more things would not give God more power to think, either: He starts out maximal in this respect, with no possibility of developing His faculties by practice. There is no inference from His thinking of more things in a world W than in a world W* to His having had more power to think in W than in W*, any more than we can infer how strong two circus strongmen are by seeing how much weight they lift in a single trial. Both may lift 300 lbs, but it does not follow that they are equally strong—this might be one's maximum, while the other might be strong enough to lift 400 lbs.

On the view I offer later, the sole difference between God having the power to make zogs and His lacking this power is His having had a thought, adopted an attitude, formed an intention, and so given Himself a chance to exercise more basic powers which are just the same whether He has the thought, etc., or not. If He does not think of zogs, He misses nothing: there is such a thing as being a zog to think about only if God thinks it up. Not thinking up zogs does not deny Him a specific power He is such as to have, either. There is no specific power to make zogs unless there is such a thing to make. If there is no such thing as a zog, it is not true that God is such as to have the specific power to make zogs. Thus lacking the thought of a zog would not leave Him less powerful. And so even if it is always in God to think up more than He has thought up, it does not follow that His range of power is less than maximal, nor then that He is not omnipotent.

11

DIVINE CONCEPTS

DIVINE concepts made their appearance in the last chapter. I do not in the end believe that there are any; to me divine concept talk is just a useful *façon de parler*. I now sketch some motivation for this stance, some ways to defend it, and a little of what I think lies behind the talk.

Concepts, Platonism, and Economy

I am setting out a theist modal theory. I would like to claim ontological economy as one of its chief advantages. But if there are divine concepts, my theory may have a luxuriant Platonic ontology. Divine concepts are distinct from God and immaterial. If God is not in space and (as I hold) not in time, they are not either, and so qualify as abstract on one standard account of abstractness. They do not seem the sort of thing to have causal powers, and so seem abstract on another standard account too.[1] And they can seem just to *be* Platonic attributes.[2] When Augustine moved Plato's Forms into the mind of God, they arguably remained Forms. If we also move propositions and worlds into God's mind, as complexes of divine concepts, these too seem as abstract as ever. So if I am committed to concepts, propositions, and worlds in the divine mind, arguably I must forfeit any claim that my theist theory is economical: it then does not eliminate ontology, but merely relocates it. Non-theist modal Platonists (and *a fortiori* modal non-Platonists) might then find a theist theory ill-motivated. They might see it this way: we have worlds and so on in our ontology anyway. On a theist theory we have these plus

---

[1] For discussion of the standard accounts see David Lewis. *On the Plurality of Worlds* (Oxford: Basil Blackwell, 1986), pp. 81–6.

[2] So Morris and Menzel, 'Absolute Creation', repr. in Thomas Morris, *Anselmian Explorations* (Notre Dame, IN: University of Notre Dame Press, 1987), pp. 163, 166, 178.

another entity: God. So parsimony rules in favor of non-theist Platonism (and *a fortiori* any viable non-theist non-Platonism), unless one is antecedently committed to theism. If on the other hand I avoid commitment to concepts, propositions, and the like, as divine mental content, I can argue theism to be Platonism without the pain of Platonism: providing the power of a Platonic theory of worlds at the price of only one concrete entity, God, and some events in His mind. Theism without divine concepts can provide an account of modal truth whose ontology is just one non-physical substance and some events. I take events to be themselves concrete particulars, concrete because they are able to cause, particular because uninstantiable. So if theism provides this, parsimony *prima facie* rules for theism against non-theist Platonism—Platonism recognizes concrete particulars and then adds abstracta—and in fact against many other approaches to possible worlds.

I cannot take up the elimination of divine concepts fully here. But I do want to indicate how I might defend my claims for economy. So I now address some questions about God's mental content. I take it (for reasons discussed later) that God's concepts of concreta other than Himself are all concepts of candidate creatures, things He can make, whether or not they can also come to be entirely without His causal contribution. That is, I take it that there is no such thing as an essentially uncreatable/unsustainable non-divine concrete thing.

Content

Some mental events have content—they are of something (as a thought of water is of the property *being water*) or about something (as a thought about Moses is about Moses) or grasp something (as the thought that Moses was Hebrew grasps that Moses was Hebrew). Some events' content is propositional—the sort a normal assertive use of 'Moses was Hebrew' expresses. Some is sub-propositional—the sort some uses of single words express, as 'Hebrew' in 'Moses was Hebrew' normally expresses the property of being Hebrew. Forming a concept is an event with sub-propositional content. Such events do not just have content, but also present it in various ways. If there are concepts, plausibly the concepts *water* and H_2O have the same property as their content. But they are not identical. People had *water* long before any of us had *hydrogen*. This was possible because the two concepts present the property in different ways, much as the predicables '— is water' and '— is H_2O' express the same property but differ in sense. The way a concept presents a property to us is the way we think of that property *qua* thinking of it under that concept. To think of water under the concept *water* is to have in mind (say) its wetness at room temperature, characteristic mouthfeel, and the like: roughly, ways water appears to the senses. To think of water *via* the concept H_2O is to have in mind its chemical constitution. That concepts can present the same property in different ways explains how it could be a significant chemical discovery that water = H_2O much as we explain how it could be a significant astronomical discovery that the morning star = the evening star.

Ontology

I now defend my claims for a theist theory's parsimony in two steps. One is an analogy. Concept nominalists claim to reduce our ontology by replacing extra-mental abstracta—universals—with concepts. They do not rest this claim on any particular ontology of concepts, beyond holding that they are mental particulars. Theist modal theorists can make the same claim if they replace extra-mental properties and worlds with divine concepts. It would be silly to say that ordinary concept nominalism is economical but a theist modal theory is not because the theist adds one particular, God, to our ontology. For we would not deny ordinary concept nominalism's claim to economy if it insisted on positing another human (perhaps on a planet beyond our ken) to host certain concepts. Concept nominalism's claim to economy rests on its ridding us of *kinds* of entity: there are concepts anyway, and so with universals dropped, there are fewer kinds of thing in its heaven and earth than are dreamt of in Russell's philosophy. So too, if one is a theist, God and His concepts are there anyway, and so every kind of independent abstract entity purged is one less kind in one's ontology. And if one is not a theist, still one may think concepts are there, and one may wonder whether adding God and subtracting propositions, worlds, and so on, is not a tempting bargain. For while adding God does add a kind to our ontology, we can eliminate many kinds of abstracta by positing God, so the theist move still simplifies our ontology overall. Further, the kind *deity* is plausibly not a highest kind, an ontological category, but rather a sub-kind of *person*, and in general kinds count less against a claim to economy the further down the tree of kinds they occur. The concepts human-concept nominalists appeal to exist in time, and in space also on some accounts of mind. But nothing in nominalism requires this. Class nominalism is a form of nominalism even if classes do not exist in space or time. And if our concepts are not spatial—if we are all Platonic souls, say—nobody would claim that for that reason, concept nominalists merely shift our ontology elsewhere, or redefine it, rather than reduce it. For the concept nominalist replaces universals with mental particulars. The theist who deals in divine concepts does the same. And many theists hold that God is just a rather impressive Platonic soul, existing too in time but not space.[3] But temporality is not essential; it would be odd to say that theism in modality is as parsimonious as concept-nominalism if God is in time but not if He is not.

---

[3] So in so many words Richard Swinburne, *The Christian God* (New York: Oxford University Press, 1994), p. 127.

My analogy supposes that there are such things as divine concepts. But I do not really believe in these, and this is a more basic reason to think my theory parsimonious. Having a concept consists in having or gives us various powers—*inter alia* to discriminate, recognize, classify, use terms, form propositions, infer, affirm and deny claims: broadly, to have a mental life of a certain sort. I recognize that you have the powers, infer that you are in whatever internal condition constitutes having the concept, and so say that you competently command the concept. But someone who grants that mental events represent the world does not automatically commit to there being things which are their representations of the world. In saying that God has concepts, the most I commit myself to is that there is in God some underlying reality making it apt to speak of concept-possession. There may be reasons to go further and posit concepts in our case, as part of an overall representational theory of mind (RTM), but these reasons do not apply to God.

The primary problem current RTM tries to solve is how physical systems can produce physical processes that encode or parallel rational relations among thought contents. This problem does not arise for the divine mind, which is not physical. In fact, it has been a widely held view that God has no need to think, no thought processes, but instead just knows immediately; so too, that He has no need to deliberate, but just sees what to do and so decides immediately.[4] The primary thought behind RTM is that the human mind is a sort of computer, a causal system that produces rational trains of thought by physical operations on physical internal symbols with semantic properties.[5] The divine mind is not a computer, and so there is no need to posit internal objects for it to 'process'. One popular argument for RTM has been the empirical success of cognitive psychology that presupposes it, but we have no divine cognitive science. Fodor points to the 'productivity' of belief-states as a point for RTM:

> There is a (potentially) infinite set of...belief-state types...This is...
> explicable on the assumption that belief-states have combinatorial structure; that they are somehow built up out of elements and that the intentional object and causal role of each such state depends on what elements it contains and how they are put together. (This is true if) believing (involves) a relation to a syntactically structured object (with) a compositional semantics...[6]

The thing to be explained is how a mind with finite capacity is able to acquire a (potential) infinity of different beliefs. The explanation is that the mind has a finite vocabulary of internal symbols which it can so manipulate as to

---

[4] So, for example, S. Thomae Aquinatis, *Summa Theologie* (Ottawa: Studii Generalis, 1941). Ia 14, 7 and 19, 5.

[5] See, for example, Jerry Fodor, *Psychosemantics* (Cambridge, MA: MIT Press, 1987), p. 16ff., and 'Propositional Attitudes', *Monist* 64 (1978).

[6] Fodor, *Psychosemantics*, pp. 147–8.

generate a potentially infinite series of distinct belief-state contents. But the divine mind does not have a finite capacity. So this inference to the best explanation has no traction in God's case, because what sets up the need for the explanation is absent. Finally, Fodor points to the way native speakers learn their languages to argue that human thought has 'systematicity', a further property RTM could explain.[7] God never learns a language. As always omniscient, He always knows all possible languages.

So far, then, we have no reason to think that divine thought involves mental representations. If so, we are free to hold that while there are contentful mental events in God, there are not items which are their contents. Rather, God causes mental events, and we can speak fictionally of them by saying that He creatively generates a range of representations. In us, what licenses talk of concept-possession is often entirely dispositional: I have the concept of a kangaroo but rarely use it. The reality behind talk of divine concept-possession may be just God's having certain powers. But it probably involves more. Perfect-being considerations suggest that God is never unaware of anything He knows—that all His knowledge is occurrent, not dispositional. If this is so, every 'divine concept' is always in use in some divine mental event. I suggest then that in the final analysis, the ontology behind talk of divine concepts is in terms of divine mental events and powers.[8] So my move is to replace abstract modal ontology with one of divine mental events and powers. There are powers and events anyway. So if I can make this move stick, I economize on kinds of entities.

Events and Powers

But I am not yet out of the woods. As we have seen, many accounts of events involve attributes. So it might seem that if we talk of events, we do not avoid abstract ontology: perhaps attributes are in the picture. But most such accounts of events are compatible with many accounts of what attributes are.[9] Most are compatible with even resemblance nominalism: it would be true that an item had an attribute at a time, for instance, if that just were just a way to say that it was then appropriately like other items.

---

[7] *Ibid.*, p. 149ff.

[8] I hold that God is timeless. So this claim commits me to the existence of atemporal events. I defend these in 'The Eternal Now', in Gregory Ganssle and David Woodruff (eds), *God and Time*, (New York: Oxford University Press, 2001). Another sort of indirect defense is in my *Time and Eternity*, (Ithaca, NY: Cornell University Press, 1991) pp. 290–7, where I argue that an atemporal God can act. Actions are events. If you do not accept my arguments for atemporal events, restate the view in terms of causation: whether it is an event or not, God's knowing that cats are mammals has causes (in my view, His having cat-thoughts as He does) and effects (His making cats mammals). If you do not think a timeless God can be causally involved, you just do not think there can be a timeless God, since God is by nature an agent. As nothing in my argument here requires that God be timeless, we can differ over this another day.

[9] Theories of events as tropes are exceptions; also perhaps Lewis's view.

Again, talk of divine powers may seem only to shift the bump in the rug rather than flatten it. For a power is one to bring it about that P, for some P. So it might seem that powers bring propositions with them. But that a power is one to bring it about that P does not entail that it involves an entity, a proposition P, in its inner constitution. It may just be a brute fact about that power that it brings it about that P. For a power to be one to bring it about that P, all that is required is that it be such that if it 'fired', its 'firing' would bring it about that P.

More basically, powers are properties. On some views, possible worlds are just properties of a certain sort, most unexemplified.[10] If I parse world-talk into talk of divine powers, and powers are also properties, I cannot claim a simpler ontology than these views', though perhaps there might be a point to substituting exemplified for unexemplified properties. So to sustain my ontological gain, I need a suitably lean account of God's powers. I construct mine from accounts of how God's powers relate to deity and of deity.

Divine Powers and Deity

God has some powers just by being divine. Because He is divine, He can think and will, is omnipotent, and so on. One might see these as supervening on deity, somehow part of the content of deity, or constituents of a logically complex *deity*. If it is logically complex, deity is quantified, negative, disjunctive or conjunctive. 'God is divine' does not look like it says something quantified. (If it did, what would that something be?) That deity is a negative is a non-starter. So is a claim that deity is a property of being F v F, not being F. But if deity's disjuncts were non-identical God would have both deity and an MDN, a claim whose problems we saw in Chapter 8. Chapters 6 and 8 also gave reason to think that deity is not conjunctive. If God's natural powers supervene on deity, deity does not have power content. Rather, it is a purely categorical base for a set of powers. But there are good general reasons to hold that where we might think there is a purely categorical property subvening a purely dispositional property, there is instead just one 'double-aspect' property, with both dispositional and categorical content.[11] As this is so, I suggest that God's natural powers are not actually distinct from deity, but instead part of its content: being omnipotent, for instance, is part of what it is to be divine. If I am right about this, giving a theory of God's natural powers is just part of giving a theory of deity.

---

[10] So Peter Forrest, 'Ways Worlds Could Be', *Australasian Journal of Philosophy* 64 (1986), 15–24, and Robert Stalnaker, 'Possible Worlds', in Michael Loux (ed.), *The Actual and the Possible* (Ithaca, NY: Cornell University Press, 1979), pp. 225–34.

[11] See, for example, John Heil, *From an Ontological Point of View* (New York: Oxford University Press, 2003).

The Nature of Deity

Let us ask, then, what theory of attributes rightly describes deity. Chapter 8 argued that concept nominalism does not apply to it. I argue elsewhere that class nominalism is false.[12] On 'ostrich' and resemblance nominalism, there is no such thing as deity; on mereological nominalism, deity is just God. Chapter 8 argued that Platonism is not the right account of deity. By arguing that deity is a haecceity, Chapter 7 argued that it is not any sort of universal: universals by definition can be had by more than one possible item, haecceities by definition cannot. I also argue elsewhere that theists should not be realists, because God or constructions involving Him can do all ontological work for which realists posit universals.[13] My arguments, then, suggest that if there is such a thing as deity, it must be a trope—as Chapter 8 argued, a non-free-floating trope, one whose nature includes its being God's. That it is by nature God's would also follow if it is a haecceity.

But if my arguments about realism are sound, they also imply that theists should not believe in tropes. For tropes 'mirror' universals: where the realist might put a universal to work, a trope theorist will employ a sum of perfectly similar tropes. As the realist will say that all dogs have doghood in common, the trope theorist will say that all dogs have dog-tropes and so have in common the sum of these tropes; as (say) there being a natural law might consist in a certain relation linking universals, the trope theorist can say that it consists in a relation-trope linking certain sums of tropes. Every trope is part of such a sum (minimally, an improper part). So if theists should eliminate universals, by the same token they should eliminate trope-sums, and so all tropes. Leaving this aside, though, let us ask whether we have reason to recognize a trope of deity—whether there is ontological work it can do which God or constructions involving God cannot do at least as well. This requires a brief look at arguments in favor of trope theories.

Arguments appealing to advantages of treating substances as complexes of tropes are non-starters here.[14] As we have seen, ultimacy considerations rule out treating God this way. Keith Campbell and E. J. Lowe contend that we need tropes properly to understand change: when a red thing turns blue, they suggest, something, a case of redness, ceases to exist.[15] But deity is an essential property only of a thing which cannot begin or cease to exist. There cannot be change with respect to such a property. For there is such change only if an item begins or cease to possess one. As nothing can exist before it gains an essential property and begin to have it, or after it loses an essential property,

[12] 'One Step Toward God', *Royal Institute of Philosophy Supplement* 68 (2011), 67–104.

[13] 'God and the Problem of Universals', *Oxford Studies in Metaphysics* 2 (2006), 325–56.

[14] For such arguments see e.g. Kris McDaniel, 'Tropes and Ordinary Physical Objects', *Philosophical Studies* 104 (2001), 269–290; Keith Campbell, *Abstract Particulars* (Oxford: Basil Blackwell, 1990), pp. 17, 20–1.

[15] Keith Campbell, 'The Metaphysics of Abstract Particulars', *Midwest Studies in Philosophy* 6 (1981), 478; E. J. Lowe, *The Four-Category Ontology* (Oxford: Oxford University Press, 2006), pp. 23–4.

an item begins or ceases to possess one only if it begins or ceases to exist. So the change argument is no reason to treat deity as a trope. Campbell suggests that we need tropes for the proper understanding of qualities' recurrence:[16] be this as it may, deity cannot recur. D. C. Williams suggests that tropes are the immediate objects of perception.[17] It is anything but clear that deity is perceptible. Douglas Ehring argues at length, and Campbell also suggests, that tropes are needed to serve as causal relata.[18] But while God causes things in virtue of His deity, it is hard to see what deity itself might cause directly, and it cannot be an effect of anything. A different sort of argument would appeal to 'ontological uniformity'. Haecceities could only be tropes, since they cannot be shared. So if any haecceity is a real attribute, there are haecceity-tropes. If there are any, there seems no good reason to treat God's haecceity differently: it is a haecceity and so should be treated like any other. But (so the argument goes) some haecceities are real attributes. So deity is a real attribute, and so a trope. Further (one might argue), even if I have a case that theists should admit no tropes that would figure in 'mirroring' universals, this does not automatically extend to haecceity-tropes.

But ontological uniformity cuts both ways. If we eliminate most tropes, the presumption of uniformity would suggest eliminating the rest. A more basic reply is that ontological uniformity is at best a defeasible presumption. There can be reason to treat items even in the same ontological category differently: Ockham, for instance, gave reasons to believe in tropes of some but not all qualities,[19] and below I give reason for trope theorists to do the same.[20] Further, theists take it as axiomatic that God is in some way 'transcendent' of the world—outside or an exception to the way it otherwise runs. Many theist thinkers take divine transcendence so far as to place God beyond even the most basic patterns in created ontology: Aquinas, for instance, places God beyond the substance–attribute dichotomy, denying both that He is a substance and that He has attributes.[21] So not only is the uniformity presumption defeasible where it does apply, but it is an open question whether it applies at all to God. Thus the uniformity argument has dim prospects.

Tropes would figure in making predications true. But we do not need a deity-trope in our account of what makes it true that God is divine. We need not hold that every grammatical predicate expresses a real attribute. The semantic paradoxes suggest strongly that not all do, and Armstrong is not implausible when he argues that we can determine what real attributes there are only *a posteriori*.[22] We can hold instead that some predicates express

[16] Campbell, *op. cit.*, 478–9.
[17] D. C. Williams, 'The Elements of Being', *Review of Metaphysics* 7 (1953), 123.
[18] Douglas Ehring, *Causation and Persistence* (Oxford: Oxford University Press, 1997); Campbell, 'The Metaphysics', 480–1; Campbell, *Abstract Particulars*, pp. 113–15.
[19] Ockham, *Quodl.* VII, q. 2, *Opera Theologica* v. 9, 707–8.
[20] Assuming that tropehood is a quality of tropes.
[21] *ST* Ia 3, 3–6.
[22] D. M. Armstrong, *A Theory of Universals* (Cambridge: Cambridge University Press, 1978), pp. 7–12.

attributes while others express aspects or ways of being we distinguish in real things, to which no special distinct attribute corresponds. Even if the presence of tropes makes many predications true, plausibly there will be cases in which tropes do not. For there are true predications about tropes. If each has a trope in its truthmaker, any true predication begins an infinite regress of tropes of tropes. Further, this regress (in true Third Man style) generates multiple types of tropehood. Each trope is a trope. So it has (we are now supposing) a tropehood trope. That latter is itself a trope. So on present assumptions it too has a tropehood trope. But things have tropes either as a sort of constituent or by tropes' inhering in them, and plausibly both relations are irreflexive. So no tropehood has itself as a trope, and so we get a second sort of tropehood, and so *ad infinitum*. This is implausible and unparsimonious. Better, surely, to say, for example, that for a trope to be a trope requires just that it exist and so be what it is, a trope: that some predications are made true simply by the existing of their subjects. Truthmaker theorists often hold that things themselves make predications of their essential properties true. Thus John Fox writes:

> If Socrates is essentially human, Socrates is a truthmaker for 'Socrates is human', and so his manhood is not anything over and above Socrates himself.[23]

This may not be the whole story if Socrates came to exist by some matter's acquiring the property of humanity. But it has a certain plausibility if nothing can gain or lose the essential property in question. In some cases the mere existing of its ontology makes a non-existential proposition true (thin sense). I suggest that this is so with God and deity. Deity is not a trope. There is just no such thing as deity. God is the whole ontology for *God is divine*. There is nothing else to which He need bear some relation for this to be true, and so all it takes for it to be true is that He exist. Divine is just the way He is, and we need not in this case reify the way. So all it takes to make it true that God is divine is that He exist.[24] Thus I have in effect argued two components of Aquinas' doctrine of divine simplicity: that God does not have an attribute of deity distinct from Himself, and that 'God's essence is His existence'—that is, that what makes it true that God has His essence is identical with what makes it true that He exists. And so, finally, to say that God has powers by nature amounts to saying, for example, that just by existing, God is able to think, that God necessarily makes it true that He can think, that what is manifested when God thinks is simply His nature, how He is, or Himself, and

---

[23] John Fox, 'Truthmaker', *Australasian Journal of Philosophy* 65 (1987), 194. See also, for example, John Bigelow, *The Reality of Numbers* (Oxford: Oxford University Press, 1988), p. 128.

[24] This does not deny that 'God is divine' has a homophonic truth-condition: it *is* true that God is divine just if God is divine. The point is that what in reality satisfies that condition does not involve an attribute of deity.

that (if powers are in general like or correlated with functions from triggering circumstances to effects) what establishes a functional connection between God's impulse to think and the appearance of divine thoughts is just God Himself. I have eliminated God's natural powers from our ontology in two steps, first folding them into deity as part of a 'double-aspect' theory of properties, then arguing that there is no reason to posit a trope of deity at all.

Non-natural Powers

God also has powers not by nature, but due to events in His mental life: for example, He has the power to create starfish only because He has thought up starfish. Powers God has in virtue of mental events just specify His natural powers—the power to create starfish is one specification of the power to create. So their modal content is just that of God's natural powers, and God (standing in for deity) is in the ontology of the claim that He has such a power. I suggest later that God has such a power to bring it about that P just if God conceives and permits that P, and that the mental events involved are the rest of the ontology for the claim that God has such a power. To vindicate my claim for parsimony, then, I must give an account of conceivings' and permittings' content without bringing in abstract entities. I suggest one below. I also owe an account of events compatible with nominalism. But again, many accounts of events *are* compatible with nominalism.

I talk of divine concepts only as a useful *façon de parler*. That said, we should note a difference between God's concepts and ours.

Externalism

Our concepts represent attributes which exist independent of us.[25] For us, representing a world involves somehow hooking our minds onto attributes which would be just as they are whether or not we thought as we do. This is not so in the case of God's pre-creative creature-concepts. If these represent creaturely attributes, they do not in so doing hook onto a reality 'given' prior to His thoughts. They capture nothing outside God's mind. Instead, they determine what creaturely attributes there are or can be. It is far from clear that we can represent to ourselves simple attributes instances of which we have not met. If there *are* simple attributes, God does this. Before He creates, He dreams up attributes not yet instanced. Thus God's pre-creative creature-concepts differ from ours dramatically. Like ours, they represent attributes.

---

[25] This is true no matter what the correct ontological assay of talk about attributes turns out to be—even a resemblance nominalist can so parse it as to accept it. So this claim and my subsequent talk of attributes are not meant to suggest any particular account of them, or meant commissively.

But they differ in their relations to the attributes they represent. Because our concepts have to hook onto pre-given attributes, it is plausible to give externalist accounts of some of our mental content—that is, to individuate it by its relations to an independent environment. For God before Creation, there is no independent environment to hook onto. So items independent of Him cannot then help individuate any of His mental content.

Platonism and Content

I claim that we can use divine mental events to eliminate Platonic entities. But Platonists can try to turn the tables on me by appeal to God's mental content. If we need Platonist entities to make sense of this, then in the end, appeal to God's mind leaves us as much reason to Platonize as we had originally. A Platonist could take at least three tacks here.

Pre-creative Intentionality

It is puzzling that anyone can have concepts genuinely *of* items which do not exist. For if Meinongian possibilism is false, what does not exist has no attributes. But then what does not exist has no converse intentional attributes, like being conceived by a concept. So if God has a concept *of* a creaturely attribute, it seems to follow that the attribute exists.[26] Before Creation, creaturely attributes are uninstanced. So there are then attributes that exist uninstanced, and are contents of divine mental events. Either they are there prior to God's conceiving them, or the conceiving brings them to be, as its own content.[27,28]

This line of thought broaches deep issues I cannot discuss here. An idea worth exploring would be that we do manage somehow to think about fictional characters, and if there is an adequate theory of this that does not deal in Platonic entities, it may admit of a transform that applies to God's pre-creative concepts. In any case, suppose that a divine pre-creative conceiving did capture an unexemplified attribute that existed independent of it, outside

---

[26] The Platonist need not say the same about possible particulars if willing to say with Plantinga that God can have a concept of a not yet existent Socrates by grasping his existent individual essence, Socrateity, and (in effect) conceiving of him under the description 'the unique instantiation of Socrateity' (Alvin Plantinga, 'Actualism and Possible Worlds', *Theoria* 42 (1976), 139–60).

[27] I think this latter thought is at work in theories of divine ideas after Aquinas (for instance, Henry of Ghent or Scotus), but I will not pursue the history here.

[28] Plantinga's just-noted move works for properties only if they too have haecceities to precede them in God's mental life. But either their haecceities are there independent of God or God generates them by a productive sort of conceiving. If we are willing to say the first of property-haecceities, we can just say it about the original properties. If He can do the latter for property-haecceities, He can do it for the properties themselves. So either way, property-haecceities turn out to be idle wheels.

God's mind. We have little idea how this would work. But it could not be perceptual. The things perceived cause perception. Abstract, uninstanced attributes could not cause God to perceive them. So God could not acquire concepts of them perceptually. Rather, God would form concepts of them by working with materials acquired elsewhere. The most reasonable view might be that He would capture attributes by imagining things that have them, or thinking through what it would be to have them. Then what would make it the case that God captures an unexemplified attribute, if ever He did so, would simply be that He got right what does in fact exist. What it is for an attribute to be a divine mental event's content would be just that if things were as God imagined, as part of their being so, that attribute would be instanced, or else that what it would be to have the attribute really is as God independently thinks.

If this is the best story, we do not need the attribute to understand God's mental content. As an entity it does not help constitute that content; it is just something a mental event happens to represent if it is there to represent. Nor does it help causally explain the event's being such as to represent it. Rather, the (very brief) causal story of this is that the event is as it is from God's own resources: God just produces the event, which is such as to represent the attribute if it is there to represent, and that's that. The independent attribute contributes nothing to explaining how the event has its content. So we do not need it in an account of the event's content. Instead, we can eliminate the independent attribute and let the event determine what the attribute will be if instanced, rather than capturing anything Platonic and independent. Nor need the event produce the attribute as a content to do so. It is enough if due to the event's being as it is, if God causes there to be a case of the attribute, that case will *be* a case of that attribute. As to how the mental event manages to be about a non-existent and perhaps never-existent attribute, perhaps this is ultimately a fact about the powers God has in virtue of producing it: for a mental event to capture *being a dog* is for it to make an appropriate contribution to God's having the power to produce dogs. I expand this thought below.

Attributes and content

A second Platonist tack runs this way. Before Creation, God formed a cat-concept—a concept whose content was what it is to be a cat. When an event has a content, it is natural to think that something is the content it has, that having a content is having a relation to some sort of object. So it is natural to think that there was an attribute which was its content. If there 'are' no non-existents, this attribute existed, unexemplified. Further, there are no multiple modes of being. Things either simply exist or simply do not. So it existed really rather than 'merely intentionally'. Perhaps God's mental activity produced it. Perhaps it merely grasped something that was there anyway. Either way, its content was something abstract and Platonic.

But we need not think that some entity gave the cat-event its content. We could treat being contentful, and contentful one way rather than another, as a primitive fact about mental events. Many ontologies involve entities not made to be as they are by other entities. Basic particles are not made to be as they are by smaller parts. Realists say that cathood makes cats cats, but nothing makes cathood cathood: it just is as it as. So it is not clear what special fact about the cat-event would make *it* require to be made as it is by cathood. If we bring the attribute into the story of God's mental content, the story goes this way: a particular event encodes what it is to be a cat because it grasps cathood. Ignoring the questions of what this means and how it is done, we can ask simply: why does it do so? Well, it just does. That is just the event's nature, as a brute fact; that is where explanation stops. All there is to the event is the grasping and the content grasped; the content grasped makes it the event it is; to be that event is to be the grasping of that content, period. Without the attribute, the story goes: a particular event encodes what it is to be a cat. Why? It just does. That is its nature, as a brute fact; that is where explanation stops. All there is to the event is God's thinking and its being contentful in a particular way; the way it is contentful makes it the event it is; to be that event is to be an event contentful that way, period; and 'way' is not ontologically commissive.[29] Either way, explanation stops at a brute fact about the nature of a mental event.[30] Why is the one resting point any better than the other? Each resting point comes down to saying that God thinks a certain way: God thinks a certain way, such that His thought grasps an attribute (whatever that means), or God simply thinks a certain way. If we rest finally in a brute fact about God's thinking either way, why prefer the more baroque story to one with cleaner, attribute-free lines?

Attributes and causal powers

Another appeal to divine mental content runs this way. Because God's cat-concept has a mammal rather than a vegetable as its content, when God made cats, they came out mammals, not vegetables. Some real thing must account for any difference in causal role, and for the cat-thinking event's giving God the power to produce mammal, not vegetable cats. The natural candidate here is an abstract entity which gives the event its content. So we should bring abstracta into our account of God's mental content.

---

[29] For one such generalized adverbial approach to mental content, see Michael Tye, *The Metaphysics of Mind* (Cambridge: Cambridge University Press, 1992).

[30] My talk of the natures of mental events is ontologically innocent. 'The nature of x' can be just a way to say 'x insofar as x makes it true that P', for some P necessarily true of x.

I am skeptical of this proposed explanation. I do not see what the abstract entity really contributes to it. Without the abstract entity, we can say: here is a mental event with certain roles in God's thinking and willing, such that when that event guides God's action, He produces mammal cats. Why? It just is that way: it just has these roles. Perhaps its having them *is* its having a particular mental content. The real thing that accounts for the difference in causal role and resulting causal power is not some constituent of the event but simply the event itself. Nothing need make this such an event. It just is one. That is its nature. With the abstract entity, we can say why the event has its roles: because it produces or grasps an abstract entity. *But why did the event produce or grasp this abstract entity, not another?* No answer: it just did. That is its nature. Here the abstract entity seems an idle wheel. (It is particularly so if we are given no account of how an event's traffic with the abstract manages to give it its roles.) Either way, the divine mental event has an ultimate brute causal role, which gives it a particular action-guiding function. On pain of infinite regress, there have to be differences in causal role that are not further accounted for. What is the advantage to seeing the ultimate brute role as one of producing or grasping an abstract entity rather than guiding action (and thought) a certain way? Why not just say directly that the event is such that God will, if it figures appropriately in His mental life, make mammal cats? Where the abstract entity is a concept, one might answer by way of general arguments for a representational theory of mind. But I have shown that those arguments do not apply in God's case.

Toward a Causal Theory of Divine Content

I can hardly hope to have exhausted arguments for an abstract-entity theory of pre-creative divine mental content. What I have tried to suggest is that there is no quick, easy argument for one—that any case for one must involve a lot of metaphysical slogging. To my knowledge, no-one has undertaken this since the Middle Ages. I now suggest a different approach, a causal theory. It is philosophically respectable to assert that mind-world relations determine at least one component of a mental event's content. The 'informational semantics' much debated in the past decades has it that

> the fact that the concept DOG means *dog*... is constituted by a nomic connection between two properties of dogs, viz. *being dogs* and *being causes of actual or possible DOG tokenings*,[31]

though it has had trouble spelling out the relevant connection. The same sort of connection might obtain between *being dog-hallucinations* and *being*

[31] Jerry Fodor, *Concepts* (New York: Oxford University Press, 1998), p. 73.

causes . . . , or *being events of imagining a dog* and *being causes . . .* , but these cases plausibly are parasitic on the one involving *being a dog.* I will take from this approach just the idea that a causal link between the presence of an F and the tokening of the concept of an F may help constitute that concept's content. Again, Aquinas reminds us that

> Natural things from which our intellect gets its knowledge measure our intellect . . . but are measured by the divine intellect, in which are all created things as all artifacts are in the intellect of (their) artificer. So the divine intellect measures and is not measured . . . our intellect . . . measures only artifacts, not natural things.[32]

> The relation involved in divine knowledge does not involve dependence of the knowledge upon the known, but rather of the known upon the knowledge. (In us) it designates dependence of our knowledge on the known.[33]

Thomas stresses that since God is Creator, the relation between His knowledge and facts of nature reverses that between our knowledge and facts of nature. We must adjust our beliefs to catch facts of nature. God instead determines what the facts of nature shall be—as it were, adjusting the facts to match how He thinks of them. God represents them causally prior to the natural facts, and the facts can be only as He affirms them to be. Thomas' account may not do for actions done with libertarian freedom (as Ockham was to point out) or for their causal consequences, but all I want to do here is abstract the general principle that relations between divine mental items and the world sometimes reverse those between our own mental items and the world.

A mental event's content may be partly constituted by a causal link between the event and particulars of a certain sort. Relations between divine mental events and the world can reverse those between our own mental events and the world. The thought these theses jointly inspire is that perhaps the content of the divine mental events we speak of as God's possession of creature-concepts involves a causal link in the opposite direction to our own: perhaps what gives such divine events their content is not that creatures' presence is apt to cause their tokening, but instead what God is apt to cause extra-mentally when 'tokening' them—that is, when these events are appropriately involved in generating His actions. That is, perhaps one mental event is such as to be spoken of as grasping the concept *dog,* not the concept *cat,* because it is such that if it is appropriately involved in generating God's actions, dogs result, not cats. Perhaps these mental events are such ways

---

[32] S. Thomae Aquinatis, *Quaestiones Disputatae de Veritate* 1, 2, in S. Thomae Aquinatis *Quaestiones Disputatae,* v. 3 (Turin: Marietti, 1931), p. 5. My tr. See also *Suma Contra Gealikes* (Tunn: Morieth, 1909), I, 62.

[33] *Quaestiones desputatae de Veritate* in *Sancti Thomae Aquinatis Questions Disputatae,* v.3 (Turin: Marietti, 1931), 2, 5 *ad* 16, p. 48. My tr.

primitively and intrinsically, just by their natures. Every physical theory involving causation accepts that some entities have causal roles in this way. There is no physical account of why basic particles have the causal roles in the world they do. If they are truly basic, they do not have them due to any more fundamental constituents; rather, these roles are just primitively theirs. There is nothing magical about this. In the modal realm, the mental events we talk about as God's possession of concepts may be among the 'basic particles'. Perhaps it is just a primitive fact that generating a particular mental event gives God the power to create dogs, and that event's having its content consists in or is a function of this. There is then this relation between our creature-kind-concepts and God's. God's concept of a K is one primitively: it is one because it is apt to contribute in the right way to causing Ks. Ours is a K-concept because it is a grip on being a K, which content it has due *inter alia* to our appropriate causal relations to Ks, or (if we derive our barn-concept in fake-barn country) things which appropriately resemble Ks. Ks are Ks *inter alia* because God conserves them as Ks—that is, because what we speak of as God's possession of a K-concept is constantly among the causal conditions of their being Ks. So if we got our K-concept from real Ks, our K-concept is a K-concept due *inter alia* to its causal dependence on the primitive K-concept, God's. This is all, of course, a sketch of the content of one *kind* of concept, concepts that can apply to creatures. Other sorts have their content in different ways. Logical concepts, for instance, have affecting the way God causes things as one role, determining at least part of their content: *and*, for instance, can lead Him to cause states of affairs to co-obtain, and $\neg(\exists x)$ can lead Him to refrain. (I do not claim that this exhausts their content; I am not trying to offer a complete theory of God's concepts.) Concepts of states of affairs without divine input have their content by consisting of concepts having content in another way. Consider the state of affairs *there being an aardvark nothing causes to exist*. God can cause existence, aardvarks, and causes. This also involves conjunction and $\neg(\exists x)$. So God's concept of this consists without remainder of concepts whose contents are either of the reverse-causal or the modification-of-causality sort.

I will continue to speak of God as having concepts. Still, again, I do not really mean it. I think the ontology of God's mental content need invoke only powers of and causings by God and divine mental events. (Events do have powers. If a rock's striking the window smashes it, it is able to. They also have unused powers: the striking could have smashed a china vase next to the window, had one been there.) A divine mental event is an employment of *cat* because of its appropriate relation to the production of cats, or of a divine conscious event appropriately characterized in terms of cats, or divine knowledge appropriately involving cats, etc. The divine mental event which is God's thinking that P is simply that part of the divine life that has or would have effects suitable to having that content: God's thinking that Fido is a dog is that part of His life that would in conjunction with certain other divine mental events bring it about that Fido is a dog.[34]

I have suggested taking divine mental content fundamentally in terms of God's and mental events' powers and causal roles. So on my view, the reality behind talk of God forming a concept is that He produces an event with a particular causal role. I suggest that the primary causal role of the events behind creature-concept-talk is to provide 'objects' for evaluation, preference, intention, and so on. God has no external facts to know until He has so willed—that is, until He has taken attitudes and executed intentions. So the first role these events could have is in proposing objects for attitudes, which in turn might explain volitions. I suggest that every divine representation—henceforth DR—of candidate creaturely items or states of affairs actually plays this role: every DR is an object of some attitude. For God's thinking about things other than Himself is first and foremost practical. God is thinking about things to make or permit and what to do with them once on the scene, about gifts to give and to whom to give them. Every possible creature, I suggest, *is* a possible creature because God permits there to be such a thing. God forms the DR *dog*. Having the DR, God finds it acceptable that there be dogs. Because He does, God permits that there be dogs. I argue later that each such permission is constitutive of a particular power God has.

One may wonder how unsatisfiable DRs have content if DRs' content is fundamentally a matter of what God is apt to cause when tokening them appropriately. For it seems to follow that if God has *round square*, He produces an event such that He is apt to cause round squares. But it can be true both that a DR has a content which would lead God to produce a certain sort of thing *if* He tokened it appropriately and that no matter what, God would not do so. This is so, for instance, with DRs of morally unacceptable worlds. If God has *round square*, God has a resource needed to cause round squares. But it is not possible that God use His power this way. Representations do not *incline* one toward using them. They are just passive resources for use. And even if they did carry some inclination with them, inclinations can be forever blocked—dispositions forever 'masked' by competing, more powerful dispositions (which perhaps means that some who have the 'masking' dispositions are forever so disposed that were these dispositions not present, a contrary disposition would be). Another sort of answer is that the content of *round square* consists, without remainder, of the contents of *round* and *square*. Each of the latter has content involving God's causal powers. So *round square* has too, for its content is just theirs. But it does not follow that God has a power to produce round squares.

<hr>

[34] This is one place where the assumption that there are no essentially uncreatable non-divine concreta goes to work.

Non-creature Concepts

If God understands Himself, God has concepts of His attributes. These have their content as creature-concepts do only if God can cause them to have instances. It is orthodox that some such thing happens within the Trinity—the Father has the divine nature 'first', in some sense, and causes the Son to have it. Yet I see no pressing reason to construe God's concepts of Himself or items in Him as just like His creature-concepts. They could have their content externalistically: as was not the case with creatures, there *is* something whose nature they could catch logically before God forms His concepts. God did not have to dream Himself up.

12

CONCEPTS, SYNTAX, AND ACTUALISM

THERE are no divine concepts. All the same, it is useful to talk about them, and I now discuss several sorts. I start with concepts simple in content. I then take up ways concepts combine. I suggest that God invents His creature-concepts' modes of combination, rather than finding them innate in Himself. I also argue that God actually makes all possible combinations of His concepts. This helps secure actualism for my theory.

Inventing Natures

As I see it, creatures' natures are what they are because God thinks as He does: being a quark consists in what it does because that is how God thinks of being a quark. God invents the nature of quarks. For God determines the content of His quark-concept. By doing so He determines how something must be to satisfy it. He settles what it is to be a quark. What makes something satisfy this concept is that it exhibits what it is to be a quark, whatever this consists in. To exhibit this is to have the nature of a quark. So God's conceiving settles the nature of quarks. Further, it is not as if God simply forms a concept, which external things may or may not satisfy. God uses the concept to make quarks. He makes them in accord with it. They are as they are because the concept in accord with which God makes them has the content it does. So by determining the content of His quark-concept, God determines what it is to be a quark, the nature of quarks— the nature any quark will have if He makes one. More generally, what concepts God has determines the content of whatever attributes there are or can be.[1]

---

[1] Thus if in particular there are vague attributes, they are so because that is how God conceived them. Further, assuming, as I am prepared to argue, that nothing in God's nature is vague, vagueness is itself

This does not settle what attributes *are*. God could invent the nature of quarks if attributes were universals or sets, or if to be a quark just *is* to satisfy God's quark-concept. But it does have an implication, that if God has simplest-content concepts, these determine the alphabet of being, the simplest attributes of all from which any complex ones are built up. There is some reason to think that God has concepts whose contents are attributes simple in all ways attributes can be simple, and I now explore this.

Simple Attributes

Attributes are logically complex just if they have some internal structure of constituents best represented in a form involving logical operators (for instance, *being red and round*). They are definitionally complex just if they have constituents corresponding in some way to the elements of a definition: if 'to be human is to be a rational animal' gave a real definition, *being human* would be definitionally complex just if there were in it something that made us animals and something else that made us rational. Definitional complexity could involve a generic attribute (*being animal*) and a 'difference' (*being rational*) which distinguishes a kind (humans) within a superkind (animals). Determinate/determinable complexity would differ: determinates of a determinable are not made so by a 'difference'. Phenomenal scarlet is a determinate color. But if it includes its determinable, being a color, it does not also include a 'difference'. Nothing other than being phenomenal scarlet distinguishes scarlet from other phenomenal colors. Attributes are structurally complex just if they contain attributes related in ways corresponding to the structural complexity of their instances: *being water*, for instance, consisting in some way of *being hydrogen* twice over and *being oxygen*.[2] Attributes are categorical/dispositional complex just if they consist of a non-dispositional 'core' and a set of powers that go with it: *being hydrogen*, perhaps, containing a structural component and also some characteristic powers, e.g. to form water together with oxygen. Finally, it is conceivable that attributes have attributes simply as parts, in a purely mereological sense.

If an attribute is not complex in one of these ways, it is in this way simple. Theories of attributes allow attributes simple in all these ways. There can be

---

something He invented. So whatever the correct semantics for the vague is, it is so because that is how God conceived it. If epistemicism is true, that is because God has 'built' vague attributes with precise cutoffs for their exemplification and 'built' us in such a way that we cannot know where that cutoff falls. If vagueness involves objective indeterminacy and truth-value gaps, that is because God has thought up attributes that way. If these gaps are to be treated by supervaluations, these work because there are various possibilities—for example, of precisifying our vague terms in various ways—and on a theist account, God provides these. And so on.

[2] See, for example, John Bigelow and Robert Pargetter, 'A Theory of Structural Universals', *Australasian Journal of Philosophy* 67 (1989), 1–11.

concepts not consisting in these ways of other concepts. Class nominalism does not make its attributes logically complex: it treats attributes as classes of their instances, and so treats being red and round not as a pair consisting of the class of red things and the class of round things, but as the intersection of these classes. Like points apply to the other modes of complexity. Within theories of tropes or universals it is an old view that there are not really any determinable attributes—just lowest-level determinates and determinable concepts we form on their basis. It is another old view that definitions explicate only concepts, rather than grasping an internal structure of the tropes or universals in virtue of which the concepts apply.[3] It is controversial that there are structural tropes or universals and that any tropes or universals are quality/power complex, and if these controversial claims are false, all tropes or universals would be simple in these respects. I have argued against conjunctive tropes or universals (and with them mereological attribute-composition) and would argue that if there are tropes or universals, none are logically complex—that logically simple ones can handle all duties. Given Ockham's Razor, that there are none is the default view on logically complex tropes and universals; we need a positive reason to think otherwise. So it is conceivable that there be wholly simple attributes, no matter what attributes turn out to be. Thus we have reason to think this possible.

Simple DRs

This in turn is reason to think that God has some concepts with simple contents. God could perhaps do without simple-content concepts. If anyone could manage to form a concept with an infinitely complex content, God could, and so it is within the realm of legitimate theories that no DR has a bottom layer of content, that each analyzes into or involves others. But if there can be simple attributes, God has simple-content concepts. For if God is omniscient, then for each possible attribute F, He has a concept that completely captures what it is be (an) F.[4] Further, He has such a concept

---

[3] See my 'Aquinas on Attributes', *Medieval Philosophy and Theology* 11 (2003), 1–41.

[4] Here I argue from generally acceptable intuitions rather than supposing my own particular view of God's mental content. But I have to show that this remains true given my view, else forfeit the argument upon challenge. There is no particular difficulty if God has simple attributes; these can just be external contents of His concepts. A divine concept of a secular attribute F is a concept such that if God uses it appropriately, He produces Fs, that is, things which embody what it is to be an F. The concept completely captures this causally, else Fs would not be what its use led to. This is enough in my terms to guarantee that its content is F. Hence God fails to have a concept completely capturing a possible secular attribute F only if there are possible secular attributes He cannot cause to be instantiated. He can cause *being an incompatibilistically free action* to be instanced, for He can do free acts and conserve free acts as they are done. He cannot cause there to be a non-deity not created or sustained by God, but I think there cannot be such a thing. I deal with further hard cases later.

that captures only what it is to be (an) F. For suppose that He did not have a concept capturing only what it is to be (an) F. Then

> HYP. for some F, God has no distinct concept of being F, but instead only a concept whose content is (say) being F·G but has no distinct representation of F within it.

(HYP) implies that God cannot discriminate being F from being G. For if He could, He would have done so (on pain of non-omniscience) and so would have a concept whose content is just F, in addition to the concept whose content is F·G. If God cannot discriminate being F from being G, yet they are distinct, He is not omniscient: He does not know that there is such a thing as being F. Again, on (HYP), God suffers either a blindspot or another sort of cognitive inability. God has a blindspot if He cannot discriminate F as a distinct attribute. He has another sort of inability if He can distinguish it but cannot represent it to Himself separately. Further, on (HYP), God cannot think of F apart from the complex F·G. He cannot form the belief there are Fs, or so much as entertain the thought that something is F but not G, or tell F·Gs from Gs. Nor then can He think that something is G but not F·G, else He'd be subject to a truly bizarre cognitive failure, being able to form the concept of something F·G and the concept of something G but unable to tell how Gs and F·Gs differ. Nor then can He recognize Fs which are not Gs as such. These inabilities are all cognitive defects. A cognitively perfect God has no such problems. These inabilities are also dubiously compatible with omnipotence. And of course, if God has them, there are many truths He does not know. Again, on (HYP), if God has any concepts that apply just to F-things, they will represent to Him only some attribute H with which F is coextensive. But there would have to be some difference in content between H and F, something about Fs which the H-concept did not catch, of which God would then be ignorant. And there also would be something God does not know about Hs, namely that they are F. Thus for each F, God has a concept of only F. But then He also has one completely capturing only F, since He has one completely capturing F and knows that it is a concept of the very attribute captured in His concept only of F. If the concept captures all of F, it has no less content than F. If it captures only F, it has no more. So if F is simple, God has a simple-content concept, one which captures only a simple attribute. And God actually has it even if nothing has any simple attribute. Thus God has a simple-content concept for every possible simple attribute.[5]

---

[5] Some might argue that there are simple attributes whose concepts He cannot possess. I discount this in the case of those involved in phenomenal consciousness, for reasons already discussed. Some argue that God cannot fully possess such concepts as fear and despair. They contend that full possession of these concepts requires being able to be in fear and despair for oneself. But God (they claim) cannot do so, for having the experiences presupposes having beliefs God cannot have: for instance, one can feel fear (they claim) only if one believes that one is in danger, and an omniscient being cannot believe that an omnipotent being is in danger, for no omnipotent being can be in danger. (So, for example, David Blumenfeld, 'On the

Simple-content concepts have as content only attributes, unless 'bare'—attri-buteless—particulars are possible. For a particular with an attribute at least contains the complexity of bearer and borne.

If God is atemporal, He does nothing later than anything else, and so does not form complex DRs after simple ones, by combining them, or simple ones after complex, by analyzing them. If He is temporal, I have argued, DRs arrive all at once;[6] if they do, the same is true. Still, simple ones determine the traits of complex ones containing them, not *vice versa*. It is because the concept *dog* is what it is that the concept *brown dog* is what it is, not *vice versa*. So simple divine concepts have a fundamental place in the nature of things. By forming them, God determines the alphabet of being. The most basic attributes there can be in non-divine reality are so because they are the simplest things God has thought up. And if simple DRs determine the content of complex ones, simple DRs set the contours of secular modal truth. By determining the most basic non-divine attributes, simple DRs determine the basic kinds of non-deities and secular states of affairs there can and cannot be.

Syntax and Complex Concepts

Concepts' syntax is the way they combine to form other concepts and what I soon call thoughts. Let us pretend for example's sake that God's conceptual syntax involves something like nouns and adjectives; let us say that noun-type concepts have substances as content and adjective-type have attributes. Then there are ways God's concepts combine: if God has *cat*, *dog*, and *striped*, *striped cat* is a combination and *dog cat* is not, for Him as for us. There is no concept of being a dog cat, because *dog* is not adjective-type. For Him as for us, 'dog cat' is a nonsense string. Rules of syntax state combination-conditions in general form. So DRs have a syntax. There are ways they do and do not combine. A question worth asking is whether that syntax is natural or a product of creative thinking. This involves difficult further issues: what sort of 'metaphysical structure' does God's own nature bring with it, and does God in fact represent Himself to Himself in knowing all about Himself? If God is by nature a substance having attributes and by nature represents Himself to Himself, He will by nature conceive this accurately, and so by nature form at

Compossibility of the Divine Attributes', in Thomas Morris (ed.), *The Concept of God* (Oxford: Oxford University Press, 1987), pp. 201–15. For further references and discussion see Yujin Nagasawa, *God and Phenomenal Consciousness* (Cambridge: Cambridge University Press, 2008.) I have doubts about the line of argument, but for present purposes I need make only one comment: being in fear or despair are not simple phenomenal qualities. They have propositional content and (as the objection supposes) essential relations to other mental states. So being fearful or despairing are complex states of affairs. And so it is dubious that the concepts of fear and despair have simple contents.

[6] On 'generalism'—of which see below—this would be true only for purely general DRs and those of any particulars existing from all eternity.

least some DRs with noun- or adjective-syntax. I propose not to answer the overall question. Even if God's concepts are guaranteed by His own nature to include some with noun- or adjective-syntax, this would not entail that His *creature*-concepts have such syntax. So let us consider a narrower question: is the syntax of God's creature-DRs natural?

Suppose, then, that DRs of creatures are such that

1. $(x)(y)$(if x is an adjective-type DR and y a noun-type DR, there is a DR xy).[7]

The naturalness hypothesis would go this way: (1) is true because God's nature encodes rules to follow in producing representations—for example,

2. Produce adjective-type and noun-type creaturely DRs, and for all adjective-type DRs x and noun-type DRs y, produce xy, or
3. Produce adjective- and noun-type creaturely DRs, and for all adjective-type DRs x and noun-type DRs y, xy is a combination.

I am reluctant to believe in innate (2)- or (3)-type rules. If these *are* natural divine rules, God's nature requires Him to think up at least some creaturely substances and attributes. But I do not see why it would. Even if we must think of creatures this way, perhaps some unimaginable alternative is open to God— God needn't have made us able to conceive all that is in Him to conceive. Even if debate in ontology consists primarily of *a priori* arguments, the concepts which drive those arguments are as they are due to the character God gives the world and our faculties. If we found *a priori* reason to think that the world must consist of substances and attributes, that would tell us nothing about what other ways it was in God to order Creation.

Because I believe that it is in God to imagine what we cannot, I do not accept an innateness hypothesis about creaturely DRs' syntax. Instead, I see it this way. God invents the natures of things. Being a cat includes what it does because God thinks of it a certain way. This is true for *everything* that is part of being a cat; a deity theory is true for none of it. But being a cat includes belonging to an ontological category. So this too is determined by how God thinks. If God invents natures, it is up to God what the categories in created ontology are. Perhaps God invents some categories. If He does, He does so as part of coming up with His DRs, and categories are up to God because it is up to Him what sorts of DRs He thinks up. Perhaps God has some categorical concepts by nature: perhaps by nature He is a substance with attributes and is omniscient, and so grasps and has the concepts of substance and attribute. Even if this is so, it is up to Him whether to conceive creatures in any category whose concept He has by nature.

In any event, being striped is a property because God's concept *striped* is adjective-type. If God formed no adjective-type creature-concepts, there

---

[7] Note that (1) has no modal element; that xy exists is compatible with its being unsatisfiable. (1) is a pretend quantification, if there really are no DRs.

would be no creaturely properties. Cats are substances because God's concept *cat* is noun-type. If created substances are just bundles of properties, God's noun-type creature-concepts just are or appropriately involve concatenations or conjunctions of adjectival (and so on) concepts. If they are not property-bundles, this is because God's noun-type creature-concepts are not like this. Created attributes and substances combine as they do because divine concepts combine as they do. Created states of affairs assemble as they do because divine concepts fit together in a particular way. The syntax of God's concepts, in short, helps determine the ontology of non-divine reality. If we live in a substance-attribute world, that is because (*inter alia*) God thought up a world in nouns and adjectives—because He came up with concepts with this sort of syntax.

Syntax need not be innate. It is perfectly possible to legislate rules for oneself and then follow them: someone invented chess and no doubt played it, and governments sometimes obey the law. It is tenable to say that the syntax of God's creature-concepts exists in God only as a function of particular DRs' contents, rather than as an abstract formal schema into which concrete contents are plugged, and so in creatively coming up with creature-concepts, God also came up with their syntax. If this is how things are, perhaps we cannot call God's syntax a choice, but neither need we say that His nature impelled Him to it. God simply did think a particular way. We can rest with that.

If there are no innate divine syntactical rules for creature-concepts, God simply dreams up not just their contents, but their syntax and syntactical categories. So God does not just creatively account for all modal facts about creatures. He creatively accounts for the modal facts about His own creature-concepts—their syntax (how they can combine with others) as well as their semantics (how they can be satisfied). God's simple concepts determine the alphabet of being. If God determines how His concepts combine, He also determines its syllabary and vocabulary. For how God's concepts combine sets how attributes (etc.) combine. God's sway also extends to sentences, for His concepts combine into thoughts, which determine states of affairs. There are the states of affairs there are because God shapes His concepts as He does—because God thinks as He does.

Syntax and Rule

I have denied that God's syntactic rules for creature-concepts are innate. I now want to explore how these rules exist in Him. To do so, let us suppose that God's mind works by first framing an abstract syntactic rule and then applying it. What I want to show is that if this were how things are, God would have made all possible applications of the rule—which ultimately makes talk of such an abstract rule otiose. To say that God's creature-concepts have a syntax, I suggest, is simply to note patterns in His fully realized combining of His concepts.

If God frames an abstract general syntactical rule, God does not just determine the rule, and how to apply it, and so know of the elements of each combination that they can combine. If He frames a rule, God actually applies it. God makes all possible applications of the rule—He forms in His mind all possible combinations of His concepts. To the extent that He did not have the combinations in mind, it would simply be indeterminate which rule He was framing. A divine syntactic rule is or includes a function, mapping sets of combinable concepts into resulting combinations. There is no fact about *which* function one has in mind unless there is a fact about what sets of arguments the function one has in mind takes and what (if any) values it outputs for each set. Whatever these facts are, they determine the identity of the function: if functions A and B take precisely the same arguments and output the same value for each argument, then A = B. God has in mind all concepts His syntactic rules would take as arguments. So if God has determinate rules in mind at all, there are facts about what (if any) output-values there are for each set of arguments. If there are, He knows them, being omniscient. And if He knows them, He has the full set of output-values in mind. If He does, He has the combined concepts in mind. Each way concepts combine is a function from concepts to more complex concepts. So for each mode of combination, God has a determinate mode of combination in mind only if there are facts about which concepts are arguments for this function and what (if any) concepts are the result of this combination. But then each such function in God's mind is determinate only if the values also exist—and there is no other place for them to exist than in God's mind. For such a function is not an independent Platonic object; it exists only in the divine mind. We can have a function in mind without having all arguments and values in mind if the function exists independent of us and we have some way of grasping it other than by having all the argument(s)/value(s) correlations in mind. The functions God has in mind exist only in His mind, and are only as determinate as He makes them—which is to say, only as determinate as the pairings of values and arguments are in His mind. God has values for each set of arguments in mind only if He actually makes the concept-combinations the rules license. So God has a determinate syntactic rule in mind only if He actually makes all possible applications of it, and so all possible combinations of His concepts.[8] Some might reply that it is enough if it is determinate what the value of the function *would be* if He inputted these arguments. But if there

---

[8] If God's base-set of concepts changes, e.g. by the addition of new singular concepts, then His rules generate a new set of outputs for these arguments. Strictly, then, every addition of new base-concepts brings a new function with it, and this and all like points should be relativized to sets of base concepts. But the new includes the old as long as the old arguments and values persist, and thus is able to count as an extension of the rule to a new set of cases.

is a fact about this, an omniscient God would know it. He could not know that the result of combining adjective A and noun N would be AN without having AN in mind.

Again, if *striped* and *cat* can combine, striped cats are *ipso facto* conceivable. So if God did not actually form the concept *striped cat*, there would be something conceivable He had not explicitly conceived—and so something about what is conceivable He would not know. Nor would He know what it is to be a striped cat. For to have it in mind that to be a striped cat, something must be both striped and a cat, one must have the concept *striped cat*. And since there is no question of effort or of finite cognitive capacity otherwise occupied, what could account for a failure to think rules' consequences through? Again, if God is by nature omniscient, God knows what can be known as soon as it is knowable. If so, no sooner would God decide on a rule and how to apply it than He would see all the consequences—and so have all the rule's applications in mind. Thus if concepts' syntax exists in God's mind in the form of abstract general rules, it also exists as a pattern fully manifest in His actual conceptual armory, which includes all possible licit combinations of His concepts.

The Payoff

I have belabored this because it has important implications. To draw them out, I introduce what I call 'divine thoughts'.

Concepts combine into the sort of thing expressed in that-clauses following verbs of propositional attitude ('believes', 'hopes'): mental representations which represent Platonic propositions if there are such. But (say I) there are not. And if there are no divine concepts, divine concepts do not combine into proposition-representations. Talk of propositions and divine mental representations is in my view convenient fiction. I call the mental events which lie behind talk of God grasping propositions divine thoughts. *Per* Chapter 11, I suggest that these have their content primitively. It is at most in other divine mental events grounded that they are events of thinking that P rather than that Q. They contain no proposition or representation to give them their content. Rather, their being contentful as they are is just part of their being the very thoughts they are. Putting it another way, the whole thought, not (in virtue of) any combined representation or relation to an independent proposition, is what makes it true that this is a thought that P.

On my account, what thoughts God can have is a function of what 'base' concepts He has and His concepts' syntax. If God has simple-content concepts, these are an absolute base for His thoughts, even if not for all of His thoughts (perhaps He also has concepts that are infinitely analyzable, with no bottom layer). If God has no simple concepts, concepts at a given level of analysis or decomposition are still a base for all combinations they permit, and so no harm will be done by simply speaking of base concepts, without supposing that God does in fact have simple-content concepts. As we see later, God has all the base concepts He can have. So if God has combined all concepts syntax permits, God has all thoughts He can have. I do not mean by this that God generates all the mental events He can. He clearly does not. Where it is a contingent truth that P, God judges that P, but might have judged that ¬P. If God actually has all thoughts He can have, my theory is actualist about general divine thoughts. It is also so about singular divine thoughts, but to show this I must introduce a complication.

Thoughts are general just if they are not singular. Thoughts are singular just if and because they employ singular concepts. Singular concepts are concepts of particular individuals: a singular concept of me, for instance, is one only I could satisfy. God certainly has singular concepts of individuals once they exist. Once I exist, I myself, in my actual concrete existence, might be the content of a divine singular concept. But some argue that God cannot have a singular concept of an individual before it exists.[9] Instead, they contend, the story of how God acquired a singular concept of me is this. When God decided to create, He decided to instance a complex general concept of something with every purely general attribute I wind up with. It did not contain an attribute of identity with any particular individual. It could be instanced more than once in the same world—at least in a world of perfect qualitative eternal recurrence, and perhaps other-wise, depending on exactly what it contained—and each time it was instanced, the result might be someone different. God willed to instance this purely general concept, and I am the particular He wound up with, for reasons beyond His control. Once I existed, He had a singular concept of me, but not before.

For such 'generalists' about the possible, being possible and being impossi-ble are contraries, not contradictories. Before I existed, it was not impossible that I exist (since here I am). But while it was possible that there be someone just like me, it was not possible precisely that *I* exist: denial of divine singular concepts entails this, for if this *were* possible, God would know it, and so have a singular concept of me. So for generalists, at any time, there are or have been all individuals there can be, though not all the individuals it is not impossible for there to be. Generalism must be actualist about individuals. If there were non-actual individuals, God would have singular concepts of them if He is omniscient, and have them though the individuals do not exist. On generalism, merely possible worlds do not contain non-actual individuals, though they may contain actual ones (there are merely possible worlds with alternate possibilities for me). Insofar as they deal in non-actual individuals

[9] C. Menzel, 'Temporal Actualism and Singular Fore Knowledge', *Philosophical Perspechives*. 5 (1991), 475–507, following A. N. Prior; Christopher Hughes, 'Negative Existentials, Omniscience and Cosmic Luck', *Religious Studies* 34 (1998), 375–401; Barry Miller, *From Existence to God* (New York: Routledge, 1992), pp. 40–62.

they are really only types of world, with maximally detailed types of individual providing 'slots' individuals will fill if a world of that type becomes actual.

If God has pre-creative singular concepts, the argument about base concepts and syntax simply shows that He has all thoughts He can have. If He does not, it shows only that actualism applies to general thoughts—God could have new singular thoughts as new particulars showed up in reality. But on generalism, actualism about singular thoughts is still preserved at every time: at every time, God has all thoughts He can have *then*, and if new thoughts become possible as new individuals come to be later, He has them as soon as they are possible.

I do not believe in states of affairs to be thoughts' contents, but I allow talk of states of affairs as convenient fiction. Within the fiction, then, I say that if God has all thoughts He can have, He thinks up all states of affairs He can and all states of affairs there can be.[10] There could not be such a thing as God stopping short, since where He stops determines the stock of states of affairs. Platonists and deity theorists have to agree that God does not stop short. Suppose that there is, built somehow into God's nature or set in Platonic heaven, a totality of possible and impossible states of affairs. God would forfeit His omniscience if He failed to conceive of any of them. So Platonists and deity theorists should grant too that God conceives of all states of affairs He can, and all states of affairs there can be. This is the right result, on my view or its competitors. And it is also the right result *simpliciter*. Intuitively, if God is omnipotent, there cannot be states of affairs God cannot think up. Omnipotence is power enough to think up whatever there can be. If God thinks up all the states of affairs He can, and there cannot be states of affairs God cannot think up, God actually thinks up all the states of affairs there can be. Again, on pain of His omniscience, there can be only states of affairs God actually has in mind.

On my view, then, there are no states of affairs in other worlds which are not thought up in ours. Within the fiction, then, my view is actualist about states of affairs: any state of affairs in another possible world is in ours at least as the content of a divine mental state. I shortly derive secular modal facts from divine permission and prevention. Permission and prevention are directed upon thoughts of states of affairs. So if there actually is a thought of every possible state of affairs, this helps secure actualism for my view by assuring that there are enough objects for attitudes to let God's actual permitting and preventing and actual dispositions to same generate all modal truth.[11] This also helps assure that my view is extensionally adequate:

---

[10] On generalism, this claim must be relativized to times: as soon as there is a new individual, God has new thoughts and so conceives new states of affairs. Note that 'there can be' does not mean 'that can be actualized'. There are impossible states of affairs (within the fiction). Since they exist, they can exist. They are states of affairs there can be. But they are not states of affairs that can be actualized.

[11] One might wonder whether this can be true if God is timeless and time is tensed. Suppose as a sample tensed thesis presentism, the thesis that only what is present exists. It is now noon. Nothing past or future exists. How can God permit this timelessly? God can permit presentism to be true by determining the

there are enough actual permissions, preventions and dispositions to provide truth-makers or explainers for every secular modal truth.

Did God Follow Rules?

One picture of how God determines concepts' syntax would say that He does so by formulating a general rule, which He then applies. I worked with this picture in the last sections. Another would dispense with rules, and say that God determines the combinations by making them: God sets His concepts' syntax by doing with them whatever is syntactically admissible. Or, better, God's combinings define what is syntactically admissible. They are admissible because they are what He does. That a rule exists as a pattern in God's conceptual armory does not entail that He followed the rule in forming His armory as He did. On this second approach, God does not follow rules, and so Wittgenstein would say that what He has in mind does not amount to a language.[12] If he is right, I would just accept the conclusion. Not every mode of representation is a language: pictures represent.

There are many ways to legislate a rule. One might say, for example, 'It is correct to move the rook vertically or horizontally but not diagonally, it is incorrect for the rook to "jump" over other pieces or share a square with a piece, but it is correct for the rook to move onto a square occupied by an opposing piece, which must then leave the board.' But a chess rule can also be viewed as a function, which takes as arguments positions of chess pieces and outputs permitted next positions of the pieces. One can specify a function *in extenso*, by giving all values for all arguments. So in the chess case, one can instead give the rule by listing all and only the valid rook moves from each square on the board, given the positions of other pieces. One gives the same rule either way, in the latter case as a pattern among the types of permitted moves. It would be close to this to say 'Every move from square to square I am about to make is permissible, and no other move is permissible,' and then *make* all and only the correct moves. There is nothing to favor one way of stating the rule over another absolutely speaking, though the first encapsulates the information about possible moves simply. On the last method, one at once states and acts in accord with the rule: if one hadn't thought about it in advance, one would be making up the game as one went along. And if one hadn't thought about it in advance, it would not be apt to say one was following the rules as one did this.

God's nature does not dictate rules He follows in thinking up creatures. If God dreams up all His creature-concepts at once, as I have suggested, He also

---

nature of time. He can timelessly prevent its now being noon by timelessly assuring that time ends before noon. If He does not, He permits it.

[12] *Philosophical Investigations*, tr. Elizabeth Anscombe (Oxford: Basil Blackwell, 1958), pp. 258–9.

dreams up their syntax all at once, and so makes all permissible combining-moves with them at once. It fits naturally with this to say that He has not thought about rules in advance. Again, if God makes all possible combinations of His concepts, and there is a way to understand this without positing further events in His mind—the formulation, grasping, and application of rules—the latter are just otiose. We do not need them to explain what God does. We can simply say that God forms His concepts with syntax built in. So I suggest that God at once states and acts in accord with, but does not follow, the rules: it is as if the inventor of chess gave the rules about piece-movements by making all and only the possible moves simultaneously, not having thought it out beforehand. There is nothing impossible in this. Chess could have been invented in a flash by someone very smart with a great many arms.

Syntax, I submit, exists in God not as a set of rules He follows, but as a pattern in His fully realized usage. God has made all the DR-combinations there can be, and made them all the ones there can be. Dummett contrasts two forms of conventionalism. On one,

> although all necessity derives from linguistic conventions we have accepted, the derivation is not always direct. Some necessary statements (register) conventions we have laid down; others are more or less remote consequences of conventions . . . the axioms of a mathematical theory are necessary in virtue of . . . being direct registers of . . . conventions we have adopted about the use of the terms of the theory; it is the job of the mathematician to discover the more or less remote consequences of our having adopted these conventions . . . This account . . . leaves unexplained the status of the assertion that certain conventions have certain consequences. It appears that if we adopt the conventions registered by the axioms, together with those registered by the principles of inference, then we *must* adhere to the ways of talking embodied in the theorem; and this necessity must be one imposed upon us, one that we meet with. It cannot itself express the adoption of a convention; the account leaves no room for any further such convention.[13]

Thus this sort of conventionalism is a half-measure. Something non-conventional accounts for some necessities—for instance, the necessity with which consequences follow from premises. A more radical sort of conventionalism extends to all necessities. On the more radical,

> the logical necessity of any statement is always the direct expression of a linguistic convention. That a given statement is necessary consists always in our having expressly decided to treat that very statement as

---

[13] Michael Dummett, 'Wittgenstein's Philosophy of Mathematics', in Paul Benecerraf and Hilary Putnam (eds), *The Philosophy of Mathematics* (Englewood Cliffs, NJ: Prentice Hall, Inc., 1964), pp. 494–5.

unassailable; it cannot rest on our having adopted certain other conventions which are found to involve our treating it so.[14]

If we cannot lean on the 'given' power of logic to determine what follows from what, then for any PQ, it is up to us whether P implies Q: whether Q is a theorem one can prove from P. And so:

> If we accept (a) proof, we confer necessity on the theorem … In doing this we are making a new decision, and not merely making explicit a decision we had already made implicitly … accepting a theorem is adopting a new rule of language, and hence our concepts cannot remain unchanged at the end of the proof. But we could have rejected the proof without doing any more violence to our concepts than is done by accepting it; in accepting it we could have remained equally faithful to the concepts with which we started out.[15]

In other words, content already given to a concept by prior decision does not uniquely determine the new decision at hand. The concept as so far determined does not tell us how to 'go on' in the next application.[16] What we have done with the rules so far does not determine how we extend them to new cases. Thus we make up the rules as we go along.

As I see it, God is the more radical sort of conventionalist in setting creature-concepts' syntax. Nothing in or outside God determines how to combine these concepts—for example, whether *striped cat* is syntactically admissible. Nor can God first give *striped* and *cat* some partial content, then let that fill the rest of the concepts out, and so determine for Him (as it were) whether *striped cat* is admissible. There is nothing beyond Him to dictate how the rest of the concept goes, and I have ruled it out that some natural rule does the job. So if God has not settled the matter directly, it is not settled. If God did not expressly rule on *striped cat*, there would be no fact about its syntactic status at all. So what God conceives determines what is conceivable: if He does not make *striped* and *cat* combinable by combining them in His mind, they simply are not combinable—*striped cat* is not so much as conceivable, even by God.

What about Nonsense?

But some things are not conceivable or conceived, even by God. God forms all possible licit combinations of His concepts. But presumably He also knows what the illicit combinations are, for example, that 'dog cat' is a nonsense

---

[14] *Ibid.*, p. 495.   [15] *Ibid.*, pp. 496, 497–8.
[16] Dummett offers this as an interpretation of Wittgenstein; whether or not it is the right one, Wittgenstein's 'rule-following considerations' are close to its surface.

string. He knows this only if He forms the illicit combinations. If this is a nonsense string, not even God conceives or can conceive a dog cat. So we must ask what distinguishes the licit from the illicit—strings that express divine concepts from those that do not, strings that accord with the rules or norms from strings that do not. There is a related question: how can a rule be just a pattern in fully realized usage when that usage includes both uses that do and uses that do not accord with the rule? One simple reply would distinguish two levels in God's usage, involving something like a use/mention distinction. Everything I have said so far applies only to the base level, at which concepts are in use in forming objects for divine attitudes. At the second level, nonsense strings occur only as mentioned, in some form which notes of them that they *are* nonsense strings. So a divine rule is a pattern in fully realized usage in a double sense: what accords with the rule is what is used in an object for a divine attitude, and also what is set apart from what does not by a use/mention pattern in the usage.

Generalism Again

We are now ready to speak of the genesis of secular modality proper. But the issue generalism raises requires a bit of discussion first. Generalists ask whether God has singular concepts of individuals before they exist. I think He does. I discuss this later. For now I just say how things are if He has them and if He does not.

Suppose first that God has them. Then He has all secular states of affairs there could ever be in mind before creating, settles His permissions, preventions, and so on, and so (say I) before Creation makes all secular modal truths true. On generalism, before God makes individuals, there are no modal truths about just them. There are only modal truths about types of individuals. On the account I soon develop, God's non-natural powers and lacks of power would settle their truth. Let T be one such type. T's being possible makes it possible that there be individuals of type T, though before there actually are some it is not the case that there are individuals such that they are T-type individuals thus made possible. When such an individual appears, the prior possibility of something T-type made it possible (in a loose sense) before it existed. So God makes this item possible in this loose sense, though He does not bring this about by thinking up it in particular. By permitting Rover's type of dog, God permits Rover to exist, though He could not know that He was doing so. Once Rover comes to be, there are singular modal truths about Rover. There are about Rover just the truths God meant there to be about *some* dog just like him, and they are all just as God meant them to be, and assured them to be by instancing the type He did.

On generalism, God also makes Rover possible in the strict sense if He causes Rover to be actual. If God had no singular concept of Rover, He could not intend that Rover be a dog: He could not form such an intention. But we can still trace Rover's being and possibly being a dog to God. Not everything we bring about is something we intend to bring about. If I throw a rock at a window, I may intend to break the window. I can do so without any intention as to precisely where the break is to begin. But still, if I cause the shattering, and the shattering starts at place P, I cause the shattering to start at place P— only not in virtue of intending that precise result. I causally explain this although I did not intend to do it. So too, I suggest, on generalism, God makes Rover a dog, and so possibly a dog. God just does not do so by intending just that or with full control of the result.[17]

Divine thought and action determine singular modal truths about creatures. The only question is how. If God has pre-creative singular concepts, He determines them prior to creating, by conceiving, permitting, etc. If not, He determines them by creating, and not quite fully intentionally. Thus though generalism raises an interesting issue, it is not one that affects God's responsibility for secular modal truth.

Finally, I note the most complex sort of divine concept. In the Bang God conceives all secular states of affairs. So He conceives maximal secular states of affairs, those whose obtaining would entail for any secular proposition P either that P is true, that $\neg$P is, or that both lack truth-value. Thus He conceives the secular portions of entire possible or impossible worlds. By adding in His own contributions, He then also frames entire world-histories.

---

[17] This paragraph is heavily indebted to Menzel, *op. cit.*

13

MODALITY: BASIC NOTIONS

My story about the modal status of secular truths begins with the biggest bang—God's thinking up all candidate secular states of affairs. I now consider why these acquire the modal status they do. My account centers on God's preventing and permitting states of affairs, and so I begin by explaining these notions. The next chapters outline my account, then explore it in further detail.

Preventing

I suggest that

x causally prevents state of affairs S[1] at t = df.

1. S or that S is not the case are the sort of thing to come about, and

2. at t, x causes an event E which suffices in the circumstances to bring it about that S is not the case, or x does not act, this causally suffices in the circumstances to bring it about that S is not the case, and S is not x's performing the omitted act.

As I see it, (1) excludes only states of affairs divine activity presupposes—God's ever existing, having His nature, and so on. These are not the sorts of thing to come about. For God is eternal. An eternal being never began to exist. So if God is eternal, it never began to be the case that God ever existed

---

[1] As I have said, I do not in the end believe in states of affairs. So 'S' is for me a non-denoting term. I use it for convenience; the more cumbersome but (as I see it) ontologically perspicuous formulation would be along the lines of 'x causally prevents things' being as sentence S says they are when used in its standard way to make an assertion.'

and so on, and so His ever existing etc. never came about. And so as God is eternal by nature, these are not the sorts of thing to come about. Everything involving, presupposing, or caused by a divine activity comes about. Thus necessarily, everything involving non-deities, concepts or natures of non-deities, or secular propositions, attributes, or states of affairs comes about, on my view, as necessarily, it all depends on some divine mental event.[2] (1) is satisfied for every secular state of affairs, even the non-obtaining of absolute impossibilities: that these are not the case is the sort of thing to come about, because it *has* come about. It has come about that it is not the case that Rover $\neq$ Rover. If God has pre-creative singular concepts, He brought this about by thinking up Rover. 'Before' He did so, there was no such content of thought as that Rover $\neq$ Rover. Once He thought Rover up, it was not the case that Rover $\neq$ Rover, because God thought up Rover as He did. As I see it, it was not in Him so to think that it turned out that Rover $\neq$ Rover. But that it was not in God to have it otherwise does not alter the fact that He made it so. If God has no pre-creative singular concepts, then it came about that it is not the case that Rover $\neq$ Rover when God made Rover.

I put (2) in terms of sufficing in the circumstances because there are three cases to consider. In one, x alone brings it about that S does not obtain, perhaps by bringing about mediating states of affairs: 'alone' is to be taken in contrast with the other two cases. In another, x completes a preventing condition: there is or will be independent of x's contribution a condition insufficient to bring it about that S does not obtain, which together with x's contribution is or will be sufficient. Here what x does suffices *in the circumstances* (given the already-present or to-come insufficient condition) to prevent S. In the last, x overdetermines that S does not obtain. This comes in two main sorts, redundant and failsafe prevention. In a case of redundant prevention, x's contribution suffices on its own to bring it about that S does not obtain, but so does some other item's; each is *a* cause for S's not obtaining, and the two together are *the* cause. Here there is clearly a legitimate sense in which x alone prevents S: given x's contribution, independent of anything else, it is guaranteed that S does not obtain. Failsafe causation is the flip-side of what the literature calls late causal pre-emption: if x and y are events each sufficient in the circumstances to bring about event E, and x manages to do this before y's input arrives, x pre-empts y in causing E, and y failsafes x: y would have brought E about had x not pre-empted y. In a case of failsafe prevention, x alone brings it about that S does not obtain, but had x not brought this about, y would have. Here there is nothing difficult about the claim that x prevented S. But the claim that y did raises a worry. If Smith dies and Jones later shoots Smith in the heart, there seems no legitimate sense in

---

[2] On my view, there are no entities of some of these sorts. In these cases the dependence is that the realities behind talk of such things involve divine mental events.

which Jones prevents Smith's continued life.[3] On the other hand, suppose that snails threaten my garden. I overreact, and surround the garden with a wall taller than any snail can climb. The wall is hideous. So I hide it with another, prettier wall, which turns out just a bit shorter. The snails attack. As it happens, none make it over even the shorter wall. So the shorter wall prevents the snails' reaching the garden. But it seems to me that erecting the taller wall also prevented their reaching the garden, even though actually only erecting the shorter wall brought it about that they did not. Perhaps the moral is that the circumstances in (2) are time-sensitive. To qualify as one, a failsafe, pre-empted preventing cause must occur (or make a relevant omission) suffi-ciently before the effect in question.

'Causally suffices' can express more than one relation. Probabilistic theor-ies of causation may say that if an event e raises the chance of an event e*, and then e* occurs, e causally sufficed for e* and brought it about, or that if e sufficiently raises the chance of e*, e causally suffices for e*, whether or not e* comes about.[4] On such an approach, then, if e (sufficiently) raises the chance that ¬S comes about, and then ¬S comes about, e brought ¬S about and thereby prevented S. E's occurring need not have made it certain that S would not come about; the occurrence of a preventing condition need not guarantee that what it is fit to prevent is in fact prevented. Rather, whether it is the case that e prevented S may wait on whether S comes about. Other approaches to causation would say that if e occurs and causally suffices for e*, it follows that e* comes about, and so whether e prevents S does not wait on whether S comes about. Rather, if a preventing condition occurs at t, it is guaranteed at t that S does not come about at whatever time the preventing condition prevents for: e's occurring makes it certain that S does not come about. I use 'causally suffices' in the second way. I do not by so doing take a stance on the viability of probabilistic theories of causation. Those who favor them can accept (2), reading 'causally suffices' as they prefer, but view me as applying it only to limiting cases of causal sufficiency and prevention, where a cause raises the chance of its outcome to 1. Even an indeterminist world can contain cases of this. The world's being indeterminist entails that not all cases of causation are so, not that none are.

(2)'s second disjunct allows for prevention by omission. Intuitively, omis-sions can prevent, just as intuitively, omissions can cause: the President's omitting to sign a bill prevents its becoming law, at least for a while. But we do not want to say that my not raising my arm prevents my raising my arm: thus the exception. One by omitting prevents some causal consequence of the

[3] My thanks here to a referee.

[4] So, for example, Paul Humphreys, *The Chances of Explanation* (Princeton, NJ: Princeton University Press, 1989), and Patrick Suppes, *Probabilistic Metaphysics* (Oxford: Basil Blackwell, 1984). Both are of course too crude, but they suffice for present purposes.

act omitted.[5] In at least one case, God's not doing something suffices to prevent. God has prevented it that

T. there are first-order states of affairs other than $S_1 \ldots S_n$,[6]

where $S_{1 \ldots n}$ are all the first-order states of affairs that are possible or impossible.[7] He has done so simply by not thinking up more. When something prevents, a state of affairs is prevented (say, that there is an accident). If God prevents (T), there are no first-order states of affairs whose existence He prevents (else He would have failed to prevent them). But He prevents a general second-order state of affairs. Again, sometimes, when something prevents S, S would have been the case but for this: if I prevent an accident, there would have been an accident but for me. When God prevents (T) by omitting, there would have been other states of affairs but for this omission, for had He not omitted to add more, He would have added more.[8]

One might be tempted to add a clause like

3. $((\neg(\text{E occurs}) \cdot \neg(x \text{ makes a causally sufficient omission}^9)) > S \text{ obtains})$ v $(((\neg(\text{E occurs}) \cdot \neg(x \text{ makes a causally sufficient omission})) > (\exists y)(y \text{ causes } E^\star (\neq E) \text{ and } E^\star \text{ causally suffices in the circumstances to bring it about that } S \text{ is not the case, or } y \text{ does not act, and this causally suffices in the circumstances to bring it about that } S \text{ is not the case})))$.[10]

But it does seem possible that an event E prevent S and yet it is not the case that S would have obtained or been prevented by something else had E not occurred. Cases involving irreducibly chancy events show this. Radioactive decay is irreducibly chancy. During no time-period in which it has not yet decayed is the chance of a particular radioactive atom A's decaying 1. If so,

---

[5] Note, with reference to my discussion of (3) below, that I am not saying 'a causal consequence the omitted act *would have had.*'

[6] Talk of non-obtaining states of affairs is fiction, on my view. The reality behind (T) would be that there are such divine mental events as make it apt to say within the fiction that (T).

[7] 'First-order' avoids a problem. Without it, (T) would be one of $S_{1 \ldots n}$, and so (as it were) non-well-founded. With it, we can say that (T) is a second-order state of affairs and so the issue does not arise.

[8] This counterpossible is true for both trivial and substantive reasons. Prevention by omission can seem puzzling. I omit to act only if I do not act. That I do not act is true simply because something is absent from reality: namely, my action. That the prevented state of affairs does not occur is also true just because something is absent. Absences are not things that exist, though we sometimes speak as if they were. So we may wonder how a causal relation can link them; if it cannot, then not every case of causal prevention is a case of causation. I incline to the latter claim. Where there is prevention by omission, an absence explains an absence, and something positive and often causal in reality grounds a counterfactual—in this case, that had God not omitted to add more, He would have added more. I suspect that what makes the absence-claims true, what makes the counterpossible substantively true, and what makes it true that no other agent's action or omission is causally relevant jointly make it true that God has causally prevented (T) by omission.

[9] Ways not to make a causally sufficient omission include performing the act omitted, making an omission which is not causally sufficient, and perhaps neither acting nor fulfilling the conditions to count as omitting an act.

[10] In the spirit of Philip Dowe, *Physical Causation* (Cambridge: Cambridge University Press, 2000), pp. 132–4.

there is before A decays no true counterfactual of the form (it is now t > A decays). For if there were, the preventing chance of A's decaying during any period including t would be 1, and so A's decay would not be irreducibly chancy. Suppose that someone plants a bomb which will be triggered by A's decay. If it is irreducibly chancy when A decays, then for any S relevantly like *the bomb explodes within the next five minutes*, it is not the case that S's objective chance is 1 and there is no true counterfactual relevantly like (nothing interferes with the bomb and five minutes pass > the bomb explodes). Still, even if no other event or omission ever would have prevented the explosion, I can prevent the explosion by dismantling the bomb. Again, I can prevent libertarian-free acts even if there are no true 'counterfactuals of freedom'[11] and nothing else backstops my prevention. So (3) is false.

Preventing S does not bring it about that ¬S obtains. Instead, it brings it about that S does not obtain. One can see that the two are distinct in at least two ways. Where S involves a vague property, it might be possible to bring it about that *S obtains* and *¬S obtains* lack determinate truth-value.[12] Something that did so would bring it about that S does not obtain (it is not the case that S obtains) but not that ¬S obtains: it would prevent the obtaining of S without bringing ¬S about. Again, on a thesis about time I accept—that the future is unreal—something similar is true for causally undetermined future contingents. Where S and ¬S are such, even if it is the case that S v ¬S, it is not the case that S obtains and it is not the case that ¬S obtains. The nature of time and the factors that render S and ¬S causally undetermined open options for the future bring this about. But these things *ex hypothesi* do not bring it about either that S obtains or that ¬S does. They prevent the obtaining of S without bringing about the obtaining of ¬S.

The notion of prevention I employ is purely causal. It does not require intention: I can prevent in this sense without knowing I do or intending to do so, and can do so despite my best efforts, if I try not to prevent but do not succeed. It does not even require intentional states: a cloud can in this sense prevent my remaining dry by raining on me. So that a preventing cause (in my sense) acts entails only that an event appropriately involving the cause has an effect. Because of the way I use the concept of prevention, I must so explicate bringing-about that it does not simply consist in necessitating or in anything else irreducibly modal. It must have a non-modal core. I suggest that this core involves a primitive causal or 'because' relation: x brings it about that P just if because x acts, P. Perhaps this non-modal core *accounts* in some or all cases for there being necessitation that P; this is compatible with my account, for it will allow that divine activity can account for the existence of what makes that activity count as necessitating its effects.

---

[11] For discussion of these see Thomas Flint, *Divine Providence* (Ithaca, NY: Cornell University Press, 1998).

[12] Not all accounts of vagueness allow for this, of course, but I incline to one which does.

Divine Prevention

By nature, God is omniscient, omnipotent, and perfectly rational. As of the Bang, God has all states of affairs in mind.[13] Someone omniscient knows which states of affairs are not such as to be prevented, by their natures or just because it is too late. Someone perfectly rational who knows this never tries to prevent these. Someone omnipotent has it in Him to prevent whatever *is* such as to be prevented. Thus by His nature, what God wills to prevent, He succeeds in preventing.

We could rest with a 'just like magic' appeal to omnipotence on this, but we can also say a bit about just how God might manage to be effective. Obviously, if God decides that there shall be no rocks, for as long as this remains His wish, He makes none. The question is how He deals with other causes for rocks and with uncaused rocks. As to other causes, creatures have at any time only powers the Creator lets them have. Thus God can head off anything He wishes to prevent. God can, for example, assure in creating the world that He does not build in a potentiality for Creation ever to develop a power to make a rock against His will. God perfectly understands the powers of anything He is such as to let exist or occur. So if He knows He might want there to be no rocks, He will not permit in Creation through ignorance anything that could cause there to be a rock despite His will, or could cause something that could do so. As God perfectly controls His power, He will not 'slip up' and permit in Creation powers that might lead to unwanted rocks. God's omniscience and perfect rationality assure that He will make no Freudian slips either: He cannot 'despite Himself' let a source for a rock-threatening power through.

(GSA) implies that nothing pops into being without divine causation, and I argue later that God has the (GSA)-property necessarily; if so, that in God which accounts for this takes care of uncaused rocks. Further, God can avoid uncaused rocks by His control of the natural laws in accord with which uncaused things appear. Such control requires much less power than omnipotence. For instance, if there being a natural law consists in there being certain relations among properties, God can control the law if He can control these relations. On a Platonism which places the existence of properties beyond His sway or a deity theory which places these properties (somehow) in His nature, He cannot control the relations if properties' natures determine or include them. He can if they are contingent. Either way, He can control what the laws are by controlling which properties are instanced, and this requires only control of actual natural processes. On my view, what secular properties there can be, and how they can be related, depends simply on how

---

[13] Again, this is just convenient talk. In terms of my actual views: there are in God's mind all the contentful mental events which would if appropriately involved in generating actions bring it about that things are as sentences say they are when used in standard ways to make assertions.

God thinks and wills, and so the only control required in determining possible laws of nature is God's control of His own thoughts and will. Again, control of instantiation will suffice for control of actual laws. If natural laws are just exceptionless regularities (Hume-style), then again control over law requires only control over actual natural events: if God wants it to be a law that Bs follow As, He need only assure that Bs follow As. He can do so by controlling what powers there are in nature (Humeanism about law does not imply Humeanism about causation,[14] so it is compatible with the existence of powers) or if need be by direct intervention.[15]

Prevention from all Eternity

Suppose now that God wills from all eternity that there shall ever after be no rocks. If He does, I now show, He cannot be too late to prevent any rock from existing. So no matter how things go, none ever do unless He changes His mind. I first show that if God is timeless, He cannot be too late to prevent rocks. I show too that if God is timeless, He does not change His mind. The upshot is that in any world in which it is always the case that God is timeless and God wills this from all eternity, no rocks ever appear. I then show that if God is temporal, He also cannot be too late to keep rocks from existing and does not change His mind about this. If so, in any world in which God is always temporal, if He wills against rocks from all eternity, no rocks ever appear. Thus nothing essential would vary if in some world God started out timeless and became temporal, or *vice versa*.[16] The upshot is that a divine attempt of this sort at prevention from eternity must succeed in excluding the prevented state of affairs from the entire history in which the attempt occurs.

---

[14] This suffices to dissolve an objection by Evan Fales (*Divine Intervention* (Abingdon: Routledge, 2010), pp. 23–4).

[15] If we adopt a regularity theory of both laws and causation, Fales argues this (*loc. cit.*): if God always wills that there be a B when an A occurs, He and the As overdetermine the A–B law, since on regularity theory terms As also cause Bs. But theists (says Fales) should want the law and Bs to depend more on God than on As. Further, on a regularity theory As cause God to will Bs, which sounds odd. But if God causes the Bs, then equally (as creator, sustainer, and so on). He causes the As, and so what we more basically have is God's willing As, coupled with an intention to establish a law, causing His willing Bs. As long as we can make sense of God's willing As being causally prior to the As' occurring, there is no difficulty here. I think the first point is actually not a problem, but a good result for theists. Theists should *want* it to be the case that God and As overdetermine Bs' occurrence, because they should want there to be real creaturely causation—they should want to avoid any hint of occasionalism. (If the term 'occasionalism' is unfamiliar, see Alfred Freddoso, 'Medieval Aristotelianism and the Case Against Secondary Causation in Nature', in Thomas Morris (ed.), *Divine and Human Action* (Ithaca, NY: Cornell University Press, 1988), pp. 74–118.) And if God is responsible for the As' making their contribution to the A–B law and also makes an independent contribution to it, He is more responsible for it than the As are; he also has sole ultimate responsibility for it.

[16] I do not myself think this possible, but mention it because William Craig holds that God was timeless '*sans* creation' and ceased to be timeless when the universe came to exist ('Timelessness and Omnitemporality', in Gregory Ganssle (ed.), *God and Time* (Wheaton, IL: InterVarsity Press, 2001)).

If God is timeless, He cannot act too late. Something acts too late to succeed only if it acts after the last period in which it could (or perhaps would) have succeeded. Something done timelessly is done at no temporal location, and so not after any time. So nothing done timelessly can be done too late. Again, a timeless God is in a position to have volitions causally prior to any point in time. For if God is timeless, then given (GSA), each time is something He creates and sustains, perhaps by creating and sustaining creatures which stand in temporal relations. What causes an effect acts causally prior to the effect's occurring—hence, causally prior to that point in time. If God wills 'Let there ever after be no rocks' causally before a rock-threatening instant, He is not too late to block rocks. A timeless God can have volitions causally prior to the universe's whole existence, even if the universe had no first instant: God's timeless will to create such a universe would be causally prior to its whole temporal span. If causally prior to the whole span God Wills 'Let there never be rocks', He wills this causally before any rock-threatening instant and so not too late to prevent all rocks. Further, if it is at all times true that God is timeless, God never changes His mind.[17] A timeless being cannot while timeless change in any intrinsic respect, as intrinsic change requires being F at one time and ¬F at another, for some intrinsic F.[18] Changing one's mind involves altering a belief or a state of will, occurrent or dispositional, and so intrinsic change in some respect.[19]

Let us now consider what is true if God is temporal. Time either did or did not have a first instant. If it did not and God is temporally eternal, then before any instant, there was another, at which God existed. So for any instant at which a rock could appear, God was on the scene before that, and so in time to prevent this. If time had a first instant, the same holds for any time after that. But that first instant needs a bit more attention. If God is never other than temporal and time had a first instant, God's life had a first instant. This is compatible with His being eternal only if it does not entail that God's life began: something eternal pastward cannot have begun to exist. If a first

[17] Leaving aside the question of whether He could do so effectively—that is, whether a volition of an omnipotent being could limit His other options.

[18] If (per impossibile) something could cease to be timeless, it would still not have been able to change while timeless. At most, its timeless state would be a change's terminus a quo; it would not have been changing until (causally?) after its timeless state.

[19] Now some passages of Scripture suggest that God does change His mind: Genesis 6: 6–7 suggests that God wills that there be humans up until the time their sin grieves Him, then decides to wipe them out. To deal with these, a defender of divine timelessness can suggest that God gets the effect of a mind-change without an actual change, and these passages are written from the perspective of those who see only the effect. One way to get this effect is to will contents with temporal limits: rather than willing that the universe contain only photons, then willing at t that it contain other items, God can will that the universe contain only photons till t, and thereafter contain other items. Another way to will a change without undergoing a change of will is to will it conditionally, on built-in 'triggers' in Creation for changes in creaturely situations. In this case, God wills that there be humans and that if their evil has reached a particular level by t, there shall then be a Flood. (In which case, in a fairly strong sense they brought their punishment upon themselves.) So it is not hard to square the claim that God never changes His mind with what might appear to be divine changes of mind.

instant of existence must be a beginning of existence, then, we need not worry further, for it simply cannot be the case both that God is temporally eternal and that time had a first instant.

But perhaps a first instant of existence need not be a beginning of existence. Perhaps a temporal God would not begin to exist at time's first instant. For perhaps only a time at which a thing comes into existence is a true beginning of its existence, and a thing comes into existence at a time only if had that time never arrived, all else remaining as nearly the same as possible, the item would not have existed. If both are true, a first instant of God's existence is a true beginning of His existence only if it is a time such that had that time not arrived, all else remaining thus the same, He would not have existed. Accept this for the nonce, and suppose now that time had a first instant and God was at all times temporal. Suppose too that God would have existed timelessly had time never begun: God makes Himself temporal by making time begin. Then time's first instant will be the first instant of God's life, but it will not be the case that had this instant not arrived, God would not have existed. Rather, had it not arrived, He would have existed timelessly.[20] If so, then on the account of beginning just given, it would not be the case that God's life began. Still, on this picture God exists causally though not temporally before the first instant, since His willing accounts for its occurring. If God's willing is causally before the first instant, then it is as if He were timeless: even at that instant, He is not too late to head off rocks, as these would exist at the earliest only once that instant occurs.

Thus if God is always temporal and wills from all eternity that there shall be no rocks, none appear unless He changes His mind. Now considering a time t in advance, God knows which events are candidates to occur then. As soon as He knows this, He knows which He is prepared to tolerate, and which He definitely, all things considered, wants to prevent. Knowing and wanting this, He must at least be disposed to will to prevent them when t arrives. Even if He waits till t to will this, doing so could not constitute changing His mind. It would be merely implementing a previously decided course of action. But then even if God is temporal and wills at different times to execute different parts of His providential plan, His doing so does not involve mind-changes. Again, God would know how things might turn out by t, so that even if at first consideration—that is, from all eternity—He did not want to prevent an event, if He might by t find its not occurring desirable enough to effect, He would know this. So, He would have planned to prevent the event by t, conditional on things' turning out that way. Once again, willing the prevention would not be a change of mind, but just an implementation.

---

[20] For the nub of this, see my *Time and Eternity* (Ithaca, NY: Cornell University Press, 1991), p. 269; but I am also indebted here to a conversation with Peter Van Inwagen. On present assumptions, a God who exists necessarily cannot begin to exist, even at time's first instant.

If God wills from all eternity that there shall ever after be no rocks, He does not change His mind about this. For He wills it only if He knows that ever after He will want no rocks. A temporal God would know how His preferences might change over time. If God knew He was too likely in future to want rocks, then as He is perfectly rational, He would not will that there shall ever after be no rocks. He would instead will at most that there not be rocks for some shorter period. For times thereafter, even if there were just a small chance that He would want them, He would at most will something with conditions: there shall in the period t- t* be no rocks, unless . . . For it would not be perfectly rational to will against rocks unconditionally if in fact His self-knowledge and knowledge of future alternatives tell Him that He might under certain conditions want them, unless some other consideration pushes Him to unconditional rejection despite this. And if some other consideration so pushes Him, He is not *too* likely to want them in future to will that there shall ever after be no rocks, for He'd be so only if His knowledge of His possible future preferences were such as to overrule this other consideration. So if a temporal God wills that there ever after be no rocks, He does not thereafter change His mind. The upshot is that whether He is temporal or timeless, if God from all eternity wills that S not obtain, S does not obtain at any point in the history in which He does so. Once He wills this, a condition is in place which will infallibly block S's obtaining. Moreover, if God so wills from all eternity, S does not obtain in any causally possible continuation of the history in which He does so. Even if there are powers which but for His action would bring S about, the presence of a preventing condition removes their opportunity to do so.

Dispositions to Prevent

I also say that

x is disposed to prevent state of affairs S = df.

4. x has the power to prevent S, and

5. x is intrinsically such that had x the opportunity, *ceteris paribus* x would probably prevent S.[21]

For God and secular states of affairs, (4) is satisfied. This is so even for such absolute necessities as that if Rover exists, Rover = Rover. God had the power never to think Rover up, though it could not have been so described had He not thought Rover up, and had He used this power, there would have been no

---

[21] (5) allows cases in which the probability is 1, and so too (8) below. Probabilistic theorists of causation can read (5) as their theories require: for example, as ' . . . would probably produce a condition that lowered the chance of S' obtaining, and so would probably prevent S if S did not in fact occur.'

truths about Rover at all. This was a full power, rather than merely something it was in Him to do, because what enabled Him not to think Rover up were powers He had by nature: to think, without constraint, and to direct His thoughts. *Per* earlier discussion, God has passed (or timelessly is passing) up His chance so to use His powers, but this does not deprive Him of any power. God brings (5) about, where He does, by settling His attitudes and will, as outlined later. (5) treats a disposition as something other than a power—as an intrinsic attribute giving one a propensity to use a power in a particular way. But many use 'power' and 'disposition' interchangeably, and I sometimes do this where the difference between them does not matter.

Impossibility and Prevention

I soon suggest that divine prevention and dispositions to prevent account for secular absolute impossibilities. On my account, the latter satisfy (1). It came about that ¬(Spot is a dog · ¬(Spot is a dog)). For it came about that there was such a thing as being Spot: God thought him up. There were no facts about what Spot was to be before He did so. This is trivially true if God is atemporal, as nothing is before anything atemporal. It is also true if God is temporally eternal and thinks up Spot in the Bang: then at every time, God is thinking of Spot, and so there is no time before He does so. If (as on generalism) there come to be individuals not thought up in the initial Bang, then this is still true. For it comes about, later, that there is such a thing as Spot: God makes him, though not fully intentionally. And there were no facts about what *Spot* was to be beforehand, though there were facts about the dog-type he turned out to instance. Now these bits of reasoning are useful in cutting off a line of response that might run 'God first thinks Spot up at t. It was true at t-1 that He would do so. So there were facts about Spot before God thought him up.' But what I mean by the claim that there were no facts about what Spot was to be beforehand cuts deeper than this. This claim is a denial of Platonism and deity theories, and an affirmation that God's creative thinking accounts for *everything* about Spot.

Further, by thinking Spot up as He did, God made it false that (Spot is a dog · ¬(Spot is a dog)).[22] So God did an act sufficient in the circumstance to bring it about that it is not the case that Spot is a dog and ¬(Spot is a dog): He thought Spot up as He did, not some other way. One might rejoin here that the facts of logic prevented this before God ever got into the picture, but this would Platonize logic in a big way. If God's thinking obeys the laws of logic before all Creation, a *Euthyphro*-type question arises: does He obey them

---

[22] If He had no pre-creative singular concepts, the act that made this false was God's making Spot. What I now say on the assumption of pre-creative singular concepts applies to the alternate, generalist scenario *mutatis mutandis*.

because it is (intellectually) right to do so (because, for instance, they are somehow there and intrinsically normative for rational beings, or because logical truths are Platonic), or is it right to obey them because He does so? Anti-Platonists cannot go the first way. Many would see the second as threatening to make logic a matter of arbitrary divine convention. I think the right move here parallels best response to the original *Euthyphro* question: ground logic in the divine nature. Doing so avoids Platonic ontology and also avoids arbitrariness; it provides necessity for logic without external constraint on God. So I issue a promissory note for such an account, and hope to complete a response to this elsewhere. Given the note, this case also satisfies (2).

Again, had God not thought up Spot, there would have been no such state of affairs as that (Spot is a dog · ¬(Spot is a dog)) to prevent. So had God not thought Spot up, it would not have been the case that (Spot is a dog · ¬(Spot is a dog)) was not the case. There being no such state of affairs, it would not have been impossible; it would not have risen to the level of impossibility. Thus God's preventing it that (Spot is a dog · ¬(Spot is a dog)) satisfies (3)'s second disjunct: His not thinking up Spot would have been the inaction needed. So this case also satisfies (3)—at least from the standpoint of our Spotty world. But had God not thought Spot up, then *per* earlier argument, our world would not have been so much as impossible. There would not have been an external perspective to be taken on what God had done, such that it would have been true from that perspective that God had prevented this by omission.

Only the contradictories of such non-secular states of affairs as those of pure logic and mathematics could escape this sort of treatment. But even here, God has a role. Pure logical states of affairs, for instance, would involve such logical operators as conjunction, disjunction, negation, material implication and identity. I would argue that even *modulo* the fiction that there are such things as states of affairs, nothing in extra-mental reality corresponds to these operators. Even within the fiction, these are just concepts. If so, then even within the fiction, pure logical and mathematical states of affairs 'exist' only in minds. They 'exist' first in God's mind. So within the fiction, even pure logical states of affairs are of a sort to come about, because there must be divine mental events for them to 'exist'—and by thinking them up as He does, God prevents their contradictories' being true. If God makes conjunction what it is, by thinking of it as He does, He sets its truth-table in place.

Now I have just shown that what God prevents from all eternity does not obtain in any causally possible continuation of the history in which He does so. So as God exists necessarily,

IMP. if necessarily from all eternity God prevents S, S is impossible.

if God necessarily eternally prevented S, God would actually eternally prevent S. Plausibly He also would actually be disposed eternally to prevent S, no matter what. One way to argue this begins from an ontology enough like Plantinga's to include world-indexed properties[23] and Platonist possible worlds. If in one of them, W, God prevents S, God actually has a world-indexed property: He prevents-S-in-W. Now *prevents-S-in-W* might be an intrinsic property, a relation to W, a relational property, or a 'mere Cambridge' property. The last plausibly do not exist, being instead (as it were) shadows cast by true predictions. Relations to necessary beings (such as a platonist W) come out intrinsic on plausible accounts of the intrinsic.[24] So then do cognate relational properties. If *prevents-S-in-W* is intrinsic, its content is really conditional. It is that W is actual $\rightarrow$ God prevents S. This property is, at least partly a disposition, to prevent S if He chooses to (help) actualize W. If in W nothing but God ever acts and nothing occurs uncaused, we can delete '(help)'. God's choice suffices to get W, and if God chooses to actualize W, God prevents S. Part of His choosing to actualize W is His choosing to do so. This is even clearer if we eliminate the world-name 'W'. For then what God chooses is not to actualize W, but to bring it about that P, Q, R and so on obtain but He prevents S. And of course, if He chooses to bring this about, as part of it He chooses to prevent S. If in W items other than God act, but none have incompatibilist freedom or occur uncaused, we reinstate '(help)' but the rest is as just laid out. If in W items other than God act with such freedom or occur uncaused, God could choose to (help) actualize W but not wind up with W, because other things do not cooperate. If in such a world preventing S does not require cooperation from anything uncaused or incompatibilist-free, this case is like the first: God's disposition to prevent S if choosing to help actualize W is just part of His being so disposed that He might try (or have tried) to actualize W. If preventing S depends on such cooperation, God can try to prevent S but not succeed. But still, as part of choosing to try to actualize W, He chooses to try to prevent S—and He succeeds if He tries and gets the cooperation He needs, so we need invoke nothing else in Him to explain why He gets S prevented if He does. So God's being disposed to try to prevent S is just part of His being so disposed that He might try (have tried) to actualize W.

Once we get this far we can see that possible worlds and world-indexed properties are idle wheels: divine prevention and dispositions to prevent are enough to account for secular impossibilities. *Per* my move on the first alternative, we can describe these without world-names, using instead exhaustive lists of propositions or states of affairs that would be actual were the supposed world actualized. That we need not so much as name worlds in describing the dispositions and preventions is good reason to see worlds as fully eliminable from such an account.

Coming at this another way, if there are world-indexed properties, that God prevents-S-in-W makes true every claim the fact that in W, God prevents S does: unsurprisingly, since the latter is that W is actual → God prevents S and the former that God is such that W is actual → God prevents S. W is part of the content of prevents-S-in-W. So if the property exists, it provides what is needed to make true any claim about W or its contents. And so if we have a truthmaker for an assertion of a world-indexed property, we have a truthmaker for the claim about worlds it parallels. Thus if we can dissolve world-indexed properties into divine dispositions not involving worlds, we can be rid of both. Of course, for the argument to go through, I need to show that the content of the world-indexed property can be expressed without using a world-name, but again, this is not hard. For illustration, suppose that the only candidate states of affairs for worlds to include are P and S, plus God's permitting or preventing P or S. Suppose too that W contains just P, that God permits P and that God prevents S. Then on the account I go on to develop, what stands behind talk of God having the world-indexed property of preventing-S-in-W is that God permits that both P (if He permits this, He permits that He permits this) and He prevents S: if God then brings about what He permits, He will permit that P, actualize P, and prevent S, which is just what it would take to actualize W if there were such an item. Now if God includes that He prevents S in the content of every permission then He issues, this gives us the equivalent of God preventing S in every possible world, but with no mention of worlds. And, finally, if God permits only that He prevents S, no matter what of all that He permits occurs, He is disposed to prevent S, no matter what of all He permits occurs. So again, worlds and the world-indexed are idle wheels. We could get to the same place from a leaner Platonism, one with worlds but no world-indexed properties, as I show in Chapter 22.

This matters because it affects how we read (IMP). Before all Creation, we can only read it in accord with Platonism, possibilism or a theist theory of modality—there is no other candidate ontology. Read Platonistically, (IMP) may not provide an account of why the secular impossible is impossible. It could just record a parallel whose fundamental explanation lies in the realm of worlds, not in God. Read theistically, it does provide such an account. What I have now suggested, in effect, is that even if we start out reading (IMP) Platonically, a theist has reason to apply Ockham's Razor and shift to a theist reading. As to possibilism, I have already suggested that its Meinongian version should not be combined with theism, and that conjoined with theism, Lewis' version amounts to a peculiar theist theory of modality—which also reads (IMP) as giving us a theist story of why the secular impossible is so. So theists, at least, should find the reading of (IMP) I offer congenial.

None of this would persuade modal Platonists. They will hang onto the worlds, and insist that such properties as being red or even being-red-in-W are part of the Platonic furniture independent of God. For the present, though, I am not trying to persuade Platonists: I attempt that with *theist* Platonism in Chapter 22, where I lay out a related case with more care and hopefully more force. Just now I am merely setting out a view. If one starts from Platonism, then the property *being Spot*, and Spot's being a dog, are on the scene before God gets to think up, permit, or prevent anything. What I go on to suggest is that if one is a theist and does not insist on starting from Platonism, there is no reason ever to get to it: there is a way to understand modal truth that will deliver just about anything the Platonist thinks Platonism delivers, but involves only God and divine mental events. In setting out my account—which is all I am so far doing—I am playing not to the Platonist, but to the theist uncommitted for or against Platonism. The Platonist will insist that when I say that if God from all eternity wills that S not obtain, S does not obtain in any causally possible continuation of the history in which He does so, the sense has to be that there are abstract Platonic possible worlds, which determine what possible continuations there are, and God's willing against S simply determines which of these are still in the running to represent actual history. I say instead that God's preventing, permitting, and disposing Himself at the Bang determine what the possible continuations are, period. There are no Platonic worlds whose relevance to continuing history God determines. Rather, God's preventing S from eternity determines that S is not causally possible; God's eternal dispositions to prevent S determine that S would not have been causally possible had things been in some respects otherwise; and the absolute possibilities just are those continuations from the Bang not ruled out by actual or dispositional prevention.

From Prevention to Impossibility

I have noted that on some views, conditions that reduce or greatly reduce the probability that S obtains, but leave some positive probability that S obtains, can count as causally preventing S. But I want to discuss only divine prevention. This is the pre-eminent case of probability-1 prevention: what God sets Himself to prevent, He cannot but succeed in preventing, and so at the point at which He does so, it is certain that what He sets Himself to prevent does not occur.[25] There is no chance that God slips up; we need not wait upon the

---

[25] Of course, God can also reduce the probability of an event, but leave it non-zero. Probabilistic theories of causation might in some cases include this under divine prevention; here I so speak that I do not. Surely if what God wants is *simpliciter* that S not obtain, He does not leave this a matter of chance: He takes the most rational means to promote it, and so assures it, reducing its probability to zero. If He does want to avoid S but nonetheless leaves some positive probability that S occurs, that has to be due to some other consideration—for example, that He wants to give us a choice about whether S obtains. In such a case

upshot and see whether He has managed it. Henceforth, then, I discuss only a restricted sort of prevention, probability 1 (1-) prevention.

Intuitively, it cannot be the case both that at t some condition 1-prevents S' obtaining then and that S obtains at t. But one may wonder whether what follows from S's being 1-prevented is merely that S will not obtain, or that S causally cannot. 'Will not' suffices for my purposes, as I am content to invoke dispositions to prevent in explaining impossibility, rather than tracing it simply to actual prevention. And here is a picture to motivate 'will not': the future is just a branching tree of histories that may unfold. At each future time, if some event may happen whose effects are not causally determined, there is a new set of branches, one for each possible outcome. Each path through the tree from the present represents a complete possible history from the present on. There is also a distinguished path, marked in red: the history the universe *will* have from the present on. Preventing S is bringing it about that the red line does not cross S. And (the picture adds) one can do this without blocking alternate paths. It is enough to make the red line take one particular non-S path.

But the picture does not really do without blocking alternate paths. Suppose I so act at t that the red line is down a particular path at t + 1. My act at t is itself a preventing condition: it prevents the line from being down other paths later. In no causally possible continuation of a history identical with ours up through t, with my act at t, does the line go down those other paths, just because my act is there. And beyond the general point made above, that prevention removes opportunity and so removes causal possibility, it is clear in at least some particular cases that actual 1-prevention entails that an outcome cannot happen, not just that it will not. If I 1-prevent S, I reduce the probability that S obtains to zero. Suppose that S can come about without cause, by chance. Then even reducing S's probability to zero does not guarantee or make it certain that S does not obtain, for if there can be uncaused events, even zero-probability events may happen. The surface of a ping-pong ball has continuum-many parts. Suppose that uncaused, the ball floats aloft and rotates, then drops onto my desk. There is nothing to physically determine which part of the ball's surface touches the desk first. It is a matter of chance. They are all equi-probable. So to find the probability of any part being the first, we assign each an equal portion of the probability '1'. On standard approaches this gives them all a zero probability of being first. Yet one winds up first, by chance. That it be first was left an open option because it was causally possible that it be—it was not guaranteed not to occur. If nothing guaranteed this, what led to there being zero chance of this occurring did not guarantee it. So it seems that to guarantee that this

---

He does not *simpliciter* want S not to obtain. He *simpliciter* wants S not to obtain (say) by our free choice, and so takes the most rational means to promote that. In the cases that concern me—those that generate secular modal status—if God prevents S, God wants *simpliciter* that S not obtain.

sort of S not obtain by chance I must not only zero out the probability that S obtains, but remove the causal possibility that S obtains. If that is right, the only way to assure that the red line does not cross S is to block off all paths that lead to S. 1-preventing such a chance S, in the sense of making it certain or guaranteed that S not occur, requires removing the causal possibility of S. Now let us approach the case in terms of non-standard analysis. On this, the equi-probable results all have infinitesimal instead of zero probability. If their being a causally open entails this, reducing their probability to zero guarantees that they do not occur. If physical possibility implies some positive probability, then if I cause an alternative to have zero probability, I render it physically impossible. So where all possible chance results have equal, infinitesimal probability, bringing a chance result's probability down to zero renders it physically impossible.

This argument extends to events with certain sorts of cause. Suppose that I can make decisions I am not causally determined to make, and sometimes have alternate possibilities of decision. Let us say, then, that I can pick up the ping-pong ball and decide in this way which part of it shall touch the desk first. It seems possible in principle that I have a Buridan's-Ass type choice about this, one where there is no reason to incline me to pick one part over another, and so all parts have an equal chance. Moreover, though this may be controversial, something similar seems to me true where there are inclining reasons, simply because I have the power to choose irrationally. My reasons may make it more probable that I choose some parts, not others, but I may simply decide to do what I have less or no reason to do. If that's right, even given inclining reasons, all parts of the ball it is physically possible for me to choose have some positive chance to be first, and so again, 1-preventing a part's being first would require rendering a choice physically impossible. Nor, finally, is the involvement of free agency essential to this sort of case. A free agent chooses by an indeterminist power, one which may or may not act, given opportunity, and may if acting act in more than one way. Any other sort of cause with such a power would be subject to similar reasoning if all options it is able to bring about are equi-probable or all have some positive chance of occurring.

The Range of Divine Prevention

I now introduce two terms of art. An indicative state of affairs is one whose obtaining one standardly asserts with an indicative sentence including no modal words. A subjunctive state of affairs is one whose obtaining one standardly asserts with a subjunctive conditional sentence. It is in God to prevent any indicative secular state of affairs involving concreta, by not letting a needed concrete creature exist or not even thinking it up. This is true too of any subjunctive states of affairs 'grounded' on these; it is in God to prevent these by preventing their grounding indicatives. Prior to the Bang, as I see it, it is in God to prevent even secular states of affairs making true cases of pure logical theses—for example, that ¬(Spot is a dog · ¬(Spot is a dog). Nothing required Him to think Spot up, and had He not done so, this would not have been the case.[26] It was in God to prevent in the same way secular cases of pure mathematical theses, secular necessary moral truths and that courage is a virtue—for it was in Him not to think up courage, or any other moral virtue only creatures can have[27]—and truths based on secular essences. Some may jib here that only contingent states of affairs can be prevented. But prior to the bang, nothing is contingent or necessary. On my view, God's activity has an explanatory priority to any full fact of modal status.[28]

Some secular states of affairs involve attributes only creatures can have—for example, that courage is a virtue or that red is a color (understood as higher-order predications). How God can prevent these depends on what attributes are. I reject Meinongian possibilia; they are just otiose if there is a God and a theist modal theory is viable. So I take it that necessarily, items have attributes only if they exist. If so, necessarily, red is a color only if red exists. If so, then necessarily, if red does not exist, it is not the case that red is a color. So on Aristotelian realism or any sort of nominalism, God can prevent red's being a color in a world by preventing the existence of red things in that world,[29] and had it in Him to prevent red's being a color altogether by not thinking redness up. Platonist attributes can exist unexemplified. So power to prevent things' having them would not give God power over their existence. But that they can exist unexemplified hardly entails that nothing can prevent their existence, for it does not entail that their existence is independent of things other than whether they are exemplified. If secular attributes are Platonic, it could still be that God causes them to exist. Perhaps being a bear is really satisfying God's concept of a bear, and God causes the attribute to exist by having the concepts of a bear and of satisfaction—which can exist even if no bears do. If so, then as it is in God not to have had the concept of a bear, it is in Him to have prevented a Platonic attribute's existence. Again, if attributes are as such exemplifiable, then if God thinks up F, He can still prevent there being an attribute F if He can prevent there being Fs in any possible world—as I am in the process of suggesting.

---

[26] Again, as above, this seems correct from our world, but would not have been true had God done it.

[27] More precisely, only creatures and beings incarnate in creatures, in virtue of their incarnations. That courage is a virtue remains a secular moral truth in that it does not provide information about God save insofar as He 'is' a creature.

[28] Though not to His having the powers which are the source of the modal element in such 'full' facts.

[29] Though it might still be true there that God's concept of red is a concept of a color, and so the *conditional* (x)(x is red ⊃ x is colored) might remain true.

The Source of Divine Prevention

God prevents some things due to His nature. His natural goodness (I submit) leads Him to deny possibility to some states of affairs. It is conceivable that there be great suffering God's permission of which is not morally justified. All the same, I submit, it is not possible, because by His nature, God does not let it occur. Something similar may apply with non-moral sorts of goodness. Again, nothing in God's nature required Him to think up squareness. So nothing in His nature dictated a specific preference to have square things appear square rather than round to normal perceivers under appropriate conditions. All the same, if He is perfectly rational and good, then if square-ness has intrinsic purely categorical content, in conceiving of squareness, He associates with this the power to appear square, and if squareness does not have this, He makes this power part of what it is to be square. It would be deceptive to have square things appear only round: at best a joke at our expense which only He would ever enjoy, and if not, perhaps a bit irrational as well. A preference to have things appear as they are rather than otherwise under appropriate conditions is one we would expect of a perfectly rational, good being. *Of course* square things look square. It could not be otherwise. But the fact that it could not be otherwise reflects something about God's nature, something which prevents there being a very different sort of squareness.

God's nature may not account for all His preventing. There may also be an element of non-natural will in the content of the possible. God might have relevant preferences deity does not dictate—though His deity will constrain these. Being morally perfect, for instance, leaves one able to prefer chocolate to vanilla, but does not leave one able to prefer the pointless suffering of the innocent to their innocent pleasure. As evils incompatible with God's exis-tence are conceivable but impossible, for any sort of conceivability they enjoy, conceivability does not imply possibility. Perhaps in some cases, what is thus-conceivable is not possible, but not due to the divine nature. Unicorns are thus-conceivable. *There is an animal conforming to the description of a unicorn* is not contrary to morality, logic, or mathematics.[30] But such animals might nonetheless be impossible.[31] Perhaps every role unicorns thus-conceivably play in a possible world is one God prefers that something else play, and deity does not determine the preference. This does not (I submit) leave the epistemology of modality worse off than it might otherwise be, for it does not imply that some sorts of conceivability are not good evidence for possi-bility. It implies only that the evidence is defeasible, and on independent grounds, I believe that we should not give it more weight than this anyway.

---

[30] Note that the phrasing avoids Kripke's thesis that if unicorns are fictional, it is in a way impossible that any real thing be a unicorn.

[31] And not for Kripke's reason, *per* the previous note.

Perhaps some conceivable morally neutral states of affairs are also neutral with reference to any divine preference. If so, God must simply decide whether to prevent them no matter what. Whichever He chooses, He chooses as a matter of sheer will. There may be a maximum possible atomic number for elements (why not?); if so, prevention of anything higher may be a matter of sheer divine will. Again, perhaps the laws of nature associated with certain properties are necessary, yet due simply to God's non-nature-determined tastes about what such properties can be involved with. It is conceivable that $E = Mc^3$ rather than Mc^2. If this is not possible, that might be ultimately for no other reason than that God preferred it so. I hasten to add that such 'taste' might be expressed in His very conceiving of properties, rather than by some sort of arbitrary combining of previously conceived elements, and that such 'taste' must be consonant with being perfectly rational and perfectly good.

Permission

Causal prevention is my first basic notion. My second is causal permission. To define this I must first define a modal notion. Its root thought is that the presence of a power to bring S about, with an opportunity to do so, makes it possible in some sense that S come about. It takes both power and opportunity to achieve this. Something that neither is, was, nor timelessly-is actual is causally possible just if the powers that be can make history so unfurl that it becomes actual. If powers do not have the chance to act, they cannot then make anything happen. I say then that

6. it is causally possible that P[32] = df,
   a. it is, was, will be or timelessly-is the case that P, or
   b. something has (or timelessly-has,[33] or some things jointly have or timelessly-have[34]) the power and opportunity to bring it about that P, or bring it about that something has the power and opportunity to bring it about that P, or bring it about that something has the power and opportunity to bring it about that something has the power and opportunity to bring it about that P (and so *ad infinitum*), or
   c. some x has the power to bring it about that P, and some y has power and opportunity to give x an opportunity to bring it about that P before x loses that power, or power and opportunity to bring it about that something

---

[32] I am defining a present-tensed claim, and so provide only clauses appropriate to that tense. It should be clear how to transform the account for the past tense. An account for the future tense is unnecessary, because on the present-tensed account, whatever will be causally possible *is* causally possible.

[33] Take this addition as read where appropriate throughout.

[34] Take this addition as read where appropriate throughout.

has power and opportunity to give x an opportunity to bring it about that P before x loses that power (and so *ad infinitum*), or

d. some x has the opportunity to bring it about that P, and some y has power and opportunity to give x power to bring it about that P before x loses the opportunity, or power and opportunity to bring it about that something has power and opportunity to give x power to bring it about that P before x loses the opportunity (and so *ad infinitum*), or

e. that P is the sort of thing to come true without cause, and nothing has power and opportunity causally to prevent it coming about without cause that P, or that there comes to be without cause something with power and opportunity to bring it about that P, or that there comes to be without cause something with power and opportunity to bring it about that something has power and opportunity to bring it about that P (and so *ad infinitum*), or

f. that P is the sort of thing to come true without cause and something has the power and opportunity causally to prevent its doing so, prevent its coming-true coming without cause to have a potential cause, etc., but has not done so.

Later chapters refer back to (6a)–(6f) as (CAUSAL POSS).

Opportunities for opportunities 'collapse' into opportunities. If there is a chance for there to be a chance that P, there is a chance for it to be the case that P. So we need not consider these separately. Powers to bring about the possession of powers do not 'collapse' into powers. I can have a power to have a power to bring it about that P, but lack power to bring it about that P. I have the powers to have the power to play a piano concerto—I have flexible fingers, the intelligence to read music, and so on. But I am not able to do so. As I have not yet learned to play the piano, I lack the opportunity to so use the powers I have as to develop this further power. Again, I can have the power to have the powers of the US President (I can get myself elected) but lack the latter (I have not done so).

Intuitively, causal possibility 'collapses'. In the most basic case, we have a power with a chance to bring its effect about. So the setup is causally primed for that effect, in the sense that nothing more need be added: whether or not the power does act, nothing internal or external prevents its 'firing'; it is simply up to the power or what bears it whether it does, and if it 'fires' we will have the effect. (If I have a libertarian-free power of choice, for instance, and at t have free choice, the setup is causally primed for my choice. No more need be added.) If it is causally possible that it be causally possible that P, powers and circumstances that be are causally primed to bring about powers and circumstances causally primed to bring it about that P (whether they do so or not). But causal priming is transitive. If a causal setup is primed to bring about a causal setup primed to bring it about that P, the first causal setup is primed to bring it about that P, by way of the second. This 'collapse' warrants (b)'s extension beyond the first clause. It also stands behind (c). As to (c)'s first clause, x has a power and it is causally possible that x have the relevant opportunity while retaining the power. So it is causally possible that it is causally possible that x bring it about that P; y need only act, and there is the full possibility. So by 'collapse' it is causally possible that P. Collapse also warrants the extension, as in (b). Obviously (d) works similarly. The thought behind the base clauses in (e) and (f) is that if that P is the sort of thing to come about without cause, all that's needed for it to be possible that history so unfurl as to include that P is that there be nothing preventing this. The only 'causal condition' required is that there be nothing to stop it. The extensions beyond the first clause cover other ways a lack of prevention of the uncaused might set up a causal possibility that P; they seem licit because it can be the case both that P is the sort of thing to come true without cause and that something can cause it to be the case that P.

Expressed formally, the modal collapse I have discussed is the fact that $\Diamond_c \Diamond_c P \rightarrow \Diamond_c P$. If this is so and it is also the case that $\Box_c P \supset P$ and $\Box_c(P \supset Q)$ $\supset (\Box_c P \supset \Box_c Q)$, the logic of my causal modality includes S4. That $\Box_c P \supset P$ seems plausible given simply that $\Diamond_c$ does express a kind of possibility, for if it does, there must be a kind of necessity interdefinable with it, and that $\Box P \supset P$ (with appropriate subscripts) should hold of anything that counts intuitively as a kind of (objective) necessity. There might seem to be a problem about cases where a causal setup that suffices to bring it about that P can do so only through bringing about intermediate states of affairs over time: then, we might think, it could be causally necessary that P but not yet the case that P. But we need to pay attention to tense here. If P says something future- or past-tensed there is no difficulty. If it says something present-tensed, the antecedent claims that in every causally possible world it is now the case that P. If that is true, it is not now the case that P only if the actual world is not causally possible. If it is not, the inference from actuality to possibility fails for causal possibility, and so something is deeply wrong with the causal modalities. But this, at least, is not wrong with them, as (6a) builds the actuality-to-possibility inference into them. So where the causal setup suffices to bring it about that P only by bringing about intermediate states over time, we do not really have $\Box_c$ prefixing a claim that P. We instead have something like that $\Box_c$P-at-some-time, and it remains that $\Box_c$P-at-some-time $\supset$ P-at-some-time or perhaps that $\Box_c$P-at-t $\supset$ P-at-t.

Given that $\Box_c P \supset P$, that $\Box_c(P \supset Q)$ implies that $P \supset Q$. $\Box_c P$ iff $\neg\Diamond_c\neg P$, i.e. iff the world's causal setup permits only that P. If the world's causal setup permits only that P, and $P \supset Q$, the world's causal setup permits only that Q: and so $\Box_c(P \supset Q) \supset (\Box_c P \supset \Box_c Q)$. Thus my causal modalities' logic includes S4.

Finally, (6) is not a reductive definition. Powers are intrinsically modal. They just are the sort of thing that *can* produce effects. So their existing, given opportunity, is just the sort of thing to non-reductively make possibility-claims true.

Some substitutions for the dummy-sentence 'P' assert a sequence of events, a history for an entire universe. S is causally possible at t just if S would occur in at least one universal history causally possible at t. Now S is causally permitted at t just if at least one causally possible history moves from the state of things at t to the obtaining of S. X causally permits S at t just if x brings it about at t that S is causally permitted or leaves S causally permitted when x could change this. If x brings this about, x renders S causally possible. If x changed it, x would prevent S. Thus I say that

> x causally permits S at t = df.

7. at t, x brings it about that S is causally possible, or has the opportunity and power to prevent S, but does not do so.[35]

(7) does not require that what permits be able to prevent, since it does not require that anything making S causally possible be able to prevent S. A weaker condition would require only power and chance to obstruct, not to prevent. But if a cause obstructs S but does not prevent it, S remains causally possible despite it, after it has done its best. If this is all the cause can do, the cause cannot affect whether S is causally permitted. What has no bearing on whether something is causally permitted does not belong in a definition of causal permission. My definitions allow cases in which God neither prevents nor permits: we can have ¬(2) and ¬(7). God's ever existing is one case of this: God never had opportunity to prevent it, nor could He make it causally possible. If God is temporal, states of affairs now past seem another. Lincoln was shot. Seemingly God is not rendering this causally possible, nor has He any longer the chance to prevent it.

Disposition to Permit

I say finally that

> x is disposed to permit S = df.

8. x has the power to render S causally possible and is intrinsically such that had x the opportunity to do so, x probably would, or x has the power to

---

[35] This may seem to create a difficulty for my treatment of (T) above: hasn't God the power and opportunity to bring it about that there are more states of affairs, even if He has not done so? But then God's existing brings it about that this was causally possible and so *per* (6b), God permits this rather than prevents it. I argue later that He does not have such a power, though it is in Him to do this.

prevent S and is intrinsically such that had x the opportunity to do so, x probably would not.

What about the Past?

I want to give a theist account of secular modality based on divine prevention, permission, and dispositions to both. The possibility of what is secular and now past poses a problem for this project: it was the case, and so is causally possible, but seems not to be the object of any divine prevention, permission, or disposition to either. I now address past possibilities.

Suppose first that God is atemporal.[36] Recall (7): God causally permits the actual past if He makes it causally possible. Recall (6b): the actual past is causally possible if something timelessly-has the power and chance to bring it about. So God timelessly causally permits the actual past if He timelessly has power and chance to bring it about. Anything God brings about, He has the power and chance to bring about. If He is atemporal, He still timelessly is bringing about that of the actual past which He brings about (for example, by creating, conserving, and cooperating). So He has the power and chance to do so. So this part of the actual past remains an object of a timeless God's causal permission.

If there is anything secular in the past God does not bring about, God is still timelessly rendering it causally possible. For if anything secular happens without direct divine input, this is either because God has thought up its so happening and not prevented it, or because God did so for its cause, its cause's cause, or something such—that is all He need do to make it causally possible, *per* (6f)—or because He creates and sustains a cause for it, and so on, making it causally possible in a thicker way. If He is timeless, these things timelessly are so. It is with these as with alternative pasts. Alternative pasts were possible: Booth could have failed to shoot Lincoln. We think these alternative pasts are still absolutely possible, though they can no longer come about. If God is atemporal, God's timeless permission that Lincoln not be shot, which made it possible that he not be, still timelessly exists. God still timelessly has the power to bring this about. He is in the act of passing up His chance, and so for Him the chance is still open, *per* earlier argument. The passage of time is irrelevant to what is true timelessly, so it cannot close off possibilities timeless divine permission establishes. A state of affairs not causally possible in time may remain causally possible timelessly, because an opportunity lost

---

[36] An atemporal God could permit tensed states of affairs. He could timelessly permit, for example, that in time, *P* was the case. The prefixed 'in time' ensures that the tenses do not refer to any temporal standpoint of His own. So too, if there is a second temporal series, we can say, for example, 'In the other temporal series, *P* was the case.' This does not imply that the other series' past is ours. 'In the other temporal series' cancels tense's usual reference to the speaker's temporal location.

to temporal agents may be one an atemporal agent still has, as He passes it up. What is causally possible timelessly is causally and so absolutely possible.

It remains to ask whether there might have been past states of affairs a timeless God lacks power or chance to bring about, or to bring it about that anything else has power and opportunity to bring about, or to let occur uncaused. The hardest cases might be the claims that

9. God never brought anything about, or

10. nothing ever brought anything about.

Obviously God cannot bring (9) about by acting. Nor can God do so by not acting. If God does bring (9) about by not acting, he does not: by not acting, God brings (9) about, and so it is not the case that God never brings something about. So there is just no possible way for Him to bring (9) about. (There is nothing peculiar to God here: substitute a name of any agent and the same result emerges.) The last question, then, is whether God could have power and opportunity to let (9) occur uncaused. Could God without cause let Himself not bring anything about—that is, omit to act without a positive event of refraining that causally explains this, just being quiescent without deciding to be? If God is timeless, no events in His life are at temporal distances from each other. It is not the case that He could at one time be quiescent and act at others; all of His acts are together, timelessly. So it is not possible that God both does anything at all and brings (9) about by this sort of omission. (9)'s being true is open to God only if He could never so much as think. But I have already argued that God's nature requires Him to think up creatures. Thinking them up is doing something. I have also argued that God must think them up from all eternity, whether He is temporal or timeless. So I conclude that (9) is just an impossibility. More simply, even an omission of the sort described would count as bringing (9) about if (9) did come about, and so again, (9) is impossible. (10) includes (9) if God exists, and so the response is the same. If God is atemporal, then, past possibilities are not a problem for my view.

Now suppose that God is temporal. Then before the shooting, God permitted that Lincoln be shot and that this become past. If the past exists, that prior time and the divine permission exist in the past to account for the prospective possibility, sadly actualized, that Lincoln was shot. So divine permission over the course of time can account for the prospective possibility of the whole actual past: divine permission always does account for what is prospectively possible, and always did account for what was prospectively possible. The actual past remains the object of God's existent prospective causal permission, which is also past. But this is at best only part of the answer. While past divine permission made the shooting possible in prospect, it is no longer in prospect. But it is still causally possible *per* (6a): having been the case suffices for being causally possible. We need, then, to show that God somehow accounts or accounted for its having been the case: for Lincoln's shooting's occurring and that event's being past. God's then-current cooperation with the relevant causes (sustaining them, their powers, and so on) helped bring about the actual shooting, and so the actual shooting traces back (*inter alia*) to God's past action. So if the passage of time was also somehow down to God—a thing I believe, though one I cannot argue here—this gives us that God's past activity accounted for the past fact that Lincoln was shot. And so if Lincoln's shooting's being part of the existent past suffices to render it now causally possible, *per* (6a), we have our answer. If on the other hand the past does not exist, how there are *any* truths about the past is a hard question. But if there is a solution to this at all, it adapts to the present case.

Thus the actual past. If God is temporal, alternative pasts are puzzling even if the past exists. If it does, there also exist in the past whatever alternative possibilities the past state of things grounded. If God permits at a past time that Lincoln not be shot, that permission exists in the past and grounds that past prospective possibility. But that is a possibility for *then*. It is no longer prospectively possible. It is now too late for it to become actual. None of us any longer has or can produce the opportunity to bring this about. Now that it is past, past permission only makes it the case that this *was* causally possible, not that it is so. So we can still ask whether such possibilities as that Lincoln not be shot disappear in later states of the world. (Many medieval philosophers thought they do.[37]) We do not want earlier absolute possibilities to disappear. What causally could have been remains possible absolutely. This just seems part of the concept of absolute possibility. We want to know, then, how something about a temporal God in the present or past can account for past unrealized possibilities remaining absolutely possible.

The answer, I think, comes in two parts. One is a definition:

11. It is absolutely possible that P = df. it is, was or atemporally-is causally possible that P.

To defend (11) I first show that any history in which God exists cannot be a purely temporal sequence of events, but must include some causal sequences which are not also temporal sequences. I then put this point to use.

I begin by showing that any history in which God is atemporal must be a purely causal sequence or a combination of temporal and purely causal sequences. If an atemporal God never creates, there are no temporal sequences—there is time only if He makes it, given (GSA)—but there are causal sequences (for example, His producing His thoughts).[38] If an atemporal God

---

[37] See, for example, S. Thomae Aquinatis, *Summa Theologia* (Ottawa: Studii Generalis, 1941), Ia 25, 4.

[38] Obviously, I am committing here to some theory of causation which does not require causes to occur temporally prior to their effects.

creates temporal things, some atemporal divine volitions cause temporal events, and so are parts of the histories in which they do so, though they stand in no temporal sequence with their effects. So such histories are combinations of temporal and causal sequences.

Histories in which God is temporal are also combinations. For either time began or it did not. If time began, God caused it to do so. Now either times are existing things, or relationalism is true and they are not. If the former, then if time began, there was a first instant and/or period, and *per* (GSA), God caused it to exist. God's causing either to exist would be causally but not temporally prior to its existing, and so stand in a causal but not a temporal sequence in that history. If relationalism is true, talk of times is to be paraphrased into talk of temporal relations' obtaining. So if relationalism is true, time begins just if there come to be events standing in temporal relations. Suppose that it is enough if an event occurs which is temporally simultaneous with some event. God thinks causally prior to creating, and so to the existence of anything else. Either these thoughts are temporally before He creates, or they are only causally prior to it. If the second, we have a purely causal sequence, and so the history is a combination. If the first, God causes time to begin by having the thoughts, but He makes His contribution to their occurring causally prior to their occurring, and so we again have a purely causal sequence and a history which is a combination. If time's beginning requires time after the first instant, then still, history will include the purely causal sequences just noted.

Suppose now that God is temporal but time never began. Then there are events causally though not temporally prior to the whole beginningless span of time, as zero is prior to the beginningless span of positive real numbers. For every time t, God wills that t occur, at or before t. If the past exists, these events of willing have a sum, E, which is God's willing that there be times $-\infty - t$, which constitute the whole span of time. The occurring of $-\infty - t$ is a single long event. That event includes E (or at any rate E occurs at the times whose occurring compose it) if God is temporal: E is not temporally prior to it. But E caused this event. So E is causally prior to it. So again we have a history which is a combination. If only the present exists, there is no sum E, since an existent event cannot have non-existent parts. But there was and is a continuing event E*, which had what we called the earlier parts of E as parts and has E's present part as its sole part. E* continued through the continuing event which was and is the occurring of $-\infty - t$, and the rest goes as before: the continuing E* was and is causally but not temporally prior to the occurring of $-\infty - t$.

Thus if God exists necessarily, as I have assumed, any possible history must be either a purely causal sequence or a combination of temporal and causal sequences. I now put this point to use.

If a history is indeterminist, in it causal possibility has a 'tree' structure: from any time at which there are indeterminist powers, there branch off multiple paths history causally could take. If a history is determinist, the tree is a log: no branches. (11) asserts that every absolute possibility is found somewhere along one tree some of whose temporal or (if I may put it so) causal past overlaps the actual past. So (11) is false if non-actual states of affairs are possible, but not compatible with any part of our past. (11) is false if there could be histories whose past is completely disjoint from—not a branch from—the actual (thus including some actually ruled-out possibilities). And it seems that there could be. If the past was of finite length, then surely there could have been a time with a longer finite past, or an infinite past. Any time before the actual beginning of time is not a branch from actual time. So nothing after such time is a branch from actual time either, since it is a branch from something which is not part of actual time—even if the events along some branch from the longer tree are just those along some branch from actual time.[39] Again, if the past was of finite length n, surely there could have been pasts of length n-1. Even if everything along the n-1-length tree is just as it is along the relevant part of the n-length tree, the shorter tree has been (so to speak) severed from its root. Since it does not go back all the way to its actual root, it is not a branch from actuality. Again, if the natural laws have always been N, surely it is possible that they have always instead been N*. But as I see it, because God is in the picture, there can be no wholly disjoint histories—and in saying this I do not prune from possibility anything we intuitively want to be there.

I have supposed that God exists necessarily. If He does, every possible history is either a causal sequence or a combination. If so, then even if some histories' non-divine portions are entirely disjoint, some finite and some infinite, etc., I submit that all histories share a common causally first segment involving God. The causally first state of reality must be God's being as He is and doing what He does by nature. Causally next comes the biggest Bang. Things diverge causally-after this. There being natural laws, or time with or without beginning, lie further downstream causally. With God in the picture and histories understood as both causal and temporal, (11) is an extensionally adequate definition.

The other part of my temporalist response to the problem of the past is what makes it the case that

12. it is now the case that some unrealized states of affairs were causally possible.

If the past exists, that suffices to let God's past permissions make (12) true, *per* earlier discussion. If the past does not exist but there are truths about the past, (12) rests partly on God's past permissions and partly on whatever provides for present truth about the past. (12) has a wholly theist truthmaker if what

---

[39] It is a good question whether there *could* be any actual events along such a non-actuality-based tree. I do not need to take a stand on it.

provides for truth about the past is theist. Theist accounts of this are available.[40] Thus (12) could in the end rest on God's past and present state.

(12) could also rest on God's present state alone. God is always omnipotent. Suppose that a no longer causally possible state of affairs S was causally possible *inter alia* because He had the intrinsic power and the opportunity to bring it about (or make a cause able to, etc.). God still has that intrinsic power, if He is still omnipotent. That is, He still has the power which then made it the case that He could bring S about given opportunity. Thus He not only then was but now is such that He could have then brought S about given the chance. So due to God's present state, S now causally-could have been actual then given opportunity. As omnipotent, God now has all powers He would have used (or did use) to give Himself the chance. So He now could have brought about the opportunity. If God now has the very powers such that could have brought about opportunity for S and God now has the very powers that could have brought S about given opportunity, S now could have been brought about, due to God's present powers. What now for this sort of reason causally-could have been brought about, once was causally possible. So present facts about God make it true that S now was causally possible.

(12) tells us that some unrealized past possibilities were causally possible. (11) tells us that this suffices for them now to be absolutely possible. So my stories about (11) and (12) together give us a metaphysics for unrealized past absolute possibilities.

---

[40] See, for example, Alan Rhoda, 'Presentism, Truthmakers and God', *Pacific Philosophical Quarterly* 90 (2009), 41–62; Dean Zimmerman, 'The A-Theory of Time, Presentism and Open Theism', in Melville Stewart (ed.), *Science and Religion in Dialogue* (Oxford: Wiley–Blackwell, 2009), v. 2.

14

THE GENESIS OF
SECULAR MODALITY

I now set out the genesis of secular modal status as a sequence, though in this context being earlier only means being presupposed by what follows.

(i) God exists, wholly alone. There are no other concreta. There is nothing abstract 'outside' Him. Meinongianism is false: it is not the case that there 'are' non-existents. God can create, and so it is possible that there be some creature or other. But there are no states of affairs involving determinate non-deities, nor has God thought any up.

(ii) The Bang: God thinks up states of affairs involving determinate non-deities.

(iii) God notes any good- or bad-making features they would have.

If (as I have argued) God thinks up some or other non-deities by nature, there is no temporal gap between (i) and (ii). There is also no temporal gap between (ii) and (iii). God is by nature omniscient, and were there some time, however small, in which He had not yet noticed a feature, He would not then be omniscient.

(iv) If they would have good- or bad-making features, God takes attitudes toward their obtaining.

If a state of affairs would have no such features, He takes no attitude.[1]

There is no temporal gap between (iii) and (iv) either. God is by nature ideally wise and good. As such He by nature perfectly loves the good and rejects the bad. He would be a less than perfect lover of the good were there

---

[1] Perhaps having no first-level good-making features is a second-level bad-making feature, or having no first-level bad-making features, is a second-level good-making feature. If either is true, there are fewer states of affairs to which God has no attitude than one might think.

any time, however small, in which He had noted a good-making feature but not formed a positive attitude toward it, and a less than perfect rejecter of the bad were there any time, however small, in which He had noted a bad-making feature but not formed a negative attitude toward it. Nor is there a temporal gap if a state of affairs has no good- or bad-making features; 'before' He noticed this He neither approved nor disapproved, and once He notices this, there is no change.

(v) Given His approval, disapproval or neutrality, God decides whether to prevent these states of affairs, either absolutely or conditionally.[2]

Just for example's sake, perhaps if He disapproves enough, He just will not allow it, and He otherwise will. God needs no time to mull over His reactions or decisions. For any period He might need, His mind would be more perfect if He needed less time than that, and if time is continuous, there would always be a period shorter than that.[3] Hence no non-zero period is short enough to be the time a perfect mind would need to reflect—even if there are really infinitesimal quantities. If this is correct, the claim that a perfect mind needs any length of time to do this is in fact logically (Ω-) inconsistent: if it needs a length of time, there is a length of time it needs, but this existential quantification has no instance, as no length of time is short enough to be this length. So a mind is perfect—unsurpassable—only if its reactions and decisions need no time, i.e. are capable of being causally but not temporally posterior to its grasp of what it reacts to. A mind is maximally efficient only if it takes no more time than it needs. So God decides instantaneously and in such a way as never to need correction. Finally,

---

[2] In this chapter, unless otherwise noted, all uses of 'prevent' express 1-prevention, which guarantees that what is prevented, does not occur, rather than merely reducing its probability to zero. That a permission is unconditional means that nothing need be the case for what it permits to be permitted; the contrast is with something of the form 'If P, I permit that Q', which does not actually permit anything if it is not the case that P. From all eternity, God has those abilities which make it apt to speak of possessing logical concepts, including if-concepts (otherwise He would not know the truths of logic). Given these, God can issue conditional permissions. Conditional permission is not equivalent to permission of a conditional. 'I permit that: Q if P' permits a conditional. Its doing so does not depend on anything but God's uttering it. Whether 'If P, I permit that Q' permits anything depends on whether P.

Conditional permissions could determine accessibility relations. They could, for example, lie behind talk of possibly possible worlds which are not possible. The reality behind this could be that for some PQ, God permits that P, and so disposes Himself that P > God permits that Q, but it is not the case that P and God does not permit that Q. By issuing this conditional permission, God would ensure that the logic of absolute modality does not include S4. God puts S4 in place if He issues only simple permissions, not permissions to permit. By so doing, He permits Himself to permit what He does. (He makes His making these permissions actual. Being actual suffices for being causally possible. So He makes it causally possible that He issue them. So He permits Himself to permit them.) As there are no 'stated' permissions to permit or not permit, nothing is not permitted but permitted to be permitted. The only things permitted to be permitted are the things permitted.

Conditional permission and prevention figure in God's establishing natural laws. If God decrees that if any body of stuff is H_2O under such-and-such conditions and at a temperature between 32°and 212° F, He permits that it is liquid and does not permit its being in any other state, God establishes a physical necessity, and a natural-law link between properties.

[3] My thanks here to Laura Garcia.

(vi) God prevents or permits, and perhaps also forms dispositions to do so.

I argue shortly that there is no temporal gap between (v) and (vi) either. So no sooner does God have situations in mind than He notes their value-relevant features, settles His attitude or lack thereof, decides about them, and prevents, permits and perhaps forms dispositions. The last three, I submit, determine a secular state of affairs' modal status. Since every secular state of affairs there is from all eternity has its modal status from all eternity,[4] this requires that God prevent or permit every such state of affairs from all eternity. I now argue that He does, then comment on (ii)–(vi).

The Eternality Claim

If

POP. necessarily, for each secular state of affairs, either God prevents it or God permits it,

then for each secular state of affairs there is from all eternity, from all eternity either God prevents it or God permits it. This is all I need to argue here, but some further points deserve note. If God permits S, He either brings it about or leaves it the case that some causally possible continuation of the history in which He does so includes S. If God prevents S, He brings it about that no causally possible continuation of the history in which He does so includes S. So God cannot both prevent and permit a state of affairs. It is not in Him to bring about a logical inconsistency (or try to: He knows His nature and so knows what His permitting and preventing involve). So if (POP) is true, from all eternity, for each secular state of affairs there is from all eternity, God prevents it or God permits it, but not both. I assume here a classical rather than a supervaluationist semantics. On such a semantics, if the disjunction is true, a disjunct is true. So on this assumption, for each such secular state of affairs, it is settled from all eternity whether God prevents it, and if He does not do so, He permits it. So its permission/prevention status is settled from all eternity. I now argue (POP). I begin by saying which secular states of affairs God prevents from all eternity.

As I see it, God prevents the truth of secular cases of logical falsehoods. To treat this fully would mean giving my full story about God and logic. That is too involved to broach here, so I simply sketch. Even if there are no logical truths due to vagueness, the propositions we call logical truths are logically non-false: no matter how the world comes out, they are non-false. So too, no

---

[4] If God has pre-creative singular concepts, all states of affairs are there from all eternity. If He does not, there are from all eternity only general states of affairs and singular ones involving items that exist from all eternity. Others come to be when new individuals come to be.

matter how the world comes out, the propositions we call logical falsehoods are non-true. Thus God cannot affect their non-truth by affecting the world. He prevents their truth only if He has an appropriate role in determining their content.

At stage (i), God exists, is perfectly good, and so on. It is not also the case that He does not exist, is not perfectly good, and so on. This is so just as a matter of His nature. To say that logic (or the contents of antecedently given possible worlds insofar as logic is written into them) prevented it would Platonize. But God also (I believe) naturally has logical concepts. These are just concepts—there is no Platonic conjunction-function.[5] They are as they are because God thinks as He does. There is no more to, for example, conjunction than what God puts into it. God so forms the concept—so thinks—that the propositions we call logical falsehoods are at least logically non-true. Concepts just do have certain satisfaction-conditions. Conjunction just is a concept such that where there is a pair of truths PQ, the satisfaction-condition for_ and _ is met, and so it is true that P and Q. This is so whether concepts are independent Platonic objects or entities in the mind of God. The like is true for the divine mental events that for me replace concepts. There is nothing fancy to all this. Those who first form concepts get to determine their satisfaction-conditions. If we first formed the concept of conjunction, we would have done this. As it happens, God beat us to it. Had He come up with any other set of logical non-truths, the result would not have been conjunction, but that conjunction could not have been otherwise does not entail that it was not made to be so. Even what is inevitable has causes. And it *is* inevitable, not just because of the point just made but also because in this respect God's nature determines how He thinks, in accord with the last chapter's *Euthyphro* move.

Thus God prevents the truth of pure logical falsehoods by thinking as He does. *Per* the last chapter's (1), their not being true comes about, due to divine thought. *Per* its (2), God causes an event which suffices in the circumstances to bring it about that they are not true: He forms logical concepts. Thus one way to the outlandish-seeming claim that God prevents the truth of pure-logical falsehoods runs thus: start with logical Platonism—logical operators represent abstract entities such as functions. Relocate the Platonic entities to the mind of God, as divine concepts. Then 'reduce' concepts away. What is left, *per* Chapter 11, is God's thinking in certain ways, and God and the events involved do the preventing. If my theist reduction of logical Platonism and my simple story about concepts and satisfaction-conditions are at least intelligible, my claim that God prevents pure logical falsehoods' truth is at least intelligible. I think it can be made attractive, even to non-theists, but that is a

[5] Thus I endorse as a significant counterpossible the claim that if there were no God, there would be no conjunction. For if conjunction is just a (non-Platonic) concept, then necessarily, if there are no minds to host concepts, there is no such thing as conjunction. But necessarily, if there were no God, there would be no minds, since necessarily any mind is either God's or the mind of some being God thought up.

story I must delay. *Per* my earlier discussion of prevention, my story does not imply that logical falsehoods might have been true.

It is also part of God's preventing the truth of pure logical falsehoods to prevent their having true secular instances: Spot is not both a dog and not a dog simply because that is how God made him. So add to the picture that if God represents to Himself Rover, who both is and is not a dog, by His nature He prevents his existing. A natural reply would be 'What needs preventing?'. Rover does not 'need preventing' in the sense that he threatens to come to be if God does not act. Rover could not but come out non-existent. But what is inevitable can be explained, and the explanatory story here counts as a case of prevention on the account I am using.

One story about the prevention involved builds on my account of pure logical non-truths. A Platonist could say that truth-tables just are as they are, a contradiction comes out non-true on any assignment of truth-values to its conjuncts; this is why *Rover exists* comes out non-true, and so this is why Rover does not exist. Start, then, with this Platonist picture. Transfer the truth-table to the mind of God. Reduce it away. Then the way God thinks rules out Rover's appearing. For the truth-tables to 'just be as they are' is for God to think a certain way. But the Platonist picture is odd: shouldn't the world determine which propositions are non-true, not *vice-versa*? Surely logical non-truths' 'independence' of the world is just that given the content of the logical constants, any possible state of the world renders them non-true, not that the mere content of Platonic objects or divine concepts does so. Conventionalists decry the whole picture of logic dictating to reality and so ruling Rover out.[6] They say that logic is just an aspect of how we think and talk. This does not explain the non-existence of anything extra-mental, but it does explain why 'Rover exists' comes out false: because of how we talk or think, there is nothing *we describe* as relevantly like Rover. Logic does not dictate to reality; it just shapes the way we describe it. Still, conventionalists must acknowledge an exception. The way we think and talk does dictate to reality when it guides what we make. If our thought and talk embeds logic within it, so then does logic.

At this point, theists can make a suggestion. There is *something* to the Platonic intuition that logic dictates to reality. Theism can accommodate this, and explicate it in a way acceptable (*modulo* theism) to conventionalists: God's bare thinking has no more direct impact on what really exists than anyone else's. It directly shapes only the way He describes reality. But—Himself apart—He describes it causally prior to its existence, in a design, a plan to make. His thinking guides what He makes, as ours does what we make. So as conventionalism must let logic dictate to reality when we make, it must let logic dictate to reality when God makes. Logic dictates to reality because God does. In place of whatever sort of abstract constraint Platonic entities would

---

[6] So too conceptualists, here and below.

provide, there is efficient causation. The way God thinks affects what He decides. Due to the abstract aspect of His thinking which logic formulates, God decides that there shall be no Rover, and this secures a Roverless world. In either story, by setting the contents of the truth-table, God's thinking prevents Rover's appearing, but the second adds a chapter about how that works itself out. Neither story should suggest that there was ever a chance that things be otherwise. God's nature dictated the result. He would have so thought no matter what. Now that God's nature dictates His activity might suggest that its existing or God's having it is the real preventing condition here; if there is no such thing as deity, it might suggest that God's bare existing is the preventing condition. But if it is, it is so only because it dictates what God *does*. So too, Booth's shooting the gun prevented Lincoln's ripe old age, but only by dictating the path of a bullet.

My story about mathematics would have the same broad outlines, and so I say that God prevents the truth of secular cases of mathematical falsehoods, again by nature. On my view, God prevents all other secular absolute impossibilities. Consider those based on definitional essences: for example, that c belong to {a, b}, assuming that c ≠ a and c ≠ b. If this is a *secular* impossibility, abc are not God, divine attributes, and so on. If so, abc and {a, b} are simply divine inventions—things God thought up. Suppose God so conceives {a, b} that to be {a, b} is to be a thing with a and b as members and no other member. {a, b} has no other nature than the one His thinking gives it. God's settling the definition prevents it that c belongs to {a, b}. If what it is to be {a, b} includes having no other member, anything with c as a member does not satisfy the definition of {a, b} and so is not {a, b}; thus it is prevented that {a, b} include c. Definitional essences are (supposed to be) relevantly like definitions. As a word can have but one definition—different meaning, different word—an item can have but one definitional essence. So in all possible worlds, God either lacks the concept of {a, b} or defines it as He does. So He necessarily prevents what He thereby prevents.

Consider now secular impossibilities reflecting merely modal essences—for example, that Socrates be a number. Socrates is a divine invention. God determines what Socrates can be. God prevents his being a number by thinking up Socrates as He does and (as I go on to show) giving him the careers across possible worlds He gives him. That he has these careers comes about: God determines what they are. Doing so suffices in the circumstances to bring it about that it is not the case that Socrates is a number, as (we soon see) it includes His denying Himself power to make him a number or empower others things to do so and preventing Socrates' being a number uncaused, and all this prevents Socrates' being a number. As an item cannot exist without a modally essential attribute, an item can have but one modal essence. So in all possible worlds, either God lacks the concept of Socrates or He gives Socrates the modal essence he has: He necessarily prevents what He thereby prevents. Again, what He does necessarily, He does from eternity. If there are impossibilities other than those of logic, mathematics or essence, there will be a similar story to tell about them.

Secular states of affairs not absolutely impossible are either necessary or contingent. If God brings about pure-logical, pure-mathematical, modal-essential and definitional necessities, *a fortiori* He permits them, again from eternity. He thus also brings it about and so permits it that they have from eternity any secular instances they have from eternity. Now consider contingent secular states of affairs. Each such S either is or is not such as to come about without cause. Suppose that S is such as to come about without cause. Given that He has conceived S, God by nature has power and opportunity to prevent S and all iterations in (e) of (CAUSAL POSS), for any such S.[7] Necessarily He does or does not use this power. If God thinks S up and does not prevent it, He brings it about that (f) of (CAUSAL POSS) is satisfied, thus rendering S causally possible. So God permits S. And since God necessarily either does or does not use His power to prevent S, necessarily, He either permits or prevents S.

Suppose now that S is not such as to come about without cause. Then upon conceiving S—that is, from eternity—God by nature has power and opportunity to prevent S and all iterations in (b)–(d) of (CAUSAL POSS). Either He does or He does not use this power. What it would take not to have used it depends on what it takes for such an S not to be prevented. If God does not render S causally possible—that is, provide Himself a power, or a power able to produce a power, and so on, to produce it—nothing else does either. From all eternity, there is nothing else to do so. But if S is not such as to come about without cause, and no cause is available, S is prevented. S cannot come about, for it needs a cause and one has not been provided. So S is not prevented only if God provides for a cause (plus opportunity) for S, rendering S causally possible. By doing so He causally permits it. So again, necessarily, He either permits or prevents S. This completes my case for (POP). Given (POP), the eternality claim follows.

I now discuss (ii)–(v). I then suggest that divine permission and dispositions to permit are the root of secular possibility and divine prevention and dispositions to prevent are the root of secular impossibility.

On (ii): Alternative Bangs?

The Bang actually had certain contents. One might wonder whether God could have had one with other contents. If He could, then given the role the

---

[7] This assumes that no secular states of affairs obtain by God's very nature, since He cannot prevent His having His nature. If God is free not to create (as is orthodox), and to be unaccompanied by other concreta, then for any non-deity c, neither that c exists nor that c does not exist obtain by God's nature, nor then any state of affairs entailing either. In particular, there being time is not a secular state of affairs which obtains by God's very nature. Either there is no such 'thing' as time, or if there is, either time is somehow at bottom an aspect of God, or time does not exist by God's very nature.

Bang plays in my metaphysic, there could have been attributes and individuals other than any that are possible or impossible—a logical space with denizens appearing nowhere in our own. And of course there could not. In no possible world is there anything that appears in no actually possible or actually impossible world. However, it is one thing to accept that this is the right conclusion, and another to show that it falls out of my view in any natural way. I now try to do the latter.

If there could have been a Bang different in some way, this' being possible would involve no determinate creaturely content not contained in the Bang as it actually was. For there is no place for such content to come from. If no deity theory is true, it could not come from God's nature. It is implausible that it could come from there even on a deity theory. On a deity theory, God's grasp of creaturely natures comes from His grasp of His own or else His nature determines the Bang to be as it is. But given one divine grasping of deity, why would deity have more content for another to get? Why would not God have grasped this part of His nature with the rest? Or why would God's nature not have included this content in the initial Bang? Nor could God think such content up in the Bang, for then it would be not an alternative Bang's contents, but part of the actual Bang's contents. There is no other source for such content. So while it is in God to have thought up different things than He has, there are no other things such that it is in God to have had a Bang including *them*. In the actual Bang, God conceives all possible and impossible fully determinate attributes, individuals, and histories.[8] If other Bangs are possible, it is possible that there be attributes and so on other than any of these. It is possible, for example, that

DOG. there is a history in which another dog than God has from all eternity actually conceived barks like Lassie.[9]

But (DOG) is a general possibility. Individual fully determinate further histories and dogs have not been conceived. So (DOG) does not bring with it particular possibly possible dogs or histories.

---

[8] If certain sorts of indeterminate entities are as such impossible, then (speaking crudely) in the Bang God thinks them up as fully determinately indeterminate.

[9] 'From all eternity' is needed if (DOG) is to be possible. Suppose that we delete it, and then God tries to instantiate (DOG). In doing so He creates a dog to bark like Lassie. If He has pre-creative singular concepts, He first conceives it and then creates it—and so it is not a dog other than any God has actually conceived, and so (DOG) is not true. So it turns out that (DOG) cannot be true. 'From all eternity' gets us around this: it lets us suppose that God conceives many dogs from all eternity, but if He wants (DOG) to be possible refrains from conceiving a further dog until He is about to instantiate it. (DOG) is formulated against a background assumption of pre-creative singular concepts. If God has none, any particular dog not yet actual is one other than God has actually conceived, for God can conceive particulars only once they appear. So (DOG) without 'from all eternity' turns out to be satisfiable even if there cannot be alternate Bangs, and so does not express something true only if there can be such Bangs. 'From all eternity' will not get us around this, since on generalism, God conceives from eternity only particulars that exist from eternity, and no dog exists from eternity. The nearest relative of (DOG) within generalism would be:

DOG*. There is a history in which another type of dog than God has actually conceived, etc.

Discussion of (DOG*) would parallel my treatment of (DOG). So I omit it.

If (DOG) is possible, an omniscient God must conceive it. If He conceives it, then as it involves candidate creatures, it is part of the content of the Bang. So a different Bang is possible just if the actual Bang includes partly—or wholly—general histories of (DOG)'s sort, which would have been filled in by particulars had there been a different Bang. If they are there, these histories represent (incompletely) the contents of an alternate Bang within the resources provided by the only one there actually is. Equivalently, God has a specific power to produce a different Bang just if the actual Bang is partly general.[10]

If there could be or have been another Bang, the actual Bang is partly general. For simplicity, let us suppose that the generality involves only individuals; adding attributes would not change things essentially. Then there are fully determinate histories involving Lassie, and if (DOG) is possible, for some of these, there are also histories otherwise identical which are not filled out with respect to what dog—perhaps even what type of dog—plays that barking-dog role, even if God has pre-creative singular concepts. Now the Bang is *inter alia practical* thinking. God is dreaming up alternatives for Himself—candidate plans for action. Given His role in them, all their details matter. Every bit has an effect on what He would do. To (so to speak) leave a blank in (DOG)'s history, He would have to not even think in full detail from all eternity about what He might do to fill in the blank were He to try to actualize a history of (DOG)'s sort. For if He did think in full detail of this, He would equally think up further particular possible dogs He might make. If He did, He would actually conceive these dogs, and so any history involving them, if actualized, would not actualize a specific possibility instancing (DOG)'s general possibility. So to leave a blank in (DOG), He would (so to speak) have to not even speculate, not even consider a plan, for some details of a (DOG)-history. But God is of perfect practical rationality. He has no limits of capacity or time. He is at a point in His life at which all conceived plans His nature permits Him to execute—that is, plans such that it is in Him once He conceives them to both have His nature and execute them—are live options, and any (DOG)-plan would be one such plan. There is no distinctive value to be realized by divine improvisation at the last minute. The eventual dog would be arrived at just as creatively either way, and the excitement *we* find in making things up as we go along is thoroughly a function of our finitude: we might well get it wrong, we do not control even our own contribution exactly, we strain to both make up a plan and execute it well at once, and so on. So how could He not plan, not even give this a thought, not be at least curious?

I see one answer to these questions. God might think up deliberately general (DOG)-histories as a sort of safeguard: as He sets Himself to think up histories, perhaps He is not assured of satisfying Himself with all His

---

[10] God has the general power to think things up—to imagine. It was in God to use this otherwise, to think up other things than He has, and so to have a different Bang. The question is whether in addition He has the specific power.

histories on the first try, and including (DOG) *et al.* among the histories He all at once frames gives Him the chance to do better, to rectify histories in specific ways. But this seems unlikely. God knows that He is perfect and that if He is perfect, He will do well enough on His first try not to have use for another. Let us explore this.

On the 'safeguard' story, the Bang contains maximally determinate histories (Ds) and others (Gs) by conceiving which He gives Himself powers to conceive alternatives to what He at first conceived. Once God has the Ds in view, He has a set of all-things-considered desires (some elicited by them) and adopts a set of purposes. The Ds are ideally sufficient for God's purposes only if at least one D lets Him ideally fulfill all His purposes and satisfy all these desires. If some of this depends on libertarian-free creatures' cooperation, it must also be the case given the set of creatures some such D involves that it is highly likely that if created these creatures give the needed cooperation, so that what results if God tries to actualize an ideally fulfilling D is highly likely to be ideally fulfilling. Now if Fred has libertarian freedom, it cannot be certain before creation that Fred will always give God exactly what He wants. God in considering His creative decision has before Him (speaking non-commissively) a set of possible worlds involving Fred. There are (so I claim) no Molinist facts about what Fred would do in possible situation C for Him to know. There are only facts about what he might do, and probabilities for each possible action. If Molinism is false, as I assume, God could have certainty before selecting an initial segment of a world to actualize that Fred would do thus-and-so in C only by causally determining him to do so—in which case Fred's act would not be libertarian-free. Perhaps once God decides, He immediately sees the future, including Fred's act in C. But it is then too late for that knowledge to inform His creative choice. All He has to go on, then, are probabilities about Fred. That being so, 'highly likely' suggests a way God could improve on the Ds: He could think up other alternatives on which the same creatures are still more likely to give Him what He wants, or there are other types of creatures more likely to do so. But there is no *a priori* limit to this. God could always get closer to 100% of creatures being certain to co-operate without reaching it. This suggests a reason for God not to go down this route: if the desire for a higher probability, just as such, is worth acting on, then as He could always get a higher one, He would never have an alternative He could take as fit to act on. God must instead stop somewhere, and say 'this probability is good enough.' But if He ever would make that judgment, not to come up with creatures and worlds yielding a good-enough probability in His first try would seem to manifest an imperfection. So a perfect being would think up a world whose creatures provide a good-enough probability on one try.

The Ds are insufficient only if none is likely enough if God tries to actualize it to yield an actuality ideally serving some divine purpose or fulfilling some divine all-things-considered desire. But to be liable to having the Ds be insufficient would involve an imperfection, a misalignment or lack of integration in God's faculties. We can fill this thought out as follows. If God's nature did not guarantee that His wants, purposes, and conceptions are each overall extremely good, this would be an imperfection: it would be better to have a nature that did guarantee this. If God's nature guaranteed only that His conceptions or that His wants and purposes are extremely good, the lack of guarantee for the other would be an imperfection and would also explain the misalignment. Even if both are guaranteed to be extremely good, liability to mismatch would involve imperfections. To keep it simple, let us vary only either the conceptions or the wants/purposes, not both at once.

First, then, let us 'fix' God's wants and purposes, keeping them constant as WP. Then liability to mismatch might be a liability not to think up alternatives good enough to satisfy WP: a liability to insufficiently good conceiving. It might be a liability to come up with only alternatives incommensurable with WP: only alternatives realizing complex of values V, while WP home in only on complexes including some value V* where V is incommensurable with V*, so that V*-desires/purposes cannot find satisfaction in some equivalent quantity or quality of V. Liability to this would be liability to appreciate V insufficiently and also to either practical paralysis (having no basis for choice among presented alternatives) or less than ideally rational decision-making (having no reason to choose any presented alternative, if God nonetheless had to choose, He would in effect flip a coin, rather than being guided by available values). Finally, there might be mismatch because the alternatives God comes up with are all too good for WP. Since WP are at least partly elicited by the alternatives, this would involve liability to fail to respond appropriately to presented value.

Now let us instead 'fix' God's alternatives as A. Then liability to mismatch would be liability for A to elicit wants and purposes for constellations of value below, incommensurable with or above the values presented in A. In the first case, liability to mismatch would entail liability to fail to respond appropriately to presented values. We would also have to say that God's character is not good enough to measure up to the possibilities for bringing about good He is able to envision. It is not clear that the second option is really coherent. Values incommensurable with any presented in A must be values not conceived in A. If God has not conceived a form of value, how can He want it or form a purpose to realize it? It cannot be a value that is a function of anything His nature contains, or else He would have conceived it in understanding Himself. Nor can He have been predetermined to want it: again, He would then have grasped it in understanding His own nature. Nor can it be a value given outside Him: then His omniscience would entail that He had understood and so conceived it. Nor can a perfect being be liable to inchoate adolescent urges for something, He knows not what—or so one would think.

The last case does not have so much obviously against it: a tendency to great aspiration is no bad thing. But if this tendency can come into play, God is liable to thinking up only alternatives not good enough for aspirations He is liable to form: to insufficiently good conceiving. Further, we must ask what would happen if God then rectified matters, coming up with alternatives good enough to satisfy His initial wants and purposes. If His aspirations would then overshoot His alternatives again, and so *ad infinitum*, His nature would lead to paralysis: He would never be able to choose any alternative He had. If He would eventually 'match' alternative to aspiration, still, it would have been better to be such as to find harmony between the two on the first try. For it would be better to be proof against initial dissatisfaction with one's alternatives.

The Ds are insufficient only if none is likely enough if God tries to actualize it to lead to a situation ideally serving some divine purpose or fulfilling some all-things-considered divine desire. This would be so only if God were in some way imperfect. So perfect-being theology rules this out. If God is perfect, He must on the first try have likely enough ideal satisfaction to hand. One might wonder whether despite this, God might have a higher-order desire or purpose, to want more than all His initial wants want, or frame a further purpose than He initially did. But if He did, either He would no matter what He wanted or purposed, or His higher-order want/purpose would have a specific motivation which could be satisfied, and so there could be an end to additions to God's wants/purposes. On the first, no totality of wants/purposes, finite or infinite, could be all of God's wants/purposes—there would always have to be more than *those*. This would deny God any determinate totality of wants and purposes. I see no reason to accept this. If there is some specific motive for an addition, it could be met with a single addition to an initial Bang, of further fully determinate possibilities. It would be simply incompetent of Him to have a second chance to assure there is a fully determinate way for it all to satisfy Him and not manage it. So we should at worst see the Bang as fully determinate in all respects, not partly general, but always consisting of two parts, one of which presupposes some form of dissatisfaction with the other. It is in God to have had other Bangs, but none are in fact possible.

On (iii): Value

In (iii), states of affairs contain good-making or bad-making features independent of divine choice. God's thinking up what He did was not a matter of choice, as we have seen, so their contents are not a matter of divine choice.[11]

---

[11] But it is not the case that their having these contents 'just happened'. It is of God's nature to think up other things. He *produces* what He comes up with, rather than having it just 'happen' to Him. His nature constrains what He comes up with. Its content accords fully with His nature and any preferences that bear on His conceiving activity. God conceives this content in light of His knowledge of His nature, preferences, purposes and desires. Because this is so and He is perfect, it is such as ideally to satisfy His purposes and desires. To the extent that He has 'given' material to take account of, He does so. Beyond that, though,

God's nature is also not a matter of His choice. As I see it, states of affairs' contents and God's nature suffice to determine what is good- or bad-making in them: as I have suggested, given the nature of God and (say) a character-trait, it is determinate that it is good, indifferent, or evil, and it is not a coherent supposition that it be otherwise.[12] If this is true, then, they have their value features independent of divine choice. But I cannot give my full story about moral value here, or discuss other forms of value at all.

On (iv): Value and Divine Attitudes

Turning to (iv), as He is perfectly wise and good, God's approval and disapproval perfectly track states of affairs' valuable or disvaluable features. With perhaps one exception, to be discussed shortly, God will approve of things' being as He imagines in the ways (moral, aesthetic, and so on) and to the extent that the states of affairs would be good, and disapprove of them in the ways and to the extent that they would be bad. One way a state of affairs can be extrinsically good is by satisfying a morally licit preference or taste; thus God will approve of things which satisfy His preferences or tastes, because they do, even if they are intrinsically value-neutral (IN).[13] If situations are evaluatively complex (involving, for example, first-order evils that enable second-order goods), God will have a correspondingly complex attitude. If a state of affairs is IN and such that God has no relevant taste or preference, but is part of states of affairs which are not IN and neutral relative to His preferences/tastes, God will approve or disapprove of those, and so approve or disapprove of the IN one insofar as it is part of these other states of affairs. Perhaps such IN states of affairs have extrinsic value due to their inclusion in these other states of affairs.

The hard case would be an entire IN possible world neutral with respect to God's preferences/tastes, as possible worlds are not parts of larger possible

---

there is irreducible creativity. He just does think as He does. It is not clear to me that our own mental operations ever involve anything quite like this. But there is at least a parallel for this lack of parallel. All our making is out of other things; God can make things out of nothing. If all our conceiving is a matter of making new content out of old, then God's differs similarly—He can think things up out of no prior content. A theist who wanted to object to the creativity of God's thinking would have to take care not thereby to impugn His ability to bring matter to be *ex nihilo* too. But it is not clear to me what sort of *a priori* objection there could really be to the creativity. As we see later, it does not, for instance, leave more about the metaphysics of modality 'brute' than Platonism or possibilism. And these are the serious rivals for accounts of from-eternity modal truth. To say that at the Big Bang, the principle of non-contradiction was true because a few billion years thence there would be speakers who recognized it deserves an incredulous stare, and even if all created powers were in some inchoate way within the Bang singularity, as noted earlier, created powers do not give us enough possibility—and their being what they are and our being as we are are on these stories just as brute as the singularity's existing and containing what it does.

[12] I earlier compared the relations involved to resemblance. Given two humans, it is not in God to have them not resemble *qua* human; He cannot make it a coherent situation that they both be human and yet not be alike *qua* human. He has no control over what His nature is, and by nature He resembles Himself perfectly. So what resemblance is and how it works are matters He cannot affect.

[13] A perfectly good and wise being will have no taste for the morally bad.

states of affairs. But we have no strong reason to think there are any. For one thing, we know little of God's preferences, save insofar as these track value and disvalue. It may seem plausible that a world could be neutral in value, but the only thing we really have much basis for a belief about is that a world could be IN. More precisely, we may have reason to think that a world's *non-divine portion* could be IN. An *overall* IN world would be one in which the intrinsic value God realizes was precisely offset by the intrinsic disvalue of the rest. But God is a good than which no greater is possible. To offset this, the rest would have to bring as much evil to a world as God does good. Plausibly a morally perfect God would not let non-divine world-portions so bad be possible, if it is up to Him; if He would not, there are no overall IN worlds. Instead, IN non-divine world-portions are parts of overall good worlds, tipped to the good side by God's presence. It does not strain credulity to suppose God to approve of them as part of such worlds—or disapprove of them, as not achieving anything relative to His purposes, which would perhaps in any non-deity-containing world include the realizing of some positive overall intrinsic value among non-deities. We need not decide which. It is enough to have reason to say that God may well have an attitude to these.

We can be unclear about whether or how much to approve of something, because we do not understand it, its consequences, the relevant standards or our own reactions fully, or we understand all this well enough but just do not apply it properly, or are 'processing' some of it, etc. A perfect mind suffers no such defects. God always has a perfectly definite degree of approval or disapproval toward every state of affairs, and knows what it is. (Neither approving nor disapproving is one such degree, a 'neutral' setting along a continuous scale.) God's attitudes will be exactly proportioned to any exact, determinate good- or bad-making properties in a state of affairs,[14] and perfectly grasped. So if the value-making properties yield sharp cutoffs—for example, if any state of affairs involving $\geq n$ units of F is good and any involving less than n is not—there will be a parallel sharp cutoff in where God has what attitude. Any increase of goodness, however small, up to or beyond some cutoff point, will make the difference about approval.

Suppose now that some states of affairs would be evaluatively vague, falling somewhere between (say) being clearly/determinately bad and being clearly/determinately neutral. What to say about God's attitudes will then depend on what the true theory of vagueness is. If a theory of vagueness involving sharp cutoffs is true, God's attitudes will (I submit) involve sharp cutoffs. On epistemicism,[15] for instance, such cutoffs exist—there is a last amount of F at which a state of affairs is bad or a first at which it is not—but the vagueness of these states of affairs' value is due to cutoff points being unknowable for us. What makes them unknowable to us may not do so for

---

[14] Including extrinsic ones—for example, how they map onto His preferences.
[15] For which see Timothy Williamson, *Vagueness* (London: Routledge, 1994).

Him. If it does not, His attitude will have a sharp cutoff. If the cutoff is unknowable to Him as to us,[16] it will be as if a theory of vagueness not generating sharp cutoffs is true.

In this case God would approve and disapprove consistently. For God cannot have irrational attitudes, and it would be irrational to (say) morally disapprove of a state of affairs for the sole reason that it has or contains (say) a moral bad-making quality F to degree n but not morally disapprove of one which also has/contains F to degree n and has/contains no other relevant attribute. So His rationality would enforce consistency. Thus He would approve and disapprove as if following at least some intuitive rules—for example, 'morally disapprove of all states of affairs with n degree Fness and no other attribute relevant to moral attitude.'[17] I suspect that God's rationality would further constrain His attitudes. It seems to me irrational morally to disapprove of something just for being F-bad to a certain degree but morally to approve of it just for being F-worse, or morally disapprove of it more just for being less F-bad. Of course, one can imagine reasons to disapprove more of something which is less F-bad—perhaps, for example, some further sort of badness supervenes on certain precise degrees of F-badness—but in such cases one would not be disapproving more *just* because the situation has a certain (lesser) precise degree of F-badness. If this is correct, it yields a stronger sense in which a perfectly rational God would approve and disapprove as if following intuitive rules, and consistently.[18]

To explore the case of vagueness without sharp cutoffs, let us think of being bad and being neutral as lying along a continuous scale of some quantity. Where the amount of that quantity associated with a state of affairs is low enough, it is bad, where it is sufficiently higher it is neutral, and on present assumptions, in part of the scale the amount is neither clearly and definitely low enough nor clearly and definitely sufficiently higher. (These areas' boundaries raise hard questions, but for present purposes we can ignore them.) I will deal only with approval or disapproval precisely in respect of that quantity, avoiding any intrusion of other reasons to take an attitude to a

---

[16] In which case the thesis that He is omniscient will have to be parsed rather as omnipotence is: not in terms of knowing everything, but in terms of knowing all that is knowable, or some suitably large part of that.

[17] Strictly, any pattern of action is in accord with *some* rule, if only one of the form 'First do A, then do B...' But these latter are unintuitive rules.

[18] Let me note one other facet of God's rationality: His permissions come out practically consistent. That is, He never at once unconditionally permits that P and unconditionally prevents that P. If God unconditionally permits S, God adds S to the stock of causally possible states of affairs. If God unconditionally prevents S, He subtracts it from that stock. If He succeeds at the one, He fails at the other, just because of the natures of the tasks (which His nature determines). So nothing comes out both permitted and prevented. Further, it would be irrational for God to try both at once, if He meant simply to succeed at both, because He could not succeed at both and as omniscient would know this. Thus if God is perfectly rational and omniscient, He does not try both with this intention. If He ever does try both, it is with some further intent the attempts serve jointly.

state of affairs: once we have the simplest case clear, more complex ones can be treated on its basis.

At every point along this scale, God must either have or lack an attitude of (some degree of) disapproval. Presumably He will disapprove in the clearly bad region of the scale and *ceteris paribus* not disapprove in the clearly neutral part. (The reason for the qualification emerges shortly.) If there is a sharp cutoff between bad and neutral, the scale is continuous and His disapproval tracks the value of states of affairs, there will be a last point at which He disapproves or a first at which He does not, a sharp cutoff. If there is no sharp bad/neutral cutoff, the facts at the bad/neutral border are vague, and so if God's attitudes track the facts, they will be as the correct no-sharp-cutoff theory of vagueness dictates. Now in the clearly/determinately bad region of the scale, states of affairs get a '1' for badness. In the clearly/determinately non-bad part they get a '0'. The question of what to say about the vague zone between can be put as that of how the badness-value fares between 0 and 1. Intuitively, there are two possibilities: maybe if shades continuously downward from 1 to 0, or maybe there is just no value in the in-between. In the former case, the degree to which a state of affairs is bad continuously decreases. This has been developed formally as the view that the degree to which 'it is bad' is true decreases.[19]

If a degree-of-truth theory is correct, then while there is no sharp cutoff between the (degree-1) bad and the (degree-0-badness, degree-1) neutral, 'it is bad' and 'it is neutral' have precise degrees of truth if the case is not degree-1 bad or degree-1 neutral. Presumably corresponding to this there will be some precise divine attitude(s?) appropriate to it. It will be precise to what degree God has an attitude, to what degree it is an attitude of a given sort, and what degree of the attitude is in question if it is degreed: on degree-of-truth theories, vagueness turns out to be precision involving degrees other than 1 and 0. As long as the state of affairs has some degree of badness, God must have an attitude involving some degree of disapproval. Neutrality purely in itself would presumably elicit no attitude. One can imagine approving of it in contrast to badness, e.g. where an improvement is being noted, or disapproving in contrast to goodness, where this is a decline, but in these cases one is reacting to a contrast and a process of change in addition to the pure, simple neutrality involved—and so these are factors extraneous to the maximally simple case we want to consider.[20] On degree-of-truth theories, then, we would have consistency, an intuitive rule and sharpness of cutoff for every degree of truth.

Finally, if a theory of vagueness involving truth-value gaps is correct, then in the in-between zone 'it is bad' and 'it is neutral' are neither true nor false (to any degree). If that is so, there is nothing to elicit the disapproval appropriate to

[19] See, for example, Nicholas J. J. Smith, *Vagueness and Degrees of Truth* (Oxford: Oxford University Press, 2008).

[20] I earlier noted the possibility that, for example, the absence of bad-making features be a good-making feature. I am assuming that this is not so, but if it were so, it would not be hard to modify my account in light of that. So for present purposes I make the simpler assumption.

badness. The lack of attitude appropriate to neutrality in itself is not an elicited response—it is what we get when no response is elicited. In this case there is nothing to elicit approval or disapproval, and accordingly a perfectly rational being will have no attitude—which is itself a non-vague state of affairs. Further, if the scale running from badness through neutrality is continuous, there will be a first point at which God has no attitude or a last at which He has one, however determined. His rational requirement of consistency would then come in to effectively generate a sharp cutoff even though there is nothing in the facts corresponding to it. So it seems to me that no matter what the right story about vagueness, God's response (or lack of it) will not involve any vagueness of attitude, and will involve sharp cutoffs, consistency, and the appearance of following an intuitive rule. This is a reasonable picture of single sorts of value and of attitudes, insofar as they track them. God's reactions to complex patterns of value will be a function of His reactions to single sorts of value and His reactions to and preferences about mixes. Again, He will have to react to these consistently and in accord with an intuitive rule.

From Attitude to Motivation

God disapproves or does not. Perhaps God's nature or preferences provide a sharp cutoff point—a degree of disapproval n such that if He disapproves to that or a greater degree He simply reacts and prevents, and otherwise not. Or perhaps the causal story runs via His knowledge that He disapproves; God knows that He disapproves to degree n + 1 and that His cutoff is n and this motivates a choice to prevent. But suppose, on the other hand, that there were no sharp cutoff about how much or what kind of disapproval God needs to motivate prevention, or that though sharp cutoffs exist, God's disapproval (which varies continuously in intensity) was not clearly and determinately on either side of them. Still, if He does not prevent, God permits, and He knows this. So however He decides such vague intermediate cases, He will decide them, knowingly, if only by default. Again, He will have to do so in accord with an intuitive rule which imposes a sharp cutoff. The remaining question concerns the clearly, definitely, intrinsically and extrinsically neutral, if such there be. Again, there must be a decision on these. There is no basis for one: God definitely neither approves nor disapproves. Presumably God treats them all alike, lacking as He does any basis for treating them differently. One way to do so would be to assign them all the same status. Another would be to in effect flip a coin for each[21]—that is, make an equally arbitrary decision about each. If He does, perhaps He permits some and prevents others.

---

[21] I briefly note questions about divine coin-flips later.

From Motivation to Decision

Either God is motivated to prevent, or He is motivated to permit.[22] Let us now ask whether, if God has enough motivation, He must at once *decide* to prevent or permit: can God's decisions be delayed? He needs no time to process information and form reactions. Perfect processing and reacting would take none. So He will by nature take none unless His equipment misfires or He decides to do so. There can be no misfire to generate a delay. So He could not decide, or delay decision, or suspend judgment, only if He decided to do so. But what He has in mind and has not yet prevented, He has permitted. He knows this, before the Bang, just by grasping what is naturally in Him to do. So a decision to take unneeded processing time, or otherwise avoid decision, would knowingly decide to permit, at least temporarily: delay could not be *just* delay. If His equipment cannot delay a decision and He cannot successfully decide not to decide, neither His nature nor His will can keep Him from moving from motivation to decision. By His nature God cannot delay decision.

From Decision to Implementation

Once God decides, the implementing of His decision cannot be delayed. If He is atemporal, this is clear: there can be no temporal separation between His decision and its implementation. But the same holds if He is temporal. I argue this first about permission, then about prevention. In what follows, 'S' is a dummy name for some state of affairs not involving a date; where I want to consider dated states of affairs, I use 'S at t'. If S includes modal content, that is to be cashed out in terms of my eventual account of modal truthmakers. So we can ignore complications due to modality. If time does not 'pass,' and if past, present, and future states of affairs are all alike real, S will be fully describable without using tensed language and we need only consider permissions of tenseless S. If time 'passes,' as e.g. if future or past states of affairs are unreal, S may not be fully describable without tense, and we must consider permission and prevention of the irreducibly tensed.

If time is tensed and God is temporal, He can permit or prevent what is present or future not the past. A time-traveler to the past could permit/prevent only the *then*-present or -future. A Mafioso may let a henchman make it the case that Fat Tony *was* a stoolie, but that is just a way to let him end a present existence. I can prevent that Spot was a dog only if that is a way to continue Spot's present or prevent his future existence. These

---

[22] Noting the wiggle in neutral cases, perhaps what is directly motivated is just some arbitrary decision or other, which turns out to be prevention or permission.

are only on the surface past-directed. As to permitting or preventing what is tenseless, one sort of tenselessness is just a disjunction of tenses: tenselessly S iff S is or was or will be the case. Such tenseless Ss do not require separate consideration. Another sort is more radically tenseless: involving tense not even disjunctively. If there are such states of affairs, they do or do not include dates. Dated radically tenseless states of affairs can be prevented or permitted only if the dates are present or future. If they do not include dates, radically tenseless states of affairs may be parasitically temporal: it is true that Socrates be bald (call this a radically tenseless construction, for discussion's sake) iff he is, was, or will be bald. Parasitically temporal states of affairs can be prevented or permitted only if the times on which they are parasites are present or future. If neither dated nor parasitically temporal, these states of affairs are atemporal. If a temporal being prevents or permits something atemporal, the effect is 'in the atemporal realm': atemporally, there are or are not certain causal possibilities. There can be no temporal separation between a temporal event and an atemporal effect. So if a temporal God can permit or prevent such states of affairs, there can be no delay between His decision to do so and its being atemporally implemented. For a temporal God in passing time, then, we need consider only present- or future-tensed Ss.[23]

I deal first with permission. There are these sorts of case to consider:

1. God has not previously prevented S and God permits S.
2. God has not previously prevented S at t and God permits S at t.
3. God has previously prevented S, permanently, and then God permits S.
4. God has previously prevented S at t, permanently, and then God permits S at t.
5. God has previously prevented S, impermanently, and then God permits S.
6. God has previously prevented S at t, impermanently, and then God permits S at t.

In each case, I now argue, even if God is temporal, God's decision is implemented without delay.

Type 1: The Simplest Case

Deciding to permit S is deciding that S is to be causally possible. If God so decides and has not previously prevented S, then as He is perfectly rational and self-aware, He does nothing then or later to prevent S, including letting

---

[23] If in 'S at t' we take 'S' to name a future-tensed state of affairs, then there are two ways to read 'S at t either as in 'At t it will be the case that Spot is a dog' or as in 'It will be the case that Spot is a dog at t.' Read it the first way. The second makes the tense a matter of how the permission relates to the state of affairs rather than part of the state of affairs' content.

other things prevent S. Now it is compatible with permitting S to prevent S at t. God can both let Boots be a cat and prevent Boots' being a cat this year, as long as Boots' cathood has His go-ahead for some other time. But if God decides to permit S, He decides to not Himself prevent or let other things prevent for every t that S obtain at t. I have argued that once God decides to prevent S, a condition is in place which will infallibly block S. If that is so, then at that point, not later, S is prevented: it is *then* true that no still-open causal path leads to S. Similarly, if at t God decides to permit S, then there is in place as of t a condition which guarantees that for some period there is no S-preventing condition. Permission prevents prevention (for the period for which permission is issued).[24] So if prevention is instantly implemented, so is permission. It is at t guaranteed that there is at some time some open causal path to S.

If S is of a sort to come about without cause, then *per* (CAUSAL POSS), to render S causally possible God need only think S up and not prevent S—as He does if He decides to permit S. So God's decision is instantly implemented—S *is* permitted—because He need do nothing for it to be so, beyond deciding to permit and so not prevent. If S requires a cause and God decides that S is to be causally possible, either S is of a sort for God to bring about alone, or the required cause(s) include some other item.

Suppose first that S is of a sort for God to bring about alone. Then God decides that S is to be causally possible only if it is in Him to both have His nature and have the power to bring S about. So God so decides only if (so to speak) S gets past His natural filters for the morally impermissible, the contralogical, and so on. That given, once God thinks S up and does not prevent it, His not preventing S gives Him a chance to bring S about. If God thinks S up at the Bang, there is then nothing created to limit His opportunities. On generalism, God may acquire chances only after the Bang: He intends to create someone of just my sort, He winds up with me, and only once I exist has He a chance to amuse me (not just someone just like me). But apart from this, nothing created limits the opportunities of a God who can do miracles. Only His own prior decisions limit His chances (suppose, say, that He has promised not to amuse me). But if God has not previously prevented S, He has not removed His opportunity to bring S about, for removing it would prevent His doing so. So He still has His chance.[25] Further, even if S is future-tensed, once God conceives S and decides not to prevent it, He has the power to give Himself the power to bring S about. So this case falls under (d) of

---

[24] If God's permission indeed prevents prevention, then if (as I later argue) where there is prevention we can introduce a '$\Box\neg$', where there is permission we can also introduce a '$\Box\neg\Box\neg$' and so a '$\Box\Diamond$'. And so if necessarily, for every possibility there is a divine permission, we have that $\Diamond P \rightarrow \Box\Diamond P$: mine is an S5 modal metaphysics. I argue later that this is indeed the case.

[25] We are dealing with undated S here, and so we need not consider cases in which God first has the concept of me in (say) 1956 and then thinks it up that I exist in 1955—something it seems He has conceived, not prevented, but not acquired the chance to bring about.

(CAUSAL POSS). And so again God's decision—in this case, not to prevent S—instantly effects it that S is causally possible.[26]

If S requires a cause other than God and God has not conceived one, that lack prevents S's coming about. We are discussing cases in which God has not previously prevented S. So if S requires a cause, God decides to permit S, and the case is type-1, God has in mind a suitable cause. He also has not prevented the cause's existing. For if He had, He would have previously prevented S, and so the case would not be type-1. By not preventing the cause's existing, He gives Himself the chance to bring it to be. (Points from the last paragraph apply here.) Further, with the cause in mind, He has the power to give Himself the power to bring the cause to be. So God has the power and chance to cause there to be something else to make its contribution to S, as well as bring about any other circumstances needed. Thus He has the chance to give Himself the chance to bring S to be, and so has the latter chance. He also has the power and chance to give Himself the power to cause that other cause to be and the power to make His own contribution to S. So He has the (intrinsic) power to have the (extrinsic[27]) power to bring S to be. This case too, then, comes under (d) of (CAUSAL POSS). So here too we have instant implementation.

Type 2: Permitting Dated S

Under type 2 there are four cases to consider: where the object of permission is of the form S at t, S might be present- or future-tensed, and t might be present or future. The present/present case differs only verbally from simple permission of an undated present-tense S: both effect just that it is now permitted that S now occur. Consider next permitting present-tensed S at future t—for example, that Obama is President at a future t. This renders it permitted that Obama will be President at t; it differs only verbally from permission of a future-tensed state of affairs at a future t. If S is future-tensed and t is the present time, there is only a verbal difference from simple permission of a future-tensed S. As to the future/future case, necessarily, at future t it will be the case that P just if now it will be the case that P, and so there is really only a verbal difference from the future/present-t case, and

---

[26] If S is dateless and present-tensed, one might raise this problem: in 'Rover is a dog', the present-tensed 'is' semantically involves a particular time, which is present. God can only bring it about that Rover is a dog for times later than His first conceiving this—and so if the Bang is at time's first instant, He lacks the opportunity to bring this about *then*. I reply that the presumption that what causes must make its contribution before the effect occurs is rooted in the physical fact that causal signals physically must have a finite velocity as they pass from a physical cause to a physical effect. There is no reason to suppose that it applies to a non-physical cause acting by non-physical means. If God conceives that Rover is a dog, He can as He first conceives it will that it be so—and His will takes no time to have an impact.

[27] If S requires the co-operation of another cause, God has the all-things-considered power to bring S about only if the other cause exists and is able to act. So the all-things-considered power includes a divine intrinsic power but is overall extrinsic.

so from simple permission of a future-tensed S. So dated cases cause no additional worries for the instant implementation thesis. If S is dated to a future t, one might wonder if God might permit S at t now but gain the chance to bring S about only later. I reply that as noted earlier, if one has a chance to have a chance to bring S at t about, one has a chance to bring S at t about. As long as God has not previously prevented and does not presently prevent S at t, He has at least the chance to give Himself the chance—and so has the chance.

Types 3 and 4: Previous Permanent Prevention

If God has already permanently prevented S, He knows it. It would be imperfectly rational to know this and yet decide to permit S.[28] For if what God has done is prevent permanently, S *is* permanently prevented. If God could still bring it about that S is permitted, S would not already have been permanently prevented. The permanence of the prevention would depend on future decisions God might or might not yet take. Its permanence (or not) would be determined later. It would not be the case that God had *already* brought it about that the prevention is permanent, unless He had already made the relevant decisions—in which case, again, it is no longer possible to permit S. So if God has permanently prevented S, God knows that He can no longer permit S, and being rational would not will to do so.[29] God decides to permit S only if He has not already permanently prevented S. As nothing in this reasoning changes if we speak instead of S at t, type 4 needs no discussion.

Types 5 and 6: Previous Impermanent Prevention

Suppose now that God has already prevented S (or S at t) impermanently. He must do so either without or with a definite end-point. If there is a definite, settled endpoint t* to the period of prevention, the case is like that of permanent prevention. If God has already brought it about that S is prevented till t*, rather than its being the case that one must wait till t* to see whether it turns out that S was prevented till then, then not even God can permit S for any earlier time. God knows this and so does not try. So again we have no challenge to the instant-implementation thesis.

---

[28] That this is perfectly rational is not up to Him. God's nature determines what is and is not perfectly rational. This is an instance of Chapter 13's approach to *Euthyphro*-type questions, which seems to me on independent grounds the best sort of move wherever what norms are to be is in question.

[29] This is not to say that God by His earlier will gave up His omnipotence. He remains able to bring about (say) all that absolutely-can be brought about then. It is just that certain things no longer can be brought about (so S. Thomae Aquinatis, *Summa Thealogiae* (Ottawa: Studii Generalis, 1941), Ia 25, 4 *ad* 2).

Suppose finally that God has already prevented S (or S at t) impermanently but without definite end-point to its being prevented. God still has the opportunity to bring S about at once, for this sort of impermanent prevention can be overruled at any point. So too, God has power and opportunity to give Himself the power to bring S about or give it to someone else; this sort of prevention does not entail having given it up. So S is causally possible. S can occur at any later time. If this is correct, there really is no prevention here at all, and this case dissolves. Again, the instant-implementation thesis survives.

Delayed Permission?

One might wonder whether God could decide at t_1 that S will be permitted at t_2, where $t_2 > t_1$. Here there are three cases to consider: God might have already prevented S, or already permitted S (thus willing just to continue the *status quo*), or have done neither. But I discuss just one; the others do not relevantly differ.

Suppose that God prevented S before t_1. One might think that if at t_1 He only willed that S be permitted at t_2, He would not at t_1 have permitted S. But what God wills at t_1 is that S be causally possible at t_2. For the simplest case, suppose what He wills is to Himself have at t_2 the power and opportunity to bring S about. Then at t_1 He has the chance to have the chance to bring S about: in fact, He takes it. So *per* earlier argument, He has the chance (though it is not yet time to use it). Further, at t_1 He has the power to have the power to bring S about before He has lost that chance: in fact He uses that power by willing that He have the power at t_2. So *per* (b) of (CAUSAL POSS), S is causally possible at t_1 because God wills it to be so at t_2, though it is not yet time to act on that possibility (if He chooses). Once again we have instant implementation. This should not surprise. What is permitted for a particular time is permitted *simpliciter*. It is causally possible—among the things that can come about—and it is true as of the time permission is given that it is among the things that can come about. If S at t_2 is now permitted, it is now permitted that S be the case (at t_2), though it is not permitted that S be the case now. This suggests that there being a definite temporary period of prevention of S really amounts to this: for every time $t^* \leq t$, it is prevented that S at t^*, for some times $t^{**} > t$ it is permitted that S at t^{**}, and *simpliciter* S is permitted, since there are times at which it is permitted to occur. Thus if God decides to permit S, *tout court* or for a particular time, then even if He does nothing else, He has permitted S.

If God decides to permit S later but does nothing else now about S, He permits it now, not later: His mere decision brings it about that S is not permanently prevented, what is not permanently prevented will at some time be permitted, and what will be permitted at some time is now among the things which absolutely speaking are permitted. So it would be possible to permit S only later only if He decided to permit S later and meanwhile (say, at t) prevented S. But on this scenario He cannot, though He prevents S-at-t, for He has within Him a sufficient condition for S's not being prevented which will not be overridden.

Implementing Prevention

Thus the possible cases of permission. I now take up prevention. The cases are:

1. God has not previously permitted S and God prevents S.
2. God has not previously permitted S at t and God prevents S at t.
3. God has previously permitted S, permanently, and then God prevents S.
4. God has previously permitted S at t, permanently, and then God prevents S at t.
5. God has previously permitted S, impermanently, and then God prevents S.
6. God has previously permitted S at t, impermanently, and then God prevents S at t.

Types 1 and 2 are easy. If God decides to prevent S (S at t) and does nothing else, and the decision itself does not suffice for prevention, He permits S despite His decision. So if He decides to prevent, He does not do nothing else, unless doing nothing else or the decision itself suffices for prevention. But of course, if God decides to prevent S, that itself suffices then for S to be prevented. Once He has decided this, He would do nothing that would let S come about, including letting other things bring S about: there is in place a condition that will infallibly block any attempt things make to bring S about, and so all causal pathways to S are closed—from that point on, any pathway containing events tending to promote S also contains divine counteractions that suffice to frustrate them. Types 3 and 4 and types 5 and 6 with a definite endpoint work like their permission analogues, *mutatis mutandis*. As to 5 and 6 with no definite endpoint, such previous permission leaves God as much opportunity as He ever had to prevent S (at t) and denies Him no power to do so. Here the permission is real, but does nothing to delay implementation of a prevention order. Thus God's decision to prevent is in all cases sufficient to prevent. This is so even if He must do something later to implement the decision—so too a remote cause can be causally sufficient for an effect even if there must be intermediate causes to transmit its input.

Delayed Prevention?

One might think God could if temporal decide to prevent S later, at t, permitting S in the meanwhile. But this scenario really involves three states of affairs, S, S-at-or-after-t, and S-before-t. If God decides to prevent S only later, at t, meanwhile permitting S, He permits S-before-t and also prevents S-at-or-after-t: just by making a decision He will implement infallibly (no mind-change can complicate the picture here), God has guaranteed that S-at-or-after-t does not come about. Further, God permits S by permitting S-before-t, for if among the permitted things is S-at-(t–1), then among the things permitted at t–1 is S. He has not decided to change His mind about S later. He has just prevented a related state of affairs, S-at-or-after-t.

Since implementation must be instantaneous, stages (i)–(vi) occur at once. If my arguments are sound, then, what one says about God's determining of modal status is indifferent to whether He is temporal. Either way, there is no temporal gap between any stages. Were it the case that if God is temporal, there had to be some such temporal gap, there might threaten to be a time when things' modal status was not yet decided. As there is not, that threat is averted. But even without this, unless there was a first instant of time, the threat would be averted, for then at any time, God would have gone through all the stages before then.

Alternate Preferences

Given His actual attitudes, preferences, and so on, God generates a complete set of permissions and preventions: every state of affairs attracts one or the other. Chapter 9 argued that God could have had different attitudes, preferences, and so on, from all eternity. All things considered—that is, taking in the full range of His alternatives and the reasons for choice they offered—He actually preferred a universe with humans to a universe of rocks drifting in the void, but (let us suppose) He was able to form an all-things-considered preference for the rocks instead. God 'starts' with a primitive general ability to prefer—that is, to form preferences that Φ rather than that Ψ. The Bang gives Him alternatives to preference-rank: God conceives contentful mental states and so can recruit the general ability to yield specific preferences. God actually prefers as He does. His nature also rules out some preferences—for example, for contradictions' being true to their being false or for morally inferior states of affairs, *just as such*, to morally superior.[30] For the rest, God has a general ability—for any $\Phi\Psi$, He can prefer Φ to Ψ. He also has in mind values for Φ and Ψ. These jointly constitute specific abilities to prefer (for

---

[30] 'Just as such' allows wiggle-room: *perhaps* there could be other reasons such that on the balance of all reasons, God would not prefer the morally superior.

eample) rocks to sentient life. It would not be true that for any remaining $\Phi\Psi$ He can prefer Φ to Ψ were there a remaining pair of values for $\Phi\Psi$ such that He did not have the ability to prefer the one to the other. But God's having these specific abilities just consists in His having the general ability and specific ways to apply it—that is, having contentful mental states which His nature leaves as candidates to be preferred to others and a general preference-faculty that can latch onto any of these to yield a preference. That God is able so to prefer—that He has this particular power—makes it true that He could have preferred the rocks. It is a modal truthmaker, a reality behind talk of possible worlds in which God prefers that there be only rocks.

Further Truthmakers

Now God both is able to have this all-things-considered preference and is by nature ideally rational. An ideally rational agent with an all-things-considered preference and no sufficiently strong countervailing reasons not to follow it would most likely do what it preferred to do. If God has an all-things-considered preference as He decides what to create, there plausibly cannot be sufficiently strong countervailing reasons. If the preference is all-things-considered, no other alternatives are equally attractive; other alternatives have been weighed and found wanting in reaching the all-things-considered preference. So other alternatives would not be providing sufficiently strong countervailing reasons to do otherwise. God's nature will have limited His alternatives already to the morally suitable, and moral factors about other alternatives will already have been weighed, so moral considerations will not provide them. *Per* (GSA), as He decides what to create, there is nothing else there to influence Him or constrain His decisions. So given God's nature—as ideally rational and morally delimiting—His ability to have an all-things-considered preference also makes true truths about what God would likely do if He did have that preference.

There are truths about what God might do if He preferred a rocky universe: if He did, He might make one rock, two, three . . . This is so because God has the power to bring about any of these alternatives. God has general powers to choose and to will that things be as He has chosen. God's nature and prevention rule out some candidates for choice. The rest are left as of the right sort to be chosen, and so for each, God also has the power to choose it and make it so. God's having a power to make a two-rock universe consists in His having general powers and a specific way to apply them—that is, having a contentful mental state envisioning such a universe and the ability so to yoke that state into His mental machinery as to recruit those powers and yield a volition to create one.

These specific powers are the reality behind talk of entire possible worlds in which God has other preferences and acts on them. That is, what these powers are powers to bring about is so detailed as to make true claims about entire possible histories for a universe. The Bang is *inter alia* part of God's practical thinking: God is thinking up states of affairs *inter alia* to decide what to bring about. As I have argued, God fills out His alternatives in full detail. So the content of God's powers also has full detail: if what God has in mind to prefer and choose among are fully detailed rocks-only universes, then what He might do is not just make one rock, two, three . . . but make this universe, or that, or that.

If God is timeless, all such powers are just timelessly there to truthmake these kinds of truths and so (speaking without commitment) keep the contents of possible worlds constant over time. If God is temporal, such truths remain true unless God's attitudes change. But if He is omniscient and perfectly rational, it is hard to see what could account for such a change, and so if these properties are His by nature it is hard to believe it possible. For even if His omniscience does not encompass that of the future which depends on the undetermined activities of creatures, He will have in mind the full content of what would be true if the future went the one way or the other, and so nothing relevant to forming His reactions will be missing.

Prevention, Permission, and Modality

I claim that what is secular and impossible is so because God prevents it and is disposed to—and so we can trace secular necessity to this. One may wonder what makes divine prevention the right thing to be on the ground floor of secular necessity. I answer as follows: if S is permanently prevented, we do not have to wait to see how things turn out. No matter how things go, it *will not* turn out that S obtains. Only so is the prevention (so to speak) up-front permanent. Now if no matter how things go, S will not obtain, there is no way around the condition preventing S. That is, it is no longer causally possible that S come to obtain. In no possible future branching out of the obtaining of the up-front preventing condition do we find S. In short, if S is up-front permanently prevented, then $\Box_c(S$ does not obtain). Coming at this another way, if S is up-front permanently prevented, the preventing condition will obtain or be effective for the rest of time, no matter how the world evolves— no matter what causal possibility is realized. And so

1. S is up-front permanently prevented $\rightarrow$ $\Box_c$(an S-preventing condition obtains or is effective).

This truth reflects the nature of this sort of prevention. But it is a conceptual truth that if a condition preventing S obtains or is effective, S does not obtain:

2. $\Box$(an S-preventing condition obtains or is effective $\rightarrow$ $\neg$(S obtains)).

(1) and (2) jointly entail that (S is up-front permanently prevented) → $\Box_c \neg$ (S obtains).

It is of the very nature of up-front permanent prevention, then, to bring causal necessity with it.[31] Thus up-front permanent prevention from all eternity can serve as an appropriate explanation for secular necessity, for if (as the last chapter suggested) we define absolute possibility in terms of causal possibility, then similarly we define absolute necessity in terms of causal: it is absolutely necessary that P just if it neither is, was, nor timelessly is causally possible that ¬P, or equivalently just if it always was, is, and (if applicable) timelessly is causally necessary that P.

Part of what makes divine prevention the right thing to be on the ground-floor of a metaphysics for secular absolute necessity, then, is that God is able to prevent permanently up-front with a range sufficient to embrace all secular absolute necessities, and as existing from all eternity is in a position to do so 'early enough' to account for them. Another part concerns the desirability of defining absolute in terms of causal modality. Prevention removes causal possibility, and so what it brings about directly is a causal necessity. Many philosophers have felt uneasy about taking 'broadly logical' modality as a primitive. This has (I think) been a factor in the emergence both of two-dimensional semantics as an alternative to the Plantinga/Kripke picture on which it is primitive, and of a more recent push against 'brute' necessities (which in some authors amount to those which do not reduce by way of definitions to narrow-logical necessities[32]). If one wants to avoid taking broadly logical modality as primitive but sees a use for broad-logical modality nonetheless, it is desirable to define it in other terms. Causal modalities are familiar, conceptually clear and relatively unproblematic metaphysically. (I have based them on powers taken as intrinsically modal. Those uneasy about *that* could in principle offer a reductive picture of powers, as modally flat properties, and take powers views as reductive theories of modality, assigning modal statements non-modal truthmakers.) But as we have seen, non-theistic causal-powers views do not give us enough powers to provide the full extension of absolute possibility, and it is an equivalent point that they yield more absolute necessity than is plausible. We need the full powers of omnipotence to get the extensions right here, and the simplest view involving them would site them all in one being. Again, some see promise in defining possibility and necessity in counterfactual terms.[33] To do so would provide

---

[31] The divine nature accounts for the connection between this sort of prevention and necessity. As prevention is one of God's natural abilities, the divine nature determines what it is to prevent. So the divine nature alone determines any truth about what it is to prevent. Any truth so determined comes to be absolutely necessary once the semantic requisites for truths to be necessary are in place, since it is necessary that God exist and have His nature.

[32] So, for example, Cian Dorr, 'Non-symmetric Relations', *Oxford Studies in Metaphysics* 1 (2004), 161–3.

[33] Boris Kment, 'Counterfactuals and the Analysis of Necessity', *Philosophical Perspectives* 20 (2006), 237–302.

real ontological gain, though, only if it let us eliminate possible worlds. This would press us for an alternative account of counterfactuals' truthmakers, and powers provide a natural candidate for this role—but again, we need the powers of omnipotence to make this work.

I claim too that what is secular and possible is so because God permits it or is disposed to. It is an intuitive, plausible claim that the presence of a power with a chance to act makes it possible that what the power is apt to produce obtain. Ordinarily, causal permission or prevention affect only causal, not absolute possibility, by (to speak with the Platonists) adjusting facts here below in such a way that certain worlds continue (or not) to represent paths history causally might take. At the Bang, secular states of affairs do not yet have modal status. God is composing the very worlds that will bear modal status, in the 'language' of divine powers. The worlds it is then in God to place S in (by permitting) or keep S from (by preventing) are, simply, all worlds.[34] Further, because God is then composing worlds, it is not then the case that God merely adjusts concrete things so as to allow some and not other worlds to continue to represent causal possibilities. There is no further modal framework in the backdrop. So at the Bang, causal possibility God permits just is the 'outermost' sort of possibility—it is absolute possibility. None of this implies that possibility *just is* divine causal permission, or that the modal reduces to anything non-modal. I claim only that divine causal permission is an appropriate entry-point for fully determinate secular possibility, a place for it to first appear at the roots of reality.

I have argued that necessarily, from all eternity, God either permits or prevents every from-eternity secular state of affairs. I have now added that His permitting it makes a state of affairs possible and His preventing it makes it impossible. This suffices, then, to make God responsible for all actual secular possibility and necessity. If it is *necessary* that God does this from all eternity, this is grounded on His dispositions to permit and prevent under other possible circumstances—whose possibility He actually determines, if they are secular.

---

[34] In so doing He will also determine all facts of more restricted modality.

15

MODAL REALITY

For me, talk of possible worlds is a convenient fiction. Unlike much fiction, though, we express facts in it. The facts are not much like what the talk seems to be about. I now build up a fuller picture of the facts behind talk about possible worlds.

'First' there is God, not yet having set off the Bang. At that point He can produce some creature or other—He has that power—but there is no specific creature He can produce: there is not 'yet' anything in His mind to be a candidate. So at that point God has no specific productive powers. God naturally can think, will, and know, but as it is natural to Him to think up, know and will about specific creatures, these general powers are not on their own the reality behind talk of any possible world. Given only these, things are not 'yet' as they are in any possible world (that is, behind world-talk). Then there is the Bang. This yields conceptions of secular states of affairs.

Permission of what is such as to be Produced

Once He has these in mind, God is such as to produce (or produce items able to produce) any His nature does not rule out. That is, He will have the power to do so if He decides to have it. But He has not yet decided to have such powers. Equivalently, He has not yet permitted such states of affairs, or consented to any candidates for production. Then He does. He had the power to produce. He decides to have the power to make cats in particular. Deciding produces the power. (I explain how shortly.) Once He does so, He is intrinsically able to produce cats. Nothing more is needed. He need only 'press the button' and there will be cats. God also has the opportunity to produce them. The presence of a power with an opportunity grounds a causal possibility: because there are both, a state of affairs can be brought about and so is causally possible. So possibly cats exist. Thus a decision issues a divine permission—that is, it brings it about that God has a specific all-things-considered power and so brings it about that a state of affairs is causally possible. The decision brings it about that it is possible; God's having the power makes it true that it is possible.

Here is the story of how decisions produce divine powers. God has by nature the general power G to bring about any state of affairs He decides to permit. God thinks a thought E which conceives a secular state of affairs S which is such as to be produced by God. Once He has S in mind, He decides whether to permit S, and so whether S will be within G's range. This is so even if His nature guarantees His decision. If He does not decide to permit S, S is not in G's range, for at least a while: S is not an available target for a power to bring about what God decides to permit. For a period or permanently, God cannot use G on S. So He lacks the power to bring S about. But He is still omnipotent. If He does not permit that S occur at t, it is not possible that S occur at t. And omnipotence at t is power only to do what at t is possible.[1] If God decides to permit S, He brings S within G's range. He then can use G to bring S about. So He has a specific intrinsic power to bring S about. Only God's decision gives Him this specific power. It links E and G. It sorts S as a candidate for production, causes God so to think of S, produces a 'This is a candidate' attitude to S, and so makes God ready to actualize S. So at one level, God's intrinsic power to bring S about has as constituents G, E, an event E*, in which He thinks of S as a candidate (which is really an event whose content in a particular way includes E) and an attitude to S. Given all these, plus opportunity, all He has to do is (so to speak) push the button and S obtains. I would push deeper than this level in two steps. God has G by nature. So I first suggest that God's having deity makes it true that God has G. I then eliminate deity, as argued earlier. So I say that God's power to bring S about consists of God, E, E*, and the attitude. If God includes the attitude, the power consists of God, E, and E*. If this is correct, though, it still does not reduce the modal to the non-modal. It just means that God, E, and E* are 'double-aspect.'[2]

Let us further fill in this story. Secular states of affairs may be of a sort to obtain if God produces them alone, if God produces them in cooperation with other things, or without divine input.

Secular States of Affairs that Obtain Only if God Produces Them Alone

For any secular S of a sort for God to bring about alone, from all eternity, God has the opportunity to bring S about if He has S in mind. There is nothing to

---

[1] Further, this is a self-imposed limitation, and so falls under my argument in Chapter 5.

[2] On double-aspect properties see John Heil, *From an Ontological Point of View* (New York: Oxford University Press, 2003).

limit His options. This is not happenstance. God has the GSA-property. Having it guarantees that there is nothing concrete He has not made, and so guarantees that before He decides to make, there is nothing concrete. Were there Platonic abstracta outside God—possible worlds, attributes, and so on—this would not alter that. It would just mean that something outside God determined what secular S were of a sort for Him to bring about. But I have argued that if God has the GSA-property, He also is the source of all abstracta. So from all eternity, before God acts, there is nothing abstract outside God to limit His opportunities. So the GSA-property helps provide God's opportunity here.

The only way it is in God to make causally possible an S of a sort to obtain only if God produces it alone is to make it causally possible that He produce S. One story about how He does so runs this way: God conceives S. Perhaps His nature prevents His permitting S—for example, S falls foul of His natural moral perfection. If God's nature prevents this, it prevents S's being permitted, and so prevents S. If so, once God conceives S, S is prevented—by God's nature and conceiving activity. If God's nature does not prevent S, once God conceives S, it is in God's power to give Himself the power to produce S. But then per (d) of (CAUSAL POSS), it is causally possible that S obtain. God's nature and conceiving render S causally possible. So God determines S's modal status simply by having His nature and conceiving S. This story overlooks the role of preferences. I've argued that God's nature permits Him different preferences, given a field of states of affairs to consider. If that is right, then once God conceives S, there is something His nature does not determine: He forms preferences about S. Only in light of these could He permit or prevent. But the mere having of a preference does not itself generate an action. One must decide to act in accord (or not) with one's preferences. So a divine decision must enter the story. God must decide whether S is to be causally possible.

If God permits Himself to produce S, He *ipso facto* permits S. He need do nothing else. A mere permission that S obtain, without permitting Himself to produce S, would be ineffective. This would be trying to render it causally possible that an S needing a cause obtain without rendering it causally possible that S be caused. If God permits Himself to produce S, permission the S obtain would be otiose. So I suggest that God permits this sort of S by self-permission—by permitting that He bring it about. So assuming what I've said about God's opportunities, the primal modal fact about this sort of S is that God has the (all things considered) power to or causally can bring S about. Now if S were there to stand in a converse relation, we might distinguish between its being the case that God causally can bring S about and the converse, that

CONV. S causally can be brought about by God.

But S is not there. It is not a Platonic abstract object and it is not some sort of constituent of God's power. So there is no converse-relational fact in the

picture. Rather, what makes (CONV) true is that God causally can bring
S about. That is, God's having His power makes (CONV) true. Now perhaps
(CONV) is really a conjunction, that S is causally possible and God can bring
S about. If so, (CONV) includes that S is causally possible. Or perhaps
(CONV) is an atomic predication of S, the predicate being — Rgod. If so, its
informational content includes that S is causally possible. For in telling us that
S has — Rgod it also tells us that S has — Rsomething, and where R is —
causally-can be brought about by —, S' having — Rsomething is S's— being such
that something causally can bring S about. By my earlier definition of absolute
possibility, this makes S absolutely possible. Even without that account,
I could still say that this includes S's being absolutely possible; the thought
would be that being causally possible consists in being absolutely possible and
something else, and facts about secular absolute possibility come to be as
embedded in these conjunctions. Thus God's having the power to produce
S and having the opportunity the GSA-property secures Him constitute a
from-eternity truthmaker for *possibly S obtains*. Let me note one sort of
objection that shouldn't arise here. Barry Smith writes:

> Suppose God wills that John kiss Mary now. (This) necessitates the truth
> of 'John is kissing Mary.' But God's act is not a truthmaker for this...
> Intuitively (its) truthmaker... must be part of what that judgment is
> *about*, must satisfy some relevance constraint... should fall within that
> portion of reality to which (it) corresponds... God's act falls outside
> (that).[3]

One should not in like manner object that God's power to bring it about that
John kisses Mary is not part of what *possibly John kisses Mary* is about. Smith's
objection is plausible in the case of *John kisses Mary* because we have firm
intuitions about what that claim is about, and what would make it true. We
do not have such intuitions in the possibility case. I claim that God's power is
what the judgment is about, or falls within the portion of reality to which it
corresponds. Others would say the like about an abstract state of affairs'
bearing a property of possibility, there being a property entire universes would
instantiate, or there being dispositions in members of a speaking community
(which make it true that their linguistic conventions allow this as possibly
true), and so on. None of these is part of the intuitive content of *possibly John
kisses Mary*. They are different theories about what it is for this to be possible.
The judgment is 'keyed' only to the intuitive content, and neutral on its
metaphysics.

Where I do not mention divine opportunity in other divine production
cases, take me to be treating it as I have here.

---

[3] Barry Smith, 'Truthmaker Realism', *Australasian Journal of Philosophy* 77 (1999), 278, 279.

Secular S of a Sort for God to Produce Alone, but also to Come to Obtain in Other Ways

If S is causally possible and of a sort for God to produce alone, but God lacks the power to do so, God is not omnipotent. So as God is omnipotent by nature, it is not in God to permit such an S but not let Himself so produce it. So again there is a divine self-permission, yielding a power. This yields the same sort of from-eternity truthmaker for *possibly S obtains.* If there are other ways for S to come to obtain, there will also be divine permissions that these occur.

Secular S of a Sort for God to Produce Cooperating with Other Causes

Let us first consider cases not involving created freedom or macro-physical randomness: for example, let S be that Neptune is moving around the sun. Some might say that having the chance to bring S about requires that Neptune exist. I disagree. God had the chance to bring S about from all eternity and purely of Himself. For from all eternity He had purely of Himself the chance to produce Neptune and bring about all other circumstances needed for Him to have this chance, and if one has a chance to have a chance to bring S about, one has a chance to bring S about. This approach to opportunity applies to the next two cases as well.

God is Neptune's (late-) Creator. Its existence is a deterministic consequence of the Big Bang He set off.[4] So are its initial impetus into motion and its subsequent states of motion, and so God is the sole ultimate source of these. For Neptune to move, there must be time for it to move in: I would argue that God alone provides this, but if He provides it along with others, we can treat this as we do other cases of cooperation, *mutatis mutandis.* The relevant natural laws must continue to hold: God alone accounts for this. To move, Neptune must continue to exist: God and Neptune jointly cause this. Neptune must continue to have the powers it uses in moving: God and Neptune jointly cause this. So in all of Neptune's motion, S included, God and Neptune jointly move Neptune.

However, God also causes Neptune to make its contribution to continuing to exist and have the relevant powers. So it is also true that God moves Neptune. God causes Neptune's contribution if everything macro-physical in the causal chain from the Big Bang to Neptune's beginning to make its contribution to its motion—event NB—is a deterministic consequence of God's setting off the Big Bang or some other divine effect or act. For as deterministic causation is transitive, anything that starts a deterministic causal

---

[4] This assumes that quantum randomness 'washes out' in such cases at the macro-physical level. Without this assumption I would have to re-work the case, but the additional complications would not affect my conclusions.

chain causes every event in the chain. But we can suppose, at least for example's sake, that each macro-physical event in every causal chain that affected the NB chain was of this sort. Again, God truly caused *everything* macro-physical in the NB chain only if God caused the existence of every macro-physical particular it involved. But this is so. He caused at least some of them alone. If He caused some in cooperation with others, then again we can treat this as we do cooperation generally—and as He set the Big Bang off alone and alone provided whatever it involved (singularity, quantum 'froth', or the like), all cooperative causal chains are set up by prior God-alone causation. So though God and Neptune move Neptune, God also moves Neptune *simpliciter*.

God makes it causally possible that He move Neptune around the sun. His power so to move Neptune includes power to make Neptune cooperate. So again self-permission is primary: God empowers Himself to move Neptune and *ipso facto* empowers Neptune to make its contribution. The primal modal fact here is that God causally can bring it about that God and Neptune bring S about. From this we get as above to the truths that it causally can be the case that S obtains, that God and Neptune move Neptune and that Neptune makes its contribution, and the truths that these things absolutely can be the case. So God's having (all-things-considered) power to cause all deterministic chains leading to His and Neptune's cooperating in bringing S about is an appropriate from-eternity truthmaker for the claim that possibly S. And corresponding to every move Neptune may make are divine powers so to move it.

Divine Cooperation with Created Libertarian Freedom[5]

If I act with libertarian freedom, God creates me, sustains me and my powers, provides time to act, and sustains the natural laws that let me freely will. As a result, I have the power to choose one way or another, and many continuations of history are causally possible. For every choice I may make, there is a divine power to enable and cooperate with it, and so on, by sustaining me, preserving my powers as I make it and not interfering. If God is to let me so choose, He must also let Himself cooperate. If God permits Himself so to cooperate, He must also permit me to do my bit: He cannot cooperate unless my bit is there to cooperate with.

Perhaps God makes two decisions. Perhaps He makes one, that I be able to cooperate, and this makes it possible that He do His bit. Still, any divine decision that I be able to cooperate presupposes decisions about God's own input. To have a decision to make about my ability to cooperate, God must 'first' decide to have powers to make me, sustain me, and grant me powers.

---

[5] Randomly acting causes, if any, do not differ in the relevant respects from free agents, and so I do not discuss them separately.

So it makes for a smoother picture, both here and in light of the previous three sections, to say that God also decides about my doing my bit by deciding about His own powers: that by permitting Himself to cooperate with me, He permits me to cooperate with Him. In empowering Himself to cooperate, He empowers me to cooperate with Him, a bit as in empowering Himself to move Neptune, He empowers Neptune to cooperate with Him. God's power to cooperate with me does not include power to make me cooperate. That would remove my freedom. But it includes power to make cooperating me:[6] power to sustain my every physical part in being at every point along all spatial paths traversing which is part of the physical portion of my free acts, all physical events involved, my possession of all my relevant physical powers, my soul, my possession of all relevant mental powers, and all soul-events as they occur to make up the rest of my free acts (if I have a soul),[7] and not prevent my choice. So if God gives Himself power to cooperate with me, this includes power to make cooperating me. This is a to bring it about that I cooperate, but not a power to make me cooperate, because it is a power whose use I, rather than God, determine: if I freely do act A, it is up to me, not up to God, that what God cooperates with is my doing A and the power called into play is a power to cooperate with A. If I bring it about that I cooperate with God in my doing A, I bring it about that God cooperates with me in this—though not against His will, since in deciding that I am to be free with respect to A, He gave this power over to me. Power to make cooperating me includes power to empower me to cooperate. The existence of my power to cooperate, with an appropriate opportunity (which God has the power to produce), would make it possible that I so cooperate with God as to do a particular free act. So God's having the (all-things-considered, i.e. opportunity including) power to cooperate with my free action, to make cooperating me doing *that*, is a from-eternity truthmaker for the claim that possibly I perform it. It grounds a causal possibility that it be causally possible that I so act, and causal possibility 'collapses'. So I suggest that God's decision about secular possibilities involving His input is always a matter of deciding what He might do.

Where S is such as to be caused *inter alia* by Him, God's decision gives Him a power, and His having this power is the relevant truthmaker. I say this even though thinking S up and omitting to prevent S suffices to render S possible. God from eternity had the chance to bring S about. If His nature does not rule out His giving Himself the right power—that is, it is in Him to have both His nature and this power—once He has S in mind, He has the power to give Himself the power to bring S about while still having the chance. *Via* (d) of (CAUSAL POSS), this makes S causally possible. Still, God must give Himself

---

[6] I owe this distinction to James Ross.

[7] That the causal role I sketch here really is compatible with my acting with libertarian freedom is obviously something that needs showing, but I must postpone this.

the S-power at this point. In parallel with an argument above, though God can make such S possible just by omitting to prevent them, once they are possible, He will not be omnipotent unless He can make His contribution to bringing them about. Further, one way to omit to prevent S is to give oneself power to bring S about. So we can simplify our account if we deal just in self-empowerment and not in an additional deliberate omission. I therefore suggest that God's permitting such S consists in deciding to give Himself the appropriate power.

States of Affairs Without Divine Input

God has the power to refrain from ever making things other than Himself. If He never made any, there would be none. And from eternity He had the chance to use this power, purely of Himself. If He is atemporal He still has the chance; if He is temporal He does not, but His having had it in the past yields a present possibility, *per* Chapter 13. So this power and chance make it true that possibly there never are such things—that it is possible that there be only God. That only God exist is not a secular state of affairs, but it is worth mentioning here because the possible non-existence of any creature at any time can be treated analogously.

There never being anything other than God is a negative state of affairs. If God has in mind positive states of affairs of a sort to come about with no positive divine input, perhaps there are some such that it is in Him to both have His nature and permit them (that is, some His nature does not rule out permitting). If He permits them, this too yields a causal possibility. Here permission could be just a decision not to prevent. But I think that in some cases there is more.

Suppose that wholly without cause, a quark moves. Even here, there is divine cooperation: God thinks this event up, creates and sustains the quark, holds in place the natural laws in accord with which this event occurs, provides time for it, and does not prevent it. By doing so, God does everything needed to promote it. So though there cannot be a divine power to cause this, there are divine powers to promote it. All such an event needs to be causally possible is that it be causally possible that a promoting situation obtain and God does not prevent it. God's having the power to produce a promoting situation and refrain from preventing in it renders all that, and so that motion, causally possible: if God has the power, it is causally possible that the motion be causally possible, and causal possibility 'collapses'. Again, giving Himself power can be the *way* God omits to prevent in these cases.

Consider finally something's coming to exist without God's or any causal input. There are no secular kind-properties till the Bang. So there is not prior to the Bang a property of being an uncaused aardvark hanging out in abstract logical space, to threaten God with an instance despite Him. Thus if any things can come to be without His or any causal input, they appear only because He thinks them up and does not prevent this. It is up to Him whether there can be or are such things—unless His nature (as it were) makes the decision for Him. Further, here too if the item is temporal there are promoting conditions: at a minimum the availability of time to appear in. So we can treat the temporal and wholly uncaused as we did the quark's motion. If it is possible that an atemporal item appear (exist) wholly uncaused, the story differs. If God thinks such an item up, prevents it and disposes Himself appropriately, it is not causally possible. If God thinks such an item up and does not prevent it, *per* (f) of (CAUSAL POSS), He thereby makes it causally possible.[8] The decision not to prevent brings it about that the existence is possible. But this does not tell us what makes it true that it is causally possible. *Per* earlier discussion, God has a specific power to conceive it only if He in fact does conceive it. If He conceives it and prevents it, He has not promoted its existence. If He conceives it and does not prevent it, He does everything that needs doing to promote its existence. So perhaps if God conceives such an item and does not prevent its existence, His specific power to conceive S also counts as a (utilized) power to promote its obtaining. Perhaps too His power to refrain from preventing it has or shares this role. It is not utilized if He prevents it, but, the power not to prevent it is a power to do all that is needed for it to be possible. It is power to contribute to the only promoting condition it has. If its promoting conditions obtain, it is causally possible. So in parallel with the quark-motion case, God's having the(se) power (s) is the truthmaker.

Let us now consider one more wrinkle: uncreated, unsustained non-divine things that are in some fashion co-eternal with God. Call one such item Harold. There are five sorts of case to consider: either (a) both Harold and God are temporal and exist uncaused for all of beginningless time before some arbitrary time;[9] or (b) both are temporal and have an uncaused first instant of existence at time's first instant; or (c) both are atemporal; or (d) God is atemporal and Harold temporal; or (e) Harold is atemporal and God temporal. (a) is straightforward. If time had no beginning, then at every time, there was a prior time. Thus for every time at which Harold exists without divine causal contribution, there was a prior time at which God let it so exist. Events involving Harold will also be permitted beforehand. (d) is also straightforward: God exists causally prior to any time at which Harold exists, and so things are relevantly as in (a).

---

[8] Sorting this under (f) treats the claim that something exists timelessly and without cause as 'coming true.' I think we can make sense of the notion of an atemporal event, and so do not jib at this. Those jarred by it can rephrase (f) as 'that P is the sort of thing to be the case without cause,' and so on.

[9] Should Harold first be uncaused, then be caused, then be uncaused for another period, nothing essential would differ.

I suspect that (b) is not possible, as an eternal being cannot have a first instant of existence. I also suspect that (c) and (e) are not possible, because I think the only plausible non-divine candidates for uncreated atemporal existence are certain abstract entities I argue later not to exist. If (b), (c), and (e) are possible, though, I suggest the following (which is also a reserve strategy for the other variations on Harold). God exists necessarily. Thus uncreated coeternal Harold possibly exists only if possibly God eternally co-exists with it. That in God which makes it true that possibly He eternally co-exists with Harold makes it true that possibly Harold eternally co-exists with God. So God's eternally thinking Harold up and not preventing its existence can truthmake *possibly Harold exists* even if God's permission is in no sense before Harold's existence. God is what is deepest in reality. His existence is the most basic fact of all. So anything else can exist only if its existing is compatible with the basic fact—God's existence—around which the rest of reality must fit. For things such as to exist uncaused, this compatibility, which is due to that in God which makes it true that possibly He eternally co-exists with uncaused Harold, is all it takes for them to be possible. However, I argue below that this sort of thing is not in fact possible: that (GSA) is in fact necessary.

I have sketched truthmakers for secular possibility-claims and how God brings it about that secular states of affairs are possible. On my account, then, divine decisions (issuing permissions) result in are the reality behind talk of the contingent secular portion of each possible world. The facts we express by talk of the contingent secular portion of a possible world W are these. God has given Himself powers: to cause alone what He would cause alone were there such a world as W and were it actualized, in the sequence He would cause it, and to cooperate with creatures just as He would were W actualized. If W would involve contingent uncaused events or existences, God has given Himself powers to produce their promoting conditions just when/where they would occur were W actualized and not prevented (not disposed Himself to prevent, no matter what) their occurring uncaused just as they would were W actualized; if atemporal existences are involved He has thought them up and not prevented them (or appropriately disposed Himself). His having these powers (plus that not to prevent) makes it causally possible that things be just as they would in W's contingent secular portion. If W would not involve created libertarian free will or randomness, God has also given Himself the power so to use other powers as to make things be just as they would in W's contingent secular portion. If W would involve either, God has given Himself the power so to use other powers as to make things be just as they would in that of W's contingent secular part that does not depend on either, and make there be powers able to bring about just what they would in all of W that does depend on these.

I now turn to necessity and divine prevention.

Divine Prevention

God brings it about in the Bang that there 'are' secular cases of general contra-mathematical and contra-logical propositions. God prevents these being true just by thinking up certain logical operators as He does.[10] Doing so guarantees that when He sets the full reality behind talk of possible worlds, He does not give Himself power to make them true (that is, within the fiction of worlds, these come out non-true in all possible worlds). He so thinks by nature, and so prior in the order of explanation to setting these contents. But because He so thinks, the general propositions and their secular cases come out impossible once He does so. What is not so due to God's nature cannot be so, as it is not in God to permit that He not have His nature.

Within the fiction of worlds, the impossibility of some P consists in there being possible worlds and P being true in none of them. So it consists in there being some worlds and the absence of a world to make it true that $\Diamond P$. (On some accounts, this absence would consist partly in the absence of a proposition or state of affairs from those worlds.) This is also the story for the necessity that $\neg P$, of course. For every world in the fiction there is a divine 'world-power'—a power so to use powers of smaller scope as to make God's contribution to a world's being actual. If God's having His nature ultimately explains a proposition's truth-value, for that truth-value V to be necessary is for it to be the case that God has world-power 1 and use of 1 would leave it the case that God has His nature and so leave V as it is, God has world-power 2 and use of 2 would do the same, and so on, and there are no world-powers other than 1, 2, and so on. Here a necessity consists in God's having world-powers of a specific character and the absence of some power(s) and is explained partly by His omission to give Himself these. If God's nature does not figure in the explanation of P's truth-value, for that truth-value to be necessary (if it is) is for it to be the case that for every world-power W, W is used $\supset$ W recruits God's power to bring it about that P. That is, it is for it to be the case that W_1 is used $\supset$ W_1 recruits . . . and W_2 is used $\supset$ W_2 recruits . . . , and so on, and there are no world-powers other than W_1, W_2, and so on. So it consists in God's having some world-powers of a specific character and the absence of some power(s) and is explained partly by His omission to give Himself these.

Chapter 16 deals with how God prevents secular contra-essentials (for example, that Socrates be a fish) and so explains essentialist necessities. But for now suppose that God thinks up a secular non-logical or non–mathematical state of affairs S, prefers and so decides to prevent S. The prevention brings it about that it is not causally possible that S come about. This might be by removing the opportunity for it to do so. Suppose too that God's alternative

---

[10] Given other logical operators there are contingent logical truths. See Edward Zalta, 'Logical and Analytic Truths That Are Not Necessary', *Journal of Philosophy* 85 (1988), 57–74.

preferences so form that every set of preferences He has the power to adopt includes a preference to prevent S. Then He is also disposed to prevent S no matter what His preferences, and this brings it about that there cannot be opportunity for S to come about. So this brings it about that no world-power's use would bring S about. It explains the lack of a certain sort of world-power. In fact, God might prevent simply by not giving Himself a certain sort of intrinsic world-power. Preventions and dispositions to prevent bring it about that impossibility-claims are true: that God has no all-things-considered power to bring S about, would not have one no matter what, and S's coming about by other means is and would no matter what be prevented. If S is such as to come about only with some divine input, it suffices to prevent S to prevent God's having the power to make His contribution. If S is such as to come about without divine input, God's prevention must have broader scope. It must, for example, assure that S does not come about wholly without cause.

God is Inescapable

It might seem odd to bring God into all this, but it should not. Consider a modal question about a state of affairs not such as to obtain only if God alone produces it.[11] Here is a cat on a mat. Can it leave the mat? It is strong enough. The laws would let it. But these do not suffice to give the cat the all-things-considered power to do so. All-things-considered power to leave the mat is not an intrinsic property of the cat. The cat has it only if there is space beyond the mat into which it can move, and so only given the right external circumstances. That

CM. the cat can leave the mat

mentions only the cat and the mat. So if we think only of what it explicitly mentions, we incompletely describe the relevant state of affairs. We ignore the state of things beyond cat and mat which partly constitutes the cat's having that power. A deeper grasp, which made explicit what it is to leave, would read (CM) along the lines 'The cat can move from the mat to some other place.' At a deeper level, (CM) tells us there are or can be places beyond the mat to which the cat can move. A second thing also makes the cat's all-things-considered power to leave extrinsic: it depends on the cat's causal as well as spatial circumstances. Were a much faster, stronger cat watching it, intent on pinning it to the mat, the cat could not leave the mat unless the other cat could slip up. So a deeper understanding of (CM) also brings in an implicit causal picture, along the lines of 'Nothing is preventing the cat from leaving

---

[11] I assume here that occasionalism is false.

the mat, and so the cat can move. . . . ' Thus God enters the picture, though not explicitly, for the cat cannot leave the mat unless God lets it. If God willed that the cat stay on the mat, the cat could not leave. If (CM) carries information about the cat's causal environment, then if God is part of that causal environment, He is involved in (CM)'s truth, though His involvement is not part of the information we can get just by explicating (CM)'s obvious surface content. Just as there at least possibly being space beyond the mat partly constitutes the cat's being able to leave the mat, so divine permission to do so at least partly constitutes this, given only that God is on the scene. God's partial involvement is ineliminable, if He exists. His deeper involvement therefore should not seem that surprising.

Modal Logic

After the Bang, God forms preferences and becomes disposed to have had others instead. *Per* Chapter 9, these are preferences He could actually have had, else they do not get possible histories involving choices only these could rationalize into the picture. Libertarian-free choice as often understood provides an analogy here. If I so choose at t to do act A, then at t, it is in all respects open to me not to choose to do A. I have the power and chance not to choose A, and *per* earlier argument, I have both at t. Thus it is causally possible at t that this choice not be made. So too, at the Bang, God has the chance and power to adopt other preferences. His doing so is causally possible. So there are alternate causally possible states for reality, in which He has these preferences *ab initio*. Despite this, I now argue, there is just one set of from-eternity specific powers God might give Himself and from-eternity preventions He might effect. It is not the case that God might have done otherwise in these respects.

On my account, all possible histories have a causally first initial segment terminating in the Bang. At any point at which an undetermined event might occur, history (so to speak) branches into further possibilities: if three undetermined events might happen at that point, there are three branches. As I see it, alternate histories branch from the Bang. Once God has in mind the content the Bang gives Him, His general power to prefer is specified: He becomes able to adopt many different sets of preferences. He has the chance and power to adopt any of these. If God is timeless, then in adopting His actual preferences He is timelessly in the act of passing up His chance to adopt the others, and so He still has it: thus His doing so is causally possible. If there was a first time and God is temporal, at that instant God adopted His actual preferences and was in the act of passing up His chance to adopt others. So He then had the chance, and so His doing so was causally and is absolutely possible. If God is temporal and there was no first time, then at any time He *is* adopting these. God always has in mind all information on which He bases these. He is always occurrently considering it (so perfect being theology suggests); considering it includes taking His attitudes to it; thus He is always occurrently preference-ranking. So He always has the chance to prefer otherwise and is always passing it up, and as He always also has the power to prefer otherwise, again, His having other preferences remains causally possible.

God's forming His actual preferences begins one branch from the Bang. God also actually acquires powers to prefer differently. Once He thinks up chocolate and vanilla, His general preferring power is specified, so that He has (say) the power to prefer chocolate to vanilla and also that to prefer vanilla to chocolate. God actually prefers chocolate, let us say, but for the reasons just noted it is causally possible that He prefer vanilla. So there is also a possible history branching from the Bang in which He does so. The absolute possibilities are just those God in some preference-state makes causally possible continuations from having that state's preferences. Such a continuation continues only as long as nothing undetermined by its past happens. Branches develop branches, perhaps *ad infinitum*. All absolute possibilities branch out of some divine preference-state, as a tree of causally possible continuations. Each possible world traces one always-forward-moving path through such a tree. If God is by nature temporal and libertarian-free, each branch eventually branches out. Even in a physically deterministic world, a God who thinks freely might do different mental acts than He has, a claim made true by His having His actual powers. This is the truthmaker whether He is temporal or timeless, but if He is timeless, we cannot model the situation in terms of branches from different times at which He has different thoughts. We can instead think of a 'bunch' consisting of the physically determinist history and many complexes of mental acts God might freely do if history goes that way. Each possible world will correspond to the sum of the determinist history and one complex from the bunch.

If to be possible is to occur in a branch continuing from actual history, a way history could go, then to be possibly possible is to occur in a way history could go from a way history could go—a branch continuing from a branch continuing from actual history. If it is right to think of possible histories as broadly analogous to continuous spatial paths, this use of 'continues' is transitive. If it *is* transitive, whatever is possibly possible is in a branch continuing from actual history, and so possible: my view seems to bring the distinctive axiom of S4 with it. Now branching and continuing are based on sharing temporal parts. Histories have temporal parts in common: in many ways things can go, I am writing this. Histories branch after the last such part they share. One branch B_2 continues another B_1 just if B_2 is later than B_1 and either B_1 and B_2 share temporal parts or there are branches $B_3, B_4 \ldots B_n$ such that B_1 shares temporal parts with B_3, B_3 shares such parts with B_4, B_4 shares such parts with $\ldots B_n$, and B_n shares such parts with B_2. But we need to qualify our talk of histories sharing temporal parts; the temporal parts histories share are in one respect incomplete. Histories include two sorts of fact. 'Hard' facts obtain independent of later events. Thus my sitting here now is a hard fact. I could be sitting here no matter what the future holds, or if there were to be no more time at all. 'Soft' facts depend on later events. If it was a fact in 1865 that on 1 January 2010 the sun would rise,—that was a fact due to what was to occur later. Partial histories 2, 3 are branches off a common past 1 at t just if the hard facts in 2 and 3 up to t are all and only those there were in 1 till t. Only in this sense can histories with different futures (1 + 2, 1 + 3) share a past part (1). Consider histories which branch at Booth's decision about shooting Lincoln: actually, in @, he pulled the trigger, but in alternative history W he did not. If histories contain future-dependent facts, @ and W strictly speaking do not share a past. For while in @'s past it was always the case that Booth was to shoot Lincoln, in W's this was never the case. If we exclude future-dependent facts, though, @ and W share a past until Booth's decision and differ only then. For @ and W share all hard facts up to this point.[12]

As I see it, then, every possible history has an initial segment (temporal or causal) in common with the actual world, @. Every possibly possible history has this segment in common with the possible history from which it branches. What when speaking intuitively we call branching off a world W consists in including all hard facts that W does up to a time t, then continuing differently than W after t. So if world W branches off the actual world @ at time t, W includes all hard facts that @ includes up to t. Suppose now that W* branches off W at t+1. W* must then include all that W includes up to t+1. So it includes what W includes of @. If so, W* is as truly a branch off @ as W is: it is a continuation from @'s earliest segment. So every branch off a branch off @ is a branch off @, and so every possibly possible world is possible. So again, on my view, the logic of absolute modality includes S4.

The distinctive semantic feature of B is that in it relative possibility is symmetric: if W is possible relative to W*, W* is possible relative to W. The branching picture of worlds sketched here delivers this feature too. If W is possible relative to W*, this is because W branches off W* at some point in W*'s history, i.e. because W is a way things might go on from part of W* instead of the way they go in W*. If that is true, there is a segment of history they share, such that W includes one and W* another possible continuation of this segment. But then it is just as true that W* is possible relative to W: one can as easily see W* as a branch off W at the point at which their common segment ends. So on my view, the logic of absolute modality includes B.

Really, there is no tree. There are no worlds, paths or possible histories. This story is to be parsed in terms of my power-based account. So it would be good to show that this result follows too in terms of what I see as the true

---

[12] My thanks to a referee here.

modal reality, causal possibility founded ultimately on God's preventions and powers. For me, absolute modality is causal modality, and Chapter 13 showed that my causal modality includes S4. So I need only show that it also includes B. The reasoning is this: what underlie talk of possible worlds are facts about causal possibility, about what power/opportunity (P/O) complexes give all-things-considered power to produce.[13] The existence of a P/O complex makes possible all states of affairs the power in it has opportunity in it to produce. Where these include the existence of further P/O complexes, and their possible effects include further P/O complexes, and so on, we have the reality underlying talk of sequences of states of affairs—that is, histories: the existence of one initiating P/O complex makes possible all chains of causally linked states of affairs it might kick off. That is, something's having that power and opportunity makes true all possibility-claims asserting states of affairs that (within the fiction) occur in a chain beginning there. Fictionally, chains branch just if something in them acts or appears indeterministically. Consider one such branch-point, the existence at t of a P/O complex whose constituent power acts indeterministically. There can stem out of it two chains of states of affairs. If one is possible relative to the other, this is because were one actualized, the other would be a way things could have gone instead. Suppose, then, that chain 1 is actualized, and includes our indeterministic P/O complex which had it acted differently at t would have brought about chain 2 instead. If so, chain 1 includes a P/O complex due to which in chain 1, chain 2 is a way things might have gone instead. But chain 2 includes the same P/O complex. It includes that complex as it actually was, in chain 1, at t; 1 and 2 branch off in different directions only *after* t. But as it actually was, it was able to produce chain 1: it actually did so. So had chain 2 been actual, chain 1 would have been a way things could have gone instead, and would have had the P/O complex acted differently. But then if 2 is possible relative to 1, equally 1 is possible relative to 2. Now consider a deterministic P/O complex. What comes out of it does not branch, so we have symmetry for what it makes possible just if we have reflexivity. But S4 includes reflexivity already. Every possible power in every possible P/O complex acts either deterministically or indeterministi-cally. So again, on my view, the logic of absolute modality includes B.

S5 is the union of S4 and B; any logic containing all S4 theses and all theses of B contains all S5 theses. So on my view, the logic of absolute modality includes S5. In S5, whatever is possible is necessarily possible. For me, this translates into the claim that there are not alternative possible sets of divine from-eternity powers and preventions. God must have the from-eternity powers He has; God is only disposed to prevent from eternity as He actually has. This may seem to sit uneasily with His being able to have alternate preferences, as it implies that no matter what God had preferred, though He might have chosen a different actuality—shaping the universe's ends in

---

[13] Understand 'P/O complexes' loosely enough to include what is appropriate to (CAUSAL POSS)'s (e) and (f). Related thoughts about chains and powers are in Jacobs, *op.cit.*; we come to them independently.

different ways, creating a different universe, or not creating—He would not have allowed different possibilities. But this is at worst only a tension, not an inconsistency, and perhaps even the tension is only apparent. As the Bang could not have differed, God must have all and only the actual candidate histories in view. He must also (of course) have the same nature. God must be morally perfect, and moral perfection must be what it actually is. Any moral truths that guide Him are necessary, being determined by His nature. God necessarily accords with them. So His moral perfection must constrain His preferences as it actually does. God must be perfect in responding to all non-moral sorts of good as well. God must be perfectly loving, and the nature of this too is necessary. So this too must constrain His preferences as it actually does. And all that constrains God's preferences constrains His filling out of the possible. If so, perhaps it is not surprising that whatever God contingently prefers, the same set of histories winds up allowed. This is particularly unsurprising if, as I have suggested, it is histories' goodness (or not) that determines whether they wind up permitted.

One might object to the S5 claim as follows. If God is temporal, He should be able to think up some worlds and enable Himself to think up more later.[14] He should be able to permit Himself to think up more later. For this can be done: a legislature can permit itself to legislate on a subject without at that time determining what the law shall later say—it can so empower itself. If this is a possible task and God cannot do it, His omnipotence comes into question. But suppose that He can do this. If God can add a world later, it is possible that there be a world there is not now. As it would not have always been possible, this world would be only contingently possible. So if new worlds can become possible, possibly some world is not necessarily possible. This is incompatible with S5. In S5, necessarily, all worlds are necessarily possible.

This argument premises that if God is omnipotent and T is a possible task, God can perform T. I deny this. It might seem plausible if one defined omnipotence as ability to do all possible tasks. But such definitions now have few fans; it is now more common to define it in terms of ability to actualize possible states of affairs.[15] Plausibly, a God omnipotent in terms of ability to actualize might be unable to do certain tasks. If immaterial, for instance, He might be unable to walk—but this would not deprive Him of the ability to actualize a possible state of affairs, because an immaterial being's

---

[14] This raises the question 'But then why has He not done better—that is, added more and better possibilities: for example, to avoid evils?' But theists already face a parallel question, 'But then why has He not added more and better actual things: for example, to avoid evils?' Neither is easy. If the second can be answered, it is by reference to God's purposes. If the first can be answered, it is also by reference to God's purposes. Any divine purposes which justify God's actual choice may not have required the existence of further possibilities. If they did require them, they have already been provided, or will be when the time comes. So my view, and even this temporalist variant of it, does not really increase the explanatory burden theists face.

[15] See my 'Omnipotence', in Thomas Flint and Michael Rea (eds), *The Oxford Handbook of Philosophical Theology* (Oxford: Oxford University Press, 2009), pp. 167–98.

walking (while immaterial) is not possible. Further, actualization definition in terms of renders an appeal to omnipotence here at best question-begging, since what is at issue is precisely whether God's thinking up a world only later *is* a possible state of affairs.

A more serious objection to the S5 claim points out that the argument goes through only if God has pre-creative singular concepts. If God lacks these and creates, there come to be new individuals which previously were not singularly possible, though they were not impossible either. This is incompatible with S5. Further, suppose that God lacks these concepts but does not create. If S5 were then true, its truth would depend on a contingency. But S5's logical theses are not supposed to be contingently true. So the argument goes through only if God has pre-creative singular concepts. I accept this point. If God lacked such concepts, my argument would have shown only that world-types—worlds without singular truths save for those about God, entities within Him, attributes He has by nature, and so on—have an S5 structure. Putting this another way, it would have shown only that if we restrict the propositions we consider to purely general ones and the singular ones just mentioned, we can correctly apply S5 in our reasoning. If generalism is true, the logic of absolute modality *tout court* is not S5.

Another problem worth raising concerns prevention. Suppose (for a simplest case) that God's creating actualizes a single, absolutely first instant-thick slice of a universe's history. By so doing, on my account of prevention, He prevents the actualization of any history not beginning with that temporal part. This could well occur at the Bang: why wait? But then if at the Bang God cannot prevent other than as He has, no history not beginning with that part is possible. I reply that the claim that God cannot prevent other than as He has was a consequence of my S5 argument, and so applies *only* to His setting the modal facts. So the argument fails. Prevention has its effect causally downstream from the preventing act. Thus if God is atemporal, timelessly other initial parts remain causally possible, but causally downstream from God's volition—that is, in time—they are not. *Per* earlier argument, as an atemporal God actualizes that first part, He still has the power and chance to do otherwise, and so His actualizing others is still causally possible. But God's atemporal volition is a causally prior preventing condition removing created causes' chance to actualize others. Next, then, a temporalist account.

If God is temporal but did not decide from all eternity which universe to create, then before He decides, God has power and chance to actualize a different initial slice than He winds up actualizing. If a temporal God did decide from all eternity, then if past eternity had a first instant, He then had the chance to do otherwise and was passing it up. If it did not, He always had the intrinsic power to decide differently, and the chance if He can change His mind. He can change His mind only if He can make a decision about this that would leave Him reason to question and overturn it, or can change it without reason. Perhaps either could be so in some cases. Suppose that God whittles His alternatives in creating down to two that are intrinsically and extrinsically equal in value, each better than any other alternative save the other. Then if He has good reason to create, He has good reason to 'just pick', without reason, *if* this is possible. Having done so, though, He has no reason to stick with what He picks beyond having picked it. If changing His pick takes no effort and has no cost, perhaps He could just do it, if He can 'just pick'. Again, suppose the two are not equal but incommensurable in value. Then the value each has gives God reason to question and overturn His pick of the other. If He can do this, or 'just pick', then at every time prior to Creation He has the chance to, and so at every time the other initial slice is causally possible.

But while God has little reason to stick with his pick, He seems to have none to change it. There are good things about the other choice. These made it a finalist. But *ex hypothesi* they had not made Him prefer it when He picked. He knows no more about it later. All that has happened since is that time has passed; this would not change His attitudes. (A perfect God doesn't get tired or bored.) So plausibly He would not have come to prefer it. If He does not prefer it, His reason to change pick would have to be something good about changing itself. But what could this be? Mind-change, just as such, is not pleasant, fun, boredom-relieving, useful, praiseworthy, character-developing, beautiful, etc. Apparently then, changing pick would be change without reason. It would just be vacillation. Liability to vacillate would make God all too human, it does not befit a perfectly rational being. And if God could switch this way even once, He could as easily vacillate infinitely before creation.

If eternity had no first instant, God decided from all eternity, and God cannot change His mind, then at every time, He has already lost His chance to decide differently, as He has earlier made an unchangeable decision. If this is true, God never presently has a chance to do otherwise, and so presently never has the all-things-considered power to do otherwise. And if it is true, at every time God has made His decision, but at no time is He making it. God's decision is always past, never present. This is at least strange but might also suggest that talk of decision does not apply here. But if it does not, He was in no real sense free in creating. Rather, He simply always had, apparently not in any sense from Himself, and never acquired, a contingent disposition to create as He has—with no explanation at all. I think the moral of this story is that temporalists should deny that God made His creative decision from all eternity. They should instead say that He 'just picked' a time to decide: He made His choice at a particular time rather than earlier arbitrarily—that is, though there could be no reason to delay or to do it at any time rather than any other. Regardless of whether temporalists define absolute in terms of causal modalities, they have the problem of what slices God had a real chance to create, and face intuitive pressure to say that at some time He had a chance to create anything omnipotence empowers Him to create (that is, that omnipotence is at some time a matter of can, not could have). Anything the temporalist does to provide this chance—I doubt I have exhausted the possible moves—will also provide a temporalist version of my view able to accommodate the full range of absolute possibility.

Modalities

If God permits a history in which P, God permits that P. He permits a conjunction including that P, and a conjunction is permitted only if every conjunct is. Equally, if God permits that P, He permits an entire history in which P (minimally one in which the only fact is that P). So for secular propositions, $\Diamond$P just if from eternity God permits a history in which P or could have preferred to do so: but given the S5 result, we can simplify and say just that $\Diamond$P just if from eternity God permits that P. Equivalently, $\Diamond$P just if from eternity God does not prevent that P. God may permit that P and also that ¬P: if He does, both are contingent.[16] Again, for secular propositions, $\Box$P just if from eternity, God permits only that P—that is, prevents that ¬P—and would have done so no matter what He preferred: but given the S5 result, we can simplify and say simply that $\Box$P just if from eternity, God permits only that P (prevents that ¬P). There is no secular P whose permission-status is ever undecided, and it is not in God not to permit either that P or that ¬P. For this would effect it that ¬(¬P v P), the latter is logically non-true, and (so I have claimed) God's nature rules out His permitting any logical non-truth. Thus for any secular P, either God permits only that ¬P, or God permits that ¬P and also permits that P, or God permits only that P. So any secular P is either impossible, contingent, or necessary: which is as it should be in S5. Because their contingency is settled explanatorily prior to His bringing them about, God can bring about contingent states of affairs leaving their contingency intact. If He brings it about that P, this prevents it that ¬P, but He has the intrinsic power and had or timelessly has the opportunity to instead bring it about that ¬P, and so it is still causally and absolutely possible that ¬P.

A Set of All Worlds?

On the usual approach, for a truth to have a sort of necessity is for it to be true in all the relevant possible worlds. So on the usual approach to absolute necessity, there is such a thing as all absolutely possible worlds. An argument due to Kaplan and Peacocke suggests that there can be no set of them all:

---

[16] If I am wrong about the S5 claim, God may prevent that P, but be disposed to permit it in a different preference-state, or *vice versa*: this too would make it contingent that P.

Suppose that there is a set of all worlds, of cardinality k. To each subset S of this set corresponds a proposition true in precisely the worlds of S, e.g. that the actual world is a member of S. For each such proposition, it is possible that someone think of that proposition and no other at a time t. There are at least as many worlds as thinking possibilities, then. But there are 2^k such propositions. So there are at least 2^k possible worlds. So no k-cardinality set is the set of all worlds.[17]

I think there being such a thing as all worlds would not require that they form a set, or even a proper class. There would be all the worlds simply because however many there were, there would be those and no others. All that would be required to make them all the worlds would be the truth of the second conjunct, a negative proposition. All that is required for *that* is the falsity of its negation—and that would be false just because nothing would be there to make it true. On my account, alethic modal talk quantifies over divine world-powers. There are all of these because there are these and no others.

The Impossible

Though it is creative, God's dreaming up candidate secular states of affairs is not arbitrary or uncontrolled. His nature constrains it, and He does it in light of all He knows about Himself, including His preferences prior to doing so and all in Him that influences what preferences things He imagines might elicit. So it is a reasonable thought that if there are simple, basic attributes, God does not think up any that He then renders impossible. The factors that control or influence His imagination assure that He comes up with nothing simple that is so repugnant to Him that He then simply prevents its being exemplified. For like reasons, God does not think up attributes that occur only in impossible combinations. And we have little or no reason to believe in either; plausibly an attribute is something that *can* be exemplified. Rather, impossibility works this way. God comes up with a vocabulary of basic attributes. It is up to Him how they combine. How they combine is part of their content, and so their content would not be entirely His doing if it were not. If God thinks up (say) basic attributes F, G, and H, it might be in Him to let all combinations of these occur. But *a priori* there is no reason He must. Perhaps He could have them if instead only two-membered combinations were possible. In this case part of their content would not be determined by God's initial conceiving. If it is the case (recalling my earlier points about

---

[17] So David Lewis, *On the Plurality of Worlds* (Oxford: Basil Blackwell, 1986) p. 104; I have changed the presentation a bit. For another argument to the same conclusion see Alexander Pruss, 'The Cardinality Objection to David Lewis's Modal Realism', *Philosophical Studies* 104 (2001), 171.

quarks and schmarks) that if He allowed only pair-combinations, the results would be not FGH but different attributes, there is *a priori* no reason for Him to think up FGH rather than these unconceived others. It would not be irrational to permit only two-membered combinations of FGH (or their unconceived kin) and rule it out that anything have all three. If He makes some use of all three in generating possible combinations, none are otiose. Nor is the generation of any an argument for a lack of integration between His imagination and His preferences. Yet if God allowed only the pair-combinations, He would know He had not permitted an FGH to exist, and so would have thought up this combination. So, more generally, once God has the vocabulary of the possible in mind, He also knows all the ways these attributes *cannot* combine.

In particular, God conceives worlds His natural moral perfection makes impossible, in which, for example, all sentient creatures suffer horribly and pointlessly forever. It is good that He do so. His conceiving them makes them conceivable, and even if they are impossible, it is good that such worlds are conceivable. For it is good for us to be able to conceive horrors God's goodness spares us: it gives us one way to appreciate that goodness, and if there are horrors God's goodness does not spare us, this is not an unimportant way. Whether or not anything conceivable lay below the moral level of any world God would permit, there would *be* a lowest-level world or a point permissible worlds approach asymptotically, and either would be just as good or bad as it is. If conceivable worlds lie lower still, this gives us one way to appreciate that lesser worlds God permits are not entirely bad.

The Necessity of (GSA)

I have so far allowed for the possibility that items appear without divine creation or remain without God's sustenance, and I hope to have shown that I can accommodate this. But I am not convinced that this *is* possible on the Biblical picture of God. I have argued elsewhere that if God exists, God exists necessarily.[18] So if there are necessary conditions on being God, if God exists, it is necessarily true that these conditions are met. I suspect that making (GSA) true is one such condition.[19] If it is, then (GSA) is necessarily true if there necessarily is a God. So if making (GSA) true is a requisite of being God, (GSA) is necessarily true if there is a God.

I do not have a knockdown case that making (GSA) true is a requisite; Biblical authors do not talk about *de dicto* necessity. But the more central and prominent an attribute is in the Biblical picture of God, the stronger the case for taking it to be necessary to being God, *ceteris paribus*: this is the only

[18] 'Divine Necessity'; in Charles Taliaferro and Chad Meister (eds), *The Cambridge Companion to Christian Philosophical Theology* (Cambridge: Cambridge University Press, 2010), pp. 15–30.
[19] Not everyone agrees: see e.g. Richard Swinburne, *The Coherence of Theism* rev. edn. (Oxford: Oxford University Press, 1999) p. 131.

reason philosophers usually treat being omniscient or omnipotent as thus necessary. Now the Bible treats creating as criterial, as making the distinction between false and true deity: 'the gods of the nations are but idols, but the Lord made the heavens.'[20] Creating everything is central to the Biblical picture of God. That He is the Creator of all is literally the first thing the Bible tells us about Him.[21] The Psalmist writes, 'The earth is the Lord's, and everything in it; the world, and all who live in it, because he founded it ... and established it ... '[22] It is because God made it all that it is all His; it is because it is all His that we owe Him gratitude for the whole world He gives us as a gift, and so owe Him obedience. That we owe God obedience is perhaps the most basic claim the Bible makes about our moral relation to God; the creation of our entire world is part of its Biblical foundation.[23] If creating everything is prominent and central in the Biblical account, and this is our only sort of reason for taking accepted necessary conditions of deity as necessary conditions, we have as good a reason to take creating everything as a requisite as we do in any other case, and so if we believe in requisites of deity at all, we should take making (GSA) true as one of them. On the other hand, if in addition we would appeal to general intuitions about worship-worthiness or perfect-being theology to support (say) omnipotence being a requisite, these will tell just as much in favor of (GSA).

There are philosophical reasons to think that (GSA) should turn out necessary, which emerge when we ask about the ontology of predication. I begin with a suggestion already mooted, that God's mere existing (as God) makes predications of His essential attributes true: in addition to earlier arguments, this is ontologically most parsimonious, and so should be our default view, one to hold unless we find positive reason to enrich the ontology in this particular case. Theists come to the ontology of predication with pre-analytic commitments to concrete objects: God, ordinary material things, and so on. If Ockham's Razor is worth respecting, they ought to make do with these till they hit problems they cannot solve with only these resources. Consider, then, what to say about truthmakers for predications true of God essentially but of other items contingently—of e.g. goodness, knowledge, and (the important case here) existence.[24] We ought to deal with this nominalistically if we can. Resemblance nominalism is ontologically too costly. In the only version that deals fairly successfully with its well-known problems, it requires the full resources of David Lewis's theory of possible

---

[20] *Psalm* 96:5; see also *I Chron.* 16:26.

[21] *Genesis* 1. [22] *Psalm* 24:1–2. See also 89: 11–12.

[23] Our moral debt for providence also plays a role, and we would owe gratitude merely for ourselves being created, whether or not our environment was.

[24] The claim that existence is not a predicate and so not predicated has little to be said for it. Consider the sentence 'Brian exists.' Rendering it into logic in the usual way, we get $(\exists x)(x = b)$. This can be analyzed into a subject-term, b, and an open sentence, $(\exists x)(x = \_)$. I know of no good reason not to take this open sentence as a predicate. For convincing dismissals of bad reasons see Alvin Plantinga, *God and Other Minds* (Ithaca, NY: Cornell University Press, 1967), p. 27ff.; Graham Oppy, *Ontological Arguments and Belief in God* (Cambridge: Cambridge University Press, 1995), pp. 130–61.

worlds[25]—a theory whose ontology is a paradigm of bloat. We see later that it is a merit of theist modal metaphysics to be able to avoid Lewis-worlds. Class nominalism has considerable difficulties of its own and in a comparison with a theory of attributes based only on God and other concreta comes off worst.[26] We might try concept nominalism, using divine concepts to get around the difficulties the view faces when limited to human ones—but there are no divine concepts to satisfy. We can, however, do something similar: we can appeal to the divine mental events that are the reality behind talk of divine concept-possession. In place of satisfaction we can appeal to causal dependence on those events. (This is a theist-nominalist recasting of 'participation' in a Platonic Form.) We then get the view that where God is essentially F, to be F is either to be God or to depend causally in the right way on the divine mental events behind talk of God's F-concept. This sort of nominalism has strong Ockhamist credentials, and yet I show elsewhere that it can do all work realists do by appeal to universals.[27] So to theists, at least, it should have a great deal to recommend it. God is essentially existent. So on this approach to predication, for a non-deity, George, to exist is for George to depend causally on the reality behind talk of a divine concept of existence. George does so just if this figures in the content of something God wills to be so about George. This would have to be something God wills to be true of George as long as he exists, and the most reasonable suggestion is just that George depends causally on this because God wills *inter alia* that George exist. If that is how things are, then for a non-deity to come or continue to be without being created or sustained would be for it to exist, and so to depend causally on the reality behind talk of a divine concept of existence, and yet not so depend. It would be impossible—a contradiction in terms.[28] And so (GSA) turns out necessary if God exists necessarily. Further, plausibly God's nature determines this. It is of God's nature that some predications (of Him) are true; so it is of God's nature what it is for a predication to be true. This would include a clause for creatures, because it is of God's nature (so I have argued) that He think up creatures.

Again, the necessity of (GSA) follows from theses already argued. I contended in Chapter 7 that whatever is divine is necessarily perfect. But I have argued that having the (GSA)-property is a perfection, and there are no evident conflict between having this property and having other candidate perfections. If there are none, then however perfect-being theology fills out the concept of God, a divine being will necessarily have the (GSA)-property.

If (GSA) is necessary, in no possible world does (say) an atom pop into being absolutely uncaused. Some may think they can imagine this. But we cannot actually sensuously imagine this—that is, produce some kind of inner

[25] Gonzalo Rodriguez-Pereyra, *Resemblance Nominalism* (Oxford: Oxford University Press, 2002).

[26] See my 'One Step Toward God', *Royal Institute of Philosophy Supplement* 68 (2010) 67–104.

[27] 'God and the Problem of Universals', *Oxford Studies in Metaphysics* 2 (2006), 325–56.

[28] Thomists who have come this far may recognize in my view a recasting of Aquinas's claim that God exists *per se*, and creatures, as such, by participation, and in this argument a reworking of one by Aquinas.

experience which depicts this. Depicting-relations rest partly on how what is depicted can look to us. We cannot depict in imagination something's not being caused by God, because there is nothing it looks like for something not to be caused by God. We may be able to depict things which are not caused by God—if God does not exist, we do this routinely. But this is not the same thing as depicting them not being caused by God: it does not 'visually' present their having that property, even if they in fact have it.

Again, some may object that we see no contradiction in the claim that something pops into being uncaused. But apparent non-contradiction is only *prima facie* evidence of non-contradiction. Some contradictions emerge only upon long reflection, or only given premises from far afield, and I have appealed to some of the latter. In any event, non-contradiction may not assure even narrow logical possibility, let alone absolute. The conjunction of an Ω-inconsistent set of sentences is narrow-logically impossible, but implies no contradiction. Again, that Socrates is a fish may imply no contradiction, but certain sorts of essentialist claims are true, it may nonetheless be absolutely impossible. Thus apparent non-contradiction is only *prima facie* evidence of absolute possibility. To be weighed against apparent lack of contradiction when viewed in a narrow context are the arguments that led us to deny it to be possible that something pop into being uncaused.

The Necessity of (GAO)

Finally, if whatever is divine necessarily is perfect, Chapter 2's perfect-being arguments for (GAO) yield that (GAO) is necessary. Again, Chapter 2 noted that abstracta themselves may be valuable. So given (GSA) and (GAO), God is in fact the source of all natural good. It would be better to be necessarily than contingently so, and to be a being without whom no good is even possible. Of course, equally, if (GSA) and (GAO) are necessary, God is necessarily the source of all natural evil, but if God is necessarily morally perfect, the permission or causation of any possible such evil has an adequate moral justification, and so does not count against His goodness. If abstracta have value, God is necessarily the source of all natural good and necessary for all good only if (GAO) is necessary, and if we square natural evil with this, this *prima facie* perfection is compatible with any other *prima facie* perfection: so here we have another perfect-being argument for (GAO)'s necessity. Also coming from Chapter 2, it would be more awesome to be necessarily, not contingently a being for whom not even abstracta are 'given'. Without this claim, it would just be a matter of luck that God faced no 'givens'. With it, it is not luck. That He does not can be a matter of His nature—a fact about Him, not about His environment. That it be so seems relevant to His perfection; it is a respect in which He is superior to us. I take it, then, that (GAO) is necessary.

16

ESSENCES

I have dealt with the necessity of secular cases of logical and mathematical truths. I now provide an account of secular essential truths.

Modal Essences

If God understands just who an individual would be (that is, is in the sort of state we speak of fictionally as possessing a singular concept of that individual), it is unproblematic that He can establish a *de re* possibility for that individual: He can let Ralph have breakfast. *De re* possibilities for attributes (if there are attributes) work similarly: He can let something striped have *cat*. These things do not require us to speak (fictionally) of one item being in more than one possible world. Some *de re* necessities do not do so either. If God does not let Ralph be a cat, and no matter what He had preferred would not have, Ralph is necessarily not a cat even if he exists in just one world. If some *de re* necessities involve items that exist in more than one world, to tackle them one must discuss how the same item can be something different world-powers would bring or permit to be—my version of transworld identity.

'Transworld' Identity of Attributes

Most theories of events surveyed earlier analyze them in terms of attributes and times;[1] Kim and Lombard add subjects. It is hard to see what else there could *be* to an event, intrinsically. If so, whatever the analysis, events are distinct only if either they differ in part of their *analysans* (thus for Kim, only if they differ in time

---

[1] Lewis appeals to classes ('Events', in *Philosophical Papers* (Oxford: Oxford University Press, 1986), v.2, pp. 241–69), but for him classes are attributes.

of occurrence, subject or the attribute they involve) or perhaps, as Davidson has argued, if their causes differ.[2] God's graspings of what H_2O would be are all God's, all caused by God, and all involve His having just the attribute of understanding what H_2O would be. If God is atemporal, they cannot occur at different times. So if God is atemporal, on any analysis of events in terms of subjects and/or attributes and/or times, or an account of their identity in terms of their causes, there is just one event which is His grasping what H_2O would be. As noted earlier, Quine calls events the filling of spacetime regions. If God is atemporal, the analogue is (I think) to call them simply parts of His life. His atemporal life is most like an instantaneous temporal part of a temporal life, and as just one proper part of one such temporal part would be someone's thinking about H_2O, just one proper part of God's life would be His grasping what H_2O would be. So if God is atemporal, on any account considered, just one event is His grasping what H_2O would be. This one understanding is part of every understanding of a world in which H_2O would appear.

If God is temporal the story is a bit more complex. If God is perfect and temporal, perhaps all His knowledge is always occurrent. If it is, there is just one continuing event of God grasping what H_2O would be. (Its time is all of time.) This event is a common part of God's occurrent graspings of how H_2O-worlds would be. If on the other hand God has knowledge dispositionally, He everlastingly has the same token dispositional grasp of what H_2O would be. If God dispositionally understands what H_2O would be, He also dispositionally understands how H_2O-worlds would be, and His one H_2O-disposition is part of every such disposition: it is part of what is manifest in His occurrent understandings of how any H_2O-world would be. So the disposition too is a common part, on the dispositional level.

For an understanding of a creaturely attribute to have content partly consists in its or its constituents being such as to lead when appropriately involved in the divine mental life to God's causing certain things (in certain ways) extra-mentally:[3] for a particular divine understanding to be of being H_2O is for it to be *inter alia* such that if it is appropriately involved in a divine volition, bodies of H_2O result. Its causal role when so employed is to lead to production of this and nothing else. If this is correct, no other causal role could do the same: it would not make something an understanding of H_2O to be such that when so involved in a divine volition, kangaroos result. So nothing could be God's understanding of H_2O and not have this causal role. Nor could something have this causal role but not be this divine understanding. If this is true, then if there are properties, the property as it were follows God's token understanding of H_2O from world-power to world-power. If the

[2] Donald Davidson, 'The Individuation of Events', in his *Essays on Actions and Events* (Oxford: Oxford University Press, 1980), p. 179. I think Davidson is wrong, but include his view for completeness.
[3] As we have seen, logical machinery *inter alia* affects the way God causes things.

same understanding is (in the right way[4]) part of a power a world-power recruits, the same attribute is part of a world, i.e. would be instanced were things as that world-power would effect: if that world becomes actual, there will be H_2O or an uninstanced created attribute, *being H_2O*.

This is what my idea about divine mental content dictates, but it is also plausible independently. Suppose that God's mental events have content in some other way. Still, necessarily, if God wills that there be H_2O, there is H_2O. His nature rules it out that He slip up or be interfered with and get something else. If God merely permits that there be H_2O but does not cause there to be any, still it results that H_2O, not something else, is possible. So if God's understanding of H_2O occurs in many world-powers, then just because God cannot slip up or be interfered with, as the understanding moves from world-power to world-power (so to speak), the property of being H_2O moves from world to world: again, same understanding, same attribute, for same attribute understood, same attribute.

That the same divine event of understanding or grasping occurs in different world-powers is the reality behind talk of one selfsame property being instanced in different worlds; as simpler graspings are components of more complex ones, if there are properties, the property is as it were an ingredient from which God mixes worlds. As different actualist worlds would if actual involve instancing the same attributes, different world-powers would in use recruit powers involving the same understandings and so produce particulars with the same attributes. If an attribute exists in many worlds, there are also truths that hold of it in every possible world it inhabits: *de re* necessities about it. But *de re* necessities need not be determined (as it were) bottom-up, from attributes' adventures in particular worlds. God can simply prevent and be disposed to prevent, top-down e.g. that something striped be a cat.

In the end, I do not believe in attributes. I have given a story about the reality behind talk of the same attribute existing in different possible worlds. To do so I have spoken about attributes, and given an account that works if there be such, but I think there are just concrete particulars. If it is a *de re* necessity about courage that courage is a virtue, I am committed to some nominalist recasting of this. I believe I can give one in terms of God's understandings of courage and of virtue, broadly along Platonist lines, but I leave this for future work on attributes.

Definitional Essences

One variety of secular essential truth may rest on God's understanding alone. God has His understandings of the secular at the Bang. Some have analyses, in

---

[4] If in W I think of doghood, but in W there are no dogs, then unless a Platonist theory of universals is true or doghood is just a concept or predicate, in W I think (somehow) of something that does not exist in W. Yet in permitting W, God permits a content including doghood: namely, that I think of doghood.

the sense that they just are others, appropriately arranged: God's grasp of what a bachelor is, say, might just be His grasp of what an unmarried man is. If so, statements of these analyses state what it is to be something satisfying these understandings: if to be a bachelor just is to be an unmarried man, what it is to be something satisfying God's understanding of what a bachelor is to be an unmarried man. So if there are any real definitional truths—truths that state what it is to be a certain kind of thing—God's understandings make them true. Definitional essential truths are necessary. They are identity-statements, that, for example, to be F = df. to be G and H. For those who accept that all identity-statements are necessary, this suffices. But the necessity of such truths falls out of my view without reliance on the necessity of identity. It is just one more case of the reasoning about modal essences just completed.

In defining a property given independent of one, one can change a definition and be redefining the same property (say) in light of new information about it. But when God dreams up creatures, He in effect stipulates the content of a concept. Someone stipulating the content of a concept is not defining some item given independently. A pure stipulation determines what the concept *is*. And different definition, different concept. A concept defined purely stipulatively has no content beyond what the stipulation gives it. Even if necessarily, featherless bipeds are risible featherless bipeds, the two descriptions differ, and so if by stipulative definition they come to be the entire content of some concepts, those are *ipso facto* two different concepts. And so if God's stipulations about creatures' natures are not capturing the natures of properties given independently, God cannot redefine His creature-concepts. For that matter, even if they *were* capturing independent properties, God could redefine only if He could fail to get it perfect the first time around. Thus if God's actual human-concept includes being a mammal, in any world in which He has this human-concept, were anything a human, it would be a mammal—and in every world, He has this concept. God's stipulative truths about creatures' natures are true in all possible worlds. If God decreed that normal humans have two legs, then later that normal humans have one, He would not have redefined any concept. He might instead have decided to use a new concept in making things to fill the human-role. (It nonetheless might come out that all humans still have two legs at birth: they would just all be abnormal humans, and the world would be statistically fluky.) If He does use a new concept, normal humans after that decree have different natures than normal humans before it, but this does not mean that any property had first had one and then another definition. It means that there is a constant role for a human-property, and different properties have played this role at different times.

Transworld Identity of Individuals

If God grasps who an individual, Jones, would be, Jones' transworld identity is like attributes': same event, same individual. If God has such a singular grasp before making Jones, this is all we need say. Jones' essential properties will again have at most three possible sources: bottom-up, top-down and (if Jones has one and it is definable) the content of Jones' haecceity. But there are complications if God does not have a pre-creative singular grasp of Jones. For then before God makes Jones, He has only a general (though exhaustive) understanding of the Jones *type* of individual; only once Jones exists does He grasp who Jones is. I now tell the generalist story, beginning with the contribution God's grasps of types of individual (TIs) make. I then use it to make a case that God has genuinely singular concepts before Creation.

Speaking intuitively, *The Red-Headed League* and *The Hound of the Baskervilles* are about the same individual, Sherlock Holmes: those who awaited each new story in the nineteenth century wanted to hear more about the same individual they had heard about. If they are about one individual, there is only one reason they are: because Conan Doyle used 'Holmes' as if it were the name of a single person who would appear in the Holmes stories and wrote as if both were about that single person. I think an author can write stories that are about the same character (though I do not think there is such a thing as a character they write about, some entity to which stories bear some literal relation, and so this claim requires careful parsing). Suppose on the contrary that characters are defined by the claims stories make about them. Then there is a Holmes of *League* and a Holmes of *Hound*, and they are not the same character—but there is also a Holmes defined by the claims made about both, and if Conan Doyle wants to write different stories about the same character, he is simply choosing to define a character by the claims made in more than one story, and nothing stops his doing so. Even on this initially inhospitable view, it is up to an author whether different stories involve the same character. Holmes in *League* and Holmes in *Hound* are not descriptively identical—perhaps one story mentions that he has a nose, the other not, or one depicts him as angry, the other not. But if they resemble in the right way and Conan Doyle stipulates that that two stories are about the same character, they are. 'Resemble in the right way' acknowledges that what Conan Doyle wrote in some stories limited what he could write in others. Suppose that after writing all the actual Holmes stories, Conan Doyle had written another which narrates a day in the life of a Holmes described as a twenty-first-century American woman employed in a bakery. There are many ways Conan Doyle could make this work—say that she is Holmes reincarnated, or the other Holmes stories are all dreams that she has had, or she is in a dream Holmes is having, and so on. Imagine that the story explicitly (and boringly) rules all these out.[5] Can Conan Doyle then *make* this a Holmes story just by saying it is? My intuitions say 'no'. If yours do not, vary the case: I jib at saying that Conan Doyle could have written a story in which Holmes was a poached egg. This is because a great many stories establish that Holmes is human, and no human can be a poached egg: we think of fictional characters as if they had natures, and these supposed natures place limits on what they can be in other stories. If Conan Doyle stipulates that Holmes can be either human-like or a poached egg, he will be assigning Holmes, in the stories, to a kind other than *human being*, which is quite likely not such that it captures in fiction any genuine kind. (He might think he is not doing so. He might think humans can be poached eggs. But if humans cannot, that is what he will be doing.) Still, if Conan Doyle *cannot* write a poached egg story and make it a human-Holmes story by mere say-so, it is Conan Doyle who limits what Holmes can be in some stories by saying what he is in others. Authorial intent determines trans-story identity-conditions, within limits not so determined (it is not Conan Doyle's doing that no human can be a poached egg). That author's intent establishes facts of trans-story identity applies too to stories God writes by permitting—possible world-histories. But the point about characters' natures in one story limiting what they can be in others does not apply to God. If I cannot write a story in which Santa is a poached egg, this is because there are constraints on Santa's nature set before I write. Creaturely natures themselves are things God makes up. When He makes them up, there are no constraints on Him at all. And He writes all His stories at once; none form a background established before and constraining the content of others.

Conan Doyle included the same character, Holmes, in many stories. But even if there are Holmes-like haecceities out there to be expressed, nothing Conan Doyle wrote latched onto any. He did not do it descriptively. The Holmes-description of each story does not describe a haecceity or express its content and is not even complete in all its general details: exactly how big was his nose? Nor can Conan Doyle have done it in thought, without writing out what he had grasped. Holmes' haecceity might be a disjunctive property each disjunct of which is a conjunction of all attributes he would have in one possible world, a conjunctive property including all Holmes' world-indexed attributes, or a property including some unique unexemplified quality that would make Holmes Holmes. If the first or second, Conan Doyle cannot have done it because no ordinary human lifespan would suffice to distinctly grasp all the disjuncts or conjuncts. (Think of all his attributes of possibly co-existing with A, with B, and so on.) If the last, Conan Doyle cannot have done it because we have no occult faculty of intuiting unexemplified properties. Nor have we reason to think that God has made us reliable in (say) imagining haecceities without literally intuiting them, nor to think that Conan Doyle

---

[5] Nor can the reader supply a connecting story, if Conan Doyle has ruled out all possible connecting stories.

(unlike the rest of us) actually could imagine a haecceitistic individuating quality. If Conan Doyle did not get his tokens of 'Holmes' to express a haecceity, then in each story Conan Doyle displays just a *type* of character, someone of the Holmes kind. (This is true *a fortiori* in that no story even gives a qualitatively complete general description of Holmes.) Even so, Conan Doyle in writing Holmes stories sets facts of trans-story identity of a fictional *individual* by authorial stipulation. 'Holmes' is used as if it were a singular term; not a type but an individual solves the mysteries of *League* and *Hound* (though the fact behind this may just be that being an individual is part of the Holmes-type).

God understands possible histories, stories of possible universes. If His understanding of them before Creation involves no singular concepts of non-divine particulars but instead only TIs, as of Holmes-type characters, generalist 'worlds' can only be world-types—different particulars would specify them in different ways to yield fully determinate worlds. Before Creation, world stories may (as it were) use empty proper names for non-divine particulars, but these names only express types. Their force is really just e.g. that someone is a detective, lives on Baker Street in London etc., and chased a mysterious hound. Even so, it is wholly up to God whether to use the same empty name in two of these stories. If He does, the stories are about the same individual, in somewhat the way different Holmes-stories are: even if there are no 'creatures of fiction'—nothing for 'Holmes' to refer to—authorial intent determines trans-story identity of an individual, not just a type. It determines that if 'Holmes' did have a referent in some story, it would have the same referent in all stories. There can of course be trans-world-type identity (the same someone Holmes-type in two Holmes worlds; the same type-character in two stories). There can also be modal facts this establishes: for a world-type to include someone Holmes-type is for it to be true in that world-type that (say) someone Holmes-type exists, and it can be true of that someone Holmes-type, whoever exactly he turns out to be, that he might have been a baker. On generalism, God's TIs ground trans-world-type identity, as ingredients from which God mixes world-*types*.

If God causes someone to satisfy the Socratic TI just once, this person—Socrates—inherits the stories involving that TI. They become possibilities for *his* existence. 'Socrates' acquires a referent in some divine world-story W, and in other stories so involving 'Socrates' as to express a divine intent to refer (if referring at all) to the same item 'Socrates' refers to in W, 'Socrates' thus acquires the same referent. Again, if it is possible that someone just like Socrates be a clown, Socrates can be a clown, for Socrates is someone just like Socrates. Again, Socrates helps bring it about that things are as they are in a world-segment involving Socrates' TI: that this segment is an actualized possibility for him. If this segment is an actualized possibility for him, its alternatives are alternate possibilities for him—ways things might have gone instead from the outset of that segment will be ways things might have gone instead for him. The other Socratic stories are meant to be of the same individual as this one, and it has turned out that this one is about Socrates. This is so even if (as generalists say) there is just no fact of the matter about whether God would have gotten Socrates or someone else just like him had someone satisfied that TI in other circumstances. We can think of generalist divine graspings of possible world-types as being coded for individuals as paint-by-numbers pictures are coded for colors. Such pictures have '1' everywhere one color is to occur, '2' everywhere a second color is to occur, and so on, but contain no information about what colors are to interpret '1', '2', etc. So too, in a generalist understanding of a possible world-type the Socrates-TI codes for a single individual, whoever he turns out to be, and God's creating Socrates is the equivalent of providing a color-chart showing what color goes in the '1' areas.[6] Given the color-chart, '1' areas are all areas for the color the chart assigns to 1, even if a different chart might have assigned something else.

So if generalism is true, we still have necessary truths *de re*. These were initially not in God's mind at all, as He had no singular understanding with which to frame them. There were just general necessary truths of a corresponding type, and there was no fact of the matter as to what individual would result if God instanced them. Then God caused (say) Socrates to exist. There were now actual truths about him. There were new truths involving other possible world-types too. God now understood world-stories involving Socrates but otherwise just like the general stories involving his TI. These were determined by Socrates' coming to be and the way God's TIs figured in His understanding of what worlds would be like. There were these *de re* truths because God caused this individual to exist and had stipulated that the same character occurs in different general world-stories. God gets causal credit for the existence of the new singular necessary truths even though He cannot have intended to get these as opposed to other such truths and was not in control of what individual He would get if He willed that someone satisfy the Socratic TI.

Consider a non-actualized world-type W with a Socratic slot. The actual world @ has Socrates in its Socratic slots, and so W is an alternative possibility for Socrates. For generalists, it is all the same indeterminate who would have shown up had God actually brought a world of W's type to be. It need not have been Socrates. God had no control over that, since He lacked a singular understanding with which to frame a controlling intention to create a particular individual. Had someone else showed up, the Socratic slot in the generalist world that @ specifies would have been an alternate possibility for that someone else. On generalism, transworld identity is determinate given a population of individuals plus possible world-types, but given the same world-types plus a different population, there would have been different facts of

---

[6] I owe the illustration (though not this use of it) to John Divers, *Possible Worlds* (London: Routledge, 2002), p. 279, and Joseph Melia, 'Reducing Possibilities to Language', *Analysis* 61 (2001), 25–6.

transworld identity. This cashes in my metaphor above: different color-chart, different cross-world colorings-in.

There is a TI of me that two individuals in the same world cannot satisfy: being the only person ever to have a particular conjunction of general attributes. But there is probably one that two individuals in the same world *can* satisfy, which lacks the note of uniqueness. It seems possible that God make duplicate universes, each containing someone very like me, save that these men lack all properties I actually have having which entails the non-existence of a duplicate universe and have instead properties dependent on the existence of a duplicate universe. If this is possible, I have such a TI, which contains just the attributes the two men would share. So let's finally consider what to say about the resulting items' transworld identity if God causes such a TI to be satisfied twice. If two individuals in the same world satisfy a TI, they have all pure general attributes it contains. Equally there is some attribute they do not share, for example, overall spatiotemporal location or identity with *that* person. So suppose God says 'let someone BL-type be' twice; there show up someone having F (BLF) and someone lacking F (BL¬F). Recall my metaphor of color-coding. BLF shows up in a space coded '1' in a world-type with two BL-type spaces. All 1-spaces across other such worlds are then alternative possibilities for BLF. In another such world containing a 1-space, it will still be BLF filling it in, even if in that world BLF lacks F and BL¬F has F. So BLF's identity across such worlds is due to divine stipulation at the type-level. If worlds with just one BL-type slot represent possibilities for both BLF and BL¬F, or if in a world with two both BLF and BL¬F can fill either, this does not entail that BL¬F and BLF are only contingently distinct. These are *general* worlds. There is not some individual in them with which both BL¬F and BLF are transworld-identical. There is instead just a type of possibility, and they could both instance that type; there are specifications of these worlds for both BLF and BL¬F. So here again, I submit, there would be no problems of transworld identity for the generalist, and all secular *de re* modal truths would trace back to God.

Stipulative Truths

Authors stipulate trans-story identity for their characters. God stipulates transworld identity for items instancing TIs if generalism is true. If it is not, He stipulates that Socrates in one world drinks hemlock, in another henbane, but is human in both: that is just how He writes the stories. Such stipulation establishes truth-in-the-story. Stipulation establishes truth *simpliciter* when inventors invent. If anything is a complete Model T Ford, it has wheels. If Ford designed the Model T, he made this true by doing so, and his doing so was just stipulating what a complete Model T would be. If Ford's plant produced cars without wheels, they would not be complete Model Ts, just because Ford designed the car as he did. If there is no God, perhaps Ford determined what it is to be a Model T, and so added a property to the nature of things.

I do not insist on the example—not least because I think God dreamed up the Model T first. God has inventor's privilege. In thinking up creatures, God designs inventions, and His inventions do add properties to the nature of things. If God so thinks that being Alpha Centaurian includes being three-headed, this is the truth about Alpha Centaurians, and part of the content of a property as real as any other. Inventor's privilege is enough to make this stipulation true. But God's stipulations also dictate to the world. For (I now argue) there can be in reality only things He conceives, as He conceives them, and how God thinks entirely determines how these things might be.

If God necessarily has the GSA-property, then necessarily, there are only things God intends to create or sustain.[7] Necessarily, if God creates or sustains, His products are just as He intends, for God can make no mistakes. God can intend to create or sustain only things He conceives.[8] So God can create or sustain only things which satisfy His concepts: His products must conform to His concepts of them. And so there can only be non-divine things that satisfy divine concepts. God has inventor's privilege in determining the nature of the invention. For those that appear due to causes, God also does or controls the manufacturing, at every level of decomposition of the artifact, and cannot slip up.

Further, to satisfy God's concept of a K is truly to be a K. Things can have no deeper, other nature God's concepts could fail to catch. For there can be no place whence such a nature could come. Necessarily, when God first creates, there is nothing outside Him to give things a nature He does not intend them to have. Nor are there unplumbed depths in God to complicate matters. Sometimes, there may be more 'in' a novelist's character than the writer's conscious thoughts and intentions can account for: there is a role for appeal to unconscious motivations, the influence of social structures, etc., in literary interpretation. But this could be so in God's case only if He could fail wholly to comprehend His nature and mind or to control Himself. So it is not the case that things might have some deeper nature God gave them which His concepts do not catch.

Nor could it be that God intends to create (say) a dog, but the dog comes also or instead causelessly to exemplify some further nature. Not instead: this would amount to God slipping up, failing to achieve what He intends. As to 'also', Fido obviously could not have properties incompatible with those God willed him to have. So this would require that God left His concept of Fido incomplete in certain ways (say, the color of his fur), and Fido came to be with the blanks causelessly filled in. Either there were in advance facts about how Fido *would* turn out if God willed Him with a blank in his concept, or there

---

[7] Or an instance of whose T1 He intends to create or sustain. Take this sort of addition as read through the next few paragraphs.

[8] Or whose T1 He conceives. Take this sort of addition too as read through the next few paragraphs.

were only facts about how he might turn out. If the first, there was not after all a blank in God's concept of Fido. God willed Fido to be, knowing and intentionally accepting how he would come out, and His concept of Fido had the blank filled in—only not because He was so to will. God's concept catches all of Fido, and Fido is only as God willed him to be, only part of that will is an intentional acceptance. If the second, the filling of Fido's blank could only be with a contingent property. As I am now sketching only a way truths about creatures wind up necessary, we can ignore this. Thus God puts into place a system of natures which is wholly as His concepts determine. The only nature things have at Creation's outset is one God conceives and intentionally gives them. If creatures once made give one another natures, they give one another natures whose lineaments God wholly sets in advance and which God sustains in accord with His concepts. For creatures act only in virtue of the natures and powers God gives them. So anything a creature does to other things' natures is just the working-out of the overall system of natures and powers God gave creatures *ab initio*.

It is up to God how He thinks of creatures, and so what the non-modal facts about creatures' kinds are. Because God has the GSA-property, God's concepts shape the world; God's stipulations come out truths about the world. Because (GSA) is necessary, they shape all possible worlds. If God stipulates that Socrates is human in every world in which He exists, then, that settles the modal-essential truth about Socrates. He stipulates this by settling a fact about His powers, that some world-power which brought Socrates to be would cause him to be human and none can contribute to a non-human Socrates. My argument appealed to the necessity of a divine attribute. This is acceptable because I am offering only an account of how secular modal truths get to be true. Finally, all this has a fairly close analogue for things that show up wholly without divine input (if they are possible—that is, if I am wrong that God necessarily has the GSA-property). For they still have only natures God thought up in the Bang, and His stipulation about these still dictates to reality—only by providing (in effect) the vocabulary of properties uncaused things can instance.

Individual Essences

If God can stipulate transworld-type identity involving TIs and thereby stipulate it for individuals, He can give Himself singular concepts before Creation—that is, manufacture haecceities.[9] Here is one procedure:

1. Establish a world-type W including only one TI for an individual that includes being F.

---

[9] I speak of attributes without commitment, as a convenience.

2. So stipulate trans-world-type identities that the satisfier of any TI that includes being F, in any type world, would be in W the individual satisfying TI that includes being F.

3. Create something with F.

With that done, God's F-concept is one some individual satisfies in some possible worlds and world-types and no possible individual distinct from that one could satisfy. Being F is an individual essence.

I am not sure (3) is needed. I think a God who can stipulate trans-world-type identity can establish haecceities before Creation. Suppose God stops at (2). (1) gives us that at least one individual can have F. Now suppose for a moment that there are merely possible individuals, and consider two: are they candidates for the F-slot in W? If they share the same world, then *per* (2), they cannot both be F: two things cannot be identical with one. (2) guarantees that at most one thing *per* world is F. So at most one is a candidate to fill the slot in W. If they do not share a world, both fill the slot in W only if both are F, and if they are, then *per* (2), they are transworld identical with what does so and so are not two candidates. But any candidates for the slot will either share or not share a world. So at most one possible individual can fill the slot. Thus if I am right about trans-world-type identity above, F is an attribute at least and at most one possible individual could have, even if God has not yet created and there is no such thing as a determinate merely possible individual who could have F. Further, F involves no individual or individual essence in its makeup. Given a rich enough language, it should be possible to express F without referring to an individual or a haecceity, without proper names, proper adjectives ('Aristotelian') or verbs ('Pegasizes'), indexicals, or referential uses of definite descriptions.[10] Let us express this by calling F qualitative. If F is a haecceity, 'qualitative' is not another term for being general, and the conditions just mentioned do not distinguish universals from non-universals.

A natural question here is what sort of quality F is. It is in God, I think, to have F be anything at all. It may have been in God to have scarlet be a haecceity of some red patch. If scarlet is as such a universal, this is not something it was in Him to do, but it was in Him to instead dream up schmarlet, which would be just like scarlet save for not being a universal. Perhaps whether an attribute is a universal depends on what's possible at a general level—whether across all world-types it figures in more than one TI. If it does depend on what is possible, then if it is up to God how attributes are instantiated across all possible worlds, it is up to God which attributes are universals. On some views, in a trope, there are the qualitative core and the fact about ownership, the redness and its being Smith's.[11] So too, in a

---

[10] For all save the first two see Robert M. Adams, 'Primitive Thisness and Primitive Identity', *Journal of Philosophy* 76 (1979), 7.

[11] This was the standard medieval view: there were substances, and tropes were accidents particular to their bearers. More recent trope ontologies (for example, Keith Campbell, *op. cit.*) are one-sorted, trying to

universal, there are the qualitative core and the fact about ownership, that more than one item can have it, that it is not a trope. A haecceity would be a trope. Now a mental grip on scarlet's qualitative core does not tell us whether it is a trope. Our grip on the core lets us imagine many things being scarlet, but does not tell us (and sensuous imagination is not determinate with respect to) whether they have numerically the same quality, or instead distinct tropes of it. That might well suggest that the qualitative core does not determine the fact about ownership. If it does not, that fact may be up to God to settle, by inclusion in TIs. If it does, that is because God so conceived it that it does, and so settled the fact about ownership in another manner. If God wants there to be qualitative haecceities of some sort, it is in Him to bring this about, and we can acknowledge this without having clear examples of haecceities to offer. We do however have terms like 'being Moses'. We naturally construe this as a property involving an individual, the sort we could also express as '__ = Moses'. But it does not seem a strange suggestion that this might be due simply to the limits of our grips on attributes or our expressive capacities, and that were either limit loosened, we might be able to express the same property without any such singular-referential device.

Given F, there is a definite description, 'the bearer of F'—empty but still definite, and legitimately so: it could not be the case that more than one thing was F, nor is it the case that, if something comes to be F, something else might have done so instead. Rather, if something comes to be F, it is the only thing that ever could have. It is the only F-thing in any possible world or world-type, and there are no world-types with slots for a second. An empty definite description is an empty singular term. In fact, given what F is, 'the bearer of F' would refer rigidly if it referred. With it, God can frame genuinely singular claims of the form 'the bearer of F is G'. Can one then make it out, as generalists contend, that there is no fact of the matter in advance about which thing would be F? We know in advance that the bearer of F would have F, and that this description, once it picks out anything, will pick out just one possible individual, and the same one in any world. Now consider a term that supposedly names a Plantingan haecceity: 'Socrateity'. We know that if there is such a property,

—only Socrates in any possible world could have it;

—'the bearer of Socrateity' refers rigidly to Socrates;

—there can be singular propositions like *the bearer of Socrateity is bald* even if there is no Socrates;

'reduce' substances to bundles or fusions of tropes. On such views owners are metaphysically composed of tropes and so cannot figure in tropes' makeups; in place of an ownership-fact, a trope is externally related to other tropes making up the same substance.

—one can use it to specify the contents of merely possible worlds in terms entirely of actual entities: it can be true in W that the bearer of Socrateity is bald, even if there is no Socrates.

If Socrateity would be fit to do these jobs, and give an adequate account of the singular possibility of the non-actual, my F can do the same. It is as good a haecceity as Socrateity. And it makes no more sense for a generalist to say that there is no fact of the matter about who or what will bear F than to say that there is none about who will bear Socrateity.

Christopher Menzel finds qualitative haecceities problematic simply because they are not general, not built up from universals.[12] He gives no case that the notion of a trope is incoherent, though, so it is hard to see more than an expression of distaste in this. He also asks whether belief in such haecceities is

> all that far from possibilism . . . there is little to distinguish such nondescript properties from possibilia save the bare assertion that they are in fact properties. Possibilia seem to have been traded for entities scarcely less problematic.[13]

Well, on my precise version of this, what has been traded for are mental events which just do primitively have singular content. Not being non-existent objects seems just as such to make them less problematic than possibilia: there is no need to make sense of the claim that something is not there and yet has attributes. The alternative to possibilia and haecceities is the generalist's view that when God instances the BL-type TI, that I and not someone else appear is just a brute fact, caused but not intended by God. For both me and the generalist, singular content is brutely there. Either way, God primitively has the power to produce it, either in a concept or in reality. On my story, He intends to get precisely what He does get. On the generalist's, He does not and cannot. So it is a bit of a mystery why He does get it, and how it just shows up. Why multiply mysteries?

Since F is not analyzable into general attributes, it escapes arguments against the existence of haecceities based on symmetrical worlds:[14] worlds symmetrical with regard to all shareable attributes could still host F in just one place. Robert M. Adams finds qualitative haecceities mysterious. He doubts that even a superhuman mind could be acquainted with them.[15] I agree, as it is hard to see how any mind could be acquainted with any uninstantiated property, but I note that I do not in fact believe in attributes. What I have described is more properly understood as a way to generate mental events it is

---

[12] Christopher Menzel, 'Actualism, Ontological Commitment and Possible World Semantics', *Synthese* 85 (1990), 366.

[13] Menzel, 'Temporal Actualism and Singular Foreknowledge', *Philosophical Perspectives* 5 (1991) 491.

[14] For which see, for example, Alan McMichael, 'A Problem for Actualism about Possible Worlds', *Philosophical Review* 92 (1983), 57, and Robert M. Adams, 'Primitive Thisness and Primitive Identity,' *Journal of Philosophy* 76 (1979), 5–26.

[15] Robert M. Adams, 'Actualism and Thisness,' *Synthese* 49 (1981), 15.

apt to speak of as the possession of singular concepts. There is no mystery about a mind's having access to these. Adams does not see why God could not reuse haecceities in making different individuals.[16] 'They would not be haecceities, then, would they?' is not to the point: the question is really what content of qualitative haecceities makes them unshareable. But this question is illegitimate. We do not look for some special quality of universals that makes them shareable. They just are so, as a brute fact. It is of the nature of redness that there can be many red things. There is nothing more to say, and that is fine: so by what right do we hold qualitative haecceities to a stricter standard? If universals can be brutely shareable, haecceities can be brutely unshareable. If some special feature of universals made them shareable, moreover, it might be answer enough to say that haecceities lack this (and in both cases, it is just going to be the nature of the attribute that it be so). Adams and others ask why haecceities are compatible with some but not all qualitative properties.[17] But universals too are compatible with only some qualitative properties: nothing can be both red and a phenomenal sound. Why? Redness is visible. We see red things; we build into our concept of redness that it be visible; we take it that in doing so we express a grip on the nature of redness. Sounds are not visible (to normal humans in normal conditions), and again we take this to express something of their nature (and that of normal humans). Being visible and being invisible are incompatible because they are contradictory. So too, nothing can both be me and be a phenomenal sound. Why? While some philosophers make bold talk about bare particulars and the remote alleged possibility that I be a sound,[18] in a fairly thick sense we can make nothing of this supposition, any more than of the supposition that sounds be visible to normal humans.[19] We see that I am not a sound; we build it into our concept of me that I not be a sound; why should we not take this as a grip on my haecceity if I have one? In each case we rely on modal intuition or an inability to imagine to jump to a necessity-claim, and it is hard to see why the one intuition or inability should be trusted more than the other. So I suggest that we can explain the compatibilities and incompatibilities of haecceities with universals in much the way, and about as well as, we can explain those of universals with universals.

Alan McMichael argues against the existence of qualitative haecceities. Let a role be a conjunction of all an individual's qualitative properties, such that for all qualitative properties P, either the role includes P or it includes its

---

[16] *Ibid.*, 15–17.

[17] Adams, *loc. cit.*; for others see, for example, Lewis, *Plurality,* p. 241.

[18] So Penelope Mackie, *op. cit.*

[19] The ways we can and cannot make sense of this, in fact, are just those in which we can and cannot make sense of the supposition that there is a round square. I earlier made a case that (if there are propositions) there is a proposition *there is a round square,* but that case is compatible with the point I make here—it is a proposition we do not fully understand.

complement. Thus if an item has a qualitative haecceity, its role includes it. The argument is this:

> Call roles R and S compossible if it is possible for there to be individuals X and Y such that both X fills role R and Y fills role S ... if two roles are sufficiently alike, then necessarily anything that fills role R could have filled role S and *vice-versa*. But there are compossible roles R and S such that (A) R and S are sufficiently alike and (B) (there could) be distinct individuals X and Y such that both X exemplifies R and Y exemplifies S. From (A) and the first premise it follows that if R and S include essences, then they must include the same essence. From (B), it follows that if R and S include essences, then they must include distinct essences. Thus R and S cannot include essences. But (if) essences (are qualitative) ... given that R and S are roles, either both R and S include essences or necessarily, anything exemplifying R or S lacks an individual essence.[20]

It might be enough here to note that the first premise sets up a *sorites* argument. It is in effect that arbitrarily small differences in property cannot make a difference with respect to containing an individual essence, so that if R contains an individual essence, S contains the same one, and this is just like the claim that arbitrarily small differences in number of grains contained cannot make a difference with respect to being a heap. Further, essentialists, at least, have reason to resist this premise. Most are willing to include an item's natural kind among its essential properties. But over evolutionary history, arbitrarily small differences in property came to constitute differences in species, and so natural kind. Further, all species have had borderline members, we may assume, and a borderline member can differ from a clear member by as small a difference as one likes. But surely if natural kind is essential, it is essential to clearly be a member of a natural kind. So over evolutionary history, arbitrarily small differences in property guarantee that one and the same individual cannot play two closely similar roles, and so may constitute difference in individual essence.[21]

Actually, F was inessential to (1)–(3). If God can stipulate trans-world-type identities, He need not have them 'follow' a simple attribute across worlds. He can simply stipulate that, for example, the someone who is F and G and H in world-type W is the same entity as the one who is F* and G* and H* in W*. Being F and G and H in a world-type W analyzes as being F and G and H and bearing relations to the bearers (whichever items they be) of other complexes of attributes: summarize this as bearing R. Then a haecceity emerges from this particular settling of a transworld identity: possibly being F and G and H and bearing R and possibly being F* and G* and H* and

---

[20] Alan McMichael, 'A Problem for Actualism about Possible Worlds', *Philosophical Review* 92 (1983), 58.

[21] As McMichael notes, Chisholm's Adam–Noah puzzle in 'Identity Through Possible Worlds', (*Noûs* 1 (1967), 1–8) is a special case of the role argument, and so I have dealt with that as well.

bearing R*. There is also a disjunction, being F and G and H and bearing R or being F* and G* and H* and bearing R*. Another sort of stipulative haecceity might be this: suppose that in every world, God has a TI of someone Socratic. God can stipulate that the result in any world of willing that someone satisfy it is identical with the result of this in every world. He can thereby turn a satisfying this general concept into a haecceity of Socrates, i.e. turn the concept singular.

I have now argued that even if we begin from generalism, if we assume that God can determine transworld-type identities, we can get to the conclusion that He has singular concepts of possible creatures before Creation. I think He does determine these, as part of settling all secular modal truth. And it seems to me that if it is in God to have pre-creative singular concepts of possible creatures, He would provide these for Himself. If His motive in thinking about creating is in part to give gifts, He will want to know to whom He is to give them, and in fact, since His primary gift to each creature is itself, He will not have fully thought out His gifts unless He gives Himself singular concepts. Again, if His thinking about prospective creatures is in part practical planning, considering His alternatives, He will want to give Himself maximum information about what His alternatives are. So I take it that God does have pre-creative singular concepts, and that before Creation there are singular possibilities involving all possible creatures. Pre-Creation, the empty names in God's world-stories have singular senses.

Conventionalism

Some sorts of conventionalism say that a decision to hold them true no matter what makes necessary truths necessary.[22] I suggest in effect that God makes non-definitional modal-essential truths necessary by deciding to hold them true no matter what. God has decided to have the power to make Socrates human. He has decided not to give anything the power to make him non-human. So He has decided to hold it true no matter what that if anything is Socrates, it is human. This is finally just a divine convention. It is what He has stipulated is to be so about Socrates, free of any need to be responsible to independent facts about him. Essential truths which are realist in relation to us—holding independent of what we think or do—are in effect conventional to God.[23]

I have explicated God's holding true in volitional terms. Michael Loux tries to do so in intellectual terms: God makes some claims true by affirming them,

---

[22] See, for example, Michael Dummett, 'Wittgenstein's Philosophy of Mathematics', in Paul Benecerraf and Hilary Putnam, eds., *The Philosophy of Mathematics* (Englewood Cliffs, NJ: Prentice-Hall, 1964), p. 494.

[23] For this combination of realism and anti-realism see Alvin Plantinga, 'How to be an Anti-Realist', *Proceedings and Addresses of the American Philosohical Association* 56 (1982), 47–70.

he says, and others necessary by strongly affirming them.[24] But affirming is not a purely intellectual matter. It is something one does. This is particularly true if (as Loux insists) things are true because God affirms them rather than *vice-versa*, for then one cannot cast God's affirming as a natural or automatic response to a perception of intellectual merit. Loux speaks of the sort of affirming involved here as belief:

> The facts stand as they do because God has the beliefs God does . . . the Earth rotates on its axis because God believes it does.[25]

But belief that the Earth rotates cannot account for its rotation. For God can have only true beliefs, and logically prior to the Earth's rotation (which is where we must locate conditions that account for it), this belief would not yet have been true. So God could not have had this belief logically prior to the Earth's rotation. Belief that the Earth *will* rotate could not do the trick either. This would have been true *because* the Earth was to rotate, rather than being what accounts for this—or else this too would have been a belief a God with only true beliefs could not have 'early enough'. And if the belief would have been true because God had decided to make the Earth rotate, the belief would reflect the true cause rather than being one. We do not decide to believe what we do; I think we cannot. But surely God decides that the Earth is to rotate. It is not clear, then, that 'belief' can be the right name for a mental state with the causal role Loux has in mind.

Beliefs simply form in us, as involuntary responses to apparent intellectual merit. If facts are as they are because God believes what He does, claims that these facts *are* facts lack the key intellectual merit of truth in advance of God's believing them. Nor then can they seem true or be made to appear true or more probably true to God: He knows that they are not true in advance of His believing them. If God is ideally rational and omniscient, then if He knows that a belief is not true, nothing can make it appear true or probably true to Him. But one role of warrant and justification, if they do not simply confer truth, is to convey to a believer that certain claims are plausibly taken to be true, or likely to be true. So it is not clear that on Loux' conception God's 'beliefs' could have warrant, justification, and so on. It is not clear that other sorts of intellectual merit ought to attract belief—is coherence a desirable property aside from its ability to confer warrant, justification or (on some views) truth? So if the mental states Loux has in mind are beliefs, they would seem to be beliefs singularly without intellectual merit. A perfect being would not have these. Surely, then, for God to affirm that the Earth rotates on its axis, in a sense which accounts for this being so, is just for Him to *decide* that it

---

[24] Michael Loux, 'Toward an Aristotelian Theory of Abstract Objects', *Midwest Studies in Philosophy* 11 (1986), 495–512.

[25] *Ibid.*, 510.

do so. But if so for affirmation, then presumably so for strong affirmation as well.

Joining the Levels

I have spoken of divine singular understandings and understandings of possible worlds. But it is not as if God first thinks up the first, complete in content, then applies them. Rather, He determines their content partly by determining the full content of possible worlds—in effect, applying them within possible worlds. Speaking fictionally, God has the concept *dog*. It either is or is not such as to admit of co-satisfaction with *brown*. God determines whether it does by determining whether He might make a brown dog—that is, determining the color-contents of dog-containing possible worlds. If He does permit this, it is a fact about *dog* that it admits co-satisfaction with *brown*. So God determines the content of *dog* partly by giving Himself powers which make possible worlds determinate as to brown dogs. It is not one thing for God fully to form all His non-world concepts and another for Him to determine the contents of all possible worlds. It could not be otherwise if a concept is something that *can be satisfied*.

17

NON-SECULAR MODALITIES

I have so far given an account only of the modal status of secular propositions. The non-secular include those of pure logic and mathematics and those involving God, divine attributes, and so on.[1] As God by nature so thinks that pure logical and mathematical theses come out non-false (or true)—I hope to give a full story about this elsewhere—one can trace the necessity of their non-falsity (or truth) to the necessity of God's having His nature. Necessarily, if God exists, He has His nature. So an account of the necessity of God's existence will cover theistic, logical, and mathematical necessities. In theories of worlds, if a possibility is not maximal, it may be intrinsically possible and has a complement, which with it composes a possible world. 'Powers' accounts of modality largely do not deal in intrinsic possibility. If what it is for a state of affairs to be possible is that there be (say) power and opportunity to bring it about, what determines a state of affairs' possibility is in most cases mostly extrinsic to it.[2] I now take up the possibility of God's existing. This turns out to be intrinsic. I then address why God's existence is necessary and assign a truthmaker to the claim that necessarily, God exists. Finally I turn to the complement for God's existing. These things complete my account of modal status.

Divine Possibility

I define absolute possibility in terms of causal. If a state of affairs cannot be caused or come about without cause, it is not the sort of thing to come

---

[1] *Per* Chapter 9, universally quantified truths whose quantifier domain includes God are also non-secular. I will not discuss these separately, but given what I say, it should be clear how to deal with them.

[2] A 'powers' account does require that a state of affairs be intrinsically apt for possibility: its content must provide one component of there being an opportunity for it to obtain. (If no complement is available for it, there is also no opportunity for it to obtain. But this too is an extrinsic matter.)

about. The (b)–(f) clauses of (CAUSAL POSS) do not apply to it. There are then just two alternatives: either it actually obtains without having come about or it is not causally or absolutely possible. If it is causally possible, it is so by satisfying (CAUSAL POSS)'s (a)-clause. The (a)-clause lets an item's existing make it true that it is causally possible. Now God cannot come to exist. So only the (a)-clause applies to His existence. His actually existing makes it true that He possibly exists.[3] This is a case of intrinsic possibility, as there is no need for an extrinsic fact, the availability of a power (and so on), to render it possible.

As existing entails being possible, it might sound like common sense to let an item's existing make it true that it is possible. It has however a hidden freight. Existing is a non-modal property. Being possible is a modal status. So for every possible thing A, I have allowed the claim that possibly A exists a non-modal truthmaker. It does not follow that I have allowed this *only* a non-modal truthmaker. In all cases but God's and another sort to be discussed shortly, temporally or causally prior to A's existing it was possible that A exist.[4] This possibility claim had a modal truthmaker, that there was a power/opportunity complex,[5] and this complex also exists while A does.[6] But in God's case there was no such thing. An eternal God cannot have been possible temporally before He existed. If there are no Platonic or Meinongian entities, nothing is causally or explanatorily prior to God's existence. So in God's case, the (a)-clause stands alone. God's existence is primitively, intrinsically, and reductively possible.[7] It is not the realization of a prior, independently established possibility. This emerges simply from my account of possibility and uncontroversial claims about God. This also applies to mental events God necessarily generates—for example, those of the Bang. There was no prior, independent possibility that just these events occur. God's existence is causally prior to theirs, but it was not possible that just these events occur till He produced them. Though a power did produce them, it could not be specified as a power to produce *them* until it had done so. Their occurring was explanatorily prior to the power's being so specified. So they did not derive their initial possibility from the existence of that power. Rather, though they are not primitively possible—their possibility is a causal consequence of something—they are intrinsically and reductively possible: what makes it true that they are actual is the first truthmaker, explanatorily speaking, of the claim that they are possible. It should be clear that these cases are one-offs.

[3] Strictly, the (a)-clause would let His only having existed or being about to exist make this true, but given His by-nature eternality, if He existed or will exist, He exists, and so this has a present truthmaker.
[4] Or (on generalism) that something A-type exists.
[5] At least, this is what it was given the necessity of (GSA). I have indicated how I would handle the uncaused if (GSA) is not in fact necessary.
[6] Or timelessly exists.
[7] We see below that *possibly God exists* also has non-primitive and non-reductive truthmakers.

That I can deal with these possibilities reductively does not entail that I can do so for any outside God.

Divine Necessity

As argued above, I need only treat the necessity of God's existence to have an account of all non-secular necessity. I have argued God's necessity elsewhere, on grounds independent of my modal theory. This has let me appeal to it in setting my theory out without fear of circularity. But these arguments, if successful, gave us only *that* God exists necessarily. They do not tell us what it consists in for His existence to be necessary, and I do not have a full theory of necessity till I explicate this.

Though I have argued it independent of my modal views, God's necessity does fall out of my views. This is not because on the view, every possible world is something God permits to obtain. For it is not part of a theist modal theory that God does not permit His own non-existence, even if in fact He does not. Again, that God writes all world-stories does not entail that every world-story claims that God exists. Authors can write stories which contain no claims about themselves or claims to authorship, stories which claim that other authors wrote them or that nobody wrote them, or stories in which they never exist. If God wrote a world-story in which He never existed, then had it come true, He would not have existed. Further, it would not have come true that a divine world-story came true: if God had never existed, He would not have written any stories. That a world is the subject of a divine story does not imply that in that story, that story's coming true *would be* a divine story's coming true.

One connection between my views and divine (strong) necessity is this: on my view, all possible histories begin (temporally or causally) with God's existence. So God possibly does not exist only if possibly He thereafter ceases to exist. He cannot cease to exist if He is and remains atemporal. But perhaps He is always temporal or He can 'first' be timeless and then become temporal. On either assumption, divine contingency would require not only that God cease to exist, but that time continue thereafter. If God ceases to exist and time ceases too, God's ceasing does not entail that at some time in some possible world, He does not exist—and if God exists at all times in all possible worlds, He exists necessarily. If (GSA) is necessary, it is not possible that God cease and time continue. So it is not possible that there be a time at which God does not exist, on my views: God exists strong-necessarily.

Again, on my views, a possibility that He not exist could not be (so to speak) imposed on God by the contents of possible worlds. Rather, possibly God does not exist only if His nature or choice make this so. God is by nature perfect, and my arguments elsewhere for His necessity include perfect-being arguments. So these are arguments that His nature makes Him necessary—and if it does,

His choice cannot alter this. Thus again, on my modal views, God exists necessarily. Further, suppose it *were* in God to choose to exist contingently. On my views, He necessarily is there at least at the start of things, so this would have to consist in choosing to permit His demise. As God is perfectly rational and good, plausibly He would not so choose without good and morally sufficient reason. So plausibly it would be in Him to have good and morally sufficient reason to permit His demise. Such a reason would have to be a matter of His demise bringing about some good which even omnipotence and omniscience could not bring about without it. If I am right that God has the GSA-property (and the cognate GAO-property) by nature, it is not in Him for there to be such a good.

Again, I have rejected Platonism about attributes on grounds independent of my modal views.[8] If Platonism is false, it is not contingently false. Any form of realism is a partial account of what it is to be an attribute. Nothing relevant to what cathood is would differ from world to world. (If there are cats, they would still resemble *qua* cats, and so on.) So there is no reason cathood would be a Platonic universal in one world but a set of tropes in another. And what it is to be something does not seem the sort of thing to be contingent. If Platonism is not contingently false, then necessarily, there are divine powers only if a divine being is there to bear them. But from eternity, there was only God, and *per* earlier argument, if God did not exist, there would be no understudy to step in. Thus if Platonism is false,

1. God never existed → from eternity, no divine powers exist.

(1) is compatible with Meinongianism. A Meinongian could grant it and just add that if God does not exist, divine powers are among the non-existent objects. And of course, (1) follows from my own positive account of divine powers as so far outlined.

Now if God exists necessarily, (1) has a necessarily false antecedent. But as it is a relevant consequence of substantive metaphysical claims, (1) is a substantive truth. It tells us something significant about the relation between God's and divine powers' existence. Further, if we are to argue God's necessity non-circularly, we cannot premise *or* presuppose His necessity. So we cannot treat (1) as also trivially true. Rather, if the argument premising (1) succeeds, among its consequences will be that (1) is trivially as well as substantively true. Another consequence will be that

2. God never existed → from eternity, there are divine powers.

A Platonist about attributes, noting that divine powers are attributes, could suggest that (2) is a substantive truth, reflecting the (supposed) fact that the absence of one necessary being, God, would not affect the presence of others (the attributes). But (again) I have rejected Platonism. Someone else might

---

[8] 'God and the Problem of Universals', *Oxford Studies in Metaphysics* 2 (2006), 325–56.

suggest, tongue perhaps slightly in cheek, that if Platonism is false and Platonic attributes would exist necessarily, among the items there cannot be are Platonic divine powers, and so in the impossible world in which God does not exist, there would be these—and (2) reflects this fact about impossibility. It might be an adequate response that if so, (1) reflects the truth about possible worlds' and (2) the truth about impossible worlds' contents, and so (1), not (2), should govern our reasoning about what is true in all possible worlds.

As I see it, every secular modal truth has a divine power in its ontology. Remove a truth's ontology and we remove its truthmakers. Had a truthmaker not been there, either what it makes true would not have been true or something else would have made it true. So

3. From eternity, no divine powers exist → from eternity there are no secular modal truths or secular modal truths have an entirely different ontology.

(3) too has an impossible antecedent if God exists necessarily, and I would answer questions about this much as I did the parallel questions about (1). Still, (3) is the right conditional to reason with only if no secular modal truth has, in addition to a truthmaker with a theist ontology, another with an ontology involving not God but non-existent objects: it is at this point that I part company with Meinongians. If some truth did have such a truthmaker, then if no divine powers existed, there would still 'be' all the non-existent objects, and so the ontology of modal truth would not be entirely different and yet there would be secular modal truths. Further, divine powers would still 'be' there, as non-existent objects. But that they do not exist would entail that modal ontology (in our sense of 'ontology') would partly differ. Meinongians insist that whether or not an item exists, it is the same object. So a Meinongian would say that non-existent divine powers are still divine powers. But even if they were, modal ontology would no longer have a 'divine powers' component. If divine powers do not exist, nor does God. (Nothing could be both divine and wholly powerless, and deity is an essential property.) If He does not exist, nothing can cause Him to exist (His essential aseity and ultimacy rule this out), nor can He come to exist uncaused (He would then not be eternal, having previously not existed). So His existence would not be causally possible, and His having His powers could not actually serve as a truthmaker for a claim of secular causal possibility. God would still 'be' there, but in the sense of 'ontology' we have used so far, He would not be part of the modal ontology. So even a Meinongian would have to say that

> from eternity, no divine powers exist → from eternity there are no secular modal truths or secular modal truths have a partly different ontology.

This claim, which does not require me to deny Meinongianism, would serve my purposes as well as (3). So having noted that, I complete the argument in terms of (3).

(3) and (1) give us

4. God never existed → from eternity there are no secular modal truths or secular modal truths have an entirely different ontology.

Given (4), if God exists contingently, either (a) it is possible that there be no secular modal truths; or (b) it is possible that secular modal truths have an entirely different from-eternity ontology. (A) seems false. If there could be no secular modal truths, 'possible' and 'impossible' express only contraries, not contradictories: for every secular possible P, it can happen that it is neither possible that P nor impossible that P, for there is a possible world with no secular modal truths, and in that world neither is true. Now some do maintain that these are contraries: on generalism, before I existed, I was not impossible, but nor was I possible, though it was possible that there be someone just like me. But still, it is unintuitive. It is a strike against generalism to be forced to it. Again, if there could be no secular modal truths, secular necessities are contingently necessary and secular possibilities are contingently possible. Thus the strong intuitions favoring S4 or S5 as the logic of absolute modality cut against this possibility. As to (b), as the Introduction noted, stating a truth's ontology is saying what real items go into its being true. For the truth to be true is for the ontology to be there and be such as to make it true, and so giving a modal truth's ontology is giving the largest part of an account of what it is for a possibility to be possible, a necessity to be necessary, and so on. Such accounts do not look like they should be contingent. Theses like 'For it to be possible that there be one more atom than ever actually exists is for there to be a property a universe might have, such that if a universe had it there would be one more atom' read like identity-statements, and even like a sort of analysis or definition, and so seem to require necessity. So in every possible world, divine powers are the ground of the secular possible. But every possible world includes some secular facts, if only negative existential facts (there being no cornflakes, and so on). And so in every possible world, God always exists, because the ontology of modality is what it is. My views again yield divine necessity.

Of course, this does not tell us why we have God rather than Platonic entities or a Meinongian menagerie at the roots of reality. But there cannot be an explanation for this, no matter what is down there. It is not self-explanatory that (say) God is the true ultimate reality. There are no literally self-explanatory facts. That is, asked 'Why P?', 'Because P' is never an explanatory answer. But there is nothing more basic than whatever is truly the ultimate reality, to provide an explanation of why it has that status. Still, I argue later that God's existence is not a brute fact. I argue that it is not brute on my theory that He exists necessarily, there being on my theory no coherent alternative; nor then is it brute that He exists, for the same reason. But my argument for this depends on my modal theory. So it does not set up a *locus* independent of the theory to explain His necessity, nor yield one to explain His existence. There is no saying why it is God's existence to which there is no coherent alternative rather than Platonic entities'. There is nothing on which it depends that God is the ultimate reality. He exists, and it is His nature to be so. The most we can say is that given that He exists, there is a reason there are not also independent Platonic attributes: the creation/conservation presumption discussed early on leads to a claim that God has (by nature) not just the GSA-property but also a cognate GAO-property.

The argument just completed appealed to secular necessities—for example, of there being no independent Platonic attributes. But this, of course, does not entail that God's necessity depends on secular ones. The order of knowing and the order of being need not coincide. And I now offer one that does not appeal to secular necessities. As the most basic fact of all, God exists. God is alone at the explanatorily basic level of things. By His nature, God is the source of all possibility His nature does not itself determine. By His nature, every possible history includes some fact His nature does not determine. More fully, God's conceiving is the ultimate root of all secular possibility. By His nature He is the source of secular possibility, as it is His nature to think up candidate secular states of affairs, and His natural perfection guarantees that He thinks up some good enough to permit. Further, by His nature, every possible history includes some secular facts. Even the possible history which is God existing alone, never creating, includes such secular facts as there being no peach pies. For it is God's nature to think up other things, and once He has, nothing is a maximal possibility which does not settle the question of whether they are there. If God thinks up Swiss cheese, then (speaking as if there are propositions) there is the proposition *there is Swiss cheese*, and nothing is a maximal possibility which does not settle this proposition's truth-status.[9] This is again by God's nature: He is considering candidate plans, and since by His nature it is up to Him whether there is Swiss cheese and He is ideally rational, in each plan He settles *inter alia* whether there is to be Swiss cheese. As every world-history includes secular facts and there are any only if God has existed, by God's nature, no matter how history goes, it is presupposed that God has existed: it is necessary that God exist for at least some period. So the only remaining questions are whether any time could precede God's existence and whether He can cease to exist. But it is of God's nature to be eternal. If God is atemporal, no time precedes His existence: only what is temporal can stand in the temporal 'before' relation. If God is temporal, He could not qualify as eternal had He not existed for *all* past time. And no by-nature eternal being can cease to exist. Further, God's conceiving does not produce anything as its content which might exist independent of it, since there *are* no entities which are its content. Were God to cease understanding what it is to be a dog, there would be no property *doghood* left behind. This is due to His nature, which determines how His mind works and so what it does and does not produce. So even the possibility that something appear and persist wholly uncaused would depend on God's continually conceiving that state of affairs. God's

---

[9] One could make an equivalent point without talk of propositions, but doing so would be cumbersome.

nature makes it the case that there would not be possibilities even of the uncaused without Him. Thus it is not in God to make it possible that a history go on independent of Him. It cannot be that anything else exists but God does not. Thus, given that God is by nature the source of secular possibility and is by nature eternal, His necessary existence follows. So God's nature accounts for His necessity (which is not to say that God's existing necessarily consists in His having His nature). God's necessity is self-derived.

This explains God's necessity. But it does not say in just what it consists for God's existence to be necessary. Because necessary truths' truth-conditions include a negative existential and these lack truthmakers, necessary truths have no truthmakers, even in my thin sense: they have only truth-explanations. What follows provides materials for one.) In theories of worlds, God's existing necessarily is His existing in all possible worlds. That is, it is God's existing in W_1, W_2, and so on, and there being no worlds other than W_1, W_2, and so on. For God to exist in W_1, taking worlds as states of affairs just for exposition's sake, is just for it to be the case that W_1 is actualized $\rightarrow$ God exists. There is a wide consensus that whatever the nature or status of possible worlds, talk of them captures something about the content and semantics of necessity-claims. It would be good, then, to mirror the worldly explication of divine necessity in my own account of it. I do so as follows.

Let us distinguish two ways to think about divine world-powers: there is what they are powers to bring about, promote, and so on, and there is also what would be so were they used. The former gives their secular content (and perhaps also some 'mixed' content: if God has the power to bring it about that P, where P is secular, perhaps it is also power to bring it about that God brings it about that P). The latter corresponds to what would be so in a possible world—that is, as W_1 is actualized $\rightarrow$ God exists, so we have that world-power P is used $\rightarrow$ God exists. If none but God could use a world-power, this conditional is a particularly evident truth, and there is reason to think this so. A world-power is a single power, so to recruit some vast subset of all possible powers that all of a particular possible world that depends on God alone, and God's own input to all of it that does not, winds up actual. If anything else could use such a power, it could coerce God into doing all this. In any event, I suggest that God's existing necessarily is its being the case that P_1 is used $\rightarrow$ God exists, P_2 is used $\rightarrow$ God exists, etc., and there are no world-powers other than P_1, P_2, etc. We needn't lean on the 'coercion' point to warrant the conditionals. God's nature explains them. This is how it is with divine powers because God is what He is; P_1 is used $\rightarrow$ God exists due to things about God we have already seen. That world-powers' being used entails His existence is determined by His nature as He has it independent of and explanatorily prior to the powers' having their contents. I add that if this is what God's necessity consists in, then by giving Himself His world-powers, He brings it about that He exists necessarily. His nature guarantees that things come out this way, but they come out this way by His activity. But that God makes Himself necessary by filling out His world-powers does not entail that His necessity depends for explanation on any secular necessity. It was in God to give Himself world-powers that are not powers to make any particular or attribute His actual powers are powers to make, and so effect no actual secular necessity, and nonetheless come out necessary.

On the worldly picture, that God exists necessarily consists in facts about worlds. On my picture, it consists in facts about His powers. We might sum up these facts a bit differently. Iff P_1 is used → God exists, P_2 is used → God exists, etc., there are no world-powers other than P_1, P_2, etc., and every divine power is recruited by some world-power, there is no divine power to bring it about that God does not exist. If that is so, we could say that God's existing necessarily consists in God's having all His powers but lacking the power to bring it about that He does not exist. We could say the like of any non-secular necessity.

Divine Possibility Again

With this backdrop I return to the possibility that God exists. This has (so I have argued) a reductive truthmaker. But that possibly God exists is also true because some divine world-power's being used entails that He exists. God's power cannot account for His ever existing. He must already be there if He is to act, and if He is there, it is too late for His power to account for it. But we need not deny this to maintain that His having His world-powers provides non-reductive truthmakers for *possibly God exists*. It is a fact about the power that if it is used, God exists, even though it is not a fact about what that power is a power to produce.

Any possible non-world state of affairs possibly co-obtains with some complement state of affairs such that the two jointly make up a possible world. This holds for God's existence too. By His nature, God possibly exists only if His existence possibly co-obtains with some complement. In no possible state of things is there no fact about what besides God exists. Either God exists alone, or He co-exists with other things He has permitted to exist. It takes the facts about accompaniment to have a maximal possibility, due finally to God's nature. God's existing makes it true that He possibly exists and His permission brings it about that He exists in a full possible world. As the power permission gives Him is intrinsic to Him, God's possibility remains intrinsic.

I have now given an account of the possibility and necessity of the non-secular. There are also contingent non-secular states of affairs—for example, that God knows that you are reading this. The story here should be clear. God so empowers Himself that it is possible that you be reading this. His nature guarantees that if you do, He will know it. So His nature and a divine power jointly make it true that He possibly knows this, and so too for the claim that possibly He does not.

18

THEISM AND MODAL
SEMANTICS

A modal metaphysics should provide for the truth of claims employing modal locutions. One can show that it does by giving a semantics for modal talk in its terms. A Kripke-style semantics for the modal locutions of a language L involves a sextuple $\langle W, w^\star, R, D, Q, V \rangle$, where W is the set of all possible worlds, $w^\star$ the actual world, R a relation on the members of W (accessibility between worlds), D the set of all possible individuals, Q a function that assigns to each world a subset of D (the individuals that exist at that world), and V a valuation function that assigns to each predicate an extension at each world, to each constant a denotation at any world at which it has one and to each sentence a truth-value at each world.[1] Given these, the semantics assigns such truth-conditions to L-sentences as that '$\Diamond$Fa' is true just in case there exist a member x of D and a member w of W such that Q assigns x to the domain of individuals existing in w (that is, $x \in Q(w)$) and V assigns x to 'a' at w (that is, x = V('a', w)) and to F's extension at w (that is, V('a,' w) $\in$ V('F', w)).[2] Thus it treats truths quantifying over worlds as determining the truth of possibility-claims (and so on). I now provide a semantics in terms of my own view.

World-powers

My attitude to possible worlds is fictionalist.[3] As I see it, possible-world accounts commit themselves existentially to things which do not exist.

---

[1] The *locus classicus* is Saul Kripke, 'Semantical Considerations on Modal Logic', in Leonard Linsky (ed.), *Reference and Modality* (Oxford: Oxford University Press, 1971), pp. 63–72.

[2] I am indebted to a referee here.

[3] It is a version of what Rosen calls 'timid fictionalism' (Gideon Rosen, 'Modal Fictionalism', *Mind* 99 (1990), 354): I hold not that the contents of our fictional world-talk determine the modal facts, but that the facts are there independently and world-talk should conform to them.

They are strictly speaking false. But we can usefully speak in possible-world terms, because beneath world-talk is a reality involving God over which we really do quantify, which is isomorphic with world-talk in obvious ways and which our putative world-descriptions correctly describe *modulo* their false existential commitments. There is not an abstract, necessarily existing God-independent possible world representing that some pigs have wings, but there is a divine power to produce winged pigs which some world-powers recruit.

A world-power is a power to will[4]—to will to bring about what other powers are powers to bring about. By willing to bring these things about, God 'fires' those other powers. A world-power is a power so to use other powers that all of a possible world that depends on God alone, and God's input to all of it that does not, winds up actual. World-powers share parts as Chapter 13's paths through the world-tree do. Where fictional worlds contain the same state, there really are world-powers set to 'fire' the same powers to produce that state, which share the power to 'fire' the latter. If God is temporal, a world-power is a power to 'fire' other powers in a sequence, a power to use this one, then that, then that. If God is atemporal, a world-power is a power so to 'fire' powers as to produce a sequential history. A world-power F recruits a power G just if F = G or F is a power to cause use of G—that is, 'fire' G. It can happen that we help determine which world-power God uses (that is, what He wills to bring about). If Michaelangelo freely carves *David*, then due to his efforts and God's prior intention to leave him free, uphold natural laws, and so on, God wills to conserve *David*. Speaking loosely, given that context, Michaelangelo brings it about that God uses a world-power recruiting a *David*-power.

World-powers have a maximality property, that

> F is a world-power = df. F is used $\rightarrow$ ((P)(P is a contingent tenseless secular proposition) $\rightarrow$ F's use brings it about or promotes it that P has a determinate truth-status).

I speak of truth-status, not truth-values, to let propositions lack truth-value (for example, some expressed by sentences with vague predicates). I use 'proposition' without commitment. There are roles philosophers ascribe to propositions—for example, being objects of belief. I do not assume that anything plays these roles, or that if played one class of entity plays all of them; I am committed only to denying that if anything plays these roles, it is abstract objects independent of God. Only tenseless sentences matter here, even if there are irreducibly tensed facts. Actualist possible worlds, were there such, would represent tenseless skeletons of full histories for tensed-time universes. For suppose that they included or precluded irreducibly tensed states of affairs. Including that P is just entailing that P. Precluding that P is just

---

[4] One does not need another volition to use such a power. One need not will to will in order to will. So if God uses a world-power, He does not will to do so. He just wills—that is, uses the power.

entailing that ¬P.[5] If a world precluded the irreducibly tensed state of affairs that noon is present, then, in that world noon would never be present: if that world contained time, its time would not include noon or be tenseless. If a world precluded all times' thus being present, it would be a tenseless or atemporal world. If a world included noon's thus being present, its history would be just an instant. If it included more than one time's thus being present, either it would include multiple temporal series or it would be impossible. Possible worlds representing only atemporal or tenseless-time universes can include all that would be so were they actualized. If universes containing single extended tensed temporal series are possible, possible worlds representing them are just tenseless skeletons, not full histories. They do not include all that would ever be true were they actualized. I leave just what to say about this as homework for those who believe in both irreducibly tensed facts and possible worlds. On my account, God thinks up a tenseless history including time t (or events in terms of which t-talk can be parsed), then permits that t be future, then present, then past. As I see it, this is empowering Himself to make time pass.

For all propositions π, if π is contingent, secular, and tenseless, God has from eternity the power and chance to bring about or promote π's truth, and some world-power recruits this power. Further,

1. $(\pi)(\pi$ is secular $\rightarrow (\Diamond \pi \equiv$ God had from eternity the power and chance to bring it about or promote it that π, or God had from eternity no power to bring it about or promote it that $\neg \pi$ and brought this lack of power about from eternity)).

The last disjunct covers secular necessities. This is not a conceptual analysis. It only correlates secular modal truths with theist truthmakers. Nor is (1) a reduction to anything non-modal, unless (as I have not supposed) one can give a purely non-modal account of powers. If God from eternity never had power and chance even to promote it that P, then from all eternity He did not even promote it that P. So unless something else could have satisfied some clause of (CAUSAL POSS) with respect to P without God in any way promoting this, that P is not causally and so not absolutely possible. Such an item would have to come to be without even indirect divine input, and so either uncaused or due only to events with no divine input. Per earlier argument, God's so much as conceiving it would promote its existence, and so it would have to be an item God had not so much as conceived (or whose type He had not conceived, on generalism). As He could not have failed to be omniscient, this is ruled out. Per the last chapter's treatment of the contingent non-secular, 'God had from eternity the power and chance to bring it about

---

[5] If worlds are propositions; otherwise a world W's including that P is that *W is actualized* entails that P. (See Alvin Plantinga, 'Two Concepts of Modality', *Philosophical Perspectives* 1 (1987), 192.) The text is as it is just for simplicity.

or promote it that π' also covers mixed propositions, those non-secular because *inter alia* referring to or quantifying over God, a divine attribute, and so on, but also with secular content. Contingent ones include that God knows that you are reading this and universal quantifications whose domains include both God and other things—for example, *everyone rejoiced that the Giants beat the Eagles.* For a hard case, suppose that from eternity, God conceives that (secular) P. That $\Diamond$(God conceives that P) is necessary and mixed. But my view might tempt one to say that He has from eternity the power never to conceive that P, counter to the claim that $\Diamond$(*God conceives that P*) falls under a disjunct in (1). Suppose, though, that He does have this power. He has it only if He conceives that P; there could not otherwise be that specific power. So He has it only if it is too late to use it. It is not in Him to have a chance to use it, and so it is not in Him to use it. He is not even possibly able to use it. So He does not after all have it. There is no such thing as having a power to do what it is impossible that one be able to do. So though there is a general divine power to conceive freely and nothing in God predetermined that He would conceive that P, God has brought it about that there is no divine power to bring it about or promote it that He never conceives that P. So that $\Diamond$(God conceives that P) does fall under (1).

Powers merely to promote raise a question. It is compatible with God's merely promoting it that P that it not come about that P. Suppose then that God has only powers to promote that P, not to bring it about. Then God's world-powers recruit only powers to promote that P. But God can promote it that P and yet have it come about that ¬P. I want world-powers to (help) do duty for possible worlds. One might wonder how a power whose use is compatible with its not being the case that P can (help) do duty for a world in which P, given that a world in which P is not one whose being actualized is compatible with its not being the case that P. I reply that as we are giving the semantics of possibility claims, not actuality-claims, the most that is required is that the power be one which given opportunity does genuinely ground the possibility in question. I hope earlier argument has shown that a power merely to promote does so.

Preconditions

Propositions can be secular, purely non-secular, or mixed. Some contingent mixed propositions are about or about consequences of God's using a world-power—for example, that God knows that some cats are striped. God's power to bring it about that some cats are striped is also a power to bring it about that He knows this. So world-powers are also maximal with respect to 'consequential' contingent mixed propositions. The rest of the contingent mixed state preconditions of God's using a world-power—for example, that

God prefers that (secular) P. The use of a world-power recruiting the P-power has a contingent precondition, His preference that P. It also has necessary ones—for example, that God exists. Some preconditions help explain a world-power's use: God's reason to use a world-power helps explain His doing so, and if it is a power *inter alia* to bring it about that P includes that all things considered He preferred that P. Some preconditions help explain God's having the world-power: He has it *inter alia* because He conceives that P. Some help explain His being able to have it: He is able to *inter alia* because He exists. Some do not help explain any of these but are in the right ways connected to things that do: it does not help explain God's bringing it about that P that He prefer that He prefers that P, but still there is some sense of priority in which, because the one preference helps explain His act, the other is in place prior to the act.[6] Preferences exist just if God actually so prefers. Otherwise, God has only a power so to prefer: to say that God has alternate preferences is to say that He can prefer this way rather than that. So the preconditions for worlds supposing alternate preferences include a power to prefer (and the power to believe that He prefers, and so on).

In Place of Worlds

I now argue, by considering cases, that an account of W in terms of world-powers and preconditions can 'cover' every proposition. Every proposition is contingent, necessary, or impossible. Impossible propositions are impossible because there necessarily is not something needed to make them true, so we need only worry about the necessary and the contingent. For every contingent P, either some divine world-power recruits a power to bring it about or promote it that P (this is so if *P* is secular or consequential mixed) or that P is a precondition of some world-power's use. There are no contingent purely non-secular propositions. If proposition is purely non-secular—about only God, divine essential attributes, and so on, with no secular content—it is necessary or impossible. So

2. $(\pi)(\pi$ is purely non-secular $\rightarrow (\Diamond \pi \equiv$ that π is a precondition of every world-power's use)).

Given (1) and (2), there are enough world-powers and preconditions to cover the contingent and the purely non-secular. Every proposition is secular,

---

[6] God has definable concepts of the secular impossible: to be a round square = df. to be both round and square. God's having these is among the necessary preconditions of world-powers' use. As I have suggested, once God has the vocabulary of the possible in mind, He also knows how these attributes cannot combine. There is no temporal gap between knowing how they can and knowing how they cannot; settling how attributes *can* combine *ipso facto* settles how they cannot and yields concepts of how they cannot. So God's having these concepts is a 'connected' precondition of any world-power's use. Propositions about the secular definitionally impossible are precondition-propositions.

purely non-secular, or mixed. So we have left to consider just necessary mixed propositions.

Necessary mixed propositions include, for instance, that God knows that possibly some cat is striped. God's knowing such things is a precondition of using any world-power; they figure in His decision about what to try to actualize. Again, it is mixed and necessary that God is omnipotent and possibly some cat is striped. God is omnipotent by nature and His having His nature is a precondition of any world-power's use; if God's knowing that P is a precondition, its being the case that P is a precondition; so the whole conjunction expresses a precondition. The necessary mixed also include logical and mathematical truths if there are such. If these are necessarily true, that is because God thinks as He does and has only powers to bring about or promote states of affairs not involving truth-value gaps (and for His every power F, His having F makes propositions only determinately true or false). God does the relevant thinking by nature, and having His nature is a precondition. His having some of His powers is a precondition of His using the world-power He uses—but as I have argued, He settles what His powers are all at once, and so His having all His powers (and no others) also counts as a precondition. So necessary logical and mathematical truths, if any, also count as preconditions of any world-power's use. It seems, then, that for every possible P there is either a world-power or a precondition of such a power's use. On the standard account, possibly P iff there is a possible world in which P. I say that possibly P iff there are a P-world-power and the preconditions of its use, and I take as W all such pluralities. This account of W undergirds the standard equivalences. It gives as truth-condition of the claim that $\Diamond P \equiv \neg\Box\neg P$ if P is secular or mixed: for instance, that

3. ((some world-power recruits a power to bring it about or promote it that P) $\equiv \neg$(no world-power recruits a power bring it about or promote it that P)) and ((it is a precondition of some world-power's use that P) $\equiv \neg$(it is a precondition of no world-power's use that P)).[7]

The truth-condition if P is pure non-secular is that

4. it is a precondition of some world-power's use that P $\equiv \neg$(it is a precondition of no world-power's use that P).

This account of W does not affect the treatment of subjunctive conditionals. Talk about worlds is natural when we Ramsey-test, and it floats free of our underlying metaphysics. That is, we can talk about what would be the case if P whether we think we are talking about properties the universe would instantiate, propositions that would be true, states of affairs that

---

[7] That God is as He is internally explains the second conjunct. It explains the first that for any P, God permits that P just if it is not the case that God prevents it that P and is disposed to do so no matter what He preferred.

would obtain—or what the firing of powers would make so. Given my views, we can talk about worlds, since we can talk about what powers are powers to produce or promote.

In Place of the Actual World

Speaking world-talk, if as I believe the future is unreal and determinism is false, there is no one actual world (that is, actualized possible world). There has instead been an actualized world-segment common to many worlds, and there having been that one segment is compatible with more than one possible future. So w* is the common actualized segment as of the present. If God is temporal, corresponding to w* are all the powers God has so far used in playing His role in history, plus the actual preconditions of their use. If God is atemporal, an entire world-power has atemporally 'fired', but corresponding to w* are just those powers whose temporal effects have so far occurred, plus the preconditions. One way or the other, then, w* is a plurality of powers together with the actual preconditions of their use.

Accessibility

For R, I take a relation on world-powers which conditional divine permissions effect. Speaking world-talk, God makes a world W accessible from a world W_2 by bringing it about that were W_2 actual, He would permit W to be actual. Moving toward my scheme, we first say that this is so disposing Himself that were W_2 actual He would give or have given Himself the W world-power. Translating fully into my scheme, one world-power W is accessible from another W_2 just if W_2 includes a power to give God W, so that in using W_2 God would give Himself W. On my view—an S5 actualism with pre-creative singular concepts—God actually has both powers. He has in every world all powers He has in any world. Thus the content of omnipotence does not vary world-to-world, which seems reasonable.

Domains

Intuitively, there are not all the objects there could have been. If there are not, there could be objects that do not actually exist. This creates pressure to let these objects into D, and so endorse possibilism; actualists cannot let such objects into D, and yet some, at least, want to provide for true singular propositions about non-actual, non-existent objects. My way to do so appropriates bits of two others. Ruth Marcus suggests applying the substitutional interpretation of the quantifiers: do without domains in non-actual worlds. Instead use a set of actually existing names for objects, and take variables in sentences as place-markers for syntactically appropriate substitutions of those names. Assign truth-values directly to atomic sentences at worlds, rather than working by way of domains of objects which satisfy predicates at worlds. Take it as true in a world that $(\exists x)(Fx)$ just if there is a name such that $(\exists x)(Fx)$ has a true substitution instance in that world and true in a world that $(x)(Fx)$ just if every name provides this a true substitution instance in that world.[8] For the actual world,

> suppose that ... objects ... are ... denoted by those names ... Where the substitution class for the quantifiers are the names assigned to the actual world, we can read the quantifiers objectually ... associating a domain of objects with the actual world and view(ing) our quantifiers as mixed; referential for this world and substitutional otherwise.[9]

One difficulty here, of course, is the assumption that there actually are enough names to provide for talk of all possible objects.

For Plantinga as for Marcus, D includes only actual objects.[10] Plantinga does not eschew domains for non-actual worlds. Rather, he lets it be contingent what Q assigns as a domain of objects to each world: there are available for assignment only those objects that happen to be actual, and had others been actual, Q would have had a different output for some worlds.[11] But there is in addition to D a set of necessarily existing haecceities.[12] There is in addition to Q a function assigning a set of haecceities to each world—those that would be exemplified were the world actual.[13] Jager—to whom Plantinga refers us for a formal semantics[14]—assigns haecceities, not objects, to constants.[15] Some read this as entailing that constants denote haecceities.[16] This has in turn led to a charge that Plantinga leaves us no way to say that an

---

[8] Ruth Barcan Marcus, 'Possibilia and Possible Worlds', in Ruth Barcan Marcus, *Modalities* (Oxford: Oxford University Press, 1993), pp. 212–13.

[9] Ruth Barcan Marcus, 'Dispensing with Possibilia', *Proceedings of the American Philosophical Association* 49 (1975–6), 48.

[10] Alvin Plantinga, 'Actualism and Possible Worlds', in Michael Loux (ed.), *The Possible and the Actual* (Ithaca, NY: Cornell University Press, 1979), pp. 268–9.

[11] *Ibid.*, p. 268. Or, taking functions *in extenso*, a different function would have been Q.

[12] *Ibid.*, pp. 266–72. Plantinga muddies the waters a bit by claiming that a semantics worked out by Thomas Jager ('An Actualistic Semantics for Quantified Modal Logic', *Notre Dame Journal of Formal Logic* 23 (1982)) reflects his general approach (Alvin Plantinga, 'Self-Profile', in James Tomberlin and Peter van Inwagen (eds), *Alvin Plantinga* (Dordrecht: D. Reidel, 1985), p. 92), because Jager turns D into a set of essences. But Plantinga does not say that every feature of Jager's system reflects his views, only that it represents his belief that unexemplified essences should be used to handle claims about non-existent individuals (*ibid.*).

[13] Plantinga, 'Actualism and Possible Worlds', 269.

[14] *Ibid.*, 272, n. 4.

[15] *Op. cit.*, 340.

[16] Edward Zalta and Bernard Linsky, 'In Defense of the Simplest Quantified Modal Logic', *Philosophical Perspectives* 8 (1994), 454, n. 30.

individual has a property.[17] But for Plantinga, names *express* essences, which
are their senses.[18] Plantinga simply adds domains of essences to the standard
Kripkean machinery.[19] We should take Plantinga's V to assign to constants
senses they express—in virtue of expressing which they denote the right
individuals if the individuals exist. Where worlds involve items that do not
actually exist, for Plantinga, Q does not yield a denotation for a name, but
V gives it a sense, and had those worlds been actual, there would have been an
object for the name to denote.[20] For Plantinga, then, W is actual → Fa just if
in W, V assigns a haecceity h of a to F.[21] If a does not exist, the content of 'a has
F in W' is that W is actual → h and F are co-exemplified. If it is true in W that
Fa, either V assigns truth in W to Fa directly—in which case Plantinga's view
resembles Marcus'—or this is true in W because W is actual → h and F are co-
exemplified. If a exists, then in any world in which it is true that Fa, h, and
F are co-exemplified, 'a' expresses h and (since only a can have h) refers to a,
and so a has F.

I say with Plantinga that D contains just actual individuals and Q's output is
contingent. In place of haecceities I say that for each possible non-divine
individual, there is in God the reality behind talk of a singular concept, a
mental event. (As God exists necessarily, we do not need such a proxy in His
case; all other individuals would be contingent.) I do not say these events are
senses of our terms. I add to the Kripke machinery a plurality E of just these
events. I also add a function 2Q which assigns to each world-power the E-
events which understand who or which the individuals would be whose
existence that world-power would cause or promote, assigns individual events
to constants (as understandings of what denotations would be), and assigns
pluralities of them to predicates' extensions (as understandings of what
extensions would be). Speaking within the fictions of divine concepts and
possible worlds, 2Q parcels out divine singular concepts to God's stipulations
about what is to be true in each world.

V assigns actual objects as denotations of terms and in extensions, and
truth-values in worlds to sentences. If a exists, D includes a, and my account is
just Kripke's *modulo* my account of W and my avoidance of sets: it is true in
W that Fa just if there exists one of D(w), x, such that x = V('a', w) and V('a',
w) is one of V('F', w). If a does not exist, it is true in W that Fa just if there
exists a member of E, x, which is one of 2Q(w) and is such that x = 2Q('a', w)
and 2Q('a', w) is one of 2Q('F', w). It is true that ◊Fa just if there is a member
w of W such that it is true in w that Fa. That is, this is true just if there is a
world-power whose content God settles *inter alia* by deciding to place a, the
individual a singular-understanding event e understands, in F's extension. If a

[17] *Ibid.*, 442.
[18] Alvin Plantinga, 'The Boethian Compromise', *American Philosophical Quarterly* 15 (1978), 129–38.
[19] Plantinga, 'Actualism', 268–9.
[20] *Ibid.*, 268.
[21] Jager, *op. cit.*, 339–40.

does not exist, V assigns truth in W to *Fa* directly—God just stipulates that (say) Fido barks at Boots in W. But it does so just if the event 2Q assigns to 'a' in W is among those 2Q assigns to 'F's extension in W. W is actual → Fa just if it is true in W that Fa. Finally, quantifiers in non-actual worlds are in effect partly substitutional; it is, for example, true in a world that (x)(Fx) just if in that world, V assigns every actual object existing there to 'F's extension and assigns *true* to every proposition predicating F of an individual, including individuals that do not actually exist.

Barcan Formulae

Mine is an S5 theory. In S5 one can easily derive the Barcan Formula (BF), $(x)\Box Fx \rightarrow \Box(x)Fx$.[22] But BF appears false. Let W be the world that happens to be actual. Let F be the predicate 'is included in W'. Then BF's antecedent is true. Every actual object is necessarily included in W, because W has all its contents necessarily. BF's consequent seems to assert that in all possible worlds, all objects are included in W. This seems false, because intuitively, there could be objects there are not.[23] We can play the same trick with 'is identical with some in-fact-actual object'. Those adopting S5, then, must either block derivation of BF and show that their semantics does not validate it, or show why BF is harmless.

The intuition that BF is false arises because we take worlds' domains to contain non-actual objects. I deny this, but I still avoid BF. On my account there are more singular truths and true existential quantifications in a world than the objects in its domain account for. I accommodate the intuition that there could be objects there are not roughly as Marcus does, by assigning truth in a world directly to propositions about such objects, treating quantifiers as non-objectual save where actual objects are in play, and noting that were these other worlds actual, there would be objects for their terms to denote. This is a natural move given my metaphysical picture: God simply stipulates what shall be true in each possible world, and that makes it true in that world. He need not do so by first finding denotations for constants in a mental language, just as Conan Doyle knows what he means by 'Sherlock Holmes' without finding it a denotation, and can stipulate what is to be true-in-the-story about him. Once we make this move, in some possible worlds it is

---

[22] See e.g. Timothy Williamson, 'Bare Possibilia', *Erkenntnis* 48 (1998), 260–1.

[23] If we insist that only in-fact-actual objects are available to quantify over in any possible world—that D includes just actual objects—and do not supplement D with something relevantly like my E or Plantinga's set of haecceities, (BF) will come out true. Just as every in-fact-actual object necessarily is included in W, so necessarily every in-fact-actual object is included in W.

true that there are objects not included in W. Thus BF is false. I have nothing original to say about how to block its derivation.[24]

In S5 one can also derive the Converse Barcan Formula (CBF), $\Box(x)Fx \rightarrow (x)\Box Fx$. What to make of CBF depends on how one reads its quantifiers. If they range only over actual objects, CBF seems true: if it is necessarily the case that all of these are F, then of course, all of them are necessarily F. But one could also read the antecedent's quantifier as ranging in each world over all of that world's objects. So read, CBF seems false. Plug in for F 'exists': it is necessarily the case that every object exists (in every possible world, all that world's objects exist), but intuitively, it is not the case that every actual object necessarily exists. Friends of S5, then, must either block derivation of CBF and show that their semantics does not validate it, or show why CBF is harmless. On my account, the only objects in any world's domain of quantification are actual objects. If D contains only actual objects and necessarily every actual object is F, then of course all of D are necessarily F. But again, on my account the semantics in other worlds goes partly substitutional, and so CBF is false. Here too I have nothing original to say on the derivation side.[25]

Generalism

This is how things are if God has pre-creative singular thoughts of possible individuals. For those who do not accept my case that God has these, I now also sketch a 'generalist' account. In one respect, it is like that just given: D contains only actual individuals. But if God has no pre-creative singular thoughts of non-actual individuals, and is omniscient from eternity, there are from eternity no singular possibilities for non-actual individuals. (Without such a thought, were it possible that Brian Leftow exist, God could not know that, and so would not be omniscient.) All that need providing for in non-actual worlds are singular truths about actual objects and truths about general possibilities. It is not the case from eternity that possibly I exist. Rather, there is from eternity just a TI of which I turn out to be an instance. The truth-maker of *possibly something BL-type exists* is God's having a power to create or sustain something instancing this TI. Once I exist, my existing makes it true that possibly Brian Leftow exists and that possibly someone BL-type exists. On the generalist account, from all eternity, E contains only understandings of TIs, or perhaps we can just delete E, and if D contains no referent for 'a', there is no such proposition as that $\Diamond Fa$.

---

[24] For a survey of ways to do so, see Christopher Menzel, 'Actualism, Ontological Commitment and possible World Semantics,' *Synthese* 85 (1990), http://plato.stanford.edu/entries/actualism/.
[25] See *ibid*.

Domain: The Competition, Briefly

The rivals to my proposal about D are possibilism, Platonism, generalism, and what has been called constant domain metaphysics. I have given some reasons for theists to reject possibilism and Platonism already; Chapter 22 argues further against Platonism, and Chapter 23 argues against both on grounds that may also appeal to atheists. Generalism's chief support comes from arguments that there is just no way there could be singular possibilities in advance of the relevant particulars' existing.[26] Chapter 16 undercut these, at least for theists; atheists can note that the argument from generalism to haecceities admits of a non-theist transform—the transform for the claim that stipulated trans-world identity need not 'follow' a simple quality world-to-world is a claim that trans-world identity can simply be brute, but if we allow this in attributes' case, why not in particulars'?—and most of my rebuttals of anti-haecceity arguments do not depend on theism. On constant domain metaphysics, all possible concrete individuals actually exist. The actual world includes all possible individuals and so do all other worlds: every world has the same domain. The rub is that at any time, most concreta exist in unusual states. On Williamson's 'constant domain' proposal, before you were born, you existed, but were nowhere in space or time.[27] Linsky and Zalta add that you were then abstract (and will be again).[28] But I do not see how your non-temporal state could be both atemporal and *before* you were born. Nor do I see how something atemporal could cease to be so. Its atemporal existence would then be over. What is over lies in the past, and what is in the past is not atemporal. And surely it cannot be the case that a state of affairs was atemporal when 'present'—and if this is not the right way to put it, I leave figuring out a better to constant domain fans—but is temporal when past. Temporality seems to be an intrinsic property; a thing does not seem able to change with respect to temporality by how other things are related to it. If despite this temporality is in fact extrinsic, then we can

---

[26] So Menzel, 'Temporal Actualism and Singular Foreknowledge' one can read Hughes (*op. cit.*) this way too, Christopher Hughes, Negative Existentials, Omniscience and Cosmic Luck; *Religious Studies* 34 (1998), 375–401: he actually contends that there is no way God could know singular truths about non-existent objects and so He cannot be essentially omniscient, but one could take the same arguments, stand pat on the claim that God is essentially omniscient, and infer that there are no singular truths about the non-existent. Prior merely appeals to an incongruity: 'Suppose (someone) living before ... Caesar or Antony ... prophesies that (someone) called "Caesar" ... will be murdered, etc., and another ... called "Antony" ... will dally with Cleopatra, etc. And then suppose this prophet to say, "No, I'm not sure now ... perhaps it is the second ... who will be called 'Caesar' ... etc., and the first who will be ... called 'Antony' etc." This ... would be a spurious switch; and after Caesar and Antony had actually come into being ... it would be quite senseless to ask "Are these ... really the people he meant?" (or) "Is it ... our man's first prophecy or his suggested alternative that has now come to pass?"' (A.N. Prior, 'Identifiable Individuals', in A.N. Prior, *Papers on Time and Tense*, ed. Per Hasle, Peter Ohrstrom, Torben Brauner, and Jack Copeland (Oxford: Oxford University Press, 2003), new edn, pp. 86–7). Chapter 16 suggests that one can believe in haecceities without allowing that this sort of switch is possible.

[27] Timothy Williamson, 'Bare Possibilia', *Erkenntnis* 48 (1988), 266.

[28] Bernard Linsky and Edward Zalta, 'In Defense of the Contingently Non-Concrete', *Philosophical Studies* 84 (1996), 283–94.

reason this way: 'before' it became temporal, this state of affairs was going to be temporal. It was going to be true of it that something had succeeded it. But then this state of affairs had a future—and so was not atemporal. Again, on the constant domain proposal, you first existed without material parts, then all at once came to have many. Either you as abstract had no parts, or you had as parts only whatever sort are appropriate to abstract objects, and so you presumably no longer have these. In other contexts—Star Trek transporter scenarios, for example—we do not believe that objects can survive having their entire composition altered at once. Again, we think our existences must be temporally continuous—that we cannot survive 'gaps' in our existence. But what sense can be made of continuity between being atemporal and being temporal? We tend to think that items are phases of our existence only if appropriate causal relations hold between them, but an abstract object cannot cause anything, and if we are concrete while not spatial or temporal, still I do not see how our non-spatiotemporal 'phase' could causally contribute to our incarnation in time, nor how any cause in time could manage to shift something from being abstract or at least non-spatiotemporal to the opposite condition. Theism (whether or not generalist) faces none of these difficulties. Thus I do not think the constant domain proposal is preferable.

19

FREEDOM, PREFERENCE, AND COST

On a non-deity theory, God's nature does not determine Him to establish the modal truths He has. If it does not, nothing else does either, since He alone existed at that point. An act God is not determined to do may be free. So I now ask whether He was in some way free in doing so. This leads me to ask to what extent He was rational in doing so. I then compare my account with my deity rivals'. I argue that my package of answers is better than theirs, and that this is reason to favor my view.

Freedom and Content-generation

On my account there are two things whose freedom we have to consider: God's initially thinking up secular states of affairs, and God's assigning these their modal status. I first address His thinking. I take up the way God's thinking up the secular involves four properties relevant to freedom or lack of it, being an ultimate source, lack of constraint, ability (or its kin) to do otherwise, and extent of control over what one does.

a. constraint and ultimacy. It is God's nature to think up creatures: that is, He did it due to what He is. Nothing made Him what He is. Nothing outside God in any way constrained Him to think up what He did, for there are no items outside God before He permits any. Nor was it necessary for God to think as He did; necessity is something His thinking helps explain, and so did not exist prior to it, in any sense of 'prior'. Thus God thought as He did under no external compulsion and was His thinking's true ultimate source. God's nature did not determine and does not explain what He thought. So God was under no internal compulsion to think what He did either, though His nature determined that He think up some creatures or other.

b. thinking otherwise. To avoid an even partial deity theory, we must say that God's nature did not determine that He think up any particular kind or individual. Thus God was not naturally determined to think up dogs. But this cannot be true of Him only on the basis of His nature. As His nature does not include the property *dog*, it cannot be true given only what is natural in God that He was not determined to think up dogs. Rather, He was naturally able not to think of any particular sort of creature. Once He thinks up dogs, we can correctly redescribe His not having been naturally determined to think up any particular sort of creature as not having been determined to think up dogs—retrospectively, once the pre-requisites for doing so exist.[1] Further, He had every endowment needed not to have thought them up. God has lost or is timelessly using the chance to have it so, but that does not affect what He is so endowed as to do. Still, He is not *able* (or able to be able, etc.) not to think up dogs. For if He were, there would be a possible (possibly possible, etc.) world containing no facts about dogs—not even that they are impossible. So God was naturally so endowed as to bring about something impossible, that there be no dog-facts in some world. This is not because God had it in Him to do something impossible given that it *is* impossible, but rather because God had it in Him not to have made this impossible to do. It is not that God's nature lets Him crash through some stone barrier at the far end of possibility. Rather, God has *de facto* thought up dogs. This only makes it impossible that He not think of them. It was up to God whether thinking up dogs would be something with respect to which He could not do otherwise.

Once God thinks up dogs, God is able to think up dogs. So once God thinks up dogs, we have these truths: God is able to think up dogs; He is so endowed naturally as not to think them up; due to what God has *de facto* done, it is impossible; it was up to Him whether this would be impossible, or whether on the contrary there would be no facts about dogs at all. This is not ability to do otherwise, but it is a cousin.

c. control. The only model we have for God's thinking these up is our own imagining. We partly control our imaginations. Though some things float in willy-nilly,[2] we can set ourselves to think up (say) blue unicorns and produce the image. But we control our imagining by intending to imagine, which requires some description of what we want to picture: we must intend to imagine such-and-such. If I do not intend to imagine anything, I do not control my imagination.[3] While

---

[1] Here I am indebted to Christopher Menzel, 'Temporal Actualism and Singular Foreknowledge', *Philosophical Perspectives* 5(1991), 475–507.

[2] We may have some unconscious control or at least influence over what seems to us to be random imagery—certainly it emerges from our brain processes, and some of these likely control others of these without the control rising to the conscious level. But God has no brain, and for reasons noted earlier no unconscious mental states. So we can ignore this sort of control in His case.

[3] Parts of my brain do so without my intention. But my brain's controlling something does not entail that I control it. My brain controls my heartbeat when I am asleep. I do not.

I am or my brain is causally responsible for what I imagine, I might not be fully morally responsible. Suppose I just let my mind drift, and something morally repellent floats to mind. It does not seem fair to blame me for the precise image I generate, just because I did not seek to imagine it. Perhaps a freely undertaken vicious course of life has disposed me to corrupt imaginings. If so, I am blame-worthy only to the extent that this course of life explains what I imagine. This might suggest a general blame for its being something nasty, but not blame for the precise content of the nastiness unless I had given myself a habit of thinking of just *that* sort of thing.

In first forming His creature-concepts, God cannot fully pre-describe what He is to get. To do so, He would need concepts He has not yet formed. At this point only innate concepts or concepts based on Himself would be available to pre-describe what He wants to think up. As we saw earlier, these will not suffice. So God cannot have intended to think up exactly what He did. He did not have the concepts to form the needed intention. From one point of view, what cannot be guided by an even partly formed intention and is not the forming of an intention is not fully intentional. If based on Himself God has, say, the concept of a spirit, He sets Himself to think up some particular kind of spirit, and then He forms the concept of an embodied spirit, He forms the concept of a kind of spirit fully intentionally, but not the concept of an embodied spirit. (So too, on generalism, God can fully intentionally create someone just like me, but not fully intentionally create me.) Still, looked at in another way, this sort of case can be fully intentional. If I intend to hit the ball to right field, and I hit it to one particular point in right field, it seems odd to say that my hitting it there was not fully intentional. I intended to hit it to right, and I did. To hit it to right, I had to hit it to some bit of right, and this was the bit I hit to: hitting it there fully fulfilled the only intention I had, which was to hit it to right. So too, God's thinking up embodied spirits fully fulfilled the only intention He had, though it involved doing something with a content not present in the governing intention. God has a kind of control of this imagining: He determines its parameters, sets it in motion and executes it Himself rather than leaving it to some module of a brain. But no fully specifying intention was there to control it, and so God lacked a sort or degree of control over it. Had God had the concept of an embodied spirit with which to form a fully controlling intention to think this up, He would have had no need to think it up—He would already have had it.

All of these points generalize. There is nothing unique to the divine case in this lack of control. It just instances a general fact about conceptual creativity, that it involves a sort of spontaneous imagination which when looked at one way cannot be fully intentionally controlled. One can perhaps intend to be creative, but intending to be creative of the concept of an F is a contradiction in terms if what is meant is that the resulting concept be *just* the concept of an F. So imaginative spontaneity seems simply to rule out the sort of intentional control involved in deciding to perform an act and then doing exactly and only what one has decided. Such spontaneity can be intentional only in a looser sense, that one sets oneself to think up a certain general sort of thing and then does.[4] Still, it does not seem that such spontaneous thoughts 'just happen to' God. Thinking them is something He does. It does not just happen to me that I hit the ball to just that spot in right, though I did not control all details of the ball's flight, and just as I hit the ball, God thought the thought.

Let us summarize. God alone causes His generation of intellectual content. He is its true ultimate source. His generation of it is wholly spontaneous and unconstrained from without. His nature constrains what He thinks up only in general terms. God was not and is not able to do otherwise, but it was up to Him whether He would not be able to do otherwise in this respect. His thinking up just what He did was spontaneous and genuinely creative, and this made the question of how it was or was not intentional or fully under His control a bit complex. So there clearly are senses in which it was free and senses in which it was not (though neither was it coerced, determined, etc.). Finally, if His nature did not determine what He thought up, nothing did. God's conceiving is a 'wild card' element in the metaphysics of modality.

Freedom and God's Permitting

I now turn to God's assigning of modal status. To begin, nothing outside God in any way influenced Him to permit what He did. Nor was it necessary for God to do as He did. Nor on my view did God's nature determine Him to permit what He did: His nature does not explain His permitting. So God issued His permissions under no external or internal compulsion and was

---

[4] A referee objected to the claim that God's generation of the possible includes spontaneous, not fully controlled imagining: our own not-fully-controlled imagination does not give us a good grip on what is really possible, he thought, and so he thought there to be little reason to think that genuine possibilities are the result of such imaginings. Now this objection may just not apply at all. If our imaginations are not modally reliable, that is because there are imagination-independent modal facts they fail to catch. On my view, there is no independent secular possibility for God to fail to get a grip on. Rather, *whatever* God thinks up and permits turns out possible. Even apart from this, both the premise and the inference are suspect. Our imaginings are not *ex nihilo*; we recombine and modify elements we have met in experience. Many philosophers, particularly Humeans, find it plausible that any recombination of such elements yields a genuine possibility—Armstrong and Lewis, for instance, elevate this to a basic metaphysical principle (David Lewis, *On the Plurality of Worlds* (Oxford: Basil Blackwell, 1986), pp. 87–8; D. M. Armstrong, *A Combinatorial Theory of Possibility* (Cambridge: Cambridge University Press, 1989), p. 21). Even if we disagree, imagination, controlled or not, is one of our main sources of belief about the possible. The claim that it does not usually get a grip on genuine possibility is a fairly extreme sort of modal skepticism, and so would need arguing. Further, even if we concede the skeptical premise, the inference is dubious. We could infer from the claim that our uncontrolled imaginings do not get a grip on genuine possibility that God's do not only by taking it that God's imagination is no more reliable than ours—and why should we believe *that*? The referee also objected that the actual world's great order and rational comprehensibility count against the claim that its possibility resulted from spontaneous imagination. Well, it certainly counts against the claim that it resulted from the imaginings of a mind very like ours. But it is not news that God's mind is in many ways unlike ours. God is by nature perfectly rational, and His nature conditions what He imagines. It is no great stretch to infer from this that He will imagine many orderly, rationally comprehensible ways for universes to be.

their true ultimate source. Given a field of secular states of affairs, God decides which to let occur. We believe that we control our decisions—though not quite as we control things we decide to do. If God is perfect, He controls His decisions perfectly. They are conscious, intentional and made in appropriate response to all relevant reasons for choice. It is in Him to decide otherwise than He does. The only reason we cannot also say that He is able to decide otherwise is that He has in fact decided one way, not another. Further, at the point at which He decided, He did not *have* full abilities in these respects. He was precisely deciding which things it is in Him to do would also be things He is able to do. So having it in Him to do otherwise is the only doing-otherwise property He could have had. Thus the permitting which establishes secular modal facts is free either in the strongest libertarian sense or in a strong analogue to this.

By contrast, on deity theories, if there is anything for God to do to establish modal facts, His nature determines all of it. So my view gives God more freedom with respect to modality. Let's now ask how the freedom I ascribe to God affects our assessment of His overall rationality.

Freedom and Rationality: First Pass

If the bounds of the possible are up to God, we do not see what reason He could have to impose one boundary rather than another. So my view may seem to suggest that God has limited the possible without reason, and so irrationally. Thus one might argue that deity theories give Him less freedom, but leave Him more rational, and perhaps then that rationality is the more important perfection. But my view does not imply that God acted irrationally. We must again consider both God's initial generation of content and His choice of what to permit.

Consider God thinking up (say) water. God's having this idea is no more irrational than it was for Conan Doyle to come up with an idea of Holmes as wearing a deerstalker hat. There is no rational standard by which giving Holmes a hat can be judged defective. It was perfectly rational, or else it was simply not the sort of thing that can be judged either rational or irrational. Again, there are many ways to have a reason to do A. I might have reason to do A, in one sense, if there are no facts that would justify doing A, but I believe that P, where *P* would help justify doing A, and I have desires I could satisfy by doing A, even though I do not believe that believing that P and having these desires would justify doing A. Before God thinks up water, there are no water-facts available to justify thinking up water. *P* in His case is that He wants to give generous gifts and is able to do so. The desire in question is the desire to give generous gifts. These jointly justify thinking up water, for if He thinks up water, He will be able to give it as a gift. But they do not justify it before

God thinks up water, because for them to justify it then, there would have to be at least a divine concept of water, to be part of an act-description which stands in a justification relation. And God does not believe that anything about Him provides a reason to think up water if He does not have the concept *water*. So this is a case of having a reason in the sense just specified. God acts on the reason He has when He thinks up water. This reason does justify His doing so. This is the only sort of reason that could be applicable here, He has it, and He acts on it.

I suggest, then, that God's content generation is perfectly rational. Let us now consider God's setting the bounds of the possible. For any orthodox Western theist, God has given the universe its total mass-energy and space-time extent. He has chosen, then, that the mass-energy total n rather than n + 1, and the extent be what it is rather than slightly larger. We see no good reason for any such number. But we cannot infer that God chose these without reason. Perhaps God had access to considerations we cannot even imagine, which made one number rather than another appropriate. Again, perhaps He had good reason to choose but no reason to pick one rather than another, and so had good reason to 'just pick'. In such a case, 'just picking' is not acting entirely without reason. It is acting as rationally as the circumstance permits, and making a selection not guided by the kind of reason provided by some alternative having more merit than another. Or perhaps one number simply pleased Him, for not much reason at all, and lacking any other basis of choice, this was reason enough. Whichever answer we pick, I submit, works equally well in the case of God's setting the bounds of the possible. I plump for the last below.

Freedom and Rationality: A Dilemma?

William Mann suggests a conflict between God's freedom and His rationality.[5] Either

1. God affirms that water = H_2O because water = H_2O, or
2. water = H_2O because God affirms that water = H_2O.

If (1), God has a reason to affirm that water = H_2O. But He is not free in affirming it; His natural omniscience and the pre-given fact jointly determine His doing so. (2) does not curtail God's freedom. But it might seem to leave God's act arbitrary and so less than ideally rational if there is no further reason for Him to affirm that water = H_2O. Mann seeks to dissolve this dilemma by identifying items *prima facie* distinct. In (1), affirming seems to be an intellect's response to a fact. In (2) it seems an act of will establishing one.

---

[5] William Mann, 'Modality, Morality, and God', *Noûs* 23 (1989), 83–99.

Mann suggests that the dilemma is false because in God knowing and willing are one:

> God's believing that water = H$_2$O just is ... God's willing that water = H$_2$O ... there is one divine activity, which in some respects from our point of view is more aptly called ... knowing, and in other respects more aptly called His willing ... God brings it about that *water = H$_2$O* is necessarily true insofar as he wills it to be so ... But his willing that (it) be necessarily true is his knowing that (it) is necessarily true.[6]

But are (1) and (2) true or false? Mann does not say. The last two sentences quoted, moreover, seem not to dissolve the dilemma, but simply to favor (2). Mann holds that

> God's will ... must be perfectly rational ... God thus operates under the 'constraint' of rational necessity. Nothing he does can be rationally sub-optimal ... the necessary truths (are) part of the creative expression of this perfectly rational will ... it is not as if we could use the necessary truths to determine whether God is perfectly rational ... they have no status independent of ... God's ... mental activity.[7]

But what makes it rational to will that water = H$_2$O in particular? The answer Mann seems to suggest is that whatever God wills is perfectly rational, because He is perfectly rational and He wills it. The identity of God's willing and knowing does no work in this. So I do not see that identifying God's knowledge and will gains us anything. But I think there is actually no dilemma here. To begin, there is more than one proposition 'water = H$_2$O' might express. The clearest cases of necessity among them are that

> if anything consists wholly of H$_2$O, it consists wholly of H$_2$O, that being H$_2$O = being H$_2$O,

and that

> (x)(x is a body of water ⊃ (∃y)(y is a body of H$_2$O and x = y)) · (x)(x is a body of H$_2$O ⊃ (∃y)(y is a body of water and x = y)).

The first two instance logical non-falsities (truths, if such there be). So does the last if—as is plausible—'__ is a body of water' and '__ is a body of H$_2$O' express the same property. So my story about these factors into my story about logic and my story about there being the property *being H$_2$O*. God's nature guarantees at least non-falsity to what we call logical truths, but there are such properties as being H$_2$O, and so on, due simply to God's conceiving. So let us consider

---

[6] *Ibid.*, 93.   [7] *Ibid.*, 94.

3. God affirms that being H_2O = being H_2O because being H_2O = being H_2O, and

4. being H_2O = being H_2O because God affirms that being H_2O = being H_2O.

(4) is true. There is such a content of thought as being H_2O simply because God freely imagines it; given His logical nature, further, He imagines (so affirming) this about it. There is no more to it than that, even if it is up to God whether H_2O turns out to be a *possible* stuff. Even if God had no further reason to affirm that being H_2O = being H_2O, God's doing so seems to me no more rationally defective than it was for Conan Doyle to affirm that Holmes = a man who often wears a deerstalker cap. (3) is true given that the nature of water is settled. Of course God accepts that being H_2O = being H_2O once He has made this the case. The dilemma dissolves because two different sorts of affirming are involved.

A Thomist deity theory accepts (3), then tries to draw its sting by saying that God's reason to affirm that being H_2O = being H_2O lies wholly in His nature: it is done in full light of all applicable reasons, automatically, given His natural omniscience and His nature, which contains the nature of water. A Scotist theory says the same, though working out the details differently. On my account, once God understands what water would be, He has as much reason to affirm that being H_2O = being H_2O as He would on a deity theory: for this correctly reflects what He has thought up. So like a Thomist or Scotist, I affirm (3) given that the nature of water is settled. I thus protect God's rationality as well as they do. *Per* earlier argument, it is not on to suggest that it was in God on my view to give H_2O another nature, so that it is somehow arbitrary that it came out as it did. The next chapter addresses the thought that perhaps on my view it is more arbitrary than on Thomism or Scotism that 'being H_2O' has the concept to express which it actually expresses. Thomist and Scotist subject God's affirming to no standard outside God. Nor do I. Unlike them, I also accept (4). This leaves God fully rational. So Thomists and Scotists accept the price of writing water into deity, denying God the ability to settle the nature of water, and a lesser degree of divine freedom, for no gain in divine rationality.

Scotus and I agree that creaturely natures do not exist till God thinks them up. The Thomist who sees deity as wholly simple, as Aquinas did, should say the same; if it has no constituents, it does not have creaturely natures as constituents, and so for such Thomists these first 'exist' when God generates concepts by (somehow) reflecting on His nature. Scotus adds that God's nature determines Him to think as He does.[8] The Thomist will agree: God must be omniscient, so He must comprehend all there is to know about His nature, and on Thomism, the natures of creatures somehow arise from His

---

[8] So, for example, *Ordinatio* I, d. 43, *passim*.

doing so. The claim that God's nature determines Him to think as He does does not add to the internally available reasons on which God acts; there are no more on Scotism or Thomism than on my view. Consider how Scotus and I answer some questions. Why these creaturely natures? We both say, 'Because God conceives them.' For neither of us is this thinking irrational. To Scotus this because it is not irrational to do as one's nature dictates, particularly if the nature does not dictate behavior irrational on other standards. On my view this is because it is not irrational to be creative (where there is no reason not to be). Why not other natures? We both say that there were no others for God to conceive. I add that it was in God for there to be, but again, this does not bring with it determinate others that it is in God to think up. Why were there no others to conceive? For us both, the answer lies in God's nature: to Scotus because it determines what it is in Him to think, for me because it determines that there are no secular natures till He thinks. Why did God think what He did? Scotus says 'It is His nature to.' I say 'He just did.' But Scotus does not say that God so thinks because there are truths His intellect must grasp or internally available reasons to do so. Rather, in his view, first God thinks this way, coming up with the truths, and then He grasps them, both simply because He must.[9] So why is Scotus' answer worth giving? Perhaps Scotus thought that only so could the truths God affirms be absolutely and necessarily necessary, but my view provides for this too. Scotus and I are on all fours as to the rationality of God's thinking, for it does not detract from God's rationality to have a creative imagination. Nor does it detract from this that His permissions are all of items He initially thinks up by sheer creativity, any more than it detracted from Conan Doyle's rationality that the characters he decided to write stories about had come to him thus. I see no reason to prefer to spontaneity, creativity, and greater freedom the claim that God's nature compels His thought. It is better to have the same degree of rationality plus added perfections. If so, I depict God as more perfect than Scotus does, which is reason to favor my view as long as it does not exact an equivalent price elsewhere. Thus I claim that my account has an edge over its deity-theoretic rivals in how it conceives of God's thinking up creatures.

On my view, modal truth emerges after God's thinking is complete, with an application of His will. So to fully evaluate God's rationality on my view, we must ask why He wills what He does. I now do so. Earlier I raised the thought that God might have access to considerations we cannot imagine, that might in every case make one rather than another choice objectively better. If He does, of course, then His willing is perfectly rational. In the discussion that follows I stipulate that this is not the case—taking chocolate and vanilla as an example, that there is nothing that makes chocolate objectively better than vanilla. For all we know, God always has a sufficient reason for what He does. If so, the following discussion is only hypothetical.

---

[9] *Ibid.*, n. 18.

However, we do not see such reasons in many cases. As long we do not, the discussion has a point. Moreover, if it is a live option on my view that God always has adequate reason, the full picture of God's rationality on my view is disjunctive: either God is perfectly rational, or He has whatever degree of rationality emerges from the discussion I now begin.

Freedom, Preference, and Rationality

God's nature gives Him preferences. For instance, because it is His nature to be morally perfect, He prefers to act with perfect justice. For His natural moral perfection includes naturally having the virtue of perfect justice. Virtues include dispositions to desire the good. In God, desires have no connection with bodily or even emotional needs. They amount instead to preferences, action-guiding attitudes. So this virtue includes a motivational state, a moral preference.

God permits what He does due to His preferences. But I hold that His natural preferences do not fully determine His will about what secular states of affairs to permit once He dreams them up. If they did, it would be written into deity that (say) God must like dogs' having tails if He thinks them up. But then what it is to be a dog would be written into deity. Thus to not slip into even a partial deity theory by the back door, we must limit God's natural preferences. Any creature-involving detail they involve *ipso facto* gives us a deity theory for the attributes involved. So they must not even contain the content of diminished-perfection concepts. The most I can grant God naturally, beyond moral preferences, may be something like general aesthetic preferences—for example, for coherence over chaos, for diversity, harmony in diversity, and so on. The less secular detail is written into God's natural preferences, the less likely it is that they uniquely determine which states of affairs God permits once He dreams them up. So if God's natural preferences are general enough to avoid an even partial deity theory, it is likely that some other basis of choice enters the picture.

God also has *ab initio* preferences not determined by His nature. But reasoning like that just given applies to these too. Were it innate though not nature-determined in God to want there to be dogs if He thinks them up, He would still (so to speak) come with *dog* written in, only not into His very nature. If it is implausible that I innately though not by my very nature have a dog-concept, I do not see why this would be more plausible in God's case. So I think we should say that all of God's innate preferences together, natural and non-natural, do not uniquely determine a set of permissions.

There are, however, other preferences to consider. Experience can make one develop new preferences. And sometimes it is not plausible that one's nature or antecedent preferences uniquely determine the new preferences, though these set boundary conditions and may make some more likely than others. Dr Gene (let us say) tampered with my DNA at my conception, to assure that I have no innate preference for chocolate or vanilla, and am not physically determined to like one more than the other when I meet them. Gene has fed me tasteless gruel for my first twenty years, giving me no chance to develop experience-based preferences for chocolate-like or vanilla-like tastes. On my 21st birthday, he lets me taste some chocolate ice-cream and some equally good vanilla ice-cream. Neither makeup nor prior experience dispose me to like one more than another. All the same, I might. I might therefore go on to finish just one bowl of ice-cream. I would be fully rational to do so. If a new preference develops, it is as rational to act on it, if nothing else outweighs it, as to act on any deeper or longer-standing preference. We discourage acting on whims—sudden new transient preferences. As whims often lead to trouble, it is good to do so. All the same, acting on a whim might at times be perfectly reasonable: it might be that even given perfect information, a whim provides the only difference relevant to making a choice. A reasonable person acts on an appropriate weighting of the reasons available. If only one reason for choice is available, giving decisive weight to that one is appropriate. One might object that a sudden transient preference may be irrational, and it is rational to respect the preferences one has only if they are rational. But that the preference has no deeper basis does not guarantee that it is irrational. It may be a-rational or non-rational. It may even be fully rational, based on a sudden fleeting glimpse of something new about the alternatives one is considering. In any case, the thesis that preferences must be rational to provide reasons cannot really be sustained. There can be a method in one's madness. One can act rationally and on the basis of reasons given one's irrational preferences. Again, if my DNA gave me a strong preference for chocolate, that would not make it a *rational* preference. Yet it could give me a fully justifying reason to choose chocolate.

Any divine preferences new mental content elicits would not have the attributes that make whims problematic. They would be based on full information, including about probable or definite consequences where this is relevant. They would reflect an ideally rational nature, not one swayed by the adventitious or bodily, and so would reflect an appropriate weighting of relevant aspects of that information. They would not inculcate or reinforce patterns of irrational behavior. And so on. It is no imperfection to be liable to likes one's innate endowment does not pre-determine. On the contrary, the ability to react in new ways to new content is desirable in those whose innate preferences do not fully determine their reactions. We might add that in God's case, these new preferences will not be transient. He is perfectly rational and by nature has perfect information. His nature guarantees a maximally good fit between His information, His pre-given stable preferences and any new preference He forms, since liability to a failure of fit would be an imperfection. So His nature is such that His new preferences will be stable once formed. When God thinks up candidate secular states of affairs, He has an experience He has not had 'before': He apprehends new content. His nature did not pre-contain what He thinks up. It thus did not 'prepare Him' for it. His innate preferences set boundary conditions for His reactions: being morally perfect, He will not like any world containing pointless suffering, say. God might have many candidate systems of worlds in mind, and these might differ only in ways between which His innate preferences do not provide a decision. He might, then, simply find Himself liking a chocolate system better than a vanilla one. If the systems are equally satisfying to His stable moral, aesthetic etc. inclinations, there seems no reason He should not simply act on the preference He finds Himself having. It is perfectly rational to respect this if nothing ought to outweigh it—and *ex hypothesi* there is nothing that should.

Perhaps, then, God just likes some things—that is, has non-innate preferences elicited by content He dreams up. If not, either God does something like flip a coin[10] or God 'just picks'. (I will call this making a bare pick.) Let us ask which picture of God makes Him out to be most rational. Imagine asking God why He made some particular feature of the world so much as possible, assuming that nothing about the feature and its competitor candidates for possibility makes one objectively better than all the rest. God could give three sorts of answer:[11]

a. I had to pick some feature from a range including this. I had no reason to pick any particular feature in the range as vs any other. I had no reason not to pick this one and none not to pick at least one other feature in the range. (*Inter alia*, each was good enough not to generate such a reason.) It is rational to flip a coin if there is reason to choose and no basis to prefer one or another alternative. That is, it is rational to set up an undetermined process which will yield a 'pick' and decide to do what it dictates. For one who acts only on reasons but has none immediately presented to Him can rationally choose to provide Himself with one if He must decide. I reasonably decided to decide by (let us say) coin-flip. The coin picked this feature. I had reason to do what the coin picked: I had chosen to choose in this way. I had no reason to flip again, since I had no reason to reject the pick, and so I had no reason not to do what I had previously chosen to do. So I accepted the verdict of one flip. But I had no reason to pick this feature beyond the coin's having dictated it.[12] I did not prefer it. Nor did I need to,

---

[10] I discuss coin-flipping only. This is for concrete illustration; obviously, any relevantly similar process would do as well.

[11] Klaas Kraay argues that (a) is not possible ('Can God Choose a World at Random?', in Yujin Nagasawa and Erik Wielenberg (eds), *New Waves in Philosophy of Religion* (London: Palgrave MacMillan, 2008)). Since I do not in the end opt for (a) I need not dispute this; if you think (a) impossible, take me to be trying to be fair—that is, making the best case I can against my eventual conclusion.

[12] There is no reason for this particular choice *apart from* this decision procedure, but it is not in general required for rationality that there always be reason for the results of a decision procedure independent of

for given that I had decided to abide by the flip and had no reason to countermand this, the flip gave me reason enough. True, I could then have chosen not to abide by it after all. But a reason weak enough to override easily can still be a reason, and as I had no more reason to favor something the coin did not pick than to favor what it picked, I had no reason not to abide by it.

b. I had to pick some feature from a range including this. I had no reason to pick any particular feature in the range as vs any other—that is, none that could explain my picking this *rather than* that. I had no reason not to pick this one and no reason not to pick at least one other. The character of each alternative and/or my liking for it could justify my picking it. I was left free to choose between them because each was good enough (and/or I liked each enough) to be my pick. So I had sufficient reason to pick 1, and sufficient reason to pick 2, but no reason to pick 1 rather than 2. I had a non-contrastive but not a contrastive justification for picking any of them; I had reason enough to pick any but no reason to prefer any. It is rational to just pick if there is reason to choose and no basis to prefer one alternative to another. So I just picked 1, though I had no reason to pick 1 rather than 2.

c. I had to pick some feature from a range including this. I had no reason not to pick this one. I liked this one best. So I picked it because I liked it best. I had no deeper-lying reason to like it best, but it is rational to respect one's preferences if there is no reason not to do so.

(A) requires comment. God is deciding which creatures are to be so much as possible. So He has not yet created anything undetermined to help Him decide. He cannot do so without settling it that some creature is possible, either beforehand or in the very choice to create. He could settle it either way only by (b) or (c), if there is no single ideal choice of coin to flip. Plausibly there is not. Some candidate-for-possibility dimes might for all we know differ only in bare identity: that is, be perfectly similar save for whatever determines that each is precisely that individual, not another. Even if none do, dimes may differ only in ways that do not affect their usefulness in flipping or appeal to any divine preference. Dimes may not differ from quarters in these respects either. So plausibly (a) in this context is parasitic on (b) or (c), and so plausibly if (a) is a possible divine procedure, so is either (b) or (c).

Let us focus on what choices God makes on (a)–(c), with what sort of reason. On (a), He must choose a picker. Even if only one conceived creature

---

that procedure. If it were, no single decision procedure could ever rationally be used to decide anything: there would always be need for a supplemental reason. But for every decision procedure D and supplemental reason R, there is a single decision procedure, adopting D and accepting R. If we adopt D and accept R, we have adopted this single procedure, and so need *another* reason to accept its result, and so *ad infinitum*. Yet surely there are cases where having a finite number of reasons to make a given choice suffices to make the choice rational.

could pick for Him, God would have to choose between using it and picking for Himself—for if (a) is possible, so is (b) or (c), and even if this implication does not hold, He would have to make this choice as long as He could in fact pick for Himself. But given the claims just made about dimes, it seems likely that there would be many candidates. It would set off a regress to choose a picker by a further coin-flip, and if the regress is not to be infinite, it must terminate in some pick made by (b) or (c)—so there is no reason to start the regress, and so a perfectly rational mind choosing to flip a coin will choose to do so by preference or bare pick. God must choose a picking-device on (b) and (c) too if (a) is possible, for then God must choose to be the picker Himself rather than farm the choice out. Plausibly if He opts for (b), this would be by an elicited preference[13] to do the picking Himself: plausibly He might just prefer not to farm the pick out. On (c), He chooses Himself by elicited preference. God finds Himself with a preference for feature A. He has no reason not to act on it, and so does—and so His preference for A dictates that He Himself choose. It would be irrational to farm the choice out given that He has a preference, for at worst He would wind up with what He does not prefer, and at best He would merely have reached the same point He could have reached without the epicycle of inserting a picking device. It would also be irrational to make a bare pick of Himself as chooser, for He has a reason to pick Himself, and He would have to ignore it to make the pick bare.

On (a), God must choose an instant for the undetermined process to begin operating. It would set off a regress to do this by a further coin-flip, and so again, the rational choice will be to do so by preference or bare pick. If God is atemporal and time is substantival, it is hard to see what basis there could be to prefer one empty instant to all others: one might think that if time had a first instant, this would make most sense, but really, why would that be so? Still, I am allowing that God may just like some things better than others, or have access to considerations beyond our ken. So while I suspect that the pick would be bare, I cannot rule out an elicited preference, even one elicited by a good reason. If God is atemporal and time is relational, the appearance of the coin He is to flip is a first event that begins time. The coin would either be in motion when it appeared or start to flip thereafter. If the first, God will have chosen to begin the process at the first instant rather than later, and equally, if He has the coin appear motionless, then begin flipping, He will have chosen that. Again, I see no way to decide between bare pick and elicited preference. If God is temporal, then I have elsewhere suggested a form of answer to the question 'Why would God create the world just then?' which would apply here too.[14] The form of answer makes God's innate endowment determine what seems to Him the best instant. So if God is temporal, on my form of answer,

---

[13]   God's attitude to Himself is natural, but until He has a second candidate chooser to compare Himself with, He can have no preference between the two.

[14]   Brian Leftow, 'Why Didn't God Create the World Sooner?', *Religious Studies* 27 (1991), 159–72.

He has a preference for an instant elicited by His consideration of time. If that form of answer be rejected, then again, I have no basis to favor elicited preference over bare pick.

On (b), if God is atemporal, having chosen Himself as a picking device, there is no need to choose an instant at which the device picks. If God is temporal, God must choose a time to pick. Again, there is no way to rule out either preference or bare pick.

Turning to (c), God does not control when His new preferences show up, and earlier reasoning suggests that they do so as soon as He considers the matter. It is one thing to like A best, another to pick A because one likes it best: liking is not an act, but picking is. But given earlier argument, it is hard to see why picking A would not follow immediately upon God's having a preference for it. So I suggest that on (c), even if God is temporal, there would be no need to choose a time to pick by any other act than just picking A. He would always have liked A best and always have picked it.

If I am right, then, the score-card on (a)–(c) is: (a), two picks (of picker and time), with it epistemically possible that both be bare if it is epistemically possible that God be timeless or my story about His temporal preferences be false; (b), if God is atemporal, two picks, one bare and one elicited; if God is temporal, three picks, one bare, one elicited and one which could be either; (c), two picks, both based on elicited preference. Only on (c) do we know that God always has a reason for the choices He makes. On (a) it is epistemically possible that God make two bare picks. On (b) God makes at least one. So (c) provides the most appealing non-deity picture of the relation between God's preferences and His choices. Not only does it always provide a reason, but the reason provides a full contrastive explanation for His choice: preference is of this over that, and so provides a reason to choose this rather than that. Thus we should say that secular content God dreams up leads Him to form non-innate preferences not determined by anything innate, and these guide His choice. One might ask here whether God is free to choose against His all-things-considered preference. Since His preference in this instance provides the only reason to choose He has, ability to do this would count as ability to choose against reason, to be irrational. To want to do A, have no sufficient countervailing reason not to do A and yet not do A given cost-free opportunity is simply to be perverse or akratic. We can be, but we do not count it a good thing. So I suggest that this is not in God's nature.

The Indiscernibles Problem

We can conceive problem cases for choice by elicited preference. In the chocolate/vanilla example, there is qualitative content on each side, which makes sense of God forming a preference. We can conceive cases where there is no such content. God has dreamed up Moses. We can conceive that God also dream up someone distinct from him but perfectly like him save for *being Moses*—we can at least conceive that there be differences in bare identity. Suppose that being Moses is not a qualitative property, with content that could ground a preference. Suppose too that God thought up not only Moses but Schmoses, who differs from Moses only over the bare property of being Moses. Then He would have in mind a system of worlds with a slot to be filled, a Mosaic role, and would have to decide whether to give the role to Moses or to Schmoses, or whether there should be worlds indiscernible save that some contain Moses and some Schmoses. God must pick. Shall He let both be possible? Just one? If so, which? It is hard to see what could possibly elicit a preference on which to base a pick.

To explore this, we must ask what else being Moses could be if it is not a qualitative property. It cannot contain Moses as a constituent or have content which in some way depends on his existence, because we are considering God's conceiving before all Creation, and so Moses does not exist. Perhaps being Moses could be a Scotist haecceity, a property added to a kind-nature to generate the nature of a particular individual.[15] If such a haecceity is really a trope of a quality, *being Moses*, it has preference-grounding content. There is then a qualitative difference between being Moses and being Schmoses. *Being Moses* accounts for it—*is* it. If the haecceities *being Moses* and *being Schmoses* had or were qualitative content but were perfectly similar, they would yield individuals perfectly similar in all respects—including their very identities. So there would be some difference between them. This difference could elicit a preference.

To make things harder, let us now suppose that a Scotist haecceity has no unique Mosaic etc. content, but is just a thisness-trope, each perfectly like the rest and only numerically different. Let us say that a haecceity just makes this human this human and that human that, with no intrinsic difference between Moses' and Schmoses' haecceities other than their bare being this and being that. If so, God's pre-creative thoughts of Moses' and Schmoses' haecceities involve the general character *thisness* and no other qualitative content. Neither has broad content, there being nothing to constitute broad content for them. Neither has any reference-relations. So it is unclear how God could have one thought just of one trope of thisness, another of just another. My theory of divine mental content might reply that there is this 'of-ness' relation due just to a brute fact, that if God acts on one thought He gets one trope and if He acts on another gets another. But equally, then, if He acts on one thought He uses a power to make one trope and if He acts on another uses a power to make another; the thoughts specify corresponding powers. God could have a preference about which power He exercises. One can prefer to exercise one's left arm or one's right. So on this

---

[15] Scotus, *Ordinatio* II, d. 3, p. 1, qq. 5–6, n. 188 [Scotus (1950–), 7: 483–4].

alternative, the Moses/Schmoses case again fails to constitute a problem for the elicited-preference view.

Let us therefore take another tack and ask what could make God's Moses-concept distinct from His Schmoses-concept before Creation. If the bare-identity, non-qualitative difference between Moses and Schmoses is not grounded on their having distinct non-qualitative haecceities, it could be primitive or be grounded on the involvement of distinct bare particulars. Other views are ruled out by the stipulation that we are discussing pre-creative concepts of things differing only in bare identity. On some readings, for instance, Aquinas holds that what makes two material individuals of the same kind two is that one involves one quantitative form and the other a numerically distinct quantitative form.[16] This is not a bare-identity difference, since it is based on possessing different quantitative forms. So let us ask how the two routes to a difference in bare identity would affect God's concepts.

Let us first consider what to say if Moses' individuality would be just primitive. On this approach, any note in God's concept of Moses or Schmoses would specify a world-indexed or non-world-indexed shareable property or a haecceity: there are no bare particulars to consider, for if there were, they would explain Moses' individuality and so it would not be primitive. If there are haecceities of some sort available to distinguish Moses and Schmoses, their difference is not primitive, but accounted for by haecceities. We can leave world-indexed properties out of the reckoning. We are considering a decision (make Moses possible, Schmoses possible, or both) that is to determine which world-indexed properties they have, so their concepts must be distinct on some other basis. Were they not, there would be no decision to take and no possibility that they come to differ in world-indexed properties. This leaves non-world-indexed shareable properties. But any of these Moses could be made to have, Schmoses could be made to have: again, they differ only in bare identity. So these cannot distinguish their concepts. So if the individuality of particulars differing in bare identity is primitive, there is no conceptual note to distinguish Moses and Schmoses before Creation.

This might have one of two consequences. Perhaps Moses' concept and Schmoses' would have the same content, and so just would not *be* two distinct concepts. They would be one purely general concept of a Mosaic-type individual, the bare-identity difference between Moses and Schmoses being something that would exist only if God actually instanced the concept twice. God's only decision would then be of how many times to satisfy that concept, and we can reasonably suppose that God might have a preference about this. If this did not follow, then there would instead just primitively be two concepts not differing in any qualitative content, each primitively such that if tokened it leads to just Moses or just Schmoses—in which case we are back

[16] Aquinas, *Sancti Thomae de Aquino Expositio super librum Boethii De Trinitate*, ed. Bruno Decker (Leiden: Brill, 1959), 4, 2 ad 3.

to my theory of divine mental content, and once again, God could have a preference about which powers to exercise.

We come finally to bare particulars. These are truly *bare*. There is nothing to them but particularity. They have no qualitative content (save perhaps particularity). There is nothing to distinguish one from another. They just are primitively distinct.[17] So they differ in bare identity. And so they merely reraise the very issue we are discussing; invoking them cannot provide any progress on it. Thus the indiscernibility of Moses and Schmoses does not seem to be a real problem for the elicited preference view.

Preference and Rationality

There is a temptation to say that if preferences elicited purely by new content and grounded in nothing innate figure in God's choice, God's acts are less than fully rational, because He has no reason to have the preferences on which He acts. But there *is* a reason to have these preferences. God prefers the features He prefers because of what they are. If after Dr Gene's preparation I find myself preferring chocolate, this is because of *how chocolate and vanilla taste.* I can appeal to that to say why I like chocolate better. Now one can still ask why, given that they taste that way, I should prefer chocolate. Given Dr Gene, my answer is 'I have already said—it is how they taste.' Without him, the answer will be the same. In each case, my reasons run out there. Without Dr Gene, there might be a further story to tell about my genetic makeup, microstructure, past experience, and so on. But these stories talk about the *causal antecedents* of my liking. They do not provide further internally available reasons for me to prefer one to another. I am not a more rational agent for having such a story available, but just an agent whose actions are more susceptible to full explanation from a third-person perspective. It is a perfection to act more rationally. I do not see why it would be a perfection to act in a way that is more causally explicable. So I do not see that the involvement of non-innate elicited preferences should impugn God's rationality or perfection.

The Balance of Costs

Let us distinguish three sorts of deity-theoretic accounts of God's rationality in choosing:

> Thomism: secular modal truths are grounded directly on deity. So God
> needed no reason to opt for these, since they were in no way up to Him.

---

[17] For the *locus classicus* see E. B. Allaire, 'Bare Particulars', in Michael Loux (ed.), *Universals and Particulars* (Garden City, NY: Doubleday Books, 1970), pp. 235–44.

Scotism: God's nature compels Him to think up secular modal truths. They are true just intrinsically, due to their own content, once He thinks them up. So God needed no reason to opt for these, since they were in no way up to Him.

Deity-voluntarism: God's nature compels Him to think up the states of affairs He does, and also fits Him with preferences which fully determine His permissions given this field of candidates. God must select, but His nature fully determines His selection.

My theory and these three alternatives ground secular modal truth ultimately in something brute about God—the content of deity, or a *de facto* imagining plus a preference. There is no full explanation for God's imagining the candidate secular states of affairs He does, nor for the preferences His imagination elicits (unless of the 'it is the way they taste' sort), but there is none for deity's containing what it does either (given the failure of the accounts discussed in Chapter 6). The non-innateness of the preference and imagination does not threaten the necessity or necessary necessity of any modal truth, or so I have argued. The deity theories and my view tie on rationality, if as I have argued the involvement of divine preferences does not impugn this. One might think that there is more just brute fact, or brute necessity, on my view than on these rivals. This is not an issue about freedom or rationality, and so does not affect the present discussion. I take it up in the next chapter.

Chapter 8 argued that *ceteris paribus*, we ought to hold a non-deity theory. I have now examined one of the *cetera*. My view gives God some freedom and control with respect to modality, at no cost in divine rationality. This is a modest point in favor of my view.

20

EXPLAINING MODAL STATUS

MANY philosophers have found absolute necessity, possibility etc. problematic. Faced with philosophically problematic concepts, there are (says Colin McGinn[1]) four sorts of approach. We might eliminate the concepts when speaking 'strictly and philosophically' as opposed to 'loosely and popularly'. We might retain them but try to 'reduce' them to less problematic concepts: in the modal case, this would roughly speaking mean continuing to use modal language, but providing modal claims with truthmakers invoking only non-modal properties. We might allow absolute modal properties but try to explain their presence (as vs reductively explaining them away): a reductionist might claim, for instance, that absolute necessity just is analyticity, while an explainer might say analyticity explains necessity but is distinct from it. Finally, we might accept absolute modal properties as real, irreducible, and inexplicable: take it as a brute fact that they are there, and just domesticate the brute by offering an orderly metaphysical account of it. I 'reduce' absolute modality to causal modality. This move is genuinely reductive and worth making. Causal modality is more familiar and better understood; we have a grip on what it means to say that we are able to do something, and even that we are able to do things we do not in fact do. But as modal reductionism seeks as a rule to rid us of modal properties altogether, a claim that I am a reductionist would likely not be taken seriously; my view fits more naturally under the third and fourth headings. Ultimately, for me, there is one entity with primitive, unexplained causal-modal attributes: God, who has natural powers. But I explain God's non-natural powers, and in so doing explain all absolute modal status other than God's possibility, which I treat reductively.

---

[1] Colin McGinn, *Problems in Philosophy* (Oxford: Basil Blackwell, 1993), pp. 15–17.

I now compare my account of secular modal status to some 'explanationist' rivals. It quickly emerges that my main competition comes from explanations of states of affairs' modal status by their intrinsic content. I argue against several versions of this which involve analyticity or kindred notions. I also consider the extent to which my view involves brute necessities.

The Rivals

On a theist theory, secular modal status must appear before, at, or after the point in our explanation of things at which God from all eternity has secular concepts. 'Before' gives us a broadly Thomist theory—secular modal facts settled by the divine nature. 'At' gives us two alternatives. In Scotus, once it is in His mind, God's mental content determines its own modal status.[2] The content is as it is because God thinks as He does, and so Scotus if correct only displays some fine structure of how *God* establishes facts of modal status. The other alternative does without this fine structure and says that the content's modal status is due simply to how God thinks of it. If secular modal status is determined neither before nor at the point of having secular concepts, it is determined 'after'. If it is 'after', God's thinking does not give the content a modal status. Once God has done His thinking, though, His intellect's contribution to modal status is complete. So on the 'after' approach, what determines modal status must be non-intellectual. On my version of this, God's decisions do so.

I suggest that we disregard the third view. It has modal status determined from beyond the content of the state of affairs bearing it, but does not let us treat that content as a reason for it. On the third view, God's thinking of goats as a possible kind of thing causally explains their being so, but He does not so think goats up that the concept *goat* itself, by its content, determines that goats are possible. Nor has He a chance to consider the notion of a goat and decide whether goats should be so. So nothing about being a goat ever contributes to explaining goats' being possible. God just thinks goats up as possible without having a reason to do so, as it were blindly. If this is genuinely a coherent story, it makes the possibility of goats given that God has conceived them wholly arbitrary. It would be better if the nature of goats helped explain their possibility, as on Scotus's or the 'after' view.

For Thomas, a secular state of affairs is possible just if it is in God's power to produce it. If we step away from Thomas's demanding doctrine of divine

[2] John Duns Scotus, *Ordinatio* I, d. 43, q. unica, nn. 14, 16; d. 36, q. unica, nn. 60–1. For discussion see Calvin Normore, 'Duns Scotus' Modal Theory', in Thomas Williams (ed.), *The Cambridge Companion to Duns Scotus* (Cambridge: Cambridge University Press, 2003), pp. 129–60; , Simo Knuuttila, 'Duns Scotus and the Foundations of Logical Modalities', in Ludger Honnefelder *et al.*, eds., *John Duns Scotus: Metaphysics and Ethics* (Leiden: Brill, 1996), pp. 127–43; Fabrizio Mondadori, 'The Independence of the Possible According to Duns Scotus', in Olivier Boulnois *et al.*, eds., *Duns Scot à Paris* (Turnhout: Brepols, 2004), pp. 313–74.

simplicity and focus instead on what he says about God's power, we can ask which is prior. Perhaps it is in God's power to bring secular S about because S is possible, just intrinsically, and it is God's nature to be able to bring about whatever is possible. If so, the Thomist, like Scotus, explains S's modal status by its intrinsic content. Or perhaps being in God's power makes S possible. If so, then since for Thomas the content of God's power is part of His nature, God's having His nature makes S possible. Chapter 6 argued that attempts to use a 'core' part of God's nature to explain its also containing secular content (and so perhaps its modal status) do not succeed. So on the second Thomist option, I suggest, there is no explanation at all of secular modal status. It is all simply primitive. God's having His nature *partly* explains the possibility that there not be (say) aardvarks, as it gives God the powers not to create and to prevent. But these are not powers to bring it about that there are no aardvarks unless there is a divine concept *aardvark*, a property *being an aardvark*, a proposition *there are aardvarks*, and so on. Were there none of these, then no matter what God did or did not do, it would not be true that there were no aardvarks. So if God's nature does not explain His having *aardvark* (and so on), neither does it on its own explain the possibility that there not be aardvarks. *Ceteris paribus*, we should prefer a view providing a good explanation of at least some secular modal status. So if my view does so, as I have tried to suggest, then unless the *cetera* tilt against it, it is preferable. The last chapter argued that some *cetera* in fact favor my view, and this chapter adds more. Thus only theist intrinsic-content explanations provide a theist competitor for the 'after' account.

Intrinsic-content Explanations

There are in the abstract three ways a purely intrinsic, non-reductionist explanation of a secular state of affairs' modal status could work: either all attributes it involves will be infinitely complex, or it will ground this status ultimately at least partly in primitive, unexplained modal facts, or it will at least partly ground the status in non-modal facts, but involve brute, unexplained supervenience of the modal on the non-modal.[3] I now argue that the primitive modal fact approach is best.

Consider a pair of incompatible attributes FG. If each is infinitely complex, they may be incompatible because $F = (H \cdot I)$, $G = (J \cdot K)$, and H and J are incompatible; H and J are incompatible because an attribute H contains is incompatible with one J contains; and so on endlessly. Again, if every secular attribute is infinitely complex, then perhaps every compatible pair FG is possibly co-instanced because $F = (H \vee J)$, $G = (H^* \vee J^*)$, and H and H^* are

---

[3] Part of that will be the brute existence of supervenience-relations, if (as is plausible) supervenience is itself a modal relation.

possibly co-instanced, and so infinitely. Every level's modal property, one might assert, is explained by a more basic level's having a modal property; since the levels are contained within F and G, this is an intrinsic-content explanation of the modal status of something's being F and G. But any n attributes are either compatible or incompatible, and it is implausible that every secular attribute is infinitely complex—in most cases we have no reason to believe in infinite complexity. Moreover, even if this truly explains modal status at each level, it does not explain there being any modal properties at all anywhere in the hierarchy. No individual modal property in the hierarchy can do so, for other modal properties explain its presence, and so its presence presupposes that there are modal properties in the hierarchy. Nor do the hierarchy's modal properties as a whole do so. Taking all of them together, it still seems perfectly apt to ask, 'Why any, rather than none?' So the presence of modal properties remains unexplained, even if the hierarchy's levels explain their distribution within it. Yet the puzzle philosophers find in modal status has as least as much to do with modal properties' mere presence as with their distribution. So the infinite-descent model's implausible view of attributes' complexity does not actually buy an answer to the entire puzzle of modal status. On the other hand, if every explanatory descent is truly infinite and such descent really does explain, this offers as complete an explanation of modal properties' distribution as can be had without explaining their mere presence.

Suppose now that some secular attributes are not infinitely complex. Then some explanatory regresses for items' modal status eventually hit bedrock, and in bedrock cases regresses do not start. If it is bedrock that being F is incompatible with being G, there is no further explanation for this. 'Incompatible' is a modal term: F and G are so just if nothing can be both F and G. So here we reach a primitive modal fact. In other cases we may hit bedrock with attributes which are possibly co-instanced, or single attributes which just can have instances. Grounding all other modal status in primitive, unexplained modal facts does not explain modal properties' presence, since it offers no explanation for the primitive modal facts. As this approach takes some modal facts as primitive, it cannot completely explain modal properties' distribution either: it has no explanation for those in the primitive facts. Still, on balance, this second approach seems preferable; as it is implausible that there really is all the complexity the first approach posits, it does not seem likely that it can explain the distribution as it promises.

Our third approach claims that the modal facts I just called primitive are not in fact bedrock: secular non-modal facts lie beneath them, and non-reductively explain modal properties. Whether this is a sort of intrinsic-content explanation depends on whether (say) Spot's being a dog is part of his being a possible being. Be this as it may, it is not easy to find examples here. Suppose to begin that it is secular and non-modal that P. Then $P \rightarrow \Diamond P$, but that P does not seem to *explain* that $\Diamond P$. It would be odd to say that it is possible that penguins swim because they actually do. Surely it is rather that their possibly doing so is one precondition of their doing so. Again, where something is possible reductively, by being actual, it is not the case that actuality explains possibility. Rather, what makes it true that it is actual just is—and so cannot explain—what makes it true that it is possible.

Now let us suppose there are logical truths,[4] and ask whether their being logically true explains their being necessary. On the standard approach, logical truth is model-theoretic validity, or truth in all models for the language in question.[5] Models are sets which include a set providing a domain of objects and a function assigning objects from that domain to non-logical vocabulary. A sentence says something true in all models for its language just if it says something true on all admissible substitutions for its variables and assignments of denotations to its singular terms and extensions to its predicates. (Re. the latter two, the requirement is that it say something true no matter how we interpret its non-logical vocabulary.[6]) Thus if a sentence is true in all models, having its logical form suffices for it to say something true. This captures a sense in which logical truths are formal, which some go on to gloss in terms of being true purely in virtue of their logical form[7] or of the meanings of their logical words. On its face, model-theoretic validity is something non-modal. It is just a fact about how actual sentences relate to actual sets: the fact that no assignment actual sets actually provide renders what the sentence says false. So we can ask whether validity is a non-modal property that explains the necessity of a logical truth. Since it is obvious that logical truths should wind up necessary and validity seems relevant to necessity, we ought to be able to find a non-modal explanation here if one is to be had anywhere.

Patricia Blanchette writes:

> On any standard reading of the language, the propositions expressed by formulas of the same syntactic form as $(\exists x)(x = a)$ ... are all true ... *There is something identical with Smith, there is something identical with Jones*, and so on, (are) true ... many of these ... are only contingently ... true. (So) we can infer from the model-theoretic truth of a formula ϕ the actual truth of ... those propositions expressible ... by formulas of the same syntactic form as ϕ. But this ... is no guarantee of the necessary truth of propositions expressible by ϕ.[8]

---

[4] Just to reiterate: whether there are depends on what the right treatment of vagueness is. (Also, I now add, on how to treat other potential generators of truth-value gaps—for example, future contingents.)

[5] The *locus classicus* is Alfred Tarski, 'On the Concept of Logical Consequence', tr. J. H. Woodger, in J. Corcoran (ed.), Alfred Tarski, *Logic, Semantics, Metamathematics*, 2nd edn. (Indianapolis, IN: Hackett, 1983), pp. 409–20.

[6] It is a substantive question just how to distinguish logical from non-logical vocabulary, but for present purposes we need not address this.

[7] Bertrand Russell, *The Principles of Mathematics*, 2nd edn. (New York: Norton, 1938), p. xii; *Introduction to Mathematical Philosophy* (New York: Simon and Schuster, 1971), pp. 196–7.

[8] Patricia Blanchette, 'Models and Modality', *Synthese* 124 (2000), pp. 59–60.

Consider the formula '$(\exists x)(x = a)$'. Interpretations of first-order languages are usually required to give non-empty sets as domains. Any such domain provides items to assign as denotations, and '$(\exists x)(x = a)$' is true on all assignments of denotations to 'a'—or at rate, only Meinongians will deny this, as all others allow only existent objects as denotations. It is thus valid—true in all models—and so (on the standard approach) logically true. Every proposition corresponding to some assignment to 'a' is true. As Blanchette notes, most propositions of this form are contingent. Apparently, then, either Meinong was right or on the usual way of interpreting first-order logic there are contingent logical truths. Edward Zalta points out a contingent logical truth in modal logics containing an actuality operator A, such that $A\phi$ is true in a world w just if ϕ is true in the world that is in fact actual. That $A\phi \rightarrow \phi$ is true on all interpretations of ϕ, hence logically true. But suppose that ϕ is contingent. It is true in every possible world that $A\phi$, as the A-operator simply looks back to the actual world, and in every possible world it is true that in this world, the one which happens to be actual ϕ. So if ϕ is contingent, it can be true that $A\phi$ but false that, and so it is not necessary that $A\phi \rightarrow \phi$.[9] The validity of a formula, then, does not even entail, let alone explain, the necessary truth of the propositions which are its 'readings'.[10] Vann McGee suggests that model-theoretic validity does not even guarantee truth. Models are sets, and so contain only sets. Suppose then that we add to

> the language of set theory... the quantifier 'There are absolutely infinitely many', where $(\exists^{AI}x)\phi$ means that there is no set which contains all the ϕs, then we find that, even though $(\exists^{AI}x)(x=x)$ is true—there are absolutely infinitely many individuals—there is no model in which $(\exists^{AI}x)(x=x)$ is true.[11]

Since no set contains all sets and so no set contains all individuals, it is true that $(\exists^{AI}x)(x=x)$. But since no set contains all individuals, no domain does so, and so it is true on every model—logically true—that $\neg(\exists^{AI}x)(x=x)$. Yet this formula's 'reading'—the proposition that there are not absolutely infinitely many individuals—is false.[12]

If there are such cases, validity never on its own explains necessity: other conditions must be met as well.[13] If

---

[9] Edward Zalta, 'Logical and Analytic Truths That Are Not Necessary', *Journal of Philosophy* 85 (1988), 63.

[10] In the sense of Blanchette, *op. cit.*, 47–8.

[11] Vann McGee, 'Two Problems with Tarski's Theory of Consequence', *Proceedings of the Aristotelian Society* 92 (1992), 279.

[12] Blanchette, *op. cit.*, 51.

[13] Blanchette's way of showing that validity in propositional logic entails necessity includes the assumption that possible worlds induce valuations for logical formulae and concludes that for each model of a language L's formulae in which it comes out true that P there will be a possible world at which it is true that P (*ibid.*, 54). Obviously, this does not let us claim that validity explains necessity; it is an argument that validity will match up with necessity. Blanchette's case that validity entails necessity in non-modal languages with first-order quantification includes the premises that logical truths are necessary and

1. the models' domains for a first-order non-modal language jointly include all possible combinations of all objects ever possible,

and we call there being none of them one possible combination, thus allowing empty domains, validity plus (1) entail and perhaps explain necessity, for then whatever is true on all actual assignments (including the 'null assignment') *ipso facto* is true on all possible assignments. Given (1) plus empty-domain models, all possible models are actual models and truth in all possible models appears to entail necessity. But (1) is a modal fact. Another thought might be that model-theoretic validity explains necessity if the actual models with respect to which a sentence is valid represent all possible worlds.[14] But the *explanans* here would include the modal fact that every possible world has a model representing it. It would not be purely non-modal. Further, the explanation's point is that 'readings' of valid sentences will be necessary because (on a particular sort of semantics) validity brings with it representation of necessity and 'readings' express what the formula 'read' represents. So the real picture here is that certain truths are necessary—for no reason, or reasons independent of validity—and the semantics of valid sentences on certain assumptions guarantees that 'readings' of logically valid formulae express them.[15]

It seems, then, that even in the case of logical truth we do not have a non-modal explanation of necessity. Suppose, further, that in fact we did. It is epistemically possible that

2. there are logical truths but no modal properties.

Reductionists and eliminationists, who assert (2), contradict nothing we know by doing so. For that there are modal properties is not self-evident. Nor is it plausibly *a priori* evident in some looser sense—say, that *a priori* arguments would eventually convince anyone with the right conceptual equipment that there are such properties: we have learned to doubt that any substantive philosophical thesis has such a property. If being a logical truth explained in an *a priori* evident way the presence of a modal property, necessity, (2) would not be epistemically possible. As (2) is, if being necessary somehow supervenes on being a logical truth, it is not *a priori* evident why it does so. The supervenience may be real, but as far as we can tell it is brute, which is why eliminationists and reductionists have room to deny it. What is *a priori* evident is at most something like this: if there is a modal property of necessity, there

---

that the theorems of this language express only necessary truths (*ibid.*, 54–5); again, there is no way to build an explanation of necessity by validity from this.

[14] Thus the 'representational' semantics of John Etchemendy, *The Concept of Logical Consequence* (Stanford, CA: CSLI Publications, 1999).

[15] Stewart Shapiro seems to acknowledge this ('Logical Consequence: Models and Modality', in Matthias Schirn, ed., *The Philosophy of Mathematics Today* (Oxford: Oxford University Press, 1998), p. 148). See also McGee, *op. cit.*, 278, where the approach is that facts of possibility (and so necessity) are pre-given and the task of semantics is to find models adequate to represent them.

are just the classical truth-values and no proposition can lack a truth-value; the claims we call logical truths have this property. This does not provide an explanation from the purely non-modal, and it explains at most a bit of what the property's distribution would be, not the presence of the property. If the supervenience would be brute in this favorable case, it would be so *a fortiori* in others. Without an explanation of the supervenience, though, what seems to be an explanation of base-level modal properties' presence really turns out to be just a survey of their distribution. For supervenience theses just assert property correlations. Of themselves they have no explanatory content.[16] If this supervenience is brute, I submit that non-modal facts give no non-reductive explanation of base-level modal properties' presence or distribution.

Analyticity

Before drawing this conclusion, though, there is another place to look for non-modal explanations of modal status. If model-theoretic validity—being a logical truth—will not explain modal status, we might appeal instead to analyticity. I now consider two versions of this.

Many philosophers have held that truths are necessary just if analytic.[17] If they were, we might explain all modal status this way: a claim is necessary because analytic, impossible because its negation is analytic, contingent because neither it nor its negation is analytic, and possible just if necessary or contingent. But this will not really do. The whole notion of analyticity is mired in controversy.[18] Chapter 1 set out some absolutely necessary truths which on many accounts of analyticity would be non-analytic. And there may even be contingent analytic truths. If logical truths are analytic—and as we see shortly, on one prominent view of analyticity, they are—we have already seen some.[19] But let us look anyway at what two prominent accounts of analyticity might get us.

'Analytic' has been used in many senses.[20] In one prominent usage,

> a proposition is analytic if and only if any sentence which expresses it expresses a (truth) solely because the words in the sentence mean what they do. The fact that the words mean what they do, that is, is by itself sufficient to make the statement true.[21]

---

[16] See, for example, John Divers, 'Recent Work on Supervenience', *Philosophical Books* 39 (1998), 81–91; Stephan Leuenberger, 'Supervenience in Metaphysics', *Philosophy Compass* 3 (2008), 749–62.

[17] See Arthur Pap, *Semantics and Necessary Truth* (New Haven, CT: Yale University Press, 1958).

[18] For a survey, see Corey Juhl and Eric Loomis, *Analyticity* (London: Routledge, 2010).

[19] For discussion of another sort of case see Ori Simchen, 'Meaningfulness and Contingent Analyticity', *Noûs* 37 (2003), 278–302.

[20] For a brief survey see George Bealer, 'Analyticity', in E. Craig (ed.), *Routledge Encyclopedia of Philosophy* (London: Routledge, 1998), http://www.rep.routledge.com/article/U002SECT1.

[21] Richard Swinburne, 'Analyticity, Necessity and Apriority', in Paul Moser (ed.), *A Priori Knowledge* (New York: Oxford University Press, 1987), p. 173.

What a sentence's words mean determine what claim (if any) it makes. If a sentence's expressing that P suffices by itself to make it express a truth, this is because *P*'s being true requires nothing of the world. If 'all bachelors are unmarried' expresses a truth just because it says what it does, its truth does not require of the world, for instance, that there are real properties of bachelorhood and being unmarried, and these stand in certain relations. If it did require this, 'All bachelors are unmarried' would express a truth because it says what it does and these properties exist and are appropriately related. Thus Quinton, equating necessity and analyticity, writes that 'If a truth is necessary it is true in itself and independently of everything outside it.'[22] So if there are sentences whose expressing what they do truly does on its own make them express a truth, some sentence-contents are true 'in themselves', just intrinsically. If it is analytically true that P, on this account, it is true that P just because *P* is the proposition it is; *P* is true just by nature.

It violates deep-seated intuitions about truth to call a proposition intrinsi-cally true; plausibly truth always derives from how something else is *somehow*. Further, if Chapter 3 was right about the way logic depends on the world, this theory rules that logical truths (if any) are not analytic: yet they are supposed to be a paradigm of analyticity. Again, a problem arises about the kind of necessity this account provides. If an analytic truth is true just by nature, regardless of how the world is, then necessarily, if an analytic proposition exists, it is true. The necessity that falls naturally out of being analytic seems to be this: if it is analytic that P,

3. $\Box(P \text{ exists} \supset P)$.

(3) is a strong necessity, but provides only a weak necessity for *P*. We could detach a strong necessity for *P* only if we had as a further premise that *P* strong-necessarily exists. That *P* is analytic does nothing to secure this, and the empiricists and Kantians who championed analytic accounts of necessity were largely adamant that no existence-claim could be analytic. (Existence-claims surely must be made true by the world—by what exists. So it is hard to see how a claim could be both intrinsically true and existential.) Even if they wavered on this, an analytic existential proposition as so far understood would itself provide only weak necessity: strong necessity would attach only to the (3)-type conditional associated with it. So this analytic theory of necessity seems unable to generate strong necessity. Yet if it accepts such claims as (3), it needs strong necessity. And we have strong intuitions that some states of affairs are strongly necessary. Either something exists (or borderline-exists, if existence is vague) or nothing (even borderline) exists: how could that fail to be so? This theory, though, cannot give more than weak necessity to this proposition, because the most it can do is guarantee truth if the proposition exists.

[22] Anthony Quinton, *The Nature of Things* (London: Routledge and Kegan Paul, 1973), p. 267.

One might try to deal with this by deflation. Talk of propositions (we might say) is just talk. The claim that a proposition exists requires nothing of reality to be true, for properly understood it neither asserts nor implies the existence of anything. It is true trivially, for free, without ontology; it is just a way of speaking. So to condition anything on the existence of a proposition is to impose a null condition, a condition reality strongly cannot not meet because it does not take anything in reality for it to be met.[23] What is true on a condition that strongly cannot not be met is strong-necessarily true. If it has a trivial truth-condition, that P exists is strong-necessarily though trivially true, and so we obtain for free the premise we need to infer a strong necessity for P. This sort of deflation, though, sits ill with an analytic *explanation* of necessity. If it is hard to grasp how a proposition can be intrinsically true, it is harder still to see how something that is not there can have any intrinsic properties at all. If P is not really there to explain P's truth, P's truth really has no explanation—or else calling P true is itself just a way of speaking, in which case calling P necessary is so too. If we deflate the *explanans*, we deflate the *explanandum*: we really have not necessary truths, but a game of talking as if there were some, and so this moves us over into an eliminative or reductive account of modal truth. Either might attract many philosophers, and I will say nothing against them here. I am comparing my view only with rivals that explain necessity rather than explain it away. So whatever the merits of thus deflating necessity, it does not provide the sort of competitor for my account which is relevant at just this point.

For present purposes, then, we can leave the conjunction of analyticity and deflationism aside. For like reasons we can also leave aside the alternative of dealing with (3) by 'naturalizing' and de-modalizing strict implication.[24] We can also ignore the thought that perhaps analytic truths are true in worlds without propositions because if they *were* there, they would be true. This would save strong necessity, but at the price of making sense of counterfactuals. The best going theories of these invoke possible worlds, and if we need possible worlds to make sense of necessity we have left behind the claim that analyticity suffices on its own to do so. Other accounts of counterfactuals invoke other ontology, appeal to which would also falsify the claim that analyticity alone explains necessity. Finally, we might consider adapting a device of Robert Adams.[25] Adams suggests that while some propositions are true in a world W, others are true *at* W—true not because W contains them and has them true, but because they exist in other worlds than W and in *those* are true of W. On some

---

[23] For 'trivialist' approaches to such truth-conditions see Ross Cameron, 'Necessity and Triviality', *Australasian Journal of Philosophy* 88 (2010), 401–15; Agustín Rayo, 'On Specifying Truth-Conditions', *Philosophical Review* 117 (2008), 385–443. Trivialism is not a theory about propositions specifically; some deflationary accounts of propositions might also yield this result.

[24] For a sample of such a view see Richard Swinburne, *The Christian God* (New York: Oxford University Press, 1994), pp. 96–116. Swinburne is happy to do without strong necessity. See also, for example, Robert Brandom, *Between Saying and Doing: Towards an Analytic Pragmatism* (Oxford: Oxford University Press, 2008).

[25] Robert M. Adams, 'Actualism and Thisness', *Synthese* 49 (1981), 3–42.

theories of propositions, if in world W Lincoln never exists, there is no such proposition in W as *Lincoln does not exist*. Even if this is correct, in our world that proposition does exist, and so in our world it is true of W that in it Lincoln never exists, and so this claim is true at, though not in, W. One might suggest, then, that analytic truths gain strong necessity because they are true at all worlds they are not true in. But then we need worlds to make sense of strong necessity: mere analyticity still does not provide it.

A theist can derive *P*'s strong-necessary existence from God's. But if it takes the strong-necessary existence of God to provide the necessary availability of *P*, the explanation of *P*'s modal status no longer comes from within the content of *P* unless God's existence is part of the content of *P*. If *P* is secular, it is not.[26] So this move does not actually provide a theist intrinsic-content explanation of secular states of affairs' necessity. Further, if God exists necessarily, this bursts the bounds of the analyticity theory, as *God exists* is not analytic on any reasonable sense of the term, and goes beyond intrinsic-content explanations altogether unless the intrinsic content of the proposition that God exists explains its strong necessity. Now one could perhaps maintain that its content lets it *entail* its strong necessity. That God exists entails that possibly God exists. It entails that God has His nature and so is a perfect being, which entails (as I have argued elsewhere) that God exists with strong necessity. And I have argued that reflection on divine ultimacy, also an aspect of God's nature, sets us moving down a path that eventually gets us to the truth of S5. But even if someone charitably granted all this, it would give us an explanation of God's strong necessity only if *God exists* explained all that it entailed. And it does not explain that possibly God exists, nor (I think) that God is perfect. Thus I do not think the necessity of God's existence lets a theist retain an overall intrinsic-content account of necessity—which leaves trying to do so for the specific case of secular necessity unmotivated.

Fregean Analyticity

Thus one account of analyticity. On another prominent account—Frege's—a truth is analytic just if it is a logical truth, a definition, or a consequence of these.[27] So if a truth is necessary just if analytic, on Frege's view we have it that

4. □P ≡ that P is a logical truth, a definition, or a consequence of logical truths and definitions.

---

[26] Chapter 15 suggested that some secular claims carry implicit information about creatures' causal environments, and that these include God: if a cat can leave a mat, part of that's being the case is that nothing prevents its doing so, and if God exists, He is one thing that does not prevent this. But this (I suggested) does not suffice to make God part of the content of *the cat can leave the mat*. No manner of penetration into what that says will reveal that God exists.

[27] Gottlob Frege, *The Foundations of Arithmetic*, tr. J. L. Austin, 2nd revised edn. (London: Blackwell, 1980), p. 4e.

A friend of (4) will need some non-question-begging way to exclude sorts of logic that generate contingent logical truths. But in any case, (4) cannot provide strong necessity *via* (1) either. For that there is such a proposition as *P* is not a logical truth, a definition, or a consequence thereof, and so not necessary on (4). Further, (4) is or is not itself necessary. If it is not, then $\Diamond \neg$(4), and so either

5. $\Diamond \neg$(that P is a logical truth, a definition, or a consequence of these $\supset \Box P$), or

6. $\Diamond \neg (\Box P \supset$ that P is a logical truth, a definition, or a consequence of these).

On (5), (4) gives only contingently a sufficient condition for necessity, and so being a logical truth, a definition, or a consequence of these does not on its own explain necessity: contingent conditions let this suffice, and a full explanation must include them. On (6), possibly some necessary truth is not a logical truth, a definition, or a consequence of these. So Frege-analyticity is not the only possible source of necessity. At best, and contingently, it is the source of all actual necessity. But it is hard to see why this alternate source of necessity would not operate actually as well. If there can be necessities based in other parts of language, why would only non-actual languages have them? If there can be necessities based in the contents of essences, why would those essences all be contingent and non-actual? So on (6), it looks as if (4) can be true only if it is necessary.

Yet if (4) is necessary, (4) courts self-referential inconsistency. (4) is not a logical truth and is of the wrong form to be a definition. So either (4) follows from a logical truth by way of definitions or it falsifies itself. The definitions would surely have to include that

7. $\Box P$ =df. that P is a logical truth, a definition, or a consequence of logical truths and definitions.

(7) is (to put it mildly) not obvious. (7) is not a definition in any ordinary sense: it does not explicate ordinary usage of 'necessarily'. (7) looks far more like a substantive, controversial, metaphysical thesis. But then (7) is either contingent or false: for if (7) is a substantive metaphysical thesis, then *per* its own strictures it cannot be necessary. Now some substantive metaphysical theses are plausibly contingent: physical determinism, the existence of physical objects, the existence of souls.[28] But (7) is of the wrong form to be one of these. The examples all are or imply existence-claims (physical determinism's truth implies that there are no events of a certain sort). (7) is not and does not. (7) looks like a definition, an identity-statement: and these should come out necessary. But again, if it is not contingent, it is false. Further, if (7) is a substantive metaphysical thesis and is itself contingent, we face questions like

---

[28] For an argument about others, see Kirstie Miller, 'Defending Contingentism in Metaphysics', *Dialectica* 63 (2009), 23–49.

those mooted earlier: why is there actually only the sort of absolute necessity thus definable, rather than some other possible sort which is not?

Finally, it is not clear that appeal to logical truths gives us in any case a form of intrinsic-content explanation. Even leaving Chapter 3's point about world-dependence aside, ours is an indeterministic world in the small: that is one lesson of quantum theory. Consider a uranium atom decaying: no antecedent physical state determines just when it spits out a particular particle. Consider a future-tensed proposition P about such an indeterminist event, that the atom will spit out a particle at t. On one view of time, that of the future which such events will settle is not just physically undetermined but simply indeterminate before they occur: there is just no fact of the matter about how it will be. If so, P's truth-value is simply indeterminate before those events occur (or fail to): it is not now the case that $\neg P$, and it is not now the case that $\neg\neg P$. Now the future simply does or does not have this indeterminate character. So either this is the true story about P, or it is not—period.

If it is the true story, classical logic is false. Instead negation works intuitionistically and there is a third truth-value, Indeterminate. Apart from the exception noted earlier, if theses of classical logic are false, they are not possibly true. But this is not because of any internal problem. Classical logic is perfectly coherent and internally consistent. There is no more to say about why its theses are not possible than that save for exceptions earlier noted, logical theses are of their nature not contingent, and in every possible world, it is true instead that in at least one world, the future is indeterminate. Whichever state of affairs is impossible—that classical logic's theses are true or that (say) intuitionist logic's are instead—is so entirely because in every world something else is true instead. So to speak, it faces an external obstacle. It fails to be included in any possible world though nothing about its content precludes this—though it has (so to speak) no internal defects to disqualify it, and so no intrinsic-content explanation of its impossibility. And if classical rather than intuitionistic logic has the truth, the reason again lies in a realm of possibility given independently, and so we again have left the field of intrinsic-content explanations. If this is so even in the case of logic, which seems to have the clearest claim to determine its modal status purely intrinsically, it is so *a fortiori* for other states of affairs.

Very Metaphysical Analyticity

Cian Dorr's variation on Frege substitutes for definitions metaphysical analyses, of the sort we give when we say that to be water is to be H_2O.[29] For Dorr,

[29]   Cian Dorr, 'Non-symmetric Relations', in Dean Zimmerman (ed.), *Oxford Studies in Metaphysics* vol. 1, (Oxford University Press, 2004), pp. 155–7, and 'There Are No Abstract Objects', in John Hawthorne, Theodore Sider, and Dean Zimmerman (eds), *Contemporary Debates in Metaphysics*, (Blackwell, 2007), p. 53.

□P ≡ that P is a logical truth, a metaphysical analysis, or a consequence of logical truths and metaphysical analyses.

If this is itself necessary, Dorr preserves self-referential consistency just if it is derivable from logical truths and metaphysical analyses, which would likely include that

8. □P = df. that P is a logical truth, a metaphysical analysis, or a consequence of these.

(8), like (4), is at least partly reductive to the non-modal. Being a logical truth, being a definition and being an analysis (a particular sort of identity-statement) are non-modal properties. Being a consequence of these is modal only if the relation of logical consequence is modal. It may not be—one can instead explicate it in terms of proof or models not construed as modeling possible worlds. If it is not, (8) is reductive, identifying a modal property with a disjunction of non-modal properties. This would place Dorr's proposal beyond our purview, as we are at present just making comparisons among non-reductive theories. If logical consequence *is* a modal relation, (8) is still partly reductive: if we accept that what makes a disjunct true makes its disjunction true, then on (8) logical truths' and metaphysical analyses' having non-modal properties of logical truth and being an analysis makes it true that the modal concept of necessity applies to them. And the non-reductive bit does not show that intrinsic content accounts for modal status. Consider a truth that is a consequence of logical truths and analyses. Nothing about its own content secures that these other things are true and bear the converse of the consequence-relation to it. So whatever the merits of Dorr's proposal, it does not in fact give us an intrinsic-content non-reductive explanation of modal status.

Take Dorr's analyses to explicate real definitional essences, and his proposal moves toward recent work by Kit Fine.[30] Fine takes essential truths about an item as those true in virtue of its identity, of its being that object, and specifying an essence to be like stating an analytic truth.[31] This is not to say that for Fine an item's identity, or what it is to be that object, is one thing, and the truth it makes true is another:

> The form of words 'it is true in virtue of the identity of x' might seem to suggest an analysis . . . into the notions of the identity of an object and of a proposition being true in virtue of the identity of an object. I do not wish to suggest (this). The notation (expresses) an unanalyzed relation between an object and a proposition . . . we should understand the identity . . . of an object in terms of the propositions rendered true by

---

[30] See, for example, 'Essence and Modality', *Philosophical Perspectives* 8 (1994), 1–16.
[31] *Ibid.*, 9.

its identity rather than the other way around . . . the . . . essence of x (is) the collection of propositions that are true in virtue of its identity.[32]

Perhaps this is just nominalism about essential predication; if it is not, I am not sure how to take it. In any event, Fine may mean to reduce, e.g. identifying metaphysical necessity with the property of being true in virtue of the nature of all objects whatsoever.[33] If so, he too falls outside our purview. If the view is not reductive, it may be just mysterious: Fine has little if anything to say about how necessity emerges from this sort of truth. As mysterious, it does not explain modal status. Finally, perhaps Fine traces truths' necessity to the necessity of self-identity: necessarily I am I, so necessarily I have my identity, so necessarily truths true in virtue of my identity (or my having it) are true. If so, this is not a case of non-modal content explaining modal status. Further, the necessity of self-identity is weak. If it is contingent that I exist, it is contingent that anything is identical with me, and so the only strong necessity in the vicinity is that $\Box((\exists x)(x = \text{Leftow}) \supset (\text{Leftow} = \text{Leftow}))$.

I have now examined four variations on the use of analyticity to give non-reductive intrinsic-content explanations of modal status. These tended to slide into reduction to the non-modal. Where they did not, they did not yield an intrinsic-content explanation for strong necessity, even in theist versions. Coupled with the problems noted at the outset, this constitutes a strong case that this approach will not do. The only other sort of intrinsic-content explanation I know of barely counts as an explanation: it is simply to say that non-modal content generates its supervening modal status somehow. By contrast, my view can explain strong necessity and is not committed to denying contingent analytic truths, affirming intrinsic truths, etc. And I have a story about how content explains possibility. It is that having conceived them, God finds states of affairs good enough to permit, and they do not run foul of any preference He has. Given this, God's permission links their content and their possibility. Other states of affairs are impossible simply because they are too bad for God to permit. They will also be impossible for any other theist who holds that God necessarily has the attributes which set up the problem of evil. Thomists, Leibnizians, and Scotists have held this, and so my view incurs no particular disadvantage here. Non-theists will see flouting their modal intuitions that these things are possible as a cost of theism, but note that this is a price of *theism* of a particular sort, not of theist modal theories *per se*. The modal theories' role is to explain what about modality makes it not *ad hoc* to say that the price is in fact paid— which is to say that the modal theories try to reduce the price.

I began by distinguishing three ways an intrinsic-content non-reductionist explanation of modal status might go. One depend on as highly implausible

---

[32] Kit Fine, 'Ontological Dependence', *Proceedings of the Aristotelian Society* 95 (1995), 273, 275.
[33] 'Essence and Modality', 9.

thesis, that all secular attributes are infinitely complex. The third, I have now argued, does not really explain base-level modal status at all, though it can use base-level modal facts to explain other modal facts. The second thus seems preferable, as it does not claim to explain the base level or commit to the failing explanatory strategies I have examined. As we can surely reflect the first approach, it seems that no intrinsic-content non-reductionist explanation of modal status can account for more than part of its distribution. My own view does not account for more than this.[34] If my rivals do not do so either, my not doing so does not count against me when compared with them. We can only be compared with respect to how much we do explain and how well we explain it. If I explain more of the distribution than they do, that is an edge for my view.

Comparison

On the intrinsic-content approach, there are infinite primitively possible propositions, states of affairs, and so on. So there are infinite bedrock modal facts. My story has bedrock primitive modal facts. God just naturally has a few powers, and can specify these by coming up with ideas about what to use them for, as we can. For reasons outlined above, this determines all secular modal facts. It just does work that way. It is just part of God's nature that it be so; I make no claim that anything more basic in His nature explains this. But there are fewer primitively modal entities in my view than in the intrinsic-content competition: just one. There are also fewer bedrock modal facts: just God's having His few primitive natural powers. And we too can generate powers by coming up with ideas about how to use natural powers, and so my story has analogues in our own case to render it somewhat plausible. As against theist intrinsic-content accounts, my story takes less as primitive and explains more, in a familiar way. This is a metaphysical advantage, if the explanations are good ones and bring no correlative disadvantages.

I have discussed modal truths not about value, and I hope the explanations I offered seem good. They are a bit incomplete at the point where value enters. For secular modal truths about value, the story is this. God thinks up candidate secular states of affairs. This content plus His nature—that is, plus God—determine their value-properties. This is like what non-theist realists about moral properties may say: there are states of affairs involving non-moral properties, there are also moral properties whose natures determine when they will supervene on such states of affairs, and the two together just do determine that the moral properties supervene where they do. The theist story has more details, and I cannot fill them out here. So I leave this part of

---

[34] I offer no account of God's primitive powers other than that He has them by nature—that is, just by existing as Himself.

the explanation incomplete. This does not affect the point about parallel structure, and it is a problem only if there is reason to think it cannot be well-completed. But the literature contains promising attempts to do so,[35] and so I do not think that case can be made. These accounts suggest, in fact, that in the moral case particularly, theists might be able to give a fuller, more satisfying account of why moral properties supervene where they do than non-theist moral realists can.

Explanation must stop somewhere. On the intrinsic-content approach, it stops with brute modal facts:

> Necessity and possibility are underived properties of propositions... propositions do not inherit their modal status from anything else.[36]

> Why is it possible for there to be lions? Golly, it just is. The concept of a lion or the property lionhood are possible. That is a part of their natures. They have possibility as an essential property. You might as well ask what makes the concept of a lion the concept of *inter alia* something that is not made of whipped cream as ask what makes it a possible concept...a concept...of something that is made of whipped cream...is not the concept of a lion, it is some other concept. If a concept is a concept of something that is impossible, it is not the concept of a lion, it is some other concept.[37]

On mine, explanation stops with things' (non-modal, non-normative) natures and the nature of God, which plays the role the natures of normative properties play for moral realists, of determining the conditions under which secular states of affairs will have normative properties; these together yield such facts as that there is nothing wrong with there being lions, that lions are in various ways valuable. I add that God's being perfectly good leads Him to recognize value and permit accordingly: so to speak, a theistic reality selects for value. Philosophers have found both normative and modal properties mysterious. One might therefore cry 'obscurum per obscurius' at my account. But intrinsic-content theists also believe in divine goodness and (of course with many others) in normative properties. They have four sorts of primitive property: non-secular and secular modal and moral. I use three to explain the fourth. This is a gain, a reduction of mystery, if the explanation is good. And normative properties are a *familiar* mystery. We recognize them even if we find them hard to explicate. Any explanation rests on something it does not itself explain; we judge explanations *inter alia* whether it is at least clear that

---

[35] See, for example, Robert M. Adams, *Finite and Infinite Goods* (Oxford: Oxford University Press, 1999), pp. 13–49, and over a narrower scope, Linda Zagzebski, *Divine Motivation Theory* (Cambridge: Cambridge University Press, 2004).

[36] Stephen Schiffer, *The Things We Mean* (Oxford: Oxford University Press, 2003), p. 79.

[37] A referee.

this final stopping-point really is there and really can explain. For theists, at least, things really do have normative properties.

God's goodness is His by nature, and so its necessity falls under my account of the necessity of God's nature. Since God has necessarily a nature which is necessarily as it is, on my story, necessarily, if the secular content exists and is just as it is, it has the value-property it actually has. So secular modal truths about value inherit (weak) necessity from the non-secular necessity that God have His nature. Since all I am aiming at here is an explanation of *secular* modal status, this move is acceptable. It both derives and explains, and our account of the necessity of God's existence and nature does not render this account circular or defeat the claim that we do get an explanation here. This story does not require that God necessarily think up the states of affairs He does. So it does not depend on a necessity that He do so to explain weak necessity. That He necessarily does so is orthogonal to this explanation. But it helps explain strong necessity, and the story does require that God strong-necessarily exist and have His nature. This raises the question of whether these necessities are brute, and one must address this fully to evaluate my view.

Brute Necessities?

Brute (unexplained) necessity is a bugaboo in recent work. Desire to avoid it has motivated nominalism, moves to restrict necessity to the logical,[38] eliminative and reductive accounts of necessity, and a variety of broadly Humean metaphysical proposals.[39] It is reasonable to try to avoid brute necessity. If it absolutely cannot be otherwise than that P, 'Why can't it be?' seems a legitimate question. It is a defect in a view that it be unable to answer a legitimate question it raises. There is disagreement on what would count as an adequate answer. Cian Dorr has the strictest standard:

> When something strikes us as impossible . . . we feel that in some important sense, the idea *just makes no sense at all* . . . It is hard to see how any notion of necessity weaker than . . . reducibility to logical truth could be absolute in this way . . . necessity (which) does not flow from real definitions plus logic . . . would seem (just) an extra-strong variety of nomological necessity . . . [40]

---

[38] See, for example, Cian Dorr, 'Non-symmetric Relations', pp. 155–92; 'There Are No Abstract Objects', pp. 32–63; Ross Cameron, 'Necessity and Triviality', 401–15; 'From Humean Truthmaker Theory to Priority Monism', *Noûs* 44 (2010), 178–98.

[39] See Jessica Wilson, 'What is Hume's Dictum, and Why Believe It?', *Philosophy and Phenomenological Research* 80 (2010), 595–637.

[40] Dorr, 'There Are No Abstract Objects', 53.

Dorr thinks that any absolute necessity with a non-nonsensical—I will say 'coherent'—alternative is unacceptably brute. For Dorr, if it is absolutely necessary that P, it is incoherent that ¬P. Putting it another way, the only acceptable explanation for an absolute necessity is displaying that there is no coherent alternative. If it is conceivably, coherently otherwise, the explanatory demand (he thinks) cannot be met, and so it is more plausible that what is in question is absolutely contingent, and necessary only in some weaker sense.

The three necessities I posit are God's having deity, existing, and generating the Bang. Chapter 7 argued that deity is essential to God. I think some of those arguments not only show *that* this is so, but give reasons *why* it is so. Conceptual truths—truths knowable *a priori* by reflection that is in some broad sense on the content of the relevant concepts—meet the Dorr standard; the idea that a bachelor not be an unmarried man 'makes no sense'. So my claim that deity is essential to God meets the Dorr standard if one of these arguments is sound and has as premises only conceptual truths. Consider, then, the premises of the first (renumbered):

9. The concept of deity is an 'Aristotelian' natural-kind concept.

10. If anything is a deity, it has always been a deity.

11. If something has always been a deity, there is no natural-kind concept under which it fell before it fell under deity.

12. If there is no natural-kind concept something fell under before it fell under deity, deity is among the first natural-kind concepts it fell under.

13. Nothing could have failed to fall under the 'Aristotelian' natural-kind concepts it first fell under.

14. If anything is a deity, it cannot cease being a deity.

15. For all x and F, if x could not have failed to be F and cannot cease to be F, x is necessarily F, and so being F is modal-essential to x.

If (9) is true, it is true by the concept's content: that content makes it the sort of concept it is. (10) and (14) are in the sense just given conceptual truths; we know them by seeing that the Western monotheist concept of deity includes eternality, that nothing could count as such a deity were it not eternal. (11) and (12) instance definitional truths involving 'always', 'before', and 'first'. (15) is obviously a matter of (modal) logic and definitions. My argument for (13) reasoned from the claim that

16. S5 is the logic of absolute modality.

Here we must distinguish two senses of 'conceivable'. It is epistemically possible that (16) be false, and so in one sense, (16) is conceivably false. However, it is part of modal concepts' content to have the logic they do. So if (16) is true, it expresses the content of these modal concepts. So if (16) is true, it is in a different sense inconceivable that things be otherwise: it would take a different set of modal concepts to have a different logic. A falsehood can be in this second sense inconceivable and yet epistemically possible because we do not both fully, clearly understand the concepts in question and know that we do. Dorr's standard must involve the second sort of inconceivability. There are logical truths too complex for any of us to 'intuit' to be true or prove in a single lifetime from any axiom-set we can grasp. So for any of us, it is epistemically possible that they are false—and yet they are logical truths, and so their negations are paradigms of Dorr-inconceivability. Now if a thesis follows from premises all having Dorr-inconceivable nega-tions, it inherits this trait from them. So I suggest that if the argument from (9)–(15) is sound, it shows the essentiality of deity not to be brute even by Dorr's standard.

This brings me to the necessity of God's existence—taken by David Chalmers to be a paradigm of brute necessity.[41] I have argued elsewhere on perfect-being grounds that God must exist necessarily; if it is of God's nature to be a perfect being, then, these arguments count as explanations of His necessity based in His nature. Chapter 17 gave a different sort of explanation of God's necessity. By some standards, being able to give such explanations is enough to render God's necessity non-brute. Whether it is in the Dorr sense conceivable that God not exist depends on whether He does exist and what sort of God we have in mind: it is not an obvious, slam-dunk sort of claim. Suppose that God exists and that as theist modal theories have it, what possible-worlds semantics quantifies over exists in God. Then to conceive God's non-existence fully (only a full conception is a true test of whether it is conceivable) would be to conceive inter alia that there is nothing for such semantics to quantify over. If there is not, no possibility-claim is true—nothing is possible. But then if God did not exist, we would have it that God does not exist, that if P then possibly P, and that it is not possible that God does not exist: an inconsistent triad. If in this circumstance it would not be true that if P then possibly P, then if God did not exist, a modal-logical truth would not be true—which is itself Dorr-inconceiv-able. Nor would the semantics in this circumstance work (letting modal claims be true) without items to quantify over: if the right way to explicate absolute modal concepts involves quantifying over some real domain, and their seman-tics in some way explicates those concepts' content, one does not have the same concepts if the semantics does not quantify over anything. One might say that absent God, there would be some other range of items to quantify over. But if God exists necessarily, this is a counterpossible, and on the standard account of counterpossibles, it is just as true that there would not be these items. For reasons discussed earlier, we ought to select at most one of any such pair of counterpossibles to guide philosophical reasoning, and for reasons seen

[41] David Chalmers, 'Does Conceivability Entail Possibility?', in Tamar Gendler and John Hawthorne (eds), Conceivability And Possibility (Oxford: Oxford University Press, 2002), p. 189.

earlier, the latter seems the one to pick. My theory includes the necessity of God's existence. Given that theory, this necessity cannot be called brute, as given that theory it is not Dorr-conceivable that God not exist. To the extent that I have a case for the theory, then, I have a case that God's existence is not a brute necessity, even by the most stringent standard. Thus a charge of involving a brute necessity of God's existence cannot without begging the question be used against the theory.

If the Bang is necessary, it is strongly necessary that God think up the content He has. One wants to know if this necessity is brute. My reply comes in two parts. The necessity of the Bang has been explained. And it is a brute fact what God thinks up, but this involves my view in no more brutality than its competitors. For Thomist and Scotist it is equally a brute fact that there are the states of affairs there are. If they ask me 'Why does God think up dogs' having tails?', I can equally ask the Thomist why God's nature contains dogs' having tails, the Scotist why God's nature contains an impulse to think this, the Platonist why there is Form of Dog with a particular relation to the Form of Tail, or the contemporary Platonist why such a state of affairs as that dogs have tails. I have no answer, nor do they. For me, God just does think up what He does, and there is no more to say; for them there just are the Platonic states of affairs or divine impulses there are, and there is no more to say. Brutality for brutality, then, they and I are on a par. The bump in the rug does not disappear. We just move it to different places. My rivals might answer, 'The question's misplaced. It just could not be any other way.' But I say that God could not have thought up other than He did—that the Bang could not have been otherwise. I only add that this modal character was not imposed by His nature, but instead was consequent on His thinking as He did. Whereas Platonists, and so on, will say that God thought as He did because He had to, I say that He had to only because He did. I add that His nature did not constrain His thinking. Rather, it was *in* Him to think otherwise. This does not imply that He could have. It implies only that He does not and could not have the power to do so only because He did not will to have it. And that there was and is no divine volition to have it, and so to have power to (say) think up schmarks in addition to quarks, is no more brute for me than it is for them that there was and is no divine impulse to do so, no Platonic state of affairs that *there being schmarks*, and so on. Reminded that we can *conceive* that schmarks, not quarks, be possible, we all reply that conceiving is a fallible guide to possibility. For the rest, there is the brute fact that there is such a content as dogs' having tails. For me the brute fact is that God thinks this up. These facts are equally brute. So how are things more arbitrary on my view? I submit, then, that at this point my story parallels and is no worse than its competitors.

Comparison Continued

I suggest, then, that my view is preferable to intrinsic-content theism. We share the theist commitment, and I leave no more brute than they do. But I explain more on a basis of fewer primitive modal facts (none secular) and I avoid their difficulties. Further, I can consistently explain strong necessities, because I can grant God's strongly necessary existence, and the rest flow from that. Fewer primitive modal facts is also one point for my view over against non-theist intrinsic-content views. For Adams, for instance, possible worlds are maximal consistent sets of propositions, sets such that possibly all their members are true together.[42] Possibly all members are true together only if each member is, individually, possibly true. Let us ask why it is so. Since its inclusion in a consistent set presupposes its being possible, on Adams' terms we cannot explain a proposition's being possible in terms of being true in a possible world or a smaller possibility. And if it has some extra-propositional explainer, that would surely be a better candidate for a possibility-truthmaker and an ingredient of worlds. So since for Adams possibilities just are sets of propositions, either an individual proposition's intrinsic content explains its possibility or this has no explanation at all. Adams rejects the analyticity story of how content explains modal status.[43] But he offers no other. We thus have infinite brute modal facts. Something similar will hold for those who take as possible worlds simple, unstructured world-attributes or -propositions. That theists can have fewer primitive modal facts will not of itself persuade non-theists who believe in worlds to consider theism, but can be part of a cumulative case for non-theist consumption whose main argument comes later.

Chapter 9 argued that those seeking a theist modal theory should *ceteris paribus* avoid a deity theory. This chapter and the last have assessed the *cetera*. They are better than are equal. They add up to a modest case for my view. However, on the other side, my view implies that God actively accounts for necessary truths. So it faces a general objection to which some broadly Thomist theories are not prey, that genuine explanation of a necessary truth is impossible. The next chapter takes this up. Dealing with it completes a case that my view is preferable to a deity theory.

---

[42] Robert M. Adams, 'Theories of Actuality', in Michael Loux (ed.), *The Possible and the Actual* (Ithaca, NY: Cornell University Press, 1979), p. 204.

[43] So Robert M. Adams, 'Divine Necessity', in Thomas Morris (ed.), *The Concept of God* (New York: Oxford University Press, 1987), pp. 41–53. Further, there are apparently analytic truths which are not necessary. See Edward Zalta, 'Logical and Analytic Truths That Are Not Necessary', *Journal of Philosophy* 85 (1988), 57–74.

21

EXPLAINING THE NECESSARY

I now take up the objection that genuine explanation of a necessary truth is impossible. Once I have discussed it, I move to the sense in which necessary truths depend on God.

Contrastive Explanation

Putnam, Van Fraassen, and others have argued that many or all explanations are explicitly or implicitly contrastive.[1] On their view, even if one seems just to explain why P, one may in fact explain why P rather than (in contrast to) Q. The implicitly contrastive nature of explanation can reveal itself in what sort of explanations one will accept. Suppose that runners 1–3 run a race. 1 wins. Jones asks why. If I answer 'Because 1 ran fast' this may not satisfy Jones, though it does say what earned 1 the victory. If this does not satisfy Jones, this may be because Jones thinks the other runners also ran fast. If runners 2 and 3 also ran fast, 1's running fast does not explain why 1 rather than 2 or 3 won, even if it explains why 1 won. So if Jones does not like my answer, this may be because Jones really wants to know not why 1 won, but why 1 rather than 2 or 3 won. If Jones wanted to know the latter, the answers '1 ran faster than 2 or 3' or '2 was out of shape and 3 had blisters' might be more to Jones' liking. An ideal contrastive explanation would spell out all the relevant alternatives, say why these were the only relevant alternatives, tell what

[1] See Bas Van Fraassen, *The Scientific Image* (New York: Oxford University Press, 1980), pp. 134–53; Hilary Putnam, *The Many Faces of Realism* (LaSalle, IL: Open Court Press, 1987), pp. 38–40; Alan Garfinkel, *Forms of Explanation* (New Haven, CT: Yale University Press, 1981), pp. 21–41.

eliminated all alternatives save the one that came about and tell what brought that one about.

Now if all genuine explanations are contrastive, only things to which there are alternatives can be explained. For one cannot explain why P rather than Q unless there is a Q to contrast with P. If a truth is necessary, there is no possible alternative to it. An impossible alternative, one might argue, is no genuine alternative at all. If this is so, then if all genuine explanations are contrastive, necessary truths are inexplicable. If they are inexplicable, nothing involving God explains them. This needs addressing. I now argue by example that necessary truths are explicable. If the examples are good enough and are not contrastive, they defeat the claim that all genuine explanations are contrastive. If they are contrastive, they defeat the claim that only things to which there are possible alternatives can be explained contrastively. Given S5, this argument extends to necessary truths' modal status: if □P, that □P is itself a necessary truth.

Some Sample Explanations

To begin, it seems plausible that what makes a truth true somehow explains its being true: that Spot's being brown explains its being true that Spot is brown.[2] This intuition has the same force when the truth involved is necessary. That God exists somehow explains its being true that God exists. If this is right, it is enough to vindicate my view. For if God produces truthmakers for necessary truths, He explains their existence—and if He explains the existence of what explains necessary truths' truth, He explains their truth.

Again, suppose that we reject Meinongian possibilism: there are only existents. Suppose too that existence-claims cannot lack determinate truth-value, but must be true or false. Then necessarily,

1. {a, b} exists ⊃ a exists.

Further, (1) has an explanation. (1) is true just if it is not the case that its antecedent is true and its consequent false. On present assumptions, necessarily, (1)'s antecedent is either true or false. Suppose that it is true. Necessarily, if {a, b} exists, then a is a member of {a, b}: sets have their members essentially.[3] And if there are only existents, then if a belongs to {a, b}, a exists. So if (1)'s antecedent is true, its consequent is also true. Member-essentialism and there being only existents do not just entail this. They explain it. They connect (1)'s antecedent and consequent (assuming the antecedent true) and

---

[2] Though see to the contrary Chris Daly, 'So Where's the Explanation?', in Helen Beebee and Julian Dodd (eds), *Truthmakers* (Oxford: Oxford University Press, 2005), pp. 85–103.

[3] For discussion, see James Van Cleve, 'Why a Set Contains its Members Essentially', *Noûs* 19 (1985), 585–602.

tell us why the consequent follows. On the other hand, if (1)'s antecedent is false, then because it is false, it is not the case that (1)'s antecedent is true and its consequent false, and so if (1)'s antecedent is false, (1) is true. Again, we have not just derived this but explained it. Conjoining explanations, we see why (1) is true. Further, (1) is necessary just if it *cannot* be the case that its antecedent is true and its consequent false. If it is necessary that there are only existents, the explanation tells us why this cannot be the case.[4]

We do not need the assumptions just made to produce an example. Let us drop one, and let existence-claims lack truth-value. If they can, (1) can fail to be true, at least within Kleene's 3-valued logic K_3.

But even if it can, if (1) is true, it is weakly necessary: (1) is true and cannot be false. Further, {a, b} *exists* is true $\supset$ ({a, b} exists $\supset$ a exists) is strongly necessary, and we can use what's just been said to help explain its truth. To get the rest, note that if {a, b} *exists* is true, the consequent follows; if it is false, the conditional's antecedent is false and so the conditional is true; and if it lacks truth-value, it is false that {a, b} *exists* is true and so the conditional is true. So to have an example, we need not assume that existence-claims must have truth-values. Let us now drop another assumption, and suppose that there 'are' non-existent possible objects. Then we say that

A is an object = df. A possibly exists.

Existing things all possibly exist, so this definition includes them. Given the reasonable claim that a set is an object just if all its members are,

{a, b} is an object $\supset$ a is an object

gives us an example minus even the restriction to existents. To allow for object-claims without truth-value, we can move to that {a, b} *is an object* is true $\supset$ ({a, b} is an object $\supset$ a is an object).

The last controversial assumption in the treatment of (1) is that truth-values are all determinate—true, false or neither, without borderline cases. One could deny this. There might be borderline cases of composition, in which 'abc compose something' is at the border between being true and lacking truth-value, and so neither determinately true nor determinately truth-valueless. Then it is indeterminate whether there is an object abc compose, and so one might suggest that *there is an object abc compose* has a truth-value at the border between true and truth-valueless: if composition is vague, perhaps truth is vague also. There are four main approaches to vagueness. On epistemicism, borderline cases really do have classical truth-values: we just cannot know which.[5] Supervaluationism sorts all propositions as true, false, or neither. The 'simple gap' approach does so too, I think, treating any case at the border of 'neither' and true as a 'neither' case. Only

---

[4] For this paragraph I am indebted to correspondence with Tom Flint.
[5] See, for example, Timothy Williamson, *Vagueness* (London: Routledge, 1994).

degree-of-truth theories allow other possibilities. On these, a conditional is simply, degree-1 true if its consequent is at least as true as its antecedent.[6] Intuitively, it could not be less true that {a, b} is an object than that a is an object. So intuitively, we do not need even this last assumption to have an example.

Again, if P, then it follows by the introduction-rule for conjunction that P · P. Intuitively, that P and the rule explain it that P · P. That the rule is valid is necessary. If we now stipulate that necessarily P, the intuition that its being the case that P and the rule explain it that P · P remains. So if necessarily P, we have an explanation of the necessary truth that P · P. Of course, equally, that P · P entails that P by simplification, which is again a matter of the logic of '·'. Some might think this undercuts the intuition that there is an explanation here: there cannot be one in both directions, and if not, how do we pick?[7] But though that P · P entails that P, it is not plausible that it explains why P: this entailment would undercut the example only if both putative directions of explanation seemed equally natural. It is a natural thought that conjuncts are basic and their conjunction derived. It is natural to think that whatever makes conjuncts true *ipso facto* makes their conjunction true.[8] The thought is even more appealing when the conjuncts are identical. The claim that conjunctions are basic and their conjuncts derived has no such appeal, particularly when the conjuncts are identical. And it is not plausible that there really is a truthmaker in some way matching up with the logical form of 'P · P,' and given that, logic accounts for it that P. For this would require us to believe that something in reality corresponds to the duplication of 'P' in 'P · P'.

A different sort of example supposes essentialism. Any veteran of Logic 1 will tell you that

2. Socrates is mortal.

Why is he so? We can derive (2) from

3. Socrates is human, and

4. all humans are mortal.

Derivation from (3) and (4) seems to explain (2). (3) tells what kind of thing Socrates is. (4) connects Socrates' being of this kind to (2). One could flesh the connection out with a biological story: something is human only if dead or alive. If dead it was mortal. Humans live only if certain processes go on, and our constitutions and environment guarantee that these processes do not continue indefinitely. But one need not flesh the connection out for (3) and (4)

---

[6] *Ibid.*, p. 117. For present purposes we can just pretend we understand what degreed truth really would be.

[7] My thanks to Timothy Williamson here.

[8] Implicit in this claim is the thesis that logical connectives do not express or refer to 'logical objects,' that '·' does not denote some *thing*, a relation of conjunction.

to explain (though perhaps they explain only if it is *possible* to flesh it out in some such way).

There are at least two ways to parse the explanation (3) and (4) give (2). One involves dispositions and the non-dispositional 'base' property on which they supervene: perhaps (3) tells us that Socrates has a base property, (4) that this is a base property for mortality, and the biological story *why* it is one. On another, (3) ascribes a complex attribute to Socrates, and (4) is true because (assuming for example's sake that medieval philosophers were right, and being human is being a rational mortal animal) this attribute contains being mortal. What the containment comes to depends on how one understands the attribute's complexity. If *rational mortal animal* is really a conjunctive property, being mortal is one conjunct of it. If its complexity is instead determinate-determinable, the overall explanation is really: Socrates has humanity. Humanity contains mortality, as species (*rational mortal animal*) include generic attributes (*mortal animal*) which exist only in their species. Whatever has humanity has all it contains. So Socrates has mortality—he is mortal. Why does Socrates have mortality? Because he has what contains it.

Given essentialism, (3) is necessary. Attributes have their contents and base-properties their superveners necessarily, so on either way of construing (4), it is necessary. If it is, (2) is also. But this does not defeat the claim that (3) and (4) explain (2). So (2)–(4) give us an example of explaining a necessary truth. Their explanatory force may come from an implicit ruling-out of conceivable alternatives. Other base-properties subvene and other species include mortality—such as felinity. To point out that Socrates is mortal because he is human is implicitly to reject such conceivable though impossible alternatives as that he is mortal because he is a cat. But the case may not be contrastive. Even if we knew that there were no alternatives to (2)–(4) other than Socrates' not existing, we would find (3) and (4) explanatory, and not by ruling this alternative out. The example might fail to persuade some because the essential property involved is substantive—that is, had by only some things. We could eliminate this:

3a. Socrates is an object,

4a. all objects are self-identical, so

2a. Socrates is self-identical.

Here (3a) and (2a) predicate essential properties and (4a) connects them by way of a necessary condition on being an object.[9]

[9] My examples might seem to count as 'explanatory proofs', and so call to mind the literature on whether there are such things in mathematics. I take no stand on the mathematical issue. For discussion of explanation within mathematics, see Paolo Mancosu, 'The Varieties of Mathematical Explanation', in J. Hafner (ed.), *Visualization, Explanation and Reasoning Styles in Mathematics* (Dordrecht: Springer. 2005); Erik Weber and Liza Verhoeven, 'Explanatory Proofs in Mathematics', *Logique et Analyse* 45 (2002), 299–307; David Sandborg, 'Mathematical Explanation and the Theory of Why-Questions', *British Journal for the Philosophy of Science*, 49 (1998), 603–24: Mark Steiner, 'Mathematical Explanation', *Philosophical Studies* 34 (1978), 135–51.

Again, set theory's truths have pure mathematics' claim to be absolutely necessary. One truth of set theory is that

5. there is no set of all sets which are not members of themselves.

We can explain (5) this way:

6. There is a set of all sets which are not members of themselves only if P.
7. That P is a contradiction. So:
8. ¬P. So:
5. there is no set of all sets which are not members of themselves.

This explanation does not invoke the necessity of (6)–(8), though they are in fact necessary. It does not depend on their having any particular modal status. It appeals to one particular *source* of necessity, being contradictory of something that entails a contradiction. Not all absolute necessities have this source. So this case is a bit like that of Socrates, mortality, and humanity. To say that Socrates is human rules out other reasons to be mortal. So too, to tell us (5)'s truth has its source in connection to a contradiction rules out other conceivable sources (connection to some essence, for instance). This explanation does not trade merely on the fact that no contradiction is true. Rather, our sense is that (7) *explains* (8), and so (5). When we see that a claim is contradictory, we feel, we see why it is not true, though we may not be clear on just what it is we're seeing. Some theories try to articulate the 'why'. Scotus spoke of a '*repugnantia terminorum*'.[10] Fans of analytic truth appeal to the meanings of 'not' and 'and'. But the intuition is there regardless. So the explanation appeals to whatever about contradictions explains their being false.

Finally, scientists sometimes do experiments to determine what the laws of nature are. An experiment confirms a set of laws L more than another L2 because L explains the experiment's result better than L2 would. Suppose that L does explain a result R better than L2 would. Then a scientist can say that the result was R, not R2, and this was because initial conditions C obtained and L, not L2, are the laws of nature. This gives a contrastive explanation. It tells why events led to R rather than R2. If the laws are L and the initial conditions were C, R2 was physically impossible. But this does not affect the genuineness of the explanation. Nor is this because R2 was absolutely possible. The explanation may well have dealt only in physical modalities; if it did, only physical possibility was relevant. Further, if physical laws reflect things' natures (as many think), physical impossibilities *are* absolute impossibilities. If they are not, still physical and absolute necessity share features that qualify both as sorts of necessity. So it is not obvious a priori that they may not also share features which make both contrastively explicable.

---

[10] So, for example, *Ordinatio* I, d. 36.

It seems, then, that one can explain a necessary fact. This should not be surprising. That □P says only that in every possible world, P. This leaves it open whether something may account for its actually being the case that P. Plausibly, sometimes, something does. Necessarily, some possible world-segment is actual. So it is actually the case that some possible world-segment is actual. But something(s) account(s) for this, namely the cause(s) (and causeless events or states of affairs, if any) involved in actualizing the particular world-segment that is actual.

Contrasts without Possible Alternatives

When things might have gone otherwise, it usually makes sense to say why they turned out as they did, rather than some other way. But this can also make sense if we only *think* things might have gone otherwise—that is, if alternatives are conceivable, even if none are truly possible, or there are none. For explanations have a pragmatic dimension. They are *inter alia* things people address to people. So a contrastive explanation can be worth giving because its audience thinks the alternatives it eliminates possible, whether or not they really are. The audience's beliefs about what the relevant alternatives are, true or not, partly determine what alternatives a good explanation will eliminate. So it can make sense to explain why things went one way, not another, even if they could not have gone the other way.

But there are not only pragmatic reasons that a contrastive explanation need not rule out genuinely possible alternatives. There may be a reason why P even if there are no alternatives to its being the case that P. For something may have brought it about that P, as above, and there may be a reason that there are none. Telling why there are none can help explain why P. This can take the form of ruling out merely conceivable alternatives. One can specify ways things seemingly could have gone, and tell why things could not have gone those ways. One can say why P rather than Q partly by saying *why* it is impossible that Q. Conventionalism and conceptualism offer accounts of how impossible alternatives get to be impossible. They site these prior (in some sense) to their being impossible, and so an objection from the alternatives' being impossible does not apply to them. The same applies to my view. Saying why an alternative is impossible might not involve explaining a necessity: if the logic of absolute modality does not include S4, Q could be impossible contingently. If Q is impossible necessarily, still asserting that we can say why it is impossible need not beg the question. For I have shown that there can be 'explanatory proofs', and perhaps Q's impossibility can be explained by an explanatory proof that ¬Q. If this is so, one can explain contrastively without eliminating a possible alternative. So even if all genuine explanation is contrastive, it may be possible to explain a necessity.

Dependence and the Necessary

I am committed to real dependence among necessary items. For I claim that necessary truths depend for their truth-value on necessary truthmakers involving God. So I now argue that necessary states of affairs can depend on other states of affairs.

Explanations of the contingent usually involve or imply some real dependence among facts. This is often causal, but it need not be. Parts' traits explain wholes', and wholes' traits depend on parts'. But this dependence is not causal: that all large-enough parts of the wall are red does not cause the wall to be red. As the sort of explanation in question differs, the sort of dependence does too. Things do not seem to differ in where what's explained is necessary. Even if both wall and parts existed necessarily, the parts' redness would explain the whole's, and the whole's would depend on its parts', not *vice versa*. If God necessarily exists and creates some universe or other, His creation explains there being some universe and there being some universe depends on God's activity, not *vice versa*. That there necessarily is a universe only because God necessarily creates heightens dependence on God, rather than canceling it: not only is there some universe only because God willed it, but there being some universe depends so completely on God that this is the only way there could be some universe.

God exists necessarily. So then does the set {God}, if there are sets. If there is such a set, its existence really depends on God's, as sets' do on their members' generally. It exists because God does. So that {God} exists depends on the fact that God exists, and not *vice versa*, though both are necessary. It is true that $1 + 1 = 2$. It is true that $2 + 2 = 4$. So it is true that $1 + 1 = 2$ and it is true that $2 + 2 = 4$. This truth derives its truth from its conjuncts', and depends for it on theirs. So its being true that $1 + 1 = 2$ and true that $2 + 2 = 4$ depends really on its being true that $1 + 1 = 2$ and its being true that $2 + 2 = 4$, and not *vice versa*, even if all alike are necessary. Such claims as that

> in all cases, just as such, wholes really depend for properties on their parts, and
>
> in all cases, just as such, sets really depend for existence on their members,

have more intuitive appeal than the claim that what is so necessarily is so independent of everything else—or so it seems to me. Thus it seems that necessary facts can depend on other facts.

Having dismissed the general claim that necessary facts are independent of all other facts, let's now consider an argument that necessary facts are independent of God. God exists either contingently or necessarily. If contingently, then

9. were there no God, it would still be the case that $2 + 2 = 4$,

in which case it seems that arithmetic does not depend on God. If necessarily, then arguably (9) is still true, as (9) is then a counterpossible, and on the orthodox treatment of these, they all are true. So whether God be contingent or necessary, it seems, (9) is true. If (9) is true, it seems that its being the case that $2 + 2 = 4$ does not depend on God.

I reply that even if God exists contingently and (9) is true, necessary states of affairs may really depend on God. For to infer that they do not, we need in addition to (9) a premise about the relation between real and counterfactual dependence. One such premise is the claim that

10. P really depends on it that $Q \rightarrow (\neg Q > \neg P)$.

This is too simple to be true. Sometimes two or more causes contribute to an event, each sufficient to cause the event by itself. If Casca and Cassius stab Caesar's heart at once and only fractions of an inch apart, Casca and Cassius together kill Caesar. It would be reasonable for a court to try both for first-degree murder. But in fact, each stab on its own would have sufficed to kill Caesar. Thus Caesar's death was redundantly caused. Both Casca's and Cassius' stab contributed to Caesar's dying. Caesar's dying depended causally on both. But neither satisfies (10). For had either not stabbed, Caesar would still have died.

A cause failsafe-causes its effect when it alone brings the effect about, but there is also a 'backup' cause which would have brought the effect about had the first cause failed. Suppose that Casca's dagger preceded Cassius' by a second or so, and Casca alone killed Caesar. (Perhaps they were both stabbing at his brain, and by freak chance Casca hit a spot in the brain wounds in which cause almost instantaneous brain-death.) Were this so, Caesar's death would have been failsafe-caused. For had Casca's thrust somehow missed, Cassius' would have done the deed. But Caesar's death still depended on Casca's thrust as effect on cause. So failsafe-causation also involves causal dependence, which does not satisfy (10).

Causal dependence is a form of real dependence. So if causes can failsafe- or redundantly cause effects, there can be failsafe or redundant real dependence. This forces us to revise (10). (10) failed because other events might play the causal role the event that made it true that Q played. So we might try that

11. P really depends on it that Q in respect of role R $\rightarrow$ (($\neg Q \cdot$ nothing plays R with respect to P) $> \neg P$).

But (11) will not do either, for sometimes roles themselves are dispensable. Given the social conventions of the day, if Sarah is to marry, her father must give permission if living. So if Abraham asks Sarah's father for her hand in marriage, his marrying Sarah really depends on her father's granting permission. Yet if nothing played the permission-granter's role, this might not keep Sarah from marrying. For this could be because Sarah had no live relatives; if there is no-one who *should* give permission, not getting permission is no bar to wedlock.

Let us now turn to a contingent God. If God plays some role in mathematical truth's being true, God is contingent and mathematical truth is necessary, then either His role is dispensable or something else plays it in other possible worlds. If the role is dispensable, it does not follow that the effect does not depend on the one who actually plays it. If there *is* someone to give permission for Sarah to marry, she needs permission (given the conventions of the day). So if God's role is dispensable, mathematical truth may still actually depend on God. Moreover, if something else plays the role in other worlds, it does not follow that the effect does not depend on the one who actually plays it. For perhaps this other is only a failsafe. Intuitively, in cases of failsafe causation, the effect depends on the actual cause in some way even if not counterfactually. If the other is not a failsafe, perhaps it is a redundant cause. Intuitively, in redundant causation, the effect depends on both causes in some way though not counterfactually. Ultimately, on my view, the role God actually plays for mathematical truth is that certain facets of His nature truthmake it. If mathematical truth necessarily has truthmakers, then if God is contingent, His nature can still play this role. The worst that follows is that mathematical truth also may have failsafe or redundant truthmakers.

Now suppose that God exists necessarily. Then (9) is true just because it is a counterpossible. But then for the same reason so is

Were God not to exist, it would not be the case that $2 + 2 = 4$.

If (9) indicates real independence, then this for the same reason indicates real dependence. But arithmetic cannot both really depend and not really depend on God. If God exists necessarily, then, we need not worry further about (9). Counterpossibles do not on their own reveal whatever is the case between God and arithmetic.

Real Dependence

If A and C compose B, were A removed, B would differ: some of B's character depends really on A's. The dependence, I now suggest, does not consist in the counterfactual's being true. If A and C compose B, A's character and C's are the source of B's. B's comes from and so really depends on theirs. There is (say I) a determinable, categorical, non-modal relation, _ is a source of the _ of _. Its converse is the relation *the _ of _ is from _* —or perhaps just as plausibly, '_ is a source of the _ of _' and 'the _ of _ is from _' are just two names for the same relation, as 'after' and 'before' may be. I suggest that '_ really depends for _ on _' is another name for whatever relation 'the _ of _ is from _' names. I suggest that real dependence just is being-from, as its etymology suggests. Where there is being-from, there will often be counterfactual dependence as well. This is why counterfactual dependence has been able to attract such attention in e.g. analyses of causal dependence. All the same, counterfactual dependence is an epiphenomenon here.

Effects come from causes. To be produced is to come from; producers—causes—are one sort of source. So the causal relation is a source-relation, one determinate of the determinable above. If e causes e*, then (I suggest) e*'s depending on e is the converse of this, or talk of the dependence is just another way to describe this fact. If the first, e* depends on e because e* comes from e, because e is its source; if the second, the dependence consists in the causation. It is because causes are sources that causal claims often support counterfactuals. If the fire's burning causes the kettle's heating and the situation is simple—no failsafes, no redundant causation, and so on—then had the fire not burned, the kettle would not have heated up. This is because the heating came from the burning. If the heating came from the burning and the situation was simple, removing the burning would have been removing the heating's source. Without the source, what came only from that source would not have come at all.

That dependence is being-from can solve puzzles in the metaphysics of causality. It tells us why an effect depends on a cause even if it does not counterfactually depend on it. For whether or not the effect depends counter-factually on its cause, the effect is *from* its cause. Again, that dependence is being-from can help explain the persuasiveness of transfer-based theories of physical causation. Yet again, this bears on discussions of Frankfurt-style cases about alternative possibilities and freedom. We sometimes think that being free in choosing whether to do A consists in having powers plus opportunity at the time of choice—that is, being in all respects able to choose to do A or not do A. In a Frankfurt-style case, an interfering mechanism will kick in and cause one to choose A if one is about to choose not to do A. Suppose such a mechanism, and that in fact, one chooses to do A, so that it never kicks in. It seems odd to many to say that in this case one did not choose freely. If one did choose freely, the present thought about dependence can help say why. Even if I could not have done other than choose A, my choice was in the relevant respects *from me* because the mechanism never actually operated. My choice depended only on me, not on the mechanism, and so (one can argue) my freedom was inviolate. If I did not choose freely, my thought about depen-dence can at least help explain intuitions that I did.

Dependence is (I am suggesting) a modally flat phenomenon. It concerns what is actually so, not what would have been so in other circumstances. So counterfactuals like (9) are just irrelevant to whether arithmetic depends in some real way on God.

Historically, most theist modal metaphysicians have held deity theories. Dispatching the objection to explaining necessities completes my case that my theory is preferable. Chapter 5's 'contingent options' may not in the end provide an alternative to deity theories and my own view. For it is compatible with either that divine contingent intrinsics of some sort be involved in making necessary truths true or necessary; all that is required is that in other worlds, other contingent entities perform the same role. A contingent option that did not make this move would agree with one reading of Descartes, that all absolute necessities are contingently so. Given the plausibility of the S4 axiom, a view able to accommodate it would be preferable. God-involving views that do not offer theist ontologies include the conjunction of theism with ordinary modal conventionalism. This would maintain that God made us and we made the modal facts. For reasons I begin to develop elsewhere I do not think such conventionalism viable.[11] Another option would be to conjoin theism with an Aristotelian 'powers' metaphysics restricted to creatures. This would be unmotivated: if creaturely powers can ground modal truth, why not God's? I have suggested reasons theists should not conjoin theism and possibilism, and more emerge in the final chapter. The main remaining sort of God-involving modal metaphysics would conjoin theism with belief in actual, existent abstract entities that provide the ontology for modal truth. I have already given what amounts to a theological case against this—the line of argument concluded in Chapter 4, that theists ought to hold theist theories of modality. I now make a philosophical case against this sort of theist Platonism.

---

[11] I argue against one version of it in 'Swinburne on Divine Necessity', *Religious Studies* 46 (2010), 141–62.

22

AGAINST THEISTIC
PLATONISM

I now make a philosophical case against the conjunction of theism with Platonism about worlds. I first consider what reasons a theist might have for holding such Platonism.

Why Platonize?

There are, I think, two sorts of reason a theist might be a world-Platonist. Worlds do philosophical work. So if the work seems worth doing, the theist might want entities to play the world-role, and given a limited menu of options to choose from, some Platonist entity might simply seem more attractive than its rivals. I address this sort of argument in the next chapter, suggesting that there is good reason to have something in God play these roles instead. The argument is not directed specifically to theists, but obviously, if one is already a theist, one chief source of resistance to it is removed. At present I consider the other sort of reason to be a Platonist about worlds. Platonist worlds might be propositions, attributes, states of affairs, or sets of these.[1] A theist may think there are good arguments for (say) Platonic propositions. The theist may then find it plausible that if there are

---

[1] For single propositions see Peter Van Inwagen, 'Two Concepts of Possible Worlds', in his *Ontology, Identity and Modality* (Cambridge: Cambridge University Press, 2001), pp. 206–42; for states of affairs see Alvin Plantinga, *Nature of Necessity*; for attributes, see Robert Stalnaker, 'Possible Worlds' and Situations; *Journal of Philosophical Logic* 15 (1986), 109–23;, and Peter Forrest, 'Ways Worlds Could Be', *Australasian Journal of Philosophy* 64 (1986), 15–24 (Forrest's attributes are structural and so equally count as complexes of attributes); for sets of propositions, see R. M. Adams, 'Theories of Actuality', in Michael Loux (ed.), *Universals and Particulars* (Garden City, NY: Doubleday Books, 1970), pp. 235–44. Some broadly Meinongian views provide more outré ways to involve properties (in the construction of 'possibilia' which would if actual be universes enacting histories)—see, for example, Josh Parsons, 'The Least Discerning and Most Promiscuous Truthmaker', *Philosophical Quarterly* 60 (2010), 309–10; or Edward Zalta, 'Twenty-Five Basic Theorems in Situation and World Theory', *Journal of Philosophical Logic* 22 (1993), 385–428—but what I say about sets applies to these too.

propositions, there are propositions suited for world-duty: if there are propositions, surely there are conjunctive propositions, and so there presumably are maximal consistent conjunctive propositions. There could be a maximal conjunctive sentence, and it would be arbitrary to deny that such a sentence expressed a proposition if one grants that non-maximal conjunctive sentences do so. As consistent, these propositions are possibly true. As consistent and maximal, they entail just one of every pair of contradictories. So they might seem able to do duty as possible worlds, and so theists might think belief in Platonic possible worlds falls out of more general Platonist commitments. I now ask whether it in fact does.

Propositions

I first take up Platonic maximal consistent propositions; what I say about them also addresses theories of worlds as sets of propositions. I will say that a proposition is Platonic just if it is abstract and exists independent of all minds, even God's.[2] I now show that arguments for the existence of propositions tell us little about their character and suggest that theists who believe in propositions should adopt a non-Platonic account of their character.

A common line of argument in favor of propositions is that certain sorts of inference treat that-clauses as noun-phrases used to refer:

> Fred believes that Sheila is stalking him. So:
>
> There is something Fred believes.
>
> George believes and Sheila denies that Sheila is stalking him. So:
>
> Sheila denies something George believes.

The arguments seem valid, and so, we are told, we should take that-clauses to have referents;[3] further, the appearance of quantification over propositions may impress fans of Quine's view of ontological commitment. Make of this what one will, it tells us nothing about the intrinsic nature of what is believed.[4] Nor do such considerations as that there 'should' be propositions to simplify semantics.[5] Such arguments alone do nothing to support distinctively Platonist *accounts* of propositions. And theism appears to undercut arguments for the latter. Consider Scott Soames' quick argument for propositions' language- and mind-independence:

---

[2] As Van Inwagen holds ('God and Other Uncreated Things', in Kevin Timpe (ed.), *Metaphysics and God* (London: Routledge, 2009)).

[3] See, for example, Andrea Iacona, 'Are There Propositions?', *Erkenntnis* 58 (2003), 326–7; George Bealer, 'Universals', *Journal of Philosophy* 90 (1993), 7–16; Stephen Schiffer, *The Things We Mean* (Oxford: Oxford University Press, 2003), pp. 12–13.

[4] So Iacona, *op. cit.*, 329–30.

[5] So Terence Parsons, 'On Denoting Propositions and Facts', *Philosophical Perspectives* 7 (1993), 441–60.

the proposition that the sun is a star could have been true even if no one and hence no sentence had existed to express it.[6]

The argument premises that possibly there are truths but no minds. Theists who believe that God exists necessarily deny this. Again, George Bealer's elaborate case that propositions are Platonic can draw that conclusion only by explicitly denying God's existence.[7] Other arguments that propositions exist necessarily imply nothing about what they are apart from this,[8] save that they are some sort of thing that can exist necessarily.

Propositions are things that can be asserted, doubted, believed, true, or false. These are extrinsic properties. As to their intrinsic character, if they are without constituents—'unstructured'—we find ourselves in the predicament Peter van Inwagen notes for abstract objects generally:

> We do not understand even the simplest . . . abstract objects very well . . . the number 4 . . . has logical properties like self-identity . . . and it has arithmetical properties . . . But what others? It is, no doubt, non-spatial and perhaps non-temporal. It is perhaps necessarily existent. At about this point . . . if we try to describe its intrinsic features, we soon trail off in puzzlement.[9]

Further, if propositions have constituents, then if those are other abstract entities (properties, say), we know no more else about their intrinsic natures than that they consist of other somethings-we-know-not-what, and if they are concrete entities (as in Russellian singular propositions), we know about their intrinsics no more else than we know about those of the concreta. We do not, in particular, have a theory of propositions' intrinsic features that would rule it out that something in God plays the proposition role, or one of their extrinsic features that would rule out their depending on God for their existence.

Van Inwagen offers the next best thing, a case that the most plausible candidate item in God for propositions to be or depend on, a divine thought, cannot take up either role. He has two arguments:

> —divine thoughts would be events. But there are no events. When someone gains a property at a time, there is no fourth thing, an event, constituted by the person, property and time. We can fully describe what happens in terms of the three, without supposing that there are objects with the property of happening.[10]

[6] Scott Soames, *Understanding Truth* (Oxford: Oxford University Press, 1999), p. 19. See also Iacona, *op. cit.*, 337; G. E. Moore, *Commonplace Book* (New York: Macmillan, 1962), p. 375.

[7] Bealer, 'Universals', 27–8.

[8] For example, Van Inwagen, 'A Theory of Properties', in Dean Zimmerman (ed.), *Oxford Studies in Metaphysics*, 137–8.

[9] Van Inwagen, 'A Theory of Properties', 111–12.

[10] Van Inwagen, 'God and Other Uncreated Things', 14–15.

—if there were events, they would contain properties, and so an elimination of Platonic propositions in favor of divine mental events would not
fully purge abstracta.[11]

Van Inwagen's first argument is really just a promissory note: he does not
survey the phenomena that lead many to believe in events. So I reply with two
similar promises. I elsewhere use divine mental events to eliminate properties.[12] As I note there, and van Inwagen in effect reminds us, this puts me on
the hook for a nominalistically acceptable account of divine mental events.
But I begin one elsewhere and—first promise—believe I can defend the view.
Further, believers in events use them to purge times from our ontology.[13] If
one of their methods succeeds and is nominalistically acceptable—second
promise—my 'gaining a property' involves just a substance, that event, and
(say I) a divine mental event. This is three token items, as in van Inwagen's
preferred story, and only two categories (substance and event), not three. So if
I can redeem my promises, positing events will produce the leaner ontology
overall. Till it is clear that I cannot pull this off and Van Inwagen has
redeemed *his* promise, Van Inwagen will not have given us reason to deny
divine thoughts or deny that divine thoughts can play the proposition role.

So far, I have addressed both simple and 'structured' propositions. But
if propositions have constituents, these include other sorts of abstract entity—
attributes, usually. The attributes would largely be universals.[14] I argue elsewhere that theists do not have reason to believe in universals, including
Platonic ones—that theism undercuts the arguments in their favor, and so
theists, as such, should not be realists.[15] Thus I submit that theism undercuts
belief in Platonic structured propositions. So theists have no reason to believe
in structured Platonic propositions, nor to believe anything about unstructured propositions or God that would rule it out that something in God plays
the role of propositional possible worlds. I thus suggest that so far, at
least, theist Platonists do not have an argument for distinctively Platonic

[11] *Ibid.*, 16.
[12] 'God and the Problem of Universals', *Oxford Studies in Metaphysics* 2 (2006), 325–56. See also my
'Divine Simplicity', *Faith and Philosophy* 23 (2006), 365–80 and 'One Step Toward God', *Royal Institute of
Philosophy Supplement* 68 (2011), 67–104.
[13] Any version of relationalism about time attempts this. For a variety of approaches see Roderick
Chisholm, 'Events Without Times', *Noûs* 24 (1990), 413–27; Bertrand Russell, 1914, *Our Knowledge of the
External World*, rev. edn. (London: Allen and Unwin, 1926); S. K. Thomason, 'Free Construction of Time
from Events', *Journal of Philosophical Logic* 18 (1989), 43–67; F. Pianesi and, A. C. Varzi, 'Events, Topology,
and Temporal Relations', *Monist* 78 (1996), 89–116; Graham Forbes, 'Time, Events and Modality', in Robin
Le Poidevin and Murray MacBeath (eds), *The Philosophy of Time* (Oxford: Oxford University Press, 1993),
pp. 80–95.
[14] If propositions are complexes of Fregean senses, these are a sort of universal: a sense is intuitively a
property of term-tokens, and numerically different tokens of terms may have the same sense.
[15] 'God and the Problem of Universals'. I there considered only the standard arguments in favor of
universals. I did not consider an argument that would run this way: we need structured propositions. So we
need universals to figure in them. So we should believe in universals. A quick answer would be that if some
construction involving God is available to take the place of universals in the structure, theism undercuts this
argument too.

propositions from which Platonic proposition-worlds fall out, because they do not have an argument for distinctively Platonic propositions at all.

There may in fact be reasons to think theism can fill the proposition-role better than Platonism does. Lewis asks the defender of propositional worlds two questions; theism's advantage emerges with the second. For Platonists, there are the abstract worlds, and what goes on in the universe somehow 'selects' one as the actual world.[16] Lewis's first question is what relation does the 'selecting'.[17] Van Inwagen suggests that if worlds are propositions, making-true 'selects' the actual (true) world.[18] On my account, pluralities consisting of a world-power and the preconditions of its use play the world-role. My 'selection' picture is non-Platonic, and so for me Lewis's question just does not arise. For me, there are the powers, and so on, and God's use of a power 'selects' a universe and concrete history to match up with what it is a power to bring about. What pairs these up with a world-power is just that the power produced them. A power to produce figs produces figs. This looks analytic. There seems to be nothing to explain about it. It is its nature to produce figs; this is just a primitive fact about it. The nature of the power determines the nature of the effect and brings about a 'match' between them. On my account, God's power to produce figs is specified as such by a mental event such as to lead to figs, and the event's being this way is primitive. Such events are concrete simples with brute causal roles. Lewis cannot say there is something 'magical' about these. It could have worked out that physical reality at the bottom level consisted of true atomic particles, smallest bits of classical matter with causal roles not further explained by any structure of particles within. These would have been concrete simples with brute causal roles. There would have been nothing magical about them; belief in them would have been sober science. If this is a possible way for things to be, further, then on Lewis's own views, somewhere in the plethora of concrete universes there are such particles. If there can be concrete simples with brute causal roles and there can be immaterial things—something Lewis was willing to concede,[19] as would any but the most dogmatic materialist—there seems no reason that there could not be concrete simple immaterial things with brute causal roles. Nor should van Inwagen pooh-pooh my leaving the causal role of these events brute. These events play the largest part in my elimination of properties; the event we speak of as God's possessing the concept *cat* is as close as my scheme gets to a Platonic form Cat, and this figures in a Platonist-style elimination of universals (literal repeatables). For me, there is such an event, and it just does produce cats (with a little help from its friends). It is in other words something with a brute nature such that items with the right relation to it are and could only be cats. For van Inwagen, there is the property cathood, and that property is itself something with a brute nature

---

[16] So David Lewis, *On the Plurality of Worlds* (Oxford: Basil Blackwell, 1986), pp. 180, 182.
[17] Lewis, *Plurality*, pp. 174–90.   [18] 'Two Concepts of Possible Worlds', 232.
[19] So, for example, Lewis, *Plurality*, p. 73.

such that items with the right relation to it are and could only be cats. He and I are on all fours here. Finally, we do somehow understand causation. If in fact the ontology of causation is in terms of powers, this is one sort of understanding of powers and their effects, though it is philosophically disputed that this *is* what it is. If so, my selection-relation is not a bad, inaccessible primitive we could understand only by magic.[20] It is empirically accessible to the extent that causation is.

Lewis' second question concerns representation. Propositions are supposed to bear truth-values. So they must represent the world as being certain ways, and be true just if the world is as they represent it. So propositions must represent the world. Here Michael Jubien objects that

> it is implausible ... that *any* genuine Platonic entity could represent on its own cuff. *Representation* is an 'intentional' ... relation. If x represents y, then x has a part that 'stands for', 'refers to', or is otherwise 'about' y ... It borders on the absurd to suppose that any inert, non-spatiotemporal entity could have a part that, in itself, plays any such referential or quasi-referential role, especially with respect to contingent, concrete entities. Representation is ultimately the business of ... beings with intentional capacities, in short, thinkers.[21]

Lewis likewise notes that defenders of propositional possible worlds seem unable to say what it is in virtue of which an abstract simple (an unstructured proposition, for instance) represents the world as one way rather than another.[22] Well, the theist can agree with Jubien. And this is equally an advantage over Lewis. Lewis' claim for his own view is that

> Another world ... can have as part a Humphrey of its own, a flesh and blood counterpart of our Humphrey ... By having such a part, a world represents *de re*, concerning Humphrey—that is, the Humphrey of our world ... that he exists and does thus-and-so ... by waving his arm ... the other-worldly Humphrey represents the this-worldly Humphrey as waving.[23]

I demur. Other-worldly Humphrey no more intrinsically 'refers to' or 'stands-for' this-worldly Humphrey than an abstract Platonic entity does. Material things do not intrinsically represent any more than propositions do. They just sit there. It is minds which use them to represent, by capitalizing on (say) resemblances to things we wish to represent.

As to Lewis's query, I earlier sketched an approach to divine mental events' content. A divine mental event has the content *cat* at least partly because it is such that its appropriate involvement with divine volition causes cats to be.

---

[20] *Ibid.*, pp. 178, 182.
[21] Michael Jubien, 'Propositions and the Objects of Thought', *Philosophical Studies* 104 (2001), 54.
[22] Lewis, *Plurality*, pp. 174–90.   [23] *Ibid.*, p. 194.

We can equally say that for this reason it represents the property of being a cat to God, who grasps what it is a power to produce. A divine thought has the content *Boots is a cat* at least partly because it is such that its appropriate involvement with divine volition brings it about that Boots is a cat; we can equally say that for this reason it represents it to God that Boots is a cat. So I have also sketched a non-Platonic account of what it is about the divine mind in virtue of which its thoughts represent the world. Further, in a sense, it does not matter if my approach ultimately does not work. For most of us, it is a datum that minds represent the world, the only question being how. The claim that Platonic propositions represent enjoys no such status. So the representation question is a problem for Platonists in a way it is not even for theists who lack a theory of divine mental representation. Minds (including God's) represent; not knowing how does not incline us to doubt it. Not knowing how Platonic propositions represent does incline many to doubt that they can.

Platonist replies to Lewis have not offered an account of representation.[24] Until they do, if a theist story fills the proposition-role without Platonic entities and leaves less mystery behind than one with Platonic entities, or leaves behind a more familiar and plausible mystery (the representing ability of minds, not that of propositions), it does better than Platonism at filling that role. One residual mystery in my own story is God's power to create and conserve, but any theist has that to deal with: by avoiding propositions, I have less mystery or more familiar mystery overall in my views. Thus I suggest that theism minus Platonism can in fact fill the proposition role better than Platonism, with divine thoughts. If that is correct, theist Platonism is not just unsupported but unmotivated as well. I note finally that my argument extends also to Platonist theories of properties such as Van Inwagen's, which see them primarily as 'things said of other things', or 'assertibles'[25] (as it were, unsaturated fragments of propositions).

Worlds as Attributes

Some Platonists take as possible worlds attributes universes would have, whose being exemplified would involve enacting entire universe-histories. These could either have other attributes as constituents or be unstructured.[26] The constituents would include universals. Again, I argue elsewhere that theists do not have reason to believe in these. If that argument is sound,

---

[24] Van Inwagen ('Two Concepts of Possible Worlds', 232, n. 31) and Zaragoza (Kevin Zaragoza, 'Bring Back the Magic', *Pacific Philosophical Quarterly* 88 (2007), 391–402) offer nothing. Jubien says only that to represent, propositions must have constituents (Michael Jubien, 'Could This Be Magic?', *Philosophical Review* 100 (1991), 249–67).

[25] 'A Theory of Properties'.

[26] Forrest, *op. cit.*, sees them as complex structural attributes. Stalnaker *op. cit.* seems to treat them as simples.

then, theists do not have reason to believe in structured Platonic world-attributes.[27]

Suppose, on the other hand, that world-attributes would be unstructured. Generalist possible world-types would be universals—more than one possible individual could have them. For universes would have such attributes. Different sets of individuals could realize a generalist world-type, and if one varies the individuals involved enough, surely one gets a different universe.[28] So world-types fall under my previous argument about universals. If possible worlds are not generalist, not just types, they involve haecceities or the equivalent for all individuals that would exist were they actual. They specify the identity of every item that ever exists, including the universe that would bear them. Only one possible individual, that universe, could bear them. So non-generalist possible-world attributes would not be universals and do not fall directly under my argument about universals.

Such world-attributes would not be haecceities either. A haecceity is an essential property. Our very universe could have existed had you sneezed one microsecond earlier this morning. But if you had, a different possible world would have been on the way to actuality. Thus non-generalist world-attributes would be accidental properties only one possible individual could have. For them to exist unexemplified (as most would) would be as if there were, floating free of all bearers, a trope which is my older brother's baldness, even though I have no older brother, or my younger brother's blondness, though he never has been or will be blond. Thus theist Platonists could not say that arguments for Platonist universals or haecceities extend to support belief in non-generalist world-attributes. These could not 'fall out of' commitment to haecceities or universals. Nor could arguments for trope theories yield them, as these do not extend to free-floating, never-borne Platonic tropes. So simple, unstructured world-attributes would require specific support *as a particular sort of attribute*—and in the present context, the support could not be that they are needed to function as possible worlds, for my claim against the Platonist is precisely that they are not.

One argument might come from arbitrariness: there are (the Platonist might say) universal and non-universal essential properties and universal accidental properties, so there should be non-universal accidents too. It would be arbitrary to call this category empty if the others are not. Here, though, my earlier argument is again a block: theists have no reason to think there are universals, and if two other categories are empty, there is nothing arbitrary about saying that a third is. Alternately, one might try to move from

[27] Or worlds which are sets containing or Meinongian constructions involving universals. An argument paralleling that in n. 14 is possible here; I would reply as I did there.

[28] If there is no such single individual as a universe, then world-attributes' bearers are the pluralities of items in a given universe. They have 'gaps' for such pluralities. So they are relations rather than qualities, but this difference does not affect the point that they are universals. The text continues to treat them as qualities to smooth exposition.

a general commitment to Platonism to unstructured world-attributes *via* some principle mandating abundance in abstract entities. But such cases as I have seen for such principles rest on their philosophical utility: on the sort of work a Platonic menagerie can do.[29] And though my argument about universals does not directly apply to unshareable accidents, it extends to worlds readily. My argument was simply that God or constructions involving God could do any philosophical work universals allegedly do; if that is correct, there is no reason to add to an ontology already containing God any further entities to do that work. If the modal theory I have laid out is coherent, I have now made that case for simple non-generalist world-attributes as well.

Finally, one might appeal to paraphrase considerations and a rejection of arbitrariness. We cannot avoid quantifying over properties, one might argue, and so to the extent that we have reason to believe claims that entail or include these quantifications, we have reason to believe in properties.[30] It is implausible that our languages manage to express all the properties there are. So to avoid arbitrariness we should grant that any non-paradox-generating predicate in any possible language would express a property, and (one might claim) some such language would have predicates for world-attributes. One might reply that there is no reason to believe this last, or none that does not illicitly assume that there are such attributes. But a more basic point is just that this argument under-determines the character of the supposed attribute. What is wanted at present is a *simple* world-attribute. This sort of argument cannot assure us of this. If the supposed predicate were logically complex it would hardly suggest a simple attribute, and if it were logically simple it would remain the case that simple predicates can express complex attributes (if there are any): if there are conjunctive properties, it is just an accident of history that English does not include the predicate 'brownd', which would apply to just those things both brown and round.

I thus suggest that the sort of support a theist would need to justify attribute-Platonism about worlds has so far not appeared. I turn finally to worlds as states of affairs.

States of Affairs

One can define logical relations on states of affairs much as on propositions.[31] If there are such relations, one can show that if there are Platonic states of

---

[29] See, for example, Bernard Linsky and Edward N. Zalta, 'Naturalized Platonism versus Platonized Naturalism', *The Journal of Philosophy* 92 (1995), 525–55; George Bealer, *Quality and Concept* (Oxford: Oxford University Press, 1992).

[30] So Van Inwagen, 'A Theory of Properties', broadly following Chisholm.

[31] See, for example, Roderick Chisholm, *Person and Object* (LaSalle, IL: Open Court, 1976), pp. 118–20; John Pollock, *The Foundations of Philosophical Semantics* (Princeton, NJ: Princeton University Press, 1984), pp. 55–6.

affairs, there are Platonic maximal consistent states of affairs, fit to do duty for possible worlds.[32] We must ask, then, whether Platonic states of affairs would have Platonic attributes as constituents. If they do, those would largely be universals, and so my argument against conjoining realism and theism would again come into play.[33] Suppose, on the other hand, that states of affairs are simple and unstructured. Then their logical relations become mysterious.[34] If *Boots' being a cat and Puff's being a cat* has no constituents, it does not contain *Boots' being a cat*. But then why should the first's obtaining entail the second's? Why should this not instead entail that *Poll's being a parrot* obtains? To the extent that logical relations between states of affairs begin to look unmotivated, though, so does the case for world-sized states of affairs, which depends on these.

Arguments for states of affairs have come from truth, elimination, and causation. *Pace* the logical atomists and truthmaker theorists, we do not need states of affairs—whether simple or complex—to make true or to correspond to truths. It is true that Boots is a cat iff Boots is a cat. The latter requires that Boots have cathood, whatever that amounts to, but on the weak account of truthmaking I have used it does not require that there be an entity, *Boots' being a cat*. As my weak account does appear to get us truth, it is up to truthmaker theorists and atomists to show why truth has to involve more. Chisholm's case for states of affairs was this: sentences stating truths appear to refer to events and propositions. We cannot paraphrase these apparent references away while preserving these truths' truth. So we should take events and propositions to exist.[35] We can define 'event' and 'proposition' in terms of states of affairs.[36] If we do, we have fewer primitive categories.[37] We also eliminate propositions understood as entities distinct from and corresponding to facts and events understood as concrete particulars. So we should take states of affairs to exist, as a genus of which event and proposition are species. Chisholm's theory and definitions had problems large and small, however,[38] and perhaps it is enough to note that he himself abandoned this argument.

Mellor plumps for facts—obtaining states of affairs—as causal relata.[39] This lets causation iterate: lets causal facts be explained causally, as when ('because' being a causal connective) Don's falling explains the causal fact that the climb

---

[32] For one such argument see John L. Pollock, 'Plantinga on Possible Worlds', in James Tomberlin and Peter van Inwagen (eds), *Alvin Plantinga* (Dordrecht: D. Reidel 1985), p. 123ff.

[33] One might try to turn states of affairs against that argument, as one might with structured propositions; the reply would be the same.

[34] This point is a relative of some of Lewis's.

[35] Chisholm, *Person and Object*, pp. 115–17.

[36] *Ibid.*, pp. 117–36.

[37] For states of affairs' being primitive, *ibid.*, pp. 21–2.

[38] For many of which see the essays by Kim, Pollock and Wolterstorff in *Grazer Philosophische Studien* 7/8 (1979).

[39] D. H. Mellor, *The Facts of Causation* (London: Routledge, 1995), p. 106ff. He seems to believe also in non-obtaining states of affairs (*ibid.*, pp. 8, 162). Given his distinction between facts and 'facta' (*ibid.*, pp. 161–2), neither is a metaphysically 'deep' commitment, but for present purposes that does not matter.

is halted because Don dies.[40] Mellor alleges that if concrete events are the only causal relata, causation cannot iterate, because that e occurs because c occurs is not an event and so (if only events are causal relata) cannot be caused.[41] Thus, he concludes, as causation does sometimes iterate, facts are at least sometimes causal relata. But c's causing e can be a concrete event or process, and these can be causes: in the sample case, the process which is Don's falling's causing his dying causes the climb to halt.[42] Mellor asserts that here 'Don's falling's causing his dying' refers not to an event/process, but to a fact, but he gives no reason to believe it.[43] In fact, it meets his own test for event status: it has temporal parts.[44] As Don's dying extends through time, so does the causing of his dying, and the whole process, beginning with the fall and ending with the death, can be what causes the whole halt. So the 'iteration' argument that at least some causal relata are facts fails. Still, taking it to have succeeded, Mellor then suggests that we unify our treatment of causal relata by saying that all causal relata are facts. He claims that this is the direction in which to seek unification because while whenever concrete event putatively causes concrete event there are also facts to serve as relata, there are cases of fact-causation without corresponding events. Consider the claim that

1. Don does not die because he does not fall.[45]

The linked sentences report facts; Mellor takes (1) to report a causal relation between them. There are no corresponding events, of non-dying and non-falling, as there are no 'negative events'. So here (says Mellor) we have fact-causation without corresponding event-causation.[46] Mellor adds that were we to say that what really goes on here is that

2. Don survives because he holds on,

surviving and holding on would be negative events—just matters of not dying and not falling—and there are again no negative events. But (1) does not seem causal to me even at an intuitive level. Getting down to the metaphysics, (1) reports no events, and negative truths are true just by the absence of truth-makers for their negations—there are no 'negative facts', merely the absence of positive truthmakers—so how could there be causation here? If no relata, no relation. Something like (2) seems to me the only causal fact in the vicinity. Mellor's claim about (2) rests on stipulative definitions of surviving as not

---

[40] The example seems questionable to me, but I will concede for argument's sake that some such example could be constructed.

[41] Ibid., pp. 106–10.

[42] This also yields a reply to Mellor's claim (ibid., p. 108) that only fact-causation would let us perceive causation.

[43] Ibid., p. 109.

[44] Ibid., p. 122–4.

[45] Just for the record, this is false: he does not die because he does not fall *and* he does not get a heart attack *and* he does not have a stroke, and so on.

[46] Ibid., p. 131–4.

dying and holding on as not falling.[47] But surviving is living which continues from past living. Living is a paradigmatic 'positive' event or process, chock-full of other events and processes; that it bears a relation to a past process does not alter this. Holding on is an action. One does it by tensing muscles, causing friction, and so on. Such actions are 'positive' events. Perhaps Mellor is gesturing at cases where omissions are said to cause omissions. Chapter 13 gave my account of these, and it does not support his argument. So it seems to me that Mellor does nothing to shake the view that causal relata are always concrete events or substances. In any case, if obtaining states of affairs ever serve as causal relata, they are not simple: Boots herself is a constituent of what causes that mewing sound.

Finally, Jan Westerhoff suggests that we primarily perceive *Gestalten*, wholes, and only then analyze them into parts or constituents; he then adds that as the perceived whole is primary in perception, so states of affairs are 'the primary epistemic point of contact between us and the world.'[48] This is true only if they cause us to perceive them. If they do not, we do not perceive them, and Gestalt phenomena are due to the mind's way of structuring its perceptual input. So my objections to Mellor carry over.

I claim, then, that theists have no good reasons to believe in states of affairs. Further, my replies to Mellor, Chisholm, and the atomists do not rest on the assumption that their states of affairs would be simple or Platonic. So I need not rest my rejection of complex states of affairs on any distinctively theist move. Thus it seems to me that more generally there *are* no good reasons to believe in states of affairs. This is itself good reason not to believe in them, but I now argue in addition that theists have particular reason not to believe in Platonic states of affairs fit to serve as possible worlds. My argument's major premise is Ockham's Razor. Many cite this in the form 'Do not multiply entities without necessity.' Now if there *were* states of affairs, they or their obtaining would be truthmakers, and one instance of the Razor is 'Do not posit overdetermining truthmakers where there is no independent need for all of them.' If this instance of the Razor should be followed, it should be followed where God and Platonic entities would provide the truthmakers. For the theist, God is non-negotiable. So in such cases, unless there is independent reason to believe in the Platonic entities, theists should not believe in them—and I have argued that theists have no such independent reason.

In making my case, as far as possible, I seek premises theist Platonists themselves will accept individually.[49] The Razor is acceptable to Platonists. It

[47] *Ibid.*, p. 132–3.
[48] Jan Westerhoff, *Ontological Categories* (Oxford: Oxford University Press, 2005), p. 71.
[49] Of course, the Platonist will resist accepting their conjunction, if it gives good reason to reject Platonism.

counsels no posits without need. Platonists just have a particular view about what we need. Still, I begin with a brief case in favor of the Razor.

Why Shave?

My argument against state-of-affairs worlds will be that the Razor rules against them. So it raises the question of why we should think the Razor a way to find true philosophical beliefs. A first response is simply that we do have powerful intuitions that it is, and we are entitled to respect them absent argument that it is not.[50] Again, we believe that physical science has been successful in finding or approximating to true theories.[51] There is good evidence that opting for theories with various sorts of parsimony has played a role in this success.[52] Ontology and physical science differ in many ways, but to the extent that a move that leads toward truth in one field transfers to another field, it is reasonable to expect it to be truth-conducive in the second field too, unless the second field has specific features that render this unlikely.

---

[50] Michael Huemer tries to cast doubt on the intuitions by arguing that one can explain why picking parsimonious theories is a good epistemic policy in science, but the explanations do not apply to philosophical appeals to parsimony ('Why is Parsimony a Virtue?', *Philosophical Quarterly* 59 (2009), 216–36). The most basic point to make here is that inability otherwise to justify an intuitive belief (that parsimony is good philosophical policy) does not entail that we are not rationally entitled to hold it: intuition itself counts as a primary source of *prima facie* justification, for the denial of this (I would argue) cannot consistently be maintained. Moreover, the differences between science and philosophy (on which Huemer insists, 228–9) make the force of Huemer's argument unclear. Given the differences, we might well expect that if anything other than intuition justifies the Razor in philosophy, it will differ from what justifies scientific parsimony. Nor does our intuition about parsimony in ontology seem to have roots in illicit generalization from parsimony's success in science: many who feel its force have no acquaintance with its role in science. In any event, Huemer's case that one of his ways of justifying scientific appeal to parsimony does not apply to, for example, the realist–nominalist debate rests on claiming that the issue between realist and nominalist is not over how many metaphysical categories there are, but over what the relationship between things and their properties is or whether 'characteristics' exist (*op. cit.*, 230). To me, this seems precisely wrong. The issue is whether in addition to particulars there are universals, which are precisely a second metaphysical category. The formulation in terms of whether characteristics exist simply misses this. Characteristics might be particular—tropes or sets—or universal. Trope and set theories are usually viewed as versions of nominalism: so a disagreement over whether characteristics exist could as easily be an intramural debate among nominalists, for example, between a trope theorist and a resemblance nominalist who does without tropes or other characteristics (for example, Gonzalo Rodriguez-Pereyra, *Resemblance Nominalism* (Oxford: Oxford University Press, 2002)). And it is hard to know what to make of the formulation about the relationship between things and properties. What the relationship is depends on what properties are, and this is just the question whether properties are universals, particulars of some sort, or non-existent. So this is not the basic issue between realist and nominalist, but a 'spoils to the victor' side-issue. Finally, my argument below is *inter alia* a counter to Huemer, since my appeal to scope could be made as well on behalf of scientific uses of the Razor. The argument involves at least a relative of Huemer's own claim that simple theories are more likely than complex on the data both explain.

[51] Huemer, to whom I owe part of this argument, raises a circularity concern about using this premise, but also identifies a strategy for avoiding it which I endorse (*op. cit.*, 218).

[52] See, for example, Daniel Nolan, 'Quantitative Parsimony', *British Journal for the Philosophy of Science*, 48 (1997), 329–43; A. Baker, 'Quantitative Parsimony and Explanation', *British Journal for the Philosophy of Science*, 54 (2003), 245–59; Richard Swinburne, *Epistemic Justification* (Oxford: Oxford University Press, 2001), pp. 83–99. This is not to imply that parsimony was a motive for these theory-choices.

But there is nothing about ontology to lead us to expect that seeking parsimony is unlikely to be truth-conducive in it.[53]

Again, scope is a virtue in explanations. If candidate explanations E and E* explain a certain fact equally well, but E is also a good explanation for some further fact, that is reason to believe E. This virtue is epistemic. An explanation is supported by what it explains; that it well-explains these facts becomes evidence for its being a true explanation. So the more an explanation explains, and the better it explains it, the more evidence there is for its truth, *ceteris paribus*. Better-supported explanations are more likely true. So wider-scope explanations are more likely true. It is relevant that scope is a virtue because sparser ontologies may offer ontological explanations of greater scope. One kind of *explanandum* in the debate over universals is of the form

R. there are particulars a and b, and a and b resemble one another in being F.

According to the resemblance nominalist, the particulars themselves make (R) true.[54] Realists let a and b (or their existing) make (R)'s first conjunct true, but in some cases have as truthmaker for the second a and b's sharing a universal, Fhood. So if the nominalist ontological explanation[55] works, it has greater scope than either explanation the realist offers: it explains both conjuncts, not just one.

In addition, if the nominalist explanation works, its scope undercuts the realist's justification for positing universals. For if a and b themselves fully explain (R)—that is, suffice to make (R) true—that a and b share a universal cannot add explanatory force. It can only overdetermine (R)'s truth. Now there can be reason to believe in overdetermination. Suppose that it takes 10 volts to light a bulb, and two streams of 10-volt current reach the bulb at once. In such cases, we see independently that the overdetermining factors are present and appear to contribute to the bulb's lighting. But this is not the case with (R). Nominalist and realist are disputing precisely whether a further factor is present. Again, there may be full, non-overdetermining explanations at different levels. Emergentists, at least, might argue that a biological event may have full explanations in terms of biology, chemistry, and physics, higher-level ones not 'reducing' to explanations at lower levels, because higher-level entities, properties, or laws do not so 'reduce.'[56] But nominalist and realist are not explaining at different levels. Rather, each has a proposal about what is at the ontologically basic level. Where we already have a full explanation and have no independent reason to believe there is overdetermination or that

---

[53] Fn. 50 noted that our intuition that parsimony is good philosophical policy is not a generalization from scientific practice. This argument offers a *prima facie* case for that generalization. That one can argue for this does not entail that the intuition depends on the generalization.

[54] So Rodriguez-Pereyra, *Resemblance Nominalism*, pp. 113–21.

[55] The next chapter offers an account of distinctively ontological explanation.

[56] Here I am indebted to a referee.

different 'levels' are in play, we have no reason to posit overdetermination or an extra 'level': there is nothing left to explain, and they do not yield a better overall explanation. If all evidence for an entity rests on what it would explain, and it neither explains what was not explained previously nor improves an explanation of what was explained previously, there is no evidence for its existence. And making posits without evidence is no more truth-conducive than guessing. It is likely that beliefs without backing turn out false. So if we avoid them, we are more likely to wind up with a higher proportion of true beliefs overall. Without Razoring, we would have had certain likely-true ontological beliefs and certain likely-false ones. The Razor removes some likely-false ones, and counsels us against replacing them with other likely-false ones. As a result, it is likely that likely-true beliefs comprise a larger portion of our ontological beliefs, and so it is likely that true beliefs do. So we now see another reason following the Razor is conducive to having a greater proportion of true philosophical beliefs: the Razor counsels us to avoid posits without evidence.

Sparser ontologies, then, are more likely true at least to the extent that they offer wider-scope explanations. And entities deserving Razoring are precisely entities whose existence there is no reason to posit. So if mere guessing in ontology is fairly likely to produce false beliefs, assertions of the existence of entities deserving to be Razored are fairly likely to be false. If the Razor-worthy is fairly likely not to exist, the fact that an entity deserves to be Razored counts as a reason to think it does not exist. Thus there is reason to wield the Razor. But even if one could not argue for this, Razoring is common practice among ontologists; the theist Platonist would probably accept the Razor unargued. Finally, if mere-guess ontological beliefs are fairly likely to be false, my arguments that theists have no reason to believe in, for example, propositional worlds take on a further character: they should turn theists from agnostics into weakly convinced atheists about such entities.

Dividing Worlds

I now set out the sample state of affairs possible worlds I will discuss. Let us suppose that God exists, and there are also abstract possible worlds, maximal ways reality could be, which are maximal states of affairs which could obtain. For convenience, let us suppose that these are conjunctive, and their conjuncts include at least one state of affairs 'corresponding' to every proposition that would be true were they actualized. Nothing turns on this. Forming these states of affairs into worlds by other means would serve as well. Nor does anything turn on using internally complex worlds rather than worlds which are single simple states of affairs. My argument proceeds by gradually emptying abstract possible worlds. If a world is a simple state of affairs, this cannot amount to removing conjuncts—that is, substituting smaller for larger conjunctions.[57] But even if a world is simple, its obtaining will entail the obtaining of what I treat as worlds' conjuncts. 'Emptying' a simple world will amount to accounting for the possibility of each entailed state of affairs on another basis. Once I have accounted for all of these, the world will be otiose. So if I worked in terms of internally simple worlds, the end result would be the same, and the path to it almost so.

I now note some broad sorts of state of affairs any such possible world contains. There are necessary states of affairs; call their conjunction N. There are contingent secular states of affairs; call their conjunction C. There are also contingent non-secular states of affairs. In any world, God has some contingent volition, if only a volition not to create. Let us call a world's conjunction of states of affairs of God's having contingent volitions V. I divide the rest of a world's contingent non-secular states of affairs by their relation to V. Any world includes

> God's being in contingent states or undergoing contingent events for which V's obtaining causally suffices. Let us call a world's conjunction of these states of affairs CS. God's willing that a squirrel exist causally suffices to bring it about that a squirrel exists. So it causally suffices for God to bring about a squirrel's existence. So I place the bringing-about under CS. If God brings a squirrel to be and wills time to continue, later He has done so. So His having done so falls under CS. God's willing that there be a squirrel causally suffices for His knowing that there is a squirrel: that too goes into CS. CS also includes God's having some attitudes. If God is disposed to approve of a squirrel, His willing it to be causally suffices for His approving of its presence. God's co-existing with concrete non-divine things He brings to be is also in CS: what He causally suffices to bring to be, He causally suffices to co-exist with. And as (GSA) is necessary, this is the only sort of co-existence we need worry about. Now suppose that I act with libertarian freedom. If God conserves or concurs with this, V includes God's willing a corresponding divine volition: I freely choose, and God wills to conserve or concur with that choice.[58] This does not cause me to choose, else I did not choose with libertarian freedom. But the willing causally suffices for my choosing to occur, in one sense: in no causally possible world is it the case that God wills this but I do not make my choice. In another, it does not: my choice determines what God wills, not *vice-versa*.[59] Perhaps in this case

---

[57] That is, replacing a conjunction C with one whose conjuncts form a proper subset of the set of C's conjuncts.

[58] On concurrence see Alfred Freddoso, 'God's General Concurrence with Secondary Causes: Pitfalls and Prospects', *American Catholic Philosophical Quarterly* 68 (1994), 131–56, and 'God's General Concurrence with Secondary Causes', *Philosophical Perspectives* 5 (1991), 553–85.

[59] There are obviously difficulties in making sense of this. For present purposes we need not try.

God's contingently knowing what I do falls under CS, perhaps not. As will be clear, I need not decide.

In any world, God also is in contingent states or undergoes contingent events for which V's obtaining is not causally sufficient. Call a world's conjunction of these states of affairs ¬CS. ¬CS may have two relevant parts:

God's having some contingent attitudes from eternity, *per* earlier argument. Call a world's conjunction of such states of affairs A.

Call a world's conjunction of anything in ¬CS which is not in A, ¬A. If God neither conserves nor concurs with creaturely actions, His knowing what we do does not fall under CS, for there is no relevant divine volition. But still, God contingently knows what I do, and may have an attitude to it.

God's other relations to concrete non-divine things fall under His knowing and willing things involving them or having attitudes directed toward them. Thus a world's contingent non-secular states of affairs divide exhaustively into V, CS, and ¬CS. ¬CS may in turn divide into A and ¬A. Thus a world's states of affairs divide exhaustively into N, C, V, CS, A, and perhaps ¬A. I now argue that all should be Razored. I assume S5 (without Barcan Formulae) to smooth exposition.

Truthmaking

I will deal in truthmakers (in my weak sense). As noted in the Introduction, one truth may have many: every donkey's existing makes it true that there are donkeys. Modal truths are no exception. Platonism provides a truthmaker *possibly there are fleas* had from all eternity. Platonists can admit that God does too without having to deny that Platonic entities do so. Thus the claim that God does so is a premise individually acceptable to Platonists, as is the Razor.

The Razor's First Stroke: Eliminating N

I now take up N. N is a conjunction. N's conjuncts are everything necessary save itself, and on our present Platonist account, their necessity consists in each possible world's including them. However, state of affairs Platonism can accommodate this necessity in another way. It could say this sort of thing: in the Actual Cosmos, God exists. No possible world has ¬(God exists) as a conjunct. So it is necessary that God exists. In the Actual Cosmos, ¬(2 + 2 = 5). No possible world has as a conjunct that 2 + 2 = 5, and there is nothing in the Actual Cosmos to make this true. So it is necessary that

$\neg(2 + 2 = 5)$—that is, that $2 + 2 = 5$ is impossible. Worlds need not contain necessary states of affairs for those states of affairs to be necessary. Rather, we need posit only contingent states of affairs. For each contingent P, some maximal contingent-only state of affairs (i.e. state of affairs which contains one and only one of each pair of a contingent state of affairs and its 'negation' and no necessary states of affairs) has as a conjunct that P and some that $\neg$P. For each necessary P, no maximal contingent-only state of affairs has as a conjunct either that P or that $\neg$P, but that P has a truthmaker or—explainer in the Actual Cosmos. Necessity consists in non-contingent actuality. For every possible P, either some maximal contingent-only state of affairs has as a conjunct that P, or actually P. This 'Platonism with holes' preserves Plantinga's account of what it is to exist in a possible world. For each world-name 'W', W is actualized → God exists. But this is true because of what the Actual Cosmos contains and what maximal contingent-only states of affairs do not. 'Platonism with holes' would treat the possibility of necessary states of affairs as partly a (negative) fact about merely possible states of affairs, and so not treat it reductively. It would lose a certain smoothness in treating the contingent and the necessary differently, but plausibly these *are* two fundamentally different sorts of truth, and so deserve different treatment.

Working with holey Platonism, let us use 'Portion' as a plural referring phrase for the entities in the ontology of necessary truths' Actual-Cosmos truthmakers. Most Platonists will have entities on hand for Portion—such as attributes. Theists certainly do if the position I have worked out is tenable, or if a deity theory is. If the holey proposal is viable, theist Platonists now face a choice. They can believe only in Portion, or also in N. Given the holey proposal, they can do without N for purposes of modal semantics. The question is whether they need it for some other ontological purpose Portion will not serve. I say that they do not. We do not need N for other modal work possible worlds do: we have seen how my theory takes over possible-world roles, and a deity theory could make like moves. A Platonist cannot plausibly claim that we need N to provide an object for intentional attitudes or content for mental states. As it is opaque how our mental states would manage to hook on to conjuncts of N, how could one make it out that they could not hook on in some similar way to bits of Portion? So the Razor bids us delete either N or Portion.

For the theist, Portion includes God,[60] and if my theory or a deity theory is viable need include no more. It is not an option to reductive identify Portion with N, so that (speaking crudely) what's 'really' there is N, and God-talk has to be parsed into talk of N. That is too radical a revision of theism; whatever else God is, He is a concrete agent. The theist has reasons or grounds to believe in God, but (so I have argued) none to believe in N. Further, it is good

---

[60] Even someone who thinks God exists contingently will grant that He figures in making true (weakly) necessary truths about Him.

to have a metaphysics that underwrites knowledge-claims to which we think we are entitled. Platonists accept this, because they accept that the Benecerraf Dilemma is indeed a problem for Platonism about mathematics, and the Dilemma is precisely that if Platonism is true, then on many conceptions of knowledge it is not clear how our mathematical knowledge-claims can be sustained.[61] Because they see that the Dilemma is a problem, Platonists should also grant that *ceteris paribus*, truthmakers whose ontology we can detect are preferable to truthmakers whose ontology we cannot, and so *ceteris paribus*, ontology that can cause events is preferable to ontology that cannot: for if the relevant effects are in range of our senses, we can sometimes know that such truthmakers exist. Thus truthmakers with detectable ontology are able to underwrite knowledge-claims to which we think we are entitled. Now N cannot be detected, since it cannot cause anything. But some claim to have perceived God. God can cause, and if He exists, may well have left evidence of His existence. And every divine mental event in Portion can in principle causally contribute to a divine act: God might choose to tell someone that $1 + 1 = 2$, and if He does, His knowledge will causally contribute to what He says. So I submit that even Platonists should think Portion-truthmakers the better ones to posit, *ceteris paribus*—and if I am right that N is not independently needed, a theist should find no *cetera* here to outweigh this.

Nothing requires the Platonic realm not to have an N-shaped hole in it, as long as Portion can fill the hole. So let us be holey: remove N from Platonic Heaven. Maximal contingent-only states of affairs remain. We now say that composites consisting of Portion plus one of these play all possible-world roles. I finally note a complication. Theist Platonists who do not hold to S5 can accept the argument as it stands. But in S5, all facts of possibility are necessary, and so there are no maximal contingent-only states of affairs left in Platonic Heaven if things are as I say—and so holey Platonism as so far explained is not tenable. S5 Platonists, then, should take this section's argument to concern only necessary facts which are not facts about what is possible.

The Next Stroke: Eliminating Vs

Every world contains some particular V. Now God is necessarily omnipotent, and omnipotence is necessarily the property it is. So God necessarily satisfies whatever definition there actually is of being an omnipotent agent. I have argued that this definition includes a clause specifying a range of possible states of affairs God can bring about—and almost all contemporary work on omnipotence agrees, differing only on how to specify that range.[62] Given S5,

[61] For the dilemma, see Paul Benecerraf, 'Mathematical Truth', in Paul Benacerraf and Hilary Putnam (eds), *Philosophy of Mathematics*, 2nd edn. (Cambridge: Cambridge University Press, 1983), pp. 403–20.

[62] See my 'Omnipotence'; in Thomas Flint and Michael Rea (eds), *The Oxford Handbook of Philosophical Theology* (Oxford: Oxford University Press, 2009), pp. 1673–98.

the content of possibility is constant from world to world. So given S5, whatever range of action is open to God in one possible world is open to Him in all possible worlds. From all eternity, in each world, God has the power He exercises in its V. So given S5, He actually has the power He exercises in any world's V—the power to will all these volitions, or His fully specified will, or (henceforth) simply His will. God has the power to will as in all Vs from all eternity. He has it even if He lacks the opportunity to use some of it.

God's having His will is a truthmaker. I want to substitute it for all Platonic Vs, *en route* to excising all Platonic states of affairs. I can do this only if powers do not include or presuppose states of affairs or worlds. So I now defend this claim. There are, I think, at least three ways one could try to involve these in the makeup of powers. I now discuss these; if I deal with them satisfactorily, I can rely on my earlier account of divine powers.

Shoemaker writes that

> for something to have a power . . . is for it to be such that its presence in circumstances of a particular sort will have certain effects. One can think of such a power as a function from circumstances to effects.[63]

Many of the relevant circumstances and effects will not obtain. A Platonist might contend that these are Platonic states of affairs. If they are, and powers are functions from circumstances to effects, powers are relations between states of affairs, and so presuppose their existence. But a power is not a function. Functions are sets. As usually conceived, powers are attributes, and there are good reasons not to identify attributes with sets.[64] I parse divine power-talk into talk about substances and mental events. These are not sets either. Nor for like reasons do powers consist partly in sets. That having a power entails the existence of a function does not make the power the function.

Again, one might involve possible worlds in powers by appeal to a conditional analysis of what it is to have a power or disposition. On the simplest such view, to say that a thing has either is just to say that appropriate counterfactual conditionals are true: for a thing to be flammable, for instance, is just for it to be the case that e.g. were a match applied to it in suitable circumstances, it would begin to burn.[65] It is widely held that the simple view has been refuted. But if one supposed (with considerable charity) that some descendant of it fares better, one might add that the semantics of counterfactuals requires possible worlds, and so possible worlds come into the analysis of powers. However, charity to even a revised conditional analysis

---

[63] Sydney Shoemaker, 'Causality and Properties', in Sydney Shoemaker, *Identity, Cause and Mind* (Cambridge: Cambridge University Press, 1984), p. 211.

[64] See my 'One Step Toward God', 67–104.

[65] So, for example, Gilbert Ryle, *The Concept of Mind* (London: Hutchinson, 1949), p. 123.

is probably misplaced.[66] Again, if any powers-based account of counterfactuals is viable, this argument is just undercut.[67] And even if some conditional analysis works and counterfactuals require parsing in possible-worlds talk, one can take the latter as useful fiction. Finally, if the Platonist retreats to the claim that the presence of powers in certain circumstances entails the truth of counterfactuals, the response will be the same.

Returning to the main thread, I now argue that for every volition 'inscribed' in a world's V, God's actually having His will from all eternity and being able to have alternate preferences make it true that possibly He has that volition. God's will is not finkish. Finkish powers disappear when they would be called-upon; if God is by nature omnipotent, He cannot lose an intrinsic power, though He may lack chances to use various powers. Nor does anything outside God deny Him the chance to use His will from all eternity. Only He can do so. If God has a specific power to do act A in circumstances in which doing A would be wrong, His moral preferences necessarily prevent His using it in those circumstances. If there cannot be such necessary intrinsic blocks on powers' use, God has no such specific power, though He is able to do A in any circumstance in which it would not be wrong.[68] If there can be such necessary intrinsic blocks, then this bit of His will, because blocked, does not ground a possibility—which is as I would like. If God's preferences only contingently block a bit of His will, or do not block it at all, His will, ability to have alternate preferences and from-eternity circumstances make it the case that He might have so used or might so use it. That is enough to make it absolutely possible that He so use it; it places His so using it within the range of His entire complex of powers. God's will is all-things-considered able to produce the full range of volitions in V. So for each volition 'inscribed' in V, it is reasonable to see God's having His will as a from-eternity truthmaker for the claim that possibly God has that volition.

We now face from-eternity truthmaker-overdetermination. We have as truthmakers for each 'possibly God wills volition v' claim God's having His will and some world's V in Platonic Heaven. We do not need the Platonic Vs for the purposes for which we did not need N. Nor (I have claimed) do we need them to write into His will, to explain its being a power to have these volitions: God's own mind suffices to guide His will, and its content does not involve Platonic Vs. Nor do we need the Vs to explain His will's being a *power*—being directed toward something possible—either. We can let being a power be a primitive fact about it. The Platonist can insist that powers must

[66] See, for discussion, C. B. Martin, *The Mind in Nature* (Oxford: Oxford University Press, 2009), pp. 19–23; Stephen Mumford, *Dispositions* (Oxford: Oxford University Press, 1998), pp. 36–63; Alexander Bird, *Nature's Metaphysics* (Oxford: Oxford University Press, 2007), pp. 24–42.

[67] For one power-based account, see Jonathan Jacobs, 'A Powers Theory of Modality', *Philosophical Studies* DOI 10.1007/s11098-009-9427-1.

[68] This obviously creates a problem about the compatibility of omnipotence and necessary moral perfection. I discuss this in my 'Omnipotence'.

presuppose rather than constitute possibilities, but I do not see how an *argument* for this is supposed to go. It might seem perverse to trim away (what the Platonist would see as) the basic truthmaker and leave the derivative one, but trimming the Platonic Vs just means turning the derivative into the primary, rather than leaving it derivative but with nothing to derive from.

I do not see where else an argument that we need Platonic Vs in addition to God's having His will and preferring power might come from. Now we do sometimes allow truthmaker overdetermination. We allow it where different 'levels' of explanation exist. Again, God has the power and opportunity to bring it about that I walk to work; so do I. Each of us having our own power and chance makes it true that possibly I walk to work. But there are good independent reasons to allow both truthmakers. If I did not have mine, not even God could make me walk to work, unless He gave me the power and chance at the instant He willed me to do it—otherwise what took place would not be my walking, but God's walking me marionette-like to work. If God did not have the power and chance, I could not have my own, for He would not be able to conserve me in walking and so I could not do it. Again, a pair of redundant causes for an event each individually has the power and (let us suppose) chance to bring the event E about. So they overdetermine the truth of *possibly E occurs*. But we can empirically establish that the circumstances that give opportunity obtain, that the causes have had the relevant powers in other such circumstances and that they do not relevantly differ now from the way they were then. None of these things is true before Creation. So the Razor bids us eliminate the Vs or God's will and preferring power, or reduce one to the other. 'Reducing' God's having His will to the Vs' being possible would 'reduce' a power to something about possible worlds, and so has already been discussed. If we delete God's having His will but leave the Vs possible in Platonic Heaven, we leave God non-omnipotent. For then it is, for example, possible that God will that Spot bark, but God lacks the power so to will, though He may have the power to gain the power—and till He does so, He cannot make Spot bark. On any reasonable analysis of omnipotence, that leaves Him short of the mark. So for orthodox Western theists only the Vs are fair game for elimination.

Nothing requires the Platonic realm not to have V-shaped holes in it, so long as the web of modal truth stays intact. Thus we now chip the Vs off our maximal contingent-only states of affairs, and say that what do world-duties are 'smaller' contingent-only states of affairs plus Portion plus God's having His will plus (in some cases) His power to have other preferences. If so, Portion fill all the holes in worlds. For God is in Portion. He is there with His will and power to prefer, and these let Him fill the V-hole. Each Portion + world-fragment composite does duty as a possible world because each composite contains a power matching the V-hole in the fragment. Of course, it also contains powers not matching the hole. But what would not yield a possible world would be composites containing *only* powers not matching a hole.

Stroke Three: CSs are Out

God's willing V-volitions would causally suffice for Him to bring things about, know what He brings about, and perhaps react to what He knows. For His nature guarantees that what He executively wills to bring about, He brings about. So His having His nature, His will, the power to have other attitudes (in some cases) and the powers to know and react can make it true for each state of affairs in CS that possibly things are as they would be were that state of affairs actualized. The arguments just run for Platonic V apply here too. So we can remove every CS from Platonic Heaven.

Eliminating As

We can eliminate each world's A as we did its V. Arguments for doing so carry over from earlier sections: the Razor point, but also that about causally relevant truthmakers. If God likes chocolate, God inclines to create chocolate, *ceteris paribus*. If He does make chocolate, His taste will then directly explain His volition. It may even causally explain it, if the taste is a complex of dispositions to choose, one of which then 'fires'. Abstracta being such that God might have this taste cannot figure in causal explanations.

With As gone, our world-substitutes involve Portion and further-reduced world-fragments. Each fragment will have a hole for an A. If God's actual attitudes do not fill a particular fragment's hole, God's power to form other attitudes does. Finally, if a world has a ¬A, what eliminates it will be a complex consisting of God's powers to contribute to relevant secular states of affairs, His power to (say) know the relevant truths, and what grounds the possibility of the secular states of affairs of which He would know. I have now expunged all Platonic states of affairs save the Cs and their conjuncts. I now turn to these.

Dispensing with Cs

I have argued that God's having powers can make it true that possibly things are as they would be were there a C and were it actualized. If the Platonist at least understands my non-Platonist story, at least finds it coherent, the Platonist should accept that God provides at least a 'failsafe' truthmaker for all Cs, one which does not actually make it true, but (*per impossibile*) would do so were it not already settled in the Platonic realm. A Platonist could accept this, as it is compatible with the Platonist insistence that something in Platonic Heaven is the sole actual truthmaker. The arguments for eliminating the Cs in favor of a theist truthmaker are by now familiar. So theists should also drop the Cs from Platonic Heaven. Secular truths about possibility would be no less secular for that, for being secular is a matter of the information a truth communicates, not of what makes it true.

I have now 'emptied' the conjunctive states of affairs that did duty for possible worlds, and so eliminated possible worlds on this conception of them. If a possible world would be a single simple state of affairs, I have now for all of N, C, and so on, provided truthmakers for the relevant truths within an ontology to which the theist is committed before coming to metaphysics. So theists who take the Razor seriously should not be state of affairs Platonists about possible-worlds. There is, however, another issue.

Modal Status

Let us now consider how God accounts for modal status on my proposal. Suppose that necessarily,

3. if anything is Rocky, it is a stone.

On the usual account, (3)'s being necessary is its being true in each of $W_1 \ldots W_n$ and W_{1-n} being all the possible worlds. Part of this being so is its being true in W_1. Were W_1 actual, God would make Rocky a stone (let us say[69]). As omnipotent, God actually has the power to make Rocky a stone if there obtains that of W_1 which obtains when Rocky is to appear in W_1. So the Razor gives us that a divine power provides this part of (3)'s necessity-maker. We can extend this to Rocky's being a stone in all other Rocky-worlds, and to all like truths in N.

That $W_{1 \ldots n}$ are all the possible worlds is the 'closure condition' for a truth's being necessary. I have so far argued that theists can and should provide theist truthmakers for everything but the closure-condition for all necessary truths. If this is correct, then even if God does not determine the closure condition, theists should hold that facts about God determine which truths are necessary. If we stopped here, theists could say this: God somehow inherits templates for a totality of worlds. God's powers fill out the templates. So they set what is necessary, even if they do not account for that which ensures that God's having the power to make Rocky a stone in each of *these* worlds makes (3) necessary (the closure condition, or that there are just these templates). That is, even without closure, we have at this point the conclusion that God is responsible for the necessity of secular necessary truth.

---

[69] Permission of uncaused stones could be factored in as previous discussion suggests, so there is no need to complicate the exposition here.

Closure

But I do not want to stop short. I now offer a theist account of the closure-condition. Where P is an existential claim, what makes a negative existential $\neg P$ true is there being no truthmaker for P.[70] What makes P false—there being no truthmaker—makes $\neg P$ true. In such a case $\neg P$ is true but has no truthmaker. So my story about the closure condition is this. God has certain powers. He has no more than these. They are all the divine powers. What makes them all the divine powers is that there are no more. 'There are no more' is a negative existential. It is true, but has no truthmaker. So too its equivalent, 'There do not exist divine powers other than these.' So God's power-state provides closure for God's powers.

I have eliminated worlds, but I now continue to talk about them fictionally, without commitment. God's having the power to make His contribution to actualizing a world *makes* it possible. God's powers account for what distinguishes one world from another. By so doing they determine what worlds there are, and how many they are. And God's powers make these worlds all the worlds. These are all the worlds because those are all the divine powers. So God's power-state provides the closure condition for worlds. W_{1-n} *are all the worlds* is equivalent to *there are no worlds that are not either* W_1 *or* W_2 *or*... W_n. It is really a negative existential, and so falls under my account of those. As I see it, then, fictional assertions of world-existence express facts about divine powers, and there not being a divine power is the fact behind a negative existential about worlds. So what lies behind the claim that $W_{1...n}$ are all the worlds is God's having no other powers than He does, to be behind further assertions of world-existence. This general closure condition yields a simple specific account of (3) including closure. If He is omnipotent, God has no power to falsify (3) only if $\neg$(3) is not possible. So if He has no such power, is omnipotent, and has the power to make (3) true, then necessarily (3). I say not just this, but that God's having His powers (with opportunity) and lacking the other power truthmakes it that necessarily (3).

---

[70] While I arrived at this independently, this idea applied to negative truths generally has seen print in, for instance, A. D. Woozley, *Theory of Knowledge* (London: Hutchinson's University Library, 1949), pp. 138–9; Stephen Read, 'Truthmakers and the Disjunction Thesis', *Mind* 109 (2000), 73; David Lewis, 'Armstrong on Combinatorial Possibility', in David Lewis, *Papers in Metaphysics and Epistemology* (Cambridge: Cambridge University Press, 1999), p. 204. Some claim to find the view in Wittgenstein's *Tractatus*, but I am not convinced it is there. I have no good criterion to offer for being positive or negative. For existential truths, the difference is between really asserting that something is there and really asserting that something is not there. Negation and being negative do not go in tandem. Intuitively, a negated existential is not necessarily also a negative existential. 'There are no vacuums anywhere' is negated in form, but arguably it is really positive, asserting that everywhere there is something. 'There is a void in the room' arguably really asserts that there is nothing in the room. It is not negated in form, but it is negative. It is true because there is nothing in the room. Still, we are rarely if ever unsure about whether an existential is negative on reflection. That being so, it is not clear that we need a criterion, since a criterion—as distinct from a definition or analysis—simply serves to decide hard cases. (For discussion of criteria see Richard Gale, *Negation and Non-being* (Oxford: Basil Blackwell, 1976), pp. 19–35.)

Cheyne and Pigden object that such an account leaves universally quantified truths like *all the worlds are either* W_1 *or* W_2 *or* ... W_n without sufficient truth-makers. On my account, if only Tom and Dick exist, the claim that

MM. all men are mortal

is true because Tom is mortal, Dick is mortal, and there are no other men. The latter is true without truthmaker. So (they reason) (MM) as a whole has either no truthmaker or only a partial truthmaker (Tom's and Dick's mortality). This is insufficient because it does not necessitate (MM)'s truth:[71] it could be true that Tom and Dick are mortal, but false that all men are mortal, were there also an immortal Harry.[72] But in some cases, truth without a truthmaker is compatible with the underlying intuition of the truthmaker project. D. M. Armstrong—the project's foremost contemporary proponent—puts the intuition this way: 'a truth, any truth, should depend for its truth for (*sic*) something "outside" it, in virtue of which it is true.'[73] The demand here is surely that truths' being true have a certain sort of explanation from outside themselves. Sometimes the lack of a factor that could have made a positive contribution contributes to an explanation: the pilot's absence helps explain the crash. So too, what explains a truth in the right way can be a combination of truthmakers plus the lack of a further truthmaker. Even if the truthmakers on their own do not necessitate the truth, the truthmakers plus the lack do. This retains the intuition that truth must always have a certain sort of explanation. Further, appeal to the lack handles the Cheyne–Pigden argument about (MM)—were there a Harry, we would not lack men other than Tom and Dick, and so it would not be true that all men are mortal. On my proposal, universally quantified truths are an ontological free lunch. But a free lunch can nourish. Those who favor more ontologically commissive accounts of universally quantified truths must find another explanation than Cheyne–Pigden's of why this sort of thing will not do. I submit, then, that the Razor rules against state-of-affairs worlds, and theists should not be world-Platonists.

---

[71] Armstrong would add that as truthmakers must necessitate their truths, it simply is not a truthmaker for this at all (D. M. Armstrong, *Truth and Truthmakers* (Cambridge: Cambridge University Press, 2004), p. 54).
[72] Colin Cheyne and Charles Pigden, 'Negative Truths from Positive Facts', *Australasian Journal of Philosophy* 84 (2006), 263–4.
[73] Armstrong, *Truth and Truthmakers*, p. 7.

23

WORLDS AND THE EXISTENCE OF GOD

I have argued that mine is the best God-involving modal metaphysics. I now argue that it should be preferred to any non-theist theory dealing in possible worlds. This is, of course, an argument that realists about possible worlds should become theists. Thus what I now offer counts as at least part of an argument for God's existence. I first explain what sort of argument for God this is, then develop it.

Ontological Explanation

Much natural theology deals in causal explanation—for example, of the universe's existence and hospitality to intelligent life. Ontology deals in a different sort of explanation. It does not say why things are as they are. It instead tries to clarify how things are. It explains by telling us what sorts of thing figure in making certain broad classes of truths true—what the ontology of these truths is. Set theorists talk set-talk; ontology asks what, if anything, they are talking about. It asks whether there are really sets; if there are, what they are; what it is for a set to exist; and if there are no sets, what makes set-theoretic statements true. It is possible that Blair win a fifth term in office. But in what does it consist for this to be possible? Such truths, we are told, concern possible worlds. Ontology asks whether there are any; if so, what they are; and if not, what makes possibility-claims true. Ontological explanations answer such questions.

One rule many cite in ontology is Ockham's Razor: posit no entity unless you must.[1] I have offered a general case for the Razor, but I now note further that economy helps an ontological scheme clarify how things are, *ceteris paribus*. Economy helps clarify if one prunes away primitive entities whose natures are ill-understood and makes do with those better understood, or defines previously primitive entities in better-understood terms.[2] But it helps even when these conditions are not met. Ontological economy as such consists in positing fewer primitive entities and kinds. If there are fewer, but there is the same amount of ontological work to do, a leaner ontology puts the same items to work in more contexts than one more luxuriant. Seeing an entity at work in more contexts gives us a better grip on its nature. Again, the fewer our entities and kinds, the more complex our theory of their relations must be if it is to be adequate to the facts: to eliminate physical objects in favor of sense data, for instance, we need a complex account of sense data's relations to one another and to us in making our intuitive physical-object beliefs true *modulo* their existential commitments. This account again increases our understanding of the primitive types of entities, and clarifies how things are at non-primitive levels.

The formulation of the Razor above is not apt. An entity necessary in no one place can be useful in many, and our understanding of both it and the many contexts in which we use it increases when we put it to work this way. It is short-sighted to assess ontological economy only with reference to single philosophical problems. It is wiser to think globally. Suppose one shows that one entity (or type of entity) can provide many ontological explanations, replacing many other sorts of entity, even though one need not make the replacement in any one case. Then one has shown that we get an overall economy and a concomitant gain in ontological clarity by making an initial investment. If we can eliminate many sorts of being by positing one sort or one being, and we are left with explanations at least as illuminating, that is a good buy.

Global economy arguments can persuade even if the sort of entity they commend is strange. Sets are strange. They are some sort of collection, but no ordinary sort. For sets come in strange varieties. The null set is a collection that does not collect anything. If I own one painting, I do not have enough to have an art collection, but for every painting there is a unit set, a one-member collection containing just it. Again, there is nothing to a set but its members. But even if the members are concrete, on the usual account, their set is abstract. Though the paintings are in spacetime, it is often said that the set is not. While I can show you my art collection, I cannot show you the set of my

---

[1] For a variety of historical formulations of 'the' Razor, see W. Thornburn, 'The Myth of Occam's Razor', *Mind* 27 (1918), 345–53. For an important distinction made more recently, see E. C. Barnes, 'Ockham's Razor and the Anti-Superfluity Principle', *Erkenntnis* 53 (2000), 353–74.

[2] Given van Inwagen's point about the opacity of the abstract, this is one more reason nominalism has the edge on realism if one can make it work.

paintings. The paintings are parts of the art collection, but members are not parts of sets—and it is unclear just what their relation to their sets *is*.

Despite all this (and more besides), most philosophers believe in sets. One main reason is their role in mathematical ontology. To Frege and many Platonists, numbers were *sui generis* abstract particulars. When the view became popular that mathematics in some way 'reduces' to set theory, it became popular to eliminate such abstract particulars in favor of sets. Some simply identified numbers with certain sets. It is now more popular to treat mathematics as a study of structures sets instantiate, with such natures as 'numbers' have only as determinate as the structures make them. Either way, given sets, one need not believe in Frege-style numbers, and yet mathematics has a real subject-matter. Now one might try to move from set theory's mathematical role to realism about sets by way of arguments for scientific realism (if mathematics is a science) or the indispensability of mathematical truth to science. But the most the first yields is that we must be realistic about set theory or mathematics, not about any particular proposed ontology for them. And the most the other yields is that there must be *some* ontology beneath set theory or mathematics sufficient to undergird their truth. It must be argued on other grounds that the ontology involves sets. Global economy is chief among these.[3] Some possibilists use sets to explicate the nature of possibilia.[4] Some actualists use sets to explain the nature of possible worlds.[5] Some take attributes to be sets.[6] Many philosophers have believed in sets because by positing them, one could (they thought) eliminate numbers, possibilia, worlds, universals, and/or other *sui generis* sorts of thing in favor of a single sort of entity. Sets' global economy outweighs their strangeness.

An economy-claim of this sort requires either that there are independent reasons to believe in sets or that sets take over at least two other kinds' roles. If we eliminate Frege-numbers in favor of sets, then for every number, there must be a corresponding set (else the reduction fails). So if we have no independent reason to believe in sets, it appears that we are merely switching entities one for one—before we posited numbers but (having no reason to do so) not sets, and after we posit sets but not numbers. After we make the move, we have as many particulars and kinds as we had before. But if we do have independent reason to believe in sets, it appears that we are eliminating numbers in favor of something that exists anyway, and so reducing our overall ontology. Thus absent independent reason to believe in sets, the set ontologist

[3] Or at least among the *good* ones. I suspect that many philosophers have poor reasons to believe in sets—for example, unjustified assimilation of them to common-sense collections.

[4] So Terence Parsons, *Non-Existent Objects* (New Haven, CT: Yale University Press, 1980), p. 101.

[5] So R. M. Adams, 'Theories of Actuality', in Michael Loux (ed.), *The Possible and the Actual* (Ithaca, NY: Cornell University Press, 1979).

[6] So e.g. Anthony Quinton, 'Properties and Classes', *Proceedings and Addresses of the Aristotelian Society* 58 (1957–58), 33–58.

can claim economy only if sets do numbers' ontological work and also the work of some other kind that does not 'reduce' to numbers, leaving us with fewer individuals and kinds than we had before.[7]

Intuitively, economy in higher-level kinds matters more than economy at lower levels. For dropping a higher-level kind entails dropping its sub-kinds, and perhaps dropping more individuals. One sometimes meets the view that in measuring ontological economy, only economy in kinds matters.[8] But consider two highest-level kinds without sub-kinds—one with three members, and one with $\aleph_0$. Surely an ontology that pares the latter and its members away is more economical than one otherwise identical which instead pares away the former and its members. The reason it is economical to do without sets, if we can, is not just that we thereby lose a highest-level kind and all its sub-kinds, but also that we thereby lose all the sets. If it seems that only kind-economy matters, that may be because it sometimes seems that only kind-economy can be had (as, for instance, in a one-for-one reduction of numbers to sets).

Cost/benefit

If an ontology cannot claim a straightforward edge in economy, there can still be cost/benefit arguments for it, for there are more sorts of epistemic cost than being uneconomical. Positing intuitively strange sorts of entity is an epistemic cost, for the more intuitively strange a sort of entity, the more positing it flouts intuitions that there just cannot be that sort of thing. Such intuitions are good reasons not to make the posit. Good reasons against a view add to the justificatory burden it must meet; *ceteris paribus* they should lower our credence in it. True, not everyone finds the same things strange: but the fact that others of equal intelligence, rationality, and so on, have intuitions that items are too strange to bear arguably constitutes a problem even for those who do not share them. Again, an entity's strangeness consists in its being unlike things we already recognize. The less like items we already recognize a new posit is, the more it faces an inductively based objection against its existence.

If two ontological explanations have equal scope, but one sort of entity provides an explanation in some cases only less naturally, that too is an epistemic cost, on the reasonable assumption that apparently more strained accounts are less likely true. Finally, if two explanations are equal in scope and equally natural, but all the same one is better in some other way, accepting the lesser explanation is an epistemic cost if the respect of superiority is

---

[7] If the individuals involved are finite in number, use of 'fewer' is unproblematic. If they are same-order infinite, understand it in terms of one infinite set being a subset of another.

[8] So David Lewis, *Counterfactuals* (Cambridge, MA: Harvard University Press, 1973), p. 87.

relevant to likelihood of truth. If one's view incurs fewer such costs than others, then *ceteris paribus* one's view is more likely true. If one's cost equals others' but one 'buys' a greater scope of explanation with it, then again one's view is more likely true if greater scope brings greater likelihood of truth, as suggested above.

My overall case for God's existence applies the strategies above. It tries to show that God can provide a variety of ontological explanations, and so let us dispense with less globally relevant rivals. Where it contends with a rival of equal scope, it tries to show that God has this scope more naturally, or that theist explanations surpass their rivals in some other way. Plainly this is a larger project than one chapter can complete, since to do it fully must involve global comparisons over a range of ontological issues between theist ontologies and their many rivals (including such no-ontology rivals as fictionalism and conventionalism, in some cases). Still, I present a bit of the case here, and perhaps a bit can recommend the project as a whole, and my modal metaphysics.

Some Assumptions

I have shown elsewhere that theism can provide a theory of attributes whose sole posit is God.[9] The view substitutes divine concepts (or relations to them[10]) for attributes, rather as Augustine did with Plato's Forms, then gets rid of the concepts. This could be enough for a global-economy argument for God, for given attributes, we get a great deal else. As we have seen, one can treat attributes of a special sort as possible–worlds. Attributes can also replace sets, as Russell intimated and George Bealer has shown.[11] Propositions can be constructions from attributes, and in any case we have already seen another theist proposition-substitute. So a God who provides a theory of attributes can do any ontological work numbers, sets, propositions, and possible–worlds do, and more besides. However, I here assume only that the theory of attributes is available. Christopher Menzel has shown that theists can replace sets with divine mental acts of collecting-together.[12] Here I assume that this elimination too is available to theists. I now argue that my view is preferable to possibilist theories of worlds. Once I have done so, I take up actualism.

---

[9] 'God and the Problem of Universals', *Oxford Studies in Metaphysics* 2 (2006), 325–56.

[10] If all attributes are relations to divine concepts and relations are themselves attributes, this can seem to touch off a nasty infinite regress. I acknowledge the problem, but the story I tell to deal with it is too long to go into here.

[11] George Bealer, *Quality and Concept* (New York: Oxford University Press, 1982). Russell spoke repeatedly of eliminating class-names in favor of 'propositional functions'. These express attributes.

[12] Christopher Menzel, 'Theism, Platonism and the Metaphysics of Mathematics', in Michael Beaty (ed.), *Christian Theism and the Problems of Philosophy* (Notre Dame, IN: University of Notre Dame Press. 1990), pp. 208–29.

Against Possibilism

Possibilists' possibilia come in two varieties. Lewis's exist but are not actual. For Lewis, all possible concrete individuals of all possible kinds exist, composing all the possible worlds. Lewis was in some moods happy to grant that across all worlds there are gods of all sorts[13]—he just did not think there were any hereabouts. Admit as much and it is obvious that making do with just one deity and one universe is more economical than positing infinities of both. But even if we insist dogmatically that Zeus *et al.* are not so much as possible, making do with one deity is more economical than making do with untold infinities of concrete universes. There is (to begin) the sheer number of existing extra-mental items. Lewis, as mentioned earlier, wanted to say that only economy of kind counts.[14] I cannot see why economy of individual is supposed to be irrelevant. My arguments that the Razor is truth-conducive and aids ontological understanding apply equally to kinds and individuals. And if one theory of planetary motion explains perturbations in an orbit by positing one undiscovered planet and another does so with two, the first is surely more parsimonious. But even if we waive this, in Lewis's multiverse there is also a profusion of kinds—every possible sort of particle, animal, plant—natural laws and *types* of natural laws, and types of complexity.

Now Lewis might reply this way: what matter most in ontology are highest-level natural kinds. At this level I (Lewis) posit just concrete particulars and sets.[15] This is highly economical. Adding a deity entails adding a highest-level kind, deity. Adding universes adds many instances but no highest-level kinds. So my view is most economical in the sense that matters most to ontology. This reply fails, though. For one thing, even if highest-level kinds matter most, one cannot say that only highest-level kinds matter; an ontology with a highest kind *abstract entity* and just the sub-kinds *attribute* and *set* is clearly more parsimonious than one that also posits Fregean numbers. Further, a god is just one sort of immaterial person.[16] An immaterial person is a person, and *person* is not a highest-level kind. So a theist view can be equally economical at the highest level. And adding a deity lets one do without sets, attributes, and propositions.[17] So theism has *concrete particular* as its sole

---

[13] So, for example, David Lewis, *On the Plurality of Words* (Oxford: Basil Blackwell, 1986), p. 73.

[14] So too D. C. Williams, *Principles of Empirical Realism*, (Springfield, IL: Charles C. Thomas, 1966), p. 133.

[15] Lewis sees classes as composing other classes (*Parts of Classes* (Oxford: Blackwell, 1991)), but he also sees them as entities whose smallest parts, singletons, are related to their elements by a mysterious membership relation (54), and no concrete thing has members in this sense. Thus classes, though particular, are not concrete.

[16] At least, this would be a common view today. It was equally common medieval lore that God belongs to no kinds at all (so, for example, S. Thomae Aquinatis, *Summa Theologiae* (Ottawa: Studii Generalis, 1941), Ia 3, 5). I will not go into what lies behind this claim; suffice it to say that if it is true, then again, positing a deity adds no highest-level kinds, and a deity continues to fall under the *concept* person.

[17] Lewis does not believe in states of affairs, so these would create a difference in economy only if theism required them—as it obviously does not.

highest-level kind, beating Lewis at the highest level. For reasons noted, theism beats Lewis by a wide margin in regard to lower-level kinds. At the lowest level, a theist theory adds *a priori* to our ontology one existent substance, Lewis's uncountably many. These do matter in ontology. Theism's added item is unusual. But Lewis' universes include infinitely many things perhaps equally unusual. Some might reply that God is Himself complex. But that's debatable—Aquinas and his heirs would give you a fight on it. God has no material parts or literal mereological parts of any sort. On my account He has no essential properties distinct from Himself, and 'His essence is identical with His existence.' He has many thoughts, but this only makes His mind more complex, not Himself. Adding smart people to the universe does not have a greater ontological cost than adding dumb ones. Now one might suggest (perhaps with tongue a bit in cheek) that Lewis' ontology is more parsimonious than mine as follows: for each of his possible individuals I have a divine thought of just that individual. For each of his classes I have a divine thought of just its members. I have in addition a deity. So I have one more particular than he does. In reply, let us compare two world-pictures. One has every physical thing there actually is, but does not include a particular disembodied mind. The other is a solipsism with the disembodied mind as the sole existing thing and all physical things merely as parts of its very elaborate illusory world-story. Would anyone seriously claim that the solipsist story involves the larger ontology? But this is a good analogy to the claim that I have the larger modal ontology: Lewis has a modal universe which is a huge physical thing, and by comparison my God is a modal solipsist, in that the whole modal universe exists within Him.

The other sort of possibilia—Meinong's—are actual but do not exist.[18] So Meinongians add no existents to our ontology. But for every existent particular or kind Lewis adds, Meinongians add a 'subsistent' one.[19] Meinongian and Lewis's unrestricted quantifiers range over exactly the same things.[20] Meinongians and Lewis think we must add exactly the same things to our universe to get a full picture of reality. So I submit that Meinongians bloat our ontology just as Lewis does.[21] If they do, my argument against Lewis carries over. Theism is also a more conservative revision of our general ontology than Meinongianism. Theism requires only belief that there actually is one unusual being. Meinongians must accept that some things actually are horses although they do not exist. If non-existent horses actually have causal powers to affect

---

[18] Instead, they 'subsist'—a term he did not well explain (*op. cit.*).

[19] And the historical Meinong adds impossibilia beyond all the possibilia—but I will ignore this.

[20] Meinong calls his a 'subsistence' quantifier. But as we have no real explanation of what that means, this hardly confers a theoretical advantage.

[21] Albeit their terminology does not sit well with the 'onto' in ontology. Even leaving impossibilia aside, the bloat may be greater for the historical Meinong, who had no interest in parsing away intensions; my point is that a leaner Meinongian position is possible which parallels Lewis's. Meinongians can, of course, reply that their view does not bloat our story about what *exists*—but I fail to see why that matters, given that on their view we quantify unrestrictedly over more than the existent.

existing concreta, it is remarkable that no-one has ever been kicked by one: so while the Meinongian may insist that non-existent horses are just like existent ones save for existing, most of us will infer that they lack causal powers to affect the existent. Similarly, while the Meinongian may say that non-existent horses have such properties as standing in doorways, their presence in the doorway does not exclude anything else from their supposed location in space, and so most will infer that non-existents do not really have spatial locations. Thus on Meinongian terms, most actual horses are abstract objects, on standard ways of drawing the abstract/concrete distinction. For a Meinongian, one is privileged to meet a concrete or existing horse; they are rare. Theists need say no such things.

Still, a fair discussion of possibilism must include both benefit and cost. We must ask what the possibilist *does* with possibilia: are they worth the pain? Lewis uses his to 'construct' attributes;[22] I argue elsewhere that this theory is unacceptable even apart from its ontological cost.[23] Possibilia appear in Lewis' accounts of counterfactuals and of propositions as sets of worlds, but these accounts cannot count as benefits for which they are needed. Actualists also use possible-worlds to parse counterfactuals and in theories of propositions. Possibilists use possibilia in accounts of singular possibility, and Lewis taxes actualists with being unable to handle singular possibilities for non-actual individuals—some (he claims) conflate possibilities for indiscernible possible individuals into single possibilities,[24] while others have one individual actualizing all possibilities for multiple indiscernible possible individuals.[25] If I provide divine singular concepts, I get around both charges. Lewis also charges some actualist theories of singular possibility with lack of an adequate account of representation;[26] hopefully I have suggested that I can handle this.

Finally, Lewis uses his worlds to give a reductive account of modal discourse.[27] As Lewis sees it, the claim that $\Diamond P$ asserts something completely non-modal, that there *exists* a world in which P, 'exists' being a wholly non-modal concept and worlds being defined in wholly non-modal terms.

But Lewis's account of worlds does not manage to 'reduce' the modal, because it does not 'reduce' all of the modal: it does not provide all the possibilities we intuitively think there are. Consider all the Lewis-worlds, however many they be, each a concrete physical universe in splendid spatio-temporal isolation. It seems to us that however many physical objects there are, there could be others. It also seems to us independently that any physical object or array could have a qualitative duplicate. So intuitively, there could be a larger multiverse, consisting of Lewis' initial array and a qualitative duplicate of it. Every way we have of judging possibility chimes in that this

---

[22] *Plurality,* pp. 50–69.

[23] 'One Step Toward God', *Royal Institute of Philosophy Supplement* 68 (2011), 67–104.

[24] *Plurality,* pp. 157–8.

[25] *Ibid.,* pp. 170–1.

[26] *Ibid.,* pp. 174–91.

[27] *Ibid.,* pp. 150–6; John Divers, *Possible Worlds* (London: Routledge, 2002), p. 106ff.

is possible. This multiverse is, however, on Lewis' terms impossible, since it does not exist, and so none of these worlds is part of logical space. Obviously this cannot be fixed by adding Lewis-worlds; the problem recurs however many we add. If Lewis does not have sufficient entities to 'reduce' all possibilities, his reduction fails. Of course, Lewis might contend that his rivals also do not have enough entities: Platonists, for instance, might lack alien Platonic universals.[28] But Lewis does not believe in alien *worlds* (as distinct from worlds all of whose entities are alien to us) and so he cannot claim that a Platonist should and cannot allow for alien Platonic attribute-worlds. And most of Lewis's rivals do not have the problem of worlds that are qualitative duplicates. Platonic attributes, propositions, and states of affairs cannot differ only in number: there cannot be two universals *redness*, two propositions that there are toucans, etc. Nor can there be distinct eternal divine events of conceiving redness, either intuitively or on any developed theory of events.

This is enough to show that Lewis's view fails and cannot be fixed. But let us ask a more basic question: is Lewis's reduction even worth attempting? What is so bad about primitive modality? Perhaps its epistemology is problematic;[29] thus one might try to reduce necessity to analyticity because we know how we know about analyticity. On one level, Lewis's account does not improve matters. It leaves the Benacerraf problem unsolved, it does not 'reduce' the merely possible or the necessary to anything with which we have epistemic contact, and it offers no help in explaining how we know modal truths, if we do. By contrast, if there are such things as powers, our access to them is unproblematic: we learn what powers things have by learning the causal structure of the world. Reduction of absolute to causal modalities thus turns the reality behind absolute modal claims into something to which we have epistemic access. At another level, Lewis' views respond to an epistemological worry Quine raises. Quine objects to quantified modal logic that it forces one to sort items' traits as necessary and contingent, and there is no principled or plausible way to do so.[30] Lewis' response, I think, comes to this: one has a trait necessarily just if all one's counterparts have it, contingently if only some do. But which other-worldly items are an item's counterparts depends on context, and in particular how one specifies the item: there is some matter, and specified as a statue it has only statue-counterparts, while specified as a lump it has other, lumpier ones.[31] So necessity is relative to how one describes the object—a conclusion Quine could love, but liberated (as Quine would wish) from involvement with analyticity. But this move does not

---

[28] For example, *Plurality*, pp. 159–65.

[29] This is clearly Peacocke's concern (John Peacocke, *Being Known* (Oxford: Oxford University Press, 1999).

[30] W. V. O. Quine, 'Reference and Modality', in Leonard Linsky, ed., *Reference and Modality* (Oxford: Oxford University Press, 1971), pp. 30–1.

[31] *Plurality*, pp. 248ff.

require one to reduce modality. Primitivists and actualists can play counterpart games. So Lewis cannot count it as motivation to reduce the modal.

Lewis wants to have fewer primitives and thinks he can manage it.[32] But he offers no argument that massive ontological bloat is a price worth paying for reduction of one otherwise-primitive concept. The modal deserves reduction if modal concepts are somehow intrinsically mysterious or problematic, and the properties invoked in the reduction somehow clearer, better understood or unproblematic. But Lewis never offers a case that modal concepts are problematic. (Some other reductionists do no more than gesture at one.[33]) Quine does make a case against modal concepts, connected closely with a skepticism about intensional notions, and whether or not this played a motivating role; in fact Lewis restricts himself to thoroughly unintensional basic concepts—spatiotemporal, mereological, set-theoretic, and such unproblematic notions as existence. But Quine's skepticism about intensionality is a hard sell these days.

Lewis may be moved to reduce the modal to the non-modal to secure the place of modal truth within an overarching naturalism or physicalism[34] and yet give himself other worlds over which to quantify. But other theories of worlds are acceptable to naturalists of various stripes; these others might, for instance, be friendlier to Platonic universals, and so Platonic world-types, than Lewis is. So at this point Lewis's reductive motivations come to include his case against 'ersatz' worlds, which constitutes his best effort to show that his is the way for a naturalist to go, rather than, say, a naturalist Platonism about worlds.[35] Part of this case is that 'ersatzers' cannot reduce modality, and so cannot be used to motivate the reduction. Another part consists of queries about how 'ersatz' worlds represent, and (for 'magical' ersatzers) the question about 'selection' already discussed. I think theism has answers here, as should be clear. The rest raises difficulties about singular possibilities for non-existent objects. We might sum its thrust up this way: we need possibilia, and Lewis's are not (quite) as crazy as Meinongians'. But if we can provide haecceities, we do not need possibilia. So I do not see a case for reducing the modal; the strongest argument for doing so may be epistemological, and I have suggested that a reduction of absolute to causal modalities is all the help we need here. Thus I do not see a case that Lewis' huge expansion of our ontology buys us anything worth having, and I conclude that economy considerations strongly favor theism over possibilism.

---

[32] *Ibid.*, p. 157.

[33] See, for example, Theodore Sider, 'Reductive Theories of Modality', in Michael Loux and Dean Zimmerman (eds), *The Oxford Handbook of Metaphysics* (Oxford: Oxford University Press, 2003), p. 185.

[34] See his Introduction to David Lewis, *Philosophical Papers*, v. 2 (New York: Oxford University Press, 1986), pp. ix–xi.

[35] Michael Tooley, *Causation* (New York: Oxford University Press, 1987), makes a case for uninstantiated universals that appears compatible with the strictest naturalism. From here it would be a short step to possible worlds.

Against Platonism

Platonic actualists treat worlds as propositions, attributes, states of affairs, or sets.[36] I now suggest that it would be ontologically profitable to trade these for God. Or, perhaps better, that if one were starting from zero, with an ontology only of ordinary physical particulars, containing neither God nor these, it would be better to add God than to add these.

In one respect, God and Platonic entities are on all fours. The standard semantics brings possible worlds into modal claims' truth-conditions. It thus involves them in what these claims assert—what they mean, in one parsing of 'meaning.' I bring in divine powers. It is no doubt surprising to hear that claims as homely as that the Giants might win on Sunday assert something which entails the existence of God. But it is no less so to hear that the Giants' possible win commits us to abstract entities of various *outré* sorts. None is a particularly natural explication of what we say. All involve items whose relevance to what we say is not initially obvious. All seem bizarre to some serious thinkers. We pre-philosophically talk about ways things might go; we do not pre-philosophically have views on what these 'ways' *are*, as distinct from what their contents are, and so it is not surprising if these turn out to surprise us. So the surprise, as such, does not tell against one proposal more than another. For that matter, talk of the Giants does not on its surface commit us to quantum entities, fields, curved spacetime, and so on, but if current physics is correct, what will make our claim true or false on the day entails claims about many such things.[37] Of course, some will be more or less surprised by particular entities: you may find God's involvement more surprising, I universals'. But why? Perhaps it is that one seems less relevant to modality than the other—if so, my argument about relevance below is to the point. But probably our reactions reflect assigning lower prior epistemic probability to there being the one or the other. If God seems the more surprising, this may be because of other evidence you take yourself to have against His existence. This will probably come chiefly from evil. I address this below.

A second consideration that does not favor one view over another is strangeness. God is personal; worlds, to Platonists, may be attributes, propositions, or states of affairs. We are familiar with homely, ordinary persons and (say Platonists) universals or propositions. But modal metaphysics deals in large-scale versions of each. We do not ordinarily meet omniscient, omnipotent persons or grasp propositions able to imply a possible world's worth of truth. In each case, the kind is familiar, the instance not. In each case, further, we know little of the intrinsic nature of the entity involved. If anything, we

---

[36] John Bigelow, 'Real Possibilities', *Philosophical Studies* 53 (1988), 37–64, has sets of universals; M. J. Cresswell, 'The World is Everything that Is the Case', in Michael Loux (ed.), *The Actual and the Possible* (Ithaca. NY: Cornell University Press, 1979), pp. 129–45, has sets of 'basic situations.'
[37] My thanks to a referee for this point.

have (surprisingly) a bit more grasp of what goes on inside God. As Van Inwagen notes, we do not know much at all about abstract entities' intrinsic properties. Perhaps we are best off relative to sets, but worlds would be sets *of* other entities, and the other entities are mysterious. On the other hand, we know a lot about some intrinsic properties God would have (personhood, power, moral perfection, self-knowledge, various mental properties), though we do not know how they are realized in an immaterial being. Some will protest that the concept of God is strange, but nominalists usually find realists' entities strange, and so this too seems a standoff. In any case, as noted earlier with the example of sets, it is precisely the role of a global economy argument to overcome strangeness with utility.

Platonists may observe that there is no problem of evil about propositions, and so theism is automatically disfavored in the comparison. But if you think that evil currently provides any very strong argument against the existence of God, you have not been paying attention. Purely deductive ('logical') versions of the problem of evil are very widely conceded to be 'dead', killed off by Plantinga's free-will defense.[38] It is not so much that the details of Plantinga's argument persuade—they do not persuade *me*—but that once one sees the sort of thing a defense has to be to work, it seems pretty clear that some kind of free-will defense has to be available and adequate. The debate has shifted to 'evidential' versions of the problem of evil, and my own view, which is not uncommon, is that these are pretty thoroughly on the ropes—what's called skeptical theism provides an effective counter.[39] So I suggest that the prior epistemic probability for God's existence you bring to considering the present argument should not be particularly low. But even if you do your homework and still disagree, any argument for God's existence is *ipso facto* a counter to such problem as evil poses, for any good argument for God is good reason to think that God exists and so to think that there is some effective counter to arguments from evil, even if one does not have it to hand. Of course, by the same token, to the extent that evil seems an unsolved problem, it is reason to think that any strong-seeming argument for God must be less strong than it appears. All this means is that no case for God's existence is complete without addressing evil, which is hardly a surprising thought. By the same token, no case for Platonism is complete without addressing the epistemological worries it entrains and those versions of naturalism which might preclude it. Any modal metaphysics faces objections, some known in advance of considering particular new arguments for it. I do not claim that any one argument settles the question of God's existence, and my present reasoning does not even complete the global economy argument for God's existence.

---

[38] For one version of this see Alvin Plantinga, *God, Freedom and Evil* (Grand Rapids: William B. Eerdmans, 1974).
[39] For some of the debate see Daniel Howard-Snyder (ed.), *The Evidential Argument from Evil* (Bloomington: Indiana University Press, 1996).

My current claim is merely that if we keep our attention on modal metaphysics, God looks like a better buy than Platonism does.

I now turn to reasons to prefer a theist view. Scott Shalkowski notes:

> The key concern for . . . any (modal) approach framed in terms of a set of objects is: What have these objects to do with modality? Why are they . . . relevant? Simply admitting that there is more to the world than our spacetime continuum no more automatically accounts for necessity than does admitting that there is more to the world than the contents of my toolbox.[40]

Thus too Tony Roy:

> If I were suddenly to find out that there are no possible worlds, my response would not be 'So much the worse for its being possible that I take a walk', but 'So much the worse for the relevance of possible worlds.' *This* world makes it possible for me to take a walk . . . modal facts . . . 'located' somehow in the actual world (are) what determines which states of affairs are the possible worlds . . . we need to know that there is an appropriate connection between the possible worlds and the actual world before a worlds analysis can seem to be so much as relevant to modality.[41]

If its being possible that Roy walks is relevant to whether he walks, the ontology of this possibity should be relevant to his walking. Propositions, attributes, and states of affairs cannot causally constrain Roy's legs. How else can they be relevant to his walk? An obvious reply is that if the propositions (and so on) are not there, it simply is not possible that he walk, and that impossibility, though not a causal fact, is nonetheless relevant.[42] But this misses the point. We can agree pre-analytically that an impossibility would be a non-causal constraint, or is relevant. But does the appearance of relevance remain on the ontological picture that Platonism provides? It is not puzzling that impossibility should constrain Roy somehow, but it is puzzling that a property or a Platonic proposition should be able to dictate what he does and does not do. Some might say that world-talk is just talk about ways things can go, and if there is no way things can go in which Roy walks, this certainly affects whether he walks. But this is sleight of hand. 'There is no way things can go in which he walks'—or more simply 'He cannot walk'—makes a non-metaphysical modal claim. Its truth (or not) is relevant to how things actually go. Roy's suggestion is that when we parse this in terms of a

[40] Scott Shalkowski, 'Conventions, Cognitivism and Necessity', *American Philosophical Quarterly* 33 (1996), 376.
[41] Tony Roy, 'Worlds and Modality', *Philosophical Review* 102 (1993), 337, 338, 339. See also Michael Jubien, 'Problems with Possible Worlds', in David Austin, (ed.), *Philosophical Analysis* (Boston: Kluwer, 1988), pp. 303–4.
[42] So a referee.

metaphysics of worlds, the relevance evaporates. It is no answer to this to say that the pre-analytic claim is relevant. That a proposition is possibly true may be reason to think it possible that Roy walk, but (so it seems to us) does not *make* it possible for him to do so. A truth represents the way things are. So too, a possible truth possibly represents the way things are. It possibly represents them because things possibly are that way. It gets things backwards to say that things possibly are that way because it possibly represents them. It is because it is possible that Roy walk that the proposition *Roy walks* is possibly true. Possibly-true propositions represent possibilities for our universe. *Prima facie*, what merely represents a possibility reflects something else—whatever else makes this possible. If there is relevance here, it runs the wrong way for a 'worlds' theory. Again, told that there is a property of entire universes such that were it exemplified, Roy would walk, one wants to say that whether Roy can walk will be part of what determines whether this universe can have the property, rather than being determined by it: the part's powers determine what character the whole can have, not *vice versa*. Again, if there is relevance here at all, it runs in the wrong direction for worlds accounts.

My theist theory has no relevance problem. On my account, if it is true that there is no way things might go in which Roy walks, what makes it true is just that nothing, not Roy, not even God, has the power to bring this about, and it is not something that can come about uncaused. (If Roy walks, it must be that Roy does something to bring this about, namely walk.) Concrete this-worldly lack of power is obviously relevant to how things might go. Further, God has brought this about, and so prevented Roy's walking. What makes it true that Roy might walk, if that's true, is that Roy has the power to do so (God giving it to Him) or God has the power and chance to give Roy the power (and so on)—that is, permits Himself to do so. Preventing, permitting, and empowering are actual causal facts, and their relevance to Roy's walking is obvious. I now add that Lewis's universes and Meinongian entities also face relevance problems. If it is odd to hear that the lack of a Platonic proposition prevents Roy's walking, it is even odder to hear that how things go in other physical universes does so, because one expects that physical entities will be relevant to the spacetime paths of other physical entities only causally, and Lewis' universes are causally isolated from our own. The picture gets only stranger if one adds that the universes in question do not exist.

In modal matters, the non-physical has an explanatory priority to the physical. For there could fail to be anything physical at all.[43] Were there nothing physical, there would still be positive modal truths: that necessarily $2 + 2 = 4$, and that possibly there is something physical. But then these would have an ontology. Their ontology could only be non-physical entities

---

[43] Lewis would demur (*Plurality*, pp. 73–4), but not plausibly, and we noted earlier that Rodriguez-Pereyra (among others) has a way to bring even the possibility of a physically empty universe into Lewis's framework.

of some sort. And it would be odd if these things would be there only if nothing physical existed. So there are in addition to physical entities items which suffice to ground modal truth without them. The physical at best overdetermines a portion of modal truth. And if it could fail to do even that, but truth would then remain the same, its contribution is inessential and secondary. So in modal matters, the non-physical is primary. But what form must it take? What seems desirable is that there be something non-physical but not a mere representing entity, something that can get in on the ground floor of the modal realm rather than reflecting or being determined by modal facts established elsewhere, and be relevant causally to what goes on in the physical world. God fits the bill, and (*per* earlier argument) provides a fuller range of possibilities than any assembly of actual non-divine powers can.

There is in addition a Razor case for theism. Theists can do without abstracta, as Menzel showed for sets and I have argued for the rest. So theists can avoid the highest-level kind *abstract entity*, all its subkinds, and its countless instances. They can be nominalists. They add not a highest-level kind but a sub-kind: a deity is a kind of person. Of course, for every abstract world a Platonist might add, there will be something in God, on my account. But these decompose into God and mental events, and again, it would be hard to claim that an ontology of one solipsist with his thoughts is really less parsimonious than one of uncountable infinities of abstract substances.

Here a Platonist might offer a comeback: I have an independent case that we should add to our purely concrete ontology (say) propositions. We need these for purposes unrelated to modality. And worlds fall out of a commitment to propositions, as you have noted. So there is no need to add God: we have propositions anyway, and they will do. But what the Platonist has, again, is at most a case that a particular role is played. Theists can grant that, and then ask what plays the role. Any adequate nominalist account of this expands our ontology less than Platonism does. So if a theist account is adequate, as I have suggested, the case for Platonic propositions is undercut, on Razor grounds. And so I claim that God would make a better addition to our ordinary ontology both on Ockhamist grounds and because He does not have a relevance problem. As noted in Chapter 3, He also does not create a Benacerraf Dilemma for modal knowledge.

I have not taken up all the ontological issues a cost/benefit argument for God must address. But even so, I submit that I have given a case, on ontological grounds, that my theory is preferable to worlds-theories. If the case works, atheist modal realists' best move might try to do without worlds (or equivalent possibilia) on a non-theist basis, by speaking instead of situations or world-fragments. But situations or world-fragments are abstract, and so do not escape the Platonist limb of my argument, which does not depend on abstract entities' being world-sized. Jubien offers a different sort of Platonism, resting not on world-fragments but on entailment-relations between abundant Platonic properties.[44] But this theory either does or does not deliver world-sized possibilities in its own way. If it does not it is inadequate to our intuitive modal conceptions—for as suggested in Chapter 1, we do intuitively recognize a natural maximum size for possibilities, the world-size. If it does, its properties and the appropriate relations between them simply become world-substitutes and inherit the disadvantages sketched here.

If theism provides a better modal metaphysic than worlds theories, non-world abstract-entity theories or non-theist 'power' views (my case for the last came in Chapter 2), theism yields the best realist account of modality. The anti-realist options include conventionalism, fictionalism, and projectivism. I argue against one form of conventionalism elsewhere.[45] But my full treatment of modal anti-realism must await another occasion. Instead, I close with this. Possible worlds have a place in our intuitive modal beliefs, and the best modal semantics we have quantifies over them. This is reason to be realistic about them, at least to the extent of maintaining that real entities play the possible-world role. My present case for my theory, and God's existence, is that we do best to include among these entities divine powers.

---

[44]   Michael Jubien, *Possibility* (Oxford: Oxford University Press, 2009).
[45]   'Swinburne on Divine Necessity', *Religious Studies* 46 (2010) 141–62.

BIBLIOGRAPHY

ADAMS, M. M. *William Ockham* (Notre Dame, IN: University of Notre Dame Press, 1987).

ADAMS, R. M. 'Must God Create the Best?', *Philosophical Review* 81 (1972), 317–32.

—— 'Theories of Actuality', in Michael Loux (ed.), *The Possible and the Actual* (Ithaca, NY: Cornell University Press, 1979).

—— 'Primitive Thisness and Primitive Identity', *Journal of Philosophy* 76 (1979), 5–26.

—— 'A Modified Divine Command Theory of Ethical Wrongness', in Paul Helm (ed.), *Divine Commands and Morality* (Oxford: Oxford University Press, 1981), pp. 83–108.

—— 'Actualism and Thisness', *Synthese* 49 (1981), 3–42.

—— 'Divine Necessity', in Thomas Morris (ed.), *The Concept of God* (New York: Oxford University Press, 1987), pp. 41–53.

—— 'Presumption and the Necessary Existence of God', *Noûs* 22 (1988), 19–32.

—— *Leibniz* (New York: Oxford University Press, 1994).

—— *Finite and Infinite Goods* (Oxford: Oxford University Press, 1999).

ALLAIRE, E. B. 'Bare Particulars', in Michael Loux (ed.), *Universals and Particulars* (Garden City, NY: Doubleday Books, 1970), pp. 235–44.

ALSTON, W. P. 'Does God Have Beliefs?', in *Divine Nature and Human Language* (Ithaca, NY: Cornell University Press, 1989), pp. 178–93.

—— 'Some Suggestions for Divine Command Theorists' (Ithaca, NY: Cornell University Press, 1989), pp. 253–73.

—— 'Perception and Conception', in Kenneth Westphal (ed.), *Pragmatism, Reason, and Norms* (New York: Fordham University Press, 1998), pp. 59–87.

—— 'Back to the Theory of Appearing', *Philosophical Perspectives* 13 (1999), 181–203.

ANSELM. *Proslogion*.

AQUINATIS, S. THOMAE. *Summa Contra Gentiles* (Turin: Marietti, 1909).

—— *Quaestiones de Potentia Dei*, in *Sancti Thomae Aquinatis Quaestiones Disputatae*, v. 1 (Turin: Marietti, 1931).

—— *Quaestiones Disputatae de Veritate*, in *Sancti Thomae Aquinatis Quaestiones Disputatae*, v. 3 (Turin: Marietti, 1931).

—— *Summa Theologiae* (Ottawa: Studii Generalis, 1941).

—— *Sancti Thomae de Aquino Expositio super libram Boethii De Trinitate*, ed. Bruno Decker (Leiden: Brill, 1959).

ARMSTRONG, D. M. *A Theory of Universals* (Cambridge: Cambridge University Press, 1978).

—— *Nominalism and Realism* (Cambridge: Cambridge University Press, 1978).

—— *What Is a Law of Nature?* (Cambridge: Cambridge University Press, 1983).

—— 'In Defence of Structural Universals', *Australasian Journal of Philosophy* 64 (1986), 85–8.

—— *A Combinational Theory of Possibility* (Cambridge: Cambridge University Press, 1989), p. 21.

—— 'Classes Are States of Affairs', *Mind* 100 (1991), 189–200.

—— *A World of States of Affairs* (Cambridge: Cambridge University Press, 1997).

—— *Truth and Truthmakers* (Cambridge: Cambridge University Press, 2004).

AUGUSTINE, ST. *Eighty-Three Different Questions*, tr. David Mosher (Washington: Catholic University of America Press, 2002).

AUNE, BRUCE. *Metaphysics* (Minneapolis, MN: University of Minnesota Press, 1985).

AVICENNA, *Compendium of Metaphysics.*

—— *Metaphysica.*

AYER, A. J. *Language, Truth and Logic*, 2nd edn. (New York: Dover Publications, 1952).

—— 'The A Priori', in Paul Moser (ed.), *A Priori Knowledge* (Oxford: Oxford University Press, 1987).

BACON, JOHN. *Universals and Property Instances* (Oxford: Basil Blackwell, 1995).

BAKER, A. 'Quantitative Parsimony and Explanation', *British Journal for the Philosophy of Science*, 54 (2003), 245–59.

BAKER, LYNNE RUDDER. *The Metaphysics of Everyday Life* (Cambridge: Cambridge University Press, 2007).

BARNES, E. C. 'Ockham's Razor and the Anti-Superfluity Principle', *Erkenntnis* 53 (2000), 353–74.

BAYLE, PIERRE *Historical and Critical Dictionary* (first published, 1695), quoted in G. W. Leibniz. *Theodicy*, sec. 150, tr. Diogenes Allen in his *Leibniz: Theodicy* (Indianapolis, IN: Bobbs-Merrill, 1962), pp. 104–5.

BEALER, GEORGE. *Quality and Concept* (New York: Oxford University Press, 1982).

—— 'Universals', *Journal of Philosophy* 90 (1993), 5–32.

—— 'Analyticity', in *The Encyclopedia of Philosophy* (New York: Routledge, 1998), v. 1, pp. 234–9.

BEALL, J. C. 'Is the Observable World Consistent?', *Australasian Journal of Philosophy* 78 (2000), 113–18.

—— 'Introduction: At the Intersection of Truth and Falsity', in Graham Priest, J. C. Beall, and Bradley Armour-Garb (eds), *The Law of Non-Contradiction* (Oxford: Oxford University Press, 2004), pp. 1–19.

—— and COLYVAN, MARK. 'Looking for Contradictions', *Australasian Journal of Philosophy* 79 (2001), 564–9.

BEEBEE, HELEN. and DODD, JULIAN, (eds), *Truthmakers* (Oxford: Oxford University Press, 2005).

BENACERRAF, PAUL 'Mathematical Truth', in Paul Benacerraf and Hilary Putnam (eds), *Philosophy of Mathematics*, 2nd edn. (Cambridge: Cambridge University Press, 1983), pp. 403–20.

BENNETT, JONATHAN. *Events and Their Names* (Oxford: Oxford University Press, 1988).

—— 'Farewell to the Phlogiston Theory of Conditionals', *Mind* 97 (1988), 509–27.

—— 'Descartes' Theory of Modality', *Philosophical Review* 103 (1994), 639–67.

BERGMANN, MICHAEL. 'Skeptical Theism and Rowe's New Evidential Argument from Evil', *Noûs* 35 (2001), 278–96.

BIGELOW, JOHN. *The Reality of Numbers* (Oxford: Oxford University Press, 1988).

—— 'Real Possibilities', *Philosophical Studies* 53 (1988), 37–64.

—— 'Sets Are Universals', in A. D. Irvine, (ed.), *Physicalism in Mathematics* (Dordrecht: Kluwer, 1990), pp. 291–306.

—— and PARGETTER, ROBERT. 'A Theory of Structural Universals', *Australasian Journal of Philosophy* 67 (1989), 1–11.

—— and—— *Science and Necessity* (Cambridge: Cambridge University Press, 1990).

BIGGER, CHARLES. *Participation: a Platonic Inquiry* (Baton Rouge, LA: Louisiana State University Press, 1968).

BIRD, ALEXANDER. 'Dispositions and Antidotes', *The Philosophical Quarterly* 48 (1998), 227–234.

—— *Nature's Metaphysics* (Oxford: Oxford University Press, 2007).

BLACKBURN, SIMON. 'Morals and Modals', in Simon Blackburn, *Essays in Quasi-Realism* (Oxford: Oxford University Press, 1993), pp. 52–74.

BLANCHETTE, PATRICIA. 'Modals and Modality', *Synthese* 124 (2000), 59–60.

DAVID BLUMENFELD,'On the Compossibility of the Divine Attributes, in Thomas Morris, (ed.) *The Concept of God* (Oxford: Oxford University Press, 1987), pp. 201–15.

BRANDOM, ROBERT. *Between Saying and Doing: Towards an Analytical Pragmatism* (Oxford: Oxford University Press, 2008).

BORGHINI, ANDREA. and WILLIAMS, NEIL. 'A Dispositional Theory of Possibility', *Dialectica* 62 (2008), 21–41.

CAMERON, ROSS. 'What's Metaphysical about Metaphysical Modality?', *Philosophy and Phenomenological Research* 79 (2009), 1–16.

—— 'From Humean Truthmaker Theory to Priority Monism', *Noûs* 44 (2010), 178–98.

—— 'Necessity and Triviality', *Australasian Journal of Philosophy* 88 (2010), 401–15.

CAMPBELL, KEITH. 'The Metaphysics of Abstract Particulars', *Midwest Studies in Philosophy* 6 (1981), 478.

—— *Abstract Particulars* (Oxford: Basil Blackwell, 1990).

CARNAP, RUDOLPH. 'The Logicist Foundations of Mathematics', in Paul Benacerraf and Hilary Putnam, (eds), *Philosophy of Mathematics*, 2nd edn. (Cambridge: Cambridge University Press, 1983), pp. 41–52.

CARTWRIGHT, RICHARD. 'Speaking of Everything', *Noûs* 28 (1994), 1–20.

CASULLO, ALBERT. 'Conjunctive Properties Revisited', *Australasian Journal of Philosophy* 62 (1984), 289–191.

CHALMERS, DAVID. 'Does Conceivability Entail Possibility?', in Tamar Gendler and John Hawthorne (eds), *Conceivability and Possibility* (Oxford: Oxford University Press, 2002), pp. 149–51.

CHEYNE, COLIN. and PIGDEN, CHARLES. 'Negative Truths from Positive Facts', *Australasian Journal of Philosophy* 84 (2006), 249–65.

CHIHARA, CHARLES. *The Worlds of Possibility* (Oxford: Oxford University Press, 1998).

CHISHOLM, RODERICK. *Person and Object* (LaSalle, IL: Open Court Publishing, 1976).

—— *On Metaphysics* (Minneapolis, MN: University of Minnesota Press, 1989).

—— 'Events Without Times', *Noûs* 24 (1990), 413–27.

—— *A Realistic Theory of Categories* (Cambridge: Cambridge University Press, 1996).

CLARK, STEPHEN. 'God's Law and Morality', *Philosophical Quarterly* 32 (1982), 339–47.

CLARKE, SAMUEL. *A Demonstration of the Being and Attributes of God* (London: John and Paul Knapton, 1738).

CLOUSER, ROY. *The Myth of Religious Neutrality* (Notre Dame, IN: University of Notre Dame Press, 1991).

CONEE, EARL. 'The Possibility of Power Beyond Possibility', *Philosophical Perspectives* 5 (1991), 447–73.

COVER, J. A. and O'LEARY-HAWTHORNE, JOHN. *Substance and Individuation in Leibniz* (Cambridge: Cambridge University Press, 1999).

CRAIG, WILLIAM LANE. 'Timelessness and Omnitemporality', in Gregory Ganssle (ed.) *God and Time* (Wheaton, IL: InterVarsity Press, 2001), pp. 129–60.

CRESSWELL, M. J. 'The World is Everything that Is the Case', in Michael Loux (ed.), *The Actual and the Possible* (Ithaca, NY: Cornell University Press, 1979), pp. 129–45.

CURLEY, E.J. 'Descartes on the Creation of the Eternal Truths', *Philosophical Review* 53 (1984), 569–97.

DALY, CHRIS. 'So Where's the Explanation?', In Helen Beebee and Julian Dodd (eds), *Truthmakers* (Oxford: Oxford University Press, 2005), pp. 85–103.

DAVIDSON, DONALD. 'The Individuation of Events', in his *Essays on Actions and Events* (Oxford: Oxford University Press, 1980).

DAVIS, RICHARD. 'God and Modal Concretism', *Philosophia Christi* 10 (2008), 37–54.

DAVIS, STEPHEN. *Logic and Nature of God* (Grand Rapids, MI: William B. Eerdmans, 1983), pp. 94–5.

DESCARTES. *Descartes: Philosophical Letters*, tr. Anthony Kenny (New York: Oxford University Press, 1970), p. 11.

DEUTSCH, HARRY. 'Real Possibility', *Noûs*, 24 (1990), 751–5.

DEVITT, MICHAEL. ' "Ostrich Nominalism" or "Mirage Realism"?', *Pacific Philosophical Quarterly* 61 (1980), 433–9.

DIVERS, JOHN. 'Recent Work on Supervenience', *Philosophical Books* 39 (1998), 81–91.
—— *Possible Worlds* (London: Routledge, 2002).

DORR, CIAN. 'Non-symmetric Relations', in Dean Zimmerman (ed.), *Oxford Studies in Metaphysics*, vol. 1, (Oxford University Press, 2004), pp. 155–92.
—— 'There Are No Abstract Objects', in John Hawthorne, Theodore Sider, and Dean Zimmerman (eds). *Contemporary Debates in Metaphysics*, (Blackwell, 2007), pp. 32–63.

DOWE, PHILIP. *Physical Causation* (Cambridge University Press, 2000).

DUDMAN, VICTOR. 'Indicative and Subjunctive', *Analysis* 48 (1988), 113–22.

DUMMETT, MICHAEL. 'Wittgenstein's Philosophy of Mathematics', in Paul Benecerraf and Hilary Putnam, (eds), *The Philosophy of Mathematics* (Englewood Cliffs, NJ: Prentice-Hall, 1964).
—— *Frege: Philosophy of Language*, 2nd edn. (London: Duckworth, 1981).

EDGINGTON, DOROTHY. 'Do Conditionals Have Truth-Conditions?', in Frank Jackson (ed.), *Conditionals* (New York: Oxford University Press, 1991), pp. 176–201.
—— 'On Conditionals', *Mind* 104 (1995), 235–329.

EHRING, DOUGLAS. *Causation and Persistence* (Oxford: Oxford University Press, 1997).

ELDER, CRAWFORD. 'Realism and Determinable Properties', *Philosophy and Phenomenological Research* 56 (1996), 149–59.

ELLIS, BRIAN. 'A Unified Theory of Conditionals', *Journal of Philosophical Logic* 7 (1978), 107–24.

ETCHEMENDY, JOHN. *The Concept of Logical Consequence* (Stanford, CA: CSLI Publications, 1999).

EVANS, C. STEPHEN (ed.), *Exploring Kenotic Christology* (Oxford: Oxford University Press, 2006).

EWING, A. C., *Value and Reality* (London: George, Allen and Unwin, 1973).

FALES, EVAN. *Causation and Universals* (New York: Routledge, 1990).

—— *Divine Intervention* (Abingdon: Routledge, 2010).

FALLS-CORBIT, MARGARET and McCLAIN, F. MICHAEL. 'God and Privacy', *Faith and Philosophy* 9 (1992), 369–86.

FIELD, HARTRY. *Science Without Numbers* (Princeton, NJ: Princeton University Press, 1980).

—— *Realism, Mathematics and Modality* (Oxford: Basil Blackwell, 1989).

FINDLAY, J. N. 'Can God's Existence Be Disproved?', in Antony Flew and Alasdair MacIntyre (eds), *New Essays in Philosophical Theology* (New York: Macmillan, 1955), pp. 47–56.

FINE, KIT. 'Essence and Modality', *Philosophical Perspectives* 8 (1994), 1–16.

—— 'Ontological Dependence', *Proceedings of the Aristotelian Society* 95 (1995), 273, 275.

—— 'Senses of Essence', in Walter Sinnott-Armstrong (ed.), *Modality, Morality and Belief* (Cambridge: Cambridge University Press, 1995), pp. 52–73.

—— 'Vagueness, Truth and Logic', in Rosanna Keefe and Peter Smith (eds), *Vagueness* (Cambridge, MA: MIT Press, 1996), pp. 119–50.

FISHER, JOHN. 'On Perceiving the Impossible', *British Journal of Aesthetics* 18 (1978), 19–30.

FLINT, THOMAS. *Divine Providence* (Ithaca, NY: Cornell University Press, 1998).

—— and FREDDOSO, ALFRED. 'Maximal Power', in Alfred Freddoso (ed.), *The Existence and Nature of God* (Notre Dame, IN: University of Notre Dame Press, 1983), pp. 81–113.

FODOR, JERRY. 'Propositional Attitudes', *Monist* 64 (1978), 501–23.

—— *Psychosemantics* (Cambridge, MA: MIT Press, 1987).

—— *Concepts* (Oxford: Oxford University Press, 1998).

FORBES, GRAHAM. 'Time, Events and Modality', in Robin Le Poidevin and Murray MacBeath (eds), *The Philosophy of Time* (Oxford: Oxford University Press, 1993), pp. 80–95.

FORREST, PETER. 'Neither Magic Nor Mereology', *Australasian Journal of Philosophy* 64 (1986), 89–91.

—— 'Ways Worlds Could Be', *Australasian Journal of Philosophy* 64 (1986), 15–24.

FOX, JOHN. 'Truthmaker', *Australasian Journal of Philosophy* 65 (1987), 188–207.

FRANKFURT, HARRY. 'Freedom of the Will and the Concept of a Person', *Journal of Philosophy* 68 (1971), 5–20.

—— 'On God's Creation', in Eleonore Stump (ed.), *Reasoned Faith* (Ithaca, NY: Cornell University Press, 1993), pp. 128–41.

—— *The Reasons of Love* (Princeton, NJ: Princeton University Press, 2004), pp. 44, 46.

FREDDOSO, ALFRED. 'Accidental Necessity and Power Over the Past', *Pacific Philosophical Quarterly,* 63 (1982), 54–68.

—— 'Accidental Necessity and Logical Determinism', *Journal of Philosophy* 80 (1983), 257–78.

—— 'Medieval Aristotelianism and the Case Against Secondary Causation in Nature', in Thomas Morris (ed.), *Divine and Human Action* (Ithaca, NY: Cornell University Press, 1988), pp. 74–118.

——— 'God's General Concurrence with Secondary Causes', *Philosophical Perspectives* 5 (1991), 553–85.

——— 'God's General Concurrence with Secondary Causes: Pitfalls and Prospects', *American Catholic Philosophical Quarterly* 68 (1994), 131–56.

FREGE, GOTTLOB. *The Foundations of Arithmetic*, tr. J. L. Austin, 2nd revised edn. (London: Blackwell, 1980), p. 40.

FULMER, GILBERT. 'The Concept of the Supernatural', *Analysis* 37 (1977), 113–16.

GALE, RICHARD. *Negation and Non-being* (Oxford: Basil Blackwell, 1976).

GÄRDENFORS, PETER. 'Belief Revisions and the Ramsey Test for Conditionals', *Philosophical Review* 95 (1986), 81–93.

GARFINKEL, ALAN. *Forms of Explanation* (New Haven, CT: Yale University Press, 1981).

GENDLER, TAMAR-SZABO, and HAWTHORNE, JOHN (eds), *Conceivability and Possibility* (Oxford: Oxford University Press, 2002).

GERT, JOSHUA. 'A Realistic Colour Realism', *Australasian Journal of Philosophy* 84 (2006), 565–89.

GIBBARD, ALAN. 'Two Recent Theories of Conditionals', in William Harper, Robert Stalnaker, and Glenn Pearce (eds), *Ifs* (Dordrecht: D. Reidel, 1981), pp. 211–47.

GOODMAN, NELSON. *The Structure of Appearance*, 3rd edn. (Dordrecht: Reidel, 1977).

GRIM, PATRICK. *The Incomplete Universe* (Cambridge, MA: MIT Press, 1991).

——— 'Worlds By Supervenience: Some Further Problems', *Analysis* 57 (1997), 146–51.

——— 'The Being That Knew Too Much', *International Journal for Philosophy of Religion* 47 (2000), 141–54.

GULESERIAN, THEODORE. 'God and Possible Worlds: the Modal Problem of Evil', *Noûs* 17 (1983), 221–38.

——— 'Divine Freedom and the Problem of Evil', *Faith and Philosophy* 17 (2000), 348–66.

——— 'Can God be Trusted?', *Philosophical Studies* 103 (2001), 296.

HAACK, SUSAN. *Deviant Logic, Fuzzy Logic* (Chicago, IL: University of Chicago Press, 1996).

HALE, BOB. *Abstract Objects* (Oxford: Basil Blackwell, 1987).

——— 'On Some Arguments for the Necessity of Necessity', *Mind* 108 (1999), 23–52.

HALE, SUSAN. 'Spacetime and the Abstract—Concrete Distinction', *Philosophical Studies* 53 (1988), 85–102.

HARTSHORNE, CHARLES. *The Divine Relativity* (New Haven, CT: Yale University Press, 1947).

HAWTHORNE, JOHN. 'Identity', in Michael Loux and Dean Zimmerman (eds), *The Oxford Handbook of Metaphysics* (Oxford: Oxford University Press, 2003), pp. 99–130.

HAZEN, A. P. 'Worlds as Complete Novels', *Analysis* 56 (1996), 33–8.

HEIL, JOHN. *The Nature of True Minds* (Cambridge: Cambridge University Press, 1992), p. 64.

——— *From an Ontological Point of View* (New York: Oxford University Press, 2003).

HELM, BENNETT. 'Love', http://plato.stanford.edu/entries/love.

HICK, JOHN. *Evil and the God of Love*, rev. edn. (New York: Harper and Row, 1978).

HIRSCH, ELI. 'Physical-Object Ontology, Verbal Dispute and Commonsense', *Philosophy and Phenomenological Research* 70 (2005), 1–30.

HOCHBERG, HERBERT. *Thought, Fact and Reference* (Minneapolis, MN: University of Minnesota Press, 1978).

HERBERT HOCHBERG. 'Negation and Generality', in *Logic, Ontology and Language* (Munich: Philosophia Verlag, 1984).

HOFFMAN, JOSHUA and ROSENKRANTZ, GARY. 'Omnipotence Redux' *Philosophy and Phenomenological Research* 49 (1988), 283–301.

HOWARD-SNYDER, DANIEL (ed.), *The Evidential Argument from Evil* (Bloomington, IN: Indiana University Press, 1996).

HUEMER, MICHAEL. 'Why is Parsimony a Virtue?', *Philosophical Quarterly* 59 (2009), 216–36.

HUGHES, CHRISTOPHER. 'Negative Existentials, Omniscience and Cosmic Luck', *Religious Studies* 34 (1998), 375–401.

HUGHES, G. E. and CRESSWELL, M. J. *An Introduction to Modal Logic* (London: Methuen, 1968).

HUMBERSTONE, I. L. 'From Worlds to Possibilities', *Journal of Philosophical Logic* 10 (1981), 313–40.

HUMPHREYS, PAUL. *The Chances of Explanation* (Princeton, NJ: Princeton University Press, 1989).

IACONA, ANDREA. 'Are There Propositions?', *Erkenntnis* 58 (2003), 325–51.

JACKSON, FRANK. 'A Causal Theory of Counterfactuals', *Australasian Journal of Philosophy* 55 (1977), 3–21.

JACOBS, JONATHAN. 'A Powers Theory of Modality', *Philosophical Studies*, DOI 10.1007/S11098-009-9427-1 14.

JAGER, THOMAS. 'An Actualistic Semantics for Quantified Modal Logic', *Notre Dame Journal of Formal Logic* 23 (1982), 338.

JAGO, MARK. 'The Conjunction and Disjunction Theses', *Mind* 118 (2009), 411–15.

JOHANSSON, INGVAR. 'Determinables As Universals', *Monist* 83 (2000), 101–21.

JUBIEN, MICHAEL. 'Problems with Possible Worlds', in David Austin (ed.), *Philosophical Analysis* (Dordrecht: Kluwer, 1988), pp. 299–322.

—— 'Could This Be Magic?', *Philosophical Review* 100 (1991), 249–67.

—— 'Propositions and the Objects of Thought', *Philosophical Studies* 104 (2001).

—— *Possibility* (Oxford: Oxford University Press, 2009).

JUHL, COREY and LOOMIS, ERIC. *Analyticity* (London: Routledge, 2010).

KANT, IMMANUEL. *Critique of Practical Reason*, tr. Lewis White Beck (Indianapolis, IN: Bobbs-Merrill, 1956).

KENNY, ANTHONY (ed. and tr.), *Descartes' Philosophical Letters* (New York: Oxford University Press, 1970).

KIM, JAEGWON. 'Events as Property-Exemplifications', in Jaegwon Kim, *Supervenience and Mind* (New York: Cambridge University Press, 1993), pp. 33–52.

KMENT, BORIS. 'Counterfactuals and the Analysis of Necessity', *Philosophical Perspectives* 20 (2006), 237–302.

KNUUTTILA, SIMO. 'Time and Modality in Scholasticism', in Simo Knuuttila (ed.) *Reforging the Great Chain of Being* (Dordrecht: Reidel, 1981), pp. 163–257.

—— 'Duns Scotus and the Foundations of Logical Modalities', in Ludger Honnefelder *et al.* (eds), *John Duns Scotus: Metaphysics and Ethics* (Leiden: Brill, 1996), pp. 127–43.

KRAEMER, ERIC. R. 'Conjunctive Properties and Scientific Realism', *Analysis* 37 (1977), 85–6.

KRAPY, KLAAS. 'Can God Choose a World at Random?', in Yujin Nagasawa and Erik Wielenberg (eds), *New Waves in Philosophy of Religion* (London: Palgrave Macmillan, 2008).

KRIPKE, SAUL. 'Identity and Necessity', in Milton K. Munitz (ed.), *Identity and Individuation* (New York: NYU Press, 1971), p. 137.

—— 'Semantical Considerations on Modal Logic', in Leonard Linsky, (ed.) *Reference and Modality* (Oxford: Oxford University Press, 1971), pp. 63–72.

—— 'Naming and Necessity', in Donald Davidson and Gilbert Harman, (eds) *Semantics of Natural Language*, 2nd edn. (Dordrecht: Reidel, 1972), pp. 253–355.

LAORTE, JOSEPH. *Natural Kinds and Conceptual Change* (Cambridge: Cambridge University Press, 2004).

LE POIDEVIN, ROBIN. *Arguing for Atheism* (London: Routledge, 1996).

LEEDS, STEPHEN. 'Possibility: Physical and Metaphysical', in Carl Gillett and Barry Loewer (eds), *Physicalism and its Discontents* (Cambridge: Cambridge University Press, 2001).

—— 'Physical and Metaphysical Necessity', *Pacific Philosophical Quarterly* 88 (2007), 458–85.

LEFTOW, BRIAN. 'A Leibnizian Cosmological Argument', *Philosophical Studies* 57 (1989), 135–55.

—— 'Necessary Moral Perfection', *Pacific Philosophical Quarterly* 70 (1989), 240–60.

—— 'God and Abstract Entities', *Faith and Philosophy* 7 (1990), 193–217.

—— 'Is God an Abstract Object?', *Noûs* 24 (1990), 581–98.

—— *Time and Eternity* (Ithaca, NY: Cornell University Press, 1991).

—— 'Why Didn't God Create the World Sooner?', *Religious Studies* 27 (1991), 159–72.

—— 'Concepts of God', *The Encyclopedia of Philosophy* (New York: Routledge, 1998), v. 4, pp. 93–102.

—— 'Necessary Being', *The Encyclopedia of Philosophy* (New York: Routledge, 1998), v. 6, pp. 743–7.

—— 'Anti Social Trinitarianism', in Steven Davis and Daniel Kendall (eds), *The Trinity* (New York: Oxford University Press, 1999), pp. 203–48.

—— 'A Timeless God Incarnate', in Daniel Kendall and Steven Davis (eds), *The Incarnation* (New York: Oxford University Press, 2002), pp. 273–99.

—— 'Anselm's Neglected Argument', *Philosophy* 77 (2002), 331–47.

—— 'The Eternal Now', in Gregory Ganssle and David Woodruff (eds), *God and Time* (New York: Oxford University Press, 2002).

—— 'Aquinas on Attributes', *Medieval Philosophy and Theology* 11 (2003), 1–41.

—— 'A Latin Trinity', *Faith and Philosophy* 21 (2004), 304–33.

—— 'Eternity and Immutability', in William Mann, (ed.) *The Blackwell Companion to Philosophy of Religion* (New York: Basil Blackwell, 2004).

LEFTOW, BRIAN. 'Aquinas on God and Modal Truth' *The Modern Schoolman* 82 (2005), 171–200.

—— 'No Best World: Moral Luck', *Religious Studies* 41 (2005), 165–81.

—— 'No Best World: Creaturely Freedom', *Religious Studies* 41 (2005), 269–85.

—— 'Power, Possibilia and Non-Contradiction', *The Modern Schoolman* 83 (2005), 231–43.

—— 'Divine Simplicity', *Faith and Philosophy* 23 (2006), 365–80.

—— 'God and the Problem of Universals', *Oxford Studies in Metaphysics* 2 (2006), 325–56.

—— 'Impossible Worlds', *Religious Studies* 42 (2006), 393–402.

—— 'Omnipotence', in Thomas Flint and Michael Rea (eds), *The Oxford Handbook of Philosophical Theology* (Oxford: Oxford University Press, 2009), pp. 167–98.

—— 'Aquinas, Divine Simplicity and Divine Freedom', in Kevin Timpe (ed.), *Metaphysics and God* (London: Routledge, 2009), pp. 21–38.

—— 'Divine Necessity', in Charles Taliaferro and Chad Meister (ed.), *The Cambridge Companion to Christian Philosophical Theology* (Cambridge: Cambridge University Press, 2010), pp. 15–30.

—— 'Swinburne on Divine Necessity', *Religious Studies* 46 (2010), 141–62.

—— 'One Step Toward God', *Royal Institute of Philosophy Supplement* 68 (2011), 67–104.

—— 'Why Perfect Being Theology?', *International Journal of Philosophy of Religion* 69 (2011), 103–18.

LEIBNIZ, G. W. 'Fifth Paper', in H. G. Alexander (ed.), *The Leibniz-Clarke Correspondence* (Manchester: Manchester University Press, 1956), p. 56.

—— 'Divine Freedom' (forthcoming).

—— 'God, Vagueness, and Logical Truth' (forthcoming).

—— *Theodicy*, tr. Diogenes Allen (Indianapolis, IN: Bobbs-Merrill, 1962).

—— 'On the Ultimate Origination of the Universe', tr. Paul and Anne Schrecker, in *Leibniz: Monadology and Other Philosophical Essays* (Indianapolis, IN: Bobbs-Merrill, 1965).

—— 'Monadology', in Nicholas Rescher (ed.), *The Monadology: An Edition for Students* (Pittsburgh, PA: University of Pittsburgn Press, 1991).

—— 'On Nature's Secrets', tr. in Nicholas Rescher (ed.), *The Monadology: An Edition for Students* (Pittsburgh, PA: University of Pittsburgn Press, 1991).

LEUENBERGER, STEPHAN. 'Supervenience in Metaphysics', *Philosophy Compass* 3 (2008), 749–62.

LEWIS, DAVID. *Counterfactuals* (Cambridge, MA: Harvard University Press, 1973).

—— 'Counterpart Theory and Quantified Modal Logic', in Michael Loux (ed.), *The Possible and the Actual* (Ithaca, NY: Cornell University Press, 1979).

—— *On the Plurality of Worlds* (Oxford: Basil Blackwell, 1986).

—— 'Events', in David Lewis, *Philosophical Papers* (Oxford: Oxford University Press, 1986), v. 2, pp. 241–69.

—— 'Against Structural Universals', *Australasian Journal of Philosophy* 64 (1986), 25–46.

—— *Parts of Classes* (Oxford: Basil Blackwell, 1991).

—— 'Armstrong on Combinatorial Possibility', in David Lewis, *Papers in Metaphysics and Epistemology* (Cambridge: Cambridge University Press, 1999).

—— 'Truthmaking and Difference-making', *Noûs* 35 (2001), 602–15.

LINSKY, BERNARD and ZALTA, EDWARD. 'In Defence of the Simplest Quantified Modal Logic', *Philosophical Perspectives* 8 (1994), 431–58.

—— and —— 'Naturalized Platonism versus Platonized Naturalism', *The Journal of Philosophy* 92 (1995), 525–55.

—— and —— 'In Defence of the Contingently Non-Concrete', *Philosophical Studies* 84 (1996), 283–94.

LLOYD, A. C. 'Plotinus on the Genesis of Thought and Existence', *Oxford Studies in Ancient Philosophy* 5 (1987), 155–86.

LOCKE, JOHN. 'Of Identity and Diversity', reprinted in John Perry (ed.), *Personal Identity* (Berkeley, CA: University of California Press, 1975).

LOMBARD, LAWRENCE BRIAN. *Events* (London: Routledge and Kegan Paul, 1986).

LÓPEZ DE SA, DAN. 'Disjunctions, Conjunctions, and Their Truthmakers', *Mind* 118 (2009), 417–25.

LOUX, MICHAEL. (ed.), *The Possible and the Actual* (Ithaca, NY: Cornell University Press, 1979).

—— 'Toward an Aristotelian Theory of Abstract Objects', *Midwest Studies in Philosophy* 11 (1986), 495–512.

—— 'Aristotle's Constituent Ontology', *Oxford Studies in Metaphysics* 2 (2006), 207–50.

LOWE, E. J. 'The Truth about Counterfactuals', *Philosophical Quarterly* 45 (1995), 41–59.

—— *The Four-Category Ontology* (Oxford: Oxford University Press, 2006), pp. 23–4.

—— and A. RAMI (eds), *Truth and Truth-Making* (Stocksfield: Acumen, 2009).

LUDLOW, PETER. and MARTIN, NORAH, (eds), *Externalism and Self-Knowledge* (Stanford, CA: CSLI Publications, 1998).

—— NAGASAWA, YUJIN and DANIEL STOLJAR, (eds). *There's Something About Mary* (Cambridge, MA: MIT Press, 2004).

MACKIE, J. L. 'Omnipotence', in Linwood Urban and Douglas Walton (eds), *The Power of God* (Oxford: Oxford University Press, 1978), pp. 73–88.

MACKIE, PENELOPE. *How Things Might Have Been* (Oxford: Oxford University Press, 2006).

MADDY, PENELOPE. 'A Naturalistic Look at Logic', *Proceedings and Addresses of the American Philosophical Association* 76 (2002), 61–90.

MANCOSU PAOLO, 'The Varieties of Mathematical Explanation', in J. Hafner (ed.), *Visualization, Explanation and Reasoning Styles in Mathematics* (Dordrecht: Springer, 2005).

MANN, WILLIAM. 'Modality, Morality, and God' *Noûs* 23 (1989), 83–99.

MARCUS, RUTH BARCAN. 'Dispensing with Possibilia', *Proceedings of the American Philosophical Association* 49 (1975–76), 39–51.

—— 'Possibilia and Possible Worlds', in Ruth Barcan Marcus, *Modalities* (Oxford: Oxford University Press, 1993), pp. 212–13.

MARION, JEAN-LUC. *Sur la théologie blanche de Descartes* (Paris: Presses universitaires de France, 1981).

MARKOSIAN, NED. 'Brutal Composition', *Philosophical Studies* 92 (1998), 211–49.

MARTIN, C. B. *The Mind in Nature* (Oxford: Oxford University Press, 2008).

McDANIEL, KRIS. 'Tropes and Ordinary Physical Objects', *Philosophical Studies* 104 (2001), 269–90.

McGEE, VANN, 'Two Problems with Tarski's Theory of Consequence', *Proceedings of the Aristotelian Society* 92 (1992), 279.

McGINN, COLIN. *Problems in Philosophy* (Oxford: Basil Blackwell, 1993).

McMICHAEL, ALAN. 'A Problem for Actualism about Possible Worlds', *Philosophical Review* 92 (1983).

MEINONG, ALEXIUS. 'The Theory of Objects', tr. Isaac Levi, D. B. Terrell, and Roderick Chisholm, in Roderick Chisholm (ed.), *Realism and the Background of Phenomenology* (New York: Free Press, 1960), pp. 76–117.

MELIA, JOSEPH. 'Reducing Possibilities to Language', *Analysis* 61 (2001), 19–29.

MELLOR, D. H. *The Facts of Causation* (London: Routledge, 1995).

MENZEL, CHRISTOPHER. 'Actualism, Ontological Commitment and Possible World Semantics', *Synthese* 85 (1990), 355–89.

—— 'Theism, Platonism and the Metaphysics of Mathematics', in Michael Beaty (ed.), *Christian Theism and the Problems of Philosophy* (Notre Dame, IN: University of Notre Dame Press, 1990), pp. 208–29.

—— 'Temporal Actualism and Singular Foreknowledge', *Philosophical Perspectives* 5 (1991), 475–507.

MENZIES, PETER. 'Possibility and Conceivability', *European Review of Philosophy* 3 (1998), 255–77.

MERRICKS, TRENTON. *Truth and Ontology* (Oxford: Oxford University Press, 2007).

—— 'Truth and Freedom', *Philosophical Review* 118 (2009), 29–57.

MILLER, BARRY. *From Existence to God* (New York: Routledge, 1992).

MILLER, KIRSTIE. 'Defending Contingentism in Metaphysics', *Dialectica* 63 (2009), 23–49.

MOLNAR, GEORGE. 'Truthmakers for Negative Truths', *Australasian Journal of Philosophy* 78 (2000), 72–86.

—— *Powers* (Oxford: Oxford University Press, 2003).

MONDADORI, FABRIZIO. 'The Independence of the Possible According to Duns Scotus', in Oliver Boulnois *et al.* (eds), *Duns Scotus a Paris* (Turnhout: Brepols, 2004), pp. 313–74.

—— and MORTON, ADAM. 'Modal Realism: the Poisoned Pawn', *Philosophical Review* 85 (1976), 3–20.

MONTAGUE, RICHARD. 'On the Nature of Certain Philosophical Entities', *Monist* 53 (1969), 159–93.

MOORE, G. E. *Commonplace Book* (New York: Macmillan, 1962).

MORRIS, THOMAS. 'The Necessity of God's Goodness', *The New Scholasticism* 59 (1985), 418–48.

—— *Anselmian Explorations* (Notre Dame, IN: University of Notre Dame Press, 1989).

MORRISTON, WESLEY. 'Is God "Significantly Free"?', *Faith and Philosophy* 2 (1985), 257–64.

—— 'What's So Good About Moral Freedom?', *Philosophical Quarterly* 50 (2000), 344–58.

MUMFORD, STEPHEN. *Dispositions* (Oxford: Oxford University Press, 1998)

—— 'The True and the False', *Australasian Journal of Philosophy* 83 (2005), 263–9.

NAGASAWA, YUJIN. *God and Phenomenal Consciousness* (Cambridge: Cambridge University Press, 2008).

NOLAN, DANIEL. 'Impossible Worlds: A Modest Approach', *Notre Dame Journal of Formal Logic* 38 (1997), 535–73.

—— 'Quantitative Parsimony', *British Journal for the Philosophy of Science*, 48 (1997), 329–43.

NORMORE, CALVIN. 'Duns Scotus' Modal Theory', in Thomas Williams (ed.), *The Cambridge Companion to Duns Scotus* (Cambridge: Cambridge University Press, 2003), pp. 129–60.

NUTE, DONALD. 'Conditional Logic', in D. Gabbay and F. Guenther (eds), *Handbook of Philosophical Logic*, v. 2 (Dordrecht: D. Reidel, 1984), pp. 387–440.

NYGREN, ANDERS. *Agape and Eros* (London: SPCK, 1939).

OCKHAM, WILLIAM. *In 1 sent* d. 43, q. 2, in *Opera Philosophica et Theologica*.

O'LEARY-HAWTHORNE, JOHN. 'The Epistemology of Possible Worlds: A Guided Tour', *Philosophical Studies* 84 (1996), 183–202.

OPPY, GRAHAM. *Ontological Arguments and Belief in God* (Cambridge: Cambridge University Press, 1995).

OVE HANSSON, SVEN. 'In Defense of the Ramsey Test', *Journal of Philosophy* 89 (1992), 522–40.

PARSONS, JOSH. 'The Least Discerning and Most Promiscuous Truthmaker', *The Philosophical Quarterly* 60 (2010), 307–24.

PARSONS, TERENCE. *Non-Existent Objects* (New Haven, CN: Yale University Press, 1980).

—— 'On Denoting Propositions and Facts', *Philosophical Perspectives* 7 (1993), 441–60.

PAP, ARTHUR. *Semantics and Necessary Truth* (New Haven, CT: Yale University Press, 1958).

PARSONS, JOSH. 'The Least Discerning and Most Promiscuous Truthmaker', *Philosophical Quarterly* 60 (2010), 309–10.

PARSONS, TERENCE. 'On Denoting Propositions and Facts', *Philosophical Perspectives* 7 (1993), 441–60.

PASEAU, ALEXANDER. 'Defining Ultimate Ontological Basis and the Fundamental Layer', *Philosophical Quarterly* 60 (2010), 169–75.

PEACOCKE, JOHN. *Being Known* (Oxford: Oxford University Press, 1999).

PERRY, JOHN. 'From Worlds to Situations', *Journal of Philosophical Logic* 15 (1986), 83–107.

PIANESI, F. and VARZI, A. C. 'Events, Topology, and Temporal Relations', Monist 78 (1996), 89–116.

PIKE, NELSON. *God and Timelessness* (New York: Schocken Books, 1970).

PLANTINGA, ALVIN. *God and Other Minds* (Ithaca, NY: Cornell University Press, 1967).

—— *God, Freedom and Evil* (Grand Rapids, MI: William B. Eerdmans, 1974).

—— *The Nature of Necessity* (New York: Oxford University Press, 1974).

—— 'Actualism and Possible Worlds', *Theoria* 42 (1976), 139–60.

—— 'The Boethian Compromise', *American Philosophical Quarterly* 15 (1978), 129–38.

—— *Does God have a Nature?* (Milwaukee, WI: Marquette University Press, 1980).

—— 'How to be an Anti-Realist', *Proceedings and Addresses of the American Philosohical Association* 56 (1982), 47–70.

—— 'Self-Profile, in James Tomberlin and Peter Van Inwagen (eds), *Alvin Plantinga* (Dordrecht: D. Reidel, 1985), p. 92.

—— 'Two Concepts of Modality', *Philosophical Perspectives* 1 (1987), 192.

—— and Patrick Grim, 'Truth, Omniscience, and Cantorian Arguments: An Exchange', *Philosophical Studies* 71 (1993), 267–306.

PLOTINUS. *Enneads*, tr. A. H. Armstrong, 7 vols. (Cambridge, MA: Harvard University Press, 1988).

POLLARD, STEPHEN. *Philosophical Introduction to Set Theory* (Notre Dame, IN: University of Notre Dame Press, 1990).

POLLOCK, JOHN. L. *The Foundations of Philosophical Semantics* (Princeton, NJ: Princeton University Press, 1984).

—— 'Plantinga on Possible Worlds', in James Tomberlin and Peter van Inwagen, (eds), *Alvin Plantinga* (Dordrecht: D. Reidel 1985), pp. 121–44.

POST, JOHN. *The Faces of Existence* (Ithaca, NY: Cornell University Press, 1987).

PRICE, H. H. *Thinking and Experience* (Cambridge, MA: Harvard University Press, 1953).

PRIEST, GRAHAM. *In Contradiction* (Dordrecht: Kluwer, 1987).

—— *An Introduction to Non-Classical Logic* (Cambridge: Cambridge University Press, 2001).

—— *Toward Non-Being* (Oxford: Oxford University Press, 2005).

PRIOR, A. N. 'Identifiable Individuals', in A. N. Prior, *Paperson Time and Tense*, ed. Per Hasle, Peter Oberstrom, Torben Brauser, and Jack Copeland (Oxford: Oxford University Press, 2003), new edn, pp. 86–7.

—— 'The Notion of the Present', in Peter Van Inwagen and Dean Zimmerman, (eds), *Metaphysics: The Big Questions* (Oxford: Blackwell, 1998), pp. 80–2.

PROCLUS. *Commentary on Plato's Parmenides*, tr. Glenn Morrow and John Dillon (Princeton, NJ: Princeton University Press, 1983).

PRUSS, ALEXANDER. 'The Cardinality Objection to David Lewis's Modal Realism', *Philosophical Studies* 104 (2001), 169–78.

—— 'The Actual and the Possible', in Richard Gale (ed.), *The Blackwell Guide to Metaphysics* (London: Basil Blackwell, 2002), p. 330.

PUTNAM, HILARY. *The Many Faces of Realism* (LaSalle, IL: Open Court Press, 1987).

QUINE, W. V. O. *Word and Object* (Cambridge, MA: MIT Press, 1960).

—— *From a Logical Point of View*, 2nd edn. (New York: Harper and Row, 1961).

—— 'Reference and Modality', in Leonard Linsky (ed.), *Reference and Modality* (Oxford: Oxford University Press, 1971), pp. 30–1.

QUINN, PHILIP. *Divine Commands and Moral Requirements* (Oxford: Oxford University Press, 1978).

—— 'Divine Command Theory', in Hugh LaFollette, (ed.), *The Blackwell Guide to Ethical Theory* (Oxford: Basil Blackwell, 1999).

QUINTON, ANTHONY. 'Properties and Classes', *Proceedings of the Aristotelian Society* 58 (1957–58), 33–58.

—— *The Nature of Things* (London: Routledge and Kegan Paul, 1973).

RAYO, AGUSTIN. 'On Specifying Truth-Conditions', *Philosophical Review* 117 (2008), 385–443.

—— 'Towards a Trivialist Account of Mathematics', in Otávio Bueno and Øystein Linnebo, (eds), *New Waves in Philosophy of Mathematics* (Palgrave MacMillan, 2009), pp. 239–60.

REA, MICHAEL. (ed.), *Material Constitution* (Lanham, MD: Rowman and Littlefield, 1997).

—— 'Sameness Without Identity: An Aristotelian Solution to the Problem of Material Constitution', *Ratio* 11 (1998), 316–28.

READ, STEPHEN. 'Truthmakers and the Disjunction Thesis', *Mind* 109 (2000), 67–79.

—— and EDGINGTON, DOROTHY. 'Conditionals and the Ramsey Test, I', *Proceedings of the Aristotelian Society* supp. vol. 69 (1995), 47–65.

—— 'Ontology and the Disjunction Thesis', *Mind* 109 (2000), 67–79.

RESCHER, NICHOLAS. *A Theory of Possibility* (Pittsburgh, PA: University of Pittsburgh Press, 1975).

RESTALL, GREG. 'Truthmakers, entailment and necessity', *Australasian Journal of Philosophy* 74 (1996), 331–40.

RHODA, ALAN. 'Presentism, Truthmakers and God', *Pacific Philosophical Quarterly* 90 (2009) 41–62.

RODRIGUEZ-PEREYRA, GONZALO. *Resemblance Nominalism* (Oxford: Oxford University Press, 2002).

—— 'Modal Realism and Metaphysical Nihilism', *Mind* 113 (2004), 683–704.

—— 'Truthmaking, Entailment and the Conjunction Thesis', *Mind* 115 (2006), 957–82.

—— 'The Disjunction and Conjunction Theses', *Mind* 118 (2009), 427–43.

ROSEN, GIDEON. 'Modal Fictionalism', *Mind* 99 (1990), 327–54.

—— 'Abstract Objects', *The Stanford Encyclopedia of Philosophy* (online).

ROSENKRANTZ, GARY and HOFFMAN, JOSHUA. 'What an Omnipotent Agent Can Do', *International Journal for Philosophy of Religion* 11 (1980), 1–19.

ROSS, JAMES. 'Eschatological Pragmatism', in Thomas Morris (ed.), *Philosophy and the Christian Faith* (Notre Dame, IN: University of Notre Dame Press, 1988), 279–300.

ROUTLEY, RICHARD. *Exploring Meinong's Jungle* (Canberra: Australian National University, 1980), p. 203.

ROWE, WILLIAM. *The Cosmological Argument* (Princeton, NJ: Princeton University Press, 1975).

—— *Can God Be Free?* (Oxford: Oxford University Press, 2004).

ROY, TONY. 'Worlds and Modality', *Philosophical Review* 102 (1993), 335–62.

—— 'In Defense of Linguistic Ersatzism', *Philosophical Studies* 80 (1995), 217–42.

RUSSELL, BERTRAND. *The Problems of Philosophy* (New York: Oxford University Press, 1912).

—— *Our Knowledge of the External World*, rev. edn. (London: Allen and Unwin, 1926).

—— *The Principles of Mathematics*, 2nd edn. (New York: Norton, 1938), p. xii.

—— *Human Knowledge: Its Scope and Limits* (London: Allen and Unwin, 1948).

—— 'Lectures on Logical Atomisation', in Robert Marsh (eds), *Logic and Knowledge* (New York: G. P. Putnam's Sons, 1956), pp. 262, 265ff.

—— 'Logical Atomism', in Robert Marsh (ed.), *Logic and Knowledge* (New York: G. P. Putnam's Sons, 1956), pp. 321–44.

—— 'The Philosophy of Logical Atomism', in Robert Marsh (ed.), *Logic and Knowledge* (New York: G. P. Putnam's Sons, 1956), pp. 175–282.

RYLE, GILBERT. *The Concept of Mind* (London: Hutchinson, 1949).

SALMON, NATHAN. 'The Logic of What Might Have Been', *Philosophical Review* 98 (1989), 3–34.

SANDBORG, DAVID. 'Mathematical Explanation and the Theory of Why-Questions', *British Journal for the Philosophy of Science* 49 (1998), 603–24.

SCHAFFER, JONATHAN. 'The Least Discerning and Most Promiscuous Truthmaker', *Philosophical Quarterly* 60 (2010), 307–12.

SCHIFFER, STEPHEN. *The Things We Mean* (Oxford: Oxford University Press, 2003).

SCOTUS, JOHN DUNS. *Ordinatio*.

SERENE, EILEEN. 'Anselm's Modal Conceptions', in Simo Knuuttila (ed.), *Reforging the Great Chain of Being* (Dordrecht: Reidel, 1981), pp. 117–62.

SHALKOWSKI, SCOTT. 'Conventions, Cognitivism, and Necessity', *American Philosophical Quarterly* 33 (1996), 375–92.

SHAPIRO, STEWART. 'Logical Consequence: Modals and Modality', in Matthias Schirm (ed.), *The Philosophy of Mathematics Today* (Oxford: Oxford University Press, 1998), p. 148.

SHEEHY, PAUL. 'Theism and Modal Realism', *Religious Studies* 42 (2006), 315–28.

SHOEMAKER, SYDNEY. 'Causality and Properties', in Sydney Shoemaker (ed.), *Identity, Cause and Mind* (New York: Cambridge University Press, 1984), pp. 206–33.

—— 'Causal and Metaphysical Necessity', *Pacific Philosophical Quarterly* 79 (1998), 59–77.

—— *Physical Realization* (Oxford: Oxford University Press, 2007), pp. 11–18.

SIDELLE, ALAN. *Necessity, Essence and Individuation* (Ithaca, NY: Cornell University Press, 1989).

SIDER, THEODORE. 'Reductive Accounts of Modality', in Michael Loux and Dean Zimmerman (eds), *The Oxford Handbook of Metaphysics* (Oxford: Oxford University Press, 2003), pp. 180–208.

SIMCHEN, ORI. 'Meaningfulness and Contingent Analycity', *Noûs* 37 (2003), 278–302.

SMITH, BARRY. 'Truthmaker Realism', *Australasian Journal of Philosophy* 77 (1999), 274–91.

SMITH, NICHOLAS J. J. *Vagueness and Degreees of Truth* (Oxford: Oxford University Press, 2008).

SOAMES, SCOTT. *Understanding Truth* (Oxford: Oxford University Press, 1999).

SOSA, ERNEST. 'Persons and Other Beings', *Philosophical Perspectives* 1 (1987), 155–87.

SPINOZA, BENEDICT. *Ethics*, tr. E. Curley, in *The Collected Works of Spinoza* (Princeton, NJ: Princeton University Press, 1985).

STALNAKER, ROBERT. 'A Theory of Conditionals', in Nicholas Rescher (ed.), *Studies in Logical Theory* (Oxford: Basil Blackwell, 1968), pp. 98–112.

—— *Inquiry* (Cambridge, MA: MIT Press, 1984).

—— 'Possible Worlds and Situations', *Journal of Philosophical Logic* 15 (1986), 109–23.

—— 'On What Possible Worlds Could Not Be', in Robert Stalnaker, *Ways a World Might Be* (Oxford: Oxford University Press, 2003), pp. 40–54.

STEINER, MARK. 'Mathematical Explanation', *Philosophical Studies* 34 (1978), 135–51.

—— 'Possible Worlds', in Michael Loux (ed.), *The Actual and the Possible* (Ithaca, NY: Cornell University Press, 1979), pp. 225–34.

STRAWSON, P. F. *Individuals* (London: Methuen, 1959).

STRICKLAND, LLOYD. 'God's Problem of Multiple Choice', *Religious Studies* 42 (2006), 141–57.

STUMP, ELEONORE. *Aquinas* (London: Routledge, 2003).

—— and KRETZMANN, NORMAN. 'Eternity', *Journal of Philosophy* 78 (1981), 429–58.

SUAREZ, FRANCISCO. *Disputationes Metaphysicae* (1597).

SUPPES, PATRICK. *Probabalistic Metaphysics* (Oxford: Basil Blackwell, 1984).

SWINBURNE, RICHARD. 'Analyticity, Necessity and Apriority', in Paul Moser (ed.), *A Priori Knowledge* (New York: Oxford University Press, 1987), p. 173.

—— *The Coherence of Theism*, rev. edn. (Oxford: Oxford University Press, 1993).

—— *The Christian God* (New York: Oxford University Press, 1994).

—— *Epistemic Justification* (Oxford: Oxford University Press, 2001).

TALIAFERRO, CHARLES and MEISTER, CHAD (eds), *The Cambridge Companion to Christian Philosophical Theology* (Cambridge: Cambridge University Press, 2010), pp. 15–30.

TARSKI, ALFRED. *Logic, Semantics, Metamathematics*, 2nd edn. (Indianapolis, IN: Hackett, 1983), pp. 409–20.

TAYLOR, RICHARD. 'Negative Things', *Journal of Philosophy* 49 (1952), 433–48.

THOMASON, S. K. 'Free Construction of Time from Events', *Journal of Philosophical Logic* 18 (1989), 43–67.

THORNBURN, W. 'The Myth of Occam's Razor', *Mind* 27 (1918), 345–53.

TOOLEY, MICHAEL. *Causation* (New York: Oxford University Press, 1987).

TYE, MICHAEL. *The Metaphysics of Mind* (Cambridge: Cambridge University Press, 1989).

—— 'Sorites Paradoxes and the Semantics of Vagueness', in *Philosophical Perspectives* 8 (1994), 189–206.

VAN CLEVE, JAMES. 'Why a Set Contains Its Members Essentially', *Noûs* 19 (1985), 585–602.

VAN FRAASSEN, BAS. 'Singular Terms, Truth-Value Gaps and Free Logic', *Journal of Philosophy* 63 (1966), 481–95.

—— 'Presuppositions, Supervaluations and Free Logic', in Karel Lambert (ed.), *The Logical Way of Doing Things* (New Haven, CT: Yale University Press, 1969), pp. 67–91.

—— *The Scientific Image* (New York: Oxford University Press, 1980).

VAN INWAGEN, PETER. *Material Beings* (Ithaca, NY: Cornell University Press, 1990).

—— 'Two Concepts of Possible Worlds', in his *Ontology, Identity and Modality* (Cambridge: Cambridge University Press, 2001), pp. 206–42.

—— 'A Theory of Properties', in Dean Zimmerman (ed.), *Oxford Studies in Metaphysics* 1 (2004), pp. 107–38.

—— 'God and Other Uncreated Things', in Kevin Timpe (ed.), *Metaphysics and God* (London: Routledge, 2009), 3–20.

VANDER LAAN, DAVID. 'Counterpossibles and Similarity', in Frank Jackson and Graham Priest (eds), *Lewisian Themes* (Oxford: Oxford University Press, 2004), pp. 258–75.

—— 'Persistence and Divine Conservation', *Religious Studies* 42 (2006), 159–76.

WAINWRIGHT, WILLIAM. *Religion and Morality* (Aldershot: Ashgate, 2005).

WEBER, ERIK. and VERHOEVEN, LIZA. 'Explanatory Proofs in Mathematics', *Logique et Analyse* 45 (2002), 299–307.

WELLS, NORMAN. 'Descartes' Uncreated Eternal Truths', *New Scholasticism* 56 (1982), 185–99.

WERNER, LOUIS. 'Some Omnipotent Beings', in Linwood Urban and Douglas Walton (eds), *The Power of God* (Oxford: Oxford University Press, 1978), pp. 94–106.

WESTERHOFF, JAN. *Ontological Categories* (Oxford: Oxford University Press, 2005).

WIELENBERG, ERIK. 'Omnipotence Again', *Faith and Philosophy* 17 (2000), 26–47.

WIERENGA, EDWARD. 'Omnipotence Defined', *Philosophy and Phenomenological Research* 43 (1983), 363–76.

—— *The Nature of God* (Ithaca, NY: Cornell University Press, 1989).

—— 'Theism and Counterpossibles', *Philosophical Studies* 89 (1998), 87–103.

WILKERSON, T. E. *Natural Kinds* (Aldershot: Avebury, 1995).

WILLIAMS, D. C. 'The Element of Being', *Review of Metaphysics* 7 (1953), 123.

—— *Principles of Empirical Realism* (Springfield, IL.: Charles C. Thomas, 1966).

WILLIAMS, J. R. G. 'Fundamental and Derivative Truths', *Mind* 119 (2010), 103–41.

WILLIAMS, THOMAS and VISSER, SANDRA. 'Anselm's Account of Freedom', in Brian Davies and Brian Leftow (eds), *The Cambridge Companion to Anselm* (Cambridge: Cambridge University Press, 2004), pp. 179–203.

WILLIAMSON, TIMOTHY. *Vagueness*. (London: Routledge, 1994).

—— 'Bare Possibilia', *Erkenntnis* 48 (1998), 257–73.

WILSON, JESSICA. 'What is Hume's Dictum, and Why Believe It?', *Philosophy and Phenomenological Research* 80 (2010), 595–637.

WITTGENSTEIN, LUDWIG. *Philosophical Investigations*, tr. Elizabeth Anscombe (Oxford: Basil Blackwell, 1958).

WOLTERSTORFF, NICHOLAS. *Universals* (Chicago, IL: University of Chicago Press, 1970).

WOOZLEY, A. D. *Theory of Knowledge* (London: Hutchinson's University Library, 1949).

WRIGHT, CRISPIN. *Wittgenstein on the Foundations of Mathematics* (London: Duckworth, 1980).

YABLO, STEPHEN. 'Intrinsicness', *Philosophical Topics* 26 (1999), 479–505.

ZAGZEBSKI, LINDA. *Divine Motivation Theory* (Cambridge: Cambridge University Press, 2004).

ZALTA, EDWARD. 'Logical and Analytic Truths That Are Not Necessary', *Journal of Philosophy* 85 (1988), 57–74.

—— 'Twenty-Five Basic Theorems in Situation and World Theory', *Journal of Philosophical Logic* 22 (1993), 385–428.

—— and BERNARD LINSKY, 'In Defense of the Simplest Quantified Modal Logic', *Philosophical Perspectives* 8 (1994), 431–58.

—— 'Naturalized Platonism versus Platonized Naturalism', *The Journal of Philosophy* 92 (1995), 525–55.

ZARAGOZA, KEVIN. 'Bring Back the Magic', *Pacific Philosophical Quarterly* 88 (2007), 391–402.

ZIMMERMAN, DEAN. 'Immanent Causation', *Philosophical Perspectives* 11 (1997), 433–71.

—— 'The A-Theory of Time, Presentism and Open Theism', in Melville Stewart (ed.), *Science and Religion in Dialogue* (Oxford: Wiley–Blackwell, 2009), v. 2.

INDEX